THE **CJ** SOLUTION

Print + Online

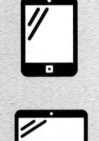

CJ⁴ delivers all the key terms and core concepts for the **Criminal Justice** course.

CJ Online provides the complete narrative from the printed text with additional interactive media and the unique functionality of **StudyBits**—all available on nearly any device!

What is a StudyBit™? Created through a deep investigation of students' challenges and workflows, the StudyBit™ functionality of **CJ Online** enables students of different generations and learning styles to study more effectively by allowing them to learn their way. Here's how they work:

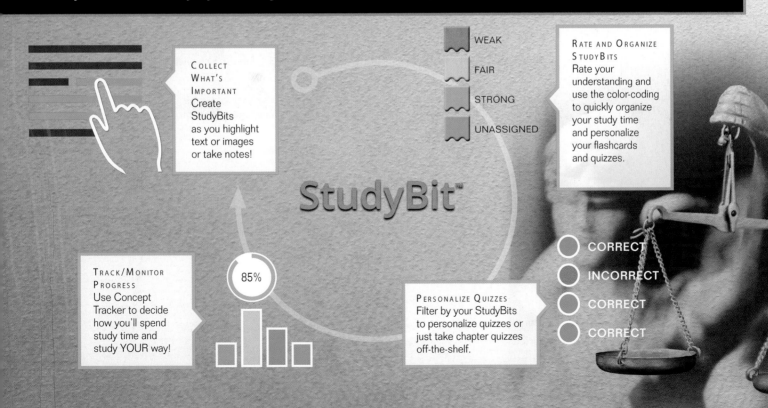

COLLECT WHAT'S IMPORTANT
Create StudyBits as you highlight text or images or take notes!

WEAK
FAIR
STRONG
UNASSIGNED

RATE AND ORGANIZE STUDYBITS
Rate your understanding and use the color-coding to quickly organize your study time and personalize your flashcards and quizzes.

StudyBit™

TRACK/MONITOR PROGRESS
Use Concept Tracker to decide how you'll spend study time and study YOUR way!

85%

PERSONALIZE QUIZZES
Filter by your StudyBits to personalize quizzes or just take chapter quizzes off-the-shelf.

CORRECT
INCORRECT
CORRECT
CORRECT

CJ⁴

Larry Gaines

Roger LeRoy Miller

Vice President, General Manager,
   4LTR Press and the Student Experience:
   Neil Marquardt

Product Director, 4LTR Press: Steven E. Joos

Product Manager: Clinton Kernen

Content Developer: Victoria Castrucci

Product Assistant: Lauren Dame

Marketing Manager: Valerie Hartman

Sr. Content Project Manager: Ann Borman

Manufacturing Planner: Ron Montgomery

Art Director: Bethany Casey

Cover and Internal Designer:
   Joe Devine/Red Hangar Design

Cover Image: imagedb.com/ShutterStock.com

Intellectual Property:

   Analyst: Alex Ricciardi

   Project Manager: Betsy Hathaway

Indexer: Terry Casey

Production Service: Lachina

Design elements: fingerprint and magnifying
   glass: imagineerinx/ShutterStock.com;
   gavel: Nata-Lia/ShutterStock.com

For product information and technology assistance, contact us at
Cengage Learning Customer & Sales Support 1-800-354-9706

For permission to use material from this text or product,
submit all requests online at **www.cengage.com/permissions**
Further permissions questions can be emailed to
permissionrequest@cengage.com

Library of Congress Control Number: 2015949775

Student Edition ISBN: 978-1-305-66119-6

Cengage Learning
20 Channel Center Street
Boston, MA 02210
USA

Cengage Learning is a leading provider of customized learning solutions with employees residing in nearly 40 different countries and sales in more than 125 countries around the world. Find your local representative at **www.cengage.com**

Cengage Learning products are represented in Canada by Nelson Education, Ltd.

To learn more about Cengage Learning Solutions, visit **www.cengage.com**

Purchase any of our products at your local college store or at our preferred online store **www.cengagebrain.com**

Printed in the United States of America

Print Number: 01   Print Year: 2015

GAINES / MILLER
CJ⁴

BRIEF CONTENTS

imagedb.com/ShutterStock.com

CONTENTS

Part 2
THE POLICE AND
LAW ENFORCEMENT

Bill Clark/CQ Roll Call/Getty Images

4 Law Enforcement Today 70

5 Problems and Solutions in Modern Policing 92

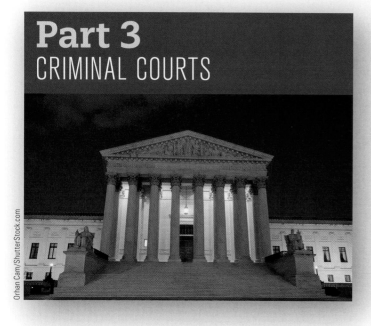

Part 3
CRIMINAL COURTS

Orhan Cam/ShutterStock.com

**Part 4
CORRECTIONS**

Travis Dove/*The New York Times*/Redux Pictures

Scott Olson/Getty Images

Part 5
SPECIAL ISSUES

14 Today's Challenges in Criminal Justice 294

SKILL PREP

A Study Skills Module

Welcome!

With this course and this textbook, you've begun what we hope will be a fun, stimulating, and thought-provoking journey into the world of criminal justice.

In this course, you will learn all the basics about crime, law enforcement, the court system, corrections, and other special issues like justice for juveniles, homeland security, and cyber crime. Knowledge of these basics will get you well on your way to a great future in criminal justice.

We have developed this study skills module to help you gain the most from this course and this textbook. Whether you are a recent high school graduate or an adult returning to the classroom after a few years, you want RESULTS when you study. You want to be able to

understand the issues and ideas presented in the textbook, talk about them intelligently during class discussions, and remember them as you prepare for exams and papers.

This module is designed to help you develop the skills and habits you'll need to succeed in this course. With tips on how to be more engaged when you study, how to get the most out of your textbook, how to prepare for exams, and how to write papers, this guide will help you become the best learner you can be!

STUDY PREP

What does it take to be a successful student? Although you may think success depends on how naturally smart you are, the truth is that successful students aren't born, they're made. Even if you don't consider yourself "book smart," you can do well in this course by developing study skills that will help you understand, remember, and apply key concepts.

Reading for Learning

Your textbook is the foundation for information in a course. It contains key concepts and terms that are important to your understanding of the subject. For this reason, it is essential that you develop good reading skills. As you read your textbook with the goal of learning as much of the information as possible, work on establishing the following habits:

FOCUS

Make an effort to focus on the book and tune out other distractions so that you can understand and remember the information it presents.

TAKE TIME

To learn the key concepts presented in each chapter, you need to read slowly, carefully, and with great attention.

REPEAT

To read for learning, you have to read your textbook a number of times. Follow a preview-read-review process:

1. **PREVIEW: Look over the chapter title, section headings, and highlighted or bold words. This will give you a good preview of important ideas in the chapter.** Notice that each major section heading in this textbook has one or more corresponding **Learning Objectives.** By turning headings or subheadings in all of your textbooks into questions—and then answering them—you will increase your understanding of the material. Note graphs, pictures, and other visual illustrations of important concepts.

   QUICK TIP! Log in to CJ4 Online with the access code in the front of your textbook to find interactive figures and tables from the chapters, to quiz yourself on the important material in the book!

2. **READ: During this phase, it is important to read with a few questions in mind:** What is the main point of this paragraph or section? What does the author want me to learn from this? How does this relate to what I read before? Keeping these questions in mind will help you be an attentive reader who is actively focusing on the main ideas of the passage.

   QUICK TIP! In CJ4 Online, create StudyBits from Key Terms and definitions, photos, figures, and your text highlights. You can include notes in your StudyBits, and add your own tags—such as "Midterm Exam"—so you can collect them all later.

It is helpful to take notes while reading in detail. You can mark your text or write an outline, as explained next. Taking notes will help you read actively, identify important concepts, and remember them. Then when it comes time to review for the exam, the notes you've made will make your studying more efficient.

QUICK TIP! In CJ4 Online, create practice quizzes from filtered StudyBits or use all quiz questions from the chapter to test yourself before exams.

3. REVIEW: Review each section of the text and the notes you made, asking this question: What was this section about? You'll want to answer the question in some detail, readily identifying the important points. Use the Learning Objectives in the text to help focus your review.

QUICK TIP! Tear out the Chapter Review cards in the back of the textbook for on-the-go review!

A reading group is a great way to review the chapter. After completing the reading individually, group members should meet and take turns sharing what they learned. Explaining the material to others will reinforce and clarify what you already know. Getting a different perspective on a passage will increase your knowledge, since different people will find different things important during a reading.

Diego Cervo/ShutterStock.com

Take Notes

Being *engaged* means listening to discover (and remember) something. One way to make sure that you are listening attentively is to take notes. Doing so will help you focus on the professor's words and will help you identify the most important parts of the lecture.

The physical act of writing makes you a more efficient learner. In addition, your notes provide a guide to what your instructor thinks is important. That means you will have a better idea of what to study before the next exam if you have a set of notes that you took during class.

Make an Outline

As you read through each chapter of your textbook, you might want to make an outline—a simple method for organizing information. You can create an outline as part of your reading or at the end of your reading. Or you can make an outline when you reread a section before moving on to the next one. The act of physically writing an outline for a chapter will help you retain the material in this text and master it.

To make an effective outline, you have to be selective. Your objectives in outlining are, first, to identify the main concepts and, then, to add the details that support those main concepts.

Your outline should consist of several levels written in a standard format. The most important concepts are assigned Roman numerals; the second most important, capital letters; and the third most important, numbers. Here is a quick example:

I. What Is the Criminal Justice System?
   A. The Purpose of the Criminal Justice System
      1. Controlling and Preventing Crime
      2. Maintaining Justice
   B. The Structure of the Criminal Justice System
      1. Law Enforcement
      2. The Courts
      3. Corrections
   C. The Criminal Justice Process
      1. The Assembly Line
      2. The Formal Criminal Justice Process
      3. The Informal Criminal Justice Process

Mark Your Text

If you own your own textbook for this course, you can greatly improve your learning by marking your text. By doing so, you will identify the most important concepts of each chapter, and at the same time, you'll be making a handy study guide for reviewing material at a later time. Marking allows you to become an active participant in the mastery of the material. Researchers have shown that the physical act of marking, just like the physical acts of note-taking during class and outlining, increases concentration and helps you better retain the material.

WAYS OF MARKING

The most common form of marking is to underline important points. The second most commonly used method is to use a felt-tipped highlighter, or marker, in yellow or some other transparent color. Put a check mark next to material that you do not understand. Work on better comprehension of the checkmarked material after you've finished the chapter. Marking also includes circling, numbering, using arrows, jotting brief notes, or any other method that allows you to remember things when you go back to skim the pages in your textbook prior to an exam.

QUICK TIP! Reminder!! Don't forget about the StudyBit functionality when highlighting in CJ4 Online! Change colors of your highlights to rate your understanding of each StudyBit, and use them in your review in the Studyboard.

TWO POINTS TO REMEMBER WHEN MARKING

▶ **Read one section at a time before you do any extensive marking.** You can't mark a section until you know what is important, and you can't know what is important until you read the whole section.

▶ **Don't overmark.** Don't fool yourself into thinking that you have done a good job just because each page is filled up with arrows, circles, and underlines. The key to marking is selective activity. Mark each page in a way that allows you to see the most important points at a glance. You can follow up your marking by writing out more in your subject outline.

Try These Tips

Here are a few more hints that will help you develop effective study skills.

▶ **Do schoolwork as soon as possible after class.** The longer you wait, the more likely you will be distracted by television, video games, texts from friends, or social networking.

> Researchers have shown that the physical act of marking, just like the physical acts of note-taking during class and outlining, increases concentration and helps you better retain the material.

▶ **Set aside time and a quiet, comfortable space where you can focus on reading.** Your school library is often the best place to work. Set aside several hours a week of "library time" to study in peace and quiet. A neat, organized study space is also important. The only work items that should be on your desk are those that you are working on that day.

▶ **Reward yourself for studying!** Rest your eyes and your mind by taking a short break every twenty to thirty minutes. From time to time, allow yourself a break for doing something else that you enjoy. These interludes will refresh your mind, give you more energy required for concentration, and enable you to study longer and more efficiently.

▶ **To memorize terms or facts, create flash (or note) cards.** On one side of the card, write the question or term. On the other side, write the answer or definition. Then, use the cards to test yourself or have a friend quiz you on the material.

QUICK TIP! In CJ4 Online, flash cards are already ready for all key terms (with definitions). Create more flash cards from your StudyBits or anything in the online narrative, and rate your understanding on each while you study!

▶ **Mnemonic (pronounced ne-mon-ik) devices are tricks that increase our ability to memorize.** A well-known mnemonic device is the phrase ROY G BIV, which helps people remember the colors of the rainbow—Red, Orange, Yellow, Green, Blue, Indigo, Violet. You can create your own for whatever you need to memorize. The more fun you have coming up with mnemonics for yourself, the more useful they will be.

▶ **Take notes twice.** First, take notes in class. Writing down your instructor's key points will help you be a more active, engaged listener. Taking notes will also give you a record of what your instructor thinks is important. Later, when you have a chance, rewrite your notes. The rewrite will act as a study session by forcing you to think about the material again.

TEST PREP

You have worked hard throughout the term, reading the book, paying close attention in class, and taking good notes. Now it's test time, and you want to show mastery of the material you have studied. To be well prepared, you should know which reading materials and lectures will be covered. You should also know whether the exam will contain essays, objective questions, or both. Finally, you should know how much time will be allowed. By taking these steps, you will reduce any anxiety you feel, and you can approach the test with confidence.

Follow Directions

Students are often in a hurry to start an exam, so they take little time to read the instructions. The instructions can be critical, however. In a multiple-choice exam, for example, if there is no indication that there is a penalty for guessing, then you should never leave a question unanswered. Even if only a few minutes are left at the end of an exam, you should guess on the questions that you remain uncertain about.

Additionally, you need to know the weight given to each section of an exam. In a typical multiple-choice exam, all questions have equal weight. In other types of exams, particularly those with essay questions, different parts of the exam carry different weights. You should use these weights to apportion your time. If the essay portion of an exam accounts for 20 percent of the total points on the exam, you should not spend 60 percent of your time on the essays.

Finally, you need to make sure you are marking the answers correctly. Some exams require a No. 2 pencil to fill in the dots on a machine-graded answer sheet. Other exams require underlining or circling. In short, you have to read and follow the instructions carefully.

Objective Exams

An objective exam consists of multiple-choice, true/false, fill-in-the-blank, or matching questions that have only one correct answer. Students usually commit one of two errors when they read objective exam questions: (1) they read things into the questions that do not exist, or (2) they skip over words or phrases. Most test questions include key words such as:

> >ALL   >NEVER
> >ALWAYS   >ONLY

If you miss any of these key words, you may answer the question wrong even if you know the information.

Whenever the answer to an objective question is not obvious, start with the process of elimination. Throw out the answers that are clearly incorrect. Typically, the easiest way to eliminate incorrect answers is to look for those that are meaningless, illogical, or inconsistent. Often, test authors put in choices that make perfect sense and are indeed true, but they are not the answer to the question under study.

Here are a few more tips that will help you become an efficient, results-oriented student.

▸ **Review your notes thoroughly** as part of your exam preparation. Instructors usually lecture on subjects they think are important, so those same subjects are also likely to be on the exam.

- **Create a study schedule** to reduce stress and give yourself the best chance for success. At times, you will find yourself studying for several exams at once. When this happens, make a list of each study topic and the amount of time needed to review that topic.

- **Form a small group for a study session.** Discussing a topic out loud can improve your understanding of that topic and will help you remember the key points that often come up on exams.

- **Study from old exams.** Some professors make old exams available, either by posting them online or by putting them on file in the library. Old tests can give you an idea of the kinds of questions the professor likes to ask.

- **Avoid cramming just before an exam.** Cramming tires the brain unnecessarily and adds to stress, which can severely hamper your testing performance. If you've studied wisely, have confidence that you will be able to recall the information when you need it.

- **Be sure to eat** before taking a test so you will have the energy you need to concentrate.

- **Be prepared.** Make sure you have everything you will need for the exam, such as a pen or pencil. Arrive at the exam early to avoid having to rush, which will only add to your stress. Good preparation helps you focus on the task at hand.

- **When you first receive your exam, make sure that you have all the pages.** If you are uncertain, ask your professor or exam proctor. This initial scan may uncover other problems as well, such as illegible print or unclear instructions.

- **With essay questions, look for key words** such as "compare," "contrast," and "explain." These will guide your answer. Most important, get to the point without wasting your time (or your professor's) with statements such as "There are many possible reasons for . . . ."

- **Review your answers** when you finish a test early. You may find a mistake or an area where some extra writing will improve your grade.

- **Keep exams in perspective.** Worrying too much about a single exam can have a negative effect on your performance. If you do poorly on one test, it's not the end of the world. Rather, it should motivate you to do better on the next one.

WRITE PREP

A key part of succeeding as a student is learning how to write well. Whether writing papers, presentations, essays, or even e-mails to your instructor, you have to be able to put your thoughts into words and do so with force, clarity, and precision. In this section, we outline a three-phase process that you can use to write almost anything.

Phase 1: Getting Ready to Write

First, make a list. Divide the ultimate goal—a finished paper—into smaller steps that you can tackle right away. Estimate how long it will take to complete each step. Start with the date your paper is due and work backward to the present: For example, if the due date is December 1, and you have about three months to write the paper, give yourself a cushion and schedule November 20 as your targeted completion date. Then, list what you need to get done by October 1 and November 1.

PICK A TOPIC

To generate ideas for a topic, any of the following approaches work well:

- **Brainstorm with a group.** There is no need to create in isolation. You can harness the energy and the natural creative power of a group to assist you.

- **Speak it.** To get ideas flowing, start talking. Admit your confusion or lack of clear ideas. Then just speak. By putting your thoughts into words, you'll start thinking more clearly.

- **Use free writing.** Free writing, a technique championed by writing teacher Peter Elbow, is also very effective when trying to come up with a topic. There's only one rule in free writing: Write without stopping. Set a time limit—say, ten minutes— and keep your fingers dancing across the keyboard the whole time. Ignore the urge to stop and rewrite. There is no need to worry about spelling, punctuation, or grammar during this process.

> There is no need to create in isolation. Brainstorm ideas for a topic with a group. Ask for feedback from your instructor or a friend as you prepare an outline and revise your first draft.

REFINE YOUR IDEA

After you've come up with some initial ideas, it's time to refine them:

- **Select a topic and working title.** Using your instructor's guidelines for the paper, write down a list of topics that interest you. Write down all of the ideas you think of in two minutes. Then choose one topic. The most common pitfall is selecting a topic that is too broad. "Terrorism" is probably not a useful topic for your paper. Instead, consider "The Financing of Terrorist Activities."

- **Write a thesis statement.** Clarify what you want to say by summarizing it in one concise sentence. This sentence, called a *thesis statement,* refines your working title. A thesis is the main point of the paper—it is a declaration of some sort. You might write a thesis statement such as "Drug trafficking and other criminal activities are often used to finance terrorism."

SET GOALS

Effective writing flows from a purpose. Think about how you'd like your reader or listener to respond after considering your ideas.

- If you want to persuade someone, make your writing clear and logical. Support your assertions with evidence.

- If your purpose is to move the reader into action, explain exactly what steps to take, and offer solid benefits for doing so.

To clarify your purpose, state it in one sentence—for example, "The purpose of this paper is to discuss and analyze the role of women and minorities in law enforcement."

BEGIN RESEARCH

At the initial stage, the objective of your research is not to uncover specific facts about your topic. That comes later. First, you want to gain an overview of the subject. Say you want to advocate for indeterminate sentencing. You must first learn enough about determinate and indeterminate sentencing to describe the pros and cons of each one.

MAKE AN OUTLINE

An outline is a kind of map. When you follow a map, you avoid getting lost. Likewise, an outline keeps you from wandering off topic. To create your outline, follow these steps:

1. **REVIEW YOUR THESIS STATEMENT** and identify the three to five main points you need to address in your paper to support or prove your thesis.

2. **NEXT, FOCUS ON THE THREE TO FIVE MAJOR POINTS** that support your argument and think about what minor points or subtopics you want to cover in your paper. Your major points are your big ideas. Your minor points are the details you need to fill in under each of those ideas.

3. **ASK FOR FEEDBACK.** Have your instructor or a classmate review your outline and offer suggestions for improvement. Did you choose the right points to support your thesis? Do you need more detail anywhere? Does the flow from idea to idea make sense?

DO IN-DEPTH RESEARCH

Dig in and start reading. Keep a notebook, tablet, or laptop handy and make notes as you read. It can help to organize your research into three main categories:

1. **SOURCES** (bibliographical information for a source),

2. **INFORMATION** (nuggets of information from a correctly quoted source), and

3. **IDEAS** (thoughts and observations that occur to you as you research, written in your own words).

You might want to use these categories to create three separate documents as you work. This will make it easy to find what you need when you write your first draft.

When taking research notes, be sure to:

▶ Copy all of the information correctly.

▶ Always include the source and page number while gathering information. With Internet searches, you must also record the date a site was accessed.

▶ Stay organized; refer to your outline as you work.

Jacob Lund/ShutterStock.com

Phase 2: Writing a First Draft

To create your draft, gather your notes and your outline (which often undergoes revision during the research process). Then write about the ideas in your notes. It's that simple. Just start writing. Write in paragraphs, with one idea per paragraph. As you complete this task, keep the following suggestions in mind:

▶ **Remember that the first draft is not for keeps.** You can worry about quality later. Your goal at this point is simply to generate words and ideas.

▶ **Write freely.** Many writers prefer to get their first draft down quickly and would advise you to keep writing, much as in free writing. You may pause to glance at your notes and outline, but avoid stopping to edit your work.

▶ **Be yourself.** Let go of the urge to sound "scholarly" and avoid using unnecessary big words or phrases. Instead, write in a natural voice.

▶ **Avoid procrastination.** If you are having trouble getting started, skip over your introduction and just begin writing about some of your findings. You can go back later and organize your paragraphs.

▶ **Get physical.** While working on the first draft, take breaks. Go for a walk. From time to time, practice relaxation techniques and breathe deeply.

▶ **Put the draft away for a day.** Schedule time for rewrites, and schedule at least one day between revisions so that you can let the material sit. After a break, problems with the paper or ideas for improvement will become more evident.

Phase 3: Revising Your Draft

During this phase, keep in mind the saying, "Write in haste; revise at leisure." When you are working on your first draft, the goal is to produce ideas and write them down. During the revision phase, however, you need to slow down and take a close look at your work. One guideline is to allow 50 percent of writing time for planning, researching, and writing the first draft. Then use the remaining 50 percent for revising.

Here are some good ways to revise your paper:

1. **READ IT OUT LOUD.** The combination of voice and ears forces us to pay attention to the details. Is the thesis statement clear and supported by enough evidence? Does the introduction tell your reader what's coming? Do you end with a strong conclusion that expands on your introduction rather than just restating it?

2. **HAVE A FRIEND LOOK OVER YOUR PAPER.** This is never a substitute for your own review, but a friend can often see mistakes you miss. With a little practice, you will learn to welcome feedback because it provides one of the fastest ways to approach the revision process.

3. **CUT.** Look for excess baggage. Also, look for places where two (or more) sentences could be rewritten as one. By cutting text you are actually gaining a clearer, more polished product. For maximum efficiency, make the larger cuts first—sections, chapters, pages. Then go for the smaller cuts—paragraphs, sentences, phrases, words.

4. **PASTE.** The next task is to rearrange what's left of your paper so that it flows logically. Look for consistency within paragraphs and for transitions from paragraph to paragraph and section to section.

5. **FIX.** Now it's time to look at individual words and phrases. Define any terms that the reader might not know. In general, focus on nouns and verbs. Too many adjectives and adverbs weaken your message and add unnecessary bulk to your writing. Write about the details, and be specific. Also, check your writing to ensure that you:

   ▶ **Use the active voice.** Write *"The research team began the project"* rather than (passively) *"A project was initiated."*

   ▶ **Write concisely.** Instead of *"After making a timely arrival and observing the unfolding events, I emerged totally and gloriously victorious,"* be concise with *"I came, I saw, I conquered."*

   ▶ **Communicate clearly.** Instead of *"The speaker made effective use of the television medium, asking in no uncertain terms that we change our belief systems,"* you can write specifically, *"The reformed criminal stared straight into the television camera and said, 'Take a good look at what you are doing! Will it get you what you really want?'"*

wavebreakmedia/ShutterStock.com

6. **PREPARE.** Format your paper following accepted standards for margin widths, endnotes, title pages, and other details. Ask your instructor for specific instructions on how to cite the sources used in writing your paper. You can find useful guidelines in the *MLA Handbook for Writers of Research Papers.* If you are submitting a hard copy (rather than turning it in online), use quality paper for the final version. For an even more professional appearance, bind your paper with a plastic or paper cover.

7. **PROOFREAD.** As you ease down the home stretch, read your revised paper one more time, and look for the following:

   ▶ A clear thesis statement.

   ▶ Sentences that introduce your topic, guide the reader through the major sections of your paper, and summarize your conclusions.

   ▶ Details—such as quotations, examples, and statistics—that support your conclusions.

   ▶ Lean sentences that have been purged of needless words.

   ▶ Plenty of action verbs and concrete, specific nouns.

   ▶ Spelling and grammar mistakes. Use contractions sparingly, if at all. Use spell-check by all means, but do not rely on it completely, as it will not catch everything.

Academic Integrity: Avoiding Plagiarism

Using another person's words, images, or other original creations without giving proper credit is called *plagiarism*. Plagiarism amounts to taking someone else's work and presenting it as your own—the equivalent of cheating on a test. The consequences of plagiarism can range from a failing grade to expulsion from school.

To avoid plagiarism, ask an instructor where you can find your school's written policy on this issue. Don't assume that you can resubmit a paper you wrote for another class for a current class. Many schools will regard this as plagiarism even though you wrote the paper. The basic guidelines for preventing plagiarism are to cite a source for each phrase, sequence of ideas, or visual image created by another person. While ideas cannot be copyrighted, the specific way that an idea is *expressed* can be. You also need to list a source for any idea that is closely identified with a particular person. The goal is to clearly distinguish your own work from the work of others. There are several ways to ensure that you do this consistently:

▶ **Identify direct quotes.** If you use a direct quote from another source, put those words in quotation marks. If you do research online, you might copy text from a Web page and paste it directly into your notes. This is the same as taking direct quotes from your source. Always identify such passages in an obvious way.

▶ **Paraphrase carefully.** Paraphrasing means restating the original passage in your own words, usually making it shorter and simpler. Students who copy a passage word for word and then just rearrange or delete a few phrases are running a serious risk of plagiarism. Remember to cite a source for paraphrases, just as you do for direct quotes. When you use the same sequence of ideas as one of your sources—even if you have not paraphrased or directly quoted—cite that source.

▶ **Note details about each source.** For books, include the author, title, publisher, publication date, location of publisher, and page number. For articles from print sources, record the author, date, article title, and the name of the magazine or journal as well. If you found the article in an academic or technical journal, also include the volume and number of the publication. A librarian can help identify these details.

▶ **Most professors don't regard Wikipedia as a legitimate source.** If your source is a Web page, record as many identifying details as you can find—author, title, sponsoring organization, URL, publication date, and revision date. In addition, list the date that you accessed the page. Be careful when using Web resources, as not all Web sites are considered legitimate sources.

▶ **Cite your sources as endnotes or footnotes to your paper.** Ask your instructor for examples of the format to use. You do not need to credit wording that is wholly your own. Nor do you need to credit general ideas, such as the suggestion that people use a to-do list to plan their time. But if you borrow someone else's words or images to explain the idea, do give credit.

▶ **When in doubt, don't.** Sometimes you will find yourself working against a deadline for a paper, and in a panic, you might be tempted to take "shortcuts." You'll find a source that expressed your idea perfectly, but you must cite it or completely rephrase the idea in your own words. Professors are experts at noticing a change in tone or vocabulary that signals plagiarism. Often, they can simply Google a phrase to find its source online. Do not let a moment's temptation cause you to fail the course or face an academic integrity hearing.

Dragon Images/ShutterStock.com

DEDICATION

This book is dedicated to my good friend and colleague, Lawrence Walsh, of the Lexington, Kentucky Police Department. When I was a rookie, he taught me about policing. When I became a researcher, he taught me about the practical applications of knowledge. He is truly an inspiring professional in our field.

L.K.G.

To Charley French,

You continue to
inspire me.

R.L.M.

1 Criminal Justice Today

LEARNING OBJECTIVES

After studying this chapter, you will be able to . . .

1-1 Define crime, and identify the different types of crime.

1-2 Outline the three levels of law enforcement.

1-3 List the essential elements of the corrections system.

1-4 Define ethics, and describe the role that it plays in discretionary decision making.

1-5 Contrast the crime control and due process models.

After you finish this chapter, go to PAGES 19–20 for STUDY TOOLS

Deadly Force in Ferguson

The way Dorian Johnson tells it, he and his friend Michael Brown were walking down the middle of a street in Ferguson, Missouri, on the afternoon of August 14, 2014, when white police officer Darren Wilson pulled up beside them. From inside his police vehicle, according to Johnson, Wilson ordered the pair to "get the 'F' on the sidewalk." Then, unprovoked, Wilson grabbed Brown around the neck and shot the eighteen-year-old African American. After a brief attempt to escape, Brown stopped, raised his hands, and faced the police officer, who by now was also on foot. Wilson proceeded to shoot Brown several times in the chest, killing him, in Johnson's words, "like an animal."

Appearing before a grand jury, Wilson gave a markedly different version of the events that led to Brown's death. The police officer testified that he stopped Brown and Johnson because they fit the description of two suspects who had just stolen cigarillos from a nearby convenience store. In Wilson's telling, an altercation followed during which Brown punched him numerous times in the face and tried to grab his service weapon. Brown then fled the scene, with Wilson in pursuit on foot. After a short chase, Brown turned and charged Wilson, who felt he had no choice but to shoot the other man in self-defense.

On November 24, 2014, a grand jury determined that Wilson would not face criminal charges for killing Brown. Although the jurors heard testimony from dozens of eyewitnesses and had access to physical evidence supporting Wilson's account of the incident, the decision sparked demonstrations—some violent—nationwide. "The system failed us again," said one protester expressing the outrage felt by many African Americans over what they perceive as a pattern of unchecked police brutality against young black men. Countering allegations of racial bias in the Wilson case, one criminal justice expert said, "It's really pretty straightforward—a police officer can use deadly force when it's necessary to prevent bodily injury or death."

On November 25, 2014, New York City police control protesters following a Missouri grand jury's decision not to charge Ferguson police officer Darren Wilson in the shooting death of Michael Brown. *If Officer Wilson's version of the incident is correct, do you feel that he was justified in shooting Brown? Why or why not? What additional information might you need to make your decision?* a katz/ShutterStock.com

1-1 WHAT IS CRIME?

Many observers—and not just those who took to the streets—were shocked that Darren Wilson was able to escape criminal punishment for his role in the death of Michael Brown. In fact, though, American law enforcement agents commit about four hundred "justifiable homicides" each year.[1] To determine whether Wilson's killing of Brown was justified, and therefore not a potential crime, the grand jury relied on Missouri's "use of force" law. This law states that a law enforcement agent may use "deadly force" against a suspect if the suspect is resisting a lawful arrest or "may otherwise endanger life or inflict serious physical injury unless arrested without delay."[2]

Because Brown's actions could reasonably be seen as posing a threat of injury to Wilson, the police officer's response was, according to Professor David Klinger of the University of Missouri at St. Louis, "awful but lawful."[3] As this dramatic example shows, a *crime* is not simply an act that seems dishonest or dangerous or taboo, even if that act involves the death of a human being. A **crime** is a wrong against society that is *proclaimed by law* and that, if committed under specific circumstances, is punishable by the criminal justice system.

One problem with the definition of crime just provided is that it obscures the complex nature of societies. A society is not static—it evolves and changes, and its concept of criminality evolves and changes as well. Furthermore, different communities can have different

Crime An act that violates criminal law and is punishable by criminal sanctions.

ideas of what constitutes a crime. Missouri's "use of force" statute is particularly favorable for law enforcement agents. If the scenario described in the opening of this chapter had taken place in a different state, Darren Wilson might have been charged with criminal wrongdoing.

International examples can be even more striking. In 2014, six Iranians (three men and three women) were arrested for posting a YouTube video of themselves dancing to Pharrell Williams's hit song "Happy" on a Tehran rooftop. They were charged with making a "vulgar" video that "hurt public chastity." It is highly unlikely that American courts, bound by American traditions of freedom of speech and expression, would allow any police action in such circumstances. To more fully understand the concept of crime, it will help to examine the two most common models of how society "decides" which acts are criminal: the consensus model and the conflict model.

Consensus Model A criminal justice model in which the majority of citizens in a society share the same values and beliefs. Criminal acts are acts that conflict with these values and beliefs and that are deemed harmful to society.

Morals Principles of right and wrong behavior, as practiced by individuals or by society.

1-1a The Consensus Model

The term *consensus* refers to general agreement among the majority of any particular group. Thus, the **consensus model** rests on the assumption that as people gather together to form a society, its members will naturally come to a basic agreement with regard to shared norms and values. Those individuals whose actions deviate from the established norms and values are considered to pose a threat to the well-being of society as a whole and must be sanctioned (punished). The society passes laws to control and prevent unacceptable behavior, thereby setting the boundaries for acceptable behavior within the group.[4]

The consensus model, to a certain extent, assumes that a diverse group of people can have similar **morals.** In other words, they share an ideal of what is "right" and "wrong." Consequently, as public attitudes toward morality change, so do laws. In seventeenth-century America, a person found guilty of *adultery* (having sexual relations with someone other than one's spouse) could expect to be publicly whipped, branded, or even executed. Furthermore, a century ago, one could walk into a pharmacy and purchase heroin. Today, social attitudes have shifted to consider adultery a personal issue, beyond the reach of the state, and to consider the sale of heroin a criminal act.

1-1b The Conflict Model

Some people reject the consensus model on the ground that moral attitudes are not constant or even consistent. In large, democratic societies such as the United States, different groups of citizens have widely varying opinions on controversial issues of morality and criminality such as abortion, the war on drugs, immigration, and assisted suicide. These groups and their elected representatives are constantly coming into conflict with one another. According to the **conflict model,** then, the most politically powerful segments of society—based on class, income, age, and race—have the most influence on criminal laws and are therefore able to impose their values on the rest of the community.

Consequently, what is deemed criminal activity is determined by whichever group happens to be holding power at any given time. Because certain groups do not have access to political power, their interests are not served by the criminal justice system. In the wake of Darren Wilson's fatal shooting of Michael Brown, discussed earlier, many observers saw the grand jury's decision as further evidence of a national power structure that systematically protects police officers who kill young black men. In one poll conducted after Brown's death, 57 percent of African Americans said that Wilson's actions were unjustified, compared with 18 percent of the survey's white respondents.[5]

1-1c An Integrated Definition of Crime

LO1-1   Considering both the consensus and conflict models, we can construct a definition of crime that will be useful throughout this textbook. For our purposes, crime is an action or activity that is:

1. Punishable under criminal law, as determined by the majority or, in some instances, by a powerful minority.

2. Considered an *offense against society as a whole* and prosecuted by public officials, not by victims and their relatives or friends.

3. Punishable by sanctions based on laws that bring about the loss of personal freedom or life.

At this point, it is important to understand the difference between crime and **deviance,** or behavior that does not conform to the norms of a given community or society. Deviance is a subjective concept. For example, some segments of society may think that smoking marijuana or killing animals for clothing and food is deviant behavior. Deviant acts become crimes only when society

E-cigarettes, such as the one shown in this photo, deliver the drug nicotine to users without some of the tobacco-related health risks of traditional cigarettes. Nicotine is, however, highly addictive. *Why might e-cigarette use be considered deviant behavior by minors, but not by adults?*

Tibanna79/ShutterStock.com

as a whole, through its legislatures, determines that those acts should be punished—as is the situation today in the United States with using certain drugs but not with eating meat. Furthermore, not all crimes are considered particularly deviant—little social disapproval is attached to those who fail to follow the letter of parking laws. In essence, criminal law reflects those acts that we, as a society, agree are so unacceptable that steps must be taken to prevent them from occurring.

1-1d Types of Crime

The manner in which crimes are classified depends on their seriousness. Federal, state, and local legislation has provided for the classification and punishment of hundreds of thousands of different criminal acts, ranging from jaywalking to first degree murder. For general purposes, we can group criminal behavior into six categories: violent crime, property crime, public order crime, white-collar crime, organized crime, and high-tech crime.

VIOLENT CRIME Crimes against persons, or *violent crimes,* have come to dominate our perspectives on

Conflict Model A criminal justice model in which the content of criminal law is determined by the groups that hold economic, political, and social power in a community.

Deviance Behavior that is considered to go against the norms established by society.

CAREER TIP Universities and community colleges, hospitals, mental health clinics, and social service agencies often hire *rape crisis counselors* to help victims of sexual assault cope with the physical, emotional, and legal consequences of sexual violence.

Murder The unlawful killing of one human being by another.

Sexual Assault Forced or coerced sexual intercourse (or other sexual acts).

Assault A threat or an attempt to do violence to another person that causes that person to fear immediate physical harm.

Battery The act of physically contacting another person with the intent to do harm, even if the resulting injury is insubstantial.

Robbery The act of taking property from another person through force, threat of force, or intimidation.

Larceny The act of taking property from another person without the use of force with the intent of keeping that property.

Burglary The act of breaking into or entering a structure (such as a home or office) without permission for the purpose of committing a felony.

Public Order Crime Behavior that has been labeled criminal because it is contrary to shared social values, customs, and norms.

crime. There are four major categories of violent crime:

▶ **Murder,** or the unlawful killing of a human being.

▶ **Sexual assault,** or *rape*, which refers to coerced actions of a sexual nature against an unwilling participant.

▶ **Assault** and **battery,** two separate acts that cover situations in which one person physically attacks another (battery) or, through threats, intentionally leads another to believe that he or she will be physically harmed (assault).

▶ **Robbery,** or the taking of funds, personal property, or any other article of value from a person by means of force or fear.

As you will see in Chapter 3, these violent crimes are further classified by *degree*, depending on the circumstances surrounding the criminal act. These circumstances include the intent of the person committing the crime, whether a weapon was used, and (in cases other than murder) the level of pain and suffering experienced by the victim.

PROPERTY CRIME The most common form of criminal activity is *property crime*, or those crimes in which the goal of the offender is some form of economic gain or the damaging of property. There are three major forms of property crime:

1. Pocket picking, shoplifting, and the stealing of any property without the use of force are covered by laws against **larceny,** also known as theft.

2. **Burglary** refers to the unlawful entry of a structure with the intention of committing a serious crime such as theft.

3. *Motor vehicle theft* describes the theft or attempted theft of a motor vehicle. Motor vehicles include any vehicle commonly used for transportation, such as a motorcycle or motor scooter, but not farm equipment or water craft.

Arson is also a property crime. It involves the willful and malicious burning of a home, automobile, commercial building, or any other construction.

PUBLIC ORDER CRIME The concept of **public order crimes** is linked to the consensus model discussed earlier. Historically, societies have always outlawed activities that are considered contrary to public values and morals. Today, the most common public order crimes include public drunkenness, prostitution, gambling, and illicit drug use. These crimes are sometimes referred to as *victimless crimes* because they often harm only the offender. As you will see throughout this textbook, however, that term is rather misleading. Public order crimes may create an environment that gives rise to property and violent crimes.

WHITE-COLLAR CRIME Business-related crimes are popularly referred to as **white-collar crimes.** The term *white-collar crime* is broadly used to describe an illegal act or series of acts committed by an individual or business entity using some nonviolent means to obtain a personal or business advantage. As you will see in Chapter 14, when we consider the topic in much greater detail, certain property crimes fall into this category when committed in a business context. Although the extent of this criminal activity is difficult to determine with any certainty, the Association of Certified Fraud Examiners estimates that white-collar crime costs businesses worldwide as much as $3.7 trillion a year.[6]

ORGANIZED CRIME White-collar crime involves the use of legal business facilities and employees to commit illegal acts. For example, a teller can't steal funds from, or *embezzle* from, a bank unless he or she is first hired as a legal employee of the bank. In contrast, **organized crime** describes illegal acts by illegal organizations, usually geared toward satisfying the public's demand for unlawful goods and services. Organized crime broadly implies a conspiratorial and illegal relationship among any number of persons engaged in unlawful acts. More specifically, groups engaged in organized crime employ criminal tactics such as violence, corruption, and intimidation for economic gain.

The hierarchical structure of organized crime operations often mirrors that of legitimate businesses, and, like any corporation, these groups attempt to capture a sufficient percentage of any given market to make a profit. For organized crime, the traditional preferred markets are gambling, prostitution, illegal narcotics, and loan sharking (lending funds at higher-than-legal interest rates), along with more recent ventures into counterfeiting and credit-card scams.

HIGH-TECH CRIME The newest variation on crime is directly related to the increased presence of computers in everyday life. The Internet, with approximately 2.9 billion users worldwide, is the site of numerous *cyber crimes,* such as selling pornographic materials, soliciting minors, and defrauding consumers through bogus financial investments. The dependence of businesses on computer operations has left corporations vulnerable to

sabotage, fraud, embezzlement, and the theft of proprietary data. We will cover this particular criminal activity in much greater detail in Chapter 14.

1-2 WHAT IS THE PURPOSE OF CRIMINAL JUSTICE?

Defining which actions are to be labeled "crimes" is only the first step in safeguarding society from criminal behavior. Institutions must be created to apprehend alleged wrongdoers, to determine whether these persons have indeed committed crimes, and to punish those who are found guilty according to society's wishes. These institutions combine to form the **criminal justice system.** As we begin our examination of the American criminal justice system in this introductory chapter, it is important to have an idea of its purpose.

1-2a Maintaining Justice

As its name implies, the explicit goal of the criminal justice system is to provide *justice* to all members of society. Because **justice** is a difficult concept to define, this goal can be challenging, if not impossible, to meet. Broadly stated, justice means that all individuals are equal before the law and that they are free from arbitrary arrest or seizure as defined by the law. In other words, the idea of justice is linked with the idea of fairness. Above all, we want our laws and the means by which they are carried out to be fair.

Justice and fairness are subjective terms, which is to say that people may have different concepts of what is just and fair. If a woman who has been beaten by her husband retaliates by killing him, what is her just punishment? Reasonable persons could disagree. Some might think that the homicide was justified and that she should be treated leniently. Others might

White-Collar Crime Nonviolent crimes committed by business entities or individuals to gain a personal or business advantage.

Organized Crime Illegal acts carried out by illegal organizations engaged in the market for illegal goods or services, such as illicit drugs or firearms.

Criminal Justice System The interlocking network of law enforcement agencies, courts, and corrections institutions designed to enforce criminal laws and protect society from criminal behavior.

Justice The quality of fairness that must exist in the processes designed to determine whether individuals are guilty of criminal wrongdoing.

insist that she should not have taken the law into her own hands. Police officers, judges, prosecutors, prison administrators, and other employees of the criminal justice system must decide what is "fair." Sometimes, their course of action is obvious, but often, as we shall see, it is not.

1-2b Protecting Society

Within the broad mandate of "maintaining justice," Megan Kurlychek of the University at Albany, New York, has identified four specific goals of our criminal justice system:

1. To protect society from potential future crimes of the most dangerous or "risky" offenders.

2. To determine when an offense has been committed and provide the appropriate punishment for that offense.

3. To rehabilitate those offenders who have been punished so that it is safe to return them to the community.

4. To support crime victims and, to the extent possible, return them to their pre-crime status.[7]

Featureflash/ShutterStock.com

Defending the use of the Internet to post violent threats against his wife in the form of rap lyrics, Anthony Elonis compared himself to hip-hop artists such as Eminem, pictured here. *Do you agree with Elonis's argument? Under what circumstances, if any, should placing violent threats against a specific person online be a crime? Explain your answers.*

Again, though these goals may seem straightforward, they are fraught with difficulty. Take the example of Anthony Elonis, from eastern Pennsylvania, who became distraught after he lost his job and his wife left him. Elonis took his frustration onto Facebook, where he wrote rap lyrics promising the "most heinous school shooting ever imagined" and telling his wife, "I'm not going to rest until your body is a mess, soaked in blood and dying from all the little cuts."[8]

Elonis was convicted of using interstate communications to threaten harm and sentenced to forty-four months behind bars. Using a process we will discuss in Chapter 8, Elonis appealed his conviction, claiming that his words were merely an expression of grief and depression, and that he never intended to harm anyone. Elonis compared himself to well-known rap artists such as Eminem who routinely use violent imagery in their lyrics.

In 2014, Elonis's appeal reached the United States Supreme Court, which had to answer several crucial questions regarding the case. When is the act of making threats using the Internet a crime? How much freedom should individuals such as Elonis have to express themselves in cyberspace? How should we protect potential victims such as Elonis's wife, for whom such online threats can be psychologically damaging? As will be shown repeatedly throughout this textbook, cases and questions without easy answers reveal a great deal about the workings of the American criminal justice system.

1-3 # HOW DOES THE CRIMINAL JUSTICE SYSTEM WORK?

To understand the structure of the criminal justice system, you must understand the concept of **federalism,** which means that government powers are shared by the national (federal) government and the states. The framers of the U.S. Constitution, fearful of tyranny and a too-powerful central government, chose the system of federalism as a compromise.

The appeal of federalism was that it established a strong national government capable of handling large-scale problems while allowing for state powers and local traditions. For example, physician-assisted suicide, though banned in most of the country, is legal in Oregon. It is also legal in Montana, New Mexico, Vermont, and Washington. About a decade ago, the federal government challenged the decision made by voters in Oregon and Washington to allow the practice. The United States Supreme Court sided with the states, ruling that the principle of federalism supported their freedom to differ from the majority viewpoint in this instance.[9]

The Constitution gave the national government certain express powers, such as the power to coin money, raise an army, and regulate interstate commerce. All other powers were left to the states, including police power, which allows the states to enact whatever laws are necessary to protect the health, morals, safety, and welfare of their citizens. As the American criminal justice system has evolved, the ideals of federalism have ebbed somewhat. Specifically, the powers of the national government have expanded significantly. In the early 1900s, only about one hundred specific activities were illegal under federal criminal law. Today, there are more than 4,500 federal criminal statutes, meaning that Americans are increasingly likely to come in contact with the federal criminal justice system.[10]

1-3a Law Enforcement

The ideals of federalism can be clearly seen in the local, state, and federal levels of law

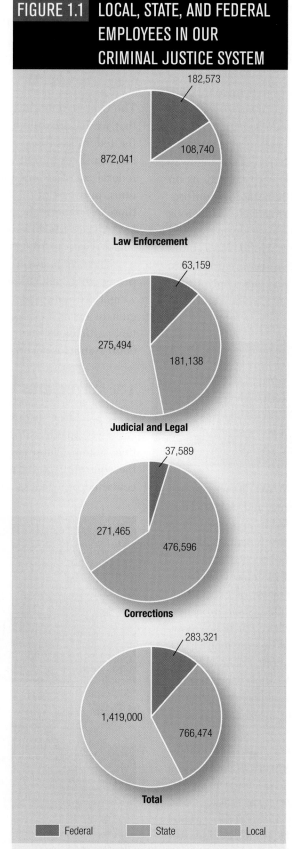

FIGURE 1.1 LOCAL, STATE, AND FEDERAL EMPLOYEES IN OUR CRIMINAL JUSTICE SYSTEM

Law Enforcement
182,573
108,740
872,041

Judicial and Legal
63,159
275,494
181,138

Corrections
37,589
271,465
476,596

Total
283,321
1,419,000
766,474

■ Federal ■ State ■ Local

Source: Bureau of Justice Statistics, *Justice Expenditure and Employment in the United States, 2010* (Washington, D.C.: U.S. Department of Justice, July 2013), Table 2.

enforcement. Though agencies from the different levels cooperate if the need arises, they have their own organizational structures and tend to operate independently of one another. We briefly introduce each level of law enforcement here and cover them in more detail in Chapters 4, 5, and 6.

LOCAL LAW ENFORCEMENT

On the local level, the duties of law enforcement agencies are **LO1-2** split between counties and municipalities. The chief law enforcement officer of most counties is the county sheriff. The sheriff is usually an elected post, with a two- or four-year term. In some areas, where city and county governments have merged, there is a county police force, headed by a chief of police. As Figure 1.1 shows, the bulk of all police officers in the United States are employed on a local level. The majority of these work in departments that consist of fewer than 10 officers, though a large city such as New York may have a police force of tens of thousands.

Local police are responsible for the "nuts and bolts" of law enforcement work. They investigate most crimes and attempt to deter crime through patrol activities. They apprehend criminals and participate in trial proceedings, if necessary. Local police are also charged with "keeping the peace," a broad set of duties that includes crowd

Federalism A form of government in which a written constitution provides for a division of powers between a central government and several regional governments.

and traffic control and the resolution of minor conflicts between citizens. In many areas, local police have the added obligation of providing social services such as dealing with domestic violence and child abuse.

STATE LAW ENFORCEMENT Hawaii is the only state that does not have a state law enforcement agency. Generally, there are two types of state law enforcement agencies, those designated simply as "state police" and those designated as "highway patrols." State highway patrols concern themselves mainly with infractions on public highways and freeways. Other state law enforcers include fire marshals, who investigate suspicious fires and educate the public on fire prevention, and fish, game, and watercraft wardens, who police a state's natural resources and often oversee its firearms laws. Some states also have alcoholic beverage control officers, as well as agents who investigate welfare and food stamp fraud.

> *CAREER TIP* Eighteen state governments completely or partially control the sale of alcoholic beverages. These states rely on *alcoholic beverage control officers* to enforce regulations on beer, wine, and distilled spirits within their borders.

FEDERAL LAW ENFORCEMENT The enactment of new national antiterrorism, gun, drug, and violent crime laws over the past forty years has led to an expansion in the size and scope of the federal government's participation in the criminal justice system. The Department of Homeland Security, which we will examine in detail in Chapter 4, combines the police powers of twenty-four federal agencies to protect the United States from terrorist attacks. Other federal agencies with police powers include the Federal Bureau of Investigation (FBI), the Drug Enforcement Administration (DEA), the U.S. Secret Service, and the Bureau of Alcohol, Tobacco, Firearms and Explosives (ATF). In fact, almost every federal agency, including the postal and forest services, has some kind of police power.

Federal law enforcement agencies operate throughout the United States. Often, they work in cooperation with their local and state counterparts. There can be tension between the different branches of law enforcement, however, when state criminal law and federal criminal law are incompatible. For example, even though states such as Alaska, Colorado, Oregon, and Washington have legalized the sale and possession of small amounts of marijuana, the drug is still illegal under federal law.

Consequently, federal officers are authorized to make marijuana arrests in those states, regardless of any changes to the states' criminal codes.

1-3b The Courts

The United States has a *dual court system,* which means that we have two independent judicial systems, one at the federal level and one at the state level. In practice, this translates into fifty-two different court systems: one federal court system and fifty different state court systems, plus that of the District of Columbia. In general, those defendants charged with violating federal criminal law will face trial in federal court, while those defendants charged with violating state law will appear in state court.

The *criminal court* and its work group—the judge, prosecutors, and defense attorneys—are given the weighty responsibility of determining the innocence or guilt of criminal suspects. We will cover these important participants, their roles in the criminal trial, and the court system as a whole in Chapters 7, 8, and 9.

1-3c Corrections

LO1-3 Once the court system convicts and sentences an offender, she or he is delegated to the corrections system. (Those convicted in a state court will be under the control of that state's corrections system, and those convicted of a federal crime will find themselves under

On any given day, America's jails hold approximately 730,000 inmates, including these residents of the Orange County jail in Santa Ana, California. *What are the basic differences between jails and prisons?*

Lucy Nicholson/Reuters/Landov

the control of the federal corrections system.) Depending on the seriousness of the crime and their individual needs, offenders are placed on probation, incarcerated, or transferred to community-based correctional facilities.

▶ *Probation,* the most common correctional treatment, allows the offender to return to the community and remain under the supervision of an agent of the court known as a probation officer. While on probation, the offender must follow certain rules of conduct. When probationers fail to follow these rules, they may be incarcerated.

▶ If the offender's sentence includes a period of incarceration, he or she will be remanded to a correctional facility for a certain amount of time. *Jails* hold those convicted of minor crimes with relatively short sentences, as well as those awaiting trial or involved in certain court proceedings. *Prisons* house those convicted of more serious crimes with longer sentences. Generally speaking, counties and municipalities administer jails, while prisons are the domain of federal and state governments.

▶ *Community-based corrections* have increased in popularity as jails and prisons have been plagued with problems of funding and overcrowding. Community-based correctional facilities include halfway houses, residential centers, and work-release centers. They operate on the assumption that some convicts do not need, and are not benefited by, incarceration in jail or prison.

The majority of those inmates released from incarceration are not finished with the corrections system. The most frequent type of release from a jail or prison is *parole,* in which an inmate, after serving part of his or her sentence in a correctional facility, is allowed to serve the rest of the term in the community. Like someone on probation, a parolee must conform to certain conditions of freedom, with the same consequences if these conditions are not followed. Issues of probation, incarceration, community-based corrections, and parole will be covered in Chapters 10, 11, and 12.

1-3d The Criminal Justice Process

In its 1967 report, the President's Commission on Law Enforcement and Administration of Justice asserted that the criminal justice system

is not a hodgepodge of random actions. It is rather a continuum—an orderly progression of events—some of which, like arrest and trial, are highly visible and some of which, though of great importance, occur out of public view.[11]

The commission's assertion that the criminal justice system is a "continuum" is one that many observers would challenge.[12] Some liken the criminal justice system to a sports team, which is the sum of an indeterminable number of decisions, relationships, conflicts, and adjustments.[13] Such a volatile mix is not what we generally associate with a "system." For most, the word **system** indicates a certain degree of order and discipline. That we refer to our law enforcement agencies, courts, and correctional facilities as part of a "system" may reflect our hopes rather than reality. Still, it will be helpful to familiarize yourself with the basic steps of the *criminal justice process,* or the procedures through which the criminal justice system meets the expectations of society. These basic steps are provided in Figure 1.2.

In his classic study of the criminal justice system, Herbert Packer, a professor at Stanford University, compared the ideal criminal justice process to an assembly line "down which moves an endless stream of cases, never stopping."[14] In Packer's image of assembly-line justice, each step of the **formal criminal justice process** involves a series of "routinized operations" with the end goal of getting the criminal defendant from point A (his or her arrest by law enforcement) to point B (the criminal trial) to point C (if guilty, her or his punishment).[15] As Packer himself was wont to point out, the daily operations of criminal justice rarely operate so smoothly. In this textbook, the criminal justice process will be examined as the end product of many different decisions made by many different criminal justice professionals in law enforcement, the courts, and corrections.

1-4 HOW DO CRIMINAL JUSTICE PROFESSIONALS MAKE DECISIONS?

Practically, the formal criminal justice process suffers from a serious drawback: it is unrealistic. Law enforcement agencies do not have the staff or funds to investigate *every* crime, so they must decide where to direct their limited resources. Increasing caseloads and a limited amount of time in which to dispose of them constrict

System A set of interacting parts that, when functioning properly, achieve a desired result.

Formal Criminal Justice Process The model of the criminal justice process in which participants follow formal rules to create a smoothly functioning disposition of cases from arrest to punishment.

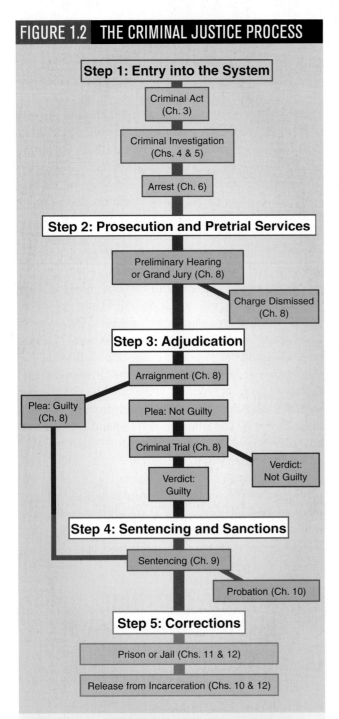

FIGURE 1.2 THE CRIMINAL JUSTICE PROCESS

Step 1: Entry into the System

Criminal Act
(Ch. 3)

Criminal Investigation
(Chs. 4 & 5)

Arrest (Ch. 6)

Step 2: Prosecution and Pretrial Services

Preliminary Hearing
or Grand Jury (Ch. 8)

Charge Dismissed
(Ch. 8)

Step 3: Adjudication

Arraignment (Ch. 8)

Plea: Guilty
(Ch. 8)

Plea: Not Guilty

Criminal Trial (Ch. 8)

Verdict:
Not Guilty

Verdict:
Guilty

Step 4: Sentencing and Sanctions

Sentencing (Ch. 9)

Probation (Ch. 10)

Step 5: Corrections

Prison or Jail (Chs. 11 & 12)

Release from Incarceration (Chs. 10 & 12)

This diagram provides a simplified overview of the basic steps of the criminal justice process, from criminal act to release from incarceration. Next to each step, you will find the chapter of this textbook in which the event is covered.

Discretion The ability of individuals in the criminal justice system to make operational decisions based on personal judgment instead of formal rules or official information.

Informal Criminal Justice Process A model of the criminal justice system that recognizes the informal authority exercised by individuals at each step of the criminal justice process.

many of our nation's courts. Overcrowding in prisons and jails affects both law enforcement agencies and the courts—there is simply not enough room for all convicts.

The criminal justice system relies on *discretion* to alleviate these pressures. By **discretion,** we mean the authority to choose between and among alternative courses of action, based on individual judgment and conscience. Collectively, the discretionary decisions made by criminal justice professionals are said to produce an **informal criminal justice process** that does not operate within the rigid confines of formal rules and laws.

1-4a Informal Decision Making

By its nature, the informal criminal justice system relies on the discretion of individuals to offset the rigidity of criminal statutes and procedural rules. For example, even if a prosecutor believes that a suspect is guilty, she or he may decide not to bring charges against the suspect if the case is weak or the police erred during the investigative process. In many instances, prosecutors will not squander the scarce resource of court time on a case they might not win. Some argue that the informal process has made our system more just. Given the immense pressure of limited resources, the argument goes, only rarely will an innocent person end up before a judge and jury.[16]

LAW ENFORCEMENT DISCRETION The use of discretion in law enforcement is also widespread, and this informal decision making often directly impacts the public. For example, both New York and Los Angeles have local ordinances prohibiting pedestrians from *jaywalking*, or crossing the street outside of a crosswalk or against a traffic light. Although jaywalking is quite common in New York, police rarely issue tickets to punish such behavior. In Los Angeles, however, where an automobile culture dominates, police handed out more than 31,000 jaywalking citations over a recent six-month period in the downtown area alone.[17] Evidently, New York police officers are using their discretion to ignore this illegal behavior, while their counterparts in Los Angeles have decided to expend considerable resources in an effort to reduce it.

In Chapters 4, 5, and 6, we will examine many other circumstances that call for discretionary decision making by law enforcement officers. (See Figure 1.3 for a description of some of the important discretionary decisions that make up the informal criminal justice process.)

THE PITFALLS OF DISCRETION Unfortunately, the informal criminal justice system does not always benefit from measured, rational decision making. Individual

FIGURE 1.3   DISCRETION IN THE CRIMINAL JUSTICE SYSTEM

Police	Judges
• Enforce laws	• Set conditions for pretrial release
• Investigate specific crimes	• Accept pleas
• Search people or buildings	• Dismiss charges
• Arrest or detain people	• Impose sentences

Prosecutors	Correctional Officials
• File charges against suspects brought to them by the police	• Assign convicts to prison or jail
• Drop cases	• Punish prisoners who misbehave
• Reduce charges	• Reward prisoners who behave well

Criminal justice officials must make decisions every day concerning their duties. The officials listed above, whether they operate on a local, state, or federal level, rely heavily on discretion when meeting the listed responsibilities.

judgment can be tainted by personal bias, erroneous or irrational thinking, and plain ill will. When this occurs, discretion becomes "the power to *get away with* alternative decisions [emphasis added]."[18] Indeed, many of the rules of the formal criminal justice process are designed to keep its employees from substituting their own judgment for that of the general public, as expressed by the law.

Recently, the American Civil Liberties Union of Michigan accused police officers in Saginaw of improperly using their discretion to racially profile recipients of jaywalking citations.[19] As you will learn in Chapter 6, racial profiling is the police practice of improperly targeting members of minority groups based on personal characteristics such as race or ethnicity. Furthermore, associate Supreme Court justice Antonin Scalia has criticized discretion in the courts for its tendency to cause discriminatory and disparate criminal sentences, a subject we will discuss in Chapter 9. According to Scalia, the need for fairness and certainty in the criminal justice system outweighs the practical benefits of widespread and unpredictable discretionary decision making.[20]

1-4b Ethics and Justice

LO1-4   How can we reconcile the need for some sort of discretion in criminal justice with the ever-present potential for abuse? Part of the answer lies in our initial definition of discretion, which mentions not only individual judgment but also *conscience*. Ideally, actors in the criminal justice system will make moral choices about what is right and wrong based on the norms that have been established by society. In other words, they will behave *ethically*.

Ethics in criminal justice is closely related to the concept of justice. Because criminal justice professionals are representatives of the state, they have the power to determine whether the state is treating its citizens fairly. If some law enforcement officers in fact make the decision to issue a jaywalking citation on the basis of the offender's race, then they are acting not only unethically but also unjustly.

ETHICS AND THE LAW The line between ethics and justice is often difficult to discern, as ethical standards are usually not written into criminal statutes. Consequently, individuals must often "fill in" the ethical blanks. To make this point, ethics expert John Kleinig uses the real-life example of a police officer who refused to arrest a homeless person for sleeping in a private parking garage. A local ordinance clearly prohibited such behavior. The officer, however, felt it would be unethical to arrest a homeless person under those circumstances unless he or she was acting in a disorderly manner. The officer's supervisors were unsympathetic to this ethical stance, and he was suspended from duty

---

Ethics The moral principles that govern a person's perception of right and wrong.

without pay.[21] (To further consider the possible tensions between a police officer's personal values and the law, see the feature *Discretion in Action—Stirring the Pot*.)

ETHICS AND CRITICAL THINKING Did the police officer in the preceding example behave ethically by inserting his own beliefs into the letter of the criminal law? Would an officer who arrested peaceful homeless trespassers be acting unethically? In some cases, the ethical decision will be *intuitive*, reflecting an automatic response determined by a person's background and experiences. In other cases, however, intuition is not enough. *Critical thinking* is needed for an ethical response. Throughout this textbook, we will use the principle of critical thinking—which involves developing analytical skills and reasoning—to address the many ethical challenges inherent in the criminal justice system.

Crime Control Model A criminal justice model that places primary emphasis on the right of society to be protected from crime and violent criminals.

Due Process Model A criminal justice model that places primacy on the right of the individual to be protected from the power of the government.

1-5 WHAT'S HAPPENING IN CRIMINAL JUSTICE TODAY?

In describing the general direction of the criminal justice system as a whole, many observers point to two models introduced by Professor Herbert Packer: the *crime control model* and the *due process model*.[22] The underlying value of the **crime control model** is that the most important function of the criminal justice process is to punish and repress criminal conduct. The system must be quick and efficient, placing as few restrictions as possible on the ability of law enforcement officers to make discretionary decisions in apprehending criminals.

Although not in direct conflict with crime control, the underlying values of the **due process model** focus more on protecting the rights of the accused through formal, legal restraints on the police, courts, and corrections. That is, the due process model relies **LO1-5** on the courts to make it more difficult to prove guilt. It rests on the belief that it is more desirable for society that ninety-nine guilty suspects go free than that a single innocent person be condemned.[23]

Discretion in Action

STIRRING THE POT

THE SITUATION Several years ago, Washington residents voted to legalize the sale of small amounts of marijuana to adults in the state. Among those Washingtonians who oppose the new law are a large number of police officers, many of whom see it as a surrender to the criminal element. There is also a sense in the law enforcement community that the new law is unethical. Even though the legal sale of marijuana will certainly lead to profits for some and increased tax revenues, it will also allow more young people to gain access to the drug. As with cigarettes and alcohol, this access will have health and social consequences for the community.

THE LAW Washington police officers no longer have the ability to make arrests for possession of small amounts of marijuana. The public use of marijuana is, however, still illegal in the state. Consequently, if a law enforcement agent sees a person smoking pot in public, he or she has the discretion to issue that person a ticket. In Seattle, the fine for such behavior is $27.

WHAT WOULD YOU DO? Suppose you are a Seattle police officer who strongly disagrees with the legalization of marijuana on ethical grounds. You can no longer make arrests for possession of small amounts of marijuana, but you have the discretion to issue tickets and fines for public use of the drug. Would you do so, even though such steps defy the spirit of the new law? (In the first six months of 2014, a single Seattle police officer wrote about 80 percent of the one hundred public marijuana use tickets issued in the city. Displeased, Seattle officials reassigned the officer—who felt the new law was "silly"—and rescinded all the fines he had levied against public marijuana users.)

1-5a Crime and Law Enforcement: The Bottom Line

It is difficult to say which of Packer's two models has the upper hand today. As we will see throughout the textbook, homeland security concerns have brought much of the criminal justice system in line with crime control values. At the same time, decreasing arrest and imprisonment rates suggest that due process values are strong as well. In any case, national rates of violent and property crimes are at historically low levels.[24] In Chapter 2, we will discuss some reasons for this phenomenon, as well as concerns on the part of some experts that crime rates in the United States have "plateaued" and are likely to rise in the near future.[25]

SMARTER POLICING Just as law enforcement inevitably gets a great deal of the blame when crime rates are high, American police forces have received much credit for the apparent decline in criminality. The consensus is that the police have become smarter and more disciplined over the past two decades, putting into practice strategies that allow them to more effectively prevent crime. For example, the widespread use of *proactive policing* promotes more rigorous enforcement of minor offenses—such as drunkenness and public disorder—with an eye toward preventing more serious wrongdoing. In addition, *hot-spot policing* has law enforcement officers focusing on high-crime areas rather than spreading their resources evenly throughout metropolitan areas. These and other innovative policing strategies will be explored more fully in Chapter 5.

IDENTIFYING CRIMINALS Technology has also played a significant role in improving law enforcement efficiency. Police investigators are enjoying the benefits of perhaps the most effective new crime-fighting tool since fingerprint identification: DNA profiling. This technology allows law enforcement agents to identify a suspect from body fluid evidence (such as blood, saliva, or semen) or biological evidence (such as hair strands or fingernail clippings). As we will also see in Chapter 5, by collecting DNA from convicts and storing the information in databases, investigators have been able to reach across hundreds of miles and back in time to catch wrongdoers.

BIOMETRICS

CJ and Technology

The science of *biometrics* involves identifying a person through her or his unique physical characteristics. In the criminal justice context, the term refers to the various technological devices that read a person's unique physical characteristics and report his or her identity to authorities. The most common biometric devices record a suspect's fingerprints, but hand geometry, facial features, and the minute details of the human eye can also provide biometric identification.

As far back as the 2001 Super Bowl, the federal government has been experimenting with facial recognition software that would allow video cameras to identify individuals within large crowds of people. Finally, it seems, the technology is close to becoming operational. The Biometric Optical Surveillance System (BOSS) uses 3-D cameras mounted on the tops of two towers to take photos of a subject from different angles. A computer then reads the features of the subject's face and matches those features against those stored in a database. The goal, according to researchers, is for BOSS to provide a near-instant match at a range of more than three hundred feet. The technology is being developed primarily for counterterrorism purposes. For example, BOSS could be used to search for terrorist suspects at a presidential inaugural parade or in an airport lounge.

Kodda/ShutterStock.com

Thinking about Biometrics

How could local police departments implement BOSS to identify and apprehend criminal suspects or fugitives? Should law enforcement agencies wait until BOSS's successful match rate is close to 100 percent, or would an 80 or 90 percent certainty be acceptable? Explain your answer.

1-5b Issues of Race and Public Trust

In the introduction to this chapter, we discussed the fallout after a grand jury decided that a white police officer should not face criminal charges for fatally shooting a young black man in Ferguson, Missouri. Shortly thereafter, in early December 2014, another grand jury similarly declined to charge a white New York City police officer who accidentally killed a black suspect named Eric Garner using a chokehold. For many African Americans, these two incidents seemed to underscore a growing mistrust between their communities and law enforcement in the United States.

According to a poll taken following the shooting of Michael Brown in Ferguson, nearly half the African American respondents said that they had experienced racial discrimination by a police officer. (Virtually none of the white respondents responded in the same manner.)[26] Examining racial tensions between blacks and law enforcement in Cleveland, a recent federal report stated that the city's police force sees itself as an "occupying force" and that the various local departments "must undergo a cultural shift at all levels to change an 'us-against-them' mentality."[27]

In Chapters 4 and 5, we will take a comprehensive look at the possible root causes of this climate and explore some of the ways in which tensions between police and members of minority groups might be defused. In particular, we will focus on diversity in law enforcement, a crucial issue in today's criminal justice system.

1-5c Homeland Security and Domestic Terrorism

Without question, the attacks of September 11, 2001—when terrorists hijacked four commercial airlines and used them to kill nearly three thousand people in New York City, northern Virginia, and rural Pennsylvania—are still the most significant events of the 2000s as far as

---

LOCAL POLICE OFFICER

CareerPrep

John Roman Images/ShutterStock.com

Job Description:

▶ Protect the lives and property of citizens in the community.

▶ Maintain order, catch those who break the law, and strive to prevent crimes.

▶ Testify at trials and hearings.

What Kind of Training Is Required?

▶ Almost every police department requires that applicants be high school graduates, and an increasing number of departments expect a college degree.

▶ Minimum height, weight, eyesight, and hearing requirements, as well as the passage of physical examinations and background checks.

▶ Graduation from a police academy.

Annual Salary Range?

▶ $31,000–$82,000

> **GETTING LINKEDIN**
> A recent job posting by the City of Farmington, New Mexico, noted that all its police officers are required to work "days, evenings, and nights, including weekends and holidays." Irregular hours are one of the most challenging aspects of a career in law enforcement.

crime fighting is concerned. As we will see throughout this textbook, the resulting **homeland security** movement has touched nearly every aspect of criminal justice. This movement has the ultimate goal of protecting America from **terrorism,** which can be broadly defined as the random use of staged violence to achieve political goals.

COUNTERTERRORISM AND CIVIL LIBERTIES
Several years ago, disclosures that federal antiterrorism agencies had secretly acquired the phone records of millions of Americans caused many to reassess their views on privacy and national security. Following these revelations, which we will explore in Chapter 14, a national poll showed that 47 percent of Americans said that the federal government had gone too far in restricting *civil liberties* in its efforts to fight terrorism.[28] The term **civil liberties** refers to the personal freedoms guaranteed to all Americans by the U.S. Constitution, particularly the first ten amendments, known as the Bill of Rights.

Concerns about balancing personal freedoms and personal safety permeate our criminal justice system. In fact, an entire chapter of this textbook—Chapter 6—is needed to discuss the rules that law enforcement must follow to protect the civil liberties of crime suspects. Many of the issues that we will address in these pages are particularly relevant to counterterrorism efforts. For example:

1. **The First Amendment to the U.S. Constitution states that the government shall not interfere with citizens' "freedom of speech." Does this mean that individuals should be allowed to support terrorist causes on the Internet?**

2. **The Fourth Amendment protects against "unreasonable searches and seizures." Does this mean that law enforcement agents should not be able to seize the computer of a terrorist subject without any actual proof of wrongdoing?**

3. **The Sixth Amendment guarantees a trial by jury to a person accused of a crime. Does this mean that the U.S. military cannot find a suspect guilty of terrorist actions without providing a jury trial?**

CAREER TIP If you are interested in ensuring that all Americans are treated equally by federal, state, and local governments, you should consider becoming a *civil liberties lawyer.*

Critics of counterterrorism measures that include increased surveillance of Internet activity (including e-mails), phone records, and citizens' daily movements believe that limits should be placed on the government's ability to collect "Big Data." Supporters counter that, for the most part, such tactics have been effective and therefore are worth any minimal privacy intrusions.

DOMESTIC TERRORISM For most of the first decade of the 2000s, America's counterterrorism strategies focused on international terrorism, represented by foreign terrorist organizations that possess the resources to carry out large-scale, coordinated attacks. According to James Comey, director of the FBI, because of these strategies, "the risk of that spectacular attack in the homeland is significantly lower than it was before 9/11." At the same time, Comey warned against the "risk of smaller attacks" by *domestic terrorists.*[29] Though the label covers a variety of illegal activities, **domestic terrorism** generally refers to acts of terror that are carried out within one's own country, against one's own people, and with little or no direct foreign involvement.

1-5d Inmate Population Trends

After increasing by 500 percent from 1980 to 2008, the inmate population in the United States has leveled off and, as you can see in Figure 1.4, has even decreased slightly since 2009. Certainly, this decrease has been small, and the American corrections system remains immense. More than 2.2 million offenders are in prison or jail in this country, and another 4.7 million are under community supervision.[30] Still, the new trend reflects a series of crucial changes in the American criminal justice system.

THE ECONOMICS OF INCARCERATION There is no question that economic considerations have played a role in the nation's shrinking inmate population. Federal, state, and local governments spend $80 billion a

Homeland Security A concerted national effort to prevent terrorist attacks within the United States and reduce the country's vulnerability to terrorism.

Terrorism The use or threat of violence to achieve political objectives.

Civil Liberties The basic rights and freedoms for American citizens guaranteed by the U.S. Constitution, particularly in the Bill of Rights.

Domestic Terrorism Acts of terrorism that take place on U.S. soil without direct foreign involvement.

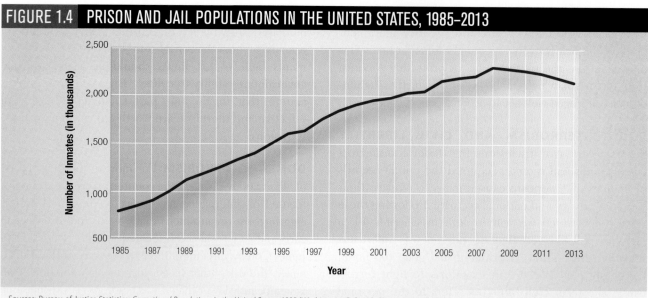

FIGURE 1.4 PRISON AND JAIL POPULATIONS IN THE UNITED STATES, 1985–2013

Sources: Bureau of Justice Statistics, *Correctional Populations in the United States, 1995* (Washington, D.C.: U.S. Department of Justice, June 1997), Table 1.1, page 12; and Bureau of Justice Statistics, *Correctional Populations in the United States, 2013* (Washington, D.C.: U.S. Department of Justice, December 2014), Table 1, page 2.

year on prisons and jails, and many corrections officials are under pressure to reduce costs.[31] Increasingly, however, downsizing efforts reflect "the message that locking up a lot of people doesn't necessarily bring public safety," says Joan Petersilia, co-director of Stanford University's Criminal Justice Center.[32] To reduce prison populations, therefore, federal and state correctional officials are taking measures such as these:

1. Granting early release to nonviolent offenders, particularly low-level drug offenders.

2. Diverting offenders from jail and prison through special courts that promote rehabilitation rather than punishment.

3. Implementing a number of programs to reduce the *recidivism* rate of ex-convicts.

Recidivism refers to a person's committing another crime (and possibly returning to incarceration) after having already been punished for previous criminal behavior. We will examine these policies and the ramifications for the nation's prisons and jails in Chapters 10, 11, and 12.

Recidivism The act of committing a new crime after a person has already been punished for a previous crime by being convicted and sent to jail or prison.

Capital Crime A criminal act that makes the offender eligible to receive the death penalty.

DECLINING USE OF THE DEATH PENALTY Another interesting corrections trend involves death row inmates, who are in prison awaiting execution after having been found guilty of committing a **capital crime.** Near the end of 2014, the death row population in American prisons stood at 3,035, down from 3,653 in 2000.[33] During that same time period, the number of annual executions in this country dropped from 85 to 35, a twenty-year low.

INCARCERATION AND RACE One troublesome aspect of capital punishment is that a black defendant is much more likely to be sentenced to death for killing a white victim than a white defendant is for killing a black victim.[34] Indeed, looking at the general statistics, a bleak picture of minority incarceration emerges. Even though African Americans make up only 13 percent of the general population in the United States, the number of black men in state and federal prisons (526,000) is significantly larger than the number of white men (454,000).[35] In federal prisons, one in every three inmates is Hispanic,[36] a ratio that has increased dramatically over the past decade as law enforcement and homeland security agencies have focused on immigration law violations. The question of whether these figures reflect purposeful bias on the part of certain members of the criminal justice community will be addressed at various points in this textbook.

1-5e Criminal Justice and the Mentally Ill

Another socially and statistically significant segment of the inmate population is the mentally ill. According to the National Alliance on Mental Illness, 40 percent

An inmate suffering from mental illness speaks to his attorney through a cell door at the Stanislaus County Public Safety Center in Modesto, California. *Why do many experts blame the large number of mentally ill jail and prison inmates on reductions in government spending on community mental health services?*

Photo by Debbie Noda/*Modesto Bee*/MCT via Getty Images

of adults with serious mental health problems will be arrested at some point in their lives, often for petty crimes.[37] About 56 percent of all state prison inmates and 64 percent of all jail inmates are suffering from some sort of mental illness.[38] States reduced their spending on mental health services by about $5 billion from 2009 to 2012,[39] meaning that those suffering from poor mental health often wind up in the "care" of the criminal justice system. "We have replaced the hospital bed with the jail cell," says Tim Murphy, a Republican congressman from Pennsylvania.[40]

Prison programs have been shown to improve the situation, both for the corrections system and for those suffering from mental illness. When Georgia began providing comprehensive health services to mentally ill jail inmates, the state was able to reduce the number of days these inmates spent behind bars by 78 percent.[41] Such treatment also makes it less likely that these offenders will reoffend after being released back into the community. In Chapter 12 we will examine how prison and jail treatment programs impact the *reentry process* for the approximately 620,000 inmates who exit prisons in the United States each year.

STUDY TOOLS 1

READY TO STUDY? IN THE BOOK, YOU CAN:

☐ Rip out the Chapter Review Card, which includes key terms and chapter summaries.

ONLINE AT WWW.CENGAGEBRAIN.COM, YOU CAN:

☐ Learn about race and crime in a short video.

☐ Dig deeper into social media in criminal justice by exploring your local Crimestoppers Facebook page.

☐ Interact with figures from the text, and watch quick animation clips.

☐ Prepare for tests with quizzes.

☐ Review the key terms with Flash Cards.

Quiz

1. Murder, assault, and robbery are labeled _____ crimes because they are committed against persons.

2. The category of crime that includes larceny, motor vehicle theft, and arson is called _____ crime.

3. To protect against a too-powerful central government, the framers of the U.S. Constitution relied on the principle of _____ to balance power between the national government and the states.

4. The United States has a dual court system, with parallel court systems at the federal level and at the _____ level.

5. At every level, the criminal justice system relies on the _____ of its employees to keep it from being bogged down by formal rules.

6. Ideally, criminal justice professionals rely on a strong sense of _____ to make moral and just decisions as part of their daily routines.

7. The _____ model of criminal justice places great importance on high rates of apprehension and conviction of criminal suspects.

8. The _____ model emphasizes the rights of individual criminal defendants over the powers of the government.

9. America's homeland security system has been designed to protect the country from violent acts committed to further political goals, otherwise known as _____.

10. To reduce inmate populations, corrections officials are implementing programs aimed at reducing the _____ rate, or the rate at which ex-inmates are rearrested and returned to jail or prison.

Answers can be found in the Answers section in the back of the book.

YOUR FEEDBACK MATTERS.

Follow us at
www.facebook.com/4ltrpress

2

The Crime Picture: Theories and Trends

LEARNING OBJECTIVES

After studying this chapter, you will be able to . . .

2-1 Discuss the difference between a hypothesis and a theory in the context of criminology.

2-2 Contrast the medical model of addiction with the criminal model of addiction.

2-3 Distinguish between the National Crime Victimization Survey (NCVS) and self-reported surveys.

2-4 Describe the three ways victims' rights legislation increases the ability of crime victims to participate in the criminal justice system.

2-5 Identify the three factors most often used by criminologists to explain changes in the nation's crime rate.

After you finish

this chapter, go

to **PAGES 44–45**

for **STUDY TOOLS**

The Hater

While Elliot Rodger could be shy and withdrawn in the real world, he had no trouble expressing himself on the Internet. A self-labeled "incel," or "involuntary celibate," the twenty-two-year-old college dropout spent hours online ranting about his lack of success with the opposite sex. At one Web site, he exhorted his fellow incels to "start imagining a world where WOMEN FEAR YOU." At another, he posted a video titled "Why Do Girls Hate Me So Much?" that, according to one comment, made him look like a serial killer.

On the night of May 23, 2014, as reports of a shooting spree near the campus of the University of California, Santa Barbara, spread through the media, members of Rodger's online community speculated that he was the gunman. Their concerns were justified. Before taking his own life that night, Rodger killed six people and wounded thirteen others. Among his victims were two young women outside a sorority house. In an e-mail he sent

out minutes before the carnage, Rodger vowed to kill "all those beautiful girls" who had rejected him and "make them suffer, just as they have made me suffer."

Looking back, Rodger's Internet postings were not the only warning signs of potential violence. He had been seeing therapists regularly since he was eight years old to help deal with a variety of emotional problems. Three weeks before the killings, Rodger's family contacted local law enforcement expressing

concerns about his mental health. Six police officers visited Rodger's apartment to perform a "welfare check." They found Rodger "timid and polite," and concluded that there was no reason to search his home. Had they done so, they likely would have found the three semiautomatic weapons Rodger used in his rampage. "For a few horrible seconds I thought it was all over," Rodger admitted in his final e-mail. "When they left, the biggest wave of relief swept over me."

Elliot Rodger, shown here in a photo released by the Santa Barbara Sheriff's Department, killed six people in Isla Vista, California, before committing suicide. *Given what they knew of the situation, should the police officers described in the text have searched Rodger's apartment? Why do you think they failed to do so?*

Robyn Beck/AFP/Getty Images

2-1 WHAT IS A THEORY?

The study of crime, or **criminology,** is rich with different explanations for why people commit crimes. At the same time, *criminologists,* or those who study the causes of crime, warn against using models or profiles to predict violent behavior. After all, not every sexually frustrated and depressed young man who spends an inordinate amount of time venting on the Internet should be treated as a future multiple-victim shooter. Most people with the same behavior patterns as Elliot Rodger "never act out in a violent way," says J. Reid Meloy, an editor at the *International Handbook of Threat Assessment*. "You can't predict who will or who won't."[1]

Still, in the case of Elliot Rodger, there does seem to be some connection between his characteristics and his violent outburst, particularly when one considers that

he may have been suffering from mental illness. That is, there appears to be a *correlation* between his behavior and his crimes, a concept that is crucial to criminology.

2-1a Correlation and Cause

Correlation between two variables means that they tend to vary together. **Causation,** in contrast, means that one variable is responsible for the change in the other. As

---

Criminology The scientific study of crime and the causes of criminal behavior.

Correlation The relationship between two variables that tend to move in the same direction.

Causation The relationship in which a change in one variable creates a recognizable change in another variable.

we will see later in the chapter, there is a correlation between drug abuse and criminal behavior: statistically, many criminals are also drug abusers. But drug abuse does not cause crime: not everyone who abuses drugs is a criminal.

To give another example, a recent study led by Scott Wolfe, a criminologist at the University of South Carolina, looked at crime rates in counties where the megastore Walmart added new stores during the 1990s. Wolfe and his co-author found that crime rates in those counties were significantly higher than in those neighboring counties with no Walmart expansion.[2] Despite these results, few criminologists would assert that new Walmart stores *caused* the higher crime rates. Other factors, such as unemployment, poverty, and zoning patterns, must also be taken into account to get a fuller understanding of the crime picture in the studied areas.

So, correlation does not equal cause. Such is the quandary for criminologists. We can say that there is a correlation between many factors and criminal behavior, but it is quite difficult to prove that the factors directly cause criminal behavior. Consequently, the question that is the underpinning of criminology—What causes crime?—has yet to be definitively answered.

2-1b The Role of Theory

Criminologists have, however, uncovered a wealth of information concerning a different, and more practically applicable, inquiry: Given a certain set of circumstances, why do individuals commit criminal acts? This information has allowed criminologists to develop a number of *theories* concerning the causes of crime.

THE SCIENTIFIC METHOD Most of us tend to think of a *theory* as some sort of guess or a statement that is lacking in credibility. In the academic world, and therefore for our purposes, a **theory** is an explanation of a happening or circumstance that is based on observation, experimentation, and reasoning. Scientific and academic researchers observe facts and their consequences to develop *hypotheses* about what will occur when a similar

LO2-1

fact pattern is present in the future. A **hypothesis** is a proposition that can be tested by researchers or observers to determine if it is valid. If enough authorities do find the hypothesis valid, it will be accepted as a theory. See Figure 2.1 for an example of this process, known as the *scientific method,* in action.

THEORY IN ACTION Criminological theories are primarily concerned with attempting to determine the reasons for criminal behavior. For example, two criminologists from Arizona State University, Matthew Larson and Gary Sweeten, wanted to test their hypothesis that young people involved in romantic breakups are at high risk for destructive behavior. Relying on a survey of high school and college students who were asked about issues in their personal lives, Larson and Sweeten found some support for their hypothesis. According to the data, breakups do indeed correlate with higher rates of criminal offending and substance abuse among young men and higher rates of substance abuse among young women.[3]

FIGURE 2.1 THE SCIENTIFIC METHOD

The scientific method is a process through which researchers test the accuracy of a hypothesis. This simple example should provide an idea of how the scientific method works.

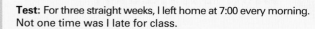 **Observation:** I left my home at 7:00 this morning, and I was on time for class.

 Hypothesis: If I leave home at 7:00 every morning, then I will never be late for class.
(Hypotheses are often presented in this "If . . . , then . . ." format.)

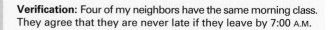 **Test:** For three straight weeks, I left home at 7:00 every morning. Not one time was I late for class.

 Verification: Four of my neighbors have the same morning class. They agree that they are never late if they leave by 7:00 A.M.

 Theory: As long as I leave home at 7:00 A.M., I don't have to worry about being late for class.

 Prediction: Tomorrow morning I'll leave at 7:00, and I will be on time for my class.

Note that even a sound theory supported by the scientific method, such as this one, does not *prove* that the prediction will be correct. Other factors not accounted for in the test and verification stages, such as an unexpected traffic accident, may disprove the theory. Predictions based on complex theories, such as the criminological ones we will be discussing in this chapter, are often challenged in such a manner.

WHICH THEORIES OF CRIME ARE MOST WIDELY ACCEPTED?

As you read this chapter, keep in mind that theories are not the same as facts, and most, if not all, of the criminological theories described in these pages have their detractors. Over the past century, however, a number of theories of crime have gained wide, if not total, acceptance. We now turn our attention to these theories, starting with those that focus on the psychological and physical aspects of criminal behavior.

2-2a The Brain and the Body

Perhaps the most basic answer to the question of why a person commits a crime is that he or she makes a willful decision to do so. This is the underpinning of the **rational choice theory** of crime, summed up by criminologist James Q. Wilson (1931–2012) as follows:

> At any given moment, a person can choose between committing a crime and not committing it. The consequences of committing a crime consist of rewards (what psychologists call "reinforcers") and punishments; the consequences of not committing the crime also entail gains and losses. The larger the ratio of the net rewards of crime to the net rewards of [not committing a crime], the greater the tendency to commit a crime.[4]

In other words, a person, before committing a crime, acts as if she or he is weighing the benefits (which may be money, in the case of a robbery) against the costs (the possibility of being caught and going to prison

Rational Choice Theory A school of criminology that holds that wrongdoers act as if they weigh the possible benefits of criminal or delinquent activity against the expected costs of being apprehended.

CRIMINOLOGIST

CareerPrep

Leah-Anne Thompson/ShutterStock.com

Job Description:

▶ Analyze criminal and delinquent behavior and provide theoretical explanations for such behavior.

▶ Work with and for law enforcement agencies to prevent crime by offering profiles of criminal behavior and scrutinizing crime statistics.

What Kind of Training Is Required?

▶ Research skills, computer proficiency, and expertise in statistics.

▶ An undergraduate degree in a field relating to criminal justice with, preferably, a minor in psychology or sociology. A postgraduate degree is necessary for an academic career in criminology.

Annual Salary Range?

▶ $40,000–$122,000

SOCIAL MEDIA CAREER TIP
Social media technologies are about connecting and sharing information—which means privacy is an important issue. Make sure you understand who can see the material you post and how you can control it. Facebook has numerous privacy settings, for example, as does Google+.

or jail). If the perceived benefits are greater than the potential costs, the person is more likely to commit the crime.

"THRILL OFFENDERS" Expanding on rational choice theory, sociologist Jack Katz has stated that the "rewards" of crime may be sensual as well as financial. The inherent danger of criminal activity, according to Katz, increases the "rush" a criminal experiences on successfully committing a crime. Katz labels the rewards of this "rush" the *seduction of crime*.[5] For example, one of the three teenagers charged with randomly and fatally shooting a jogger in Duncan, Oklahoma, several years ago told police that he and his friends were "bored and didn't have anything to do, so we killed somebody."[6] Katz believes that such seemingly "senseless" crimes can be explained by rational choice theory only if the intrinsic (inner) reward of the crime itself is considered.

RATIONAL CHOICE THEORY AND PUNISHMENT

The theory that wrongdoers choose to commit crimes is a cornerstone of the American criminal justice system. Because crime is seen as the end result of a series of rational choices, policymakers have reasoned that severe punishment can deter criminal activity by adding another variable to the decision-making process. Supporters of the death penalty—now used by thirty-one states and the federal government—emphasize its deterrent effects, and legislators have used harsh mandatory sentences to control illegal drug use and trafficking.

TRAIT THEORIES OF CRIME If society is willing to punish crimes that are the result of a rational decision-making process, what should be its response to criminal behavior that is irrational or even unintentional? What if, for example, a schoolteacher who made sexual advances to young girls, including his stepdaughter, could prove that his wrongdoing was actually caused by an egg-sized tumor in his brain? Somewhat in contrast to rational choice theory, *trait theories* suggest that certain

biological or *psychological* traits in individuals could incline them toward criminal behavior given a certain set of circumstances. **Biology** is a very broad term that refers to the scientific study of living organisms, while **psychology** pertains more specifically to the study of the mind and its processes. "All behavior is biological," pointed out geneticist David C. Rowe. "All behavior is represented in the brain, in its biochemistry, electrical activity, structure, and growth and decline."[7]

Hormones and Aggression One trait theory holds that *biochemistry*, or the chemistry of living matter, can influence criminal behavior. For example, chemical messengers known as **hormones** have been the subject of much criminological study. Criminal activity in males has been linked to elevated levels of hormones—specifically, **testosterone,** which controls secondary sex characteristics and has been associated with traits of aggression. Testing of inmate populations shows that those incarcerated for violent crimes exhibit higher testosterone levels than other prisoners.[8] Elevated testosterone levels have also been used to explain the age-crime relationship (to be discussed later), as the average testosterone level of men under the age of twenty-eight is double that of men between thirty-one and sixty-six years old.[9]

A very specific form of female violent behavior is believed to stem from hormones. In 2014, Inakesha Armour was charged with attempted murder for throwing her three-month-old baby into a lake in Miramar, Florida. Armour's defense attorney claimed his client was suffering from *postpartum psychosis* at the time of her alleged crime. This temporary illness, believed to be caused partly by the hormonal changes that women experience after childbirth, triggers abnormal behavior in a small percentage of new mothers.[10]

The Brain and Crime Dr. Margaret Spinelli, a women's health expert at New York City's Columbia University, explains that during pregnancy, a pregnant woman's hormones increase "more than a hundredfold." Then, following birth, hormone levels plummet. This roller coaster of hormonal activity can "disrupt brain chemistry," contributing to postpartum psychosis, as described above.[11] The study of how brain activity influences criminal behavior is called neurocriminology. Its practitioners have contributed a great deal to the understanding of what predisposes humans to violent behavior.

As we mentioned in the previous chapter, more than half of all prison and jail inmates in the United States have mental health problems, with smaller percentages suffering from severe brain disorders.[12] In recent years, thanks to several high-profile murders, violent crime has

Biology The science of living organisms, including their structure, function, growth, and origin.

Psychology The scientific study of mental processes and behavior.

Hormone A chemical substance, produced in tissue and conveyed in the bloodstream, that controls certain cellular and body functions, such as growth and reproduction.

Testosterone The hormone primarily responsible for the production of sperm and the development of male secondary sex characteristics, such as the growth of facial and pubic hair and the change of voice pitch.

been linked to *schizophrenia*, a chronic brain disorder that can lead to erratic, uncontrollable behavior. Persons suffering from this disease are at an unusually high risk for committing suicide or harming others. Psychiatrist E. Fuller Torrey estimates that schizophrenics commit about a thousand homicides each year.[13]

Further research shows that even moderate use of alcohol or drugs increases the chances that a schizophrenic will behave violently.[14] Still, it is important to note that about 3.5 million Americans—1 percent of the adult population—have been diagnosed with schizophrenia, and the vast majority of them will never become criminal offenders. Overall, according to Richard Friedman, a professor of clinical psychiatry at New York's Weill Cornell Medical College, only about 4 percent of violence in the United States can be attributed to those with mental illnesses.[15] Consequently, there may be a correlation between mental conditions such as schizophrenia and violence, but such conditions cannot be said to cause violent behavior.

CJ and Technology

BRAIN SCIENCE AND CRIME

 Using various techniques, from X-ray technology to magnetic resonance imaging (MRI) to measuring oxygen flow, specialists have become quite skilled at mapping the human brain. Among other uses, these approaches can identify functional abnormalities and physical deformities in the brain that correlate with violent behavior.

For example, violent criminals tend to have impaired prefrontal cortexes—the part of the brain that manages our impulses and emotions. Furthermore, brain scanning shows that criminal behavior is often associated with a smaller-than-average amygdala, a cranial region that has been linked to moral decision making. Finally, Kent Kiehl of the University of New Mexico recently mapped the brains of ninety-six offenders in the state's prison system. Kiehl found that, in the four years after these men had been released from prison, those with low activity in the anterior cingulate cortex were twice as likely to commit a crime as those with high activity in this area of the brain.

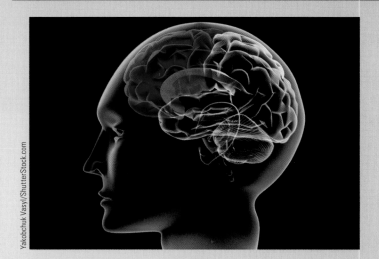

Yakobchuk Vasyl/ShutterStock.com

Thinking about Brain Science and Crime
Brain scans cannot *predict* future criminal offending. They can only indicate a *possibility* of future criminal offending. With this proviso in mind, what use should the criminal justice system make of brain mapping technology, if any?

PSYCHOLOGY AND CRIME Like biological theories of crime, psychological theories of crime operate under the assumption that individuals have traits that make them more or less predisposed to criminal activity. To a certain extent, however, psychology rests more heavily on abstract ideas than does biology. Even Sigmund Freud (1856–1939), perhaps the most influential of all psychologists, considered the operations of the mind to be, like an iceberg, mostly hidden.

One influential branch of psychology—*social psychology*—focuses on human behavior in the context of how human beings relate to and influence one another. **Social psychology** rests on the assumption that

Social Psychology The study of how individual behavior is influenced by the behavior of groups in social situations.

On November 25, 2014, a firefighter surveys the rubble of a strip mall in Ferguson, Missouri. An angry crowd destroyed the property after learning that a local white police officer would not face criminal charges for killing an African American suspect. *How does social psychology explain acts of violence or disorder by large groups of people?*

2-2b Bad Neighborhoods and Other Economic Disadvantages

For decades, the neighborhood of Liberty City in Miami, Florida, has endured one hardship after another. In the 1980s, it was racked by riots. In the 1990s, it was decimated by crack cocaine and AIDS. In the first decade of the 2000s, it was burdened by recession. Today, the area is marked by high levels of poverty, unemployment, and—not surprisingly— crime. After fifteen people were recently wounded during a shootout at a local nightclub, one resident reacted with resignation. "It's a shame," he said. "You hear gunshots every night and every day, and it becomes the norm."[18] Indeed, criminologists focusing on **sociology** have long argued that neighborhood conditions are perhaps the most important variable in predicting criminal behavior.

the way we view ourselves is shaped to a large degree by how we think others view us. Generally, we act in the same manner as those we like or admire because we want them to like or admire us. Thus, to a certain extent, social psychology tries to explain the influence of crowds on individual behavior.

About three decades ago, psychologist Philip Zimbardo highlighted the power of group behavior in dramatic fashion. Zimbardo randomly selected some Stanford University undergraduate students to act as "guards" and other students to act as "inmates" in an artificial prison environment. Before long, the students began to act as if these designations were real, with the "guards" physically mistreating the "inmates," who rebelled with equal violence. Within six days, Zimbardo was forced to discontinue the experiment out of fear for its participants' safety.[16] One of the basic assumptions of social psychology is that people are able to justify improper or even criminal behavior by convincing themselves that it is actually acceptable behavior. This delusion, researchers have found, is much easier to accomplish with the support of others behaving in the same manner.[17]

Sociology The study of the development and functioning of groups of people who live together within a society.

SOCIAL DISORGANIZATION THEORY In the early twentieth century, juvenile crime researchers Clifford Shaw and Henry McKay popularized sociological explanations for crime with their social disorganization theory. Shaw and McKay studied various high-crime neighborhoods in Chicago and discovered certain "zones" that exhibited high rates of crime. These zones were characterized by "disorganization," or a breakdown of the traditional institutions of social control, such as family, school systems, and local businesses. In contrast, in the city's "organized" communities, residents had developed certain agreements about fundamental values and norms. Shaw and McKay found that residents in high-crime neighborhoods had to a large degree abandoned these fundamental values and norms. Also, a lack of social controls had led to increased levels of antisocial, or criminal, behavior.[19] According to social disorganization theory, factors that lead to crime in these neighborhoods are:

1. **High levels of high school dropouts.**
2. **Chronic unemployment.**
3. **Deteriorating buildings and other infrastructures.**
4. **Concentrations of single-parent families.**

FIGURE 2.2 THE STAGES OF SOCIAL DISORGANIZATION THEORY

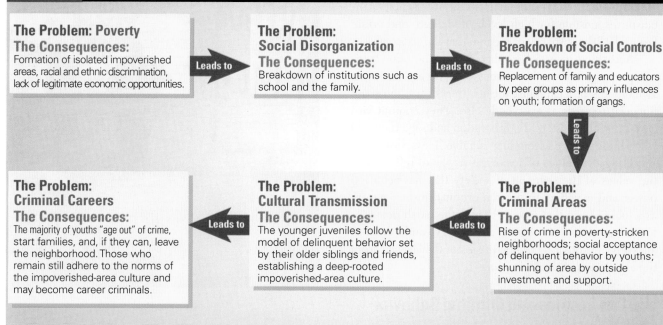

The Problem: Poverty
The Consequences:
Formation of isolated impoverished areas, racial and ethnic discrimination, lack of legitimate economic opportunities.

Leads to

The Problem: Social Disorganization
The Consequences:
Breakdown of institutions such as school and the family.

Leads to

The Problem: Breakdown of Social Controls
The Consequences:
Replacement of family and educators by peer groups as primary influences on youth; formation of gangs.

Leads to

The Problem: Criminal Careers
The Consequences:
The majority of youths "age out" of crime, start families, and, if they can, leave the neighborhood. Those who remain still adhere to the norms of the impoverished-area culture and may become career criminals.

Leads to

The Problem: Cultural Transmission
The Consequences:
The younger juveniles follow the model of delinquent behavior set by their older siblings and friends, establishing a deep-rooted impoverished-area culture.

Leads to

The Problem: Criminal Areas
The Consequences:
Rise of crime in poverty-stricken neighborhoods; social acceptance of delinquent behavior by youths; shunning of area by outside investment and support.

Social disorganization theory holds that crime is related to the environmental pressures that exist in certain communities or neighborhoods. These areas are marked by the desire of many of their inhabitants to "get out" at the first possible opportunity. Consequently, residents tend to ignore the important institutions in the community, such as businesses and education, causing further erosion and an increase in the conditions that lead to crime.

Source: Adapted from Larry J. Siegel, *Criminology,* 10th ed. (Belmont, CA: Thomson/Wadsworth, 2009), 180.

See Figure 2.2 to better understand social disorganization theory.

STRAIN THEORY Another self-perpetuating aspect of disorganized neighborhoods is that once residents gain the financial means to leave a high-crime community, they usually do so. This desire to escape the inner city is related to the second branch of social structure theory: **strain theory.** Most Americans have similar life goals, which include gaining a certain measure of wealth and financial freedom. The means of attaining these goals, however, are not universally available. Many citizens do not have access to the education or training necessary for financial success. This often results in frustration and anger, or *strain*.

Strain theory has its roots in the works of French sociologist Emile Durkheim (1858–1917) and his concept of **anomie** (derived from the Greek word for "without norms"). Durkheim believed that *anomie* resulted when social change threw behavioral norms into a flux, leading to a weakening of social controls and an increase in deviant behavior.[20] Another sociologist, American Robert K. Merton, expanded on Durkheim's ideas in his own theory of strain. Merton believed that *anomie* was caused by a social structure in which all citizens have

similar goals without equal means to achieve them.[21] One way to alleviate this strain is to gain wealth by the means that are available to the residents of disorganized communities: drug trafficking, burglary, and other criminal activities.

CAREER TIP A *sociologist* is someone who studies human social behavior. Because crime is such an important—and interesting—facet of human behavior, sociologists often study criminality.

SOCIAL CONFLICT THEORIES Strain theory and the concept of *anomie* seem to suggest that the unequal structure of our society is, in part, to blame for criminal behavior. This argument forms the bedrock of

Strain Theory The assumption that crime is the result of frustration felt by individuals who cannot reach their financial and personal goals through legitimate means.

Anomie A condition in which the individual feels a disconnect from society due to the breakdown or absence of social norms.

social conflict theories of crime. These theories, which entered mainstream criminology in the 1960s, hold capitalism responsible for high levels of violence and crime because of the disparity of income that it encourages.

According to social conflict theory, the poor commit property crimes for reasons of need and because, as members of a capitalist society, they desire the same financial rewards as everybody else. They commit violent crimes because of the frustration and rage they feel when these rewards seem unattainable. Laws, instead of reflecting the values of society as a whole, reflect only the values of the segment of society that has achieved power and is willing to use the criminal justice system as a tool to keep that power.[22] Thus, the harsh penalties for "lower-class" crimes such as burglary can be seen as a means of protecting the privileges of the "haves" from the aspirations of the "have-nots."

2-2c Life Lessons and Criminal Behavior

Some criminologists find class theories of crime overly narrow. Surveys that ask people directly about their criminal behavior have shown that the criminal instinct is pervasive in middle- and upper-class communities, even if it is expressed differently. Anybody, these criminologists argue, has the potential to act out criminal behavior, regardless of class, race, or gender.

THE ABANDONED CAR EXPERIMENT Philip Zimbardo conducted a well-known, if rather unscientific, experiment to show the broad potential for misbehavior. The psychologist placed an abandoned automobile with its hood up on the campus of Stanford University. The car remained in place, untouched, for a week. Then, Zimbardo smashed the car's window with a sledgehammer. Within minutes, passersby had joined in the destruction of the automobile, eventually stripping its valuable parts.[23]

Social process theories function on the same basis as Zimbardo's "interdependence of decisions experiment":

Two law enforcement officers investigate a murder in the Desire neighborhood of New Orleans. *How would a criminologist who advocates social conflict theories of criminal behavior explain high crime rates in low-income neighborhoods such as Desire?*

Michael DeMocker/The Times-Picayune/Landov

the potential for criminal behavior exists in everyone and will be realized depending on an individual's interaction with various institutions and processes of society. Two major branches of social process theory are (1) learning theory and (2) control theory.

LEARNING THEORY Popularized by Edwin Sutherland in the 1940s, **learning theory** contends that criminal activity is a learned behavior. In other words, a criminal is taught both the practical methods of crime (such as how to pick a lock) and the psychological aspects of crime (how to deal with the guilt of wrongdoing). Sutherland's *theory of differential association* held that individuals are exposed to the values of family and peers such as school friends or co-workers. If the dominant values a person is exposed to favor criminal behavior, then that person is more likely to mimic such behavior.[24] Sutherland's focus on the importance of family relations in this area is underscored by research showing that sons of fathers who have been incarcerated are at an increased risk of delinquency and arrest.[25]

More recently, learning theory has been expanded to include the growing influence of the media. In the latest in a long series of studies, researchers released data in 2013 showing that children or adolescents who watched "excessive" amounts of violent television content faced an elevated risk of exhibiting antisocial behavior, such as criminality, in early adulthood.[26] Elliot Rodger, whose crimes were described at the beginning of this chapter, was obsessed with the violent video game World of Warcraft as a high school student.

Social Conflict Theories A school of criminology that views criminal behavior as the result of class conflict.

Social Process Theories A school of criminology that considers criminal behavior to be the predictable result of a person's interaction with his or her environment.

Learning Theory The theory that delinquents and criminals must be taught both the practical and the emotional skills necessary to participate in illegal activity.

of the crime of arson have certainly been met, but can the manager be charged with murder? In some jurisdictions, the act might be considered a form of murder, but according to the U.S. Department of Justice, arson-related deaths and injuries of police officers and firefighters due to the "hazardous natures of their professions" are not murders.[43]

The distinction is important because the Department of Justice provides us with the most far-reaching and oft-cited set of national crime statistics. Each year, the department releases the **Uniform Crime Report (UCR).** Since its inception in 1930, the UCR has attempted to measure the overall rate of crime in the United States by organizing "offenses known to law enforcement."[44] To produce the UCR, the Federal Bureau of Investigation (FBI) relies on the voluntary participation of local law enforcement agencies. These agencies—approximately 18,400 in total, covering most of the population—base their information on three measurements:

1. **The number of persons arrested.**
2. **The number of crimes reported by victims, witnesses, and the police themselves.**
3. **Police employee data.**[45]

Once this information has been sent to the FBI, the agency presents the crime data in two important ways:

1. **As a *rate* per 100,000 people. So, for example, suppose the crime rate in a given year is 3,500. This means that, for every 100,000 inhabitants of the United States, 3,500 *Part I offenses* were reported to the FBI by local police departments. The crime rate is often cited by media sources when discussing the level of crime in the United States.**
2. **As a *percentage* change from the previous year or over other time periods. From 2004 to 2013, there was a 14.5 percent decrease in violent crime and a 16.3 percent decrease in property crime. Thus, according to the UCR, that decade saw a significant reduction in criminal behavior in the United States.**[46]

The Department of Justice publishes its data annually in *Crime in the United States.* Along with the basic statistics, this publication offers an exhaustive array of crime information, including breakdowns of crimes committed by city, county, and other geographic designations and by the demographics (gender, race, age) of the individuals who have been arrested for crimes.

2-4b Part I Offenses

The UCR divides the criminal offenses it measures into two major categories: Part I and Part II offenses. **Part I offenses** are those crimes that, due to their seriousness and frequency, are recorded by the FBI to give a general idea of the "crime picture" in the United States in any given year. For a description of the seven Part I offenses, see Figure 2.4.

Part I violent offenses are those most likely to be covered by the media and, consequently, inspire the most fear of crime in the population. These crimes have come to dominate crime coverage to such an extent that, for most Americans, the first image that comes to mind at the mention of "crime" is one person physically attacking another person or a robbery taking place with the use or threat of force.[47] Furthermore, in the stereotypical crime, the offender and the victim usually do not know each other.

Given the trauma of violent crimes, this perception is understandable, but it is not accurate. According to UCR statistics, a relative or other acquaintance of the victim commits at least 45 percent of the homicides in the United States.[48] Furthermore, as is evident from Figure 2.4, the majority of Part I offenses committed are property crimes. Notice that 61 percent of all reported Part I offenses are larceny/thefts, and another 20 percent are burglaries.[49]

2-4c Part II Offenses

Not only do violent crimes represent the minority of Part I offenses, but Part I offenses are far outweighed by **Part II offenses,** which include all crimes recorded

Uniform Crime Report (UCR) An annual report compiled by the FBI to give an indication of criminal activity in the United States.

Part I Offenses Crimes reported annually by the FBI in its Uniform Crime Report. Part I offenses include murder, rape, robbery, aggravated assault, burglary, larceny, and motor vehicle theft.

Part II Offenses All crimes recorded by the FBI that do not fall into the category of Part I offenses. These crimes include both misdemeanors and felonies.

FIGURE 2.4 PART I OFFENSES

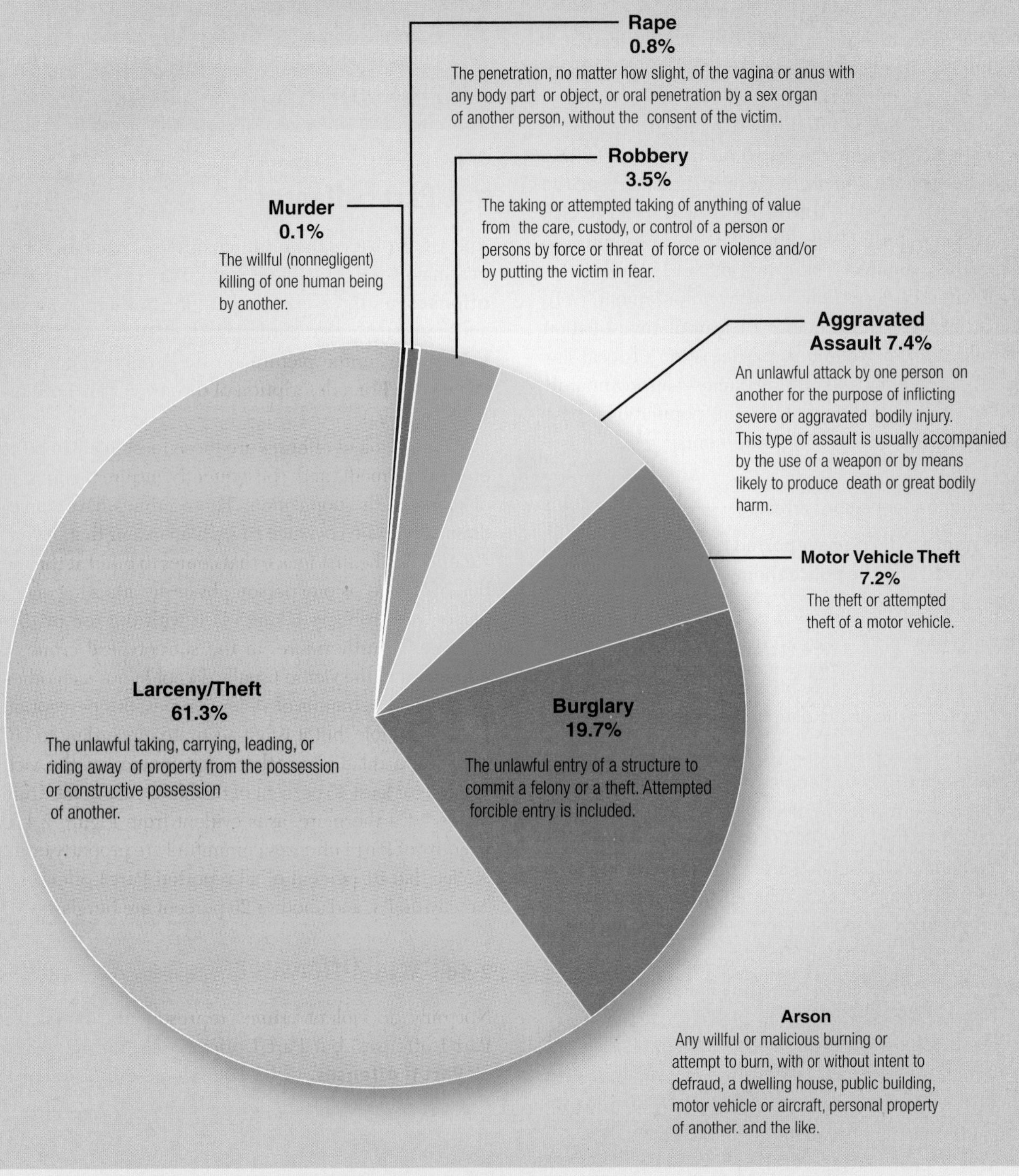

Rape
0.8%

The penetration, no matter how slight, of the vagina or anus with any body part or object, or oral penetration by a sex organ of another person, without the consent of the victim.

Robbery
3.5%

The taking or attempted taking of anything of value from the care, custody, or control of a person or persons by force or threat of force or violence and/or by putting the victim in fear.

Murder
0.1%

The willful (nonnegligent) killing of one human being by another.

Aggravated Assault 7.4%

An unlawful attack by one person on another for the purpose of inflicting severe or aggravated bodily injury. This type of assault is usually accompanied by the use of a weapon or by means likely to produce death or great bodily harm.

Motor Vehicle Theft
7.2%

The theft or attempted theft of a motor vehicle.

Larceny/Theft
61.3%

The unlawful taking, carrying, leading, or riding away of property from the possession or constructive possession of another.

Burglary
19.7%

The unlawful entry of a structure to commit a felony or a theft. Attempted forcible entry is included.

Arson

Any willful or malicious burning or attempt to burn, with or without intent to defraud, a dwelling house, public building, motor vehicle or aircraft, personal property of another. and the like.

Every month, local law enforcement agencies voluntarily provide information on serious offenses in their jurisdiction to the FBI. These serious offenses, known as Part I offenses, are defined here. (Arson is not included in the national crime report data, but it is sometimes considered a Part I offense nonetheless, so its definition is included here.) As the graph shows, most Part I offenses reported by local police departments in any given year are property crimes.

Sources: Federal Bureau of Investigation, *Crime in the United States, 2013* (Washington, D.C.: U.S. Department of Justice, 2014), at **www.fbi.gov/about-us/cjis/ucr/crime-in-the-u.s/2013/crime-in-the-u.s.-2013/resource-pages/offense-definitions/13-offensedefinitions_final** and **www.fbi.gov/about-us/cjis/ucr/crime-in-the-u.s/2013/crime-in-the-u.s.-2013/tables/1tabledatadecoverviewpdf/table_1_crime_in_the_united_states_by_volume_and_rate_per_100000_inhabitants_1994-2013.xls.**

by the FBI that do not fall into the category of Part I offenses. While Part I offenses are almost always felonies, Part II offenses include criminal behavior that is often classified as a misdemeanor. Of the nineteen categories that make up Part II offenses, the most common are drug abuse violations, simple assaults (in which no weapons are used and no serious harm is done to the victim), driving under the influence, and disorderly conduct.[50]

Information gathered on Part I offenses reflects those offenses "known," or reported to the FBI by local agencies. Part II offenses, in contrast, are measured only by arrest data. In 2013, the FBI recorded about 2 million arrests for Part I offenses in the United States. That same year, about 9.3 million arrests for Part II offenses took place.[51] In other words, a Part II offense was about four and one-half times more common than a Part I offense. Such statistics have prompted Marcus Felson, a professor at Rutgers University School of Criminal Justice, to comment that "most crime is very ordinary."[52]

2-4d The National Incident-Based Reporting System

In the 1980s, the Department of Justice began seeking ways to revise its data-collecting system. The result was the National Incident-Based Reporting System (NIBRS). In the NIBRS, local agencies collect data on each single crime occurrence within twenty-three offense categories made up of forty-nine specific crimes called Group A offenses. These data are recorded on computerized record systems provided—though not completely financed—by the federal government.

The NIBRS became available to local agencies in 1989. Twenty-six years later, thirty-three states have been NIBRS certified, and fifteen of those states now submit all their crime data to the federal government using this program.[53] Criminologists are responding enthusiastically to the NIBRS because the system provides information about four "data sets"—offenses, victims, offenders, and arrestees—unavailable through the UCR. The NIBRS also presents a more complete picture of crime by monitoring all criminal "incidents" reported to the police, not just those that lead to an arrest. For example, the 2013 NIBRS, which recorded more than 5.6 million criminal incidents, found that sex offenses were most likely to take place between midnight and 12:59 A.M., and that nearly 100,000 aggravated assaults resulted from arguments.[54]

2-4e Victim Surveys

One alternative method of data collecting attempts to avoid the distorting influence of the "intermediary," or the local police agencies. In **victim surveys,** criminologists or other researchers ask the victims of crime directly about their experiences, using techniques such as interviews or e-mail and phone surveys. The first large-scale victim survey took place in 1966, when members of 10,000 households answered questionnaires as part of the President's Commission on Law Enforcement and the Administration of Justice. The results indicated a much higher victimization rate than had been previously expected, and researchers felt the process gave them a better understanding of the **dark figure of crime,** or the actual amount of crime that occurs in the country.

Criminologists were so encouraged by the results of the 1966 experiment that the federal government decided to institute an ongoing victim survey. The result was the National Crime Victimization Survey (NCVS), which started in 1972. Conducted by the U.S. Bureau of the Census in cooperation with the Bureau of Justice Statistics of the Justice Department, the NCVS conducts an annual survey of approximately 90,000 households with about 160,000 occupants over twelve years of age. Participants are interviewed twice a year concerning their experiences with crimes in the prior six months. As you can see in Figure 2.5, questions are quite detailed in determining the experiences of crime victims.

2-4f Self-Reported Surveys

LO2-3 Based on many of the same principles as victim surveys, but focusing instead on offenders, **self-reported surveys** are another source of information for criminologists. In this form of data collection, persons are asked directly—through personal interviews or questionnaires, or over the telephone—about specific criminal activity to which they may have been a party.

Victim Surveys A method of gathering crime data that directly surveys participants to determine their experiences as victims of crime.

Dark Figure of Crime A term used to describe the actual amount of crime that takes place. The "figure" is "dark," or impossible to detect, because a great number of crimes are never reported to the police.

Self-Reported Survey A method of gathering crime data that relies on participants to reveal and detail their own criminal or delinquent behavior.

FIGURE 2.5 SAMPLE QUESTIONS FROM THE NCVS (NATIONAL CRIME VICTIMIZATION SURVEY)

36a. Was something belonging to YOU stolen, such as

    a. Things that you carry, like luggage, a wallet, purse, briefcase, book

    b. Clothing, jewelry, or cell phone

    c. Bicycle or sports equipment

    d. Things in your home—like a TV, stereo, or tools

    e. Things outside your home, such as a garden hose or lawn furniture

    f. Things belonging to children in the household

    g. Things from a vehicle, such as a package, groceries, camera, or CDs?

41a. Has anyone attacked or threatened you in any of these ways

    a. With any weapon, for instance, a gun or knife

    b. With anything like a baseball bat, frying pan, scissors, or stick

    c. By something thrown, such as a rock or a bottle

    d. Include any grabbing, punching, or choking

    e. Any rape, attempted rape, or other type of sexual attack

    f. Any face to face threats OR

    g. Any attack or threat or use of force by anyone at all? Please mention it even if you are not certain it was a crime.

43a. Incidents involving forced or unwanted sexual acts are often difficult to talk about. Have you been forced or coerced to engage in unwanted sexual activity by

    a. Someone you didn't know

    b. A casual acquaintance OR

    c. Someone you know well?

45. During the last six months, did anything you thought was a crime happen to YOU, but you did NOT report it to the police?

    a. Yes

    b. No

Source: Adapted from U.S. Department of Justice, *National Crime Victimization Survey 2009* (Washington, D.C.: Bureau of Justice Statistics, 2013).

Self-reported surveys are most useful in situations in which the group to be studied is already gathered in an institutional setting, such as a juvenile facility or a prison. One of the most widespread self-reported surveys in the United States, the Drug Use Forecasting Program, collects information on narcotics use from arrestees who have been brought into booking facilities.

Because there is no penalty for admitting to criminal activity in a self-reported survey, subjects tend to be more forthcoming in discussing their behavior. Researchers often use self-reported studies to get a better idea of the actual amount of sexual assault that takes place in our society. These studies invariably show that many more rapes take place than are reported to the police.[55] Such conclusions underscore the most striking finding of self-reported surveys: the dark figure of crime, referred to earlier as the *actual* amount of crime that takes place, appears to be much larger than the UCR or NCVS would suggest.

2-5 WHAT ROLE DO VICTIMS PLAY IN CRIMINAL JUSTICE?

Thirty years ago, a presidential task force invited federal and state legislatures to "address the needs of the millions of Americans and their families who are victimized by crime every year and who often carry its scars into the years to come."[56] This call to action was, in large part, a consequence of the rather peculiar position of **victims** in our criminal justice system. That is, once a crime has occurred, the victim is relegated to a single role: being a witness against the suspect in court. Legally, he or she has no say in the prosecution of the offender, or even whether such a prosecution is to take place. Such powerlessness can be extremely frustrating, particularly in the wake of a traumatic, life-changing event.

2-5a Legal Rights of Crime Victims

LO2-4 To remedy this situation, all states have passed legislation creating certain rights for victims. On a federal level, such protections are encoded in the Crime Victims' Rights Act of 2004 (CVRA), which gives victims "the right to participate in the system."[57] This participation primarily focuses on three categories of rights:

1. The right to be *informed*. This includes receiving information about victims' rights in general, as well as specific information such as the dates and time of court proceedings relating to the relevant crime.

2. The right to be *present*. This includes the right to be present at those court hearings involving the case at hand, as long as the victim's presence does not interfere with the rights of the accused.

Victim Any person who suffers physical, emotional, or financial harm as the result of a criminal act.

3. **The right to be *heard*.** This includes the ability to consult with prosecutorial officials before the criminal trial (addressed in Chapter 8), to speak during the sentencing phase of the trial (Chapter 9), and to offer an opinion when the offender is scheduled to be released from incarceration (Chapter 10).[58]

Some jurisdictions also provide victims with the right of law enforcement protection from the offender during the time period before a criminal trial. In addition, most states require *restitution,* or monetary payment, from offenders to help victims repay any costs associated with the crime and rebuild their lives. In 2014, for instance, a federal judge ordered three men who illegally started a two-thousand-acre fire in Southern California to pay several million dollars to the residents whose homes the blaze destroyed.

Crystal King, left, addresses a criminal court in Chardon, Ohio, during the sentencing of T. J. Lane for murdering her brother. *Should crime victims and their families have the right to participate in criminal justice proceedings? Why or why not?*

NATIONAL VICTIM ADVOCATE

CareerPrep

Job Description:

▶ Provide direct support, advocacy, and short-term crisis counseling to crime victims.

▶ Act as a liaison between victims or witnesses and district attorneys or law enforcement, and provide court support for victims.

What Kind of Training Is Required?

▶ A bachelor's degree in criminal justice, social work/psychology, or a related field.

▶ A minimum of two years' experience in the criminal justice system, one year of which should have involved direct services with victims.

Annual Salary Range?

▶ $45,000–$65,000

GETTING LINKEDIN

Victim advocates must be comfortable working with a wide range of victims. For example, the University of Colorado at Boulder's recent posting for this position referenced an applicant's ability to respond to "hazing, bias motivated incidents, death, discrimination and harassment."

2-5b The Risks of Victimization

Anybody can be a victim of crime. This does not mean, however, that everybody is at an equal risk of being victimized. For instance, residents of neighborhoods with heavy concentrations of payday-lending businesses are targeted by criminals at unusually high rates.[59] To better explain the circumstances surrounding this type of victimization, criminologists Larry Cohen and Marcus Felson devised the *routine activities theory*. According to Cohen and Felson, most criminal acts require the following:

1. **A likely offender.**

2. **A suitable target (a person or an object).**

3. **The absence of a capable guardian—that is, any person (not necessarily a law enforcement agent) whose presence or proximity prevents a crime from happening.[60]**

When these three factors are present, the likelihood of crime rises. Cohen and Felson cite routine activities theory in explaining the link between payday lenders and crime. People who use payday lenders often leave those establishments with large sums of cash, late at night or during weekends when there is less street traffic. Consequently, they act as suitable targets, attracting likely offenders to neighborhoods where the payday lenders are located.[61]

REPEAT VICTIMIZATION Cohen and Felson also hypothesize that offenders attach "values" to suitable targets. The higher the value, the more likely that target is going to be the subject of a crime.[62] A gold watch, for example, would obviously have a higher value for a thief than a plastic watch and therefore is more likely to be stolen. Similarly, people who are perceived to be weak or unprotected can have high value for criminals. Law enforcement officials in southern Florida, for example, believe that undocumented immigrants in the area have elevated victimization rates because criminals know that these immigrants are often afraid to report crimes to authorities for fear of being removed from the country.

Resources such as the National Crime Victimization Survey provide criminologists with an important tool for determining which types of people are most valued as potential victims. Statistics clearly show that a relatively small number of victims are involved in a disproportionate number of crimes. These findings support an approach to crime analysis known as **repeat victimization.** This theory is based on the premise that certain populations—mostly low-income residents of urban areas—are more likely to be victims of crimes than others and, therefore, past victimization is a strong predictor of future victimization.[63] Further criminological research shows that factors such as drug and alcohol use and depression also increase the possibility that a crime victim will be revictimized.[64]

THE VICTIM-OFFENDER CONNECTION Not only does past victimization seem to increase the risk of future victimization, but so does past criminal behavior. "The notion that [violent crimes] are random bolts of lightning, which is the commonly held image, is not the reality at all," says David Kennedy, a professor at New York's John Jay College of Criminal Justice.[65]

Kennedy's point is further made by Figure 2.6, which identifies young minority males from urban neighborhoods as the most common victims of crimes. This

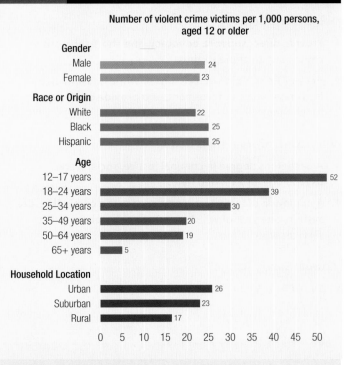

FIGURE 2.6 CRIME VICTIMS IN THE UNITED STATES

Number of violent crime victims per 1,000 persons, aged 12 or older

Gender
Male — 24
Female — 23

Race or Origin
White — 22
Black — 25
Hispanic — 25

Age
12–17 years — 52
18–24 years — 39
25–34 years — 30
35–49 years — 20
50–64 years — 19
65+ years — 5

Household Location
Urban — 26
Suburban — 23
Rural — 17

According to the U.S. Department of Justice, minorities, residents of urban areas, and young people are most likely to be victims of violent crime in this country.

Source: Bureau of Justice Statistics, *Criminal Victimization, 2013* (Washington, D.C.: U.S. Department of Justice, September 2014), 9, 10.

Repeat Victimization The theory that certain people and places are more likely to be subject to repeated criminal activity and that past victimization is a strong indicator of future victimization.

demographic, as will become clear later in the chapter, is also at the highest risk for criminal behavior. Increasingly, law enforcement agencies are applying the lessons of repeat victimization and other victim studies to concentrate their attention on "hot spots" of crime, a strategy we address in Chapter 5.

2-6 WHAT IS THE STATE OF CRIME IN THE UNITED STATES?

The UCR, NCVS, and other statistical measures we have discussed so far in this chapter, though important, represent only the tip of the iceberg of crime data. Thanks

LO2-5

to the efforts of government law enforcement agencies, educational institutions, and private individuals, more information on crime is available today than at any time in the nation's history. When interpreting and predicting general crime trends, experts tend to rely on what University of California at Berkeley law professor Franklin Zimring calls the three "usual suspects" of crime fluctuation:

1. *Imprisonment,* based on the principle that (a) an offender in prison or jail is unable to commit a crime on the street, and (b) a potential offender on the street will not commit a crime because he or she does not want to wind up behind bars.

2. *Youth populations,* because offenders commit fewer crimes as they grow older.

3. The *economy,* because when legitimate opportunities to earn income become scarce, some people will turn to illegitimate methods, such as crime.[66]

Pure statistics do not always tell the whole story, however, and crime rates often fail to behave in the ways that the experts predict.

2-6a Looking Good: Crime in the 1990s and 2000s

In 1995, eminent crime expert James Q. Wilson, noting that the number of young males in the United States was set to increase dramatically over the next decade, predicted that "30,000 more young muggers, killers, and thieves" would be on the streets by 2000. "Get ready," he warned.[67] Fortunately for the country, Wilson was wrong. As is evident from Figure 2.7, starting in 1994 the United States experienced a steep crime decline that we are still enjoying today.

THE GREAT CRIME DECLINE The crime statistics of the 1990s are startling. Even with an upswing at the beginning of the decade, from 1990 to 2000 the homicide rate dropped 39 percent, the robbery rate 44 percent, the burglary rate 41 percent, and the auto theft rate 37 percent. By most measures, this decline was the longest and deepest of the twentieth century.[68] In retrospect, the 1990s seem to have encompassed a "golden era" for the leading indicators of low crime rates. The economy was robust. The incarceration rate was skyrocketing. Plus, despite the misgivings of James Q. Wilson and many of his colleagues, the percentage of the population in the high-risk age bracket in 1995 was actually lower than it had been in 1980.[69]

CONTINUING DECREASES According to the UCR, the United States is presently enjoying historically low levels of crime. Since the mid-1990s, the violent crime rate has declined by about 50 percent (see Figure 2.7), and the property crime rate has dropped about

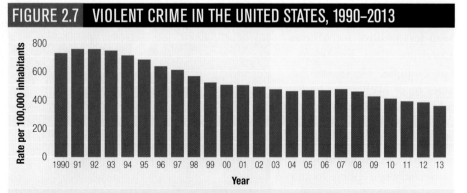

FIGURE 2.7 VIOLENT CRIME IN THE UNITED STATES, 1990–2013

Rate per 100,000 inhabitants (y-axis: 0, 200, 400, 600, 800)
Year (x-axis: 1990, 91, 92, 93, 94, 95, 96, 97, 98, 99, 00, 01, 02, 03, 04, 05, 06, 07, 08, 09, 10, 11, 12, 13)

According to statistics gathered each year by the FBI, American violent crime rates dropped steadily in the second half of the 1990s, leveled off for several years, and now have begun to decrease anew.

Source: Federal Bureau of Investigation.

40 percent.[70] Experts have put forth a number of theories to explain this fall in crime, including

1. Continued improvements in law enforcement, particularly DNA fingerprinting and information-based policing techniques that focus crime prevention tactics on "hot spots" of criminal activity.

2. An aging population: the median age in the United States is around thirty-seven years, the highest of any time in the nation's history.[71] As noted earlier, older people commit fewer crimes than younger people.

3. Improvements in digital technology that have increased the use and effectiveness of security cameras. Also, the public, armed with mobile phones with cameras, has become something of a complementary police force, sending immediate crime alerts and recording videos of criminal activity.

4. The gentrification of many formerly high-crime neighborhoods, which has contributed significantly to a 64 percent crime-rate reduction in America's largest cities.[72]

Another possible factor in the crime decline may be the large number of offenders who have been locked up in prison over the past two decades. The relationship between inmate populations and crime rates is controversial, however, and will be revisited in Chapter 11.

2-6b Crime, Race, and Poverty

Although crime and victimization rates have decreased across racial lines over the past twenty years, the trends have been less positive for African Americans than for whites. For example, blacks are 6.3 times more likely to be homicide victims than whites,[73] and almost 20 percent more likely to be homicide offenders.[74] African Americans are particularly susceptible to gun violence, with firearm murder rates of 14.6 per 100,000 adults, compared with 1.9 for whites and 4.0 for Hispanics.[75]

A large part of this violence is taking place within the African American community—nationwide, most murder victims are killed by someone of the same race (90 percent for blacks and 83 percent for whites).[76]

RACE AND CRIME Homicide rates are not the only area in which there is a divergence in crime trends between the races. Official crime data seem to indicate a strong correlation between minority status and crime: African Americans—who make up 13 percent of the population—constitute 39 percent of those arrested for violent crimes and 29 percent of those arrested for property crimes.[77] In five states that recently reformed their drug laws, the Center of Juvenile and Criminal Justice found that African Americans were still five times more likely than all other races and ethnicities to be arrested for marijuana-related crimes.[78] Furthermore, a black juvenile in the United States is more than twice as likely as a white juvenile to wind up in delinquency court.[79]

CLASS AND CRIME The racial differences in the crime rate are one of the most controversial areas of the criminal justice system. At first glance, crime statistics seem to support the idea that the subculture of African Americans in the United States is disposed toward criminal behavior. Not all of the data, however, support that assertion. A research project led by sociologist Ruth

American Spirit/ShutterStock.com

What is your opinion of the theory that economic disadvantage, rather than skin color, accounts for the disproportionate number of African Americans in U.S. prisons, such as this inmate at the Dade County (Florida) Men's Correctional Facility?

D. Peterson of Ohio State University gathered information on nearly 150 neighborhoods in Columbus, Ohio. Peterson and her colleagues separated the neighborhoods based on race and on levels of disadvantage, such as poverty, joblessness, lack of college graduates, and high levels of female-headed families. She found that whether the neighborhoods were predominantly white or predominantly black had little impact on violent crime rates. Those neighborhoods with higher levels of disadvantage, however, had uniformly higher violent crime rates.[80]

INCOME LEVEL AND CRIME Peterson's research suggests that, regardless of race, a person is at a much higher risk of violent offending or being a victim of violence if he or she lives in a disadvantaged neighborhood. Given that African Americans are two times more likely than whites to live in poverty and hold low-wage-earning jobs, they are, as a group, more susceptible to the factors that contribute to criminality.[81]

Indeed, an abundance of information suggests that income level is more important than skin color when it comes to crime trends. A 2002 study of nearly 900 African American children (400 boys and 467 girls) from neighborhoods with varying income levels showed that family earning power had the only significant correlation with violent behavior.[82] More recent research conducted by William A. Pridemore of Indiana University found a "positive and significant association" between poverty and homicide.[83] Lack of education, another handicap most often faced by low-income citizens, also seems to correlate with criminal behavior. Forty-one percent of all inmates in state and federal prisons failed to obtain a high school education, compared with 18 percent of the population at large.[84]

2-6c Women and Crime

To put it bluntly, crime is an overwhelmingly male activity. Almost 62 percent of all murders involve a male victim and a male perpetrator, and in only 2.5 percent of homicides are both the offender and the victim female.[85] Only 14 percent of the national jail population and 7 percent of the national prison population are female, and in 2013 only 26 percent of all arrests involved women.[86]

A GROWING PRESENCE The statistics just cited fail to convey the startling rate at which the female presence in the criminal justice system has been increasing. Between 1991 and 2013, the number of men arrested each year declined about 12 percent. Over that time period, annual arrests for women increased by 34 percent.[87] In 1970, there were about 6,000 women in federal and state prisons, but today, there are more than 111,000.[88] There are two possible explanations for these increases. Either (1) the life circumstances and behavior of women have changed dramatically in the past forty years, or (2) the criminal justice system's attitude toward women has changed over that time period.[89]

In the 1970s, when female crime rates started surging upward, many observers accepted the former explanation. "You can't get involved in a bar fight if you're not allowed in the bar," said feminist theorist Freda Adler in 1975.[90] It has become clear, however, that a significant percentage of women arrested are involved in a narrow band of wrongdoing, mostly drug- and alcohol-related offenses or property crimes.[91] Research shows that as recently as the 1980s, many of the women now in prison would not have been arrested or would have received lighter sentences for their crimes.[92] Consequently, more scholars are convinced that rising female criminality is the result of a criminal justice system that is "more willing to incarcerate women."[93]

WOMEN AS CRIME VICTIMS In general, about six of every ten crimes in the United States are committed by someone known to the victim. Those crimes that usually involve strangers, such as robbery and assault, most often target male victims. In contrast, women have a greater chance of being victimized in nonstranger crimes, such as sexual assault.[94] Indeed, women are the victims in 86 percent of all intimate partner violence prosecutions.[95] The highest rate of victimization occurs among women between the ages of twelve and thirty-four, and one study estimates that between one-fifth and one-quarter of female college students have experienced a rape or attempted rape.[96] (The feature *Discretion in Action—"Yes" Means "Yes"* explores efforts to reduce the incidence of sexual assault on college campuses.)

Statistically, women are also at a greater risk of being victims of **domestic violence.** This umbrella term covers a wide variety of maltreatment, including physical violence and psychological abuse, inflicted among family members and others in close relationships. Though government data show that women are significantly more likely to be victims of domestic violence than men, these

Domestic Violence Willful neglect or physical violence that occurs within a familial or other intimate relationship.

Discretion in Action

"YES" MEANS "YES"

THE SITUATION According to a White House task force, nearly one in five college female students have been the victims of sexual assault, with only 12 percent of those cases reported to school authorities. Attempts to reduce campus sexual assaults have generally relied on educating incoming students about the problem and discouraging binge drinking. As these efforts seem to have failed, victims' rights advocates are demanding stronger measures.

THE LAW As we saw earlier in the chapter, the legal definition of rape hinges on the concept of consent. If both parties to sexual activity are willing, then no crime has occurred. If one party is unwilling, then perhaps there has been a crime. Given the complexity of sexual relationships, school administrators and student disciplinary bodies often find it difficult to determine whether a rape has taken place and whether the perpetrator should be expelled. In response to this problem, about eight hundred postsecondary institutions have implemented *affirmative consent* policies on their campuses. These policies are designed to make consent

obvious by requiring each party to indicate—either verbally with a "yes" or through actions—that she or he is willing to engage in sexual activity.

WHAT WOULD YOU DO? Assume you are a politician in a state that has recently gone through several on-campus sexual assault controversies. One of your colleagues has proposed a bill making affirmative consent state law, meaning that all postsecondary school students would be required to actively indicate willingness to have sex. Proponents insist that, by removing the possibility that "silence equals consent," the proposed legislation would reduce the incidence of coerced sex and remove the burden from victims of having to prove that they said "no." Opponents counter that it is unrealistic to expect sex partners to ask, "*May* I do this now?" and that the proposed bill unfairly shifts the burden to the accused. Would you support the proposed affirmative consent legislation? Explain your answer.

[To see how one state has reacted to the problem of sexual assault on campus, go to Example 2.1 in Appendix A.]

STUDY TOOLS 2

READY TO STUDY? IN THE BOOK, YOU CAN:

☐ Rip out the Chapter Review Card, which includes key terms and chapter summaries.

ONLINE AT WWW.CENGAGEBRAIN.COM, YOU CAN:

☐ Learn about campus sex crimes in a short video.

☐ Explore the National Center for Victims of Crime home page.

☐ Interact with figures from the text, and watch quick animation clips.

☐ Prepare for tests with quizzes.

☐ Review the key terms with Flash Cards.

findings are not unquestioned. Men, many observers assume, are less likely to report abuse because of the social stigma surrounding female-on-male violence.[97]

A third crime that appears to involve mainly female victims is **stalking,** or a course of conduct directed at a person that would reasonably cause that person to feel fear. Such behavior includes unwanted phone calls, following or spying, and a wide range of online activity that we will address in Chapter 14. Stalkers target women at about three times the rate they target men, and seven out of ten stalking victims have had some prior relationship with their stalkers.[98]

Stalking The criminal act of causing fear in a person by repeatedly subjecting that person to unwanted or threatening attention.

Quiz

1. Researchers who study the causes of crime are called _____ .

2. If a hypothesis proves valid, it can be used to support a _____ that explains a possible cause of crime.

3. _____ _____ theory holds that criminals make a deliberate decision to commit a crime after weighing the possible rewards or punishments involved.

4. Social _____ focuses on how individuals justify their own antisocial or criminal behavior by patterning it after similar behavior by others.

5. Social _____ theory examines living conditions to explain the crime rate in any given neighborhood or community.

6. Among social process theories, _____ theory could be used to explain why the younger sibling of a gang member would be at a particular risk to join a gang him- or herself.

7. Drug _____ is defined as the use of any drug that causes harm to the user or a third party.

8. To produce its annual _____ _____ _____ , the Federal Bureau of Investigation relies on the cooperation of local law enforcement agencies.

9. _____ surveys rely on those who have been the subjects of criminal activity to discuss the incidents with researchers.

10. _____- _____ surveys ask participants to detail their own criminal behavior.

Answers can be found in the Answers section in the back of the book.

3 Inside Criminal Law

LEARNING OBJECTIVES

After studying this chapter, you will be able to . . .

3-1 List the four written sources of American criminal law.

3-2 Discuss the primary goals of civil law and criminal law and explain how these goals are realized.

3-3 List and briefly define the most important excuse defenses for crimes.

3-4 Describe the four most important justification criminal defenses.

3-5 Explain the importance of the due process clause in the criminal justice system.

After you finish this chapter, go to **PAGES 68–69** for **STUDY TOOLS**

sergign/ShutterStock.com

When Dogs Attack

According to witnesses who testified at his murder trial, Alex Jackson's dogs had menaced or bitten people near his home in Littlerock, California, on at least nine different occasions. One witness, an animal control officer, said that Jackson told him, "If you mess with me, you're coming into the lion's den." So, prosecutors argued, it could hardly have been a surprise to the defendant when four of his pit bulls leaped over the fence and attacked and killed sixty-three-year-old retiree Pamela Devitt during her morning walk.

About thirty people die from dog attacks each year in the United States, but criminal charges against the owners of these animals are rare. To gain conviction in such cases, prosecutors must prove that the defendants both knew that their pets were dangerous *and* failed to control them. In September 2014, a jury decided that Jackson had consciously disregarded the threat his dogs posed to the community and found him guilty

of second degree murder. A judge subsequently sentenced him to fifteen years behind bars.

Depending on the circumstances, other dog-related deaths may not warrant such serious punishment. One month after Jackson's conviction, a Saline County, Arkansas, judge sentenced Brande Coy to sixty days in jail when a bull mastiff she was looking after killed a neighbor. Unlike Jackson, Coy was apparently unaware that the dog had any violent tendencies.

Similarly, that summer Steven Hayashi of Concord, California, was sent to jail for one year after his three pit bulls mauled his grandson to death. Previously, those dogs had only attacked other animals. Besides being criminally careless, the three defendants discussed here had one other characteristic in common: they had no intent to harm their dogs' victims. "This isn't anything I orchestrated or planned," said Jackson during his trial. "I feel terrible about it."

One of Alex Jackson's pit bulls is held at a Lancaster, California, animal shelter following its owner's arrest on murder charges. Do you think it is fair that criminal law holds Jackson accountable for deaths caused by dogs under his control? Why or why not?

AP Images/The Antelope Valley Press, Claudia Lopez

3-1

WHAT ARE THE WRITTEN SOURCES OF AMERICAN CRIMINAL LAW?

In any society that is, like our own, governed by the **rule of law,** all persons and institutions, including the government itself, must abide by the law. Furthermore, the law must be applied equally and enforced fairly, and must not be altered arbitrarily by any individual or group, no matter how powerful. As the rule of law has evolved over the course of U.S. history, Americans and their government have come to rely on several written sources of criminal law, also known as "substantive" criminal law. These sources include:

LO3-1

1. The U.S. Constitution and the constitutions of the various states.

2. Statutes, or laws, passed by Congress and by state legislatures, plus local ordinances.

3. Regulations created by administrative agencies, such as the federal Food and Drug Administration.

4. Case law (court decisions).

Rule of Law The principle that the rules of a legal system apply equally to all persons, institutions, and entities—public or private—that make up a society.

We describe each of these important written sources of law in the remainder of this section. (For a preview, see Figure 3.1.)

3-1a Constitutional Law

The federal government and the states have separate written constitutions that set forth the general organization and powers of, and the limits on, their respective governments. **Constitutional law** is the law as expressed in these constitutions.

The U.S. Constitution is the supreme law of the land. As such, it is the basis of all law in the United States. Any law that violates the Constitution, as ultimately determined by the United States Supreme Court, will be declared unconstitutional and will not be enforced. The Tenth Amendment, which defines the powers and limitations of the federal government, reserves to the states all powers not granted to the federal government. Under our system of federalism (see Chapter 1), each state also has its own constitution. Unless it conflicts with the U.S. Constitution or a federal law, each state's constitution is supreme within that state's borders. (You will learn more about how constitutional law applies to our criminal justice system throughout this textbook.)

Constitutional Law Law based on the U.S. Constitution and the constitutions of the various states.

Statutory Law The body of law enacted by legislative bodies.

Supremacy Clause A clause in the U.S. Constitution establishing that federal law is the "supreme law of the land" and shall prevail when in conflict with state constitutions or statutes.

3-1b Statutory Law

Statutes enacted by legislative bodies at any level of government make up another source of law, which is generally referred to as **statutory law.** *Federal statutes* are laws that are enacted by the U.S. Congress. *State statutes* are laws enacted by state legislatures, and statutory law also includes the ordinances passed by cities and counties. A federal statute, of course, applies to all states. A state statute, in contrast, applies only within that state's borders. City or county ordinances (statutes) apply only to those jurisdictions where they are enacted.

LEGAL SUPREMACY It is important to keep in mind that there are essentially fifty-two different criminal codes in this country—one for each state, the District of Columbia, and the federal government. Originally, the federal criminal code was quite small. The U.S. Constitution mentions only three federal crimes: treason, piracy, and counterfeiting. Today, according to a recent study, federal law includes about 4,500 offenses that carry criminal penalties.[1] Inevitably, these federal criminal statutes are bound to overlap or even contradict state statutes. In such cases, thanks to the **supremacy clause** of the Constitution, federal law will almost always prevail. Simply put, the supremacy clause holds that federal law is the "supreme law of the land."

So, for example, at least 330 individuals have been charged with violating federal law for possessing or selling medical marijuana in states where such use is legal under state law.[2] As we discussed earlier in the textbook, marijuana use—for medicinal purposes or otherwise—remains illegal under federal law, and, in the words of one federal judge, "we are all bound by federal law, like it or not."[3] Along the same lines, any statutory

---

FIGURE 3.1 SOURCES OF AMERICAN LAW

Constitutional law	**Definition:** The law as expressed in the U.S. Constitution and the various state constitutions.	**Example:** The Fifth Amendment to the U.S. Constitution states that no person shall "be compelled in any criminal case to be a witness" against himself or herself.
Statutory law	**Definition:** Laws or *ordinances* created by federal, state, and local legislatures and governing bodies.	**Example:** Texas state law considers the theft of cattle, horses, or exotic livestock or fowl a felony.
Administrative law	**Definition:** The rules, orders, and decisions of federal or state government administrative agencies.	**Example:** The federal Environmental Protection Agency's rules criminalize the use of lead-based paint in a manner that causes health risks to the community.
Case law	**Definition:** Judge-made law, including judicial interpretations of the other three sources of law.	**Example:** A federal judge overturns a Nebraska state law making it a crime for sex offenders to use social networking sites on the ground that the statute violates the constitutional right of freedom of speech.

In Oregon, because of a ballot initiative, any person who fails a field sobriety test, such as the one shown here, and is convicted of drunk driving for a third time must spend ninety days in jail. *What are some of the pros and cons of using ballot initiatives to create criminal law?*

3-1c Administrative Law

A third source of American criminal law consists of **administrative law**—the rules, orders, and decisions of *regulatory agencies*. A regulatory agency is a federal, state, or local government agency established to perform a specific function. The Occupational Safety and Health Administration (OSHA), for example, oversees the safety and health of American workers. The Environmental Protection Agency (EPA) is concerned with protecting the natural environment, and the Food and Drug Administration (FDA) regulates food and drugs produced in the United States.

Disregarding certain laws created by regulatory agencies can be a criminal violation. Federal statutes, such as the Clean Water Act, authorize a specific regulatory agency, such as the EPA, to enforce regulations to which criminal sanctions are attached.[6] So, in 2014, following a criminal investigation led by EPA agents, a Longview, Washington, septic tank–pumping business was found to have illegally dumped two million gallons of pollutants and waste into the city's sewage system. A federal judge sentenced the business's owner to twenty-seven months in prison and a fine of $250,000.

law—federal or state—that violates the Constitution will be overturned. In the late 1980s, for example, the United States Supreme Court ruled that any state laws banning the burning of the American flag were unconstitutional because they impinged on the individual's right to freedom of expression.[4]

BALLOT INITIATIVES On a state and local level, voters can write or rewrite criminal statutes through a form of direct democracy known as the **ballot initiative.** In this process, a group of citizens draft a proposed law and then gather a certain number of signatures to get the proposal on that year's ballot. If a majority of the voters approve the measure, it is enacted into law. Currently, twenty-four states and the District of Columbia accept ballot initiatives, and these special elections have played a crucial role in shaping criminal law in those jurisdictions. Changes in state law regarding assisted suicide, marijuana legalization, and victims' rights, discussed earlier in this text, resulted from ballot initiatives.

Like other state laws, laws generated by ballot initiatives are not immune from review by state and federal courts. In late 2014, for example, Oklahoma and Nebraska filed a joint lawsuit asking the United States Supreme Court to find Colorado's recreational marijuana law, passed as a ballot initiative, unconstitutional. The two states claimed that marijuana flowing from Colorado over their borders has unfairly "stressed" state and local law enforcement resources.[5]

> **CAREER TIP** The federal government employs law enforcement agents called *consumer safety officers* to investigate reports of injury, illness, or death caused by certain consumer products.

3-1d Case Law

Another basic source of American law consists of the rules of law announced in court decisions, or **precedents.** These rules of law include interpretations of constitutional provisions, of statutes enacted by legislatures, and

Ballot Initiative A procedure in which the citizens of a state, by collecting enough signatures, can force a public vote on a proposed change to state law.

Administrative Law The body of law created by administrative agencies (in the form of rules, regulations, orders, and decisions) in order to carry out their duties and responsibilities.

Precedent A court decision that furnishes an example of authority for deciding subsequent cases involving similar facts.

of regulations created by administrative agencies. Today, this body of law is referred to variously as the common law, judge-made law, or **case law.**

Case law is the basis for a doctrine called *stare decisis* ("to stand on decided cases"). Under this doctrine, judges are obligated to follow the precedents established within their jurisdiction. For example, any decision of a particular state's highest court will control the outcome of future cases on that issue brought before all the lower courts within that same state. Per the supremacy clause, discussed earlier, all U.S. Supreme Court decisions involving the U.S. Constitution are binding on *all* courts, because the U.S. Constitution is the supreme law of the land.

The doctrine of *stare decisis* does not require the U.S. Supreme Court *always* to follow its own precedent, though the Court often does so. At times, a change in society's values will make an older ruling seem obsolete, at least in the eyes of the Supreme Court justices. In 1986, for example, the Court upheld a state law that banned certain homosexual acts that were lawful when performed by a man and a woman.[7] Seventeen years later, the Court overturned that decision, ruling that the government does not have the ability to treat one class of citizens differently from the rest of society when it comes to sexual practices between consenting adults. The original case "was not correct when it was decided, and it is not correct today," wrote Justice Anthony Kennedy.[8]

 # WHY DO SOCIETIES NEED LAWS?

3-2

Why do societies need laws? Many criminologists believe that criminal law has two basic functions: one relates to the legal requirements of a society, and the other pertains to the society's need to maintain and promote social values.

3-2a Protect and Punish: The Legal Function of the Law

The primary legal function of the law is to maintain social order by protecting citizens from *criminal harm.* This term refers to a variety of harms that can be generalized to fit into two categories:

1. Harms to individual citizens' physical safety and property, such as the harm caused by murder, theft, or arson.

2. Harms to society's interests collectively, such as the harm caused by unsafe foods or consumer products, a polluted environment, or poorly constructed buildings.[9]

The first category is self-evident, although even murder, as you shall soon see, involves different degrees, or grades, of offense to which different punishments are assigned. The second category, however, has proved more problematic, for it is difficult to measure society's "collective" interests.

3-2b Maintain and Teach: The Social Function of the Law

If criminal laws against acts that cause harm or injury to others are almost universally accepted, the same cannot be said for laws that criminalize "morally" wrongful activities that may do no obvious, physical harm outside the families of those involved. Why criminalize gambling or prostitution if the participants are consenting?

EXPRESSING PUBLIC MORALITY The answer lies in the social function of criminal law. Many observers believe that the main purpose of criminal law is to reflect the values and norms of society, or at least of those segments of society that hold power. Legal scholar Henry Hart has stated that the only justification for criminal law and punishment is "the judgment of community condemnation."[10]

Take, for example, the misdemeanor of bigamy, which occurs when someone knowingly marries a second person without terminating her or his marriage to an original husband or wife. Apart from moral considerations, there would appear to be no victims in a bigamous relationship, and indeed many societies have allowed and continue to allow bigamy to exist. In the American social tradition, however, as John L. Diamond of the University of California's Hastings College of the Law points out:

> Marriage is an institution encouraged and supported by society. The structural importance of the integrity of the family and a monogamous marriage requires unflinching enforcement of the criminal laws against bigamy. The immorality is not in choosing to do wrong, but in transgressing, even innocently, a fundamental social boundary that lies at the core of social order.[11]

Consider the following scenario: Jasmine, a graduate school student, exchanges intimate photos with Josh, her boyfriend. Then they break up. Several months later, Josh begins posting nude pictures of Jasmine online. Although she is mortified, there is little Jasmine can do to stop Josh, because such behavior is not illegal in most of the United States. For the most part, Web site operators are not responsible for content provided by others, unless that content happens to be in violation of federal law, such as child pornography.

Technology often moves faster than criminal law, allowing for behavior that seems as if it should be illegal but is not. When this occurs, criminal law must adjust accordingly. In December 2014, Illinois became the fourteenth state within a two-year period to ban "revenge porn," or the "non-consensual dissemination of private sexual images." Under the state law, a person convicted of sharing such images online faces one to three years in prison and a maximum $25,000 fine.

Chris Rout/Alamy

Thinking about Revenge Porn

Illinois's revenge porn law has no provision for intent, as is the case in other states. For example, in California the crime requires "the intent to cause serious emotional distress." Why might civil liberties advocates support the inclusion of an intent provision? Which version of revenge porn legislation—Illinois's or California's—do you favor? Why?

Of course, public morals are not uniform across the entire nation, and a state's criminal code often reflects the values of its residents. In Kentucky, for example, someone who uses a reptile as part of a religious service is subject to up to $100 in fines, and New Hampshire prohibits any person or agency from introducing a wolf into the state's wilds.[12] Sometimes, local values and federal law will conflict with one another. Nine states, mostly in the western half of the country, have passed "nullification" laws that seek to void federal gun legislation within their borders.[13] For example, in 2014, Idaho passed a new law under which state law enforcement officers could be charged with a misdemeanor and fined up to $1,000 dollars for enforcing a federal gun law.[14]

TEACHING SOCIETAL BOUNDARIES Some scholars believe that criminal laws not only express the expectations of society, but "teach" them as well. Professor Lawrence M. Friedman of Stanford University thinks that just as parents teach children behavioral norms

through punishment, criminal justice "'teaches a lesson' to the people it punishes, and to society at large." Making burglary a crime, arresting burglars, putting them in jail—each step in the criminal justice process reinforces the idea that burglary is unacceptable and is deserving of punishment.[15]

This teaching function can also be seen in traffic laws. There is nothing "natural" about most traffic laws: Americans drive on the right side of the street, the British on the left side, with no obvious difference in the results. Following these laws, such as by stopping at intersections, using headlights at night, and following speed limits, does lead to a more orderly flow of traffic and fewer accidents—certainly socially desirable goals. The laws can also be updated when needed. Over the past few years, several states have banned the use of handheld cell phones while driving because of the safety hazards associated with that behavior. Various forms of punishment for breaking traffic laws teach drivers the social order of the road.

Many gun activists support state "nullification" laws that aim to void federal gun legislation. *Why does the supremacy clause, discussed earlier in the chapter, make it unlikely that such state laws would withstand a court challenge?*

Mark Van Scyoc/ShutterStock.com

3-3 WHAT IS THE DIFFERENCE BETWEEN CIVIL AND CRIMINAL LAW?

LO3-2 All law can be divided into two categories: civil law and criminal law. These two categories of law are distinguished by their primary goals. The criminal justice system is concerned with protecting society from harm by preventing and prosecuting crimes. A crime is an act so reprehensible that it is considered a wrong against society as a whole, as well as against the individual victim. Therefore, the state prosecutes a person who commits a criminal act. If the state is able to prove that a person is guilty of a crime, the government will punish her or him with imprisonment or fines, or both.

Civil law, which includes all types of law other than criminal law, is concerned with disputes between private individuals or other private entities. Proceedings in civil lawsuits are normally initiated by an individual or a corporation (in contrast to criminal proceedings, which are initiated by public prosecutors). Such disputes may involve, for example, the terms of a contract, the ownership of property, or an automobile accident. Under civil law, the government provides a forum for the resolution of *torts*—or private wrongs—in which the injured party, called the **plaintiff,** tries to prove that a wrong has been committed by the accused party, or the **defendant.** (Note that the accused party in both criminal and civil cases is known as the *defendant.*)

3-3a Guilt and Responsibility

A criminal court is convened to determine whether the defendant is *guilty*—that is, whether the defendant has, in fact, committed the offense charged. In contrast, civil law is concerned with responsibility, a much more flexible concept. For example, nearly a decade ago Adam Jones started a melee in a Las Vegas strip club by tossing hundreds of dollar bills into the air. During the ensuing brawl, doorman Tommy Urbanski was shot and paralyzed from the waist down. Jones did not pull the trigger nor was he charged with any crime. Nonetheless, in 2015 a civil appeals court decided that he was **liable,** or legally responsible, for Urbanski's injuries because of his irresponsible behavior.

Most civil cases involve a request for monetary damages to compensate for the wrong that has been committed. Thus, the civil court ordered Jones to pay Tommy Urbanski and his ex-wife, Kathy, about $11.2 million to cover medical costs and loss of earnings, as well as for infliction of emotional distress.

3-3b The Burden of Proof

Although criminal law proceedings are completely separate from civil law proceedings in the modern legal system, the two systems do have some similarities.

Civil Law The branch of law dealing with the definition and enforcement of all private or public rights, as opposed to criminal matters.

Plaintiff The person or institution that initiates a lawsuit in civil court proceedings by filing a complaint.

Defendant In a civil court, the person or institution against whom an action is brought. In a criminal court, the person or entity who has been formally accused of violating a criminal law.

Liability In a civil court, legal responsibility for one's own or another's actions.

Both attempt to control behavior by imposing sanctions on those who violate society's definition of acceptable behavior. Furthermore, criminal and civil law often supplement each other. In certain instances, a victim may file a civil suit against an individual who is also the target of a criminal prosecution by the government.

Because the burden of proof is much greater in criminal trials than civil ones, it is almost always easier to win monetary damages than a criminal conviction. The most famous (or infamous) example of such a situation in recent memory occurred about twenty years ago. After former professional football player O. J. Simpson was acquitted of murder charges in the deaths of his ex-wife, Nicole, and Ronald Goldman, the families of the two victims sued Simpson. In 1997, a civil court jury found Simpson liable for the wrongful deaths of his ex-wife and Goldman, and ordered him to pay their families $33.5 million in damages.

During the criminal trial, the jury did not find enough evidence to prove **beyond a reasonable doubt** (the burden of proof in criminal cases) that Simpson was guilty of any crime. In contrast, the civil trial established by a **preponderance of the evidence** (the burden of proof in civil cases) that Simpson had killed his victims in a fit of jealous rage. (See Figure 3.2 for a comparison of civil and criminal law.)

 3-4 ## WHAT ARE THE DIFFERENT CATEGORIES OF CRIME?

Depending on their degree of seriousness, crimes are classified as *felonies* or *misdemeanors*. **Felonies** are crimes punishable by death or by imprisonment in a federal or state prison for one year or longer (though some states, such as North Carolina, consider felonies to be punishable by at least two years' incarceration). For the most part, felonies involve crimes of violence, such as armed robbery or sexual assault, or other "serious" crimes, such as stealing a large amount of money or selling illegal drugs.

3-4a Types of Misdemeanors

Under federal law and in most states, any crime that is not a felony is considered a **misdemeanor.** Misdemeanors are crimes punishable by a fine or by confinement for up to a year. If imprisoned, the guilty party goes to a local jail instead of a prison. Disorderly conduct and trespassing are common misdemeanors. Most states distinguish between *gross misdemeanors,* which are offenses punishable by thirty days to a year in jail, and *petty misdemeanors,* or offenses punishable by fewer than thirty days in jail. Probation and community service are often imposed on those who commit misdemeanors, especially juveniles. As you will see in Chapter 7, whether a crime is a felony or misdemeanor can also determine in which criminal court the case will be tried.

Beyond a Reasonable Doubt The degree of proof required to find the defendant in a criminal trial guilty of committing the crime. The defendant's guilt must be the only reasonable explanation for the criminal act before the court.

Preponderance of the Evidence The degree of proof required to decide in favor of one side or the other in a civil case. In general, this requirement is met when a plaintiff shows that a claim more likely than not is true.

Felony A serious crime, usually punishable by death or imprisonment for a year or longer.

Misdemeanor A criminal offense that is not a felony; usually punishable by a fine and/or a jail term of less than one year.

FIGURE 3.2 CIVIL LAW VERSUS CRIMINAL LAW

Issue	Civil Law	Criminal Law
Area of concern	Rights and duties between individuals	Offenses against society as a whole
Wrongful act	Harm to a person or business entity	Violation of a statute that prohibits some type of activity
Party who brings suit	Person who suffered harm (plaintiff)	The state (prosecutor)
Party who responds	Person who supposedly caused harm (defendant)	Person who allegedly committed a crime (defendant)
Standard of proof	Preponderance of the evidence	Beyond a reasonable doubt
Remedy	Damages to compensate for the harm	Punishment (fine or incarceration)

3-4b Infractions

The least serious form of wrongdoing is often called an **infraction** and is punishable only by a small fine. Even though infractions, such as parking tickets and traffic violations, technically represent illegal activity, they generally are not considered "crimes." Therefore, infractions rarely lead to jury trials and are deemed to be so minor that they do not appear on the offender's criminal record.

In some jurisdictions, the terms *infraction* and *petty offense* are interchangeable. In others, however, they are different. Under federal guidelines, for example, an infraction can be punished by up to five days behind bars, while a petty offender is only liable for a fine.[16] Finally, those who string together a series of infractions (or fail to pay the fines that come with such offenses) are in danger of being criminally charged. In Illinois, having three or more speeding violations in one year is considered criminal behavior.[17]

3-4c *Mala in Se* and *Mala Prohibita*

Criminologists often express the social function of criminal law in terms of *mala in se* or *mala prohibita* crimes. A criminal act is referred to as **mala in se** if it would be considered wrong even if there were no law prohibiting it. *Mala in se* crimes are said to go against "natural laws"—that is, against the "natural, moral, and public" principles of a society. Murder, rape, and theft are examples of *mala in se* crimes. These crimes are generally the same from country to country and culture to culture.

In contrast, the term **mala prohibita** refers to acts that are considered crimes only because they have been codified as such through statute—"human-made" laws. A *mala prohibita* crime is considered wrong only because it has been prohibited. It is not inherently wrong, though it may reflect the moral standards of a society at a given time. Thus, the definition of a *mala prohibita* crime can vary from country to country and

even from state to state. Bigamy, or the offense of having two legal spouses, could be considered a *mala prohibita* crime.

Some observers question the distinction between *mala in se* and *mala prohibita*. In many instances, it is difficult to define a "pure" *mala in se* crime. That is, it is difficult to separate a crime from the culture that has deemed it a crime.[18] Even murder, under certain cultural circumstances, is not considered a criminal act. In a number of poor, traditional areas of the Middle East and Asia, the law excuses "honor killings," in which men kill female family members suspected of sexual indiscretion.

Our own legal system excuses homicide in extreme situations, such as self-defense or when a law enforcement agent kills in the course of upholding the law. Therefore, "natural" laws can be seen as culturally specific. Similar difficulties occur in trying to define a "pure" *mala prohibita* crime. More than 150 countries, including most members of the European Union, have legalized prostitution. With the exception of seven rural counties of Nevada, prostitution is illegal in the United States.

3-5 WHAT ARE THE ELEMENTS OF A CRIME?

In fictional accounts of police work, the admission of guilt is often portrayed as the crucial element of a criminal investigation. Although an admission is certainly useful to police and prosecutors, it alone cannot establish the innocence or guilt of a suspect. Criminal law normally requires that the **corpus delicti,** a Latin phrase for "the body of the crime," be proved before a person can be convicted of wrongdoing.[19]

Corpus delicti can be defined as "proof that a specific crime has actually been committed by someone."[20] It consists of the elements of any crime, which include:

1. The *actus reus,* or guilty act.
2. The *mens rea,* or guilty intent.
3. Concurrence, or the coming together of the criminal act and the guilty mind.
4. A link between the act and the legal definition of the crime.
5. Any attendant, or accompanying, circumstances.
6. The harm done by the crime.

Infraction In most jurisdictions, a noncriminal offense for which the penalty is a fine rather than incarceration.

Mala in Se A descriptive term for acts that are inherently wrong, regardless of whether they are prohibited by law.

Mala Prohibita A descriptive term for acts that are made illegal by criminal statute and are not necessarily wrong in and of themselves.

Corpus Delicti The body of circumstances that must exist for a criminal act to have occurred.

3-5a Criminal Act: *Actus Reus*

Suppose Mr. Smith walks into a police department and announces that he has just killed his wife. In and of itself, the confession is insufficient for conviction unless the police find Mrs. Smith's corpse, for example, with a bullet in her brain and establish through evidence that Mr. Smith fired the gun. (This does not mean that an actual dead body has to be found in every homicide case. Rather, it is the fact of the death that must be established in such cases.)

Most crimes require an act of *commission,* meaning that a person must *do* something in order to be accused of a crime. The prohibited act is referred to as the **actus reus,** or guilty act. Furthermore, the act of commission must be voluntary. For example, if Mr. Smith had an epileptic seizure while holding a hunting rifle and accidentally shot his wife, he normally would not be held criminally liable for her death.

A LEGAL DUTY In some cases, an act of *omission* can be a crime, but only when a person has a legal duty to perform the omitted act. One such legal duty is assumed to exist based on a "special relationship" between two parties, such as a parent and child, adult children and their aged parents, and spouses.[21] Those persons involved in contractual relationships with others, such as physicians and lifeguards, must also perform legal duties to avoid criminal penalty. Hawaii, Minnesota, Rhode Island, Vermont, and Wisconsin have even passed "duty to aid" statutes requiring their citizens to report criminal conduct and help victims of such conduct if possible.[22] Another example of a criminal act of omission is failure to file a federal income tax return when required by law to do so.

A PLAN OR ATTEMPT The guilty act requirement is based on one of the premises of criminal law—that a person is punished for harm done to society. Planning to kill someone or to steal a car may be wrong, but the thoughts do no harm and are therefore not criminal until they are translated into action. Of course, a person can

---

Actus Reus (pronounced *ak*-tus *ray*-uhs). A guilty (prohibited) act.

PARALEGAL/LEGAL ASSISTANT

CareerPrep

Job Description:

▶ Assist lawyers in many aspects of legal work, including preparing for trial, researching legal documents, drafting contracts, and investigating cases.

▶ In addition to criminal law, work includes civil law, corporate law, intellectual property, bankruptcy, immigration, family law, and real estate.

What Kind of Training Is Required?

▶ A community college–level paralegal program that leads to an associate degree.

▶ For those who already have a college degree, a certificate in paralegal studies.

Annual Salary Range?

▶ $40,000–$77,000

JHDT Stock Images LLC/ShutterStock.com

GETTING LINKEDIN

In a recent posting, a Houston law firm noted that potential paralegal candidates must be able to "research, analyze, and summarize relevant legal precedents for applicability to assigned cases." Precedents, discussed earlier in this chapter, are crucial judicial decisions that criminal lawyers often must either rely on or overcome to best serve their clients.

be punished for *attempting* murder or robbery, but normally only if he or she took substantial steps toward the criminal objective and the prosecution can prove that the desire to commit the crime was present. Furthermore, the punishment for an **attempt** normally is less severe than if the act had succeeded.

3-5b Mental State: *Mens Rea*

A wrongful mental state—**mens rea**—is usually as necessary as a wrongful act in determining guilt. The mental state, or requisite *intent*, required to establish guilt of a crime is indicated in the applicable statute or law. For theft, the wrongful act is the taking of another person's property, and the required mental state involves both the awareness that the property belongs to another and the desire to deprive the owner of it.

THE CATEGORIES OF *MENS REA* A guilty mental state includes elements of purpose, knowledge, negligence, and recklessness.[23] A defendant is said to have *purposefully* committed a criminal act when he or she desires to engage in certain criminal conduct or to cause a certain criminal result. For a defendant to have *knowingly* committed an illegal act, he or she must be aware of the illegality, must believe that the illegality exists, or must correctly suspect that the illegality exists but fail to do anything to dispel (or confirm) his or her belief.

EdwinAC/ShutterStock.com

Suppose a seventeen-year-old babysitter falls asleep while smoking a cigarette, accidentally starting a fire that burns down the clients' home. (Nobody is harmed in the blaze.) *Has the babysitter acted negligently or recklessly, or neither? Would your answer change if she had sneaked into the clients' liquor cabinet and was drunk at the time of the accident? Why or why not?*

Negligence Criminal **negligence** involves the mental state in which the defendant grossly deviates from the standard of care that a reasonable person would use under the same circumstances. The defendant is accused of taking an unjustified, substantial, and foreseeable risk that resulted in harm.

In 2015, for example, Greeley, Colorado, prosecutors charged Kristen Braig and her boyfriend, Dustin Blanchard, with negligent homicide after the death of Braig's three-year-old daughter in a mobile home fire. Just before the fire started, Braig and Blanchard, who had been drinking and smoking marijuana, left the child alone in the mobile home while they visited a neighbor. The couple obviously did not intend for Braig's daughter to die. At the same time, there is a foreseeable risk in leaving a child of that age unattended for any amount of time, especially when one's judgment is impaired by alcohol and marijuana.

Recklessness A defendant who commits an act recklessly is more blameworthy than one who is criminally negligent. The Model Penal Code defines criminal **recklessness** as "consciously disregard[ing] a substantial and unjustifiable risk."[24] In 2015, Ryan Jorgenson pleaded guilty to reckless homicide in an Oshkosh, Wisconsin, court for causing the death of his fiancée's three-year-old daughter. Jorgenson, annoyed that the little girl would not stop crying, had fatally pushed her down a flight of stairs. Although

Attempt The act of taking substantial steps toward committing a crime while having the ability and the intent to commit the crime, even if the crime never takes place.

Mens Rea (pronounced mehns ray-uh). Mental state, or intent. A wrongful mental state is usually as necessary as a wrongful act to establish criminal liability.

Negligence A failure to exercise the standard of care that a reasonable person would exercise in similar circumstances.

Recklessness The state of being aware that a risk does or will exist and nevertheless acting in a way that consciously disregards this risk.

Jorgenson—like Kristen Braig and Dustin Blanchard in the previous example—had no intention of killing his victim, the substantial risk of harm in treating a child in such a manner is evident to any reasonable person.

DEGREES OF CRIME Crimes are graded by degree. Generally speaking, the degree of a crime is a reflection of the seriousness of that crime and is used to determine the severity of any subsequent punishment.

With many crimes, degree is a function of the criminal act itself, as determined by statute. For example, most criminal codes consider a burglary that involves a nighttime forced entry into a home to be a burglary in the first degree. If the same act takes place during the day and involves a nonresidential building, then it is burglary in the second degree. As you might expect, burglary in the first degree carries a harsher penalty than burglary in the second degree.

First Degree Murder With murder, the degree of the crime is, to a large extent, determined by the mental state of the offender. Murder is generally defined as the willful killing of a human being. It is important to emphasize the word *willful*, as it precludes homicides caused by accident or negligence. A death that results from negligence or accident generally is considered a private wrong and therefore a matter for civil law.

In addition, criminal law punishes those who plan and intend to do harm more harshly than it does those who act wrongfully because of strong emotions or other extreme circumstances. First degree murder—usually punishable by life in prison or the death penalty—occurs under two circumstances:

1. When the crime is premeditated, or contemplated beforehand by the offender, instead of being a spontaneous act of violence.
2. When the crime is deliberate, meaning that it was planned and decided on after a process of decision making. Deliberation does not require a lengthy planning process. A person can be found guilty of first degree murder even if she or he made the decision to kill only seconds before committing the crime.

Second Degree Murder As you may recall, in this chapter's opening we discussed Alex **Jackson,** who was convicted of second degree murder for failing to control his dangerous dogs. In California, where Jackson's case was tried, second degree murder is defined as any murder that is not first degree murder.[25] Jackson's behavior does, nonetheless, fall within the boundaries set by the two general definitions of second degree murder:

1. An intentional killing in which no premeditation or deliberation was present.
2. A killing resulting from the offender's dangerous conduct and an obvious lack of concern for human life.

Second degree murder is usually punishable by fifteen to twenty-five years in prison.

The difference between first and second degree murder is illustrated in a case involving a California man who beat a neighbor to death with a partially full brandy bottle. The crime took place after Ricky McDonald, the victim, complained to Kazi Cooksey, the offender, about the noise coming from a late-night barbecue Cooksey and his friends were holding. The jury could not find sufficient evidence that Cooksey's actions were premeditated, but he certainly acted with wanton disregard for his victim's safety. Therefore, the jury convicted Cooksey of second degree murder rather than first degree murder.

Types of Manslaughter A homicide committed without *malice* toward the victim is known as *manslaughter* and is commonly punishable by up to fifteen years in prison. **Voluntary manslaughter** occurs when the intent to kill may be present, but malice is lacking. (*Malice* means "wrongful intention" or "the desire to do evil.") Voluntary manslaughter covers crimes of passion, in which the

Voluntary Manslaughter A homicide in which the intent to kill was present in the mind of the offender, but malice was lacking.

emotion of an argument between two friends may lead to a homicide. Voluntary manslaughter can also occur when the victim provoked the offender to act violently.

Involuntary manslaughter covers incidents in which the offender's acts may have been careless, but he or she had no intent to kill. In 2014, for instance, a grand jury charged Hillary Schwartz with involuntary manslaughter following a fatal train collision. Schwartz was the assistant director on *Midnight Rider,* a film being made in rural Wayne County, Georgia. The filmmakers had been refused legal permission to shoot a scene on a particular railroad bridge, but, with Schwartz behind the camera, the decision was made to do so anyway. A freight train then crashed into the film set on the bridge, killing a camera assistant named Sarah Jones.

Although Schwartz had certainly not intended for Jones to die in the accident, local law enforcement authorities believed that she and several other members of the production crew were criminally responsible for the woman's death. (As the feature *Discretion in Action—Murder or Manslaughter?* shows, the distinction between various homicide charges is not always clear and often rests on the issue of intent.)

STRICT LIABILITY For some crimes, criminal law holds the defendant to be guilty even if intent to commit the offense is lacking. These acts are known as **strict liability crimes** and generally involve endangering the public welfare in some way.[26] Drug-control statutes, health and safety regulations, and traffic laws are all strict liability laws.

To a certain extent, the concept of strict liability is inconsistent with the traditional principles of criminal law, which hold that *mens rea* is required for an act to be criminal. The goal of strict liability laws is to protect the public by eliminating the possibility that wrongdoers could claim ignorance or mistake to absolve themselves of criminal responsibility.[27] Thus, a person caught dumping waste in a protected pond or driving 70 miles per hour in a 55 miles-per-hour zone cannot plead a lack of intent in his or her defense.

One of the most controversial strict liability crimes is **statutory rape,** in which an adult engages in a sexual relationship with a minor. In most states, even if the minor consents to the sexual act, the act is still a crime because, being underage, the minor is considered incapable of

---

Involuntary Manslaughter A homicide in which the offender had no intent to kill her or his victim.

Strict Liability Crimes Certain crimes, such as traffic violations, in which the defendant is guilty regardless of her or his state of mind at the time of the act.

Statutory Rape A strict liability crime in which an adult engages in a sexual act with a minor.

Discretion in Action

MURDER OR MANSLAUGHTER?

THE SITUATION It is after midnight, and George, drunk and angry, decides to pay a visit to Yeardley, his ex-girlfriend. When Yeardley refuses to let George in her apartment, he kicks the door down, grabs Yeardley by the neck, and wrestles her to the floor before leaving. Several hours later, Yeardley's roommate finds her dead, lying face down on a pillow soaked with blood.

THE LAW George can be charged with one of three possible crimes: (1) first degree murder, which is premeditated and deliberate; (2) second degree murder, which means he acted with wanton disregard for the consequences of his actions; or (3) involuntary manslaughter, which involves extreme carelessness but no intent to kill.

WHAT WOULD YOU DO? Further investigation shows that, two years prior to Yeardley's death, a jealous George put her in a chokehold in public. Furthermore, just days before breaking into her apartment, George sent Yeardley an e-mail in which he reacted to news that she was dating someone else by threatening, "I should have killed you." In his defense, George says that although he did have a physical confrontation with Yeardley, she did not seem injured when he left the apartment. George's lawyer claims that Yeardley died from suffocation, not from any wound caused by George. If it were your decision, would you charge George with first degree murder, second degree murder, or involuntary manslaughter? Why?

[To see how prosecutors in Virginia handled a similar situation, go to Example 3.1 in Appendix A.]

making a rational decision on the matter.[28] Therefore, statutory rape has been committed even if the adult was unaware of the minor's age or was misled to believe that the minor was older.

ACCOMPLICE LIABILITY Under certain circumstances, a person can be charged with and convicted of a crime that he or she did not actually commit. This occurs when the suspect has acted as an *accomplice,* helping another person commit the crime. Generally, to be found guilty as an accomplice, a person must have had "dual intent." This level of *mens rea* includes *both:*

1. The intent to aid the person who committed the crime, and
2. The intent that such aid would lead to the commission of the crime.[29]

So, assume that Jerry drives Jason to a bank that Jason intends to rob. If Jerry had no knowledge of Jason's criminal plan, he would not fulfill the second prong of the "dual intent" test. As for the *actus reus*, the accomplice must have helped the primary actor in either a physical sense (for example, by providing the getaway car) or a psychological sense (for example, by encouraging her or him to commit the crime).[30]

In some states, a person can be convicted as an accomplice even without intent if the crime was a "natural and probable consequence" of his or her actions.[31] This principle has led to a proliferation of **felony-murder** legislation. Felony-murder is a form of first degree murder that applies when a person participates in any of a list of serious felonies that results in the death of a human being. Under felony-murder law, if two men rob a bank, and the first man intentionally kills a security guard, the second man can be convicted of first degree murder as an accomplice to the bank robbery, even if he had no intent to hurt anyone.

Along these same lines, if a security guard accidentally shoots and kills a customer during a bank robbery, the bank robbers can be charged with first degree murder because they committed the underlying felony. These kinds of laws have come under criticism because they punish individuals for an unintended act or acts committed by others. Nevertheless, the criminal codes of more than thirty states include some form of the felony-murder rule.

3-5c Concurrence

According to criminal law, there must be *concurrence* between the guilty act and the guilty intent. In other words, the guilty act and the guilty intent must occur together.[32] Suppose, for example, that a woman intends to murder her husband with poison in order to collect his life insurance. Every evening, this woman drives her husband home from work. On the night she plans to poison him, however, she swerves to avoid a cat crossing the road and runs into a tree. She survives the accident, but her husband is killed. Even though her intent was realized, the incident would be considered an accidental death because she had not planned to kill him by driving the car into a tree.

3-5d Causation

Criminal law also requires that the criminal act cause the harm suffered. In 1998, for example, thirteen-year-old Don Collins doused eight-year-old Robbie Middleton with gasoline and set him on fire, allegedly to cover up a sexual assault. Thirteen years later, after years of skin grafts and other surgeries, Middleton died from his burns. In 2014, a Montgomery County, Texas, judge ruled that, despite the passage of time, Collins could be charged with Middleton's murder.

3-5e Attendant Circumstances

In certain crimes, **attendant circumstances**—also known as accompanying circumstances—are relevant to the *corpus delicti.* Most states, for example, differentiate between simple assault and the more serious offense of aggravated assault depending on the attendant circumstance of whether the defendant used a weapon such as a gun or a knife while committing the crime. Criminal law also classifies degrees of property crimes based on the attendant circumstance of the amount stolen. According to federal statutes, the theft of less than $1,000 from a bank is a misdemeanor, while the theft of any amount over $1,000 is a felony.[33] (To get a better understanding of the role of attendant circumstances in criminal statutes, see Figure 3.3.) Attendant circumstances must be proved beyond a reasonable doubt, just like any other element of a crime.

In most cases, a person's motive for committing a crime is irrelevant—a court will not try to read the accused's mind. Over the past few decades, however, nearly every state and the federal government have passed

Felony-Murder An unlawful homicide that occurs during the attempted commission of a felony.

Attendant Circumstances The facts surrounding a criminal event that must be proved to convict the defendant of the underlying crime.

FIGURE 3.3 ATTENDANT CIRCUMSTANCES IN CRIMINAL LAW

Intent	Act	Attendant Circumstances

Whoever intentionally confines, restrains, or detains another against that person's will is guilty of felony false imprisonment.

Most criminal statutes incorporate three of the elements we have discussed in this section: the act (*actus reus*), the intent (*mens rea*), and attendant circumstances. This diagram of the federal false imprisonment statute should give you an idea of how these elements combine to create the totality of a crime.

hate crime laws that make the suspect's motive an important attendant circumstance to his or her criminal act. In general, **hate crime laws** provide for greater sanctions against those who commit crimes motivated by bias against a person based on race, ethnicity, religion, gender, sexual orientation, disability, or age. According to the federal government's Crime Victimization Survey, nearly 300,000 nonfatal hate crime offenses take place each year.[34]

3-5f Harm

For most crimes to occur, some harm must have been done to a person or to property. A certain number of crimes are actually categorized depending on the harm done to the victim, regardless of the intent behind the criminal act. Take two offenses, both of which involve one person hitting another in the back of the head with a tire iron. In the first instance, the victim dies, and the offender is charged with murder. In the second, the victim is only knocked unconscious, and the offender is charged with battery. Because the harm in the second instance was less severe, so was the crime with which the offender was charged, even though the act was exactly the same. Furthermore, most states have different degrees of battery depending on the extent of the injuries suffered by the victim.

Acts may be deemed criminal if they could result in a harm that a law is intended to prevent—even if that harm does not actually occur. Such acts are called **inchoate offenses.** They exist when only an attempt at a criminal act was made. If Jenkins solicits Peterson to murder Jenkins's business partner, this is an inchoate

offense on the part of Jenkins, even though Peterson fails to carry out the act. Threats and conspiracies also fall into the category of inchoate offenses. In 2014, two teenage boys were arrested on suspicion of *conspiracy* and making criminal threats after local officials found evidence online that they were planning a mass shooting at South Pasadena High School in southern California. The United States Supreme Court has ruled that a person could be convicted of criminal **conspiracy** even though police intervention made the completion of the illegal plan impossible.[35]

3-6 WHICH DEFENSES ARE AVAILABLE UNDER CRIMINAL LAW?

Several years ago, sixteen-year-old Ethan Couch, driving with a blood-alcohol level three times the legal limit, killed four pedestrians in Burleson, Texas. During Couch's trial, a psychiatrist testified that the teenager should receive a lenient sentence because he suffered from "affluenza," a condition that "afflicts" irresponsible children of rich, lenient parents.

Although the "spoiled brat" excuse has not been embraced in the American legal system, defendants can raise a number of other, established defenses for wrongdoing in our criminal courts. These defenses generally rely on one of two arguments: (1) the defendant is not responsible for the crime, or (2) the defendant was justified in committing the crime.

3-6a Criminal Responsibility and the Law

LO3-3 The idea of responsibility plays a significant role in criminal law. In certain circumstances, the law recognizes that even though an act is inherently criminal, society will not punish the actor because he or she does not have the requisite mental condition. In other words, the law "excuses" the person for his or her

Hate Crime Law A statute that provides for greater sanctions against those who commit crimes motivated by bias against an individual or a group based on race, ethnicity, religion, gender, sexual orientation, disability, or age.

Inchoate Offense Conduct deemed criminal without actual harm being done, provided that the harm that would have occurred is a harm the law tries to prevent.

Conspiracy A plot by two or more people to carry out an illegal or harmful act.

behavior. Insanity, intoxication, and mistake are the most important excuse defenses today, but we start our discussion of the subject with one of the first such defenses recognized by American law: infancy.

INFANCY Under the earliest state criminal codes of the United States, children younger than seven years of age could never be held legally accountable for crimes. Those between seven and fourteen years old were presumed to lack the capacity for criminal behavior, while anyone over the age of fourteen was tried as an adult. Thus, early American criminal law recognized **infancy** as a defense in which the accused's wrongdoing is excused because he or she is too young to fully understand the consequences of his or her actions.

With the creation of the juvenile justice system in the early 1900s, the infancy defense became redundant, as youthful delinquents were automatically treated differently than adult offenders. Today, most states either designate an age (eighteen or under) under which wrongdoers are sent to juvenile court or allow judges and prosecutors to decide whether a minor will be charged as an adult on a case-by-case basis. We will explore the concept of infancy as it applies to the modern American juvenile justice system in much greater detail in Chapter 13.

INSANITY After Cody Metzker-Madsen beat his five-year-old brother with a brick and drowned him, the Iowa teenager told law enforcement agents that he thought he had been doing battle with a goblin. In 2014, a district court judge ruled Metzker-Madsen suffered from a severe mental illness that prevented him from knowing that his actions were wrong. As a result, Metzker-Madsen was sent to a psychiatric hospital rather than prison. Thus, **insanity** may be a defense to a criminal charge when the defendant's state of mind is such that she or he cannot claim legal responsibility for her or his actions.

Measuring Sanity The general principle of the insanity defense is that a person is excused for his or her criminal wrongdoing if, as a result of a mental disease or defect, he or she

▶ Does not perceive the physical nature or consequences of his or her conduct;

▶ Does not know that his or her conduct is wrong or criminal; or

▶ Is not sufficiently able to control his or her conduct so as to be held accountable for it.[36]

Although criminal law has traditionally accepted the idea that an insane person cannot be held responsible for criminal acts, society has long debated what standards should be used to measure sanity for the purposes of a criminal trial. This lack of consensus is reflected in the diverse tests employed by different American jurisdictions to determine insanity. The tests include the following:

1. *The* M'Naghten *rule.* Derived from an 1843 British murder case, the *M'Naghten* rule states that a person is legally insane and therefore not criminally responsible if, at the time of the offense, he or she was not able to distinguish between right and wrong.[37] As Figure 3.4 shows, half of the states still use a version of the *M'Naghten* rule. One state, New Hampshire, uses a slightly different version of this rule called the "product test." Under this standard, a defendant is not guilty if the unlawful act was the product of a mental disease or defect.

2. *The ALI/MPC test.* In the early 1960s, the American Law Institute (ALI) included an insanity standard in its Model Penal Code (MPC). Also known as the **substantial-capacity test**, the ALI/MPC test requires that the defendant lack "substantial capacity" to either "appreciate the wrongfulness" of his or her conduct or to conform that conduct "to the requirements of the law."[38]

3. *The irresistible-impulse test.* Under the **irresistible-impulse test**, a person may be found insane even if he or she was aware that a criminal act was "wrong," provided that some "irresistible impulse" resulting from a mental deficiency drove him or her to commit the crime.[39]

Infancy The status of a person who is below the legal age of majority. Under early American law, infancy excused young wrongdoers of criminal behavior because presumably they could not understand the consequences of their actions.

Insanity A defense for criminal liability that asserts a lack of criminal responsibility due to mental instability.

***M'Naghten* Rule** A common law test of criminal responsibility, derived from *M'Naghten's* Case in 1843, that relies on the defendant's inability to distinguish right from wrong.

Substantial-Capacity Test (ALI/MPC Test) A test for the insanity defense that states that a person is not responsible for criminal behavior when he or she "lacks substantial capacity" to understand that the behavior is wrong or to control the behavior.

Irresistible-Impulse Test A test for the insanity defense under which a defendant who knew his or her action was wrong may still be found insane if he or she was unable, as a result of a mental deficiency, to control the urge to complete the act.

FIGURE 3.4   INSANITY DEFENSES

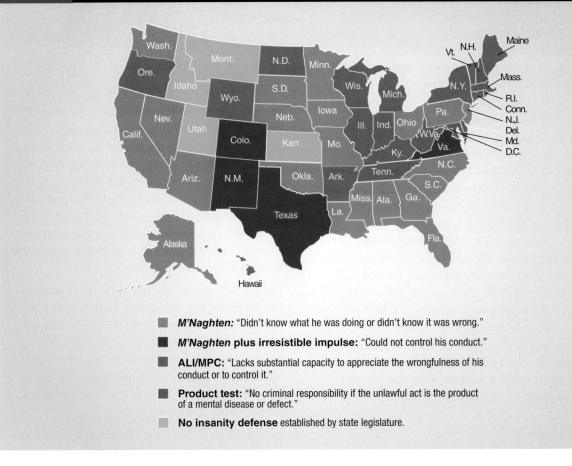

■ *M'Naghten:* "Didn't know what he was doing or didn't know it was wrong."

■ *M'Naghten* plus irresistible impulse: "Could not control his conduct."

■ **ALI/MPC:** "Lacks substantial capacity to appreciate the wrongfulness of his conduct or to control it."

■ **Product test:** "No criminal responsibility if the unlawful act is the product of a mental disease or defect."

■ **No insanity defense** established by state legislature.

The ALI/MPC test is considered the easiest standard of the three for a defendant to meet because the defendant needs only to show a lack of "substantial capacity" to be released from criminal responsibility. Defense attorneys generally consider it more difficult to prove that the defendant could not distinguish "right" from "wrong" or that he or she was driven by an irresistible impulse.

Determining Competency Whatever the standard, the insanity defense is rarely entered and is even less likely to result in an acquittal, as it is difficult to prove.[40] Psychiatry is far more commonly used in the courtroom to determine the "competency" of a defendant to stand

trial. If a judge believes that the defendant is unable to understand the nature of the proceedings or to assist in his or her own defense, the trial will not take place.

When **competency hearings** (which may also take place after the initial arrest and before sentencing) reveal that the defendant is in fact incompetent, criminal proceedings come to a halt. For example, in November 2014, a San Diego, California, judge ruled that because Carlo Mercado suffered from severe mental illness, he was not fit to stand trial. Mercado was charged with three counts of murder resulting from a shooting spree outside a shopping mall the previous Christmas Eve. As a result of the judge's decision, Mercado would receive psychiatric treatment to restore his competency. When this goal was achieved, the criminal proceedings would continue.

INTOXICATION The law recognizes two types of **intoxication,** whether from drugs or from alcohol: *voluntary* and *involuntary.* Involuntary intoxication occurs when a person is physically forced to ingest or is injected

Competency Hearing A court proceeding to determine whether the defendant is mentally well enough to understand the charges filed against him or her and cooperate with a lawyer in presenting a defense.

Intoxication A defense for criminal liability in which the defendant claims that the taking of intoxicants rendered him or her unable to form the requisite intent to commit a criminal act.

with an intoxicating substance, or is unaware that a substance contains drugs or alcohol. Involuntary intoxication is a viable defense to a crime if the substance leaves the person unable to form the mental state necessary to understand that the act committed while under the influence was wrong.[41] For example, Montana's Supreme Court recently ruled that a woman could use the involuntary intoxication defense to counter a drunken driving charge. The defendant claimed that she had unwittingly consumed a drink laced with GHB, known as the "date rape drug," before being arrested during her drive home from a bar.[42]

Voluntary drug or alcohol intoxication is also used to excuse a defendant's actions, though it is not a defense in itself. Rather, it is used when the defense attorney wants to show that the defendant was so intoxicated that *mens rea* was negated. In other words, the defendant could not possibly have had the state of mind that a crime requires. Many courts are reluctant to allow voluntary intoxication arguments to be presented to juries, however. After all, the defendant, by definition, voluntarily chose to enter an intoxicated state. Thirteen states have eliminated voluntary intoxication as a possible defense, a step that has been criticized by many legal scholars but was upheld by the United States Supreme Court in *Montana v. Egelhoff* (1996).[43]

MISTAKE Everyone has heard the saying, "Ignorance of the law is no excuse." Ordinarily, ignorance of the law or a *mistaken idea* about what the law requires is not a valid defense. Such was the case when retired science teacher Eddie Leroy Anderson and his son dug for arrowheads near their favorite campground site in Idaho, unaware that the land was a federally protected archaeological site. Facing two years in prison for this mistake, they pleaded guilty and were given a year's probation and a $1,500 fine each. "Folks need to pay attention to where they are," said U.S. attorney Wendy Olson.[44]

Mistake of Law As the above example suggests, strict liability crimes specifically preclude the *mistake of law* defense, because the offender's intent is irrelevant. For practical reasons, the mistake of law defense is rarely allowed under any circumstances. If "I didn't know" was a valid defense, the courts would be clogged with defendants claiming ignorance of all aspects of criminal law. In some rare instances, however, people who claim

Reuters/Eduardo Munoz

In 2014, Kerry Kennedy exits a White Plains, New York, courtroom after a jury acquitted her of driving while impaired. Several years earlier, Kennedy drove her car into another vehicle because, she claims, she mistakenly took a sleeping pill instead of her thyroid medication. *Why do you think Kennedy was able to successfully raise the involuntary intoxication defense?*

that they honestly did not know that they were breaking a law may have a valid defense if (1) the law was not published or reasonably known to the public or (2) the person relied on an official statement of the law that was erroneous.[45]

Mistake of Fact A *mistake of fact*, as opposed to a *mistake of law*, operates as a defense if it negates the mental state necessary to commit a crime. If, for example, Oliver mistakenly walks off with Julie's briefcase because he thinks it is his, there is no theft. Theft requires knowledge that the property belongs to another. The mistake-of-fact defense has proved very controversial in rape and sexual assault cases in which the accused claims a mistaken belief that the sex was consensual, while the victim insists that he or she was coerced.

3-6b Justification Criminal Defenses and the Law

LO3-4 In certain instances, a defendant will accept responsibility for committing an illegal act, but contend that—given the circumstances—the act was justified. In other words, even though the guilty act and the guilty intent are present, the particulars of the case relieve the defendant of criminal liability. In 2013, for example, there were 742 "justified" killings of persons who were in the process of committing a felony: 461 were killed by law enforcement officers and

281 by private citizens.[46] Four of the most important justification defenses are duress, self-defense, necessity, and entrapment.

DURESS Duress exists when the *wrongful* threat of one person induces another person to perform an act that she or he would otherwise not perform. In such a situation, duress is said to negate the *mens rea* necessary to commit a crime. For duress to qualify as a defense, the following requirements must be met:

> 1. The threat must be of serious bodily harm or death.
>
> 2. The harm threatened must be greater than the harm caused by the crime.
>
> 3. The threat must be immediate and inescapable.
>
> 4. The defendant must have become involved in the situation through no fault of his or her own.[47]

Note that some scholars consider duress to be an excuse defense, because the threat of bodily harm negates any guilty intent on the part of the defendant.[48]

When ruling on the duress defense, courts often examine whether the defendant had the opportunity to avoid the threat in question. In one case, the defendant claimed that an associate threatened to kill him and his wife unless he participated in a marijuana deal. Although this contention was proved true during the course of the trial, the court rejected the duress defense because the defendant made no apparent effort to escape, nor did he report his dilemma to the police. In sum, the drug deal was avoidable—the defendant could have made an effort to extricate himself, but he did not, thereby surrendering the protection of the duress defense.[49]

JUSTIFIABLE USE OF FORCE—SELF-DEFENSE A person who believes he or she is in danger of being harmed by another is justified in defending himself or herself with the use of force, and any criminal act

committed in such circumstances can be justified as **self-defense.** Other situations that also justify the use of force include the defense of another person, the defense of one's dwelling or other property, and the prevention of a crime. In all these situations, it is important to distinguish between deadly and nondeadly force. Deadly force is likely to result in death or serious bodily harm.

The Amount of Force Generally speaking, people can use the amount of nondeadly force that seems necessary to protect themselves, their dwellings, or other property or to prevent the commission of a crime. Deadly force can be used in self-defense if there is a *reasonable belief* that imminent death or bodily harm will otherwise result, if the attacker is using unlawful force (an example of lawful force is that exerted by a police officer), if the defender has not initiated or provoked the attack, and if there is no other possible response or alternative way out of the life-threatening situation.[50]

Deadly force normally can be used to defend a dwelling only if the unlawful entry is violent and the person believes deadly force is necessary to prevent imminent death or great bodily harm. In some jurisdictions, it is also a viable defense if the person believes deadly force is necessary to prevent the commission of a felony (such as arson) in the dwelling. Authorities will often take an expansive view of lawful deadly force when it is used to protect another person. So, in 2014, a New Orleans man was not charged with any crime after he fatally shot an offender who was sexually assaulting a woman—the first man's companion—at gunpoint.

The Duty to Retreat When a person is outside the home or in a public space, the rules for self-defense change somewhat. Until relatively recently, almost all jurisdictions required someone who is attacked under these circumstances to "retreat to the wall" before fighting back. In other words, under this **duty to retreat** one who is being assaulted may not resort to deadly force if she or he has a reasonable opportunity to "run away" and thus avoid the conflict. Only when this person has run into a "wall," literally or otherwise, may deadly force be used in self-defense.

Recently, however, several states have changed their laws to eliminate this duty to retreat. For example, a Florida law did away with the duty to retreat outside the home, stating that citizens have "the right to stand [their] ground and meet force with force, including deadly force," if they "reasonably" fear for their safety.[51] The Florida law also allows a person to use deadly force

---

Duress Unlawful pressure brought to bear on a person, causing the person to perform an act that he or she would not otherwise perform.

Self-Defense The legally recognized privilege to protect one's self or property from injury by another.

Duty to Retreat The requirement that a person claiming self-defense prove that she or he first took reasonable steps to avoid the conflict that resulted in the use of deadly force.

against someone who unlawfully intrudes into her or his house (or vehicle), even if that person does not fear for her or his safety.[52] More than thirty states now have passed legislation that removes the duty to retreat before using force in self-defense.

Debating Self-Defense "Stand your ground" statutes gained national attention when, in February 2012, George Zimmerman shot and killed unarmed seventeen-year-old Trayvon Martin in Sanford, Florida. Zimmerman told police that he had encountered Martin during his rounds as a neighborhood watchman, and that he had pulled the trigger only after being attacked by the younger man. Zimmerman was eventually acquitted of second degree murder when a jury decided that he could have been acting reasonably by defending himself against great bodily harm or death.[53]

During the furor that surrounded this case—caused in large measure because Zimmerman is Hispanic and Martin was black—"stand your ground" laws came under a great deal of criticism. According to one opponent, they have created a "nation where disputes are settled by guns instead of gavels, and where suspects are shot by civilians instead of arrested by the police."[54] In Texas, which passed its version of this legislation in 2007, the number of justifiable homicides increased from eighteen in 1999 to sixty-two in 2013.[55]

Proponents of "stand your ground" laws contend that they allow people who face serious bodily harm or death the opportunity to defend themselves without first having to retreat as far as possible. Supporters also argue that the laws strengthen the concept of self-defense by making it less likely that a person defending him- or herself will be charged with a crime.

NECESSITY The **necessity** defense requires courts to weigh the harm caused by the crime actually committed against the harm that would have been caused

Necessity A defense against criminal liability in which the defendant asserts that circumstances required her or him to commit an illegal act.

CRIMINAL COURT JUDGE

CareerPrep

Job Description:

▶ Preside over trials and hearings in federal, state, and local courts. Ensure that all proceedings are fair and protect the legal rights of everyone involved.

▶ Rule on admissibility of evidence, monitor the testimony of witnesses, and settle disputes between prosecutors and defense attorneys.

What Kind of Training Is Required?

▶ A law degree and several years of legal experience.

▶ Depending on the jurisdiction, judges are either appointed or elected.

Annual Salary Range?

▶ $104,000–$180,000

Junial Enterprises, 2010/Used under license from ShutterStock.com

SOCIAL MEDIA CAREER TIP

Find groups on Facebook and LinkedIn in which people are discussing the criminal justice career or careers that interest you. Participate in the discussions to get information and build contacts.

by the criminal act avoided. If the avoided harm is greater than the committed harm, then the defense has a chance of succeeding. A San Francisco jury, for example, acquitted a defendant of illegally carrying a concealed weapon because he was avoiding the "greater evil" of getting shot himself. The defendant had testified that he needed the gun for protection while entering a high-crime neighborhood to buy baby food and diapers for his crying niece.[56] Murder is the one crime for which the necessity defense is not applicable under any circumstances.

ENTRAPMENT Entrapment is a justification defense that criminal law allows when a police officer or government agent deceives a defendant into wrongdoing. Although law enforcement agents can legitimately use various forms of subterfuge—such as informants or undercover agents—to gain information or apprehend a suspect in a criminal act, the law places limits on these strategies. Police cannot persuade an innocent person to commit a crime, nor can they coerce a suspect into doing so, even if they are certain she or he is a criminal.

The guidelines for determining entrapment were established in the 1932 case of *Sorrells v. United States.*[57] The case, which took place during Prohibition, when the sale of alcoholic beverages was illegal, involved a federal law enforcement agent who repeatedly urged the defendant to sell him bootleg whiskey. The defendant initially rejected the agent's overtures, stating that he "did not fool with whiskey." Eventually, however, he sold the agent a half-gallon of the substance and was summarily convicted of violating the law. The United States Supreme Court held that the agent had improperly induced the defendant to break the law and reversed the conviction.

Entrapment A defense in which the defendant claims that he or she was induced by a public official—usually an undercover agent or police officer—to commit a crime that he or she would otherwise not have committed.

Substantive Criminal Law Law that defines the rights and duties of individuals with respect to one another.

Procedural Criminal Law Rules that define the manner in which the rights and duties of individuals may be enforced.

Bill of Rights The first ten amendments to the U.S. Constitution.

3-7 HOW DO CRIMINAL PROCEDURES PROTECT OUR CONSTITUTIONAL RIGHTS?

To this point, we have focused on **substantive criminal law,** which defines the acts that the government will punish. We will now turn our attention to **procedural criminal law.** (The section that follows will provide only a short overview of criminal procedure. In later chapters, many other constitutional issues will be examined in more detail.)

Criminal law brings the force of the state, with all its resources, to bear against the individual. Criminal procedures, drawn from the ideals stated in the Bill of Rights, are designed to protect the constitutional rights of individuals and to prevent the arbitrary use of this power by the government.

3-7a The Bill of Rights

For various reasons, proposals related to the rights of individuals were rejected during the framing of the U.S. Constitution in 1787. The need for a written declaration of rights of individuals eventually caused the first Congress to draft twelve amendments to the Constitution and submit them for approval by the states. Ten of these amendments, commonly known as the **Bill of Rights,** were adopted in 1791. Since then, seventeen more amendments have been added.

The Bill of Rights, as interpreted by the United States Supreme Court, has served as the basis for procedural safeguards of the accused in this country. These safeguards include the following:

1. **The Fourth Amendment protection from unreasonable searches and seizures.**

2. **The Fourth Amendment requirement that no warrants for a search or an arrest can be issued without probable cause.**

3. **The Fifth Amendment requirement that no one can be deprived of life, liberty, or property without "due process" of law.**

4. **The Fifth Amendment prohibition against *double jeopardy* (trying someone twice for the same criminal offense).**

5. The Fifth Amendment guarantee that no person can be required to be a witness against (incriminate) himself or herself.

6. The Sixth Amendment guarantees of a speedy trial, a trial by jury, a public trial, the right to confront witnesses, and the right to a lawyer at various stages of criminal proceedings.

7. The Eighth Amendment prohibitions against excessive bails and fines and cruel and unusual punishments.

The Bill of Rights initially offered citizens protection only against the federal government. Over the years, however, the procedural safeguards of most of the provisions of the Bill of Rights have been applied to the actions of state governments through the Fourteenth Amendment.[58] Furthermore, the states, under certain circumstances, have the option to grant even more protections than are required by the federal Constitution. As these protections are crucial to criminal justice procedures in the United States, they will be afforded much more attention in Chapter 6, with regard to police action, and in Chapter 8, with regard to the criminal trial.

3-7b Due Process

Both the Fifth and Fourteenth Amendments provide that no person should be deprived of "life, liberty, or property without due process of law." This **due process clause** basically requires that the government not act unfairly or arbitrarily. In other words, the government cannot rely on individual judgment and impulse when making decisions, but must stay within the boundaries of reason and the law. Not surprisingly, disagreements as to the meaning of these provisions have plagued courts, politicians, and citizens since this nation was founded, and will undoubtedly continue to do so.

To understand due process, it is important to consider its two types: procedural due process and substantive due process.

LO3-5 **PROCEDURAL DUE PROCESS** According to **procedural due process,** the law must be carried out by a *method* that is fair and orderly. It requires that certain procedures be followed in administering and executing a law so that an individual's basic freedoms are not violated.

Comstock/PhotoLibrary

Why do most Americans accept certain security precautions taken by the federal government—such as full body scans at airports—that restrict our individual freedom or compromise our privacy?

The American criminal justice system's adherence to due process principles is evident in its treatment of the death penalty. To ensure that the process is fair, as we will see in Chapter 9, a number of procedural safeguards have been built into capital punishment. Much to the dismay of many victims' groups, these procedures make the process expensive and lengthy. The average time between sentencing and execution for those convicted of capital crimes is almost sixteen years, and some inmates spend well over twenty years on death row.[59]

Due Process Clause The provisions of the Fifth and Fourteenth Amendments to the Constitution that guarantee that no person shall be deprived of life, liberty, or property without due process of law.

Procedural Due Process A provision in the Constitution that states that the law must be carried out in a fair and orderly manner.

SUBSTANTIVE DUE PROCESS

Fair procedures would obviously be of little use if they were used to administer unfair laws. For example, suppose a law requires everyone to wear a red shirt on Mondays. You wear a blue shirt on Monday, and you are arrested, convicted, and sentenced to one year in prison. The fact that all proper procedures were followed and your rights were given their proper protections would mean very little because the law that you broke was unfair and arbitrary.

Thus, **substantive due process** requires that the laws themselves be reasonable. The idea is that if a law is unfair or arbitrary, even if properly passed by a legislature, it must be declared unconstitutional. In the 1930s,

Mark Andersen/Rubberball/Getty Images

The United States Supreme Court, pictured here, often has the responsibility of determining whether federal laws violate the due process clause of the U.S. Constitution. *What are the pros and cons of a system where a court can overrule decisions collectively made by elected representatives of the people?*

Substantive Due Process The constitutional requirement that laws used in accusing and convicting persons of crimes must be fair.

for example, Oklahoma instituted the Habitual Criminal Sterilization Act. Under this statute, a person who had been convicted of three felonies could be "rendered sexually sterile" by the state (that is, the person would no longer be able to produce children). The United States Supreme Court held that the law was unconstitutional, as there are "limits to the extent which a legislatively represented majority may conduct biological experiments at the expense of the dignity and personality and natural powers of a minority."[60]

Quiz

1. The U.S. _____ is the supreme law of the United States.

2. The body of law created by judicial decisions is known as _____ law.

3. In contrast to criminal law, _____ law is concerned with disputes between private individuals or other private entities.

4. A _____ is a serious crime punishable by more than a year in prison or the death penalty.

5. A person found guilty of a _____ will usually spend less than a year in jail or pay a fine.

6. With strict liability crimes, a defendant is guilty even if he or she lacked the _____ to perform a criminal act.

7. Criminal law recognizes that a defendant may not be responsible for a criminal act if her or his mental state was impaired by _____, or mental instability.

8. Defendants may claim that they were justified in committing a crime because they were acting in _____ - _____ to protect themselves or others from serious bodily harm.

9. _____ occurs when a government agent deceives a defendant into committing a crime.

10. The _____ _____ clause requires that the U.S. government follow certain procedures to ensure fairness and reasonableness before depriving its citizens of "life, liberty, or property."

Answers can be found in the Answers section in the back of the book.

4 Law Enforcement Today

Bill Clark/CQ Roll Call/Getty Images

LEARNING OBJECTIVES

After studying this chapter, you will be able to . . .

4-1 List the four basic responsibilities of the police.

4-2 Identify the differences between the police academy and field training as learning tools for recruits.

4-3 Describe the challenges facing women who choose law enforcement as a career.

4-4 Indicate some of the most important law enforcement agencies under the control of the Department of Homeland Security.

4-5 Analyze the importance of private security today.

After you finish this chapter, go to **PAGES 89–90** for **STUDY TOOLS**

Starting Over

Year after year, Camden, New Jersey—population 77,000—ranked as one of the nation's most violent and dangerous cities. Illegal drug buyers and sellers would commute using light rail to take advantage of the city's nearly two hundred open drug markets. Residents spent most of their days safely inside homes barricaded by iron bars, known as "bird cages." In 2011, a bad situation became worse when city officials were forced to lay off half of Camden's police force due to budget cuts. In response, local drug dealers printed tee-shirts that read, "It's Our Time."

A number of the social factors linked to crime are present in Camden, such as high unemployment, urban blight, and youth gangs. For many, however, the local police department was a significant part of the problem. After the layoffs, the city had only 230 active officers. Understaffed, the Camden police stopped responding to 911 calls and let shooting investigations lag. Asked one frustrated observer, "What happens when the city can no longer pay" to fight crime?

In May 2013, Camden officials responded by disbanding the city's entire police department. This unprecedented step allowed Camden County to hire a completely new force without the restrictions of the previous department's police union labor contract. As a result, per-officer costs were cut in half, and the city was eventually able to nearly double its number of police officers. Law enforcement officials also increased the use of crime-fighting technology and trained the new officers to be more involved in the community. By the summer of 2014, even though the city's murder rate was still considerably higher than the national average, shootings were down 43 percent and overall violent crime was down 22 percent from two years earlier. "A lot of the old officers, all they did was ride around and not do anything," said one Camden resident. "These are soldiers we have here now."

Camden, New Jersey, police officers interact with residents during a day dedicated to cleaning up local parks. Under the circumstances, do you think that Camden's plan to lay off an entire police force for financial reasons was ethical? Why or why not?

Andrew Burton/Getty Images

4-1 WHAT DO POLICE DO?

Before the city's "reboot" of its police department, residents of Whitman Park, a high-crime neighborhood in Camden, New Jersey, would shout obscenities at patrol cars. After the changes, the locals were more welcoming. One little girl even yelled out, "Hi, cop!" when she saw an officer approaching her family's front porch.[1] The difference in attitudes is important, as police officers are the most visible representatives of our criminal justice system. Indeed, they symbolize the system for many Americans who may never see the inside of a courtroom or a prison cell. Still, the general perception of a "cop's life" is often shaped by television dramas such as the *CSI* series and *Hawaii Five-O.* In reality, police spend a great deal of time on such mundane tasks as responding to noise complaints, confiscating firecrackers, and poring over paperwork.

Sociologist Egon Bittner warned against the tendency to see the police primarily as agents of law enforcement and crime control. A more inclusive accounting of "what the police do," Bittner believed, would recognize that they provide "situationally justified force in society."[2] In other words, the function of the police is to solve any problem that may *possibly,* though not *necessarily,* require the use of force.

Within Bittner's rather broad definition of "what the police do," we can pinpoint four basic responsibilities of the police:

LO4-1

1. **To enforce laws.**
2. **To provide services.**
3. **To prevent crime.**
4. **To preserve the peace.**

As will become evident over the next two chapters, there is a great deal of debate among legal and other scholars and law enforcement officers over which responsibilities deserve the most police attention and what methods should be employed in meeting those responsibilities.

4-1a Enforce Laws

In the public mind, the primary role of the police is to enforce society's laws—hence, the term *law enforcement officer*. In their role as "crime fighters," police officers have a clear mandate to seek out and apprehend those who have violated the law. The crime-fighting responsibility is so dominant that all police activity—from the purchase of new automobiles to a plan to hire more minority officers—must often be justified in terms of its law enforcement value.[3]

Police officers also see themselves primarily as crime fighters, or "crook catchers," a perception that often leads people into what they believe will be an exciting career in law enforcement. Although the job certainly offers challenges unlike any other, police officers normally do not spend the majority of their time in law enforcement duties. After surveying a year's worth of dispatch data from the Wilmington (Delaware) Police Department, researchers Jack Greene and Carl Klockars found that officers spent only about half of their time enforcing the law or dealing with crimes. The rest was spent on order maintenance, service provision, traffic patrol, and medical assistance.[4]

Furthermore, information provided by the Uniform Crime Report shows that most arrests are made for "crimes of disorder" or public annoyances rather than violent or property crimes.[5] In 2013, for example, police made about 9.3 million arrests for drunkenness, liquor law violations, disorderly conduct, vagrancy, loitering, and other minor offenses, but only about 480,000 arrests for violent crimes.[6] (See the feature *Discretion in Action—Soft Power* to consider one of the many challenges police face in trying to enforce criminal laws.)

4-1b Provide Services

The popular emphasis on crime fighting and law enforcement tends to overshadow the fact that a great deal of a police officer's time is spent providing services for the

---

Discretion in Action

SOFT POWER

THE SITUATION Every day, about fifty men gather in a small park, waiting to get picked up by employers for hourly menial work. The situation at this impromptu day-laborer camp has become chaotic and, at times, dangerous. Many of the men are homeless and use the park as a bedroom and a toilet. Prostitutes frequent the area, as do alcohol sellers and drug dealers. You are a police sergeant, and your superiors have ordered you to "clean up" the park.

THE LAW These men are committing numerous infractions and minor crimes, including disorderly conduct, vagrancy, drunkenness, and public urination. Once arrested, the offenders—most of whom are recent immigrants, in the country illegally—could be reported to the federal government and potentially removed from the country.

WHAT WOULD YOU DO? Many of the day workers are breaking the law, and you would be justified in having the police officers under your command make a sweep of arrests. In the long term, however, this strategy would likely present problems. Because their offenses are minor, most of the men would be released quickly, and, needing work, would find their way back to the park. Also, the federal government is focusing on removing undocumented immigrants who have committed serious crimes, not petty offenders.

When faced with a similar problem, police officers in Kansas City, Missouri, decided to use a less confrontational approach. They helped set up a day-laborer program at a nearby community center that provided the men with bathrooms, showers, food, and help finding work. Within a year, 911 calls in the area went down by more than 50 percent. "We couldn't arrest our way out of the problem," one Kansas City police officer told a reporter. "[So] we started treating them like human beings."

community. The motto "To Serve and Protect" has been adopted by thousands of local police departments, and the *Law Enforcement Code of Ethics* recognizes the duty "to serve the community" in its first sentence.[7] The services that police provide are numerous—a partial list would include directing traffic, performing emergency medical procedures, counseling those involved in domestic disputes, providing directions to tourists, and finding lost children.

As we will see in the next section, many police departments have adopted a strategy called *community policing*. This strategy requires officers to provide assistance in areas that are not, at first glance, directly related to law enforcement. Often, regardless of official policy, the police are forced into providing certain services. For example, in many instances, law enforcement officers are first on the scene when a person has been seriously injured. As a result, officers increasingly are becoming proficient in emergency medical procedures. Some cities even allow police officers to take injured persons to the hospital in a squad car rather than wait for an ambulance.[8]

4-1c Prevent Crime

Perhaps the most controversial responsibility of the police is to *prevent* crime. According to Jerome Skolnick, co-director of the Center for Research in Crime and Justice at the New York University School of Law, there are two predictable public responses when crime rates begin to rise in a community. The first is to punish convicted criminals with stricter laws and more severe penalties. The second is to demand that the police "do something" to prevent crimes from occurring in the first place. Is it, in fact, possible for the police to "prevent" crimes? The strongest response that Professor Skolnick is willing to give to this question is "maybe."[9]

On a limited basis, police can certainly prevent some crimes. If a rapist is dissuaded from attacking a solitary woman because a patrol car is cruising the area, then the police officer behind the wheel has prevented a crime. Furthermore, exemplary police work can have a measurable effect. "Quite simply, cops count," says William Bratton, who has directed police departments in Boston, Los Angeles, and New York. "[T]he quickest way to impact crime is with a well-led, managed, and appropriately resourced police force."[10] In Chapter 5, we will study a number of policing strategies that have been credited, by some, with decreasing crime rates in the United States.

In general, however, the deterrent effects of police presence are unclear. One recent study found no relationship between the size of the police presence in a neighborhood and the residents' perceived risk of being arrested for wrongdoing.[11] Furthermore, Carl Klockars has written that the "war on crime" is a war that the police cannot win because they cannot control the factors—such as unemployment, poverty, immorality, inequality, political change, and lack of educational opportunities—that contribute to criminal behavior in the first place.[12]

4-1d Preserve the Peace

To a certain extent, the fourth responsibility of the police, that of preserving the peace, is related to preventing crime. Police have the legal authority to use the power of arrest, or even force, in situations in which no crime has yet occurred, but might occur in the immediate future.

In the words of James Q. Wilson, the police's peace-keeping role (which Wilson believed to be the most important role of law enforcement officers) often takes on a pattern of simply "handling the situation."[13] For example, when police officers arrive on the scene of a loud, late-night house party, they may feel the need to disperse the party and even arrest some of the partygoers for disorderly conduct. By their actions, the officers have lessened the chances of serious and violent crimes taking place later in the evening. The same principle is often used when dealing with domestic disputes, which, if escalated, can lead to homicide. Such situations are in need of, to use Wilson's terminology again, "fixing up," and police can use the power of arrest, or threat, or coercion, or sympathy, to do just that.

4-1e Policing Trends Today

Even as the four basic responsibilities of the police just discussed have remained fairly stable, the manner in which these duties are carried out is constantly changing. American law enforcement today faces challenges that would have been unfamiliar even fifteen years ago, and it has had to develop new areas of expertise to meet these challenges effectively. In particular, the process of collecting, analyzing, and mapping crime data has become a hallmark of law enforcement in the twenty-first century.

INTELLIGENCE-LED POLICING "Humans are not nearly as random as we think," says Jeff Brantingham, an anthropologist at the University of California, Los Angeles. "Crime is a physical process, and if you can explain how offenders move and how they mix with victims, you can understand an incredible amount."[14] Relying on this basic principle, Brantingham and several colleagues developed PredPol, a software program that strives to predict when and where crimes are most likely to occur. Each day, the software identifies a geographic area—sometimes as small as 500 square feet—that is likely to experience a certain type of criminal activity. For example, local police applied PredPol to a neighborhood in the foothills of Los Angeles. Within six months, they reported a 12 percent drop in property crimes compared with the previous year.[15]

The PredPol approach is known as predictive policing, or **intelligence-led policing** (IPL), because it relies on data—or intelligence—concerning past crime patterns to predict future crime patterns. In theory, IPL is relatively simple. Just as commercial fishers are most successful when they concentrate on the areas of the ocean where the fish are, law enforcement does well to focus its scarce resources on the areas where the most crime occurs. With programs such as PredPol and other "hot spot" technologies that we will discuss in the next chapter, police administrators are able to deploy small forces to specific locations, rather than blanketing an entire city with random patrols. Doing "more with less" in this manner is a particularly important consideration as police budgets shrink around the country.[16]

THE CHALLENGES OF COUNTERTERRORISM When basic IPL principles are applied to the issue of terrorism, it quickly becomes clear that terrorists, like other criminals, are likely to choose targets close to their homes. At the same time, when terrorist attacks occur great distances from those homes, the attacks are more deadly. Consequently, counterterrorism provides three specific challenges for American law enforcement:

Boston Globe/Getty Images

On March 4, 2015, a victim of the 2013 Boston Marathon bombing leaves the courthouse after the first day of suspect Dzhokhar Tsarnaev's trial. *Why are local police such as the Watertown, Massachusetts, officers who initially apprehended Tsarnaev so important to national counterterrorism efforts?*

1. The need to focus scarce resources to prevent and fight crimes that are relatively uncommon.

2. The scrutiny that comes with crimes that sometimes have international implications.

3. The difficult task of gathering intelligence about crimes before they happen.[17]

Each year, the U.S. Department of Homeland Security awards about $1.5 billion in grants for homeland security preparedness.[18] These funds have helped support more than one hundred local and state police intelligence units, with at least one in each state. The New York Police Department, in a class by itself, has more than one thousand personnel assigned to homeland security and has stationed agents in six foreign countries. The Los Angeles Police Department operates the National Counter-Terrorism Academy, offering a five-month course that trains police officers to prevent, rather than respond to, terrorist attacks.

The shifting nature of terrorism makes such training a necessity. Initially, the primary homeland security concern was a large-scale attack such as those that occurred in September 2001. Then, law enforcement

Intelligence-Led Policing An approach that measures the risk of criminal behavior associated with certain individuals or locations so as to predict when and where such criminal behavior is most likely to occur in the future.

attention shifted to "lone wolf" domestic terrorists motivated by grievances nurtured on the Internet. Now, homeland security officials in the United States and Europe are also focusing on citizens who receive training from extremists in the Middle East but return home to carry out their plans. In response to these various threats, all police officers are expected to prepare for a terrorist attack in their communities, and counterterrorism has become part of the day-to-day law enforcement routine.

LAW ENFORCEMENT 2.0 Fortunately, just as more intelligence has become crucial to police work, the means available to gather such intelligence have also increased greatly. Nearly every successful anti-terrorism investigation has relied on information gathered from the Internet. Furthermore, at least 90 percent of law enforcement agencies monitor social media to find leads on criminal activity.[19] Several years ago, for instance, the New York Police Department set up a new unit dedicated to preventing violence between groups of neighborhood adolescents knows as "crews." Because most of these youths use social media to communicate with each other, police officers monitoring Facebook and Twitter are often able to learn about potential conflicts before they take place. New York officials credit Operation Crew Cut with contributing to a record-low number of murders in the city in 2013.[20]

As might be expected, technology also continues to improve the capabilities of officers in the field. In this section's *CJ and Technology* feature, we see that law enforcement agents can use smartphones and tablets to access a wealth of crime information and have turned their patrol cars into command centers on wheels. Officers are also able to use less lethal weapons (such as laser beams), monitor suspects via satellite, and incorporate

dozens of other technological innovations into their day-to-day-duties.

Some law enforcement veterans are concerned that the "art" of policing is being lost in an era of intelligence-led policing and increased reliance on technology. "If it becomes all about the science," says Los Angeles Police Department Deputy Chief Michael Downing, "I worry we'll lose the important nuances."[21] As the remainder of this chapter and the two that follow show, however, the human element continues to dominate all aspects of policing in America.

CAREER TIP A number of law enforcement agencies are now hiring *social media strategists* to develop and maintain systems for using this technology to communicate with the public.

4-2 HOW DOES SOMEONE BECOME A POLICE OFFICER?

In 1961, police expert James H. Chenoweth commented that the methods used to hire police officers had changed little since 1829 when the Metropolitan Police of London was created.[22] The past half-century, however, has seen a number of improvements in the way that police administrators handle the task of **recruitment,** or the development of a pool of qualified applicants from which to select new officers. Efforts have been made to diversify police rolls, and recruits in most police departments undergo a substantial array of tests and screens—discussed next—to determine their aptitude. Furthermore, annual starting salaries that can exceed $70,000, along with the opportunities offered by an interesting profession in the public service field, have attracted a wide variety of applicants to police work.

4-2a Basic Requirements

The selection process involves a number of steps, and each police department has a different method of choosing candidates. Most agencies, however, require at a minimum that a police officer:

Recruitment The process by which law enforcement agencies develop a pool of qualified applicants from which to select new employees.

▶ Be a U.S. citizen.

▶ Not have been convicted of a felony.

▶ Have or be eligible to have a driver's license in the state where the department is located.

▶ Be at least twenty-one years of age.

▶ Meet weight and eyesight requirements.

In addition, few departments will accept candidates older than forty-five years of age.

BACKGROUND CHECKS AND TESTS Beyond these minimum requirements, police departments usually engage in extensive background checks, including drug tests; a review of the applicant's educational, military, and driving records; credit checks; interviews with spouses, acquaintances, and previous employers; and a background search to determine whether the applicant has been convicted of any criminal acts. Police agencies generally require certain physical attributes in applicants: normally, they must be able to pass a physical agility or fitness test. (For an example of one such test, see Figure 4.1).

In some departments, particularly those that serve large metropolitan areas, the applicant must take a psychological screening test to determine if he or she is suited to law enforcement work. Generally, such suitability tests measure the applicant's ability to handle stress, follow rules, use good judgment, and avoid off-duty behavior that would reflect negatively on the department.[23]

Along these same lines, more than one-third of American police agencies now review an applicant's social media activity on sources such as Facebook, Instagram, and Twitter.[24] "A single posting on Facebook in poor taste won't automatically eliminate someone from our hiring process," explains Arlington (Texas) Deputy Chief Lauretta Hill. "But if we see a pattern of behavior or something that raises a red flag, it lets us know that we need to dig a little deeper during our background investigation."[25]

EDUCATIONAL REQUIREMENTS One of the most dramatic differences between today's police recruits and those of several generations ago is their level of education. In the 1920s, when August Vollmer began promoting the need for higher education in police officers, few had attended college. In the 2000s, 82 percent of all local police departments require at least a high school diploma, and 9 percent require a degree from a two-year college.[26] Although a four-year degree is necessary for certain elite law enforcement positions, such as

1. Applicant begins test seated in a police vehicle, door closed, seat belt fastened.
2. Applicant must exit vehicle and jump or climb a six-foot barrier.
3. Applicant then completes a one-quarter mile run or walk, making various turns along the way, to simulate a pursuit run.
4. Applicant must jump a simulated five-foot culvert/ditch.
5. Applicant must drag a "human simulator" (dummy) weighing 175 pounds a distance of 50 feet (to simulate a situation in which an officer is required to pull or carry an injured person to safety).
6. Applicant must draw his or her weapon and fire five rounds with the strong hand and five rounds with the weak hand.

Those applying for the position of police officer must finish this physical agility exam within 3 minutes, 30 seconds. During the test, applicants are required to wear the equipment worn by patrol officers, which includes the police uniform, leather gun belt, firearm, baton, portable radio, and ballistics vest (with a total weight of between 9 and 13 pounds).

Federal Bureau of Investigation special agent, only about 5 percent of large local police departments have such a requirement.[27] Those officers with four-year degrees do, however, generally enjoy an advantage in hiring and promotion, and often receive higher salaries than their less educated co-employees.

Not all police observers believe that education is a necessity for police officers, however. In the words of one police officer, "[E]ffective street cops learn their skills on the job, not in a classroom."[28] By emphasizing a college degree, say some, police departments discourage those who would make solid officers but lack the education necessary to apply for positions in law enforcement.

4-2b Training

If an applicant successfully navigates the application process, he or she will be hired on a *probationary* basis. During this **probationary period,** which can last from six to eighteen months depending on the department, the recruit is in jeopardy of being fired without cause if he or she proves inadequate to the challenges of police work. Almost every state requires that police recruits pass through a training period while on probation. During this time, they are taught the basics of police work and are under constant supervision by superiors. The training period usually has two components: the police academy and field training. On average, local police departments serving populations of 250,000 or more require 1,648 hours of training—972 hours in the classroom and 676 hours in the field.[29]

LO4-2 ACADEMY TRAINING The *police academy,* run by either the state or a police agency, provides recruits with a controlled, militarized environment in which they receive their introduction to the world of the police officer. They are taught the laws of search, seizure, arrest, and interrogation; how and when to use weapons; the procedures of securing a crime scene

Probationary Period A period of time at the beginning of a police officer's career during which she or he may be fired without cause.

A recruit goes through an exercise routine at a police academy for the U.S. Capitol Police in Cheltenham, Maryland. *Why are police academies an important part of the learning process for a potential police officer?*

and interviewing witnesses; first aid; self-defense; and other essentials of police work. Nine in ten police academies also provide terrorism-related training to teach recruits how to respond to terrorist incidents, including those involving weapons of mass destruction.[30] Academy instructors evaluate the recruits' performance and send intermittent progress reports to police administrators.

IN THE FIELD Field training takes place outside the confines of the police academy. A recruit is paired with an experienced police officer known as a field training officer (FTO). The goal of field training is to help rookies apply the concepts they have learned in the academy "to the streets," with the FTO playing a supervisory role to make sure that nothing goes awry. According to many, the academy introduces recruits to the formal rules of police work, but field training gives the rookies their first taste of the informal rules. In fact, the initial advice to recruits from some FTOs is often along the lines of "O.K., kid. Forget everything you learned in the classroom. You're in the real world now." Nonetheless, the academy is a critical component in the learning process, as it provides rookies with a road map to the job.

4-3 WHAT IS THE STATUS OF WOMEN AND MINORITIES IN POLICING?

For most of this nation's history, the typical American police officer was white and male. As recently as 1968, African Americans represented only 5 percent of all sworn officers in the United States, and the percentage of "women in blue" was even lower.[31] Only within the past thirty years has this situation been addressed, with many police departments actively trying to recruit women, African Americans, Hispanics, Asian Americans, and members of other minority groups. The result, as you will see, has been a steady though not spectacular increase in the diversity of the nation's police forces. When it comes to issues of gender, race, and ethnicity, however, mere statistics rarely tell the entire story.

Field Training The segment of a police recruit's training in which he or she is removed from the classroom and placed on the beat, under the supervision of a senior officer.

4-3a Working Women: Gender and Law Enforcement

In 1987, about 7.6 percent of all local police officers were women. Twenty-six years later, that percentage had risen to almost 12 percent—17 percent in departments serving populations of more than one million people.[32] That increase seems less impressive, however, when one considers that women make up more than half of the population of the United States, meaning that they are severely underrepresented in law enforcement.

LO4-3 **ADDED SCRUTINY** There are several reasons for the low levels of women serving as police officers. First, relatively few women hold positions of high rank in American police departments,[33] and only about 3 percent of the police chiefs in the United States are women.[34] Consequently, female police officers have few superiors who might be able to mentor them in what can be a hostile work environment.

In addition to the dangers and pressures facing all law enforcement agents, which we will discuss in the next chapter, women must deal with an added layer of scrutiny. Many male police officers feel that their female counterparts are mentally soft, physically weak, and generally unsuited for the rigors of the job. At the same time, male officers often try to protect female officers by keeping them out of hazardous situations, thereby denying the women the opportunity to prove themselves.[35]

TOKENISM Women in law enforcement also face the problem of *tokenism*, or the belief that they have been hired or promoted to fulfill diversity requirements and have not earned their positions. Tokenism creates pressure to prove the stereotypes wrong. When comparing the arrest patterns of male and female officers over a twelve-month period in Cincinnati, Ohio, for example, researchers noted several interesting patterns. Although overall arrest rates were similar, female officers were much more likely than their male counterparts to arrest suspects who were "non-deferential" or hostile. Also, the presence of a supervisor greatly increased the likelihood that a female officer would make an arrest.

Such patterns, the researchers concluded, show that female officers feel pressure to demonstrate that they are "good cops" who cannot be intimidated because of their gender.[36] One officer said that her female colleagues "go into that physical-arrest mode quicker [because] you want to prove that you can do it."[37] Similarly, women who rise through the law enforcement ranks often face questions concerning their worthiness. According to Tampa (Florida) police chief Jane Castor, "No matter how qualified you are or how much experience you have . . . people will say that you were promoted—in part, if not fully—because you're a woman."[38] In fact, most of the negative attitudes toward women police officers are based on prejudice rather than actual experience. A number of studies have shown that there is very little difference between the performances of men and women in uniform.[39]

SEXUAL HARASSMENT According to a female officer interviewed by researcher Teresa Lynn, "The guys can view you as a sex object."[40] Anecdotal evidence suggests that this attitude is commonplace in police departments and often leads to **sexual harassment** of female police officers. Sexual harassment refers to a pattern of behavior that is sexual in nature, such as inappropriate touching or lewd jokes, and is unwelcome by its target. Such conduct can impact the recipient's career. One victim of sexual comments and physical contact by a superior said that when she rebuffed his advances, "he would retaliate by criticizing my reports or judgment."[41]

Over a nine-month period in 2010, the National Police Misconduct Statistics and Reporting Project confirmed eighty-six incidents of sexual harassment in police departments nationwide.[42] Self-reported surveys, however, suggest that the actual incidence is much higher, with most incidents going unreported.[43] Despite having to deal with problems such as sexual harassment, outdated stereotypes, and tokenism, female police officers have generally shown that they are capable law enforcement officers, willing to take great risks if necessary to

do their job. The names of nearly three hundred women are included on the National Law Enforcement Memorial in Washington, D.C.

4-3b Minority Report: Race and Ethnicity in Law Enforcement

Like women, members of minority groups have been slowly increasing their presence in local police departments since the late 1980s. The latest available data show that African American officers comprise about 12 percent of the nation's police officers; Hispanic officers, about 10 percent; and other minority groups such as Asians, American Indians, and Pacific Islanders, about 3 percent.[44] By some measures, members of minority groups are better represented than women in policing. Cities such as Detroit and Washington have local police departments that closely match their civilian populations in terms of diversity, and in recent years, a majority of police recruits in New York City have been members of minority groups. On other measures, such as promotion, minorities in law enforcement continue to seek parity.[45]

DOUBLE MARGINALITY According to Peter C. Moskos, a professor at the John Jay College of Criminal Justice in New York, "Black and white police officers remain two distinct shades of blue, with distinct attitudes toward each other and the communities they serve."[46] While that may be true, minority officers generally report that they have good relationships with their white fellow officers.[47] Often, though, members of minority groups in law enforcement—particularly African Americans and Hispanics—do face the problem of **double marginality.** This term refers

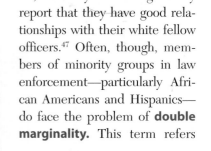

Do you believe that female police officers can be just as effective as men in protecting citizens from criminal behavior? Why or why not?

John Roman Images/ShutterStock.com

Sexual Harassment A repeated pattern of unwelcome sexual advances and/or obscene remarks in the workplace. Under certain circumstances, sexual harassment is illegal and can be the basis for a civil lawsuit.

Double Marginality The double suspicion that minority law enforcement officers face from their white colleagues and from members of the minority community to which they belong.

to a situation in which minority officers are viewed with suspicion by both sides:

1. **White police officers believe that minority officers will give members of their own race or ethnicity better treatment on the streets.**

2. **Those same minority officers face hostility from members of their own community who are under the impression that black and Hispanic officers are traitors to their race or ethnicity.**

In response, minority officers may feel the need to act more harshly toward minority offenders to prove that they are not biased in favor of their own racial or ethnic group.[48]

THE BENEFITS OF A DIVERSE POLICE FORCE In 1986, Supreme Court justice John Paul Stevens spoke for many in the criminal justice system when he observed that "an integrated police force could develop a better relationship [with a racially diverse citizenry] and therefore do a more effective job of maintaining law and order than a force composed of white officers."[49] Indeed, despite the effects of double marginality, African American officers may have more credibility in a

predominantly black neighborhood than white police officers, leading to better community-police relations and a greater ability to solve and prevent crimes.

Certainly, in the Mexican American communities typical of border states such as Arizona, Texas, and California, many Hispanic officers are able to gather information that would be very difficult for non-Spanish-speaking officers to collect. Finally, the best argument for a diverse police force is that members of minority groups represent a broad source of talent in this country, and such talent can only enhance the overall effectiveness of American law enforcement. The lack of such diversity in a number of jurisdictions, underscored by the information in Figure 4.2, continues to be a problem for the criminal justice system.

4-4 WHAT ARE THE DIFFERENT KINDS OF LAW ENFORCEMENT AGENCIES?

On September 12, 2014, Eric Frein allegedly killed Corporal Bryon Dickson and wounded Trooper Alex Douglass with a high-powered rifle outside a state police

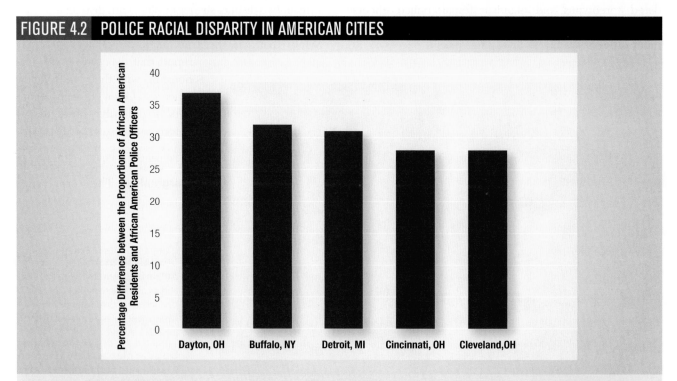

FIGURE 4.2 POLICE RACIAL DISPARITY IN AMERICAN CITIES

This graph shows the five cities in the United States with the largest negative gaps between the percentage of African American residents and the percentage of African Americans working as officers with the local police department.

Source: U.S. Census Bureau and *USA Today*.

barracks in northeastern Pennsylvania. Over the next forty-eight days, hundreds of law enforcement agents took part in the manhunt for Frein, including officers from the Federal Bureau of Investigation; the U.S. Marshals Service; the New Jersey, New York, and Pennsylvania state police; and sheriffs' departments in Monroe County (Penn.) and Schuyler County (N.Y.). Frein was finally captured by three deputy U.S. marshals at an abandoned airstrip near Tannersville, Pennsylvania.

As the effort to capture Frein shows, Americans are served by a multitude of police organizations. Overall, there are about 18,000 law enforcement agencies in the United States, employing about 880,000 officers.[50] For the most part, these agencies operate on three different levels: local, state, and federal. Each level has its own set of responsibilities, which we shall discuss starting with local police departments.

4-4a Municipal Law Enforcement Agencies

According to federal statistics, there is one local or state police officer for every 400 residents of the United States.[51] About two-thirds of all *sworn officers*, or those officers with arrest powers, work in small- and medium-sized police departments serving cities with populations from 10,000 to one million.[52] While the New York City Police Department employs about 35,000 police personnel, 50 percent of all local police departments have 10 or fewer law enforcement officers.[53]

Of the three levels of law enforcement, municipal agencies have the broadest authority to apprehend criminal suspects, maintain order, and provide services to the community. Whether the local officer is part of a large force or the only law enforcement officer in the community, he or she is usually responsible for a wide spectrum of duties, from responding to noise complaints to investigating homicides.

Larger police departments will often assign officers to specialized task forces or units that deal with a particular crime or area of concern. For example, in Washington, D.C., the police department features a Gay and Lesbian Liaison Unit that deals with anti-homosexual crimes in the city. The Knoxville (Tennessee) Police

Department has a squad devoted to combating Internet crimes against children, while the three hundred officers assigned to the New York Police Department's Emergency Services Unit are trained in suicide rescue, hostage negotiation, and SCUBA operations.

4-4b Sheriffs and County Law Enforcement

The **sheriff** is a very important figure in American law enforcement. Almost every one of the more than three thousand counties in the United States (except those in Alaska) has a sheriff. In every state except Rhode Island and Hawaii, sheriffs are elected by members of the community for two- or four-year terms and are paid a salary set by the state legislature or county board.

As elected officials who do not necessarily need a background in law enforcement, modern sheriffs often must respond to pressures that have little to do with criminal justice. Simply stated, the sheriff is also a politician. When a new sheriff is elected, she or he will sometimes repay political debts by appointing new deputies or promoting those who have given her or him support.

Sheriff The primary law enforcement officer in a county, usually elected by popular vote.

AP Images/*The Register-Guard*, Brian Davies

Lane County (Oregon) sheriff's deputies take part in an "active shooter" training exercise to protect local grade school students. *Why do sheriffs' departments and municipal police agencies often find themselves policing the same geographical areas?*

SIZE AND RESPONSIBILITY OF SHERIFFS' DEPARTMENTS Like municipal police forces, sheriffs' departments vary in size. The largest is the Los Angeles County Sheriff's Department, with more than 9,000 deputies. Of the 3,063 sheriffs' departments in the country, thirteen employ more than 1,000 officers, while forty-five have only one.[54]

Keep in mind that cities, which are served by municipal police departments, often exist within counties, which are served by sheriffs' departments. Therefore, police officers and sheriffs' deputies often find themselves policing the same geographical areas. Police departments, however, are generally governed by a local political entity such as a mayor's office, while most sheriffs' departments are assigned their duties by state law. About 80 percent of all sheriffs' departments are responsible for investigating violent crimes in their jurisdictions. Other common responsibilities of a sheriff's department include:

▶ Investigating drug crimes.

▶ Maintaining the county jail.

▶ Carrying out civil and criminal processes within county lines, such as serving eviction notices and court summonses.

▶ Keeping order in the county courthouse.

▶ Enforcing orders of the court, such as overseeing the isolation of a jury during a trial.[55]

It is easy to confuse sheriffs' departments and local police departments. Both law enforcement agencies are responsible for many of the same tasks, including crime investigation and routine patrol. There are differences, however. Sheriffs' departments are more likely to be involved in county court and jail operations and to perform certain services such as search and rescue. Local police departments, for their part, are more likely to perform traffic-related functions than are sheriffs' departments.[56]

THE COUNTY CORONER Another elected official on the county level is the **coroner,** or medical examiner. Duties vary from county to county, but the coroner has a general mandate to investigate "all sudden, unexplained, unnatural, or suspicious deaths" reported to the office. The coroner is ultimately responsible for determining the cause of death in these cases. Coroners also perform autopsies and assist other law enforcement agencies in

homicide investigations. For example, after actor Philip Seymour Hoffman died in February 2014 of an apparent heroin overdose, the New York City medical examiner needed to determine the exact cause of death. After a two-month investigation, the medical examiner confirmed that Hoffman had died because of a toxic mix of heroin and other drugs, including cocaine and amphetamines.

4-4c State Police and Highway Patrols

The most visible state law enforcement agency is the state police or highway patrol agency. Historically, state police agencies were created for three reasons:

1. **To assist local police agencies, which often did not have adequate resources or training to handle their law enforcement tasks.**

2. **To investigate criminal activities that crossed jurisdictional boundaries (such as when bank robbers committed a crime in one county and then fled to another part of the state).**

3. **To provide law enforcement in rural and other areas that did not have local or county police agencies.**

Today, there are twenty-three state police agencies and twenty-six highway patrols in the United States. State police agencies have statewide jurisdiction and are authorized to perform a wide variety of law enforcement tasks. Thus, they provide the same services as city or county police departments and are restricted only by the boundaries of their respective states. In contrast, highway patrols have limited authority. Their duties are generally defined either by their jurisdiction or by the specific types of offenses they have the authority to control. As their name suggests, most highway patrols concentrate primarily on regulating traffic. Specifically, they enforce traffic laws and investigate traffic accidents. Furthermore, they usually limit their activity to patrolling state and federal highways.

Trying to determine what state agency has which duties can be confusing. The Washington State Highway Patrol, despite its name, also has state police powers. In addition, thirty-five states have investigative agencies that are independent of the state police or highway patrol. Such agencies are usually found in states with highway patrols, and they have the primary responsibility of investigating criminal activities. For example, in addition to its highway patrol, Oklahoma runs a State Bureau of Investigation and a State Bureau of Narcotics and Dangerous Drugs. Each state has its own methods of determining the jurisdictions of these various organizations.

Coroner The medical examiner of a county, usually elected by popular vote.

4-4d Federal Law Enforcement Agencies

Statistically, employees of federal agencies do not make up a large part of the nation's law enforcement force. In fact, the New York City Police Department has about one-fifth as many employees as all of the federal law enforcement agencies combined. Nevertheless, the influence of these federal agencies is substantial.

Unlike local police departments, which must deal with all forms of crime, federal agencies have been authorized, usually by Congress, to enforce specific laws or attend to specific situations. The U.S. Coast Guard, for example, patrols the nation's waterways, while U.S. Postal inspectors investigate and prosecute crimes perpetrated through the use of the U.S. mails. In this section, you will learn the elements and duties of the most important federal law enforcement agencies, which are grouped according to the federal department or bureau to which they report. (See Figure 4.3 for the current federal law enforcement "lineup.")

THE DEPARTMENT OF HOMELAND SECURITY

LO4-4 Comprising twenty-two federal agencies, the Department of Homeland Security (DHS) coordinates national efforts to protect the United States against international and domestic terrorism. While most of the agencies under DHS control are not specifically linked with the criminal justice system, the department does oversee three agencies that play an important role in counterterrorism and fighting crime: U.S. Customs and Border Protection, U.S. Immigration and Customs Enforcement, and the U.S. Secret Service.

FIGURE 4.3 FEDERAL LAW ENFORCEMENT AGENCIES

Department of Homeland Security

DEPARTMENT NAME	APPROXIMATE NUMBER OF OFFICERS	MAIN RESPONSIBILITIES
U.S. Customs and Border Protection (CBP)	37,000	(1) Prevent the illegal flow of people and goods across America's international borders; (2) facilitate legal trade and travel
U.S. Immigration and Customs Enforcement (ICE)	12,400	Uphold public safety and homeland security by enforcing the nation's immigration and customs laws
U.S. Secret Service	4,500	(1) Protect the president, the president's family, former presidents and their families, and other high-ranking politicians; (2) combat currency counterfeiters

Department of Justice

DEPARTMENT NAME	APPROXIMATE NUMBER OF OFFICERS	MAIN RESPONSIBILITIES
Federal Bureau of Investigation (FBI)	13,600	(1) Protect national security by fighting international and domestic terrorism; (2) enforce federal criminal laws such as those dealing with cyber crime, public corruption, and civil rights violations
Drug Enforcement Administration (DEA)	4,700	Enforce the nation's laws regulating the sale and use of drugs
Bureau of Alcohol, Tobacco, Firearms and Explosives (ATF)	2,500	(1) Combat the illegal use and trafficking of firearms and explosives; (2) investigate the illegal diversion of alcohol and tobacco products
U.S. Marshals Service	4,000	(1) Provide security at federal courts; (2) protect government witnesses; (3) apprehend fugitives from the federal court or corrections system

Department of the Treasury

DEPARTMENT NAME	APPROXIMATE NUMBER OF OFFICERS	MAIN RESPONSIBILITIES
Internal Revenue Service (IRS)	2,500	Investigate potential criminal violations of the nation's tax code

A number of federal agencies employ law enforcement officers who are authorized to carry firearms and make arrests. The most prominent ones are under the control of the U.S. Department of Homeland Security, the U.S. Department of Justice, and the U.S. Department of the Treasury.

U.S. Customs and Border Protection (CBP) The federal government spends about $18 billion annually to enforce immigration law.[57] A large chunk of these funds go to **U.S. Customs and Border Protection (CBP)**, which polices the flow of goods and people across the United States' international borders. In general terms, this means that the agency has two primary goals:

1. To keep undocumented immigrants, illegal drugs, and drug traffickers from crossing our borders.
2. To facilitate the smooth flow of legal trade and travel.

Consequently, CBP officers are stationed at every port of entry to and exit from the United States. The officers have widespread authority to investigate and search all international passengers, whether they arrive on airplanes, ships, or other forms of transportation.

The U.S. Border Patrol, a branch of the CBP, has the burden of policing the Mexican and Canadian borders between official ports of entry. Every year, hundreds of thousands of non–U.S. citizens attempt to enter the country illegally by crossing these large, underpopulated regions, particularly in the southern part of the country. In 2013, Border Patrol agents apprehended about 490,000 illegal border crossers, down from a high of nearly 1.7 million in 2000.[58]

To a large degree, this decrease reflects the recent economic downturn, which has removed some of the monetary incentives for foreign nationals looking for work in the United States. In addition, CBP has "shrunk" the border, focusing the efforts of many of the nation's 20,000 Border Patrol agents on areas where illegal crossings are most likely to occur. Agents working those areas are supported by helicopters, surveillance towers, reconnaissance planes with infrared radar, and highly sensitive cameras. Eventually, CBP hopes to cover 45 percent of the border with these "dense" arrays of agents and technology, while monitoring the remaining, lightly trafficked 55 percent of the U.S.-Mexican border primarily with surveillance drones.[59]

U.S. Customs and Border Protection (CBP) The federal agency responsible for protecting U.S. borders and facilitating legal trade and travel across those borders.

U.S. Immigration and Customs Enforcement (ICE) The federal agency that enforces the nation's immigration and customs laws.

U.S. Secret Service A federal law enforcement organization with the primary responsibility of protecting the president, the president's family, the vice president, and other important political figures.

U.S. Immigration and Customs Enforcement (ICE) The CBP shares responsibility for locating and apprehending those persons illegally in the United States with special agents from **U.S. Immigration and Customs Enforcement (ICE).** While the CBP focuses almost exclusively on the nation's borders, ICE has a broader mandate to investigate and to enforce our country's immigration and customs laws. Simply stated, the CBP covers the borders, and ICE covers everything else. The latter agency's duties include detaining undocumented aliens and deporting (removing) them from the United States, ensuring that those without permission do not work or gain other benefits in this country, and disrupting human trafficking operations.

The U.S. Secret Service When it was created in 1865, the **U.S. Secret Service** was primarily responsible for combating currency counterfeiters. In 1901, the agency was given the added responsibility of protecting the president of the United States, the president's family, the vice president, the president-elect, and former presidents. These duties have remained the cornerstone of the agency, with several expansions. After a number of threats against presidential candidates in the 1960s and early 1970s, including the shootings of Robert Kennedy of New York and Governor George Wallace of Alabama, in 1976 Secret Service agents became responsible for protecting those political figures as well.

In addition to its special plainclothes agents, the agency also directs two uniformed groups of law enforcement officers. The Secret Service Uniformed Division protects the grounds of the White House and its inhabitants, and the Treasury Police Force polices the Treasury Building in Washington, D.C. To aid its battle against counterfeiters and forgers of government bonds, the agency has the use of a laboratory at the Bureau of Engraving and Printing in the nation's capital.

Additional DHS Agencies Besides the three already discussed—CBP, ICE, and the U.S. Secret Service—three other DHS agencies play a central role in preventing and responding to crime and terrorist-related activity:

▶ The *U.S. Coast Guard* defends the nation's coasts, ports, and inland waterways. It also combats illegal drug shipping and enforces immigration law at sea.

▶ The *Transportation Security Administration* is responsible for the safe operation of our airline, rail, bus, and ferry services. It also operates the Federal Air Marshals program, which places undercover federal agents on commercial flights.

▶ The *Federal Emergency Management Agency* holds a position as the lead federal agency in preparing for and responding to disasters such as hurricanes, floods, terrorist attacks, and *infrastructure* concerns. Our national **infrastructure** includes all of the facilities and systems that provide the daily necessities of modern life, such as electric power, food, water, transportation, and telecommunications.

THE DEPARTMENT OF JUSTICE The U.S. Department of Justice, created in 1870, is still the primary federal law enforcement agency in the country. With the responsibility of enforcing criminal law and supervising the federal prisons, the Justice Department plays a leading role in the American criminal justice system. To carry out its responsibilities to prevent and control crime, the department has a number of law enforcement agencies, including the Federal Bureau of Investigation, the federal Drug Enforcement Administration, the Bureau of Alcohol, Tobacco, Firearms and Explosives, and the U.S. Marshals Service.

The Federal Bureau of Investigation (FBI) Initially created in 1908 as the Bureau of Investigation, this agency was renamed the **Federal Bureau of Investigation (FBI)** in 1935. One of the primary investigative agencies of the federal government, the FBI has jurisdiction over

Infrastructure The services and facilities that support the day-to-day needs of modern life, such as electricity, food, transportation, and water.

Federal Bureau of Investigation (FBI) The branch of the Department of Justice responsible for combating terrorism and investigating violations of federal law.

FEDERAL BUREAU OF INVESTIGATION (FBI) AGENT

CareerPrep

Job Description:

▶ Primary role is to oversee intelligence and investigate federal crimes. Agents might track the movement of stolen goods across state lines, examine accounting and business records, listen to legal wiretaps, and conduct undercover investigations.

▶ Special agent careers are divided into five paths: intelligence, counterintelligence, counterterrorism, criminal, and cyber crime.

What Kind of Training Is Required?

▶ A bachelor's and master's degree, plus three years of work experience, along with a written and oral examination, medical and physical examinations, a psychological assessment, and an exhaustive background investigation.

▶ Critical skills required in one or more of the following areas: accounting, finance, computer science/information technology, engineering, foreign language(s), law, law enforcement, intelligence, military, and/or physical sciences.

Annual Salary Range?

▶ $61,000–$70,000

Courtesy Federal Bureau of Investigation/Department of Justice

SOCIAL MEDIA CAREER TIP

Don't forget about your phone! Every week, call at least three people from your social media networks and talk with them about your career interests. This kind of personal contact can be far more useful than an exchange of posts.

nearly two hundred federal crimes, including white-collar crimes, espionage (spying), kidnapping, extortion, interstate transportation of stolen property, bank robbery, interstate gambling, and civil rights violations.

With its network of agents across the country and the globe, the FBI is also uniquely positioned to combat worldwide criminal activity such as terrorism and drug trafficking. In fact, since 2001, the agency has shifted its focus from traditional crime to national security. Between that year and 2009, the FBI doubled its roster of counterterrorism agents, while reducing its number of criminal investigations. In 2014, the agency even officially changed its primary function from "law enforcement" to "national security."[60]

The FBI is also committed to providing valuable support for local and state law enforcement agencies. Its Identification Division maintains a large database of fingerprint information and offers assistance in finding missing persons and identifying the victims of fires, airplane crashes, and other disfiguring disasters. The services of the FBI Laboratory, the largest crime laboratory in the world, are available at no cost to other agencies. Finally, the FBI's National Crime Information Center (NCIC) provides lists of stolen vehicles and firearms, missing license plates, vehicles used to commit crimes, and other information to local and state law enforcement officers.

The Drug Enforcement Administration (DEA) The mission of the **Drug Enforcement Administration (DEA)** is to enforce domestic drug laws and regulations and to assist other federal and foreign agencies in combating illegal drug manufacture and trade on an international level. The agency also enforces the provisions of the Controlled Substances Act, which governs the manufacture, distribution, and dispensing of legal drugs, such as prescription drugs.

The DEA operates a network of six regional laboratories used to test and categorize seized drugs. Local law enforcement agencies have access to the DEA labs and often use them to ensure that information about particular drugs that will be presented in court is accurate and up to date. The agency also conducts extensive operations with law enforcement entities in other drug-producing countries.

Drug Enforcement Administration (DEA) The federal agency responsible for enforcing the nation's laws and regulations regarding narcotics and other controlled substances.

The Bureau of Alcohol, Tobacco, Firearms and Explosives (ATF) As its name suggests, the Bureau of Alcohol, Tobacco, Firearms and Explosives (ATF) is primarily concerned with the illegal sale, possession, and use of firearms and the control of untaxed tobacco and liquor products. The Firearms Division of the agency has the responsibility of enforcing the Gun Control Act of 1968, which sets the circumstances under which firearms may be sold and used in this country. The bureau also regulates all gun trade between the United States and foreign nations and collects taxes on all firearm importers, manufacturers, and dealers. In keeping with these duties, the ATF is also responsible for policing the illegal use and possession of explosives. Furthermore, the ATF is charged with enforcing federal gambling laws.

Because it has jurisdiction over such a wide variety of crimes, especially those involving firearms and explosives, the ATF is a constant presence in federal criminal investigations. So, following Elliot Rodger's May 2014 shooting spree in Isla Vista, California (described in Chapter 2), ATF agents searched his parents' house to determine whether the guns Rodger used were legally obtained. In addition, the ATF is engaged in an ongoing and crucial operation to keep American firearms out of the hands of Mexican drug cartels. The ATF has also formed multijurisdictional antigang task forces with other federal and local law enforcement agencies to investigate gang-related crimes involving firearms.

The U.S. Marshals Service The oldest federal law enforcement agency is the U.S. Marshals Service. In 1789, President George Washington assigned thirteen U.S. Marshals to protect his attorney general. That same year, Congress created the office of the U.S. Marshals and Deputy Marshals. Originally, the U.S. Marshals acted as the main law enforcement officers in the western territories. Following the Civil War (1861–1865), when most of these territories had become states, these agents were assigned to work for the U.S. district courts, where federal crimes are tried. The relationship between the

Job Description:

▶ Provide security at federal courts, control property that has been ordered seized by federal courts, and protect government witnesses who put themselves in danger by testifying against the targets of federal criminal investigations.

▶ Transport federal prisoners to detention institutions and hunt and capture fugitives from federal law.

What Kind of Training Is Required?

▶ A bachelor's degree or three years of qualifying experience, which includes work in law enforcement, correctional supervision, and volunteer teaching or counseling.

▶ A rigorous seventeen-and-a-half-week basic training program at the U.S. Marshals Service Training Academy in Glynco, Georgia.

Annual Salary Range?

▶ $40,000–$50,000

iStockPhoto.com/Stephen Mulcahey

GETTING LINKEDIN

Employment as an FBI or DEA agent or a U.S. Marshal is reserved for applicants with significant law enforcement experience. On LinkedIn, the most common federal law enforcement position advertised is that of a Transportation Security Officer—a recent search found thirty such postings, from Bellingham, Washington, to Arlington, Virginia.

U.S. Marshals Service and the federal courts continues today and forms the basis for the officers' main duties, which include:

1. Providing security at federal courts for judges, jurors, and other courtroom participants.

2. Controlling property that has been ordered seized by federal courts.

3. Protecting government witnesses who put themselves in danger by testifying against the targets of federal criminal investigations. This protection is sometimes accomplished by relocating the witnesses and providing them with different identities.

4. Transporting federal prisoners to detention institutions.

5. Investigating violations of federal fugitive laws.[61]

THE DEPARTMENT OF THE TREASURY The Department of the Treasury, formed in 1789, is mainly responsible for all financial matters of the federal government. It pays all the federal government's bills, borrows funds, collects taxes, mints coins, and prints paper currency. The largest bureau of the Treasury Department, the Internal Revenue Service (IRS), is concerned with violations of tax laws and regulations. The bureau has three divisions, only one of which is involved in criminal investigations. The examination branch of the IRS audits the tax returns of corporations and individuals. The collection division attempts to collect taxes from corporations or citizens who have failed to pay the taxes they owe. Finally, the criminal investigation division investigates cases of tax evasion and tax fraud. Criminal investigation agents can make arrests.

The IRS has long played a role in policing criminal activities such as gambling and selling drugs for one simple reason: those who engage in such activities almost never report any illegally gained income on their tax returns. Therefore, the IRS is able to apprehend them for tax evasion. The most famous example took place in the early 1930s, when the IRS finally arrested famed crime boss Al Capone—responsible for numerous violent crimes—for not paying his taxes.

4-4e Private Security

LO4-5 Even with increasing numbers of local, state, and federal law enforcement officers, the police do not have the ability to prevent every crime. Recognizing this, many businesses and citizens have decided to hire private guards for their properties and homes. In fact, according to a 2013 study released by ASIS International, an organization for security professionals, demand for **private security** generates revenues of more than $300 billion a year.[62] More than 10,000

> **Private Security** Security services, such as guard and patrol services, provided by private corporations or individuals rather than police officers.

firms employing around 1.9 million people provide private security services in this country, compared with about 1.1 million public law enforcement employees.

PRIVATIZING LAW ENFORCEMENT As there are no federal regulations regarding private security, each state has its own rules for this form of employment. In several states, including California and Florida, prospective security guards must have at least forty hours of training. Ideally, a security guard—lacking the extensive training of a law enforcement agent—should only observe and report criminal activity unless use of force is needed to prevent a felony.[63]

As a rule, private security is not designed to replace law enforcement. It is intended to deter crime rather than stop it. A uniformed security guard patrolling a shopping mall parking lot or a bank lobby has one primary function—to convince a potential criminal to search out a shopping mall or bank that does not have private security. For the same reason, many citizens hire security personnel to drive marked cars through their neighborhoods, making them a less attractive target for burglaries, robberies, vandalism, and other crimes.

Mario Tama/Getty Images News/Getty Images

A private security guard patrols the Manhattan Mall in New York City. *Why is being visible such an important aspect of many private security jobs?*

SECONDARY POLICING Although many states have minimum training requirements for private security officers, such training lags far behind the requirements to be a public officer. Consequently, there is a high demand for *secondary policing,* an umbrella term that covers the work that off-duty cops do when "moonlighting" for private companies or government agencies.

Generally speaking, police officers operate under the same rules whether they are off duty or on duty. In addition, 83 percent of local police departments in the United States have written policies for secondary policing.[64] For example, among other restrictions, Seattle police officers cannot work (on duty or off duty) longer than eighteen consecutive hours in a twenty-four-hour period and must clear all private employment with a superior.[65] Off-duty police officers commonly provide traffic control and pedestrian safety at road construction sites, as well as crowd control at large-scale functions such as music festivals and sporting events. They are also often hired to protect private properties and businesses, just like their nonpublic counterparts.

CONTINUED HEALTH OF THE INDUSTRY Indicators point to continued growth for the private security industry. The *Hallcrest Report II,* a far-reaching overview of private security trends funded by the National Institute of Justice, identifies four factors driving this growth:

1. An increase in fear on the part of the public triggered by media coverage of crime.

2. The problem of crime in the workplace. According to the University of Florida's National Retail Security Survey, American retailers lose about $34 billion a year because of shoplifting and employee theft.

3. Budget cuts in states and municipalities that have forced reductions in the number of public police, thereby raising the demand for private ones.

4. A rising awareness of private security products (such as home burglar alarms) and services as cost-effective protective measures.[66]

Another reason for the industry's continued health is terrorism. Private security is responsible for protecting more than three-fourths of the nation's likely terrorist targets, such as power plants, financial centers, dams, malls, oil refineries, and transportation hubs.

STUDY TOOLS 4

READY TO STUDY? IN THE BOOK, YOU CAN:

☐ Rip out the Chapter Review Card, which includes key terms and chapter summaries.

ONLINE AT WWW.CENGAGEBRAIN.COM, YOU CAN:

☐ Learn about what it takes to become a Secret Service agent in a short video.

☐ Explore the Department of Justice's ATF home page and Twitter feed.

☐ Interact with figures from the text, and watch quick animation clips.

☐ Prepare for tests with quizzes.

☐ Review the key terms with Flash Cards.

Quiz

1. In the opinion of many civilians and law enforcement officers, the primary duty of the police is to _____ criminal law.

2. In reality, police officers spend a great deal of their time providing _____ such as directing traffic and providing emergency medical aid.

3. _____-led policing is an umbrella term referring to the law enforcement practice of relying on data concerning past crime patterns to predict future crimes.

4. During the _____ period, which can last as long as eighteen months, police recruits attend a police academy to learn the rules of police work.

5. Minority law enforcement officers often face the problem of _____ marginality, which means that they are viewed with suspicion by both white colleagues and members of their home communities.

6. Municipal police departments and _____ departments are both considered "local" organizations and have many of the same responsibilities.

7. On the state level, the authority of the _____ patrol is usually limited to enforcing traffic laws.

8. Nationally, agents from the _____ have the authority to investigate and make arrests regarding all federal crimes.

9. A federal law enforcement agency called the _____ regulates the sale and possession of guns in the United States.

10. Private security is designed to _____ crime rather than stop it.

Answers can be found in the Answers section in the back of the book.

YOUR
FEED-
BACK
YOUR
BOOK

Our research never ends. Continual feedback from you ensures that we keep up with your changing needs.

5

Problems and Solutions in Modern Policing

Jewel Samad/AFP/Getty

LEARNING OBJECTIVES

After studying this chapter, you will be able to . . .

5-1 Explain why police officers are allowed discretionary powers.

5-2 List the three primary purposes of police patrol.

5-3 Describe how forensic experts use DNA fingerprinting to solve crimes.

5-4 Determine when police officers are justified in using deadly force.

5-5 Explain what an ethical dilemma is and name four categories of ethical dilemmas that a police officer typically may face.

After you finish this chapter, go to **PAGES 112–113** for **STUDY TOOLS**

The Camera's Eye

The video starts with Albuquerque, New Mexico, police officer Matthew Fisher in his squad car, his rifle drawn. "Did you guys see him go into that . . . Is he up on that street?" Fisher asks his colleagues about John Okeefe, a convicted felon with narcotics and armed robbery charges dating back fifteen years. The video then shows Fisher jumping out of his car and running. "Show me your hands!" Fisher yells several times before several faint pops of gunfire are audible. Fisher responds by shooting his rifle a total of eight times before calling for an ambulance. "He [expletive] shot at us," Fisher says. "I think he shot at us."

The January 2015 recording of this incident, in which Okeefe was killed, came from a small video camera that Fisher was wearing on his lapel. Albuquerque is one of dozens of police departments—including those in large cities such as Houston, New York, and Los Angeles—that require its officers to wear such video cameras on their uniforms.

At a time of often tense community-police relations, these devices seem to promise much-needed transparency and accountability for American law enforcement. "When you put a camera on a police officer, they tend to behave a little better," says Rialto, California, police chief William Farrar. "And if a citizen knows the officer is wearing a camera, chances are the citizen will behave a little better."

As documents of "the truth," police videos can be somewhat ambiguous. For example, the footage described above does not actually show Okeefe fleeing or shooting at Officer Fisher. One day before that incident, however, prosecutors did decide to pursue murder charges against two other Albuquerque police officers whose killing of a homeless man was captured by a helmet camera. "Everyone here agrees that that the officer-worn video made the difference," said one observer of that decision. "Now, the public will get to see the evidence and judge for [themselves.]"

A Washington, D.C., police officer models one of her department's new body-worn cameras, designed to record officer interactions with the public. Should evidence of police shootings taken by officer-worn video cameras be made available to the public? Why or why not?

Win McNamee/Getty Images

5-1 HOW DO LAW ENFORCEMENT AGENTS USE DISCRETION?

Certainly, the Albuquerque police officers just discussed would have preferred not to have shot and killed the suspects in the videotaped incidents, regardless of the consequences. Their decisions were made in a split second, under stressful circumstances, and without the benefit of hindsight. That is, the officers relied on their discretion, a concept you were introduced to in Chapter 1. Not all police discretion involves situations as serious as the ones that led to the deaths in Albuquerque, but it is a crucial aspect of all areas of law enforcement.

5-1a Justification for Police Discretion

LO5-1 Despite the possibility of mistakes, courts generally have upheld the patrol officer's freedom to decide "what law to enforce, how much to enforce it, against whom, and on what occasions."[1] This judicial support of police discretion is based on the following factors:

▶ Police officers are considered trustworthy and are therefore assumed to make honest decisions, regardless of contradictory testimony by a suspect.

▶ Experience and training give officers the ability to determine whether certain activity poses a threat to society, and to take any reasonable action necessary to investigate or prevent such activity.

▶ Due to the nature of their jobs, police officers are extremely knowledgeable in human, and, by extension, criminal, behavior.

▶ Police officers may find themselves in danger of personal, physical harm and must be allowed to take reasonable and necessary steps to protect themselves.[2]

Dr. Anthony J. Pinizzotto, a psychologist with the Federal Bureau of Investigation (FBI), and Charles E. Miller, an instructor in the bureau's Criminal Justice Information Services Division, take the justification for discretion one step further. These two experts argue that many police officers have a "sixth sense" that helps them handle on-the-job challenges. Pinizzotto and Miller believe that although "intuitive policing" is often difficult to explain to those outside law enforcement, it is a crucial part of policing and should not be discouraged by civilian administrators.[3]

5-1b Factors of Police Discretion

There is no doubt that subjective factors influence police discretion. The officer's beliefs, values, personality, and background all enter into his or her decisions. To a large extent, however, a law enforcement agent's actions are determined by the rules of policing set down in the U.S. Constitution and enforced by the courts. These rules are of paramount importance and will be discussed in great detail in Chapter 6.

ELEMENTS OF DISCRETION Assuming that most police officers stay on the right side of the Constitution in most instances, four other factors generally enter the discretion equation in any particular situation. First, and most important, is the nature of the criminal act. The less serious a crime, the more likely a police officer is to ignore it. A person driving 60 miles per hour in a 55-miles-per-hour zone, for example, is much less likely to be ticketed than someone doing 80 miles per hour.

A second element often considered is the attitude of the wrongdoer toward the officer. A motorist who is belligerent toward a highway patrol officer is much more likely to be ticketed than one who is contrite and apologetic. Third, the relationship between the victim and the offender can influence the outcome. If the parties are in a familial or other close relationship, police officers may see the incident as a personal matter and be hesitant to make an arrest.

LIMITING POLICE DISCRETION The fourth factor of the discretion equation is departmental policy. A **policy** is a set of guiding principles that law enforcement agents must adhere to in stated situations. For example, nearly every local police department in the United States has a policy limiting its officers' discretion to engage in high-speed automobile chases of suspects, which can place other drivers and pedestrians in grave danger.[4] The success of such policies can be seen in the results from Los Angeles, which features more high-speed chases than any other city in the country by a wide margin. In 2003, Los Angeles police officers were ordered to conduct dangerous pursuits only if the fleeing driver was suspected of a serious crime. Within a year, the number of high-speed pursuits decreased by 62 percent, and injuries to third parties dropped by 58 percent.[5]

DISCRETION AND BODY-WORN CAMERAS Policies regarding the use of body-worn police cameras vary, as law enforcement experts have not yet reached a consensus on how best to implement this new technology. Many departments have no body-worn camera policy whatsoever, allowing the devices to be employed at the discretion of the officer. This lack of standards can be problematic, as it leaves the police open to charges of selectively recording only those incidents free of any officer wrongdoing.

SV/Lumagraphica/ShutterStock.com

Why might police officers dislike policies restricting their discretion to engage in high-speed chases? Why might officers welcome such policies?

Policy A set of guiding principles designed to influence the behavior and decision making of police officers.

One civil liberties expert believes that officers should be required to turn the cameras on during all traffic stops and arrests, as these often are the situations in which force is used.[6] The Albuquerque Police Department goes even further. Its policy orders officers to record almost all interactions with the public. In December 2014, Albuquerque officials dismissed an officer for insubordination because he consistently failed to turn on his lapel recording device as required. Eight months earlier, the officer's camera had been off when he fatally shot a nineteen-year-old woman suspected of stealing a truck.[7]

5-2 HOW DO POLICE OFFICERS FIGHT CRIME?

Albuquerque police administrators placed Officer Matthew Fisher, whose fatal shooting of suspect John Okeefe was discussed in the opening of this chapter, on *administrative leave* pending an investigation into the incident. In other words, Fisher was temporarily relieved of his duties, with pay. This step does not imply that Fisher was suspected of any wrongdoing. Most law enforcement agencies react similarly when a firearm is fired in the line of duty, both to allow for a full investigation of the event and to give the officer a chance to recover from what can be a traumatic experience.

Administrative leave is a *bureaucratic* response to an officer-involved shooting. In a **bureaucracy,** formal rules govern an individual's actions and relationships with co-employees. The ultimate goal of any bureaucracy is to reach its maximum efficiency—in the case of a police department, to provide the best service for the community within the confines of its limited resources, such as staff and budget. Although some police departments are experimenting with alternative structures based on a partnership between management and the officers in the field, most continue to rely on the hierarchical structure described next.

5-2a The Structure of the Police Department

Each police department is organized according to its environment: the size of its jurisdiction, the type of crimes it must deal with, and the demographics of the population it must police. The Metropolitan Police Department of Washington, D.C., operates an Asian Liaison Unit that works within that city's Asian community, while the Evansville, Indiana, Police Department has set up a "No Meth" task force. Geographic location also influences police organization. The San Diego Police Department has a Harbor Patrol Unit, which would be unproductive in Grand Forks, North Dakota—as would the Grand Forks Police Department's snowmobile patrol in Southern California.

CHAIN OF COMMAND Whatever the size or location of a police department, it needs a clear rank structure and strict accountability to function properly. One of the goals of police reformers, particularly in the 1950s, was to lessen the corrupting influence of politicians. The result was a move toward a militaristic organization of police.[8] As you can see in Figure 5.1, a typical police department is based on a "top-down" chain of command that leads from the police chief down to detectives and patrol officers. In this formalized structure, all persons are constantly aware of their place in the chain and of their duties and responsibilities within the organization.

Delegation of authority is a critical component of the chain of command, especially in larger departments. The chief of police delegates authority to division chiefs, who delegate authority to commanders, and on down through

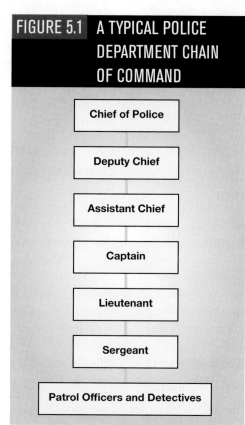

FIGURE 5.1 A TYPICAL POLICE DEPARTMENT CHAIN OF COMMAND

- Chief of Police
- Deputy Chief
- Assistant Chief
- Captain
- Lieutenant
- Sergeant
- Patrol Officers and Detectives

Most American police departments follow this model of the chain of command, though smaller departments with fewer employees often eliminate several of these categories.

Bureaucracy A hierarchically structured administrative organization that carries out specific functions.

Delegation of Authority The principles of command on which most police departments are based, in which personnel take orders from and are responsible to those in positions of power directly above them.

the organization. This structure creates a situation in which nearly every member of a police department is directly accountable to a superior. As was the original goal of police reformers, these links encourage discipline and control and lessen the possibility that any individual police employee will have the unsupervised freedom to abuse her or his position.[9] Furthermore, experts suggest that no single supervisor should be responsible for too many employees. The ideal number of subordinates for a police sergeant, for example, is eight to ten patrol officers. This number is often referred to as the *span of control.* If the span of control rises above fifteen, then it is assumed that the superior officer will not be able to effectively manage his or her team.[10]

LAW ENFORCEMENT IN THE FIELD To a large extent, the main goal of any police department is the most efficient organization of its *field services.* Also known as "operations" or "line services," field services include patrol activities, investigations, and special operations. According to Henry M. Wrobleski and Karen M. Hess, most police departments are "generalists." Thus, police officers are assigned to general areas and perform all field service functions within the boundaries of their beats. Larger departments may be more specialized, with personnel assigned to specific types of crime, such as illegal drugs or white-collar crime, rather than geographic locations. Smaller departments, which make up the bulk of local law enforcement agencies, rely almost exclusively on general patrol.[11]

5-2b Police on Patrol: The Backbone of the Department

Every police department has a patrol unit, and patrol is usually the largest division in the department. More than two-thirds of the sworn officers, or those officers authorized to make arrests and use force, in local police departments in the United States have patrol duties.[12]

"Life on the street" is not easy. Patrol officers must be able to handle any number of difficult situations, and experience is often the best and, despite training programs, the only teacher. As one patrol officer commented:

> You never stop learning. You never get your street degree. The person who says . . . they've learned it all is the person that's going to wind up dead or in a very compromising position. They've closed their minds.[13]

It may take a patrol officer years to learn when a gang is "false flagging" (trying to trick rival gang members into the open) or what to look for in a suspect's eyes to sense

if he or she is concealing a weapon. This learning process is the backdrop to a number of different general functions that a patrol officer must perform on a daily basis.

LO5-2 **THE PURPOSE OF PATROL** In general, patrol officers do not spend most of their shifts chasing, catching, and handcuffing suspected criminals. The vast majority of patrol shifts are completed without a single arrest.[14] Officers spend a great deal of time meeting with other officers, completing paperwork, and patrolling with the goal of preventing crime in general rather than focusing on any specific crime or criminal activity.

As police accountability expert Samuel Walker has noted, the basic purposes of the police patrol have changed very little since 1829, when Sir Robert Peel founded the modern police department. These purposes include:

1. **The deterrence of crime by maintaining a visible police presence.**

2. **The maintenance of public order and a sense of security in the community.**

3. **The twenty-four-hour provision of services that are not crime related.[15]**

The first two goals—deterring crime and keeping order—are generally accepted as legitimate police functions. The third, however, has been more controversial.

COMMUNITY CONCERNS The extent to which non-crime incidents dominate patrol officers' time is evident in the Police Services Study, a survey of 26,000 calls to police in sixty different neighborhoods. The study found that only one out of every five calls involved the report of criminal activity.[16]

There is some debate over whether community services should be allowed to dominate patrol officers' duties. The question, however, remains: If the police do not handle these problems, who will? Few cities have the financial resources to hire public servants to deal specifically with, for example, finding shelter for homeless persons. Furthermore, the police are on call twenty-four hours a day, seven days a week, making them uniquely accessible to citizen needs.

LAW ENFORCEMENT AND MENTAL ILLNESS Of particular concern is the frequency with which police officers on patrol find themselves acting as psychiatric social workers. According to various studies, between

7 percent and 10 percent of all police-public contacts involve people with mental illness.[17] If law enforcement officers are not properly trained or otherwise prepared for these encounters, the results can be disastrous. By one estimate, at least half of the people justifiably killed by the police each year are mentally ill.[18]

A number of law enforcement agencies have set up *crisis intervention teams* designed to improve this situation. Although the programs vary, many of them include:

1. Specialized training for law enforcement officers in managing encounters with mentally ill members of the community.

2. Access to mental health professionals who are "on call" to respond to police requests for assistance.

3. Drop-off locations, such as hospitals or mobile crisis vehicles, that provide mental health services beyond the expertise of law enforcement agencies.[19]

Given that most patrol shifts end without an officer making a single arrest, what activities take up most of a patrol officer's time?

Leonard Zhukovsky/ShutterStock.com

On the positive side, it appears that the crisis intervention model is favorably viewed by police officers and can result in reduced arrest rates of the mentally ill.[20] At the same time, such programs may be beyond the limited financial and personnel resources of small law enforcement agencies in rural areas.

PATROL ACTIVITIES To recap, the purposes of police patrols are to prevent and deter crime and also to provide social services. How can the police best accomplish these goals? Of course, each department has its own methods and strategies, but William Gay, Theodore Schell, and Stephen Schack are able to divide routine patrol activity into four general categories:[21]

1. *Preventive patrol.* By maintaining a presence in a community, either in a car or on foot, patrol officers attempt to prevent crime from occurring. This strategy, which O. W. Wilson called "omnipresence," was a cornerstone of early policing philosophy and still takes up roughly 40 percent of patrol time.

2. *Calls for service.* Patrol officers spend nearly a quarter of their time responding to 911 calls for emergency service or other citizen problems and complaints.

3. *Administrative duties.* Paperwork takes up nearly 20 percent of patrol time. In Albuquerque, officers now spend 15 percent to 20 percent of their shifts saving and logging footage from their lapel cameras.[22]

4. *Officer-initiated activities.* Incidents in which the patrol officer initiates contact with citizens, such as stopping motorists and pedestrians and questioning them, account for 15 percent of patrol time.

The category estimates made by Gay, Schell, and Schack are not universally accepted. Professor of law enforcement Gary W. Cordner argues that administrative duties account for the largest percentage of patrol officers' time. According to Cordner, when officers are not consumed with paperwork and meetings, they are either answering calls for service (which takes up 67 percent of the officers' time on the street) or initiating activities themselves (the remaining 33 percent).[23]

5-2c Detective Investigations

Investigation is the second main function of police, along with patrol. Whereas patrol is primarily preventive, investigation is reactive. After a crime has been committed and the patrol officer has gathered the preliminary

Job Description:

▶ Protect the integrity of America's natural habitat by policing the millions of acres of public land in this country, including wildlife refuges, fish hatcheries, waterfowl management areas, and wetland districts.

▶ Investigate wildlife crimes, particularly the illegal hunting, poaching, and sale of federally protected resources such as endangered species, migratory birds, marine mammals, and species of international concern.

What Kind of Training Is Required?

▶ Completion of an eighteen-week basic Land Management Police Training Academy course, a two-week Refuge Officer Basic School course, and a ten-week Field Training and Evaluation Program.

▶ The U.S. Fish and Wildlife Service offers students summer jobs that provide the experience necessary for a career in this field, with either a federal or a state agency.

Annual Salary Range?

▶ $38,000–$62,000

John Hollingsworth & Karen/National Conservation Training Center Publications & Training Materials/U.S. Fish and Wildlife Service

---

SOCIAL MEDIA CAREER TIP
When people search for your name, they generally won't click past the first page. Regularly check to see where your online material appears and whether you want this material to be on the Internet.

---

information from the crime scene, the responsibility of finding "who dunnit" is delegated to the investigator, generally known as the **detective.**

The most common way for someone to become a detective is to be promoted from patrol officer. Detectives have not been the focus of nearly as much reform attention as their patrol counterparts, mainly because the scope of the detective's job is limited to law enforcement, with less emphasis given to social services or order maintenance.

Detective The primary police investigator of crimes.

5-2d Aggressive Investigation Strategies

Detective bureaus have the option of implementing aggressive strategies. For example, if detectives suspect that a person was involved in the robbery of a Mercedes-Benz parts warehouse, one of them might pose as a "fence"—or purchaser of stolen goods. In what is known as a "sting" operation, the suspect is deceived into thinking that the detective (fence) wants to buy stolen car parts. After the transaction takes place, the suspect can be arrested.

UNDERCOVER OPERATIONS Perhaps the most dangerous and controversial operation a law enforcement agent can undertake is to go *undercover,* or to assume a false identity in order to obtain information concerning illegal activities. Though each department has its own guidelines on when undercover operations are necessary, all that is generally required is the suspicion that illegal activity is taking place. Today, undercover officers are commonly used to infiltrate large-scale narcotics operations or those run by organized crime.

In some situations, a detective bureau may not want to take the risk of exposing an officer to undercover work or may believe that an outsider cannot infiltrate an organized crime network. When the police need access and information, they have the option of turning to a **confidential informant (CI).** A CI is a person who is involved in criminal activity and gives information about that activity and those who engage in it to the police. As many as 80 percent of all illegal drug cases in the United States involve confidential informants. "They can get us into places we can't go," says one police administrator. "Without them, narcotics cases would practically cease to function."[24]

PREVENTIVE POLICING AND DOMESTIC TERRORISM Aggressive investigative strategies also play a crucial role in the federal government's efforts to combat domestic terrorism. Because would-be terrorists often need help to procure the weaponry necessary for their schemes, they are natural targets for well-placed informants and undercover agents. According to the Center on Law and Security at New York University, about two-thirds of the federal government's major terrorism prosecutions have relied on evidence provided by informants.[25]

The recent arrest of Christopher Cornell provides an example of *preventive policing*, a popular counterterrorism strategy employed by the federal government. On January 14, 2015, FBI agents arrested Cornell in the parking lot of a Cincinnati gun shop where he had just purchased two semiautomatic rifles and six hundred rounds of ammunition. About a month earlier, Cornell had met with an FBI informant and discussed plans to attack "enemies" working in the U.S. Capitol Building.

With preventive policing, then, the goal is not to solve the crime after it has happened. Rather, the goal is to prevent the crime from happening in the first place. Inevitably, such tactics raise the issue of entrapment. As you learned in Chapter 3, entrapment is a possible defense for criminal behavior when a government agent plants the idea of committing a crime in the defendant's mind. In the Cornell case, the suspect's father claimed that his son could not have afforded to purchase the weaponry he was caught with, and that the funds to do so must have been provided by the FBI.[26] Although the

entrapment defense has been raised often in domestic terrorism cases involving informants and undercover agents, it has yet to succeed. The government has been uniformly successful in proving that these defendants were predisposed to commit the crime regardless of any outside influence.

5-2e Clearance Rates and Cold Cases

The ultimate goal of all law enforcement activity is to *clear* a crime, or secure the arrest and prosecution of the offender. Even a cursory glance at **clearance rates,** which show the percentage of reported crimes that have been cleared, reveals that investigations succeed only part of the time. In 2013, just 64 percent of homicides and 46 percent of total violent crimes were solved, while police cleared only 20 percent of property crimes.[27] For the most part, the different clearance rates for different crimes reflect the resources that a law enforcement agency expends on each type of crime. The police generally investigate a murder or a rape more vigorously than the theft of an automobile or a computer.

As a result of low clearance rates, police departments are saddled with an increasing number of **cold cases,** or criminal investigations that are not cleared after a certain amount of time. (The length of time before a case becomes "cold" varies from department to department. In general, a cold case must be "somewhat old" but not "so old that there can be no hope of ever solving it."[28]) Even using the various technologies we will explore in the next section, cold case investigations rarely succeed. A RAND study found that only about one in twenty cold cases results in an arrest, and only about one in a hundred results in a conviction.[29]

5-2f Forensic Investigations and DNA

Although the crime scene typically offers a wealth of evidence, patrol officers and detectives often need assistance in interpreting it. For that aid, law enforcement

---

Confidential Informant (CI) A human source for police who provides information concerning illegal activity in which he or she is involved.

Clearance Rate A comparison of the number of crimes cleared by arrest and prosecution with the number of crimes reported during any given time period.

Cold Case A criminal investigation that has not been solved after a certain amount of time.

officers rely on experts in **forensics,** or the use of science and technology to investigate crimes. Forensic experts apply their knowledge to items found at the crime scene to determine crucial facts such as:

▶ The cause of death or injury.

▶ The time of death or injury.

▶ The type of weapon or weapons used.

▶ The identity of the crime victim, if that information is unavailable.

▶ The identity of the offender (in the best-case scenario).[30]

To assist forensic experts, many police departments operate or are affiliated with crime laboratories. Indeed, there are approximately 400 publicly funded crime laboratories in the United States. As we noted in the previous chapter, the FBI also offers the services of its crime lab to agencies with limited resources. The FBI's aid is crucial, given that the nation's crime labs are burdened with a crippling backlog of hundreds of thousands of requests for forensic services.[31]

CRIME SCENE FORENSICS The first law enforcement agent to reach a crime scene has the important task of protecting any **trace evidence** from contamination. Trace evidence is generally very small—often invisible to the naked human eye—and often requires technological aid for detection. Hairs, fibers, blood, fingerprints, broken glass, and footprints are all examples of trace evidence. A study released by the National Institute of Justice confirmed that when police are able to link such evidence to a suspect, the likelihood of a conviction rises dramatically.[32]

Police will also search a crime scene for bullets and spent cartridge casings. These items can provide clues as to how far the shooter was from the target. They can also be compared with information stored in national firearms databases to determine, under some circumstances, the gun used and its most recent owner. The study of firearms and its application to solving crimes goes under the general name **ballistics.** A new generation of ballistics technology allows technicians to create a 3D image of a bullet and match that image to the gun from which the original was fired.

For more than a century, the most important piece of trace evidence has been the human fingerprint. Because no two fingerprints are alike, they are considered reliable sources of identification. Forensic scientists compare a fingerprint lifted from a crime scene with that of a suspect and declare a match if there are between eight and sixteen "points of similarity." This method of identification is not infallible, however. It is often difficult to lift a suitable print from a crime scene, and researchers have uncovered numerous cases in which innocent persons were convicted based on evidence obtained through faulty fingerprinting procedures.[33]

CAREER TIP A *bloodstain pattern analyst* can learn a great deal about a violent crime by examining where blood landed at the scene, the size and consistency of the drops, and the pattern of the blood spatter.

Why is it so important that forensic experts be able to collect trace evidence from crime scenes such as the one shown here?

Forensics The application of science to establish facts and evidence during the investigation of crimes.

Trace Evidence Evidence such as a fingerprint, blood, or hair found in small amounts at a crime scene.

Ballistics The study of firearms, including the firing of the weapon and the flight of the bullet.

Job Description:

▶ Examine, test, and analyze tissue samples, chemical substances, physical materials, and ballistics evidence collected at a crime scene.

▶ Testify as an expert witness on evidence or laboratory techniques in criminal trials.

What Kind of Training Is Required?

▶ A bachelor's degree in science, particularly chemistry, biology, biochemistry, or physics.

▶ Certification programs (usually two years' additional study) can help prospective applicants specialize as forensic consultants, fingerprint technicians, forensic investigators, and laboratory technicians.

Annual Salary Range?

▶ $52,000–$85,000

iStockPhoto.com/Nancy Catherine Walker

GETTING LINKEDIN

Although openings for forensic scientists at law enforcement agencies are scarce, LinkedIn consistently features postings for such positions at private laboratories. Such laboratories assist clients—such as doctors' offices, drug-testing facilities, and hospitals—that have a need for forensic laboratory services.

THE DNA REVOLUTION The technique of **DNA fingerprinting,** or using a suspect's DNA to match the suspect to a crime, emerged in the mid-1990s and has now all but replaced fingerprint evidence in many types of criminal investigations. The shift has been a boon to crime fighters: one law enforcement agent likened DNA fingerprinting to "the finger of God pointing down" at a guilty suspect.[34]

DNA, which is the same in each cell of a person's body, provides a "genetic blueprint" or "code" for every living organism. DNA fingerprinting is useful in criminal investigations because no two people, save for identical twins, have the same genetic code. Therefore, lab technicians can compare the DNA sample of a suspect to the evidence found at the crime scene. If the match is negative, it is certain that the two samples did not come from the same source. If the match is positive, the lab will determine the odds that the DNA sample could have come from someone other than the suspect. Those odds are so high—sometimes reaching 30 billion to one—that a match is practically conclusive.[35]

The DNA fingerprinting process begins when forensic technicians gather blood, semen, skin, saliva, or hair from

LO5-3 the scene of a crime. Blood cells and sperm are rich in DNA, making them particularly useful in murder and rape cases, but DNA has also been extracted from sweat on dirty laundry, skin cells on eyeglasses, and saliva on used envelope seals. Once a suspect is identified, her or his DNA can be used to determine whether she or he can be placed at the crime scene. In 2014, for example, investigators connected Dennis Wilson to a bank robbery in Ansonia, Connecticut, by obtaining his DNA from a cigarette left in the abandoned getaway car.

DNA IN ACTION The ability to "dust" for genetic information on such a wide variety of evidence, as well as that evidence's longevity and accuracy, greatly increases the

DNA Fingerprinting The identification of a person based on a sample of her or his DNA, the genetic material found in the cells of all living things.

chances that a crime will be solved. Indeed, police no longer need a witness or even a suspect in custody to solve crimes. What they do need is a piece of evidence and a database.

In 1974, for example, Eileen Ferro was stabbed to death in her Shrewsbury, Massachusetts, home. For four decades, local police were unable to establish any useful leads concerning Ferro's killer. In 2014, however, investigators asked a crime lab to reevaluate evidence from the crime scene for the presence of DNA. The traces they found matched a sample recently taken from parole violator Lonzo Guthrie in California. Due to the match, Guthrie—who had delivered furniture to Ferro's house the day before her death—was arrested for murder.

Databases and Cold Hits The identification of Lonzo Guthrie is an example of what police call a **cold hit,** which occurs when law enforcement finds a suspect "out of nowhere" by comparing DNA evidence from a crime scene against the contents of a database. The largest and most important database is the National Combined DNA Index System (CODIS). Operated by the FBI since 1998, CODIS gives local and state law enforcement agencies access to the DNA profiles of about 14.1 million people who have been connected to criminal activity. As of February 2015, the database had produced approximately 277,000 cold hits nationwide.[36]

DNA Collection Policies Privacy and civil rights advocates protest that DNA collection has gone too far. Specifically, authorities in many states now collect samples from those who have been convicted of nonviolent crimes and, in some instances, from those who have merely been arrested for crimes but not convicted. In 2013, the U.S. Supreme Court upheld the practice of taking DNA samples from arrestees, as practiced in twenty-eight states and by the federal government, reasoning that such procedures are necessary to identify suspects.[37] The ruling is having the practical effect of greatly increasing DNA profiles stored in CODIS and other law enforcement databases.

Cold Hit The establishment of a connection between a suspect and a crime, often through the use of DNA evidence, in the absence of an ongoing criminal investigation.

Incident-Driven Policing A reactive approach to policing that emphasizes a speedy response to calls for service.

Computer-Aided Dispatch (CAD) A method of dispatching police patrols units to the site of 911 emergencies with the assistance of a computer program.

5-2g Patrol Strategies

While law enforcement officers do not like to think of themselves as being at the "beck and call" of citizens, that is the operational basis of much police work. All police departments practice **incident-driven policing,** in which calls for service are the primary instigators of action. Between 40 and 60 percent of police activity is the result of 911 calls or other citizen requests, which means that police officers in the field initiate only about half of their contacts with the public.[38]

911 TECHNOLOGY Nearly all the police departments in the country use **computer-aided dispatch (CAD)** systems to manage their incidence response strategies. With CAD, a 911 dispatcher enters the information from a caller into his or her computer, which prioritizes the emergency based on its nature. CAD also verifies the caller's address and phone number, and determines the closest patrol unit to the site of the emergency. In many jurisdictions, the details, including any previous 911 calls from the location, are then sent to a *mobile digital terminal* in the police officer's patrol car.

A growing number of 911 calls come from mobile phones rather than landlines. In fact, four in ten American homes now use mobile devices only, a figure that is sure to increase in the near future.[39] This trend has forced police departments across the country to adopt Next Generation 911 (NG911) systems, which make it possible for officers to receive text messages, videos, photos, and location data about crime incidents. For example, using NG911, a store clerk who has just been robbed at gunpoint will be able to take a photo of the offender's getaway car and send that photo to police along with the emergency call for service.

CAREER TIP Although they are responsible for a crucial aspect of policing, *911 dispatchers* generally are not sworn police officers and do not need any law enforcement experience. Rather, they receive special training in dealing with emergency calls.

RANDOM AND DIRECTED PATROL Of course, officers to do not sit at the station waiting for incident calls. Earlier in this chapter, we noted that the majority of police officers are assigned to patrol duties. Most of

CJ and Technology

For reasons ranging from disinterest to fear, the general public fails to report about 80 percent of gunfire incidents to police. Now, thanks to ShotSpotter, a gunshot detection system, law enforcement has the means to overcome this civic shortcoming. Placed on a rooftop, a ShotSpotter sensor unit uses microphones, computer software, a clock, and satellite positioning technology to pinpoint the precise time and location of gunfire.

When a unit detects gunfire, it sends an image of the sound wave to the local police department, where a specialist confirms that a weapon has been fired. (The sound wave of a gun blast looks something like a Christmas tree.) Ideally, police officers are dispatched to the scene within forty seconds of the initial shot. Between 2006 and 2014, ShotSpotter detected about 39,000 shooting incidents in Washington, D.C., helping the police fight violent crime and providing valuable information about gun use in the city.

Val Lawless/ShutterStock.com

Thinking about Gunshot Detection Systems
As you will see in the next chapter, many cities have placed surveillance cameras in high-crime neighborhoods. How could ShotSpotter be linked with these cameras to provide further evidence of criminal activity?

---

these officers work **random patrol,** making the rounds of a specific area with the general goal of detecting and preventing crime. Every police department in the United States randomly patrols its jurisdiction using automobiles. In addition, 53 percent utilize foot patrols, 32 percent bicycle patrols, 16 percent motorcycle patrols, 4 percent boat patrols, and 1 percent horse patrols.[40]

In contrast to random patrols, **directed patrols** target specific areas of a city and often attempt to prevent a specific type of crime. Directed patrols have found favor among law enforcement experts as being a more efficient use of police resources than random patrols, as indicated by the Philadelphia Foot Patrol Experiment. During this experiment, extra foot patrols were utilized in sixty Philadelphia locations plagued by high levels of violent crime. During three months of directed patrols, arrests increased by 13 percent in the targeted areas, and violent crime decreased by 23 percent. In addition, an estimated fifty-three violent crimes were prevented over the three-month period.[41]

"HOT SPOTS" AND CRIME MAPPING The target areas for directed patrols are often called **hot spots** because they contain greater numbers of criminals and have higher-than-average levels of victimization. Needless to say, police administrators are no longer sticking pins in maps to determine where hot spots exist. Rather, police departments are using **crime mapping**

Random Patrol A patrol strategy that relies on police officers monitoring a certain area with the goal of detecting crimes in progress or preventing crime due to their presence. Also known as *general* or *preventive patrol.*

Directed Patrol A patrol strategy that is designed to focus on a specific type of criminal activity in a specific geographical location.

Hot Spots Concentrated areas of high criminal activity that draw a directed police response.

Crime Mapping Technology that allows crime analysts to identify trends and patterns of criminal behavior within a given area.

technology to locate and identify hot spots and "cool" them down. Crime mapping uses geographic information systems (GIS) to track criminal acts as they occur in time and space. Once sufficient information has been gathered, it is analyzed to predict future crime patterns.

Computerized crime mapping was popularized when the New York Police Department launched Comp-Stat in the mid-1990s. Still in use, CompStat starts with police officers reporting the exact location of crime and other crime-related information to department officials. These reports are then fed into a computer, which prepares grids of a particular city or neighborhood and highlights areas with a high incidence of serious offenses. (See Figure 5.2 for an example of a GIS crime map.)

In New York and many other cities, the police department holds "Crime Control Strategy Meetings" during which precinct commanders are held accountable for CompStat's data-based reports in their

districts. In theory, this system provides the police with accurate information about patterns of crime and gives them the ability to "flood" hot spots with officers at short notice. About two-thirds of large departments now employ some form of computerized crime mapping,[42] and Wesley Skogan, a criminologist at Northwestern University, believes that CompStat and similar technologies are the most likely cause of recent declines in big-city crime.[43]

5-2h Arrest Strategies

Like patrol strategies, arrest strategies can be broken into two categories that reflect the intent of police administrators. **Reactive arrests** are those arrests made by police officers, usually on general patrol, who observe a criminal act or respond to a call for service. **Proactive arrests** occur when the police take the initiative to target a particular type of criminal or behavior. Proactive arrests are often associated with directed patrols of hot spots, and thus are believed by many experts to have a greater influence on an area's crime rates.[44]

The popularity of proactive theories was solidified by a magazine article that James Q. Wilson and George L. Kelling wrote in 1982.[45] In their piece, entitled "Broken

Reactive Arrests Arrests that come about as part of the ordinary routine of police patrol and responses to calls for service.

Proactive Arrests Arrests that occur because of concerted efforts by law enforcement agencies to respond to a particular type of criminal or criminal behavior.

FIGURE 5.2 **A GIS CRIME MAP FOR A NEIGHBORHOOD IN NEW ORLEANS**

This crime map shows the incidence of various crimes during a two-week period in a neighborhood near downtown New Orleans.

Windows," Wilson and Kelling argued that police strategies were focused on violent crime to the detriment of the vital police role of promoting the quality of life in neighborhoods. As a result, many communities, particularly in large cities, had fallen into a state of disorder and disrepute, with two very important consequences.

First, these neighborhoods—with their broken windows, dilapidated buildings, and lawless behavior by residents—were sending out "signals" that criminal activity was tolerated. Second, this disorder was spreading fear among law-abiding citizens, dissuading them from leaving their homes or attempting to improve their surroundings. Thus, the **broken windows theory** is based on maintaining order in neighborhoods by cracking down on "quality-of-life" crimes such as panhandling, public drinking and urinating, loitering, and graffiti painting. Only by encouraging directed arrest strategies with regard to quality-of-life crime, the two professors argued, could American cities be rescued from rising crime rates.

A Boston police officer shows off her dance moves at a summit for inner-city youth in Roxbury, Massachusetts. *How can establishing friendly relations with citizens help law enforcement agencies reduce crime?*

5-2i Community Policing

In "Broken Windows," Wilson and Kelling insisted that, to reduce fear and crime in high-risk neighborhoods, police had to rely on the cooperation of citizens. Today, a majority of police departments rely on a broad strategy known as **community policing** to improve relations with citizens and fight crime at the same time.

Community policing can be defined as an approach that promotes community-police partnerships, proactive problem solving, and community engagement to address issues such as fear of crime and the causes of such fear in a particular area. Neighborhood watch programs, in which police officers and citizens work together to prevent local crime and disorder, are a popular version of a community policing initiative. Under community policing, patrol officers have the freedom to improvise. They are expected to develop personal relationships with residents and to encourage those residents to become involved in making the community a safer place.

To improve trust within their communities, a number of police departments have turned to *collaborative reform*. In this offshoot of community policing, law enforcement officials form partnerships with local leaders to address

difficult issues such as police use of force and arrest policies. Policing experts call this strategy "putting good will in the bank" for use at times of crisis.[46] In South Los Angeles, for example, officers are in constant contact with community organizers and church leaders. These efforts were partially credited for the public reaction in August 2014 when Los Angeles police officers fatally shot an unarmed African American. Although local residents expressed concern, the response was relatively calm in comparison to other cities that had experienced similar incidents that year.

5-2j Problem-Oriented Policing

Similar in spirit to communiy policing, **problem-oriented policing** is a strategy based on the premise that police departments devote too many of their resources

Broken Windows Theory Wilson and Kelling's theory that a neighborhood in disrepair signals that criminal activity is tolerated in the area. By cracking down on quality-of-life crimes, police can reclaim the neighborhood and encourage law-abiding citizens to live and work there.

Community Policing A policing philosophy that emphasizes community support for and cooperation with the police in preventing crime.

Problem-Oriented Policing A policing philosophy that requires police to identify potential criminal activity and develop strategies to prevent or respond to that activity.

to reacting to calls for service and too few to "acting on their own initiative to prevent or reduce community problems."[47] To rectify this situation, problem-oriented policing moves beyond simply responding to incidents and attempts instead to control or even solve the root causes of criminal behavior.

Problem-oriented policing encourages police officers to stop looking at their work as a day-to-day proposition. Rather, they should try to shift the patterns of criminal behavior in a positive direction. For example, instead of responding to a 911 call concerning illegal drug use by simply arresting the offender—a short-term response—the patrol officers should also look at the long-term implications of the situation. They should analyze the pattern of similar arrests in the area and interview the arrestee to determine the reasons, if any, that the site was selected for drug activity.[48] Then additional police action should be taken to prevent further drug sales at the identified location.

5-3 WHAT ARE THE CHALLENGES OF BEING A POLICE OFFICER?

On December 3, 2014, a grand jury cleared Daniel Pantaleo of the New York City Police Department in the chokehold death of Eric Garner, who was killed several months earlier while resisting arrest for selling contraband cigarettes. Seventeen days later, a vigilante assassinated New York City police officers Wenjian Liu and Rafael Ramos as they sat in their patrol car. Earlier, the killer had posted, "I'm Putting Wings on Pigs Today. They Take 1 of Ours . . . Let's Take 2 of Theirs," on social media.[49] Reacting to the officers' murders, a New York City police union official said that there was "blood on many hands."[50] Specifically, he was referring to New York mayor Bill de Blasio, who many law enforcement agents felt had gone too far in supporting anti-police protests following the grand jury's decision not to charge Pantaleo with a crime.

Police Subculture The values and perceptions that are shared by members of a police department and, to a certain extent, by all law enforcement agents.

Socialization The process through which a police officer is taught the values and expected behavior of the police subculture.

In the weeks to come, New York City police officers used their discretion to ignore low-level offenses in the city. As a result of this work slowdown, the number of summonses for minor crimes and traffic violations dropped more than 90 percent below normal.[51] Hundreds of these officers also turned their backs on Mayor de Blasio during Lui's and Ramos's funerals. These conflicts highlight many of the on-the-job issues that bind police officers together while at the same time potentially alienating them from the society that they are sworn to protect and serve.

5-3a Police Subculture

As a rule, police officers do not appreciate being second-guessed when it comes to their decisions on when to use force against a civilian. "A majority of people don't understand what officers face on a daily basis," said one retired detective. "There were a lot of situations where I almost got killed."[52] Feelings of frustration and mistrust toward civilians are hallmarks of **police subculture,** a broad term used to describe the basic assumptions and values that permeate law enforcement agencies and are taught to new members of these agencies as the proper way to think, perceive, and act.

Every organization has a subculture, with values shaped by the particular aspects and pressures of that organization. In the police subculture, those values are formed in an environment characterized by danger, stress, boredom, and violence.

From the first day on the job, rookies begin the process of **socialization,** in which they are taught the values and rules of police work. This process is aided by a number of rituals that are common to the law enforcement experience. Police theorist Harry J. Mullins believes that the following rituals are critical to the police officer's acceptance, and even embrace, of police subculture:

▶ Attending a police academy.

▶ Working with a senior officer, who passes on the "lessons" of police work and life to the younger officer.

▶ Making the initial felony arrest.

▶ Using force to make an arrest for the first time.

▶ Using or witnessing deadly force for the first time.

▶ Witnessing major traumatic incidents for the first time.[53]

Each of these rituals makes it clear to the police officer that this is not a "normal" job. The only other people who can understand the stresses of police work are fellow officers, and consequently law enforcement officers tend to insulate themselves from civilians. Eventually, the insulation breeds mistrust, and the police officer develops an "us versus them" outlook toward those outside the force. In turn, this outlook creates what sociologist William Westly called the **blue curtain,** also known as the "blue wall of silence" or simply "the code."[54] This curtain separates the police from the civilians they are meant to protect.

5-3b The Physical Dangers of Police Work

Police officers learn early in their careers that nothing about their job is "routine"—they face the threat of physical harm every day. According to the Officer Down Memorial Page, 121 law enforcement agents died in the line of duty in 2014.[55] In addition, about 50,000 assaults were committed against police officers in 2013, with 29 percent of these assaults resulting in an injury.[56] These numbers are hardly surprising. As police experts John S. Dempsey and Linda S. Forst point out, police "deal constantly with what may be the most dangerous species on this planet—the human being."[57]

Despite perceptions to the contrary, a high percentage of deaths and injuries suffered by police officers are not the result of assaults by criminal suspects. Generally speaking, half of all law enforcement officer injuries are due to accidents, and about two-thirds of those injuries occur when officers are doing something other than making an arrest.[58] In particular, traffic accidents cause as many line-of-duty deaths as do firearms.[59] One reason for the fatalities is that a number of law enforcement officers do not take simple precautions when behind the wheel. A recent study conducted by the National Highway Traffic Safety Administration found that 42 percent of police officers killed in vehicle crashes were not wearing seat belts.[60]

5-3c Stress and the Mental Dangers of Police Work

In addition to physical dangers, police work entails considerable mental pressure and stress. The conditions that cause stress—such as worries over finances or relationships—are known as **stressors.** Each profession has its own set of stressors, but police are particularly vulnerable to occupational pressures and stress factors such as the following:

Fellow officers escort the casket of New York City police officer Wenjian Lui, who was shot by an assailant while on patrol. *How might violence against police officers contribute to the "blue curtain" between law enforcement and the public?*

▶ The constant fear of being a victim of violent crime.

▶ Exposure to violent crime and its victims.

▶ The need to comply with the law in nearly every job action.

▶ Lack of community support.

▶ Negative media coverage.

Police officers may face a number of internal pressures as well, including limited opportunities for career advancement, excessive paperwork, and low wages and benefits.[61] Both male and female law enforcement agents experience these stressors, as well as others, such as lack of sleep and chaotic private lives. Some stressors are, however, unique to female police officers, for reasons we touched on in the last chapter. These challenges include sexism, sexual harassment, the constant demand to prove oneself, and lack of acceptance in the male-dominated police subculture.[62]

Blue Curtain A metaphorical term used to refer to the value placed on secrecy and the general mistrust of the outside world shared by many police officers.

Stressors The conditions that cause stress.

Police stress can manifest itself in different ways. A University at Buffalo study found that the stresses of law enforcement often lead to high blood pressure and heart problems.[63] Other research shows that 18 percent of male police officers and 16 percent of female police officers report "adverse consequences" from alcohol use.[64] If stress becomes overwhelming, an officer may suffer from **burnout,** becoming listless and ineffective as a result of mental and physical exhaustion. Another problem related to stress is *post-traumatic stress disorder (PTSD)*. Though some studies suggest that police officers have higher rates of suicide than the general population, it appears that most develop an extraordinary ability to handle the difficulties of the profession and persevere.[65]

5-3d Authority and the Use of Force

If the police subculture is shaped by the dangers of the job, it often finds expression through authority. The various symbols of authority that decorate a police officer—including the uniform, badge, nightstick, and firearm—establish the power she or he holds over civilians. For better or for worse, both police officers and civilians tend to equate terms such as *authority* and *respect* with the ability to use force.

USE OF FORCE IN LAW ENFORCEMENT In general, the use of physical force by law enforcement personnel is very rare, occurring in only about 1.4 percent of the 40 million annual police-public encounters that occur annually. Still, the Department of Justice estimates that law enforcement officers threaten to use force or use force in encounters with 770,000 civilians a year, and nearly 14 percent of those incidents result in an injury.[66] Federal authorities also report that about 690 deaths occur in the process of an arrest on an annual basis.[67] Of course, police officers are often justified in using force

to protect themselves and other citizens. As we noted previously, they are the targets of thousands of assaults each year. Law enforcement agents are also usually justified in using force to make an arrest, to prevent suspects from escaping, to restrain suspects or other individuals for their own safety, or to protect property.[68]

At the same time, few observers would be naïve enough to believe that the police are *always* justified in the use of force. A survey of emergency room physicians found that 98 percent believed that they had treated patients who were victims of excessive police force.[69] How, then, is "misuse" of force to be defined? To provide guidance for officers in this tricky area, nearly every law enforcement agency designs a *use of force matrix*. As the example in Figure 5.3 shows, such a matrix presents officers with the proper force options for different levels of contact with a civilian.

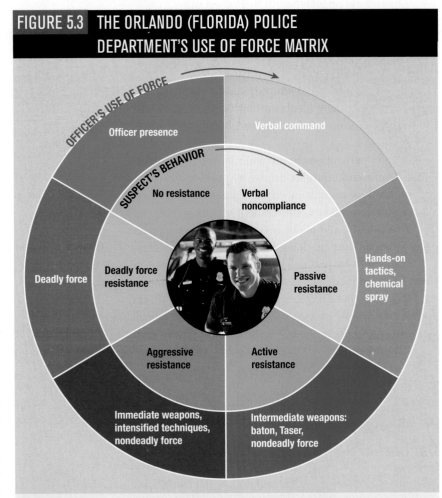

FIGURE 5.3 THE ORLANDO (FLORIDA) POLICE DEPARTMENT'S USE OF FORCE MATRIX

OFFICER'S USE OF FORCE

Officer presence

Verbal command

SUSPECT'S BEHAVIOR

No resistance

Verbal noncompliance

Deadly force

Deadly force resistance

Passive resistance

Hands-on tactics, chemical spray

Aggressive resistance

Active resistance

Immediate weapons, intensified techniques, nondeadly force

Intermediate weapons: baton, Taser, nondeadly force

Like most local law enforcement agencies, the Orlando Police Department has a policy to guide its officers' use of force. These policies instruct an officer on how to react to an escalating series of confrontations with a civilian and are often expressed visually, as shown here.

Source: Michael E. Miller, "Taser Use and the Use-of-Force Continuum," *Police Chief* (September 2010), 72. Photo credit: iStockPhoto.com/Susan Chiang

Burnout A mental state that occurs when a person suffers from exhaustion and has difficulty functioning normally as a result of overwork and stress.

TYPES OF FORCE To comply with the various, and not always consistent, laws concerning the use of force, a police officer must understand that there are two kinds of force: *nondeadly force* and *deadly force.* Most force used by law enforcement is nondeadly force. In most states, the use of nondeadly force is regulated by the concept of **reasonable force,** which allows the use of nondeadly force when a reasonable person would assume that such force was necessary. Police officers act within the law when they use reasonable force in making an arrest. For example, Daniel Pantaleo, the New York police officer who killed Eric Garner with a chokehold, could not reasonably have been expected to know that Garner suffered from health issues such as asthma that made his death more likely. This is the probable reason that a grand jury decided Pantaleo was not criminally responsible for killing Garner.[70]

In contrast, **deadly force** is force that an objective police officer realizes will place the subject in direct threat of serious injury or death. A law enforcement agent is justified in using deadly force if she or he reasonably believes that such force is necessary to protect herself, himself, or another person from serious harm.[71] Generally speaking, the key question in use-of-force cases is: Did the officer behave reasonably, under the circumstances?

THE UNITED STATES SUPREME COURT AND USE OF FORCE The United States Supreme Court set the

> **LO5-4**

standards for the use of deadly force by law enforcement officers in *Tennessee v. Garner* (1985).[72] The case involved an incident in which Memphis police officer Elton Hymon shot and killed a suspect who was trying to climb over a fence after stealing ten dollars from a residence. Hymon testified that he had been trained to shoot to keep a suspect from escaping, and indeed Tennessee law at the time allowed police officers to apprehend fleeing suspects in this manner.

In reviewing the case, the Supreme Court focused not on Hymon's action but on the Tennessee statute itself, ultimately finding it unconstitutional:

> When the suspect poses no immediate threat to the officer and no threat to others, the use of deadly force is unjustified. . . . It is not better that all felony suspects die than that they escape.[73]

The Court's decision forced twenty-three states to change their fleeing felon rules, but it did not completely eliminate police discretion in such situations. Police officers still may use deadly force if they have probable cause to believe that the fleeing suspect poses a threat of serious injury or death to the officers or others. (We will discuss the concept of probable cause in the next chapter.)

In essence, the Court recognized that police officers must be able to make split-second decisions without worrying about the legal ramifications. Four years after the *Garner* case, the Court tried to clarify this concept in *Graham v. Connor* (1989), stating that the use of any force should be judged by the "reasonableness of the officer on the scene, rather than with the 20/20 vision of hindsight."[74] In 2004, the Court modified this rule by suggesting that an officer's use of force could be "reasonable" even if, by objective measures, the force was not needed to protect the officer or others in the area.[75] (See the feature *Discretion in Action—High-Speed Force.*)

USE OF FORCE AND RACIAL BIAS When polled, African Americans consistently express less confidence in police than do whites.[76] This mistrust can be at least partially attributed to a number of recent high-profile

---

Reasonable Force A degree of force that is appropriate to protect the police officer or other citizens and is not excessive.

Deadly Force Force applied by a police officer that is likely or intended to cause death.

Photo by Mike McGregor/Contour by Getty Images

In many large cities, "hot spots" of crime—discussed earlier in the chapter—are located in low-income, minority neighborhoods. *Given this reality, how might such data-driven policing contribute to tension between the police and members of minority communities?*

HIGH-SPEED FORCE

THE SITUATION You are a sheriff's deputy, and you have just pulled over a driver named Rickar whom you suspect of being impaired by alcohol. When you ask Rickar for his license, he takes off and, weaving through traffic, leads you and five other deputies on a dangerous automobile chase with speeds reaching 100 miles per hour. Eventually, you and your colleagues corner Rickar in a parking lot. Instead of surrendering, he smashes into several of the other patrol cars and creates an opening to escape down a side street. From your position, you have the opportunity to shoot Rickar as he speeds away.

THE LAW The use of deadly force by a law enforcement officer is based on the concept of reasonableness. In other words, would a reasonable police officer in this situation be justified in using force?

WHAT WOULD YOU DO? Do you fire your service weapon? On the one hand, by his actions Rickar is certainly placing you, your colleagues, pedestrians, and other drivers in imminent threat of serious bodily injury. On the other hand, if you let him escape, this threat of harm will be significantly reduced.

[To see how a law enforcement officer in West Memphis, Arkansas, reacted in similar circumstances, go to Example 5.1 in Appendix A.]

---

use-of-force incidents during which unarmed young black men were killed by law enforcement officers. Often, because of the deference to police discretion that we have discussed throughout this chapter, judges and prosecutors see such killings as justified. For example, in the cases of Michael Brown of Ferguson, Missouri (discussed in Chapter 1), and Eric Garner of New York City (discussed earlier in this chapter), the police officers' use of deadly force was deemed reasonable under the circumstances.

Racial Profiling Such results contribute to feelings of frustration with law enforcement within African American communities, as does the perception of widespread **racial profiling** by police in the United States. Racial profiling occurs when a police action is based on the race, ethnicity, or national origin of the suspect rather than any reasonable suspicion that he or she has broken the law. In Ferguson, Missouri, for example, African Americans make up 65 percent of the population while accounting for 86 percent of traffic stops, 93 percent of arrests, and 92 percent of searches after stops by local law enforcement.[77]

Civil Rights Violations There are several ways to hold police accountable for wrongdoing. In individual cases, a local prosecutor can bring charges against a police officer for unreasonable use of force, as occurred in April 2015 when a North Charleston, South Carolina, police officer named Michael Slager was charged with murder for shooting a fleeing African American suspect in the back. In addition, victims can sue for monetary damages in civil court. (See Chapter 3 for a review of this process.) In 2013, the city of New York spent $428 million to settle a series of civil lawsuits against its police officers.[78]

If there is a pattern of improper force against minority suspects and racial profiling, the federal government can investigate police departments for committing *civil rights violations*. A **civil rights violation** involves denial of the rights afforded to all citizens by the U.S. Constitution not to be discriminated against on the basis of race. Since 2008, the Justice Department has opened civil rights investigations in about twenty cities, including Albuquerque, New Orleans, and Portland, Oregon. In May 2015, it found pervasive discrimination against minorities by the criminal justice system in Ferguson, Missouri, and began working with local officials to reform Ferguson's police department.

Racial Profiling The practice of targeting people for police action based solely on their race, ethnicity, or national origin.

Civil Rights Violation Any interference with a citizen's constitutional rights by a civil servant such as a police officer.

5-4 HOW IMPORTANT IS ETHICS IN POLICING?

If excessive force is a "strong" misuse of authority by law enforcement, then "soft" misuse of this authority manifests itself in *police corruption*. For general purposes, **police corruption** can be defined as the misuse of authority by a law enforcement officer "in a manner designed to produce personal gain." There are three basic, traditional types of police corruption:

> 1. *Bribery,* in which the police officer accepts money or other forms of payment in exchange for "favors," which may include allowing a certain criminal activity to continue or misplacing a key piece of evidence before a trial. Related to bribery are *payoffs,* in which an officer demands payment from an individual or a business in return for certain services.
>
> 2. *Shakedowns,* in which an officer attempts to coerce money or goods from a citizen or criminal.
>
> 3. *Mooching,* in which the police officer accepts free "gifts" such as cigarettes, liquor, or services in return for favorable treatment of the gift giver.[79]

Additionally, corrupt police officers have many opportunities to engage in theft or burglary by taking money or property in the course of their duties. Vice investigations, for example, often uncover temptingly large amounts of illegal drugs and cash. Several years ago, six Philadelphia police officers were arrested for improperly "confiscating" $500,000 in cash, drugs, and personal property such as Rolex watches from suspects.

> **CAREER TIP** Within police departments, *internal affairs officers* are charged with investigating corruption, ethics violations, and other misconduct on the force.

5-4a Ethical Dilemmas

Police corruption is intricately connected with the ethics of law enforcement officers. As you saw in Chapter 1, ethics has to do with fundamental questions of the fairness, justice, rightness, or wrongness of any action. Given the significant power that police officers hold, society expects very high standards of ethical behavior from them. Some police actions are obviously unethical, such as the behavior of the Philadelphia police officers mentioned above. The majority of ethical dilemmas that a police officer will face are not so clear cut. Criminologists Joycelyn M. Pollock and Ronald F. Becker define an ethical dilemma as a situation in which law enforcement officers:

LO5-5

▶ Do not know the right course of action;

▶ Have difficulty doing what they consider to be right; and/or

▶ Find the wrong choice very tempting.[80]

Because of the many rules that govern policing—the subject of the next chapter—police officers often find themselves tempted by a phenomenon called **noble cause corruption.** This type of corruption occurs when, in the words of John P. Crank and Michael A. Caldero, "officers do bad things because they believe the outcomes will be good."[81] Examples of noble cause corruption include planting evidence or lying in court to help convict someone the officer knows to be guilty.

5-4b Elements of Ethics

Pollock and Becker, both of whom have extensive experience as ethics instructors for police departments, further identify four categories of ethical dilemmas, involving discretion, duty, honesty, and loyalty.[82]

▶ *Discretion.* The law provides rigid guidelines for how police officers must act and how they cannot act, but it does not offer guidelines for how officers *should act* in many circumstances. As mentioned at the beginning of this chapter, police officers often use discretion to determine how they should act, and ethics plays an important role in guiding discretionary actions.

▶ *Duty.* The concept of discretion is linked with **duty,** or the obligation to act in a certain manner. Society, by passing laws, can make a police officer's duty clearer and, in the process, help eliminate discretion

> **Police Corruption** The abuse of authority by a law enforcement officer for personal gain.
>
> **Noble Cause Corruption** Knowing misconduct by a police officer with the goal of attaining what the officer believes is a "just" result.
>
> **Duty** The moral sense of a police officer that she or he should behave in a certain manner.

from the decision-making process. But an officer's duty will not always be obvious, and ethical considerations can often supplement "the rules" of being a law enforcement agent.

▶ *Honesty*. Of course, honesty is a critical attribute for an ethical police officer. A law enforcement agent must make hundreds of decisions in a day, and most of them require him or her to be honest in order to properly do the job.

▶ *Loyalty*. What should a police officer do if he or she witnesses a partner using excessive force on a suspect? The choice often sets loyalty against ethics, especially if the officer does not condone the violence.

Mandel Ngan/AFP/Getty Images

Several years ago, Kitsap County (Washington) deputy sheriff Krista McDonald received the Public Safety Officer Medal of Valor for rescuing two colleagues during a shootout. *What role does the concept of duty play in a law enforcement agent's decision, regardless of her or his own safety, to protect the life of another person?*

STUDY TOOLS ⑤

READY TO STUDY? IN THE BOOK, YOU CAN:

☐ Rip out the Chapter Review Card, which includes key terms and chapter summaries.

ONLINE AT WWW.CENGAGEBRAIN.COM, YOU CAN:

☐ Learn about a unique juvenile criminal case in a short video.

☐ Dig deeper into social media in criminal justice by exploring Officer.com.

☐ Interact with figures from the text, and watch quick animation clips.

☐ Prepare for tests with quizzes.

☐ Review the key terms with Flash Cards.

Although an individual's ethical makeup is determined by a multitude of personal factors, police departments can create an atmosphere that is conducive to professionalism. Brandon V. Zuidema and H. Wayne Duff, both captains with the Lynchburg (Virginia) Police Department, believe that law enforcement administrators can encourage ethical policing by:

1. **Incorporating ethics into the department's mission statement.**

2. **Conducting internal training sessions in ethics.**

3. **Accepting "honest mistakes" and helping the officer learn from those mistakes.**

4. **Adopting a zero-tolerance policy toward unethical decisions when the mistakes are not so honest.**[83]

Quiz

1. When a police administration wants to limit officer discretion, it can institute a departmental _____ to guide the officer's decision making in certain situations, such as high-speed chases.

2. One of the primary functions of patrol officers is to _____ crime by maintaining a visible presence in the community.

3. The science of crime investigation is known as _____.

4. The technique of _____ fingerprinting involves crime labs using samples of a person's genetic material to match suspects to crimes.

5. All modern police departments practice _____-driven policing, in which officers respond to calls for service after a crime has occurred.

6. Most patrol officers are assigned to _____ patrols, in which they cover designated areas and react to incidents they encounter.

7. _____ policing is a popular strategy in which officers are encouraged to develop partnerships with citizens to prevent and combat crime.

8. The police subculture is shaped by the physical dangers, such as assault, and the mental dangers, such as high levels of _____, that officers face every day.

9. Police use of nondeadly force is regulated by the concept of _____ force, or the amount of force that a rational person would consider necessary in a given situation.

10. Police _____ is an umbrella term that covers police misconduct from taking bribes to engaging in illegal drug trafficking.

Answers can be found in the Answers section in the back of the book.

6
Police and the Constitution:
The Rules of Law Enforcement

Scott Olson/Getty Images

LEARNING OBJECTIVES

After studying this chapter, you will be able to . . .

6-1 Outline the four major sources that may provide probable cause.

6-2 Explain when searches can be made without a warrant.

6-3 Distinguish between a stop and a frisk, and indicate the importance of the case *Terry v. Ohio*.

6-4 List the four elements that must be present for an arrest to take place.

6-5 Indicate situations in which a *Miranda* warning is unnecessary.

After you finish

this chapter, go

to **PAGES**

134–135 for

STUDY TOOLS

Sniff Search

When the Miami–Dade County (Florida) Police Department received an anonymous tip that Joelis Jardines was growing marijuana in his home, they sent Franky to verify. After circling for a few minutes on Jardines's front porch, Franky, a chocolate Labrador trained to sniff out illegal drugs, sat down near the front door. This was a signal to the two officers on the scene that the dog smelled something suspicious. Relying on Franky's expertise, the officers obtained permission from a judge to search Jardines's home. They found nearly 180 marijuana plants having an estimated street value of about $700,000.

Jardines eventually pleaded not guilty to drug trafficking charges. At trial, his lawyers claimed that—by allowing Franky to sniff around the outside of Jardines's home—the Miami police had used improper means to justify their search. The United States Supreme Court agreed. To come to this conclusion, the Court relied on a concept called the *expectation of privacy,* which we will address later in this chapter. Historically, Americans have enjoyed a strong expectation of privacy inside their homes and on their *curtilage,* or the area immediately surrounding their homes.

Under certain circumstances, the Court recognized, we tolerate the presence of uninvited visitors on our property. Such visitors include Girl Scouts selling cookies, trick-or-treaters, and salespeople. This tolerance does not, however, extend to law enforcement agents with drug-sniffing dogs. "The police cannot . . . hang around on the lawn or in the side garden, trawling for evidence and perhaps peering into the windows of the home," said Justice Antonin Scalia. "And the officers [in the Jardines case] had all four of their feet and all four of their companion's planted firmly on that curtilage—the front porch is the classic example of an area intimately associated with the life of the home."

The Supreme Court has ruled that the U.S. Constitution limits the ability of law enforcement to gather evidence of criminal behavior by using narcotics-sniffing police dogs on a homeowner's private property. *Do you agree that one's home should receive added protection from police searches under American criminal law? Why or why not?*

Billy Gadbury/Shutter-Stock.com

6-1 HOW DOES THE FOURTH AMENDMENT RESTRICT POLICE DISCRETION?

In *Florida v. Jardines,* the Supreme Court did not address whether Joelis Jardines was guilty or innocent of the charges against him. That was for the trial court to decide. Rather, the Court ruled that the Miami narcotics officers had overstepped the boundaries of their authority by using a drug-sniffing dog to detect the smell of marijuana from Jardines's front porch.[1] In the previous chapter, we discussed the importance of discretion for police officers. This discretion, as we noted, is not absolute. A law enforcement agent's actions are greatly determined by the rules for policing set down in the U.S. Constitution and enforced by the courts.

To understand these rules, law enforcement officers must understand the Fourth Amendment, which reads as follows:

> The right of the people to be secure in their persons, houses, papers, and effects, against unreasonable searches and seizures, shall not be violated, and no

Warrants shall issue, but upon probable cause, supported by Oath or affirmation, and particularly describing the place to be searched, and the persons or things to be seized.

This amendment contains two critical legal concepts: a prohibition against *unreasonable* **searches and seizures** and the requirement of **probable cause** to issue a warrant. (A *warrant*, as you will learn later in the chapter, is written permission from a judge for police to engage in a search or arrest.)

6-1a Reasonableness

Law enforcement personnel use searches and seizures to look for and collect the evidence prosecutors need to convict individuals suspected of crimes. When police are conducting a search or seizure, they must be *reasonable*. Though courts have spent innumerable hours scrutinizing the word, no specific meaning for *reasonable* exists. A thesaurus can provide useful synonyms—logical, practical, sensible, intelligent, plausible—but because each case is different, those terms are relative.

In the *Jardines* case, the Supreme Court accepted the argument that the search had been so unreasonable as to violate the Fourth Amendment's prohibition against unreasonable searches and seizures. That does not mean that the police officers' actions would have been unreasonable under every circumstance. The Court has allowed evidence of illegal drugs uncovered by trained dogs sniffing the exterior of luggage in an airport and the outside of a car that the police have stopped for a traffic violation.[2] According to American case law, searches in those public places are more likely to be found reasonable than searches of the home, "the most private . . . of all the places and things the Fourth Amendment protects."[3]

6-1b Probable Cause

The concept of reasonableness is linked to probable cause. The Supreme Court has ruled, for example, that any arrest or seizure is unreasonable unless it is supported by probable cause.[4] The burden of probable cause requires more than mere suspicion on a police officer's part. The officer must know of facts and circumstances that would reasonably lead to "the belief that an offense has been or is being committed."[5]

SOURCES OF PROBABLE CAUSE If no probable cause existed when a police officer took a certain action, it cannot be retroactively applied. If, for example, a police officer stops a person for jaywalking and then finds several ounces of marijuana in that person's pocket, the arrest for marijuana possession would probably be disallowed. Remember, suspicion does not equal probable cause. If, however, an informant had tipped the officer off that the person was a drug dealer, probable cause might exist and the arrest could be valid. Several sources that may provide probable cause include:

LO6-1

1. *Personal observation.* Police officers may use their personal training, experience, and expertise to infer probable cause from situations that may not be obviously criminal. If, for example, a police officer observes several people in a car slowly circling a certain building in a high-crime area, that officer may infer that the people are "casing" the building in preparation for a burglary. Probable cause could be established for detaining the suspects.

2. *Information.* Law enforcement officers receive information from victims, eyewitnesses, informants, and official sources such as police bulletins or broadcasts. Such information, as long as it is believed to be reliable, is a basis for probable cause.

3. *Evidence.* In certain circumstances, which will be examined later in this chapter, police have probable cause for a search or seizure based on evidence—such as a shotgun—in plain view.

4. *Association.* In some circumstances, if the police see a person with a known criminal background in a place where criminal activity is openly taking place, they have probable cause to stop that person. Generally, however, association is not adequate to establish probable cause.[6]

THE PROBABLE CAUSE FRAMEWORK In a sense, the concept of probable cause allows police officers to do their job effectively. Most arrests are made without a warrant because most arrests are the result of quick police reaction to the commission of a crime. Indeed, it would not be practical to expect a police officer to obtain

Searches and Seizures The legal term, as found in the Fourth Amendment to the U.S. Constitution, that generally refers to the searching for and the confiscating of evidence by law enforcement agents.

Probable Cause Reasonable grounds to believe the existence of facts warranting certain actions, such as the search or arrest of a person.

Job Description:

▶ Enforce the nation's environmental laws protecting air, water, and land resources.

▶ Investigate cases that involve negligent, knowing, or willful violations of federal environmental laws.

What Kind of Training Is Required?

▶ Eight weeks of basic federal law enforcement and criminal investigation training at the Federal Law Enforcement Training Center in Glynco, Georgia.

▶ An additional eight weeks of training in conducting investigations of the criminal provisions of federal environmental laws.

Annual Salary Range?

▶ $43,000–$73,000

Image Source/Corbis

SOCIAL MEDIA CAREER TIP

For your profile photo, stick with a close-up, business-appropriate photo in which you are smiling and wearing something you would wear as a potential employee. Avoid symbols, party photos, long-distance shots, and baby pictures.

---

a warrant before making an arrest on the street. Thus, probable cause provides a framework that limits the situations in which police officers can make arrests, but also gives officers the freedom to act within that framework.

In 2003, the Supreme Court reaffirmed this freedom by ruling that Baltimore (Maryland) police officers acted properly when they arrested all three passengers of a car in which cocaine had been hidden in the back seat. "A reasonable officer," wrote Chief Justice William H. Rehnquist, "could conclude that there was probable cause to believe" that the defendant, who had been sitting in the front seat, was in "possession" of the illicit drug despite his protestations to the contrary.[7]

Once an arrest is made, the arresting officer must prove to a judge that probable cause existed. In *County of Riverside v. McLaughlin* (1991),[8] the Supreme Court held that this judicial determination of probable cause must be made within forty-eight hours after the arrest, even if this two-day period includes a weekend or holiday.

6-1c The Exclusionary Rule

Historically, the courts have looked to the Fourth Amendment for guidance in regulating the activity of law enforcement officers, as the language of the Constitution does not expressly do so. The courts' most potent legal tool in this endeavor is the **exclusionary rule,** which prohibits the use of illegally seized evidence. According to this rule, any evidence obtained by an unreasonable search or seizure is inadmissible (may not be used) against a defendant in a criminal trial.[9] Even highly incriminating evidence, such as a knife stained with the victim's blood, usually cannot be introduced at a trial if illegally obtained. (Due to the Supreme Court's

Exclusionary Rule A rule under which any evidence that is obtained in violation of the accused's rights, as well as any evidence derived from illegally obtained evidence, will not be admissible in criminal court.

Suppose that this gun—used by a defendant to murder a victim—was found as the result of an improper police search. *Why might the exclusionary rule keep evidence of the gun's existence out of court?*

ruling explained at the beginning of this chapter, evidence of the marijuana plants in Joelis Jardines's house was excluded from his trial because of the improper search.)

Furthermore, any physical or verbal evidence police are able to acquire by using illegally obtained evidence is known as the **fruit of the poisoned tree** and is also inadmissible. For example, if the police use the existence of the bloodstained knife to get a confession out of a suspect, that confession will be excluded as well.

One of the implications of the exclusionary rule is that it forces police to gather evidence properly. If they follow appropriate procedures, they are more likely to be rewarded with a conviction. If they are careless or abuse the rights of the suspect, they are unlikely to get a conviction. A strict application of the exclusionary rule, therefore, will permit guilty people to go free because of police carelessness or honest errors. In practice, relatively few apparently guilty suspects benefit from the exclusionary

Fruit of the Poisoned Tree Evidence that is acquired through the use of illegally obtained evidence and is therefore inadmissible in court.

"Inevitable Discovery" Exception The legal principle that illegally obtained evidence can be admissible in court if police using lawful means would "inevitably" have discovered it.

"Good Faith" Exception The legal principle that evidence obtained with the use of a technically invalid search warrant is admissible during trial if the police acted in good faith when they sought the warrant from a judge.

rule. Research shows that about 3 percent of felony arrestees avoid incarceration because of improper police searches and seizures.[10]

THE "INEVITABLE DISCOVERY" EXCEPTION

Critics of the exclusionary rule maintain that, regardless of statistics, the rule hampers the police's ability to gather evidence and causes prosecutors to release numerous suspects before their cases make it to court. Several Supreme Court decisions have mirrored this view and provided exceptions to the exclusionary rule.

The **"inevitable discovery" exception** was established in the wake of the disappearance of ten-year-old Pamela Powers of Des Moines, Iowa, on Christmas Eve, 1968. The primary suspect in the case, a religious fanatic named Robert Williams, was tricked by a detective into leading police to the site where he had buried Powers. The detective convinced Williams that if he did not lead police to the body, he would soon forget where it was buried. This would deny his victim a "Christian burial." Initially, in *Brewer v. Williams* (1977),[11] the Court ruled that the evidence (Powers's body) had been obtained illegally because Williams's attorney had not been present during the interrogation that led to his admission. Several years later, in *Nix v. Williams* (1984),[12] the Court reversed itself, ruling that the evidence was admissible because the body would eventually ("inevitably") have been found by lawful means.

THE "GOOD FAITH" EXCEPTION The scope of the exclusionary rule has been further diminished by two cases involving faulty warrants. In the first, *United States v. Leon* (1984),[13] the police seized evidence on authority of a search warrant that had been improperly issued by a judge. In the second, *Arizona v. Evans* (1995),[14] due to a computer error, a police officer detained Isaac Evans on the mistaken belief that he was subject to an arrest warrant. As a result, the officer found a marijuana cigarette on Evans's person and, after a search of his car, discovered a bag of marijuana.

In both cases, the Court allowed the evidence to stand under a **"good faith" exception** to the exclusionary rule. Under this exception, evidence acquired by a police officer using a technically invalid warrant is admissible if the officer was unaware of the error. In these two cases, the Court said that the officers acted in "good faith." By the same token, if police officers use a search warrant that they know to be technically incorrect, the good faith exception does not apply, and the evidence can be suppressed.

6-2 WHAT ARE THE RULES FOR SEARCHES AND SEIZURES?

How far can law enforcement agents go in searching and seizing private property? Consider the steps taken by Jenny Stracner, an investigator with the Laguna Beach (California) Police Department. After receiving information that a suspect, Greenwood, was engaged in drug trafficking, Stracner enlisted the aid of the local trash collector in procuring evidence. Instead of taking Greenwood's trash bags to be incinerated, the collector agreed to give them to Stracner. The officer found enough drug paraphernalia in the garbage to obtain a warrant to search the suspect's home. Subsequently, Greenwood was arrested and convicted on narcotics charges.[15]

Remember, the Fourth Amendment is quite specific in forbidding unreasonable searches and seizures. Were Stracner's search of Greenwood's garbage and her seizure of its contents "reasonable"? The Supreme Court thought so, holding that Greenwood's garbage was not protected by the Fourth Amendment.[16]

6-2a The Role of Privacy in Searches

A crucial concept in understanding search and seizure law is *privacy*. By definition, a **search** is a governmental intrusion on a citizen's reasonable expectation of privacy. The recognized standard for a "reasonable expectation of privacy" was established in *Katz v. United States* (1967).[17] That case dealt with the question of whether the defendant was justified in his expectation of privacy in the calls he made from a public phone booth. The Supreme Court held that "the Fourth Amendment protects people, not places," and Katz prevailed.

In his concurring opinion, Justice John Harlan, Jr., set a two-pronged test for a person's expectation of privacy:

1. **The individual must prove that she or he expected privacy.**

2. **Society must recognize that expectation as reasonable.**[18]

Accordingly, the Court agreed with Katz's claim that he had a reasonable right to privacy in a public phone booth. Even though the phone booth was a public place, accessible to anyone, Katz had taken clear steps to protect his privacy.

Should law enforcement be able to use police helicopters such as the one shown here to determine if people are carrying out illegal behavior in their fenced-in backyards? Why or why not?

Despite the *Katz* ruling, simply taking steps to protect one's privacy is not enough to protect against law enforcement intrusion. The steps must be reasonably certain to ensure privacy. If a person is unreasonable or mistaken in expecting privacy, he or she may forfeit that expectation. For instance, in *California v. Greenwood* (1988),[19] described at the beginning of this section, the Court did not believe that the suspect had a reasonable expectation of privacy when it came to his garbage bags. The Court noted that when we place our trash on a curb, we expose it to any number of intrusions by "animals, children, scavengers, snoops, and other members of the public."[20] In other words, if Greenwood had truly intended for the contents of his garbage bags to remain private, he would not have left them on the side of the road.

In *Florida v. Jardines*, the Supreme Court case that opened this chapter, four of the nine justices believed that the Court had gone too far in protecting the defendant's expectation of privacy. As recently as 2011, these justices noted, the Court had found that people have no such expectation regarding marijuana smells coming from their homes that can be detected by a human being.[21] Why, they asked, should the nose of a drug-sniffing dog be any different?[22]

Search The process by which police examine a person or property to find evidence that will be used to prove guilt in a criminal trial.

6-2b Search and Seizure Warrants

Remember, one of the purposes of the Fourth Amendment is to protect citizens from unreasonable police searches. To ensure that they will not be retroactively accused of unreasonably infringing on a suspect's privacy rights during a search, law enforcement officers can obtain a **search warrant.** A search warrant is a court order that authorizes police to search a certain area. Before a judge or magistrate will issue a search warrant, law enforcement officers must provide:

▶ Information showing probable cause that a crime has been or will be committed.

▶ Specific information on the premises to be searched, the suspects to be found and the illegal activities taking place at those premises, and the items to be seized.

The purpose of a search warrant is to establish, before the search takes place, that a *probable cause to search* justifies infringing on the suspect's reasonable expectation of privacy.

PARTICULARITY OF SEARCH WARRANTS The drafters of the Bill of Rights specifically did not want law enforcement officers to have the freedom to make "general, exploratory" searches through a person's belongings.[23] Consequently, the Fourth Amendment requires that a warrant describe with "particularity" the place to be searched and the things—either people or objects—to be seized.

This "particularity" requirement places a heavy burden on law enforcement officers. Before going to a

Search Warrant A written order, based on probable cause and issued by a judge or magistrate, commanding that police officers or criminal investigators search a specific person, place, or property to obtain evidence.

Affidavit A written statement of facts, confirmed by the oath or affirmation of the party making it and made before a person having the authority to administer the oath or affirmation.

Seizure The forcible taking of a person or property in response to a violation of the law.

judge to ask for a search warrant, they must prepare an **affidavit** in which they provide specific, written information on the property that they wish to search and seize. They must know the specific address of any place they wish to search. General addresses of apartment buildings or office complexes are not sufficient. Furthermore, courts generally frown on vague descriptions of goods to be seized. For example, several years ago, a federal court ruled that a warrant permitting police to search a home for "all handguns, shotguns and rifles" and "evidence showing street gang membership" was too broad. As a result, the seizure of a shotgun was disallowed for lack of a valid search warrant.[24]

A **seizure** is the act of taking possession of a person or property by the government because of a (suspected) violation of the law. In general, four categories of items can be seized by use of a search warrant:

1. **Items resulting from the crime, such as stolen goods.**

2. **Items that are inherently illegal for anybody to possess (with certain exceptions), such as narcotics and counterfeit currency.**

3. **Items that can be called "evidence" of the crime, such as a bloodstained sneaker or a ski mask.**

4. **Items used in committing the crime, such as an ice pick or a printing press used to make counterfeit bills.[25]**

See Figure 6.1 for an example of a search warrant.

REASONABLENESS DURING A SEARCH AND SEIZURE No matter how "particular" a warrant is, it cannot provide for all the conditions that are bound to come up during its service. Consequently, the law gives law enforcement officers the ability to act "reasonably" during a search and seizure in the event of unforeseeable circumstances. For example, if a police officer is searching an apartment for a stolen MacBook Pro laptop computer and notices a vial of crack cocaine sitting on the suspect's bed, that contraband is considered to be in "plain view" and can be seized.

Note that if law enforcement officers have a search warrant that authorizes them to search for a stolen laptop computer, they will not be justified in opening small drawers. Because a computer cannot fit in a small drawer, an officer will not have a reasonable basis for searching one. Hence, officers are restricted in where they can look by the items they are searching for.

FIGURE 6.1 | EXAMPLE OF A SEARCH WARRANT

United States District Court

_____DISTRICT OF_____

In the Matter of the Search of
(Name, address or brief description of person or property to be searched)

SEARCH WARRANT

CASE NUMBER:

TO:_____ and any Authorized Officer of the United States

Affidavit(s) having been made before me by_____ who has reason to
believe that ☐ on the person of or ☐ on the premises known as (name, description and/or location)

in the_____District of_____there is now
concealed a certain person or property, namely (describe the person or property)

I am satisfied that the affidavit(s) and any recorded testimony establish probable cause to believe that the person
or property so described is now concealed on the person or premises above-described and establish grounds for
the issuance of this warrant.

YOU ARE HEREBY COMMANDED to search on or before_____
                                                            Date
(not to exceed 10 days) the person or place named above for the person or property specified, serving this warrant
and making the search (in the daytime — 6:00 A.M. to 10:00 P.M.) (at any time in the day or night as I find
reasonable cause has been established) and if the person or property be found there to seize same, leaving a copy
of this warrant and receipt for the person or property taken, and prepare a written inventory of the person or property seized and promptly return this warrant to_____
as required by law.   U.S. Judge or Magistrate

Date and Time Issued_____at_____City and State_____

Name and Title of Judicial Officer_____   Signature of Judicial Officer_____

6-2c Searches and Seizures without a Warrant

LO6-2 Although the Supreme Court has established the principle that searches conducted without warrants are *per se* (by definition) unreasonable, it has set "specifically established" exceptions to the rule.[26] In fact, most searches take place in the absence of a judicial order. Warrantless searches and seizures can be lawful when police are in "hot pursuit" of a subject or when they search bags of trash left at the curb for regular collection. Because of the magnitude of smuggling activities in "border areas" such as airports, seaports, and international boundaries, a warrant normally is not needed to search property in those places.

Furthermore, in 2006 the Court held unanimously that police officers do not need a warrant to enter a private home in an emergency, such as when they reasonably fear for the safety of the inhabitants.[27] The two most important circumstances in which a warrant is not needed, though, are (1) searches incidental to an arrest and (2) consent searches.

SEARCHES INCIDENTAL TO AN ARREST The most frequent exception to the warrant requirement involves **searches incidental to arrests,** so called because nearly every time police officers make an arrest (a procedure

discussed in detail later in the chapter), they also search the suspect. As long as the original arrest was based on probable cause, these searches are valid for two reasons, established by the Supreme Court in *United States v. Robinson* (1973):

1. **The need for a police officer to find and confiscate any weapons a suspect may be carrying.**

2. **The need to protect any evidence on the suspect's person from being destroyed.**[28]

Law enforcement officers are, however, limited in the searches they may make during an arrest. These limits were established by the Supreme Court in *Chimel v. California* (1969).[29] In that case, police arrived at Chimel's home with an arrest warrant but not a search warrant. Even though Chimel refused their request to "look around," the officers searched the entire three-bedroom house for nearly an hour, finding stolen coins in the process. Chimel was convicted of burglary and appealed, arguing that the evidence of the coins should have been suppressed.

The Supreme Court held that the search was unreasonable. In doing so, the Court established guidelines as to the acceptable extent of searches incidental to an arrest. Primarily, the Court ruled that police may search any area within the suspect's "immediate control" to confiscate any weapons or evidence that the suspect could destroy. The Court found, however, that there was no justification

> for routinely searching rooms other than that in which the arrest occurs—or, for that matter, for searching through all desk drawers or other closed or concealed areas in that room itself. Such searches, in the absence of well-recognized exceptions, may be made only under the authority of a search warrant.[30]

The exact interpretation of the "area within immediate control" has been left to individual courts, but in general it has been taken to mean the area within the reach of the arrested person. Thus, the Court is said to have established the "arm's reach doctrine" in its *Chimel* decision.

SEARCHES WITH CONSENT **Consent searches,** the second most common type of warrantless searches, take place when individuals voluntarily give law enforcement

Searches Incidental to Arrests Searches for weapons and evidence that are conducted on persons who have just been arrested.

Consent Searches Searches by police that are made after the subject of the search has agreed to the action. In these situations, consent, if given of free will, validates a warrantless search.

officers permission to search their persons, homes, or belongings. The most relevant factors in determining whether consent is voluntary are

1. **The age, intelligence, and physical condition of the consenting suspect.**

2. **Any coercive behavior by the police, such as the language used to request consent.**

3. **The length of the questioning and its location.**[31]

If a court finds that a person has been physically threatened or otherwise coerced into giving consent, the search is invalid.[32] Furthermore, the search consented to must be reasonable. In 2007, the North Carolina Supreme Court invalidated a consent search that turned up a packet of cocaine. As part of this search, the police had pulled down the suspect's underwear and shone a flashlight on his groin. The court ruled that a reasonable person in the defendant's position would not consent to such an intrusive examination.[33] (Figure 6.2 provides an overview of the circumstances under which warrantless searches have traditionally been allowed.)

6-2d Searches of Automobiles

In *Carroll v. United States* (1925),[34] the Supreme Court ruled that the law could distinguish among automobiles, homes, and persons in questions involving police searches. In the years since its *Carroll* decision, the Court has established that the Fourth Amendment does not require police to obtain a warrant to search automobiles or other movable vehicles when they have probable cause to believe that a vehicle contains contraband or evidence of criminal activity.[35]

The reasoning behind such leniency is straightforward: requiring a warrant to search an automobile places too heavy a burden on police officers. By the time the officers could communicate with a judge and obtain the warrant, the suspects could have driven away and destroyed any evidence. Consequently, the Court has consistently held that someone in a vehicle does not have the same reasonable expectation of privacy as someone at home or even in a phone booth.

WARRANTLESS SEARCHES OF AUTOMOBILES For nearly three decades, police officers believed that if they lawfully arrested the driver of a car, they could legally make a warrantless search of the car's entire front and back compartments. This understanding was based on the Supreme Court's ruling in *New York v. Benton* (1981),[36] which seemed to allow this expansive interpretation of the "area within immediate control" with regard to automobiles.

In *Arizona v. Gant* (2009), however, the Court announced that its *Benton* decision had been misinterpreted. Such warrantless searches are allowed only if either of the following is true:

1. **The person being arrested is close enough to the car to grab or destroy evidence or a weapon inside the car.**

2. **The arresting officer reasonably believes that the car contains evidence pertinent to the same crime for which the arrest took place.**[37]

FIGURE 6.2 EXCEPTIONS TO THE REQUIREMENT THAT OFFICERS HAVE A SEARCH WARRANT

INCIDENT TO LAWFUL ARREST
Police officers may search the area within immediate control of a person after they have arrested him or her.

CONSENT
Police officers may search a person without a warrant if that person voluntarily agrees to be searched and has the legal authority to authorize the search.

STOP AND FRISK
Police officers may frisk, or "pat down," a person if they suspect that the person may be involved in criminal activity or pose a danger to those in the immediate area.

HOT PURSUIT
If police officers are in "hot pursuit," or chasing a person they have probable cause to believe has committed a crime, and that person enters a building, the officers may search the building without a warrant.

AUTOMOBILE EXCEPTION
If police officers have probable cause to believe that an automobile contains evidence of a crime, they may, in most instances, search the vehicle without a warrant.

PLAIN VIEW
If police officers are legally engaged in police work and happen to see evidence of a crime in "plain view," they may seize it without a warrant.

ABANDONED PROPERTY
Any property, such as a hotel room that has been vacated or contraband that has been discarded, may be searched and seized by police officers without a warrant.

BORDER SEARCHES
Law enforcement officers on border patrol do not need a warrant to search vehicles crossing the border.

In many instances, it would be impractical for police officers to leave a crime scene, go to a judge, and obtain a search warrant before conducting a search. Therefore, under the circumstances listed above, a search warrant is not required.

So, for example, a police officer will no longer be able to search an automobile for contraband if the driver has been arrested for failing to pay previous speeding tickets—unless the officer reasonably believes the suspect has the ability to reach and destroy any such contraband.

As you can imagine, the law enforcement community reacted negatively to the new restrictions outlined in the *Gant* decision.[38] Police officers, however, still can conduct a warrantless search of an automobile based on circumstances other than the incidental-to-an-arrest doctrine. These circumstances include probable cause of criminal activity, consent of the driver, and "protective searches" to search for weapons if police officers have a reasonable suspicion that such weapons exist.[39]

PRETEXTUAL STOPS What if the officer in the previous example was just using the traffic violation as an excuse to stop the car and do a drug search? It is important to understand that, as long as an officer has probable cause to believe that a traffic law has been broken, her or his "true" motivation for making a stop is irrelevant.[40] So even if the police officer does not have a legally sufficient reason to search for evidence of a crime, such as drug trafficking, the officer can use a minor traffic violation to pull over the car and investigate his or her "hunch." (To learn more about such "pretextual stops," see the feature *Discretion in Action—A Valid Pretext?*)

6-2e The Plain View Doctrine

As we have already seen several times in this chapter, the Constitution, as interpreted by our courts, provides very little protection to evidence *in plain view*. For example, suppose a traffic officer pulls over a person for speeding, looks in the driver's side window, and clearly sees what appears to be a bag of heroin resting on the passenger seat. In this instance, under the **plain view doctrine,** the officer would be justified in seizing the drugs without a warrant.

Plain View Doctrine The legal principle that objects in plain view of a law enforcement agent who has the right to be in a position to have that view may be seized without a warrant and introduced as evidence.

Discretion in Action

A VALID PRETEXT?

THE SITUATION You are a police officer patrolling an area of Washington, D.C., that is marked by extremely high rates of drug-related crime. You become suspicious of a truck with temporary plates being driven slowly by a young African American male. Although you do not consider yourself racially biased, you are well aware, from experience, that in this neighborhood many young black men in these types of vehicles with temporary plates are drug dealers. These suspicions do not, however, reach the level of probable cause needed to pull over the truck. Then, the driver fails to signal while making a right turn.

THE LAW As far as Fourth Amendment law is concerned, any subjective reasons that a police officer might have for stopping a suspect, including any motives based on racial stereotyping or bias, are irrelevant. As long as the officer has objective probable cause to believe a traffic violation or other wrongdoing has occurred, the stop is valid.

WHAT WOULD YOU DO? You are convinced that the driver of the truck is selling illegal drugs, and you want to stop and search him. The failure to signal gives you a valid pretext to pull over the truck, even though your real reasons for the stop would be the truck's slow pace, its temporary plates, the race of its driver, and the level of drug crime in the neighborhood. What do you do?

[To see how the United States Supreme Court reacted to an officer's decision in a similar situation, go to Example 6.1 in Appendix A.]

The plain view doctrine was first enunciated by the Supreme Court in *Coolidge v. New Hampshire* (1971).[41] The Court ruled that law enforcement officers may make a warrantless seizure of an item if four criteria are met:

1. **The item is positioned so as to be detected easily by an officer's sight or some other sense.**

2. **The officer is legally in a position to notice the item in question.**

3. **The discovery of the item is inadvertent. That is, the officer had not intended to find the item.**

The officer immediately recognizes the illegal nature of the item. No interrogation or further investigation is allowed under the plain view doctrine.

Advances in technology that allow law enforcement agents to "see" beyond normal human capabilities have raised new issues in regard to plain view principles. *Thermal imagers,* for example, measure otherwise invisible levels of infrared radiation. These devices are particularly effective in detecting marijuana plants grown indoors because of the heat thrown off by the "grow lights" that the plants need to survive. The question for the courts has been whether a warrantless search of a dwelling through its walls by means of a thermal imager violates Fourth Amendment protections of privacy. According to the Supreme Court, an item is not in plain view if law enforcement agents need the aid of this technology to "see" it.[42] Thus, information from a thermal imager is not by itself justification for a warrantless search.

6-2f Electronic Surveillance

During the course of a criminal investigation, law enforcement officers may decide to use **electronic surveillance,** or electronic devices such as wiretaps and hidden microphones ("bugs"), to monitor and record conversations, observe movements, and trace or record telephone calls.

BASIC RULES: CONSENT AND PROBABLE CAUSE
Given the invasiveness of electronic surveillance, the Supreme Court has generally held that the practice is prohibited by the Fourth Amendment. In *Burger v. New York* (1967),[43] however, the Court ruled that it was permissible under certain circumstances. That same year,

Electronic Surveillance The use of electronic equipment by law enforcement agents to record private conversations or observe conduct that is meant to be private.

THROUGH-THE-WALL SENSORS

CJ and Technology

If law enforcement agents need a warrant to use thermal imagers, what about radar that can "see" through walls? Such devices, employed by numerous law enforcement agencies in the United States, use radio waves to detect movement from a distance of more than fifty feet. A display shows the movement, giving officers an idea—though not an actual picture—of human activity on the other side of the wall.

In December 2014, these radar devices were mentioned for the first time during a criminal case. U.S. marshals, after tracking a fugitive to a home in Wichita, Kansas, used a sensor to establish "reasonable suspicion" that the suspect was inside before forcing the door open. A judge upheld the suspect's eventual conviction, but warned that "the government's warrantless use of such a powerful tool to search inside homes poses grave Fourth Amendment questions."

Thinking about Through-the-Wall Sensors
In this chapter, we have studied Supreme Court rulings disallowing warrantless searches based on drug-dog sniffs and thermal imaging devices. Given these precedents, how do you think the Court would rule on the use of a through-the-wall sensor to justify a warrantless search?

roberthyrons/Getty Images

Katz v. United States (discussed earlier in this section) established that recorded conversations are inadmissible as evidence unless certain procedures are followed.

In general, law enforcement officers can use electronic surveillance only if consent is given by one of the parties to be monitored, or, in the absence of such consent, with a warrant.[44] For the warrant to be valid, it must:

1. Detail with "particularity" the conversations that are to be overheard.

2. Name the suspects and the places that will be under surveillance.

3. Show probable cause to believe that a specific crime has been or will be committed.[45]

Once the specific information has been gathered, the law enforcement officers must end the electronic surveillance immediately.[46] In any case, the surveillance cannot last more than thirty days without a judicial extension.

FORCE MULTIPLYING Certain pervasive forms of electronic surveillance are allowed under the theory that people who are in public places have no reasonable expectation of privacy. This theory, generally upheld by American courts,[47] allows for the use of a number of technological *force multipliers,* or devices that allow law enforcement agencies to expand their capabilities without a significant increase in personnel. Perhaps the most pervasive force multiplier is closed-circuit television surveillance (CCTV). This form of surveillance relies on strategically placed video cameras to record and transmit all activities in a targeted area. New York City's CCTV system uses about three thousand cameras to cover much of that city's midtown and downtown areas. Several other large cities, such as Boston and Los Angeles, employ hundreds of public surveillance cameras.

Another popular force multiplier involves computerized infrared cameras that take digital photos of license plates. Usually mounted on police cars, these *automatic license place recognition (ALPR)* devices convert the images to text. Then the numbers are instantly checked against databases that contain records of the license plates of stolen cars and automobiles driven by a wide variety of targets, from wanted felons to citizens with unpaid parking tickets. In heavy-traffic areas, ALPR units can check thousands of license plates each hour.

6-2g Cell Phones and the Fourth Amendment

Given the pervasiveness of cell phones in everyday life and the amount of information stored on these "mobile computers," it should come as no surprise that the devices raise a number of questions about privacy and police searches. In 2014, the Supreme Court ruled, unanimously, that police officers need a warrant to search the contents of cell phones belonging to suspects they have just arrested.[48] As we saw earlier in this section, law enforcement agents may, in many instances, carry out a warrantless search on an arrestee's body following an arrest. Because of the vast amounts of personal information on cell phones, the Court decided that when such searches are conducted, cell phones deserve greater protections than items such as wallets or cigarette packets. Furthermore, recall that the justification for a search

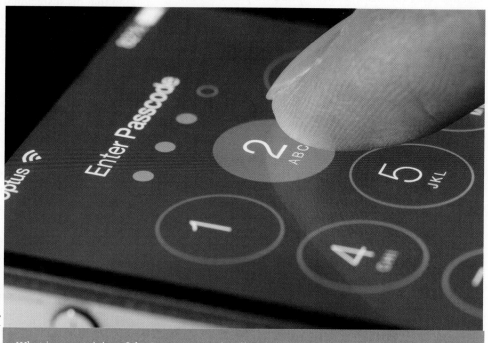

yngerman/ShutterStock.com

What is your opinion of the Supreme Court's ruling that police officers need a warrant to search the contents of arrestees' cell phones in most circumstances?

incidental to an arrest is to confiscate weapons or evidence. Once a cell phone has been secured by police, the arrestee will not be able to "delete incriminating data" and the "data on the phone can endanger no one"—so no further search of the cell phone's contents is justified.[49]

In his opinion, Chief Justice John G. Roberts acknowledged that the Court's decision would "have an impact on the ability of law enforcement to combat crime." But, he added, "Privacy comes at a cost."[50] Practically, the ruling does not mean the end of cell phone searches. Rather, it means that police will need to get a warrant before engaging in such searches or will need the consent of the cell phone owner. In many instances, such consent is given despite it being against a suspect's best interests.

6-3 WHEN CAN POLICE STOP AND FRISK SUSPECTS?

Two experienced Chicago police officers were standing by their patrol car when a woman approached. She told the officers that she had just purchased illegal drugs from a man and provided them with the suspect's physical description and the location of his drug-selling activity. The police officers went to the location—in an area known to both as a hotspot for drug dealing—and saw a man matching the suspect's description clasp hands with another man. Believing that they had just witnessed a drug deal, the officers stopped the suspect, patted him down, and, after finding heroin, made an arrest.

Under the circumstances, these two law enforcement agents believed that they had *reasonable suspicion* that the man had committed a crime. When reasonable suspicion exists, police officers may *stop and frisk* a suspect. In a stop and frisk, law enforcement officers (1) briefly detain a person they reasonably believe to be suspicious, and (2) if they believe the person to be armed, proceed to pat down, or "frisk," that person's outer clothing.[51]

6-3a The Elusive Definition of Reasonable Suspicion

Like so many elements of police work, the decision of whether to stop a suspect is based on the balancing of conflicting priorities. On the one hand, a police officer feels a sense of urgency to act when he or she believes that criminal activity is occurring or is about to occur. On the other hand, law enforcement agents do not want to harass innocent individuals, especially if doing so runs afoul of the U.S. Constitution. In stop-and-frisk law, this balancing act rests on the fulcrum of reasonable suspicion.

LO6-3 **TERRY V. OHIO** The precedent for the ever-elusive definition of a "reasonable" suspicion in stop-and-frisk situations was established in *Terry v. Ohio* (1968).[52] In that case, a detective named McFadden observed two men (one of whom was Terry) acting strangely in downtown Cleveland. The men would walk past a certain store, peer into the window, and then stop at a street corner and confer. While they were talking, another man joined the conversation and then left quickly. Several minutes later, the three men met again at another corner a few blocks away. Detective McFadden believed the trio were planning to break into the store. He approached them, told them who he was, and asked for identification. After receiving a mumbled response, the detective frisked the three men and found handguns on two of them, who were tried and convicted of carrying concealed weapons.

The Supreme Court upheld the conviction, ruling that Detective McFadden had reasonable cause to believe that the men were armed and dangerous and that swift action was necessary to protect himself and other citizens in the area.[53] The Court accepted McFadden's interpretation of the unfolding scene as based on objective facts and practical conclusions. It therefore concluded that his suspicion was reasonable.

THE "TOTALITY OF THE CIRCUMSTANCES" TEST
For the most part, the judicial system has refrained from placing restrictions on police officers' ability to make stops. In the *Terry* case, the Supreme Court did say that an officer must have "specific and articulable facts" to support the decision to make a stop, but added that the facts may be "taken together with rational inferences."[54] The Court has consistently ruled that because of their practical experience, law enforcement agents are in a unique position to make such inferences and should be given a good deal of freedom in doing so.

In the years since the *Terry* case was decided, the Court has settled on a "totality of the circumstances" test to determine whether a stop is based on reasonable suspicion.[55] In 2002, for example, the Court ruled that a U.S. Border Patrol agent's stop of a minivan in Arizona was reasonable.[56] On being approached by the Border Patrol car, the driver had stiffened, slowed down his van, and avoided making eye contact with the agent. Furthermore, the children in the van waved at the officer in a mechanical manner, as if ordered to do so. The agent pulled over the van and found 128 pounds of marijuana.

In his opinion, Chief Justice William Rehnquist pointed out that the conduct of the driver and his passengers might have been unremarkable on a busy city highway, but on an unpaved road thirty miles from the Mexican border it was enough to reasonably arouse the agent's suspicion.[57] The justices also made clear that the need to prevent terrorist attacks is part of the "totality of the circumstances," and, therefore, law enforcement agents will have more leeway to make stops near U.S. borders.

A police officer frisks a suspect in San Francisco, California. *What is the main purpose behind a frisk? When are police justified in frisking someone?*

6-3b A Stop

The terms *stop* and *frisk* are often used in concert, but they describe two separate acts. A **stop** takes place when a law enforcement officer has reasonable suspicion that criminal activity has taken place or is about to take place. Because an investigatory stop is not an arrest, there are limits to the extent police can detain someone who has been stopped. For example, in one situation an airline traveler and his luggage were detained for ninety minutes while the police waited for a drug-sniffing dog to arrive. The Supreme Court ruled that the initial stop of the passenger was constitutional, but that the ninety-minute wait was excessive.[58]

In 2004, the Court held that police officers can require suspects to identify themselves during a stop that is otherwise valid under the *Terry* ruling.[59] The case involved a Nevada rancher who was fined $250 for refusing to give his name to a police officer investigating a possible assault. The defendant argued that such requests force citizens to incriminate themselves against their will, which is prohibited, as we shall see later in the chapter, by the Fifth Amendment. Justice Anthony Kennedy wrote, however, that "asking questions is an essential part of police investigations" that would be made much more difficult if officers could not determine the identity of a suspect.[60] The ruling validated "stop-and-identify" laws in twenty states and numerous cities and towns.

6-3c A Frisk

The Supreme Court has stated that a **frisk** should be a protective measure. Police officers cannot conduct a frisk as a "fishing expedition" simply to try to find items besides weapons, such as illegal narcotics, on a suspect.[61] A frisk does not necessarily follow a stop and in fact may occur only when the officer is justified in thinking that the safety of police officers or other citizens may be endangered. So, in the case of the two Chicago police officers that opened this section, an Illinois appeals court ruled that while the initial stop was acceptable, the officers had violated the suspect's right by frisking him. The state court was unwilling to accept the contention that "drugs and guns go together" as sufficient grounds for a pat-down.[62]

Like stops, frisks must be supported by reasonable suspicion. The Illinois court rejected the argument that the Chicago police officers had objective reasons to fear for their safety. In the *Terry* case, by contrast, the Supreme Court accepted that Detective McFadden reasonably believed that the three suspects posed a threat. The suspects refused to answer McFadden's questions. Although they were within their rights to do so, because

---

Stop A brief detention of a person by law enforcement agents for questioning.

Frisk A pat-down or minimal search by police to discover weapons.

they had not been arrested, their refusal provided him with sufficient motive for the frisk. In 2009, the Court extended the stop-and-frisk authority by ruling that a police officer can order a passenger in a car that has been pulled over for a traffic violation to submit to a pat-down.[63] To do so, the officer must have a reasonable suspicion that the suspect may be armed and dangerous.

6-4 WHAT IS REQUIRED TO MAKE AN ARREST?

As happened in the *Terry* case discussed earlier, a stop and frisk may lead to an **arrest.** An arrest is the act of apprehending a suspect for the purpose of detaining him or her on a criminal charge. It is important to understand the difference between a stop and an arrest. In the eyes of the law, a stop is a relatively brief intrusion on a citizen's rights, whereas an arrest involves a deprivation of liberty. A person under arrest therefore deserves a full range of constitutional protections. (See Figure 6.3 to better understand how a stop differs from an arrest.) Consequently, while a stop can be made based on reasonable suspicion, a law enforcement officer needs probable cause, as defined earlier, to make an arrest.[64]

Arrest To deprive the liberty of a person suspected of criminal activity.

6-4a Elements of an Arrest

When is somebody under arrest? The easy—and incorrect—answer would be whenever the police officer says so. In fact, the state of being under arrest is dependent not only on the actions of the law enforcement officers but also on the perception of the suspect. Suppose Mr. Smith is stopped by plainclothes detectives, driven to the police station, and detained for three hours for questioning. During this time, the police never tell Mr. Smith he is under arrest, and in fact, he is free to leave at any time. But if Mr. Smith or any other reasonable person *believes* he is not free to leave, then, according to the Supreme Court, that person is in fact under arrest and should receive the necessary constitutional protections.[65]

LO6-4

Criminal justice professor Rolando V. del Carmen of Sam Houston State University has identified four elements that must be present for an arrest to take place:

1. The *intent* to arrest. In a stop, though it may entail slight inconvenience and a short detention period, there is no intent on the part of the law enforcement officer to deprive the suspect of her or his freedom. Therefore, there is no arrest. As intent is a subjective term, it is sometimes difficult to determine whether the police officer intended to arrest. In situations when the intent is unclear, courts often rely—as in our hypothetical case of Mr. Smith—on the perception of the arrestee.[66]

FIGURE 6.3 THE DIFFERENCE BETWEEN A STOP AND AN ARREST

	Stop	Arrest
Justification	Reasonable suspicion only	Probable cause
Warrant	None	Required in some, but not all, situations
Intent of Officer	To investigate suspicious activity	To make a formal charge against the suspect
Search	May frisk, or "pat down," for weapons	May conduct a full search for weapons or evidence
Scope of Search	Outer clothing only	Area within the suspect's immediate control or "reach"

PhotoDisc

Both stops and arrests are considered seizures because both police actions involve the restriction of an individual's freedom to "walk away." Both must be justified by a showing of reasonableness as well. You should be aware, however, of the differences between a stop and an arrest. *During a stop,* police can interrogate the person and make a limited search of his or her outer clothing. In certain circumstances, such as the discovery of an illegal weapon during the stop, the officers may arrest the person. *If an arrest is made,* the suspect is now under police control and is protected by the U.S. Constitution in a number of ways that will be discussed later in the chapter.

2. The *authority* to arrest. State laws give police officers the authority to place citizens under custodial arrest, or take them into *custody*, a concept defined later in the chapter.

3. *Seizure or detention*. A necessary part of an arrest is the detention of the subject. Detention is considered to have occurred as soon as the arrested individual submits to the control of the officer, whether peacefully or under the threat or use of force.

4. The *understanding* of the person that she or he has been arrested. Through either words—such as "you are now under arrest"—or actions, the person taken into custody must understand that an arrest has taken place. When a suspect has been forcibly subdued by the police, handcuffed, and placed in a patrol car, he or she is believed to understand that an arrest has been made. This understanding may be lacking if the person is intoxicated, insane, or unconscious.[67]

6-4b Arrests with a Warrant

When law enforcement officers have established probable cause to arrest an individual who is not in police custody, they obtain an **arrest warrant** for that person. An arrest warrant, similar to a search warrant, contains information such as the name of the person suspected and the crime he or she is suspected of having committed. (See Figure 6.4 for an example of an arrest warrant.) Judges or magistrates issue arrest warrants after first determining that the law enforcement officers have indeed established probable cause.

ENTERING A DWELLING There is a perception that an arrest warrant gives law enforcement officers the authority to enter a dwelling without first announcing themselves. This is not accurate. In *Wilson v. Arkansas* (1995),[68] the Supreme Court reiterated the requirement that police officers must knock and announce their identity and purpose before entering a dwelling. Under certain conditions, known as **exigent circumstances,** law enforcement officers need not announce themselves. These circumstances include situations in which the officers have a reasonable belief of any of the following:

▸ The suspect is armed and poses a strong threat of violence to the officers or others inside the dwelling.

▸ Persons inside the dwelling are in the process of destroying evidence or escaping because of the presence of the police.

▸ A felony is being committed at the time the officers enter.[69]

THE WAITING PERIOD The Supreme Court severely weakened the practical impact of the "knock-and-announce" rule with its decision in *Hudson v. Michigan* (2006).[70] In that case, Detroit police did not knock before entering the defendant's home with a warrant. Instead, they announced themselves and then waited only three to five seconds before making their entrance, not the fifteen to twenty seconds suggested by a prior Court ruling.[71] The defendant argued that the drugs found during the subsequent search were inadmissible because the law enforcement agents did not follow proper procedure.

By a 5–4 margin, the Court disagreed. In his majority opinion, Justice Antonin Scalia stated that an improper "knock and announce" is not unreasonable enough to provide defendants with a "get-out-of-jail-free card" by disqualifying evidence uncovered on the basis of a valid

Arrest Warrant A written order, based on probable cause and issued by a judge or magistrate, commanding that the person named on the warrant be arrested by the police.

Exigent Circumstances Situations that require extralegal or exceptional actions by the police.

FIGURE 6.4 EXAMPLE OF AN ARREST WARRANT

United States District Court

DISTRICT OF

UNITED STATES OF AMERICA
V.

WARRANT FOR ARREST

CASE NUMBER:

To: The United States Marshal
and any Authorized United States Officer

YOU ARE HEREBY COMMANDED to arrest ___
name

and bring him or her forthwith to the nearest magistrate to answer a(n)

☐ Indictment ☐ Information ☐ Complaint ☐ Order of Court ☐ Violation Notice ☐ Probation Violation Petition

charging him or her with (brief description of offense)

in violation of Title ___ United States Code, Section(s) ___

Name of Issuing Officer | Title of Issuing Officer

Signature of Issuing Officer | Date and Location

Bail fixed at $ ___ by ___
Name of Judicial Officer

RETURN

This warrant was received and executed with the arrest of the above-named defendant at ___

DATE RECEIVED | NAME AND TITLE OF ARRESTING OFFICER | SIGNATURE OF ARRESTING OFFICER

DATE OF ARREST

search warrant.[72] Thus, the exclusionary rule, discussed earlier in this chapter, would no longer apply under such circumstances. Legal experts still advise, however, that police observe a reasonable waiting period after knocking and announcing to be certain that any evidence found during the subsequent search will stand up in court.[73]

6-4c Arrests without a Warrant

Arrest warrants are not always required, and in fact, most arrests are made on the scene without a warrant. A law enforcement officer may make a **warrantless arrest** in any of these circumstances:

1. The offense is committed in the presence of the officer.
2. The officer has probable cause to believe that the suspect has committed a particular crime.
3. The time lost in obtaining a warrant would allow the suspect to escape or destroy evidence, and the officer has probable cause to make an arrest.[74]

The type of crime also comes to bear in questions concerning arrests without a warrant. As a general rule, officers can make a warrantless arrest for a crime they did not see if they have probable cause to believe that a felony has been committed. For misdemeanors, the crime must have been committed in the presence of the officer for a warrantless arrest to be valid. According to a 2001 Supreme Court ruling, even an arrest for a misdemeanor that involves "gratuitous humiliations" imposed by a police officer "exercising extremely poor judgment" is valid as long as the officer can satisfy probable cause requirements.[75] That case involved a Texas mother who was handcuffed, taken away from her two young children, and placed in jail for failing to wear her seat belt.

In certain situations, warrantless arrests are unlawful even though a police officer can establish probable cause. In *Payton v. New York* (1980),[76] for example, the Supreme Court held that when exigent circumstances do not exist and the suspect does not give law enforcement

Warrantless Arrest An arrest made without a prior warrant for the action.

Interrogation The direct questioning of a suspect to gather evidence of criminal activity and to try to gain a confession.

Coercion The use of physical force or mental intimidation to compel a person to do something—such as confess to committing a crime—against her or his will.

officers consent to enter a dwelling, the officers cannot force themselves in for the purpose of making a warrantless arrest. A year after the *Payton* ruling, the Court expanded its holding to cover the homes of third parties.[77] Thus, if police wish to arrest a criminal suspect in another person's home, they cannot enter that home to arrest the suspect without first obtaining a search warrant, a process we discussed earlier in the chapter.

CAREER TIP Once a suspect is arrested, he or she is subject to standard booking procedure, which includes providing personal information, being photographed, and being fingerprinted. This process is overseen by a *booking technician*, who may or may not be a sworn police officer.

6-5 WHAT ARE THE *MIRANDA* RIGHTS?

After the Pledge of Allegiance, there is perhaps no recitation that comes more readily to the American mind than the *Miranda* warning:

> You have the right to remain silent. If you give up that right, anything you say can and will be used against you in a court of law. You have the right to speak with an attorney and to have the attorney present during questioning. If you so desire and cannot afford one, an attorney will be appointed for you without charge before questioning.

The *Miranda* warning is not a mere prop. It strongly affects one of the most important aspects of any criminal investigation—the **interrogation,** or questioning of a suspect from whom the police want to get information concerning a crime and perhaps a confession.

6-5a The Legal Basis for *Miranda*

The Fifth Amendment guarantees protection against self-incrimination. In other words, as we shall see again in Chapter 8, a defendant cannot be required to provide information about his or her own criminal activity. A defendant's choice *not* to incriminate himself or herself cannot be interpreted as a sign of guilt by a jury in a criminal trial. A confession, or admission of guilt, is by definition a statement of self-incrimination. How, then, to reconcile the Fifth Amendment with the critical need of law enforcement officers to gain confessions? The answer involves the concept of **coercion,** or the use of physical or psychological duress to obtain a confession.

THE *MIRANDA* CASE The Supreme Court first asserted that a confession could not be physically coerced in a 1936 case concerning a defendant who was beaten and whipped until he confessed to a murder.[78] It was not until 1966, however, that the Court handed down its landmark decision in *Miranda v. Arizona*.[79]

The case involved Ernesto Miranda, a produce worker who had been arrested three years earlier in Phoenix and charged with kidnapping and rape. Detectives questioned Miranda for two hours before gaining a confession of guilt. At no time was Miranda informed that he had a right to have a lawyer present. The Court overturned Miranda's conviction, stating that police interrogations are, by their very nature, coercive and therefore deny suspects their constitutional right against self-incrimination by "forcing" them to confess.

MIRANDA RIGHTS The concept of *Miranda* rights, established in this case, is based on what University of Columbia law professor H. Richard Uviller called *inherent coercion*. This term refers to the assumption that even if a police officer does not lay a hand on a suspect, the general atmosphere of an interrogation is in and of itself coercive.[80]

Though the *Miranda* case is best remembered for the procedural requirement it spurred, at the time the Supreme Court was more concerned about the treatment of suspects during interrogation. The Court found that routine police interrogation strategies, such as leaving suspects alone in a room for several hours before questioning them, were inherently coercive. Therefore, the Court reasoned, every suspect needed protection from coercion, not just those who had been physically abused. The *Miranda* warning is a result of this need. In theory, if the warning is not given to a suspect before an interrogation, the fruits of that interrogation, including a confession, are invalid.

Photo by Chris Hondros/Getty Images

What aspects of the situation shown in this photo indicate that the Aspen (Colorado) police officer is required to "Mirandize" the suspect before asking him any questions, even if the officer never formally places the suspect under arrest?

6-5b When a *Miranda* Warning Is Required

As we shall see, a *Miranda* warning is not necessary under several conditions, such as when no questions are asked of the suspect. Generally, *Miranda* requirements apply only when a suspect is in **custody.** In a series of rulings since *Miranda*, the Supreme Court has defined custody as an arrest or a situation in which a reasonable person would not feel free to leave.[81] Consequently, a **custodial interrogation** occurs when a suspect is under arrest or is deprived of her or his freedom in a significant manner. Remember, a *Miranda* warning is only required before a custodial interrogation takes place. For example, if four police officers enter a suspect's bedroom at 4:00 A.M., wake him, and form a circle around him, then they must give him a *Miranda* warning before questioning. Even though the suspect has not been arrested, he will "not feel free to go where he please[s]."[82]

Miranda Rights The constitutional rights of accused persons taken into custody by law enforcement officials, such as the right to remain silent and the right to counsel.

Custody The forceful detention of a person or the perception that a person is not free to leave the immediate vicinity.

Custodial Interrogation The questioning of a suspect after that person has been taken into custody. In this situation, the suspect must be read his or her *Miranda* rights before interrogation can begin.

6-5c When a *Miranda* Warning Is Not Required

LO6-5 A *Miranda* warning is not necessary in a number of situations:

1. When the police do not ask the suspect any questions that are *testimonial* in nature. Such questions are designed to elicit information that may be used against the suspect in court. Note that "routine booking questions," such as the suspect's name, address, height, and eye color, do not require a *Miranda* warning. Even though answering these questions may provide incriminating evidence (especially if the person answering is a prime suspect), the Supreme Court has held that they are absolutely necessary if the police are to do their jobs.[83] (Imagine the officer not being able to ask a suspect her or his name.)

2. When the police have not focused on a suspect and are questioning witnesses at the scene of a crime.

3. When a person volunteers information before the police have asked a question.

4. When the suspect has given a private statement to a friend or some other acquaintance. *Miranda* does not apply to these statements so long as the government did not orchestrate the situation.

5. During a stop and frisk, when no arrest has been made.

6. During a traffic stop.[84]

In 1984, the Supreme Court also created a "public-safety exception" to the *Miranda* rule. The case involved a police officer who, after feeling an empty shoulder holster on a man he had just arrested, asked the suspect the location of the gun without informing him of his *Miranda* rights. The Court ruled that the gun was admissible as evidence because the police's duty to protect the public is more important than a suspect's *Miranda* rights.[85] In April 2013, federal law enforcement agents relied on this exception to question Boston Marathon bomber Dzhokhar Tsarnaev from his hospital bedside without first "Mirandizing" him. Once the agents were satisfied that Tsarnaev knew of no other active plots or threats to public safety, they read the suspect his *Miranda* rights in the presence of a lawyer.[86]

WAIVING *MIRANDA* Suspects can *waive* their Fifth Amendment rights and speak to a police officer, but only if the waiver is made voluntarily. Silence on the part of a suspect does not mean that his or her *Miranda* protections have been relinquished. To waive their rights, suspects must state—either in writing or orally—that they understand those rights and that they will voluntarily answer questions without the presence of counsel.

To ensure that the suspect's rights are upheld, prosecutors are required to prove by a preponderance of the evidence that the suspect "knowingly and intelligently" waived his or her *Miranda* rights.[87] To make the waiver perfectly clear, police will ask suspects two questions in addition to giving the *Miranda* warning:

1. Do you understand your rights as I have read them to you?

2. Knowing your rights, are you willing to talk to another law enforcement officer or me?

If the suspect indicates that she or he does not want to speak to the officer, thereby invoking her or his right to silence, the officer must *immediately* stop any questioning.[88] Similarly, if the suspect requests a lawyer, the police can ask no further questions until an attorney is present.[89]

CLEAR INTENT The suspect must be absolutely clear about her or his intention to stop the questioning or have a lawyer present. In *Davis v. United States* (1994),[90] the Supreme Court upheld the interrogation of a suspect after he said, "Maybe I should talk to a lawyer." The Court found that this statement was too ambiguous, holding that police officers should not be required to "read the minds" of suspects who make vague declarations.

Along these same lines, in *Berghuis v. Thompkins* (2010),[91] the Court upheld the conviction of a suspect who implicated himself in a murder after remaining mostly silent during nearly three hours of police questioning. The defendant claimed that he had invoked his *Miranda* rights by being uncommunicative with the interrogating officers. The Court disagreed, saying that silence is not enough—a suspect must actually state that he or she wishes to cut off questioning for the *Miranda* protections to apply.

6-5d False Confessions

While observing more than two hundred interrogations over a nine-month period in northern California, University of San Francisco law professor Richard Leo noted that more than 80 percent of the suspects waived their *Miranda* rights.[92] Apparently, the suspects wanted to appear cooperative, a "willingness to please" that contributes to the troubling phenomenon of *false confessions* in the American criminal justice system.

COERCION AND FALSE CONFESSIONS A **false confession** occurs when a suspect admits to a crime that she or he did not actually commit. Given that juries tend to place a great deal of weight on admissions, sometimes to the exclusion of other evidence, false confessions can have disastrous consequences for the defendant in court.[93] About 30 percent of wrongful convictions overturned by DNA evidence were at least partially the result of a false confession.[94]

The Reid Technique According to Saul Kassin, a professor of psychology at Williams College in Williamstown, Massachusetts, there are three general types of false confessions:

1. *Voluntary.* The suspect is seeking attention, or is delusional and thinks he or she did commit the crime.

2. *Internalized.* The suspect is a vulnerable person, suffering from the stress of the interrogation, who comes to believe that he or she committed the crime.

3. *Compliant.* The suspect knows he or she is innocent, but decides—under police influence—that it is in his or her best interests to confess to the crime.

False Confession An admission of guilt when the confessor did not, in fact, commit the crime.

DETECTIVE

Job Description:

▶ Collect evidence and obtain facts pertaining to criminal cases.

▶ Conduct interviews, observe suspects, examine records, and help with raids and busts. Some detectives are assigned to multiagency task forces that deal with specific types of crime, like drug trafficking or gang activity.

What Kind of Training Is Required?

▶ Two to five years of experience as a police officer are required before taking the test to become a detective.

▶ Larger departments require sixty units of college credit or an associate's degree.

Annual Salary Range?

▶ $40,000–$122,000

iStockPhoto.com/Karen Mower

GETTING LINKEDIN

The most common detective position offered on LinkedIn is in the field of "loss prevention," which, as you learned in Chapter 4, involves preventing shoplifting at private businesses. Like public law enforcement officers, loss prevention detectives "utilize CCTV equipment," "use the latest in advanced interviewing and interrogation techniques," and "work independently," to quote a recent posting from a retail store in Hampshire County, Massachusetts.

Kassin believes that last two categories of false confessions are often "coerced."[95] Indeed, the Reid Technique, used widely by American law enforcement, is premised on the assumption that all interrogation subjects are guilty. Police officers trained in this method reject any denials during the interrogation. They are also taught to minimize the moral seriousness of the crime, and to present the suspect's actions as the lesser of two evils. ("Was this your idea, or did your buddies talk you into it?") When the suspect finally does admit to the crime, he or she is to be congratulated and immediately asked for corroborating details.[96]

Pressure Points Critics believe that the Reid Technique creates feelings of helplessness in the suspect, and turns a confession into an "escape hatch" from the unpleasantness of the interrogation.[97] In 1983, for example, after five hours of questioning with no lawyer present, Henry Lee McCollum told police that he was involved in the rape and murder of an eleven-year-old girl. He was eventually sentenced to death for the crimes. "I had never been under this much pressure, with a person hollering at me and threatening me," McCollum said in 2014, when a North Carolina judge declared him innocent and released him from prison. "I just made up a story and gave it to them so they would let me go home."[98]

Another potential problem with the Reid Technique, noted earlier, is that it is predicated on the assumption that the suspect is guilty. Because both guilty and innocent suspects show stress when being interrogated by police, the interrogator may be "fooled" by an innocent person's evasive and nervous behavior.

The PEACE method, an alternative method of police interrogation, resembles a journalistic interview rather than psychological combat, and is part of the training of every police officer in England. Instead of relying on confrontation, this technique starts with a long series of open-ended questions to gather evidence and information. Then, the suspect is requestioned several times to determine whether there are any obvious discrepancies in his or her story.

RECORDING CONFESSIONS As with body-worn cameras (discussed in the previous chapter), the mandatory videotaping of interrogations has been offered as a means to promote police accountability. Nearly nine hundred law enforcement agencies, including the FBI and the DEA, now regularly record police interviews, particularly as part of felony investigations.[99]

In theory, such recordings will make clear any improper tactics used by law enforcement to gain a confession. In reality, this strategy might not live up to reformers' expectations. As Professor Jennifer Mnookin of the University of California, Los Angeles, points out, there is no guarantee that "judges or jurors can actually tell the difference between true and false confessions, even with the more complete record of interactions that recorded interrogations provide."[100]

Quiz

1. The Fourth Amendment has been interpreted to require _____ _____ that a crime has been or will be committed before a search warrant can be issued.

2. Judges rely on the _____ rule to keep evidence that has been improperly obtained by the police out of criminal courts.

3. A search is a government intrusion on the _____ of an individual.

4. Law enforcement agents do not need a judge's prior approval to conduct a search if the subject of the search gives her or his _____.

5. A police officer can "stop" a suspect if the officer has a _____ suspicion that a criminal act is taking place or is about to take place.

6. Following a stop, a police officer may _____ the suspect for weapons as a protective measure.

7. An arrest occurs when a law enforcement officer takes a suspect into _____ on a criminal charge.

8. If a police officer has prior knowledge of a suspect's criminal activity, he or she must obtain a _____ from a judge or magistrate before arresting the suspect.

9. In most instances, a *Miranda* warning must be read to a suspect _____ a custodial interrogation takes place.

10. A suspect can _____ her or his *Miranda* rights, but this must be done "knowingly and intentionally."

Answers can be found in the Answers section in the back of the book.

7 Courts and the Quest for Justice

Orhan Cam/Shutterstock.com

LEARNING OBJECTIVES

After studying this chapter, you will be able to . . .

7-1 Define *jurisdiction* and contrast geographic and subject-matter jurisdiction.

7-2 Explain the difference between trial and appellate courts.

7-3 Explain briefly how a case is brought to the Supreme Court.

7-4 List the different names given to public prosecutors, and indicate the general powers they have.

7-5 Explain why defense attorneys must often defend clients they know to be guilty.

After you finish this chapter, go to **PAGES 156–157** for **STUDY TOOLS**

Business as Usual

On the afternoon of October 21, 2014, without much fanfare, Ahmed Abu Khattala made his first appearance in a federal courthouse in Washington, D.C. Unshackled, wearing a black, zip-up hooded sweatshirt, unencumbered by any extra security, he heard the charges against him and swore to tell the truth, just like any other person charged with a crime. His public defender told the judge that Khattala was not guilty, bemoaning the "utter lack of evidence" against him, as she would for any client.

Khattala was not, however, your average criminal defendant. He was facing the death penalty for being the alleged ringleader of a 2012 terrorist attack that killed the U.S. ambassador and three other Americans in Benghazi, Libya. Had Khattala been captured five years earlier, there likely would have been an extensive debate over whether he should have been tried in a civilian criminal court. The alternative of sending him to the U.S. Naval Base at Guantánamo Bay, Cuba (GTMO), to appear before a military tribunal would have been presented as the better national security alternative.

Such tribunals offer fewer protections to suspected terrorists than those offered in civilian courts, and were therefore seen as more of a "sure thing" for gaining convictions.

That has not turned out to be the case. As of 2015, military tribunals have convicted only eight GTMO detainees. Furthermore, the military's efforts to prosecute Khalid Sheikh Mohammed, the self-proclaimed mastermind behind the September 11, 2001, terrorist attacks, have been plagued by numerous missteps and delays, with no end in sight. Conversely, from 2001 to 2014, federal prosecutors operating in civilian criminal courts convicted sixty-seven terrorist defendants captured on foreign soil. Voicing his support for the criminal justice system's counterterrorism role at the time of Khattala's arrest, then U.S. attorney general Eric Holder said, "We have shown, time and again, that upholding the rule of law is not inconsistent with safeguarding our national security."

In 2014, Ahmed Abu Khattala was transferred to an American courtroom to face charges for directing this terrorist attack on the U.S. Consulate in Benghazi, Libya, two years earlier. Do you think that foreign terrorist suspects like Khattala should receive the same rights under the U.S. Constitution as other criminal suspects? Explain your answer.

Reuters/Esam Al-Fetori

7-1 WHAT ROLE DO COURTS PLAY IN SOCIETY?

In 2014, angered by the slow pace of military tribunal hearings involving alleged September 11 planner Khalid Sheikh Mohammed, Charlie Clyne called the proceedings "a farce." "These parasites did it. They're guilty," said Clyne, whose wife was killed in the 2001 terrorist attacks. "Let's try them, fairly. And then kill them."[1] Clyne's frustrations—and those of many other September 11 victims and their families—are centered on the belief that *justice* has not yet been done in the case of Mohammed and his co-conspirators.

Famed jurist Roscoe Pound once characterized "justice" as society's demand "that serious offenders be convicted and punished," while at the same time "the innocent and unfortunate are not oppressed."[2] This somewhat idealistic definition obscures the fact that there are two sides to each court proceeding. While Clyne understandably has strong feelings about Mohammed's fate, American legal traditions allow a person accused of any crime, no matter how heinous, the chance to prove his or her innocence before a neutral decision maker. On a more practical level, then, a court is a place where arguments are settled. At best, the court provides a just environment in which the basis of an argument can be decided through the application of the law.

Courts have extensive powers in our criminal justice system: they can bring the authority of the state to seize property and to restrict individual liberty. Given that the rights to own property and to enjoy personal freedom are enshrined in the U.S. Constitution, a court's *legitimacy* in taking such measures must be unquestioned by society. This legitimacy is based on two factors: impartiality and independence.[3] In theory, each party involved in a courtroom dispute must have an equal chance to present its case and must be secure in the belief that no outside factors are going to influence the decision rendered by the court. In reality, as we shall see over the next three chapters, it does not always work that way.

7-1a Due Process and Crime Control in the Courts

As mentioned in Chapter 1, the criminal justice system has been seen as having two sets of underlying values: due process and crime control. Due process values focus on protecting the rights of the individual, whereas crime control values stress the punishment and repression of criminal conduct. The competing nature of these two value systems is often evident in the nation's courts.

THE DUE PROCESS FUNCTION The primary concern of early American courts was to protect the rights of the individual against the power of the state. Memories of injustices suffered at the hands of the British monarchy were still strong, and most of the procedural rules that we have discussed in this textbook were created with the express purpose of giving the individual a "fair chance" against the government in any courtroom proceedings. Therefore, the due process function of the courts is to

Why is it important that American criminal courtrooms are places of impartiality and independence?

Comstock/Thinkstock

protect individuals from the unfair advantages that the government—with its immense resources—automatically enjoys in legal battles. Seen in this light, constitutional guarantees such as the right to counsel, the right to a jury trial, and protection from self-incrimination are equalizers in the "contest" between the state and the individual.

THE CRIME CONTROL FUNCTION Advocates of crime control distinguish between the court's obligation to be fair to the accused and its obligation to be fair to society. The crime control function of the courts emphasizes punishment and retribution—criminals must suffer for the harm done to society, and it is the courts' responsibility to see that they do so. Given this responsibility to protect the public, deter criminal behavior, and "get criminals off the streets," the courts should not be concerned solely with giving the accused a fair chance. Rather than using due process rules as "equalizers," the courts should use them as protection against blatantly unconstitutional acts.

For example, a detective who beats a suspect with a tire iron to get a confession has obviously infringed on the suspect's constitutional rights. If, however, the detective uses trickery to gain a confession, the court should allow the confession to stand because it is not in society's interest that law enforcement agents be deterred from outwitting criminals.

7-1b The Rehabilitation Function

A third view of the court's responsibility is based on the "medical model" of the criminal justice system. In this model, criminals are analogous to patients, and the courts perform the role of physicians who dispense "treatment."[4] The criminal is seen as sick, not evil, and therefore treatment is morally justified. Of course, treatment varies from case to case, and some criminals require harsh penalties such as incarceration. In other cases, however, it may not be in society's best interest for the criminal to be punished according to the formal rules of the justice system. Perhaps the criminal can be rehabilitated to become a productive member of society and thus save taxpayers the costs of incarceration or other punishment.

7-1c The Bureaucratic Function

To a certain extent, the crime control, due process, and rehabilitation functions of a court are secondary to its bureaucratic function. In general, a court may have the goal of protecting society or protecting the rights of the individual, but on a day-to-day basis that court has the more pressing task of dealing with the cases brought before it. Like any bureaucracy, a court is concerned with speed and efficiency, and loftier concepts such as justice can be secondary to a judge's need to wrap up a particular case before six o'clock so that administrative deadlines can be met. Indeed, many observers feel that the primary adversarial relationship in the courts is not between the two parties involved but between the ideal of justice and the reality of bureaucratic limitations.[5]

7-2 HOW DO AMERICAN COURTS OPERATE?

One of the most often cited limitations of the American judicial system is its complex nature. In truth, the United States does not have a single judicial system, but fifty-two different systems—one for each state, the District of Columbia, and the federal government. As each state has its own unique judiciary with its own set of rules, some of which may be in conflict with the federal judiciary, it is helpful at this point to discuss some basics—jurisdiction, trial and appellate courts, and the dual court system.

7-2a Jurisdiction

 LO7-1 In Latin, *juris* means "law," and *diction* means "to speak." Thus, **jurisdiction** literally refers to the power "to speak the law." Before any court can hear a case, it must have jurisdiction over the persons involved in the case or its subject matter. The jurisdiction of every court, even the United States Supreme Court, is limited in some way.

GEOGRAPHIC JURISDICTION
One limitation is geographic. Generally, a court can exercise its authority over residents of a certain area. A state trial court, for example, normally has jurisdictional authority over crimes committed in a particular area of the state, such as a county or a district. A state's highest court (often called the state

supreme court) has jurisdictional authority over the entire state, and the United States Supreme Court has jurisdiction over the entire country. For the most part, criminal jurisdiction is determined by legislation. The U.S. Congress or a state legislature can determine what acts are illegal within the geographic boundaries it controls, thus giving federal or state courts jurisdiction over those crimes.

Federal versus State Jurisdiction Most criminal laws are state laws, so the majority of all criminal trials are heard in state courts. Many acts that are illegal under state law, however, are also illegal under federal law. What happens when more than one court system has jurisdiction over the same criminal act? As a general rule, when Congress "criminalizes" behavior that is already prohibited under a state criminal code, the federal and state courts both have jurisdiction over that crime unless Congress states otherwise in the initial legislation. Thus, **concurrent jurisdiction,** which occurs when two different court systems have simultaneous jurisdiction over the same case, is quite common.

> **Jurisdiction** The authority of a court to hear and decide cases within an area of the law or a geographic territory.
>
> **Concurrent Jurisdiction** The situation that occurs when two or more courts have the authority to preside over the same criminal case.

AP Images/Steven Mantilla

Following an extensive dogfighting investigation, animal rescue workers load pit bulls into a mobile trailer in Nathalie, Virginia. The dogs' owners were charged with violating federal dogfighting laws and faced those charges in federal criminal court. *Do you think that the federal government should have jurisdiction over a local activity like dogfighting? Why or why not?*

For instance, both the federal courts and the Massachusetts state court system have jurisdiction over Dzhokhar Tsarnaev, convicted of carrying out the Boston Marathon bombings of April 2013. First, in 2015, Tsarnaev faced federal terrorism charges in federal court. At the conclusion of this federal trial, state officials had the option to try him in state court for the killing of Massachusetts Institute of Technology police officer Sean Collier, even if they had to take him from a federal prison cell to do so.

State versus State Jurisdiction Multiple states can also claim jurisdiction over the same defendant or criminal act, depending on state legislation and the circumstances of the crime. For example, if Billy is standing in State A and fatally shoots Frances, who is standing in State B, the two states could have concurrent jurisdiction to try Billy for murder. Similarly, if a property theft takes places in State A but police recover the stolen goods in State B, concurrent jurisdiction could exist. Some states have also passed laws stating that they have jurisdiction over their own citizens who commit crimes in other states, even if there is no other connection between the home state and the criminal act.[6]

The concept of jurisdiction encourages states to cooperate with each other regarding fugitives from the law. In 2014, for example, Michael Leday was suspected of killing two people by running over them with his car in Tucson, Arizona. Leday fled to Kansas City, Missouri, where police apprehended him by following his girlfriend to a hideout. Missouri officials subsequently *extradited* Leday back to Tucson to stand trial for the two murders. **Extradition** is the formal process by which one legal authority, such as a state or a nation, transfers a fugitive or a suspect to another legal authority that has a valid claim on that person.

Extradition The process by which one jurisdiction surrenders a person accused or convicted of violating another jurisdiction's criminal law to the second jurisdiction.

INTERNATIONAL JURISDICTION Under international law, each country has the right to create and enact criminal law for its territory. Therefore, the notion that a nation has jurisdiction over any crimes committed within its borders is well established. The situation becomes more delicate when one nation feels the need to go outside its own territory to enforce its criminal law. International precedent does, however, provide several bases for expanding jurisdiction across international borders.

For example, anti-terrorism efforts have been aided by the principle that the United States has jurisdiction over persons who commit crimes against Americans even when the former are citizens of foreign countries and live outside the United States. In 2012, British authorities extradited Mostafa Kamel Mostafa to New York City to face eleven terrorism-related charges, including helping to orchestrate the kidnapping of American citizens in the Middle East. Three years later, a federal judge sentenced the British cleric to life in prison for his crimes.

SUBJECT-MATTER JURISDICTION Jurisdiction over subject matter also acts as a limitation on the types of cases a court can hear. State court systems include courts of *general* (unlimited) *jurisdiction* and courts of *limited jurisdiction*. Courts of general jurisdiction have no

Orlando Sierra/Getty Images

In 2014, Honduras extradited suspected drug dealer Carlos Lobo, shown here with members of the Honduran military police, to the United States. *Should the possibility that Lobo was shipping cocaine into this country give the American court system jurisdiction over him? Why or why not?*

restrictions on the subject matter they may address, and therefore deal with the most serious felonies and civil cases. Courts of limited jurisdiction, also known as lower courts, handle misdemeanors and civil matters under a certain amount, usually $1,000.

As we will discuss later in the chapter, many states have created special subject-matter courts that only dispose of cases involving a specific crime. For example, a number of jurisdictions have established drug courts to handle an overload of illicit narcotics arrests. Furthermore, under the Uniform Code of Military Justice, the U.S. military has jurisdiction over active personnel who commit crimes, even if those crimes occur outside the course of duty.[7] In such cases, military officials can either attempt to *court-martial* the suspect in military court or allow civilian prosecutors to handle the case in state or federal court. Congress has also passed legislation giving the military jurisdiction over certain foreign-born terrorist suspects,[8] as we saw at the beginning of this chapter.

CAREER TIP For those interested in both a military and a law enforcement career, the U.S. Army's *Criminal Investigation Command* is responsible for investigating crimes involving military personnel.

7-2b Trial and Appellate Courts

LO7-2 Another distinction is between courts of original jurisdiction and courts of appellate, or review, jurisdiction. Courts having *original jurisdiction* are courts of the first instance, or **trial courts.** Almost every case begins in a trial court. It is in this court that a trial (or a guilty plea) takes place, and the judge imposes a sentence if the defendant is found guilty. Trial courts are primarily concerned with *questions of fact.* They are designed to determine exactly what events occurred that are relevant to questions of the defendant's guilt or innocence.

Courts having *appellate jurisdiction* act as reviewing courts, or **appellate courts.** In general, cases can be brought before appellate courts only on appeal by one of the parties in the trial court. (Note that because of constitutional protections against being tried twice for the same crime, prosecutors who lose in criminal trial court *cannot* appeal the verdict.) An appellate court does not use juries or witnesses to reach its decision. Instead, its judges make a decision on whether the case should be *reversed and remanded,* or sent back to the court of original jurisdiction for a new trial. Appellate judges

present written explanations for their decisions, and these **opinions** of the court are the basis for a great deal of the precedent in the criminal justice system.

It is important to understand that appellate courts do not determine the defendant's guilt or innocence—they only make judgments on questions of procedure. In other words, they are concerned with *questions of law* and normally accept the facts as established by the trial court. Only rarely will an appeals court question a jury's decision. Instead, the appellate judges will review the manner in which the facts and evidence were provided to the jury and rule on whether errors were made in the process.

7-2c The Dual Court System

As we saw in Chapter 1, America's system of federalism allows the federal government and the governments of the fifty states to hold authority in many areas. As a result, the federal government and each of the fifty states, as well as the District of Columbia, have their own separate court systems. Because of the split between the federal courts and the state courts, this is known as the **dual court system.** (See Figure 7.1 to get a better idea of how federal and state courts operate as distinct yet parallel entities.)

Federal and state courts both have limited jurisdiction. Generally, federal courts preside over cases involving violations of federal law, and state courts preside over cases involving violations of state law. The distinction is not always clear, however. Federal courts have jurisdiction over more than 4,500 crimes, many of which also can be found in state criminal codes. As we saw earlier in this section, when such *concurrent jurisdiction* exists, both sides can try the defendant under their own laws, or one side can step aside and let the other decide the fate of the defendant. Because the federal court system has greater resources than most state court systems, federal criminal charges often take precedence over state criminal charges for practical reasons.

Trial Courts Courts in which most cases begin and in which questions of fact are examined.

Appellate Courts Courts that review decisions made by lower courts, such as trial courts; also known as *courts of appeals.*

Opinions Written statements by the judges expressing the reasons for the court's decision in a case.

Dual Court System The separate but interrelated court system of the United States, made up of the courts on the national level and the courts on the state level.

FIGURE 7.1 THE DUAL COURT SYSTEM

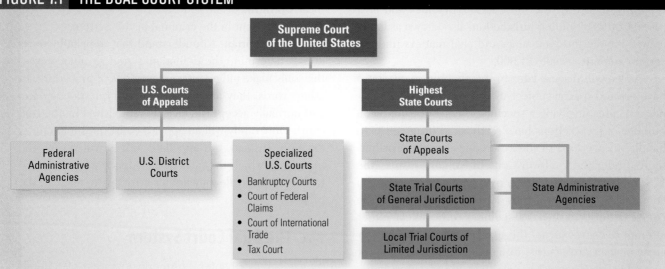

7-3 HOW DO STATES ORGANIZE THEIR COURTS?

Typically, a state court system includes several levels, or tiers, of courts. State courts may include:

1. Lower courts, or courts of limited jurisdiction.

2. Trial court of general jurisdiction.

3. Appellate courts.

4. The state's highest court.

As previously mentioned, each state has a different judicial structure, but there are enough similarities to allow for a general discussion. Figure 7.2 shows a typical state court system.

7-3a Courts of Limited Jurisdiction

Most states have local trial courts that are limited to trying cases involving minor criminal matters, such as traffic violations, prostitution, and drunk and disorderly

conduct. Although these minor courts usually keep no written record of the trial proceedings and cases are decided by a judge rather than a jury, defendants have the same rights as those in other trial courts. The majority of all minor criminal cases are decided in these lower courts. Courts of limited jurisdiction can also be responsible for the preliminary stages of felony cases. Arraignments, bail hearings, and preliminary hearings often take place in these lower courts.

MAGISTRATE COURTS Magistrates, or, in some states, municipal court judges, preside over courts whose jurisdiction is limited to disputes between private individuals and to crimes punishable by small fines or short jail terms. In certain regions, such as rural areas, *justices of the peace* perform a similar function. In most jurisdictions, magistrates are responsible for providing law enforcement agents with search and seizure warrants, discussed in Chapter 6.

SPECIALTY COURTS As mentioned earlier, many states have created **problem-solving courts** that have jurisdiction over very narrowly defined areas of criminal justice. Not only do these courts remove many cases from the existing court systems, but they also allow court personnel to become experts in a particular subject. Problem-solving courts include:

1. Drug courts, which deal only with illegal substance crimes.

2. Gun courts, which have jurisdiction over crimes that involve the illegal use of firearms.

Magistrate A public civil officer or official with limited judicial authority within a particular geographic area, such as the authority to issue an arrest warrant.

Problem-Solving Courts Lower courts that have jurisdiction over one specific area of criminal activity, such as illegal drugs or domestic violence.

FIGURE 7.2 A TYPICAL STATE COURT SYSTEM

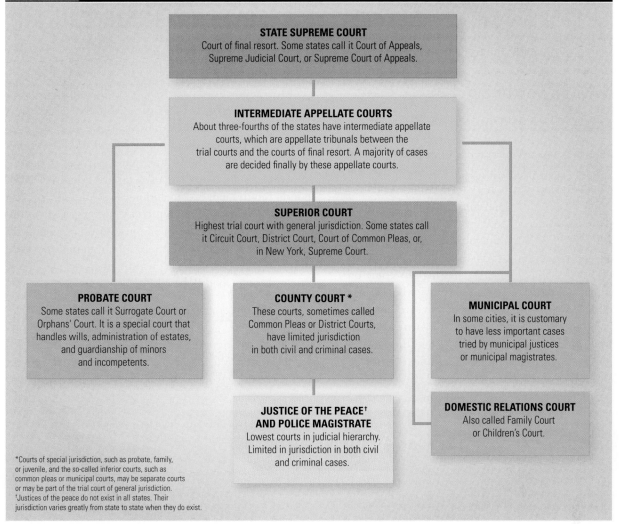

STATE SUPREME COURT
Court of final resort. Some states call it Court of Appeals, Supreme Judicial Court, or Supreme Court of Appeals.

INTERMEDIATE APPELLATE COURTS
About three-fourths of the states have intermediate appellate courts, which are appellate tribunals between the trial courts and the courts of final resort. A majority of cases are decided finally by these appellate courts.

SUPERIOR COURT
Highest trial court with general jurisdiction. Some states call it Circuit Court, District Court, Court of Common Pleas, or, in New York, Supreme Court.

PROBATE COURT
Some states call it Surrogate Court or Orphans' Court. It is a special court that handles wills, administration of estates, and guardianship of minors and incompetents.

COUNTY COURT *
These courts, sometimes called Common Pleas or District Courts, have limited jurisdiction in both civil and criminal cases.

MUNICIPAL COURT
In some cities, it is customary to have less important cases tried by municipal justices or municipal magistrates.

**JUSTICE OF THE PEACE†
AND POLICE MAGISTRATE**
Lowest courts in judicial hierarchy. Limited in jurisdiction in both civil and criminal cases.

DOMESTIC RELATIONS COURT
Also called Family Court or Children's Court.

*Courts of special jurisdiction, such as probate, family, or juvenile, and the so-called inferior courts, such as common pleas or municipal courts, may be separate courts or may be part of the trial court of general jurisdiction.
†Justices of the peace do not exist in all states. Their jurisdiction varies greatly from state to state when they do exist.

3. Juvenile courts, which specialize in crimes committed by minors. (We will discuss juvenile courts in more detail in Chapter 13.)

4. Domestic violence courts, which deal with crimes such as child and spousal abuse.

5. Mental health courts, which focus primarily on the treatment and rehabilitation of offenders with mental health problems.

As we will see in Chapter 10, many state and local governments are searching for cheaper alternatives to locking up nonviolent offenders in prison or jail. Because problem-solving courts offer a range of treatment options for wrongdoers, these courts are becoming increasingly popular in today's more budget-conscious criminal justice system. For example, about three thousand drug courts are now operating in the United States, a number that is expected to increase as the financial benefits of diverting drug law violators from correctional facilities become more attractive to politicians.

CAREER TIP Along with domestic violence courts, many cities have shelters that provide therapeutic and practical services for both victims and perpetrators of domestic violence. These organizations rely on *domestic violence counselors* to provide such services.

7-3b Trial Courts of General Jurisdiction

State trial courts that have general jurisdiction may be called county courts, district courts, superior courts, or circuit courts. In Ohio, the name is the court of common pleas and in Massachusetts, the trial court. (The name sometimes does not correspond with the court's functions. For example, in New York the trial court is called the supreme court, whereas in most states the supreme court is the state's highest court.) Courts of general jurisdiction have the authority to hear and decide cases involving many types of subject matter, and they are the setting for criminal trials (discussed in Chapter 8).

7-3c State Courts of Appeals

Every state has at least one court of appeals (known as an appellate, or reviewing, court), which may be an intermediate appellate court or the state's highest court. About three-fourths have intermediate appellate courts. The highest appellate court in a state is usually called the supreme court, but in both New York and Maryland, the highest state court is called the court of appeals. The decisions of each state's highest court on all questions of state law are final. Only when issues of federal law or constitutional procedure are involved can the United States Supreme Court overrule a decision made by a state's highest court. (See the feature *Discretion in Action—Eyewitness Identification* for an example of how the appeals process works.)

7-4 HOW DOES THE FEDERAL GOVERNMENT ORGANIZE ITS COURTS?

The federal court system is basically a three-tiered model consisting of (1) U.S. district courts (trial courts of general jurisdiction) and various courts of limited jurisdiction, (2) U.S. courts of appeals (intermediate courts of appeals), and (3) the United States Supreme Court.

Unlike state court judges, who are usually elected, federal court judges—including the justices of the Supreme Court—are appointed by the president of the United States, subject to the approval of the Senate. All federal judges receive lifetime appointments (because under Article III of the Constitution they "hold their offices during Good Behavior").

7-4a U.S. District Courts

On the lowest tier of the federal court system are the U.S. district courts, or federal trial courts. These are the courts in which cases involving federal laws begin, and a judge

Discretion in Action

EYEWITNESS IDENTIFICATION

THE SITUATION Getting ready for bed one night at an Oregon campsite, Sheryl was shot in the chest and her husband, Noris, killed by an assailant with a hunting rifle. At the scene, Sheryl told rescuers that she had not seen the shooter. On two occasions soon thereafter, police showed Sheryl a photo array that included the image of Samuel Lawson. She failed to recognize Lawson either time. Two years later, Lawson was arrested for the attack at the campsite, and a detective took Sheryl to his pretrial hearing. She then identified Lawson in a photo lineup, saying, "I'll never forget his face as long as I live." With little physical evidence linking him to the crime, Lawson was convicted of murder and sentenced to life in prison on the strength of Sheryl's testimony.

THE LAW According to previous Oregon court cases, the fact that a police officer uses "suggestive" methods to gain an eyewitness identification does not mean such evidence should be excluded from a trial. As long

as the witness makes the identification with a degree of certainty "independent of the suggestive procedure," it is valid. Following this precedent, the Oregon Court of Appeals upheld Lawson's conviction.

WHAT WOULD YOU DO? Lawson's lawyers have appealed the lower court's decision to the Oregon Supreme Court, on which you sit. His lawyers argue that Sheryl's testimony is unreliable and that state case law fails to reflect the findings of more than two thousand studies showing how memories are prone to suggestion and distortion. They also point out that eyewitness identification has played a role in nearly three-quarters of all wrongful convictions in the United States. Do you vote to uphold Lawson's conviction or, by overturning it, indicate that state case law in this area is flawed and should be changed? Explain your answer.

[To see how the Oregon Supreme Court ruled on a similar case, go to Example 7.1 in Appendix A.]

or jury decides the case (if it is a jury trial). Every state has at least one federal district court, and there is one in the District of Columbia. The number of judicial districts varies over time, primarily owing to population changes and corresponding caseloads. At the present time, there are ninety-four judicial districts. The federal system also includes other trial courts of limited jurisdiction, such as the Tax Court and the Court of International Trade.

7-4b U.S. Courts of Appeals

In the federal court system, there are thirteen U.S. courts of appeals—also referred to as U.S. circuit courts of appeals. The federal courts of appeals for twelve of the circuits hear appeals from the district courts located within their respective judicial circuits (see Figure 7.3). The Court of Appeals for the Thirteenth Circuit, called the Federal Circuit, has national appellate jurisdiction over certain types of cases, such as cases in which the U.S. government is a defendant. The decisions of

the circuit courts of appeals are final unless a further appeal is pursued and granted. In that case, the matter is brought before the Supreme Court.

7-4c The United States Supreme Court

Although it reviews a minuscule percentage of the cases decided in this country each year, the rulings of the United States Supreme Court profoundly affect our lives. The impact of Court decisions on the criminal justice system is equally far reaching: *Gideon v. Wainwright* (1963)[9] established every American's right to be represented by counsel in a criminal trial; *Miranda v. Arizona* (1966)[10] transformed pretrial interrogations; *Furman v. Georgia* (1972)[11] ruled that the death penalty was unconstitutional; and *Gregg v. Georgia* (1976)[12] spelled out the conditions under which it could be allowed. As you have no doubt noticed from references in this textbook, the Court has addressed nearly every important facet of criminal law.

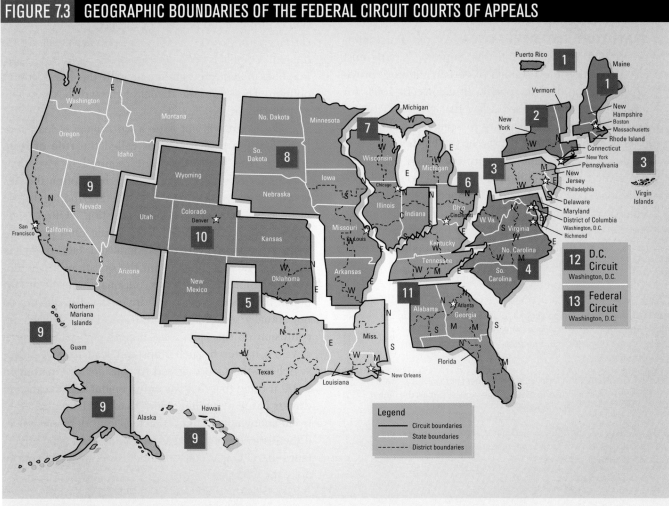

FIGURE 7.3 GEOGRAPHIC BOUNDARIES OF THE FEDERAL CIRCUIT COURTS OF APPEALS

Source: Administrative Office of the United States Courts, January 1994.

7-4d Interpreting and Applying the Law

The Supreme Court "makes" criminal justice policy in two important ways: through *judicial review* and through its authority to interpret the law. **Judicial review** refers to the power of the Court to determine whether a law or action by the other branches of the government is constitutional.

In 2005, for example, Congress passed the Stolen Valor Act, which made it a crime punishable by up to six months in prison for someone to falsely claim that he or she had earned military honors or medals.[13] Several years later, Xavier Alvarez was sentenced to three years probation and given a $5,000 fine for lying about having received the Medal of Honor. In 2012, the Court overturned Alvarez's conviction and invalidated the federal law on the ground that a false statement that does no obvious harm is protected by the First Amendment's freedom of expression.[14] (A year later, Congress passed a new version of the Stolen Valor Act that made it a crime to lie about earning military honors "with the intent to obtain money, property, or some other tangible benefit.")[15]

STATUTORY INTERPRETATION As the final interpreter of the Constitution, the Supreme Court must also determine the meaning of certain statutory provisions when applied to specific situations. In 1994, for example, Congress passed a law that gives a victim of child pornography the ability to seek restitution from offenders to the extent that he or she has been harmed by the illegal behavior.[16] Twenty years later, the Court overturned a $3.4 million award to a woman whose childhood rape had been videotaped and widely disseminated on the Internet. The Court ruled that, under the 1994 law, a single offender who had just two images of the victim on his computer could not be held responsible for all of the damages she had suffered.[17]

Judicial Review The power of a court—particularly the United States Supreme Court—to review the actions of the executive and legislative branches and, if necessary, declare those actions unconstitutional.

Writ of *Certiorari* A request from a higher court asking a lower court for the record of a case. In essence, the request signals the higher court's willingness to review the case.

Rule of Four A rule of the United States Supreme Court that the Court will not issue a writ of *certiorari* unless at least four justices approve of the decision to hear the case.

JURISDICTION OF THE SUPREME COURT The United States Supreme Court consists of nine justices—a chief justice and eight associate justices. The Supreme Court has original, or trial, jurisdiction only in rare instances (set forth in Article III, Section 2, of the Constitution). In other words, only rarely does a case originate at the Supreme Court level. Most of the Court's work is as an appellate court. It has appellate authority over cases decided by the U.S. courts of appeals, as well as over some cases decided in the state courts when federal questions are at issue.

LO7-3 WHICH CASES REACH THE SUPREME COURT? There is no absolute right to appeal to the United States Supreme Court. Although thousands of cases are filed with the Supreme Court each year, in 2013–2014 the Court heard only seventy-five. With a **writ of *certiorari*** (pronounced sur-shee-uh-*rah*-ree), the Supreme Court orders a lower court to send it the record of a case for review. A party can petition the Supreme Court to issue a writ of *certiorari,* but whether the Court will do so is entirely within its discretion. More than 90 percent of the petitions for writs of *certiorari* (or "certs," as they are popularly called) are denied. A denial is not a decision on the merits of a case, nor does it indicate agreement with the lower court's opinion. Therefore, the denial of the writ has no value as a precedent.

The Court will not issue a writ unless at least four justices approve of it. This is called the **rule of four.** Although the justices are not required to give their reasons for refusing to hear a case, most often the discretionary decision is based on whether the legal issue involves a "substantial federal question." Often, such questions arise when lower courts split on a particular issue. For example, different federal and state courts had produced varying opinions on the question of whether an anonymous tip provides reasonable suspicion for police officers to pull over a driver that the officers do not actually see breaking any traffic laws. To clear up confusion on this question—important because, as we saw in Chapter 6, such stops can lead to warrantless searches—the Court agreed to consider the matter. In 2014, it ruled that that law enforcement agents can stop drivers based on nothing more than a 911 tip phoned in by an anonymous caller.[18] Practical considerations aside, if the justices feel that a case does not address an important federal law or constitutional issue, they will vote to deny the writ of *certiorari.*

SUPREME COURT DECISIONS Like all appellate courts, the Supreme Court normally does not hear any evidence. The Court's decision in a particular case is based on the written record of the case and the written arguments (briefs) that the attorneys submit. The attorneys also present **oral arguments**—arguments presented in person rather than on paper—to the Court, after which the justices discuss the case in *conference*. The conference is strictly private—only the justices are allowed in the room.

Majorities and Pluralities When the Court has reached a decision, the chief justice, if in the majority, assigns the task of writing the Court's opinion to one of the justices. When the chief justice is not in the majority, the most senior justice voting with the majority assigns the writing of the Court's opinion. The opinion outlines the reasons for the Court's decision, the rules of law that apply, and the decision.

From time to time, the justices agree on the outcome of a case, but no single reason for that outcome gains five votes. When this occurs, the rationale that gains the most votes is called the *plurality* opinion. Plurality opinions are problematic, because they do not provide a strong precedent for lower courts to follow. Although still relatively rare, the incidence of plurality opinions has increased over the past fifty years as the Court has become more ideologically fractured.[19]

Concurrence and Dissent Often, one or more justices who agree with the Court's decision do so for different reasons than those outlined in the majority opinion. These justices may write **concurring opinions** setting forth their own legal reasoning on the issue. Frequently, too, one or more justices disagree with the Court's conclusion. These justices may write **dissenting opinions** outlining the reasons why they feel the majority erred. Although a dissenting opinion does not affect the outcome of the case before the Court, it may be important later. In a subsequent case concerning the same issue, a justice or attorney may use the legal reasoning in the dissenting opinion as the basis for an argument to reverse the previous decision and establish a new precedent.

HOW DO JUDGES FUNCTION IN THE CRIMINAL JUSTICE SYSTEM?

Supreme Court justices are the most visible and best-known American jurists, but in many ways they are unrepresentative of the profession as a whole. Few judges enjoy three-room office suites fitted with a fireplace and a private bath, as do the Supreme Court justices. Few judges have four clerks to assist them. Few judges get a yearly vacation that stretches from July through September. Most judges, in fact, work at the lowest level of the system, in criminal trial courts, where they are burdened with overflowing caseloads and must deal daily with the pettiest of criminals.

One attribute a Supreme Court justice and a criminal trial judge in any small American city do have in common is the expectation that they will be just. Of all the participants in the criminal justice system, no other person is held to the same high standards as the judge. From her or his lofty perch in the courtroom, the judge is counted on to be "above the fray" of the bickering defense attorneys and prosecutors. When the other courtroom

John G. Roberts, Jr., pictured here, is the seventeenth chief justice of the United States Supreme Court. *What does it mean to say that Roberts and the eight associate members of the Court "make criminal justice policy"?*

Collection of the Supreme Court of the United States, Photographer: Steve Petteway

Oral Arguments The verbal arguments presented in person by attorneys to an appellate court. Each attorney presents reasons why the court should rule in his or her client's favor.

Concurring Opinions Separate opinions prepared by judges who support the decision of the majority of the court but who want to make or clarify a particular point or to voice disapproval of the grounds on which the decision was made.

Dissenting Opinions Separate opinions in which judges disagree with the conclusion reached by the majority of the court and expand on their own views about the case.

contestants rise at the entrance of the judge, they are placing the burden of justice squarely on the judge's shoulders.

7-5a The Roles and Responsibilities of Trial Judges

One of the reasons that judicial integrity is considered so important is the amount of discretionary power a judge has over the court proceedings. Nearly every stage of the trial process includes a decision or action to be taken by the presiding judge.

BEFORE THE TRIAL A great deal of the work done by a judge takes place before the trial even starts, free from public scrutiny. These duties, some of which you have seen from a different point of view in the section on law enforcement agents, include determining the following:

1. Whether there is sufficient probable cause to issue a search or arrest warrant.

2. Whether there is sufficient probable cause to authorize electronic surveillance of a suspect.

3. Whether enough evidence exists to justify the temporary incarceration of a suspect.

4. Whether a defendant should be released on bail, and if so, the amount of the bail.

5. Whether to accept pretrial motions by prosecutors and defense attorneys.

6. Whether to accept a plea bargain.

During these pretrial activities, the judge takes on the role of *negotiator*. As most cases are decided through plea bargains rather than through trial proceedings, the judge often offers his or her services as a negotiator to help the prosecution and the defense "make a deal." The amount at which bail is set is often negotiated as well. Throughout the trial process, the judge usually spends a great deal of time in his or her *chambers,* or office, negotiating with the prosecutors and defense attorneys.

DURING THE TRIAL When the trial starts, the judge takes on the role of *referee*. In this role, she or he is responsible for seeing that the trial unfolds according to the dictates of the law and that the participants in the trial

Docket The list of cases entered on a court's calendar and thus scheduled to be heard by the court.

do not overstep any legal or ethical bounds. Furthermore, the judge is expected to be neutral, determining the admissibility of testimony and evidence on a completely objective basis. The judge also acts as a *teacher* during the trial, explaining points of law to the jury. If the trial is not a jury trial, then the judge must also make decisions concerning the guilt or innocence of the defendant.

At the close of the trial, if the defendant is found guilty, the judge must decide on the length of the sentence and the type of sentence. (Different types of sentences, such as incarceration, probation, and other forms of community-based corrections, will be discussed in Chapters 9 and 10.)

THE ADMINISTRATIVE ROLE Judges are also *administrators* and are responsible for the day-to-day functioning of their courts. A primary administrative task of a judge is scheduling. Each courtroom has a **docket,** or calendar of cases, and it is the judge's responsibility to keep the docket current. This entails not only scheduling the trial, but also setting pretrial motion dates and deciding whether to grant attorneys' requests for *continuances,* or additional time to prepare for the trial.

Judges must also keep track of the immense paperwork generated by each case and manage the various employees of the court. Some judges are even responsible for the budgets of their courtrooms.[20] In 1939, Congress, recognizing the burden of such tasks, created the Administrative Office of the United States Courts to provide administrative assistance for federal court judges.[21] Most state court judges, however, do not have the luxury of similar aid, though they are supported by a court staff.

CAREER TIP High-level judges, including Supreme Court justices, enjoy the services of *law clerks,* who prepare reports for the judges on the legal issues of cases and help the judges research and write opinions. Law clerks are often recent law school graduates beginning their legal careers.

7-5b Selection of Judges

In the federal court system, all judges are appointed by the president and confirmed by the Senate. It is difficult to make a general statement about how judges are selected in state court systems, however, because the procedure varies widely from state to state. In some states, such as New Jersey, all judges are appointed by the governor and confirmed by the upper chamber of the state legislature. In other states, such as Alabama,

7-5c Diversity on the Bench

In your own words, explain how a judge acts as a "referee" when he or she is presiding over a criminal trial.

According to the Brennan Center for Justice in New York City, "Americans who enter the courtroom often face a predictable presence on the bench: a white male."[24] Overall, about two-thirds of all state appellate judges are white males, and women in particular are notably absent from the highest courts of most states.[25] In many states, members of minority groups are underrepresented in comparison to the demographics of the general population. California, for example, is nearly 38 percent Hispanic and 16 percent Asian American. The state judiciary, however, is only 8.3 percent Hispanic and 4.4 percent Asian American.[26] New York is 67 percent white and 52 percent female, and its judiciary is 81 percent white and 35 percent female.[27]

Members of minority groups are also underrepresented in the federal judiciary, though not to the same extent as in the states. Of the approximately 870 federal judges in this country, about 24 percent are African American, 14 percent are Hispanic, and less than 5 percent are Asian American. Furthermore, about 45 percent are women.[28] Of the 111 justices who have served on the United States Supreme Court, two have been African American: Thurgood Marshall (1967–1991) and Clarence Thomas (1991–present). In 2009, Sonia Sotomayor became the first Hispanic appointed to the Court and the third woman, following Sandra Day O'Connor (1981–2006) and Ruth Bader Ginsburg (1993–present). A year later, Elena Kagan became the fourth woman appointed to the Court.

partisan elections are used to choose judges. In these elections, a judicial candidate declares allegiance to a political party, usually the Democrats or the Republicans, before the election. States such as Kentucky that conduct **nonpartisan elections** do not require a candidate to affiliate herself or himself with a political party in this manner. Finally, some states, such as Missouri, select judges based on a subjective definition of merit.

In 1940, Missouri became the first state to combine appointment and election in a single merit selection process. When all jurisdiction levels are counted, nineteen states and the District of Columbia now utilize the **Missouri Plan,** as merit selection has been labeled. The Missouri Plan consists of three basic steps:

▶ When a vacancy on the bench arises, candidates are nominated by a nonpartisan committee of citizens.

▶ The names of the three most qualified candidates are sent to the governor or executive of the state judicial system, and that person chooses who will be the judge.

▶ A year after the new judge has been installed, a "retention election" is held so that voters can decide whether the judge deserves to keep the post.[22]

The goal of the Missouri Plan is to eliminate partisan politics from the selection procedure, while at the same time giving the citizens a voice in the process. Regardless of how they are selected, the average term for state judges in this country is about seven years.[23]

Partisan Elections Elections in which candidates are affiliated with and receive support from political parties.

Nonpartisan Elections Elections in which candidates are presented on the ballot without any party affiliation.

Missouri Plan A method of selecting judges that combines appointment and election.

WHAT IS THE COURTROOM WORKGROUP?

Television dramas often depict the courtroom as a battlefield, with prosecutors and defense attorneys spitting fire at each other over the loud and insistent protestations of a frustrated judge. Consequently, many people are somewhat disappointed when they witness a real courtroom at work. Rarely does anyone raise his or her voice, and the courtroom professionals appear—to a great extent—to be cooperating with each other.

In Chapter 5, we discussed the existence of a police subculture, based on the shared values of law enforcement agents. A courtroom subculture exists as well, centered on the **courtroom work group.** The most important feature of any work group is that it is a *cooperative* unit, whose members establish shared values and methods that help the group efficiently reach its goals. Though cooperation is not a concept usually associated with criminal courts, it is in fact crucial to the adjudication process.

7-6a Members of the Courtroom Work Group

The courtroom work group is made up of those individuals who are involved with the defendant from the time she or he is arrested until sentencing. The most prominent members are the judge, the prosecutor, and the defense attorney. Three other court participants complete the work group:

1. The *bailiff of the court* is responsible for maintaining security and order in the judge's chambers and the courtroom. Bailiffs lead the defendant in and out of the courtroom and attend to the needs of the jurors during the trial. A bailiff, often a member of the local sheriff's department but sometimes an employee of the court, also delivers summonses in some jurisdictions.

2. The *clerk of the court* has an exhausting list of responsibilities. Any plea, motion, or other matter to be acted on by the judge must go through the clerk. The large amount of paperwork generated during a trial, including transcripts, photographs, evidence, and any other records, is maintained by the clerk. The clerk also issues subpoenas for jury duty and coordinates the jury selection process. In the federal court system, judges select clerks, while state clerks are either appointed or, in nearly a third of the states, elected.

3. *Court reporters* record every word that is said during the course of the trial. They also record any *depositions,* or pretrial question-and-answer sessions in which a party or a witness answers an attorney's questions under oath.

7-6b The Judge in the Courtroom Work Group

The judge is the dominant figure in the courtroom and therefore exerts the most influence over the values and norms of the work group. A judge who runs a "tight ship" follows procedure and restricts the freedom of attorneys to deviate from regulations, while a *"laissez-faire"* judge allows more leeway to members of the work group. A judge's personal philosophy also affects the court proceedings. If a judge has a reputation for being "tough on crime," both prosecutors and defense attorneys will alter their strategies accordingly.

Although preeminent in the work group, a judge must still rely on other members of the group. To a certain extent, the judge is the least informed member of the trio. Like a juror, the judge learns the facts of the case as they are presented by the attorneys. If the attorneys do not properly present the facts, then the judge is hampered in making rulings.

7-6c The Prosecution

LO7-4 If, as we suggested earlier, the judge is the referee of the courtroom, then the prosecutor and the defense attorney are its two main combatants. On the side of the government, acting in the name of "the people," the **public prosecutor** tries cases against criminal defendants. The public prosecutor in federal criminal cases is called a U.S. attorney. In cases tried in state or local courts, the public prosecutor may be referred to as a *prosecuting attorney, state attorney, district attorney, county attorney,*

Courtroom Work Group The social organization consisting of the judge, prosecutor, defense attorney, and other court workers.

Public Prosecutors Individuals, acting as trial lawyers, who initiate and conduct cases in the government's name and on behalf of the people.

Job Description:

▶ Maintain order and provide security in the courtroom during trials, and escort and guard jurors and prevent them from having improper contact with the public.

▶ Open and close court, call cases, call witnesses, and generally "direct the traffic" of the trial.

What Kind of Training Is Required?

▶ At minimum, a high school diploma or GED.

▶ Supplemental training at a vocational school or a police academy, or a two- or four-year college degree with an emphasis on criminal justice.

Annual Salary Range?

▶ $25,000–$67,000

iStockPhoto.com/Alina Solovyova-Vincent

SOCIAL MEDIA CAREER TIP
Networking is crucial. Develop as many useful social media contacts as possible, and cultivate those contacts. Also, reciprocate. If you help others establish online contacts, they are likely to remember you and return the favor.

or *city attorney.* Given their great autonomy, prosecutors are generally considered the most dominant figures in the American criminal justice system.

A DUTY OF FAIRNESS In some jurisdictions, the district attorney is the chief law enforcement officer, with broad powers over police operations. Prosecutors have the power to bring the resources of the state to bear against the individual and hold the legal keys to meting out or withholding punishment. Ideally, this power is balanced by a duty of fairness and a recognition that the prosecutor's ultimate goal is not to win cases, but to see that justice is done. In *Berger v. United States* (1935), Justice George Sutherland called the prosecutor

> in a peculiar and very definite sense the servant of the law, the twofold aim of which is that guilt shall not escape or innocence suffer. He may prosecute with earnestness and vigor—indeed, he should do so. But, while he may strike hard blows, he is not at liberty to strike foul ones. It is as much his duty to refrain from improper methods calculated to produce a wrongful conviction as it is to use every legitimate means to bring about a just one.[29]

THE BRADY RULE To lessen the opportunity for "foul" behavior by prosecutors, the United States Supreme Court established the *Brady rule* more than half a century ago. This rule holds that prosecutors are not permitted to keep evidence from the defendant and her or his attorneys that may be useful in showing innocence.[30]

For example, in 2000 former state trooper George Martin was convicted of burning his wife to death in Mobile, Alabama. The only eyewitness to the crime gave conflicting reports to police, including calling the killer "a big man" (Martin is 5 feet, 6 inches tall) and pointing to a different suspect in a photo lineup. Obviously, Martin's defense attorneys could have used this information to create reasonable doubt concerning their client's guilt in court. Prosecutors, however, failed to tell the defense about the eyewitness's inconsistent testimony. Consequently, in 2013 a Mobile County judge overturned Martin's conviction and ordered a new trial.[31]

THE OFFICE OF THE PROSECUTOR When he or she is acting as an *officer of the law* during a criminal trial, there are limits on the prosecutor's conduct, as we shall see in the next chapter. During the pretrial process, however, prosecutors hold a great deal of discretion in deciding the following:

1. **Whether an individual who has been arrested by the police will be charged with a crime.**

2. **The level of the charges to be brought against the suspect.**

3. **If and when to stop the prosecution.**[32]

There are more than eight thousand prosecutor's offices around the country, serving state, county, and municipal jurisdictions. Even though the **attorney general** is the chief law enforcement officer in any state, she or he has limited control (and, in some states, no control) over prosecutors within the state's boundaries.

Each jurisdiction has a chief prosecutor, who is sometimes appointed but more often elected. As an elected official, he or she typically serves a four-year term, though in some states, such as Alabama, the term is six years. In smaller jurisdictions, the chief prosecutor has several assistants, and they work closely together. In larger ones, the chief prosecutor may have numerous *assistant prosecutors*, many of whom he or she rarely meets. Assistant prosecutors—for the most part, young attorneys recently graduated from law school—may be assigned to particular sections of the organization, such as criminal prosecutions in general or areas of *special prosecution*, such as narcotics or gang crimes.

THE PROSECUTOR AS ELECTED OFFICIAL The chief prosecutor's autonomy is not absolute. As an elected official, she or he must answer to the voters. (There are exceptions: U.S. attorneys are nominated by the president and approved by the Senate, and chief prosecutors in Alaska, Connecticut, New Jersey, Rhode Island, and

Steve Petteway/Collection of the Supreme Court of the United States

Give several reasons why experience as a prosecutor would make someone, such as United States Supreme Court justice Sonia Sotomayor, a more effective judge.

the District of Columbia are either appointed or hired as members of the attorney general's office.) The prosecutor may be part of the political machine. In many jurisdictions, the prosecutor must declare a party affiliation and is expected to reward fellow party members with positions in the district attorney's office if elected.

The post of prosecutor is also considered a "stepping-stone" to higher political office, and many prosecutors have gone on to serve in legislatures or as judges. Sonia Sotomayor, the first Hispanic member of the United States Supreme Court, started her legal career in 1979 as an assistant district attorney in New York City. While at that job, she first came to public attention by helping to prosecute the "Tarzan Murderer," an athletic criminal responsible for at least twenty burglaries and four killings.

7-6d The Defense Attorney

The media provide most people's perception of defense counsel: the idealistic public defender who nobly serves the poor, the "ambulance chaser," or the celebrity attorney in the $3,000 suit. These stereotypes, though not entirely fictional, tend to obscure the crucial role that the **defense attorney** plays in the criminal justice system. Most persons charged with crimes have little or no knowledge of criminal procedure. Without assistance, they would be helpless in court. By acting as a staunch advocate for her or his client, the defense attorney (ideally) ensures that the government proves every point against that client beyond a reasonable doubt, even for cases that do not go to trial. In sum, the defense attorney provides a counterweight against the state in our adversary system.

THE RESPONSIBILITIES OF THE DEFENSE ATTORNEY The Sixth Amendment right to counsel is not limited to the actual criminal trial. In a number of instances, the United States Supreme Court has held

Attorney General The chief law officer of a state; also, the chief law officer of the nation.

Defense Attorney The lawyer representing the defendant.

In 2010, the Wayne County Prosecutor's Office found 11,000 untested rape kits in a Detroit police storage unit. These kits are prepared by forensic medical experts in the hours following a sexual assault, and often contain DNA left by the offender. In the five years following this discovery, prosecutor Kym Worthy arranged for 2,000 of the kits to be tested, identifying 188 serial rapists and obtaining fifteen convictions in the process. Though the pace of Worthy's efforts may seem slow, it isn't. A crime lab can take weeks to extract usable DNA evidence from a rape kit, at a cost of up to $1,500.

Nationwide, there is a backlog of 400,000 to 500,000 untested rape kits, meaning that innumerable sexual assault offenders have escaped arrest and conviction.

Given that most crime labs in the country are already overwhelmed with requests to test evidence, it seems that technology offers the best hope of reducing this backlog. Presently, lab technicians must laboriously separate the DNA of the victim from the DNA of the offender by slicing the cells of material in the rape kit, such as blood, semen, skin, and saliva, and testing each sample individually. A new process called *pressure cycling* immediately identifies the offender's semen, which significantly lessens the amount of time needed to get a usable DNA sample for database-matching purposes.

Thinking about Untested Rape Kits
How might the massive backlog of untested rape kits in this country discourage victims of sexual assault from reporting the crime to police?

---

that defendants are entitled to representation as soon as their rights may be denied, which includes the custodial interrogation and lineup identification procedures.[33] Therefore, an important responsibility of the defense attorney is to represent the defendant at the various stages of the custodial process, including arrest, interrogation, lineup, and arraignment. Other responsibilities include:

▸ Investigating the incident for which the defendant has been charged.

▸ Communicating with the prosecutor, which includes negotiating plea bargains.

▸ Preparing the case for trial.

▸ Submitting defense motions, including motions to suppress evidence.

▸ Representing the defendant at trial.

▸ Negotiating a sentence, if the client has been convicted.

▸ Determining whether to appeal a guilty verdict.[34]

LO7-5 **DEFENDING THE GUILTY** At one time or another in their careers, all defense attorneys will face a difficult question: Must I defend a client whom I know to be guilty? According to the American Bar Association's code of legal ethics, the answer is almost always, "yes."[35] The most important responsibility of the criminal defense attorney is to be an advocate for her or his client. As such, the attorney is obligated to use all ethical and legal means to achieve the client's desired goal, which is usually to avoid or lessen punishment for the charged crime.

As Supreme Court justice Byron White once noted, defense counsel has no "obligation to ascertain or present the truth." Rather, our adversary system insists that the defense attorney "defend the client whether he is innocent or guilty."[36] Indeed, if defense attorneys refused to represent clients whom they believed to be guilty, the Sixth Amendment guarantee of a criminal trial for all accused persons would be rendered meaningless.

THE PUBLIC DEFENDER Generally speaking, there are two different types of defense attorneys: (1) private attorneys, who are hired by individuals, and (2) **public defenders,** who work for the government. The distinction is not absolute, as many private attorneys accept employment as public defenders, too. The modern role of the public defender was established by the Supreme Court's interpretation of the Sixth Amendment in *Gideon v. Wainwright* (1963).[37]

Public Defenders Court-appointed attorneys who are paid by the state to represent defendants who cannot afford private counsel.

Job Description:

▶ Interview low-income applicants for legal services and, if they are eligible, engage in negotiation, trial, and /or appeal of legal issues on their behalf.

▶ Exercise initiative, sound judgment, and creativity in attempting to solve the legal problems of the poor.

What Kind of Training Is Required?

▶ A law degree and membership in the relevant state bar association.

▶ Commitment and dedication to the needs of low-income and elderly clients.

Annual Salary Range?

▶ $44,000–$92,000

iStockPhoto.com/BirdofPrey

GETTING LINKEDIN

Although most public defenders work on a city or county level, there are seventy-nine federal public defender organizations with 3,300 employees. Given its national reach, LinkedIn is an excellent source of information about job openings for federal public defenders.

In that case, the Court ruled that no defendant can be "assured a fair trial unless counsel is provided for him," and therefore the state must provide a public defender to those who cannot afford to hire one for themselves. Subsequently, the Court extended this protection to juveniles in *In re Gault* (1967)[38] and those faced with imprisonment for committing misdemeanors in *Argersinger v. Hamlin* (1972).[39] The impact of these decisions has been substantial: about 90 percent of all criminal defendants in the United States are represented by public defenders or other appointed counsel.[40]

Eligibility Issues Although the Supreme Court's *Gideon* decision obligated the government to provide attorneys for poor defendants, it offered no guidance on just how poor the defendant needs to be to qualify for a public defender. In theory, counsel should be provided for those who are unable to hire an attorney themselves without "substantial hardship."[41] In reality, each jurisdiction has its own guidelines, and a defendant refused counsel in one area might be entitled to it in another. A judge in Kittitas County, Washington, to give an extreme example, would frequently deny public counsel for

college student defendants. This judge believed that any person who chooses to go to school rather than work automatically falls outside the *Gideon* case's definition of indigence.[42]

Defense Counsel Programs In most areas, the county government is responsible for providing indigent defendants with attorneys. Three basic types of programs are used to allocate defense counsel:

1. *Assigned counsel programs,* in which local private attorneys are assigned clients on a case-by-case basis by the county.

2. *Contracting attorney programs,* in which a particular law firm or group of attorneys is hired to regularly assume the representative and administrative tasks of indigent defense.

3. *Public defender programs,* in which the county assembles a salaried staff of full-time or part-time attorneys and creates a public (taxpayer-funded) agency to provide services.[43]

Public defender Megan Downing makes a point to the jury during a trial in Brighton, Colorado. *Why are the rules of attorney-client privilege necessary for a defense attorney to do her or his job?*

Much to the surprise of many indigent defendants, these programs are not entirely without cost. Government agencies can charge fees for "free" legal counsel when the fees will not impose a "significant legal financial hardship" on the defendant. In at least forty-three states and the District of Columbia, therefore, local public defender offices have the option of charging some form of so-called cost recoupment.[44] Florida, North Carolina, and Virginia have mandatory public defender fees, meaning that judges cannot waive such costs under any circumstances. In Virginia, indigent defendants may be charged up to $1,235 per count for certain felonies.[45]

ATTORNEY-CLIENT PRIVILEGE To defend a client effectively, a defense attorney must have access to all the facts concerning the case, even those that may be harmful to the defendant. To promote the unrestrained flow of information between the two parties, legislatures and lawyers themselves have constructed rules of **attorney-client privilege.** These rules require that communications between a client and his or her attorney be kept confidential, unless the client consents to the disclosure.

The Privilege and Confessions Attorney-client privilege does not stop short of confessions. Indeed, if, on hearing any statement that points toward guilt, the defense attorney could alert the prosecution or try to resign from the case, attorney-client privilege would be rendered meaningless. Even if the client says, "I have just killed seventeen women. I selected only pregnant women so I could torture them and kill two people at once. I did it. I liked it. I enjoyed it," the defense attorney must continue to do his or her utmost to serve that client.[46]

> **Attorney-Client Privilege** A rule of evidence requiring that communications between a client and his or her attorney be kept confidential, unless the client consents to disclosure.

STUDY TOOLS ⑦

READY TO STUDY? IN THE BOOK, YOU CAN:

☐ Rip out the Chapter Review Card, which includes key terms and chapter summaries.

ONLINE AT WWW.CENGAGEBRAIN.COM, YOU CAN:

☐ Learn about President Obama's potential impact on *Roe v. Wade* in a short video.

☐ Dig deeper into to the United States Supreme Court's Web site.

☐ Interact with figures from the text, and watch quick animation clips.

☐ Prepare for tests with quizzes.

☐ Review the key terms with Flash Cards.

Without attorney-client privilege, observes legal expert John Kaplan, lawyers would be forced to give their clients the equivalent of the *Miranda* warning before representing them.[47] In other words, lawyers would have to make clear what clients could or could not say in the course of preparing for trial, because any incriminating statement might be used against the client in court. Such a development would have serious ramifications for the criminal justice system.

The Exception to the Privilege The scope of attorney-client privilege is not all encompassing. In *United States v. Zolin* (1989),[48] the Supreme Court ruled that lawyers may disclose the contents of a conversation with a client if the client has provided information concerning a crime that has yet to be committed. This exception applies only to communications involving a crime that is ongoing or will occur in the future. If the client reveals a past crime, the privilege is still in effect, and the attorney may not reveal any details of that particular criminal act.

Quiz

1. The due process function of American courts is to protect _____ in light of the various advantages that the prosecution enjoys during legal proceedings.

2. The _____ _____ function of the courts emphasizes punishment and the concept that criminals must suffer for the harm they do to society.

3. Before any court can hear a case, it must have _____ over the persons involved or the subject matter of the dispute.

4. The American court system is a dual court system composed of _____ courts and state courts.

5. When it agrees to hear an appeal of a lower court decision, the United States Supreme Court issues a writ of _____.

6. When a Supreme Court justice agrees with the Court's decision but for different reasons than those outlined in the majority opinion, he or she will write a _____ opinion setting forth his or her legal reasoning.

7. In some states, judges are nominated by the state's _____ and approved by the state legislature.

8. Public _____ initiate and conduct cases on behalf of society against the defendant.

9. The Sixth Amendment states that every person accused of a crime in the United States has a right to the assistance of _____.

10. Those defendants who cannot afford to hire a defense attorney are provided with _____ defenders by the government.

Answers can be found in the Answers section in the back of the book.

8 Pretrial Procedures and the Criminal Trial

Pat Greenhouse/*The Boston Globe* via Getty Images

After you finish this chapter, go to **PAGES 180–181** for **STUDY TOOLS**

LEARNING OBJECTIVES

After studying this chapter, you will be able to . . .

8-1 Identify the steps involved in the pretrial criminal process.

8-2 Indicate why prosecutors, defense attorneys, and defendants often agree to plea bargains.

8-3 Identify the basic protections enjoyed by criminal defendants in the United States.

8-4 Contrast challenges for cause and peremptory challenges during *voir dire*.

8-5 List the standard steps in a criminal jury trial.

The Love Defense

Gigi Jordan never denied killing Jude, her eight-year-old son. Her justification for giving the boy a lethal dose of drugs at a luxury midtown Manhattan hotel was, however, quite unusual. "She did it because she loved Jude," said Alan Brenner, Jordan's defense attorney. Specifically, Jordan claimed that her first husband was planning to murder her, leaving Jude in the custody of her second husband, his father. This man, she was convinced, would sexually abuse the boy, who suffers from autism, a developmental disorder that impairs one's ability to communicate.

Generally speaking, of course, love is not an acceptable legal excuse for homicide. Nevertheless, at Jordan's 2014 trial in New York City, her lawyers asked the jury to find her guilty of manslaughter rather than second degree murder. The lesser crime was appropriate, they argued, because Jordan had been under the influence of an "extreme emotional disturbance" when she killed her son.

To succeed with this defense, which is normally used for murders committed in a jealous rage, Jordan's attorneys needed to prove that, in an unstable mental state, Jordan believed that her behavior was reasonable.

Prosecutors scoffed at the notion that Jude's killing was a poignant, impulsive act of mercy. They pointed out that Jordan had not seen her ex-husbands for months and could offer no proof that either man was planning to harm her or her son. A witness for the prosecution also testified that Jordan had told her about plans to commit suicide and "take [Jude] with me" if chemotherapy treatments did not

alleviate the boy's symptoms. Even so, the jury accepted Jordan's explanation for ending Jude's life and found her guilty of manslaughter instead of murder. According to one juror, Jordan's beliefs may have been irrational or incorrect, but her actions met the definition of extreme emotional disturbance. "It was clear that she believed these stories," said the juror, explaining why the defendant did not deserve to spend the rest of her life in prison.

Jefferson Siegel/New York Daily News/Getty Images

In 2014, Gigi Jordan was convicted of manslaughter for intentionally killing her eight-year-old son in a Manhattan hotel room four years earlier. *Do you agree with the jury's decision in this case? Why or why not?*

8-1 WHAT HAPPENS AFTER ARREST?

Not surprisingly, given the extraordinary nature of the case and the defendant's significant personal wealth, estimated at more than $50 million, Gigi Jordan's murder trial attracted national attention. Those who followed the proceedings might have come away with a skewed version of how the criminal justice system works. According to the *"wedding cake" model* of our court system, only the top, and smallest, "layer" of trials comes

close to meeting constitutional standards of procedural justice.[1] In these celebrity trials, such as Jordan's, committed (and expensive) attorneys argue minute technicalities for days, with numerous (and expensive) expert witnesses taking the stand for both sides.

On the bottom, largest layer of the wedding cake, the vast majority of defendants are dealt with informally, and the end goal seems to be speed rather than justice. Indeed, as you will see in this chapter, trial by jury is quite rare. Instead, the fate of most criminal suspects in this country is decided during pretrial procedures, which start almost as soon as the police have identified a suspect.

8-1a The Initial Appearance

LO8-1 After an arrest has been made, the first step toward determining the suspect's guilt or innocence is the **initial appearance.** During this brief proceeding, the magistrate (see Chapter 7) informs the defendant of the charges that have been brought against him or her and explains his or her constitutional rights—particularly, the right to remain silent (under the Fifth Amendment) and the right to be represented by counsel (under the Sixth Amendment). At this point, if the defendant cannot afford to hire a private attorney, a public defender may be appointed, or private counsel may be hired by the state to represent the defendant.

As the U.S. Constitution does not specify how soon a defendant must be brought before a magistrate after arrest, it has been left to the judicial branch to determine the timing of the initial appearance. The Supreme Court has held that the initial appearance must occur "promptly," which in most cases means within forty-eight hours of booking.[2]

8-1b Pretrial Detention

In misdemeanor cases, a defendant may decide to plead guilty and be sentenced during the initial appearance. Otherwise, the magistrate will usually release those charged with misdemeanors on their promise to return at a later date for further proceedings. For felony cases, however, the defendant is not permitted to make a plea at the initial appearance because a magistrate's court does not have jurisdiction to decide felonies. Furthermore, in most instances the defendant will be released only if she or he posts **bail**—an amount paid by the defendant to the court and retained by the court until the defendant returns for further proceedings.

Defendants who cannot afford bail are generally kept in a local jail or lockup until the date of their trial, though many jurisdictions are searching for alternatives to this practice because of overcrowded incarceration facilities. Just under two-thirds of felony defendants in state courts are released before their trials.

SETTING BAIL Bail is provided for under the Eighth Amendment. The amendment does not, however, guarantee the right to bail. Instead, it states that "excessive

bail shall not be required." This has come to mean that the bail amount must be reasonable compared with the seriousness of the wrongdoing. It does *not* mean that the amount of bail must be within the defendant's ability to pay.

There is no uniform system for pretrial detention. Each jurisdiction has its own *bail tariffs*, or general guidelines concerning the proper amount of bail. For misdemeanors, the police usually follow a preapproved bail schedule created by local judicial authorities. In felony cases, the primary responsibility to set bail lies with the judge. Figure 8.1 shows typical bail amounts for violent offenses.

PREVENTIVE DETENTION The vagueness of the Eighth Amendment's requirement that "excessive bail shall not be required" allows the practice to serve another purpose: the protection of the community. That is, if a judge feels that the defendant poses a threat should he or she be released before trial, the judge will set bail at a level the suspect cannot possibly afford. Several years ago, for example, a King County,

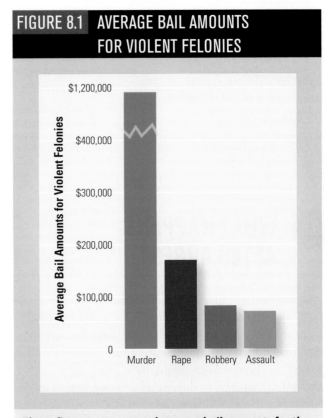

FIGURE 8.1 AVERAGE BAIL AMOUNTS FOR VIOLENT FELONIES

These figures represent the mean bail amounts for the seventy-five largest counties in the nation.

Source: Adapted from Bureau of Justice Statistics, *Felony Defendants in Large Urban Counties, 2009–Statistical Tables* (Washington, D.C.: U.S. Department of Justice, December 2013), Table 16, page 19.

Initial Appearance An accused's first appearance before a judge or magistrate following arrest.

Bail The dollar amount or conditions set by the court to ensure that an individual accused of a crime will appear for further criminal proceedings.

Washington, district court judge set bail at $2 million for indigent defendant Justin Jasper, accused of planning to firebomb three college campuses in the Seattle area.

Alternatively, more than thirty states and the federal government have passed **preventive detention** legislation to protect the community. These laws allow judges to act "in the best interests of the community" by denying bail to arrestees with prior records of violence, thus keeping them in custody prior to trial.

What ethical issues are raised by the bail system? What is your opinion of legislation that abolishes bail bonding for profit?

8-1c Release

One of the most popular alternatives to bail is **release on recognizance (ROR).** With ROR—used by almost every jurisdiction in the country—the judge, based on the advice of trained personnel, decides that the defendant is not at risk to "jump" bail and does not pose a threat to the community. The defendant is then released at no cost with the understanding that he or she will return at the time of the trial. When properly administered, ROR programs seem to be successful, with less than 5 percent of the participants failing to show for trial.[3]

POSTING BAIL Those suspected of committing a felony are rarely released on recognizance. These defendants may post, or pay, the full amount of the bail in cash to the court. The money will be returned when the suspect appears for trial. Given the large amount of funds required, and the relative lack of wealth of many criminal defendants, a defendant can rarely post bail in cash.

Another option is to use real property, such as a house, instead of cash as collateral. These **property bonds** are also rare because most courts require property valued at double the bail amount. Thus, if bail is set at $5,000, the defendant (or the defendant's family and friends) will have to produce property valued at $10,000.

BAIL BOND AGENTS If unable to post bail with cash or property, a defendant may arrange for a **bail bond agent** to post a bail bond on the defendant's behalf. The bond agent, in effect, promises the court that he or she will turn over to the court the full amount of bail if the defendant fails to return for further proceedings. The defendant usually must give the bond agent a certain percentage of the bail (frequently 10 percent) in cash.

This amount, which is often not returned to the defendant later, is considered payment for the bond agent's assistance and assumption of risk. Depending on the amount of the bail bond, the defendant may also be required to sign over to the bond agent rights to certain property (such as a car, a valuable watch, or other asset) as security for the bond.

8-2 HOW DOES A PROSECUTOR LINK A DEFENDANT TO A CRIME?

Once the initial appearance has been completed and bail has been set, the prosecutor must establish *probable cause.* In other words, the prosecutor must show that a crime was committed and link the defendant to that

Preventive Detention The retention of an accused person in custody due to fears that she or he will commit a crime if released before trial.

Release on Recognizance (ROR) A judge's order that releases an accused from jail with the understanding that he or she will return of his or her own will for further proceedings.

Property Bond Property provided to the court by the defendant as an assurance that he or she will return for trial; an alternative to cash bail.

Bail Bond Agent A businessperson who agrees, for a fee, to pay the bail amount if the accused fails to appear in court as ordered.

crime. There are two formal procedures for establishing probable cause at this stage of the pretrial process: preliminary hearings and grand juries.

8-2a The Preliminary Hearing

During the **preliminary hearing,** the defendant appears before a judge or magistrate who decides whether the evidence presented is sufficient for the case to proceed to trial. Normally, every person arrested has a right to this hearing within a reasonable amount of time after his or her initial arrest—usually, no later than ten days if the defendant is in custody or within thirty days if he or she has gained pretrial release.

THE PRELIMINARY HEARING PROCESS The preliminary hearing is conducted in the manner of a mini-trial. Typically, a police report of the arrest is presented by a law enforcement officer, supplemented with evidence provided by the prosecutor. Because the burden of proving probable cause is relatively light (compared with proving guilt beyond a reasonable doubt), prosecutors rarely call witnesses during the preliminary hearing, saving them for the trial.

During this hearing, the defendant has a right to be represented by counsel, who may cross-examine witnesses and challenge any evidence offered by the prosecutor. In most states, defense attorneys can take advantage of the preliminary hearing to begin the process of **discovery,** in which they are entitled to have access to any evidence in the possession of the prosecution relating to the case. Discovery is considered a keystone in the adversary process, as it allows the defense to see the evidence against the defendant prior to making a plea.

WAIVING THE HEARING The preliminary hearing often seems rather perfunctory. It usually lasts no longer than five minutes, and the judge or magistrate

rarely finds that probable cause does not exist. For this reason, defense attorneys commonly advise their clients to waive their right to a preliminary hearing. Once a judge has ruled affirmatively, in many jurisdictions the defendant is bound over to the **grand jury,** a group of citizens called to decide whether probable cause exists. In other jurisdictions, the prosecutor issues an **information,** which replaces the police complaint as the formal charge against the defendant for the purposes of a trial.

8-2b The Grand Jury

The grand jury does not determine the guilt or innocence of the defendant. Rather, it determines whether the evidence presented by the prosecution is sufficient to provide reasonable cause that a crime occurred. If a majority of the jurors find sufficient evidence, the grand jury will issue an **indictment** (pronounced in-*dyte*-ment). Like an information in a preliminary hearing, the indictment becomes the formal charge against the defendant.

The federal government and about one-third of the states require grand jury indictments to bring felony charges. In most of the other states, a grand jury is optional. When a grand jury is not used, the discretion of whether to charge is left to the prosecutor, who must then present his or her argument at the preliminary hearing.

SPECIAL FEATURES OF GRAND JURIES Grand juries are *impaneled*, or created, for a period of time usually not exceeding three months. For the most part, grand jury proceedings are dominated by the prosecution, which can present a wide variety of evidence against the defendant, including photographs, documents, tangible objects, and the testimony of witnesses. Generally speaking, grand jury proceedings differ from full criminal trials in that:

1. Jurors can ask the district attorney and the judge questions about relevant law, and can request that witnesses be recalled to the stand to testify a second time.

2. The defense cannot cross-examine prosecution witnesses, though it can present its own witnesses.

3. The proceedings are closed (secret). Witnesses can speak publicly, but only about their own testimony. Members of the grand jury are not allowed to speak to the media.

Preliminary Hearing An initial hearing in which a magistrate decides if there is probable cause to believe that the defendant committed the crime with which he or she is charged.

Discovery Formal investigation by each side prior to trial.

Grand Jury The group of citizens called to decide whether probable cause exists to believe that a suspect committed the crime with which she or he has been charged.

Information The formal charge against the accused issued by the prosecutor after a preliminary hearing has found probable cause.

Indictment A charge or written accusation, issued by a grand jury, that probable cause exists to believe that a named person has committed a crime.

Job Description:

▶ Oversee court operations, budget and accounting, technology, emergency management, and human resources.

▶ Establish and maintain working relationships with judges, state attorneys, public defenders, clerks, other state and federal courts (including the United States Supreme Court), law enforcement agencies, and the public.

What Kind of Training Is Required?

▶ A bachelor of arts in court administration, management, or a related area, and five years of professional experience in court administration or government administration, plus five years in a supervisory capacity.

▶ A law degree, master's degree, or certification by the Institute of Court Management may substitute for nonsupervisory experience.

Annual Salary Range?

▶ $30,000–$90,000

eurobanks/ShutterStock.com

GETTING LINKEDIN

Sheriffs' departments are often involved in operating county-level courts (see Chapter 4), and these departments also hire trial court administrators. A recent LinkedIn posting by the Hillsborough County (Florida) Sheriff's Office for a court operations assistant focused on information technology skills and "considerable knowledge of court procedures."

CAREER TIP If a grand jury needs more evidence, it can issue a document called a **subpoena**, ordering a person to appear in court and answer its questions. The task of delivering the subpoena is often left to a *process server*, whose career is based on the challenge of finding people who may not want to be found.

A "RUBBER STAMP" As we saw in Chapter 1, a grand jury chose not to indict Darren Wilson, the police officer who shot and killed Michael Brown in Ferguson, Missouri, in 2014. Following the release of the grand jury documents, a lawyer for the Brown family made a familiar complaint about the process. "If you present evidence to indict, you get an indictment," he said. "If you present evidence not to indict, you don't get an indictment."[4] Certainly, the procedural rules of the grand jury favor prosecutors. The exclusionary rule (see Chapter 6) does not apply in grand jury investigations, so prosecutors can present evidence that would be disallowed at any subsequent trial. Furthermore, the grand jury is given the prosecution's version of the facts, with the defense having only a limited ability to offer counterarguments.

In the words of one observer, a grand jury would indict a "ham sandwich" if the government asked it to do so.[5] Overall, defendants are indicted at a rate of more than 99 percent,[6] leading to the common characterization of the grand jury as little more than a "rubber stamp" for the prosecution.

8-2c Case Attrition

Prosecutorial discretion includes the power *not* to prosecute cases. Generally speaking, of every one hundred felony arrests in the United States, only thirty-five of the arrestees are prosecuted, and only eighteen of these prosecutions lead to incarceration. Consequently, fewer than one in three adults arrested for a felony sees the inside of a prison or jail cell. This phenomenon is known as **case attrition,** and it is explained in part by prosecutorial discretion.

SCARCE RESOURCES About half of the adult felony cases brought to prosecutors by police are dismissed through a *nolle prosequi* (Latin for "unwilling to pursue"). Why are these cases "nolled," or not prosecuted by the district attorney? In our earlier discussions of law enforcement, you learned that the police do not have the resources to arrest every lawbreaker in the nation. Similarly, district attorneys do not have the resources to prosecute every arrest. They must choose how to distribute their scarce resources.

In some cases, the decision is made for prosecutors, such as when police break procedural law and negate important evidence. This happens rarely—less than 3 percent of felony arrests are dropped because of the exclusionary rule, and almost all of these are the result of illegal drug searches.[7]

SCREENING FACTORS Most prosecutors have a *screening* process for deciding when to prosecute and when to "noll." This process varies a bit from jurisdiction to jurisdiction, but most prosecutors consider several factors in making the decision:[8]

▸ The most important factor in deciding whether to prosecute is not the prosecutor's belief in the guilt of the suspect, but whether there is *sufficient evidence for conviction.* If prosecutors have strong physical evidence and a number of reliable and believable witnesses, they are quite likely to prosecute.

▸ Prosecutors also rely heavily on *offense seriousness* to guide their priorities, preferring to take on felony offenses rather than misdemeanors. In other words, everything else being equal, a district attorney will prosecute a rapist instead of a jaywalker because the former presents a greater threat to society than does the latter. A prosecutor will also be more likely to prosecute someone with an extensive record of wrongdoing than a first-time offender.

▸ Sometimes a case is dropped even when it involves a serious crime and a wealth of evidence exists against the suspect. These situations usually involve *uncooperative victims.* Domestic violence cases are particularly difficult to prosecute because the victims may want to keep the matter private, fear reprisals, or have a strong desire to protect their abusers. In some jurisdictions, as many as 80 percent of domestic violence victims refuse to cooperate with the prosecution.[9]

▸ *Unreliability of victims* can also affect a charging decision. If the victim in a rape case is a crack addict and a prostitute, while the defendant is a decorated military veteran, prosecutors may be hesitant to have a jury decide which one is more trustworthy.

▸ A prosecutor may be willing to drop a case or reduce the charges against *a defendant who is willing to testify against other offenders.* Federal law encourages this kind of behavior by offering sentencing reductions to defendants who provide "substantial assistance in the investigation or prosecution of another person who has committed an offense."[10]

8-3 WHY DO SO MANY DEFENDANTS PLEAD GUILTY?

Based on the information (delivered during the preliminary hearing) or indictment (handed down by the grand jury), the prosecutor submits a motion to the court to order the defendant to appear before the trial court for an **arraignment.** Due process of law, as guaranteed by the Fifth Amendment, requires that a criminal defendant be informed of the charges brought against her or him and be offered an opportunity to respond to those charges. The arraignment is one of the ways in which due process requirements are satisfied by criminal procedure law.

At the arraignment, the defendant is informed of the charges and must respond by pleading not guilty or guilty. In some but not all states, the defendant may also enter a plea of **nolo contendere,** which is Latin for "I will not contest it." The plea of *nolo contendere* is neither an admission nor a denial of guilt. (The consequences for someone who pleads guilty and for someone who pleads *nolo contendere* are the same in a criminal trial, but the latter plea cannot be used in

Case Attrition The process through which prosecutors, by deciding whether to prosecute each person arrested, effect an overall reduction in the number of persons prosecuted.

Arraignment A court proceeding in which the suspect is formally charged with the criminal offense stated in the indictment.

Nolo Contendere Latin for "I will not contest it." A plea in which a criminal defendant chooses not to challenge, or contest, the charges brought by the government.

a subsequent civil trial as an admission of guilt.) Most frequently, the defendant pleads guilty to the initial charge or to a lesser charge that has been agreed on through *plea bargaining* between the prosecutor and the defendant. If the defendant pleads guilty, no trial is necessary, and the defendant is sentenced based on the crime he or she has admitted committing.

8-3a Plea Bargaining in the Criminal Justice System

Plea bargaining most often takes place after the arraignment and before the beginning of the trial. In its simplest terms, it is a process by which the accused, represented by the defense counsel, and the prosecutor work out a mutually satisfactory disposition of the case, subject to court approval.

Usually, plea bargaining involves the defendant pleading guilty to the charges against her or him in return for a lighter sentence, but other variations are possible as well. The defendant can agree to plead guilty in exchange for having the charge against her or him reduced from, say, felony burglary to the lesser offense of breaking and entering. Or a person charged with multiple counts may agree to plead guilty if the prosecutor agrees to drop one or more of the counts. Whatever the particulars, the results of a plea bargain are generally the same: the prosecutor gets a conviction, and the defendant a lesser punishment.

In *Santobello v. New York* (1971),[11] the Supreme Court held that plea bargaining "is not only an essential part of the process but a highly desirable part for many reasons." Some observers would agree, but with ambivalence. They understand that plea bargaining offers the practical benefit of saving court resources, but question whether it is the best way to achieve justice.[12]

8-3b Motivations for Plea Bargaining

LO8-2 Given the high rate of plea bargaining—accounting for 97 percent of criminal convictions in state courts[13]—it follows that the prosecutor, defense attorney, and defendant each have strong reasons to engage in the practice.

PROSECUTORS AND PLEA BARGAINING In most cases, a prosecutor has a single goal after charging a defendant with a crime: conviction. If a case goes to trial, no matter how certain a prosecutor may be that the defendant is guilty, there is always a chance that a jury or judge will disagree. Plea bargaining removes this risk. Furthermore, the prosecutorial screening process described earlier in the chapter is not infallible. Sometimes, a prosecutor will find that the evidence against the accused is weaker than first thought or will uncover new information that changes the complexion of the case. In these situations, the prosecutor may decide to drop the charges or, if he or she still feels that the defendant is guilty, turn to plea bargaining to "save" a questionable case.

The prosecutor's role as an administrator also comes into play. She or he may be interested in the quickest, most efficient manner to dispose of caseloads, and plea bargains reduce the time and money spent on each case. Personal philosophy can affect the proceedings as well. A prosecutor who feels that a mandatory minimum sentence for a particular crime, such as marijuana possession, is too strict may plea bargain in order to lessen the penalty. Similarly, some prosecutors will consider plea bargaining only in certain instances—for burglary and theft, for example, but not for more serious felonies such as rape and murder.

DEFENSE ATTORNEYS AND PLEA BARGAINING Political scientist Milton Heumann has said that a defense attorney's most important lesson is that "most of his [or her] clients are guilty."[14] Given this stark reality, favorable plea bargains are often the best a defense attorney can do for clients, aside from helping them to gain acquittals. Some have suggested that defense attorneys have other, less savory motives for convincing a client to plead guilty, such as a desire to increase profits by quickly disposing of cases[15] or a wish to ingratiate themselves with the other members of the courtroom work group by showing their "reasonableness."[16]

DEFENDANTS AND PLEA BARGAINING The plea bargain allows the defendant a measure of control over his or her fate. In August 2014, for example, Miranda Barbour and her husband, Elytte, pleaded guilty to second degree murder in a Northumberland County (Pennsylvania) court for killing a man they had arranged to meet using the online classified site Craigslist. Had the case gone to trial, the couple risked being convicted of first degree murder and given the death penalty. Instead, under the terms of the plea agreement, the

Plea Bargaining The process by which the accused and the prosecutor work out a mutually satisfactory conclusion to the case, subject to court approval.

Barbours will spend the rest of their lives in jail. In general, defendants who plea bargain receive significantly lighter sentences than those who are found guilty at trial.

VICTIMS AND PLEA BARGAINING One of the major goals of the victims' rights movement has been to increase the role of victims in the plea bargaining process. In recent years, the movement has had some success in this area. About half of the states now allow for victim participation in plea bargaining. Many have laws similar to North Carolina's statute that requires the district attorney's office to offer victims "the opportunity to consult with the prosecuting attorney" and give their views on "plea possibilities."[17] On the federal level, the Crime Victims' Rights Act grants victims the right to be "reasonably heard" during the process.[18]

Crime victims often have mixed emotions regarding plea bargains. On the one hand, any form of "negotiated justice" that lessens the offender's penalty may add insult to the victim's emotional and physical injuries. "No punishment will ever be long enough, harsh enough," said the widow of Miranda and Elytte Barbour's murder victim after the couple were sentenced to life in prison, as just described.[19] On the other hand, trials can bring up events and emotions that some victims would rather not have to reexperience. District Attorney Ann Targonski said that she allowed the Barbours' guilty plea to spare the victim's family the trauma of court proceedings that could have lasted decades.[20]

8-3c Pleading Not Guilty

Despite the large number of defendants who eventually plead guilty, the plea of not guilty is fairly common at the arraignment. This is true even when the facts of the case seem stacked against the defendant. Generally, a not guilty plea in the face of strong evidence is part of a strategy to do one of the following:

1. **Gain a more favorable plea bargain.**

2. **Challenge a crucial part of the evidence on constitutional grounds.**

3. **Submit one of the justification defenses that we discussed in Chapter 3.**

Of course, if either side is confident in the strength of its arguments and evidence, it will obviously be less likely to accept a plea bargain. Both prosecutors and defense attorneys may favor a trial to gain publicity, and sometimes public pressure after an extremely violent or high-profile crime will force a chief prosecutor (who is, remember, normally an elected official) to take a weak case to trial. Also, some defendants may insist on their right to a trial, regardless of their attorneys' advice. In the remainder of this chapter, we will examine what happens to the roughly 3 percent of indictments that do lead to the courtroom.

Why did Miranda Barbour, shown here being escorted out of a Sunbury, Pennsylvania, courtroom, agree to plead guilty to second degree murder for killing a man she met on Craigslist? What incentives might local prosecutors have had for accepting Barbour's guilty plea and declining to seek her execution?

AP Images/PennLive.com, Christine Baker, File

8-4 **WHAT ARE THE SPECIAL FEATURES OF CRIMINAL TRIALS?**

LO8-3 Criminal trial procedures reflect the need to protect criminal defendants against the power of the state by providing them with a number of rights. Many of the significant rights of the accused are spelled out in the Sixth Amendment, which reads, in part, as follows:

In all criminal prosecutions, the accused shall enjoy the right to a speedy and public trial, by an impartial jury of the State and the district wherein the crime shall have been committed, . . . and to be informed of the nature and cause of the accusation; to be confronted with the witnesses against him; to have compulsory process for obtaining witnesses in his favor; and to have the Assistance of Counsel for his defense.

In the last chapter, we discussed the Sixth Amendment's guarantee of the right to counsel. In this section, we will examine the other important aspects of the criminal trial, beginning with two protections explicitly stated in the Sixth Amendment: the right to a speedy trial and the right to an impartial jury.

Because Louisiana prosecutors charged Darren Sharper with a crime—aggravated rape—that carries a possible life sentence, they are not bound by state statutes of limitations in Sharper's case. *Do you agree that serious violent crimes should be free from statutes of limitations? Why or why not?*

Mark Boster/Getty Images

8-4a A "Speedy" Trial

As you have just read, the Sixth Amendment requires a speedy trial for those accused of a criminal act. The reason for this requirement is obvious: depending on various factors, the defendant may lose his or her right to move freely and may be incarcerated prior to trial. Also, the accusation that a person has committed a crime jeopardizes that person's reputation in the community. If the defendant is innocent, the sooner the trial is held, the sooner his or her innocence can be established in the eyes of the court and the public.

The Sixth Amendment does not specify what is meant by the term *speedy*. The United States Supreme Court has refused to quantify "speedy" as well, ruling instead in *Barker v. Wingo* (1972)[21] that only in situations in which the delay is unwarranted and proved to be prejudicial can the accused claim a violation of Sixth Amendment rights.

Note that the Sixth Amendment's guarantee of a speedy trial does not apply until a person has been accused of a crime. Citizens are protected against unreasonable delays before accusation by **statutes of limitations,** which are legislative time limits that require prosecutors to charge a defendant with a crime within a certain amount of time after the illegal act took place. If the statute of limitations on a particular crime is ten years, and the police do not identify a suspect until ten years and one day after the criminal act occurred, then that suspect cannot be charged with that particular offense. In general,

prosecutions for murder and other offenses that carry the death penalty do not have a statute of limitations.

8-4b The Role of the Jury

The Sixth Amendment also states that anyone accused of a crime shall be judged by "an impartial jury." In *Duncan v. Louisiana* (1968),[22] the Supreme Court solidified this right by ruling that in all felony cases, the defendant is entitled to a **jury trial.** The Court has, however, left it to the individual states to decide whether juries are required for misdemeanor cases.[23] If the defendant waives her or his right to trial by jury, a **bench trial** takes place in which a judge decides questions of legality and fact, and no jury is involved.

The typical American jury consists of twelve persons. About half the states allow fewer than twelve persons on criminal juries, though rarely for serious felony cases. In federal courts, defendants are entitled to have the case heard by a twelve-member jury unless both parties agree in writing to a smaller jury.

Statute of Limitations A law limiting the amount of time prosecutors have to bring criminal charges against a suspect after the crime has occurred.

Jury Trial A trial before a judge and a jury.

Bench Trial A trial conducted without a jury, in which a judge makes the determination of the defendant's guilt or innocence.

In most jurisdictions, jury verdicts in criminal cases must be *unanimous* for **acquittal** or conviction. As will be explained in more detail later, if the jury cannot reach unanimous agreement on whether to acquit or convict the defendant, the result is a *hung jury*, and the judge may order a new trial. The Supreme Court has held that unanimity is not a rigid requirement. It declared that jury verdicts must be unanimous in federal criminal trials, but has given states leeway to set their own rules.[24] As a result, Louisiana and Oregon continue to require only ten votes for conviction in criminal cases.

8-4c The Privilege against Self-Incrimination

In addition to the Sixth Amendment, which specifies the protections we have just discussed, the Fifth Amendment to the Constitution also provides important safeguards for the defendant. The Fifth Amendment states that no person "shall be compelled in any criminal case to be a witness against himself." Therefore, a defendant has the right not to testify at his or her own trial—in popular parlance, to "take the Fifth." Because defense attorneys often are wary of exposing their clients to prosecutors' questions in court, defendants rarely take the witness stand.

It is important to note that not only does the defendant have the right to "take the Fifth," but also that the decision to do so should not prejudice the jury in the prosecution's favor. The Supreme Court came to this controversial decision while reviewing *Adamson v. California* (1947),[25] a case involving the convictions of two defendants who had declined to testify in their own defense against charges of robbery, kidnapping, and murder. The prosecutor in the *Adamson* proceedings frequently and insistently brought this silence to the notice of the jury in his closing argument, insinuating that if the pair had been innocent, they would not have been afraid to testify.

The Court ruled that such tactics effectively invalidated the Fifth Amendment by using the defendants' refusal to testify as a ploy to insinuate guilt. Now judges are required to inform the jury that an accused's decision to remain silent cannot be held against him or her. This protection only covers post-arrest and trial silence, however. In 2013, the Supreme Court ruled that prosecutors can inform a jury that a defendant refused to answer police questions *before* being arrested, a process detailed in Chapter 6.[26]

Acquittal A declaration following a trial that the individual accused of the crime is innocent in the eyes of the law and thus is absolved from the charges.

8-4d The Presumption of a Defendant's Innocence

The presumption in criminal law is that a defendant is innocent until proved guilty. The burden of proving guilt falls on the state (the public prosecutor). Even if a defendant did in fact commit the crime, she or he will be "innocent" in the eyes of the law unless the prosecutor can substantiate the charge with sufficient evidence to convince a jury (or judge in a bench trial) of the defendant's guilt.

Sometimes, especially when a case involves a high-profile violent crime, pretrial publicity may have convinced many members of the community—including potential jurors—that a defendant is guilty. In these instances, a judge has the authority to change the venue of the trial to increase the likelihood of an unbiased jury. In 2014, for example, Dzhokhar Tsarnaev's defense attorneys requested a change of venue from Boston to Washington, D.C., for their client's trial on charges relating to the 2013 Boston Marathon bombings. They argued that "an extraordinarily high number" of Boston residents had either attended the marathon or knew someone else who had, and would therefore be "less able to set aside preconceived notions regarding guilt and punishment."[27] The presiding judge refused this request, stating, "It is doubtful whether a jury could be selected anywhere in the country whose members were wholly unaware of the marathon bombings."[28]

8-4e A Strict Standard of Proof

In a criminal trial, the defendant is not required to prove his or her innocence. As just mentioned, the burden of proving the defendant's guilt lies entirely with the state. Furthermore, the state must prove the defendant's guilt *beyond a reasonable doubt*. In other words, the prosecution must show that, based on all the evidence, the defendant's guilt is clear and unquestionable. In *In re Winship* (1970),[29] a case involving the due process rights of juveniles, the Supreme Court ruled that the Constitution requires the reasonable doubt standard because it reduces the risk of convicting innocent people and therefore reassures Americans of the law's moral force and legitimacy.

This high standard of proof in criminal cases reflects a fundamental social value—the belief that it is worse to convict an innocent individual than to let a guilty one go free. The consequences to the life, liberty, and reputation of an accused person from an erroneous conviction for a crime are substantial, and this has been factored into the process. Placing a high standard of proof on the prosecutor reduces the margin of error in criminal cases (at least in one direction).

8-5 HOW IS THE JURY SELECTED?

The initial step in a criminal trial involves choosing the jury. The main goal of jury selection is to produce a cross section of the population in the jurisdiction where the crime was committed. Besides having to live in the jurisdiction where the case is being tried, there are very few restrictions on eligibility to serve on a jury. State legislatures generally set the requirements, and they are similar in most states. For the most part, jurors must be

1. Citizens of the United States.

2. Eighteen years of age or older.

3. Free of felony convictions.

4. Healthy enough to function in a jury setting.

5. Sufficiently intelligent to understand the issues of a trial.

6. Able to read, write, and comprehend the English language (with one exception—New Mexico does not allow non-English-speaking citizens to be eliminated from jury lists simply because of their lack of English-language skills).

8-5a *Voir Dire*

At the courthouse, prospective jurors are gathered, and the process of selecting those who will actually hear the case begins. This selection process is not haphazard. The court ultimately seeks jurors who are free of any biases that may affect their willingness to listen to the facts of the case impartially. To this end, both the prosecutor and the defense attorney have some input into the ultimate makeup of the jury. Each attorney questions prospective jurors in a proceeding known as **voir dire** (French for "to speak the truth"). During *voir dire*, jurors are required to provide the court with

Master Jury List The list of citizens in a court's district from which a jury can be selected; compiled from voter-registration lists, driver's license lists, and other sources.

Venire The group of citizens from which the jury is selected.

Voir Dire The preliminary questions that the trial attorneys ask prospective jurors to determine whether they are biased or have any connection with the defendant or a witness.

The **master jury list,** sometimes called the *jury pool,* is made up of all the eligible jurors in a community. This list is usually drawn from voter-registration lists or driver's license rolls, which have the benefit of being easily available and timely.

The next step in gathering a jury is to draw together the **venire** (Latin for "to come"). The *venire* is composed of all those people who are notified by the clerk of the court that they have been selected for jury duty. Those selected to be part of the *venire* are ordered to report to the courthouse on the date specified by the notice.

Image Source/Jupiter Images

Why is it important that a defendant be tried by a jury of his or her "peers"?

a significant amount of personal information, including home address, marital status, employment status, arrest record, and life experiences.

QUESTIONING POTENTIAL JURORS The *voir dire* process involves both written and oral questioning of potential jurors. Attorneys fashion their inquiries in such a manner as to uncover any biases on the part of prospective jurors and to find persons who might identify with the plights of their respective sides. As one attorney noted, though a lawyer will have many chances to talk to a jury as a whole, *voir dire* is his or her only chance to talk with the individual jurors. (To better understand the specific kinds of questions asked during this process, see Figure 8.2.)

CHALLENGING POTENTIAL JURORS During *voir dire*, the attorney for each side may exercise a certain number of challenges to prevent particular persons from serving on the jury. Both sides can exercise two types of challenges: challenges "for cause" and peremptory challenges.

LO8-4 **Challenges for Cause** If a defense attorney or prosecutor concludes that a prospective juror is unfit to serve, the attorney may exercise a **challenge for cause** and request that that person not be included on the jury. Attorneys must provide the court with a sound, legally justifiable reason for why potential jurors are "unfit" to serve. For example, jurors can be challenged for cause if they are mentally incompetent, do not understand English, or are proved to have a prior link—be it personal or financial—with the defendant or victim.

Peremptory Challenges Each attorney may also exercise a limited number of **peremptory challenges.** These challenges are based solely on an attorney's subjective reasoning, and the attorney usually is not required to give any legally justifiable reason for wanting to exclude a particular person from the jury. Because of the rather random nature of peremptory challenges, each state limits the number that an attorney may utilize: between five and ten for felony trials (depending on the state) and between ten and twenty for trials that could possibly result in the death penalty (also depending on the state). Once an attorney's peremptory challenges are used up, he or she must accept forthcoming jurors, unless a challenge for cause can be used.

8-5b Race and Gender Issues in Jury Selection

For many years, prosecutors used their peremptory challenges as an instrument of segregation in jury selection. Prosecutors were able to keep African Americans off juries in cases in which an African American was the defendant. The argument that African Americans—or members of any other minority group—would be partial toward one of their own was tacitly supported by the Supreme Court. Despite its own assertion, made in *Swain v. Alabama* (1965),[30] that blacks have the same right to appear on a jury as whites, the Court mirrored the apparent racism of society as a whole by protecting the questionable actions of many prosecutors.

Challenge for Cause A *voir dire* challenge for which an attorney states the reason why a prospective juror should not be included on the jury.

Peremptory Challenges *Voir dire* challenges to exclude potential jurors from serving on the jury without any supporting reason or cause.

FIGURE 8.2 SAMPLE JUROR QUESTIONNAIRE

30. Do you believe that Mr. Hernandez is more likely to be guilty of the charges in this case because he has tattoos than an individual without tattoos would be?

31. Mr. Hernandez, the defendant, is Hispanic and the decedent, Odin Lloyd, was African American. Is there anything about those facts that would interfere with your ability to render a fair and just verdict?

37. Are you a fan of the New England Patriots?

39. In this case, you will hear evidence that the defendant was a professional football player for the New England Patriots. Is there anything about that fact that would impair your ability to be fair and impartial?

In 2015, Aaron Hernandez went on trial for murdering Odin Lloyd in North Attleborough, Massachusetts, two years earlier. As this excerpt from the juror questionnaire shows, lawyers in the case were interested in determining whether potential jurors had any biases that could keep them from objectively deciding the defendant's fate.

John Tlumacki/*The Boston Globe* via Getty Images

Source: Bristol County, Massachusetts, Superior Court.

THE *BATSON* REVERSAL The Supreme Court reversed this policy in 1986 with *Batson v. Kentucky*.[31] In that case, the Court declared that the Constitution prohibits prosecutors from using peremptory challenges to strike possible jurors on the basis of race. Under the *Batson* ruling, the defendant must prove that the prosecution's use of a peremptory challenge was racially motivated. Doing so requires a number of legal steps:[32]

1. First, the defendant must make a *prima facie* case that there has been discrimination during jury selection. (*Prima facie* is Latin for "at first sight." Legally, it refers to a fact that is presumed to be true unless contradicted by evidence.)

2. To do so, the defendant must show that he or she is a member of a recognizable racial group and that the prosecutor has used peremptory challenges to remove members of this group from the jury pool.

3. Then, the defendant must show that these facts and other relevant circumstances raise the possibility that the prosecutor removed the prospective jurors solely because of their race.

4. If the court accepts the defendant's charges, the burden shifts to the prosecution to prove that its peremptory challenges were race neutral. If the court finds against the prosecution, it rules that a *Batson* violation has occurred.

The Court has revisited the issue of race a number of times in the years since its *Batson* decision. In *Powers v. Ohio* (1991),[33] it ruled that a defendant may contest race-based peremptory challenges even if the defendant is not of the same race as the excluded jurors. In *Georgia v.*

McCollum (1992),[34] the Court placed defense attorneys under the same restrictions as prosecutors when making race-based peremptory challenges. Finally, in 2008, the Court, reaffirming its *Batson* decision of twenty-two years earlier, overturned the conviction of an African American death row inmate because a Louisiana prosecutor improperly picked an all-white jury for his murder trial.[35]

WOMEN ON THE JURY In *J.E.B. v. Alabama ex rel. T.B.* (1994),[36] the Supreme Court extended the principles of the *Batson* ruling to cover gender bias in jury selection. The case was a civil suit for paternity and child support brought by the state of Alabama. Prosecutors used nine of their ten challenges to remove men from the jury, while the defense made similar efforts to remove women. When challenged, the state defended its actions by referring to what it called the rational belief that men and women might have different views on the issues of paternity and child support. The Court disagreed and held this approach to be unconstitutional.

8-6 WHAT HAPPENS DURING A CRIMINAL TRIAL?

LO8-5 Once the jury members have been selected, the judge swears them in, and the trial itself can begin. (See Figure 8.3 for a preview of the stages of a jury trial that will be detailed in this section.) A rather pessimistic truism among attorneys is that every case "has been won or lost when the jury is sworn." This reflects the belief that a juror's values are the major, if not dominant, factor in the decision of guilt or innocence.[37]

FIGURE 8.3 THE STEPS OF A JURY TRIAL

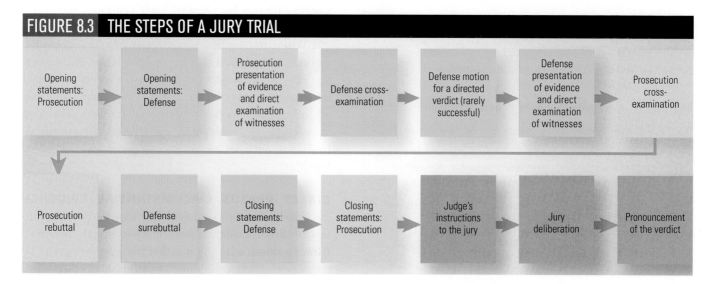

Opening statements: Prosecution → Opening statements: Defense → Prosecution presentation of evidence and direct examination of witnesses → Defense cross-examination → Defense motion for a directed verdict (rarely successful) → Defense presentation of evidence and direct examination of witnesses → Prosecution cross-examination

Prosecution rebuttal → Defense surrebuttal → Closing statements: Defense → Closing statements: Prosecution → Judge's instructions to the jury → Jury deliberation → Pronouncement of the verdict

In actuality, it is difficult to predict how a jury will go about reaching a decision. Despite a number of studies on the question, researchers have not been able to identify any definitive consistent patterns of jury behavior. Sometimes, jurors in a criminal trial will follow instructions to find a defendant guilty unless there is a reasonable doubt, and sometimes they seem to follow instinct or prejudice and apply the law any way they choose.

8-6a Opening Statements

Attorneys may choose to open the trial with a statement to the jury, though they are not required to do so. In these **opening statements,** the attorneys give a brief version of the facts and the supporting evidence that they will present during the trial. Because some trials can drag on for weeks or even months, it is extremely helpful for jurors to hear a summary of what will unfold. In short, the opening statement is a kind of "road map" that describes the destination that each attorney hopes to reach and outlines how she or he plans to reach it.

8-6b The Role of Evidence

Once the opening statements have been made, the prosecutor begins the trial proceedings by presenting the state's evidence against the defendant. Courts have complex rules about what types of evidence may be presented and how the evidence may be brought out during the trial. **Evidence** is anything that is used to prove the existence or nonexistence of a fact. For the most part, evidence can be broken down into two categories: testimony and real evidence. **Testimony** consists of statements by competent witnesses. **Real evidence,** presented to the court in the form of exhibits, includes any physical items—such as the murder weapon or a bloodstained piece of clothing—that affect the case.

Rules of evidence are designed to ensure that testimony and exhibits presented to the jury are relevant, reliable, and not unfairly prejudicial against the defendant. One of the tasks of the defense attorney is to challenge evidence presented by the prosecution by establishing that the evidence is not reliable. Of course, the prosecutor also tries to demonstrate the irrelevance or unreliability of evidence presented by the defense. The final decision on whether evidence is allowed before the jury rests with the judge, in keeping with his or her role as the "referee" of the adversary system.

CAREER TIP *Evidence technicians* help the police and prosecutors gain convictions by identifying, securing, collecting, cataloguing, and storing evidence found at a crime scene.

Opening Statements The attorneys' statements to the jury at the beginning of the trial.

Evidence Anything that is used to prove the existence or nonexistence of a fact.

Testimony Verbal evidence given by witnesses under oath.

Real Evidence Evidence that is brought into court and seen by the jury, as opposed to evidence that is described for a jury.

Lay Witness A witness who can truthfully and accurately testify on a fact in question without having specialized training or knowledge.

Expert Witness A witness with professional training or substantial experience qualifying her or him to testify on a certain subject.

Direct Evidence Evidence that establishes the existence of a fact that is in question without relying on inference.

TESTIMONIAL EVIDENCE A person who is called to testify on factual matters that would be understood by the average citizen is referred to as a **lay witness.** If asked about the condition of a victim of an assault, for example, a lay witness could relate certain facts, such as "she was bleeding from her forehead" or "she was unconscious on the ground for several minutes." A lay witness could not, however, give information about the medical extent of the victim's injuries, such as whether she suffered from a fractured skull or internal bleeding. Coming from a lay witness, such testimony would be inadmissible.

When the matter in question requires scientific, medical, or technical skill beyond the scope of the average person, prosecutors and defense attorneys may call an **expert witness** to the stand. The expert witness is an individual who has professional training, advanced knowledge, or substantial experience in a specialized area, such as medicine, computer technology, or ballistics.

DIRECT VERSUS CIRCUMSTANTIAL EVIDENCE Two types of testimonial evidence may be brought into court: direct evidence and circumstantial evidence. **Direct evidence** is evidence that has been witnessed by the person giving testimony. "I saw Bill shoot Chris" is an example of direct evidence. **Circumstantial evidence** is indirect evidence that, even if believed, does not establish the fact in question but only the degree of likelihood of the fact. In other words, circumstantial evidence can create an inference that a fact exists.

Suppose, for example, that the defendant owns a gun that shoots bullets of the type found in the victim's body. This circumstantial evidence, by itself, does not establish that the defendant committed the crime. Combined with other circumstantial evidence, however, it may do just that. For instance, if other circumstantial evidence indicates that the defendant had a motive for harming the victim and was at the scene of the crime when the shooting occurred, the jury might conclude that the defendant committed the crime.

THE "CSI EFFECT" When possible, defense attorneys will almost always make the argument that the state has failed to present any evidence other than circumstantial evidence against their client. Recently, this tactic has been aided by a phenomenon known as the "CSI effect," taking its name from the popular television series *CSI: Crime Scene Investigation* and its spin-offs. According to many prosecutors, these shows have fostered unrealistic notions among jurors as to what high-tech forensic science can accomplish as part of a criminal investigation.

> **Circumstantial Evidence** Indirect evidence that is offered to establish, by inference, the likelihood of a fact that is in question.

JURY CONSULTANT

Job Description:

▶ Pretrial: Research jurors' backgrounds, assist with juror selection, create favorable potential juror profiles, develop *voir dire* questions, and organize mock trials to aid trial attorneys.

▶ During trial: Carefully watch jurors' body language and behavior to determine if the client trial lawyer is communicating her or his arguments successfully, coach witnesses, and help trial lawyers develop strategies.

What Kind of Training Is Required?

▶ Minimum of a bachelor's degree (although a master's degree or a Ph.D. is ideal) in sociology, political science, criminology, psychology, or behavioral science. Research and data analysis skills are also crucial for this profession.

iStockphoto.com/Alina Solovyova-Vincent

▶ A strongly developed intuition. Jury consultants are not hired for their expertise in criminal law but for their insight into human behavior, decision making, and motivational patterns.

Annual Salary Range?

▶ $43,000–$110,000

> **SOCIAL MEDIA CAREER TIP**
> *You need to differentiate yourself from everyone else online by providing unique, relevant, high-quality content on a regular basis. You should network with a purpose, not just to share fun things.*

In reality, the kind of physical evidence used to solve crimes on *CSI* is often not available to the prosecution, which must rely instead on witnesses and circumstantial evidence. To test the CSI effect, researchers surveyed more than one thousand jurors in Washtenaw County, Michigan, and found that nearly half "expected the prosecutor to present scientific evidence in every criminal case." This expectation was particularly strong in rape trials and trials lacking direct evidence of a crime.[38]

RELEVANCE Evidence will not be admitted in court unless it is relevant to the case being considered. **Relevant evidence** is evidence that tends to prove or disprove a fact in question. Forensic proof that the bullets found in a victim's body were fired from a gun discovered in the suspect's pocket at the time of arrest, for example, is certainly relevant. The suspect's prior record, showing a conviction for armed robbery ten years earlier, is, as we shall soon see, irrelevant to the case at hand and in most instances will be ruled inadmissible by the judge.

PREJUDICIAL EVIDENCE Evidence may be excluded if it would tend to distract the jury from the main issues of the case, mislead the jury, or cause jurors to decide the issue on an emotional basis. In practice, this rule often precludes prosecutors from using prior purported criminal activities or actual convictions to show that the defendant has criminal propensities or an "evil character."[39] This concept is codified in the Federal Rules of Evidence, which state that evidence of "other crimes, wrongs, or acts is not admissible to prove the character of a person in order to show action in conformity therewith." Such evidence is allowed only when it does not apply to character construction and focuses instead on "motive, opportunity, intent, preparation, plan, knowledge, identity, or absence of mistake or accident."[40]

Although this legal concept has come under a great deal of criticism, it is consistent with the presumption-of-innocence standards discussed earlier. Arguably, if a prosecutor is allowed to establish that the defendant has shown antisocial or even violent traits in the past, this will prejudice the jury against the defendant in the present trial. Even if the judge instructs jurors that this prior evidence is irrelevant, human nature dictates that it will probably have a "warping influence" on the jurors' perception of the defendant.[41] Therefore, whenever possible, defense attorneys will keep such evidence from the jury.

8-6c The Prosecution's Case

Because the burden of proof is on the state, the prosecution is generally considered to have a more difficult task than the defense. The prosecutor attempts to establish guilt beyond a reasonable doubt by presenting the *corpus delicti* ("body of the offense" in Latin) of the crime to the jury. The *corpus delicti* is simply a legal term that refers to the substantial facts that show a crime has been committed. By establishing such facts through the presentation of relevant and nonprejudicial evidence, the prosecutor hopes to convince the jury of the defendant's guilt.

DIRECT EXAMINATION OF WITNESSES Witnesses are crucial to establishing the prosecutor's case against the defendant. The prosecutor will call witnesses to the stand and ask them questions pertaining to the sequence of events that the trial is addressing. This form of questioning is known as **direct examination.** During direct examination, the prosecutor will usually not be allowed to ask *leading questions*—questions that might suggest to the witness a particular desired response.

A leading question might be something like "So, Mrs. Williams, you noticed the defendant threatening the victim with a broken beer bottle?" If Mrs. Williams answers "yes" to this question, she has, in effect, been "led" to the conclusion that the defendant was, in fact, threatening with a broken beer bottle. The fundamental purpose behind testimony is to establish what actually happened, not what the trial attorneys would like the jury to believe happened. (A properly worded query would be, "Mrs. Williams, please describe the defendant's manner toward the victim during the incident.")

COMPETENCE AND RELIABILITY OF WITNESSES The rules of evidence include certain restrictions and qualifications pertaining to witnesses. Witnesses must have sufficient mental competence to understand the significance of testifying under oath. They must also be reliable in the sense that they are able to give a clear and reliable description of the events in question. If not, the prosecutor or defense attorney will make sure that the jury is aware of these shortcomings through *cross-examination.*

Relevant Evidence Evidence tending to make a fact in question more or less probable than it would be without the evidence. Only relevant evidence is admissible in court.

Direct Examination The examination of a witness by the attorney who calls the witness to the stand to testify.

8-6d Cross-Examination

After the prosecutor has directly examined her or his witnesses, the defense attorney is given the chance to question the same witnesses. The Sixth Amendment states, "In all criminal prosecutions, the accused shall enjoy the right . . . to be confronted with witnesses against him." This **confrontation clause** gives the accused, through his or her attorneys, the right to cross-examine witnesses. **Cross-examination** refers to the questioning of an opposing witness during trial, and both sides of a case are allowed to do so.

CROSS-EXAMINATION Cross-examination allows the attorneys to test the truthfulness of opposing witnesses and usually entails efforts to create doubt in the jurors' minds that the witness is reliable (see Figure 8.4). After the defense has cross-examined a prosecution witness, the prosecutor may want to reestablish any reliability that might have been lost. The prosecutor can do so by again questioning the witness, a process known as *redirect examination*. Following the redirect examination, the defense attorney will be given the opportunity to ask further questions of prosecution witnesses, or *recross-examination*. Thus, each side has two opportunities to question a witness. The attorneys need not do so, but only after each side has been offered the opportunity will the trial move on.

HEARSAY Cross-examination is also linked to problems presented by *hearsay* evidence. **Hearsay** can be defined as any testimony given about a statement made by someone else. An example of hearsay would be: "Jenny told me that Bill told her that he was the killer." Literally, it is what someone heard someone else say. For the most part, hearsay is not admissible as evidence. When a witness offers hearsay, the person making the original remarks is not in court and therefore cannot be cross-examined. If such testimony were allowed, the defendant's Sixth Amendment right to confront witnesses against him or her would be violated.

There are a number of exceptions to the hearsay rule, and as a result a good deal of hearsay evidence finds its way into criminal trials. For example, a hearsay statement is usually admissible if there seems to be little risk of a lie. Therefore, a statement made by someone who believes that his or her death is imminent—a "dying declaration" or a suicide note—is often allowed in court even though it is hearsay.[42] Similarly, the rules of most states allow hearsay when the statement contains an admission of wrongdoing *and* the speaker is not available to testify in court. The logic behind this exception is that a person generally does not make a statement against her or his own best interests unless it is true.[43]

8-6e The Defendant's Case

After the prosecution has finished presenting its evidence, the defense attorney may offer the defendant's case. Because the burden is on the state to prove the accused's guilt, the defense is not required to offer any case at all. It can simply "rest" without calling any

Confrontation Clause The part of the Sixth Amendment that guarantees all defendants the right to confront witnesses testifying against them during the criminal trial.

Cross-Examination The questioning of an opposing witness during trial.

Hearsay An oral or written statement made by an out-of-court speaker that is later offered in court by a witness (not the speaker) concerning a matter before the court.

FIGURE 8.4 | THE CROSS-EXAMINATION

During Michael Dunn's 2014 trial for the murder of Jordan Davis outside a convenience store in Jacksonville, Florida, the defendant claimed he fatally shot Davis in self-defense. Crucially, Dunn insisted that Davis had pointed a shotgun at him, though no such weapon was found at the crime scene. When Dunn took the stand, the prosecution cross-examined him about what he said to his fiancée, Rhonda Rouer, following the shooting.

Prosecutor: How did you describe the weapon [to her]? Did you say [Davis and his friends] had a sword? Did you say they had a machete?

Dunn: Gun.

Prosecutor: A gun. You used the word "gun"?

Dunn: Multiple times.

Later in the trial, the prosecution called Rouer as a witness. In her testimony, she stated that Dunn never mentioned that he had been threatened with a shotgun, or any other kind of weapon, during the confrontation.

witnesses or producing any real evidence, and ask the jury to decide the merits of the case on what it has seen and heard from the prosecution.

CREATING A REASONABLE DOUBT Defense lawyers most commonly defend their clients by attempting to expose weaknesses in the prosecutor's case. Remember that if the defense attorney can create reasonable doubt concerning the client's guilt in the mind of just a single juror, the defendant has a good chance of gaining an acquittal or at least a *hung jury,* a circumstance explained later in the chapter.

Even if the prosecution can present seemingly strong evidence, a defense attorney may succeed by creating reasonable doubt. In an illustrative case, Jason Korey bragged to his friends that he had shot and killed Joseph Brucker in Pittsburgh, Pennsylvania, and a great deal of circumstantial evidence linked Korey to the killing. The police, however, could find no direct evidence: they could not link Korey to the murder weapon, nor could they match his footprints to those found at the crime scene. Michael Foglia, Korey's defense attorney, explained his client's bragging as an attempt to gain attention, not a true statement. Though this explanation may strike some as unlikely, in the absence of physical evidence it did create doubt in the jurors' minds, and

Korey was acquitted. (For a better idea of how this strategy works in court, see the feature *Discretion in Action—Murder or Suicide?*)

OTHER DEFENSE STRATEGIES The defense can choose among a number of strategies to generate reasonable doubt in the jurors' minds. It can present an *alibi defense,* by submitting evidence that the accused was not at or near the scene of the crime at the time the crime was committed. Another option is to attempt a *justification defense,* by presenting additional facts to the ones offered by the prosecution. Possible justification defenses, which we discussed in detail in Chapter 3, include the following:

1. Self-defense.
2. Insanity.
3. Duress.
4. Entrapment.

With a justification defense strategy, the defense attempts to prove that the defendant should be found not guilty because of certain circumstances surrounding the crime. A justification strategy can be difficult to carry

Discretion in Action

MURDER OR SUICIDE?

THE SITUATION Your client is Michelle, who dialed 911 several years ago, hysterical, screaming, "My husband was shot. Somebody was in the house." When police arrived, they found her husband, Greg, lying in bed with a fatal gunshot wound to the back of his head. First, Michelle said that an intruder had knocked her unconscious and killed her husband. The police found no evidence of a forced entry. After several hours of questioning, Michelle changed her story, claiming that Greg had committed suicide and she had wiped down the crime scene—and then lied to police—to spare the couple's young daughter from knowing that her father had killed himself. Forensics showed, however, that the muzzle of the .45-caliber pistol was too far from Greg's head when it fired for him to have shot himself. Subsequently, Michelle was arrested and charged with murdering her husband.

THE LAW To find a defendant guilty, a jury must find *beyond a reasonable doubt* that he or she committed the crime.

WHAT WOULD YOU DO? As a defense attorney, your job is to create reasonable doubt in the jurors' minds that Michelle killed her husband. Besides the circumstantial evidence presented above, other important details about this case include the following: (1) the murder weapon was found near Greg's body, clean of any fingerprints; (2) Greg was heavily in debt at the time of his death; and (3) Greg's life insurance policy contained a suicide clause, meaning Michelle was not eligible to receive a payout if he took his own life. What argument will you make before the jury to create reasonable doubt?

[To see how a Fort Worth, Texas, defense attorney argued in a case with similar facts, go to Example 8.1 in Appendix A.]

out because it forces the defense to prove the reliability of its own evidence, not simply disprove the evidence offered by the prosecution.

The defense is often willing to admit that a certain criminal act took place, especially if the defendant has already confessed. In this case, the primary question of the trial becomes not whether the defendant is guilty, but what the defendant is guilty of. In these situations, the defense strategy focuses on obtaining the lightest possible penalty for the defendant. As we saw earlier, this strategy is responsible for the high percentage of proceedings that end in plea bargains.

8-6f Rebuttal and Surrebuttal

After the defense closes its case, the prosecution is permitted to bring new evidence forward that was not used during its initial presentation to the jury. This is called the **rebuttal** stage of the trial. When the rebuttal stage is finished, the defense is given the opportunity to cross-examine the prosecution's new witnesses and introduce new witnesses of its own. This final act is part of the *surrebuttal.* After these stages have been completed, the defense may offer another motion for a directed verdict, asking the judge to find in the defendant's favor. If this motion is rejected, and it almost always is, the case is closed, and the opposing sides offer their closing arguments.

8-6g Closing Arguments

In their **closing arguments,** the attorneys summarize their presentations and argue one final time for their respective cases. In most states, the defense attorney goes first, and then the prosecutor. (In Colorado, Kentucky, and Missouri, the order is reversed.) An effective closing argument includes all of the major points that support the government's or the defense's case. It also emphasizes the shortcomings of the opposing party's case.

8-7 WHAT HAPPENS AT THE END OF A CRIMINAL TRIAL?

After closing arguments, the outcome of the trial is in the hands of the jury. Before the jurors begin their deliberations, the judge gives the jury a **charge,** summing up the case and instructing the jurors on the rules of law that apply to the issues in the case. These charges, also called jury instructions, are usually prepared during a special *charging conference* involving the judge and the trial attorneys. In this conference, the attorneys suggest the instructions they would like to see be sent to the jurors, but the judge makes the final decision as to the charges submitted. If the defense attorney disagrees with the charges sent to the jury, he or she can enter an objection, thereby setting the stage for a possible appeal.

8-7a Jury Deliberation

After receiving the charge, the jury begins its deliberations. Jury deliberation is a somewhat mysterious process, as it takes place in complete seclusion. Most of what is known about how a jury deliberates comes from mock trials or interviews with jurors after the verdict has been reached. A general picture of the deliberation process constructed from this research shows that jurors are not necessarily predisposed to argue with one another over the fate of the defendant. In approximately three out of every ten cases, the initial vote by the jury led to a unanimous decision. In 90 percent of the remaining cases, the majority eventually dictated the decision.[44]

One of the most important instructions that a judge normally gives the jurors is that they should seek no outside information during deliberation. The idea is that jurors should base their verdict *only* on the evidence that the judge has deemed admissible. In extreme cases, the judge will order that the jury be *sequestered,* or isolated from the public, during the trial and deliberation stages of the proceedings. **Sequestration** is used when deliberations are expected to be lengthy, or the trial is attracting a high amount of interest and the judge wants to keep the jury from being unduly influenced. Juries are usually sequestered in hotels and kept under the watch and guard of officers of the court.

8-7b The Verdict

Once it has reached a decision, the jury issues a **verdict.** The most common verdicts are guilty and not guilty, though juries may signify different degrees of guilt if

Rebuttal Evidence given to counteract or disprove evidence presented by the opposing party.

Closing Arguments Arguments made by each side's attorney after the cases for the plaintiff and defendant have been presented.

Charge The judge's instructions to the jury following the attorneys' closing arguments.

Sequestration The isolation of jury members during a trial to ensure that their judgment is not influenced by information other than what is provided in the courtroom.

Verdict A formal decision made by the jury.

CJ and Technology

Champion Studio/ShutterStock.com

One former juror, fresh from trial, complained that the members of the courtroom work group had not provided the jury with enough information to render a fair verdict. "We felt deeply frustrated at our inability to fill those gaps in our knowledge," he added. Until recently, frustrated jury members have lacked the means to carry out their own investigations in court. Today, however, jurors with smartphones and tablet computers can easily access news stories and online research tools. With these wireless devices, they can look up legal terms, blog and tweet about their experiences, and sometimes even try to contact other participants in the trial through "friend" requests on social media Web sites.

This access can cause serious problems for judges, whose responsibility it is to ensure that no outside information taints the jury's decision. Following a Vermont trial of an immigrant from the African country of Somalia for the sexual assault of a child, one juror went online to research certain aspects of Somali culture and religion. During deliberation, the juror relied on this research to argue his position that the defendant was guilty. The judge had no choice but to overturn the defendant's eventual conviction, as this juror misconduct could have improperly influenced the final verdict.

Thinking about Wireless Devices in the Courtroom
The Sixth Amendment guarantees the accused the right to trial by an "impartial jury." How does the use of wireless devices in the courtroom threaten this right?

---

instructed to do so. Following the announcement of a guilty or not guilty verdict, the jurors are discharged, and the jury trial proceedings are finished.

When a jury in a criminal trial is unable to agree on a unanimous verdict—or a majority in certain states—it returns with no decision. This is known as a **hung jury.** Following a hung jury, the judge will declare a mistrial, and the case will be tried again in front of a different jury if the prosecution decides to pursue the matter a second time. A judge can do little to reverse a hung jury, considering that "no decision" is just as legitimate a verdict as guilty or not guilty.

Hung Jury A jury whose members are so irreconcilably divided in their opinions that they cannot reach a verdict.

Allen Charge An instruction by a judge to a deadlocked jury with only a few dissenters that asks the jurors in the minority to reconsider the majority opinion.

Appeal The process of seeking a higher court's review of a lower court's decision for the purpose of correcting or changing this decision.

In some states, if there are only a few dissenters to the majority view, a judge can send the jury back to the jury room under a set of rules set forth more than a century ago by the Supreme Court in *Allen v. United States* (1896).[45] The **Allen charge,** as this instruction is called, asks the jurors in the minority to reconsider the majority opinion. Many jurisdictions do not allow *Allen* charges on the ground that they improperly coerce jurors with the minority opinion to change their minds.[46]

8-7c Appeals

Even if a defendant is found guilty, the trial process is not necessarily over. In our criminal justice system, a person convicted of a crime has a right to appeal. An **appeal** is the process of seeking a higher court's review of a lower court's decision for the purpose of correcting or changing the lower court's judgment.

A defendant who loses a case in a trial court cannot automatically appeal the conviction. The defendant normally must first be able to show that the trial court acted improperly on a question of law. Common reasons for appeals include the introduction of tainted evidence by the prosecution or faulty jury instructions delivered by the trial judge. In federal courts, about 18 percent of criminal convictions are appealed.[47]

DOUBLE JEOPARDY The appeals process is available only to the defense. If a jury finds the accused not guilty, the prosecution cannot appeal to have the decision reversed. To do so would infringe on the defendant's Fifth Amendment rights against multiple trials for the same offense. This guarantee against being tried a second time for the same crime is known as protection from **double jeopardy.** The prohibition against double jeopardy means that once a criminal defendant is found not guilty of a particular crime, the government may not reindict the person and retry him or her for the same crime.

The American prohibition against double jeopardy is not absolute. There are several circumstances in which, for practical purposes, a defendant can find herself or himself back in court after a jury has failed to find her or him guilty of committing a particular crime:

1. One state's prosecution will not prevent a different state or the federal government from prosecuting the same crime.

2. Acquitted defendants can be sued in *civil court* for circumstances arising from the alleged wrongdoing on the theory that they are not being tried for the same *crime* twice.

3. A hung jury is not an acquittal for purposes of double jeopardy. So, if a jury is deadlocked, the government is free to set a new trial.

As a consequence of the final listed exception to double jeopardy, Michael Dunn found himself back in court only seven months after his first murder trial for fatally shooting Jordan Davis outside a Jacksonville, Florida, convenience store. At Dunn's first trial, referenced earlier in Figure 8.4, the jury could not decide whether he acted in self-defense. In November 2014, however, a second jury rejected his self-defense claim and convicted Dunn of first degree murder, sending to him prison for the remainder of his life.

THE APPEALS PROCESS It is important to understand that once the appeals process begins, the defendant is no longer presumed innocent. The burden of proof has shifted, and the defendant is obligated to prove that her or his conviction should be overturned. The method of filing an appeal differs slightly among the fifty states and the federal government, but the five basic steps are similar enough for summarization in Figure 8.5. For the most part, defendants are not required to exercise their right to appeal. The one exception involves the death sentence. Given the seriousness of capital punishment, the defendant is required to appeal the case, regardless of his or her wishes.

8-7d Wrongful Convictions

The appeals process is primarily concerned with "legal innocence." That is, appeals courts focus on how the law was applied in a case, rather than on the facts of the case. But what if a defendant who is factually innocent

Double Jeopardy The prosecution of a person twice for the same criminal offense; prohibited by the Fifth Amendment to the Constitution.

FIGURE 8.5 THE STEPS OF AN APPEAL

1. The defendant, or *appellant*, files a **notice of appeal**—a short written statement outlining the basis of the appeal.

2. The appellant transfers the trial court record to the appellate court. This record contains items such as evidence and a transcript of the testimony.

3. Both parties file **briefs.** A brief is a written document that presents the party's legal arguments.

4. Attorneys from both sides present **oral arguments** before the appellate court.

5. Having heard from both sides, the judges of the appellate court retire to deliberate the case and make their decision. As described in Chapter 7, this decision is issued as a **written opinion.** Appellate courts generally do one of the following:
   - **Uphold** the decision of the lower court.
   - **Modify** the lower court's decision by changing only a part of it.
   - **Reverse** the decision of the lower court.
   - **Reverse and remand** the case, meaning that the matter is sent back to the lower court for further proceedings.

has been found guilty at trial? For the most part, such **wrongful convictions** can be righted only with the aid of new evidence suggesting that the defendant was not, in fact, guilty. When such new evidence is uncovered, a prosecutor's office can choose to reopen the case and redress the initial injustice.

In Chapter 5, we saw how DNA fingerprinting has been a boon for law enforcement. According to the Innocence Project, a New York–based legal group, as of March 2015, the procedure has also led to the exoneration of 325 convicts in the United States.[48] The five most common reasons for wrongful convictions eventually overturned by DNA evidence are:[49]

1. *Eyewitness misidentification,* which may occur in as many as one-third of all cases in which it is used to identify criminal suspects.[50]

2. *False confessions,* which are often the result of overly coercive police interrogation techniques (see Chapter 6) or a suspect's mental illness.

3. *Faulty forensic evidence* produced by crime labs, which analyze evidence ranging from bite marks to handwriting samples to ballistics.

4. *False informant testimony,* provided by "jailhouse snitches" and other offenders who are motivated to lessen their own punishment by incriminating other suspects.

5. *Law enforcement misconduct* by overzealous or corrupt police officers and prosecutors.

Wrongful Conviction The conviction, either by verdict or by guilty plea, of a person who is factually innocent of the charges.

Habeas Corpus An order that requires corrections officials to bring an inmate before a court or a judge and explain why he or she is being held in prison.

STUDY TOOLS 8

READY TO STUDY? IN THE BOOK, YOU CAN:

☐ Rip out the Chapter Review Card, which includes key terms and chapter summaries.

ONLINE AT WWW.CENGAGEBRAIN.COM, YOU CAN:

☐ Learn about false confessions in a short video.

☐ Explore The Innocence Project's Web page and Facebook page to learn more about preventing wrongful convictions.

☐ Interact with figures from the text, and watch quick animation clips.

☐ Prepare for tests with quizzes.

☐ Review the key terms with Flash Cards.

HABEAS CORPUS In 2009, the United States Supreme Court ruled that convicts have no constitutional right to DNA testing that may prove their innocence.[51] Nonetheless, most states allow prisoners access to such testing if there is a reasonable possibility of a wrongful conviction.

In addition, even after the appeals process is exhausted, a convict may have access to a procedure known as **habeas corpus** (Latin for "you have the body"). *Habeas corpus* is a judicial order that commands a corrections official to bring a prisoner before a federal court so that the court can hear the convict's claim that he or she is being held illegally. A writ of *habeas corpus* differs from an appeal in that it can be filed only by someone who is imprisoned. In recent years, defense attorneys have successfully used the *habeas corpus* procedure for a number of their death row clients who have new DNA evidence proving their innocence.[52]

Quiz

1. Following the initial appearance, in most cases the defendant will be detained until trial unless he or she can post _____.

2. In some states, a group of citizens called a _____ _____ determines whether the prosecution has established probable cause that the defendant committed the crime in question.

3. A _____ _____ occurs when the prosecution and the defense work out an agreement that resolves the case with the defendant admitting guilt.

4. If a defendant waives his or her right to a jury trial, a _____ trial takes place in which the judge decides questions of law and fact.

5. To gain a "guilty" verdict, the prosecution must prove that the defendant is guilty beyond a _____ _____.

6. The process by which the prosecution and defense choose a jury is called _____ _____.

7. Evidence will not be admitted into a criminal trial unless it is relevant and does not unfairly _____ the jury against the defendant.

8. _____ examination takes places when, for example, the prosecution questions those witnesses that it has called to strengthen its case.

9. _____-examination takes place when, for example, defense attorneys question those witnesses that have been called to the stand by the prosecution.

10. If a defendant is convicted, she or he has the option of filing an _____ claiming that the trial court acted improperly on a question of law during the proceedings.

Answers can be found in the Answers section in the back of the book.

9 Punishment and Sentencing

Peter Kunasz, 2009/Used under license from ShutterStock.com

LEARNING OBJECTIVES

After studying this chapter, you will be able to . . .

9-1 List and contrast the four basic philosophical reasons for sentencing criminals.

9-2 Contrast indeterminate with determinate sentencing.

9-3 Explain some of the reasons why sentencing reform has occurred.

9-4 Identify the arguments for and against the use of victim impact statements during sentencing hearings.

9-5 Identify the two stages that make up the bifurcated process of death penalty sentencing.

After you finish this chapter, go to **PAGES 203–204** for **STUDY TOOLS**

A Long Time Gone

In 1996, Scott Walker was arrested for being a low-level pusher of LSD, cocaine, marijuana, and methamphetamine. If his arrests for this nonviolent offense had happened today, Walker—lacking a criminal record—would have been punished with a relatively short prison sentence. Instead, he is still behind bars, and can expect to spend the rest of his life there.

"Over the years, the absolute nature of his sentence has often weighed on my mind," wrote John Gilbert, the judge who sentenced Walker, in 2012. Gilbert did not, however, have any choice in the matter. Under a formula adopted by the United States government in 1987, federal judges could not deviate from strict sentencing guidelines for nonviolent crimes. This discretion was returned to them by the United States Supreme Court in 2005, but the consequences of harsh federal and state sentencing laws are still evident in our corrections system. According to the American Civil Liberties Union, more than 3,200 inmates presently are serving life prison sentences without the possibility of parole for nonviolent drug and property crimes.

For these offenders, the best hope for freedom is clemency, a process through which the president of the United States or a state governor essentially forgives an inmate's wrongdoing and sets her or him free from prison. In 2014, recognizing the unfair nature of many life prison sentences, the federal government announced changes to its clemency criteria. The new regulations offer federal prisoners a chance at freedom if they are low-level, nonviolent offenders who have served at least ten years of their sentences, with no history of violence before or during their prison terms. Scott Walker hopes that he can benefit from the updated clemency standards. "I believe in my right to liberty," he says, "and I continue to wait for the moment when I receive the call."

Reynolds Wintersmith, sentenced to life in prison without parole on a nonviolent drug charge, spent twenty years behind bars before being freed by presidential clemency in 2014. Are there any circumstances under which you think a nonviolent criminal deserves to spend his or her life in prison? Explain your answer.

Chicago Tribune/Getty Images

9-1 WHY DO WE PUNISH CRIMINALS?

Professor Herbert Packer has said that punishing criminals serves two ultimate purposes: the "deserved infliction of suffering on evil doers" and "the prevention of crime."[1] Even this straightforward assessment raises several questions. How does one determine the sort of punishment that is "deserved"? How can we be sure that certain penalties "prevent" crime? Should criminals be punished solely for the good of society, or should their well-being also be taken into consideration? Why is Scott Walker spending his life in prison for a nonviolent drug offense committed in the 1990s, when the same crime committed in the 2010s would be punished much less harshly?

Sentencing laws indicate how any given group has answered these questions, but they do not tell us why they were answered in that manner. To understand why, we must first consider the four basic philosophical reasons for sentencing—retribution, deterrence, incapacitation, and rehabilitation.

9-1a Retribution

LO9-1 The oldest and most common justification for punishing someone is that he or she "deserved it"—as the Old Testament states, "an eye for an eye and a tooth for a tooth." Under a system of justice that favors **retribution,** a wrongdoer who has freely chosen to violate society's rules must be punished for the infraction.

> **Retribution** The philosophy that those who commit criminal acts should be punished for breaking society's rules to the extent required by just deserts.

Retribution relies on the principle of **just deserts,** which holds that the severity of the punishment must be in proportion to the severity of the crime. Retributive justice is not the same as *revenge.* Whereas revenge implies that the wrongdoer is punished only with the aim of satisfying a victim or victims, retribution is more concerned with the needs of society as a whole.

One problem with retributive ideas of justice lies in proportionality. Whether or not one agrees with the death penalty, the principle behind it is easy to fathom: the punishment (death) often fits the crime (murder). But what about the theft of an automobile? How does one fairly determine the amount of time the thief must spend in prison for that crime? Should the type of car or the wealth of the car owner matter? Theories of retribution often have a difficult time providing answers to such questions.

Orlando Sentinel/Getty Images

In 2015, former Florida A&M University band member Jessie Baskin, right, was sentenced to six years in prison for his role in the hazing death of drum major Robert Champion. *How does the theory of deterrence justify Martin's punishment?*

9-1b Deterrence

The concept of **deterrence** (as well as incapacitation and rehabilitation) takes a different approach than does retribution. That is, rather than seeking only to punish the wrongdoer, the goal of sentencing should be to prevent future crimes. By "setting an example," society is sending a message to potential criminals that certain actions will not be tolerated.

Deterrence can take two forms: general and specific. The basic idea of *general deterrence* is that by punishing one person, others will be discouraged from committing a similar crime. *Specific deterrence* assumes that an individual, after having been punished once for a certain act, will be less likely to repeat that act because she or he does not want to be punished again. Proponents of harsh sentences for nonviolent drug crimes, addressed in the opening of this chapter, often rely on general deterrence principles to argue that such punishments discourage illegal drug possession and distribution by others.[2]

Both forms of deterrence have proved problematic in practice. General deterrence assumes that a person commits a crime only after a rational decision-making process, in which he or she implicitly weighs the benefits of the crime against the possible costs of the punishment. This is not necessarily the case, especially for young offenders who tend to value the immediate rewards of crime over the possible future consequences. The argument for specific deterrence is somewhat weakened by the fact that a relatively small number of habitual offenders are responsible for the majority of certain criminal acts.

9-1c Incapacitation

"Wicked people exist," said James Q. Wilson. "Nothing avails except to set them apart from innocent people."[3] Wilson's blunt statement summarizes the justification for **incapacitation** as a form of punishment. As a purely practical matter, incarcerating criminals guarantees that they will not be a danger to society, at least for the length

Just Deserts A sanctioning philosophy based on the assertion that criminal punishment should be proportionate to the severity of the crime.

Deterrence The strategy of preventing crime through the threat of punishment.

Incapacitation A strategy for preventing crime by detaining wrongdoers in prison, thereby separating them from the community and reducing criminal opportunities.

of their prison terms. Such reasoning is partially responsible for the dramatic increase of life sentences without the possibility of parole in the criminal justice system. Since 1984, the inmate population serving life without parole has quadrupled, to nearly 160,000, encompassing one of every nine individuals behind bars in the United States.[4]

Several studies do support incapacitation's efficacy as a crime-fighting tool. Criminologist Isaac Ehrlich of the University at Buffalo estimated that a 1 percent increase in sentence length will produce a 1 percent decrease in the crime rate.[5] More recently, Avinash Singh Bhati of the Urban Institute in Washington, D.C., found that higher levels of incarceration lead to fewer violent crimes but have little impact on property crime rates.[6]

Incapacitation as a theory of punishment does suffer from several weaknesses. Unlike retribution, it offers no proportionality with regard to a particular crime. Giving a burglar a life sentence would certainly ensure that she or he would not commit another burglary. Does that justify such a severe penalty? Furthermore, incarceration protects society only until the criminal is freed.

Many studies have shown that, on release, offenders may actually be more likely to commit crimes than before they were imprisoned.[7] In that case, incapacitation may increase likelihood of crime, rather than diminish it.

9-1d Rehabilitation

For many, **rehabilitation** is the most "humane" goal of punishment. This line of thinking reflects the view that crime is a "social phenomenon" caused not by the inherent criminality of a person, but by factors in that person's surroundings. By removing wrongdoers from their environment and intervening to change their values and personalities, the rehabilitative model suggests that criminals can be "treated" and possibly even "cured" of their proclivities toward crime. Although studies of the effectiveness of rehabilitation are too varied to be easily

> **Rehabilitation** The philosophy that society is best served when wrongdoers are provided the resources needed to eliminate criminality from their behavioral pattern.

CJ and Technology

ELECTRONIC EAVESDROPPING

"Our society is going through a technological transformation," notes Adam Schwartz, a civil liberties lawyer. "We are at a time where tens of millions of Americans carry around a telephone or other device in their pocket that has an audio-video capacity. Ten years ago, [we] weren't walking around with all these devices." This widespread ability to record interactions with others has increased the possibility that Americans are breaking the law, often without their knowledge. The criminal codes of twelve states require the consent of all parties involved before any conversation can be recorded.

In some cases, the penalties for breaking these laws can be quite harsh. Under the Illinois Eavesdropping Act, audio-recording a civilian without consent is a Class 4 felony, punishable by up to three years in prison. Audio-recording an Illinois law enforcement

1000 words/ShutterStock.com

official who is performing her or his duties without consent is a Class 1 felony, punishable by up to fifteen years in prison.

Thinking about Electronic Eavesdropping
What is the purpose behind making electronic eavesdropping a criminal act deserving of punishment?

summarized, it does appear that, in most instances, criminals who receive treatment are less likely to reoffend than those who do not.[8]

9-1e Restorative Justice

On many reservations across the United States, Native Americans practice a "peacemaking" approach to criminal justice. Unlike the adversary system of the mainstream court system, peacemaking focuses on dispute resolution and the needs of the community rather than the rights of individual offenders. In a Navajo peacemaking session, members of the community, including the

> **Restorative Justice** An approach to punishment designed to repair the harm done to the victim and the community by the offender's criminal act.

victim, describe the harm suffered because of the act in question. Then, the participants, as a group, decide on the proper *nalyeeh*, loosely translated as payment, that the offender (or the offender's family) owes the community.[9]

The goal of *nalyeeh*, which may or may not include money, is to make the injured party and the community "feel better," in the words of one Navajo judge.[10] In Native American jurisdictions, these principles have been applied to resolve criminal issues from domestic violence to gang activity to driving while intoxicated. They are also spreading to the nontribal criminal justice system as part of the **restorative justice** movement in this country.

Restorative justice strategies attempt to repair the damage that a crime does to the victim, the victim's family, and society as a whole. This outlook relies on the efforts of the offender to "undo" the harm caused by the criminal

---

MEDIATION SPECIALIST

Job Description:

▶ Complement the standard adjudication of a crime by acting as a third party facilitator between the victim and the offender. Help resolve their conflicts through a face-to-face discussion of the criminal act.

▶ Encourage the increased presence of restorative justice in the criminal justice system.

What Kind of Training Is Required?

▶ No formal licensing or certification process exists for mediators. Rather, training is available through independent mediation programs and mediation organizations. Some colleges and universities offer advanced degrees in conflict management and dispute resolution.

Golden Pixels LLC/ShutterStock.com

▶ Skills required include the ability to communicate, negotiate, solve problems, and analyze difficult situations. Successful mediators are also highly intuitive and able to meet clients' emotional needs during difficult times.

Annual Salary Range?

▶ $45,000–$70,000

> **SOCIAL MEDIA CAREER TIP**
> *Be aware of your e-mail address/screen name/login name and what it represents. Stay away from nicknames. Use a professional and unique name to represent yourself consistently across social media platforms.*

act through an apology and **restitution,** or monetary compensation for losses suffered by the victim or victims. Restorative justice has five separate components that differentiate it from the mainstream criminal justice system:

1. *Offender involvement.* Offenders are given the opportunity to take responsibility for and address the reasons behind their behavior in ways that do not involve the corrections system.

2. *Victim involvement.* Victims have a voice in determining how the offender should atone for her or his crime.

3. *Victim-offender interaction.* On a voluntary basis, victims and offenders meet to discuss and better understand the circumstances of the crime. This meeting allows victims to express their feelings about the offense.

4. *Community involvement.* Community members also affected by the crime can participate in the process and request an apology and restitution from the offender.

5. *Problem-solving practices.* Participants in the process—including victims, offenders, and community members—can develop strategies for solving the problems that led to the crime in question.[11]

Although restorative justice is theoretically available for all types of criminal behavior, it almost always involves property crime, public order crime, and, particularly, offenses committed by juveniles. Rarely, if ever, will restorative justice principles be applied to violent crime.

9-2 WHAT IS THE STRUCTURE OF THE SENTENCING PROCESS?

Philosophy not only is integral to explaining *why* we punish criminals, but also influences *how* we do so. The history of criminal sentencing in the United States has been characterized by shifts in institutional power between different branches of the government. When public opinion moves toward more severe strategies of retribution, deterrence, and incapacitation, legislatures have responded by asserting their power over determining sentencing guidelines. In contrast, periods of rehabilitation are marked by a transfer of this power to judges.

9-2a Legislative Sentencing Authority

Because legislatures are responsible for making laws, these bodies are also initially responsible for passing the criminal codes that determine the length of sentences.

LO9-2 **INDETERMINATE SENTENCING** Penal codes with **indeterminate sentencing** policies set a minimum and maximum amount of time that a person must spend in prison. For example, the indeterminate sentence for aggravated assault could be three to nine years, or six to twelve years, or twenty years to life. Within these parameters, a judge can prescribe a particular term, after which an administrative body known as the *parole board* decides at what point the offender is to be released. A prisoner is aware that he or she is eligible for *parole* as soon as the minimum time has been served and that good behavior can further shorten the sentence.

DETERMINATE SENTENCING Disillusionment with the somewhat vague nature of indeterminate sentencing often leads politicians to support **determinate sentencing,** or fixed sentencing. As the name implies, in determinate sentencing an offender serves exactly the amount of time to which she or he is sentenced (minus "good time," described below). For example, if the legislature deems that the punishment for a first-time armed robber is ten years, then the judge has no choice but to impose a sentence of ten years, and the criminal will serve ten years minus good time before being freed.

"GOOD TIME" AND TRUTH IN SENTENCING Often, the amount of time prescribed by a judge bears little relation to the amount of time the offender actually spends behind bars. In states with indeterminate sentencing, parole boards have broad powers to release prisoners once they have served the minimum portion of their sentence. Furthermore, most states offer prisoners the opportunity to reduce their sentences by doing

Restitution Monetary compensation for damages done to the victim by the offender's criminal act.

Indeterminate Sentencing Imposition of a sentence that prescribes a range of years rather than a definite period of years to be served.

Determinate Sentencing Imposition of a sentence that is fixed by a sentencing authority and cannot be reduced by judges or other corrections officials.

"**good time**"—or behaving well—as determined by prison administrators. (See Figure 9.1 for an idea of the effects of good-time regulations and other early-release programs on state prison sentences.)

Sentence-reduction programs promote discipline within a correctional institution and reduce overcrowding, so many prison officials welcome them. The public, however, may react negatively to news that a violent criminal has served a shorter term than ordered by a judge and pressure elected officials to "do something." In Illinois, for example, some inmates were serving less than half their sentences by receiving a one-day reduction in their term for each day of "good time." Under pressure from victims' groups, the state legislature passed a **truth-in-sentencing law** in 1995 that requires murderers and others convicted of serious crimes to complete at least 85 percent of their sentences with no time off for good behavior.[12]

As their name suggests, the primary goal of these laws is to provide the public with more accurate information about the actual amount of time an offender will spend behind bars. The laws also keep convicts incapacitated for longer periods of time. Fifteen years after Illinois passed its truth-in-sentencing law, those murderers

> **"Good Time"** A reduction in time served by prisoners based on good behavior, conformity to rules, and other positive behavior.
>
> **Truth-in-Sentencing Laws** Legislative attempts to ensure that convicts will serve approximately the terms to which they were initially sentenced.

subject to the legislation were spending an average of seventeen years more in prison than those not subject to the legislation. For sex offenders in the state, the difference was 3.5 years.[13] Today, forty states have instituted some form of truth-in-sentencing laws, though the continued popularity of such statutes is being undermined by the pressures of overflowing prisons.

9-2b Judicial Sentencing Authority

During the pretrial procedures and the trial itself, the judge's role is somewhat passive and reactive. She or he is primarily a "procedural watchdog," ensuring that the rights of the defendant are not infringed while the prosecutor and defense attorney dictate the course of action. At a traditional sentencing hearing, however, the judge is no longer an arbiter between the parties. She or he is now called on to exercise the ultimate authority of the state in determining the defendant's fate.

From the 1930s to the 1970s, when theories of rehabilitation held sway over the criminal justice system, indeterminate sentencing practices were guided by the theory of "individualized justice." Just as a physician gives specific treatment to individual patients depending on their particular health needs, the hypothesis goes, a judge needs to consider the specific circumstances of each individual offender in choosing the best form of punishment.

Taking the analogy one step further, just as the diagnosis of a qualified physician should not be questioned, a qualified judge should have absolute discretion in making the sentencing decision. *Judicial discretion* rests on

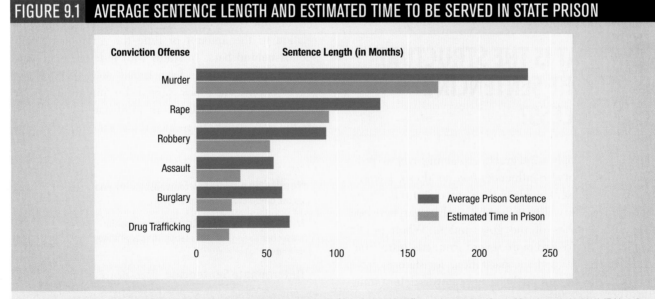

FIGURE 9.1 AVERAGE SENTENCE LENGTH AND ESTIMATED TIME TO BE SERVED IN STATE PRISON

Source: Bureau of Justice Statistics, *National Corrections Reporting Program: Sentence Length of State Prisoners, by Offense, Admission Type, Sex, and Race* (January 20, 2011), "Table 9: First Releases from State Prison, 2008," at **bjs.ojp.usdoj.gov/index.cfm?ty=pbdetail&iid=2056.**

the assumption that a judge should be given ample leeway in determining punishments that fit both the crime and the criminal.[14] As we shall see later in the chapter, the growth of determinate sentencing has severely restricted judicial discretion in many jurisdictions.

JUDICIAL DISPOSITIONS Within whatever legislative restrictions apply, the sentencing judge has a number of options when it comes to choosing the proper form of punishment. These sentences, or *dispositions*, include:

1. *Capital punishment.* Reserved normally for those who commit first degree murder—that is, a premeditated killing—capital punishment is a sentencing option in thirty-one states. It is also an option in federal court, where a defendant can be put to death for murder, as well as for trafficking in a large amount of illegal drugs, *espionage* (spying), and *treason* (betraying the United States).

2. *Imprisonment.* Whether for the purpose of retribution, deterrence, incapacitation, or rehabilitation, a common form of punishment in American history has been imprisonment. In fact, it is used so commonly today that judges—and legislators—are having to take factors such as prison overcrowding into consideration when making sentencing decisions. The issues surrounding imprisonment will be discussed in Chapters 11 and 12.

3. *Probation.* One of the effects of prison overcrowding has been a sharp rise in the use of probation, in which an offender is permitted to live in the community under supervision and is not incarcerated. (Probation is covered in Chapter 10.) *Alternative sanctions* (also discussed in Chapter 10) combine probation with other dispositions, such as electronic monitoring, house arrest, boot camps, and shock incarceration.

4. *Fines.* Fines can be levied by judges in addition to incarceration and probation or independently of other forms of punishment. When a fine is the only punishment, it usually reflects the judge's belief that the offender is not a threat to the community and does not need to be imprisoned or supervised. In some instances, mostly involving drug offenders, a judge can order the seizure of an offender's property, such as his or her home.

OTHER FORMS OF PUNISHMENT Whereas fines are payable to the government, restitution and community service are seen as reparations to the injured party or to the community. As noted earlier, restitution is a direct payment to the victim or victims of a crime. Community service consists of "good works"—such as cleaning up highway litter or tutoring disadvantaged youths—that benefit the entire community. Along with restitution, *apologies* play an important role in restorative justice, discussed previously in this chapter. An apology is seen as an effort by the offender to recognize the wrongness of her or his conduct and acknowledge the impact that it has had on the victim and the community.

In some jurisdictions, judges have a great deal of discretionary power and can impose sentences that do not fall into any of these categories. This "creative sentencing," as it is sometimes called, has produced some interesting results. A judge in South Euclid, Ohio, ordered a man who had harassed his neighbor for fifteen years to stand at a local intersection carrying a sign that said, "I AM A BULLY! I pick on children that are disabled, and I am intolerant of those that are different from myself."[15] In Broward County, Florida, a man who shoved his wife was sentenced to "take her to Red Lobster," go bowling with her, and then undergo marriage counseling.[16] Though these types of punishments are often ridiculed, many judges see them as a viable alternative to incarceration for less dangerous offenders.

9-2c The Sentencing Process

The decision of how to punish a wrongdoer is the end result of what Yale Law School professor Kate Stith and federal appeals court judge José A. Cabranes call the "sentencing ritual."[17] The two main participants in this ritual are the judge and the defendant, but prosecutors, defense attorneys, and probation officers also play a role in the proceedings. Individualized justice requires that the judge consider all the relevant circumstances in making sentencing decisions. Therefore, judicial discretion is often tantamount to *informed* discretion—without the aid of the other members of the courtroom work group, the judge would not have sufficient information to make the proper sentencing choice.

THE PRESENTENCE INVESTIGATIVE REPORT For judges operating under various states' indeterminate sentencing guidelines, information in the **presentence investigative report** is a valuable component of the

Presentence Investigative Report An investigative report on an offender's background that assists a judge in determining the proper sentence.

sentencing ritual. Compiled by a probation officer, the report describes the crime in question, notes the suffering of any victims, and lists the defendant's prior offenses (as well as any alleged but uncharged criminal activity). The report also contains a range of personal data such as family background, work history, education, and community activities—information that is not admissible as evidence during trial. In putting together the presentence investigative report, the probation officer is supposed to gain a "feel" for the defendant and communicate these impressions of the offender to the judge.

The report also includes a sentencing recommendation. This aspect has been criticized as giving probation officers too much power in the sentencing process, because less diligent judges would simply rely on the recommendation in determining punishment.[18] For the most part, however, judges do not act as if they were bound by the presentence investigative report.

SENTENCING AND THE JURY Juries also play an important role in the sentencing process. As we will see later in the chapter, it is the jury, and not the judge, that generally decides whether a convict eligible for the death penalty will in fact be executed. Additionally, six states—Arkansas, Kentucky, Missouri, Oklahoma, Texas, and Virginia—allow juries, rather than judges, to make the sentencing decision even when the death penalty is not an option. In these states, the judge gives the jury instructions on the range of penalties available, and then the jury makes the final decision.[19]

After Jason Householder, left, and John Stockum were convicted of criminal damaging for throwing beer bottles at a car, municipal court judge David Hostetler of Coshocton, Ohio, gave them a choice: jail time or a walk down Main Street in women's clothing. As you can see, they chose the dresses. *What reasons might a judge have for handing down this sort of "creative" sentence?*

AP Images/ Dante Smith/ Coshocton Tribune

9-2d Factors of Sentencing

The sentencing ritual strongly lends itself to the concept of individualized justice. With inputs—sometimes conflicting—from the prosecutor, attorney, and probation officer, the judge can be reasonably sure of getting the "full picture" of the crime and the criminal. In making the final decision, however, most judges consider two factors above all others: the seriousness of the crime and any mitigating or aggravating circumstances.

THE SERIOUSNESS OF THE CRIME As would be expected, the seriousness of the crime is the primary factor in a judge's sentencing decision. The more serious the crime, the harsher the punishment, for society demands no less. Each judge has his or her own methods of determining the seriousness of the offense. Many judges simply consider the "conviction offense," basing their sentence on the crime for which the defendant was convicted.

Other judges—some mandated by statute—focus instead on the **"real offense"** in determining the punishment. The "real offense" is based on the actual behavior of the defendant, regardless of the official conviction. For example, through a plea bargain, a defendant may plead guilty to simple assault when in fact he hit his victim in the face with a baseball bat. A judge, after reading the presentence investigative report, could decide to sentence the defendant as if he had committed aggravated assault, which is the "real offense." Though many prosecutors and defense attorneys are opposed to "real offense" procedures, which can render a plea bargain meaningless, there is considerable belief in criminal justice circles that they bring a measure of fairness to the sentencing decision.[20]

MITIGATING AND AGGRAVATING CIRCUMSTANCES When deciding the severity of punishment, judges and juries are often required to evaluate the *mitigating* and *aggravating circumstances* surrounding the case. **Mitigating circumstances** are circumstances, such as

"Real Offense" The actual offense committed, as opposed to the charge levied by a prosecutor as the result of a plea bargain.

Mitigating Circumstances Any circumstances accompanying the commission of a crime that may justify a lighter sentence.

the fact that the defendant was coerced into committing the crime, that allow a lighter sentence to be handed down. In contrast, **aggravating circumstances,** such as a prior record, blatant disregard for the safety of others, or the use of a weapon, can lead a judge or jury to inflict a harsher penalty than might otherwise be warranted.

Aggravating circumstances play an important role in a prosecutor's decision to charge a suspect with capital murder. The criminal code of every state that employs the death penalty contains a list of aggravating circumstances that make an offender eligible for execution. Most of these codes require that the murder take place during the commission of a felony, or create a grave risk of death for multiple victims, or interfere with the duties of law enforcement. As you will see later in the chapter, mitigating factors such as mental illness and youth can spare an otherwise death-eligible offender from capital punishment.

Generally speaking, jurors hand down harsher sentences than judges, particularly for drug-related crimes and sexual assaults. *Why do you think this is the case?*

CAREER TIP To emphasize the mitigating circumstances that might have contributed to a client's criminality, defense attorneys often rely on *behavioral specialists* as expert witnesses. These health-care experts focus on diagnosing and treating problem behavior.

JUDICIAL PHILOSOPHY Most states and the federal government spell out mitigating and aggravating circumstances in statutes, but there is room for judicial discretion in applying the law to particular cases. Judges are not uniform, or even consistent, in their opinions of which circumstances are mitigating or aggravating. One judge may believe that a fourteen-year-old is not fully responsible for his or her actions, while another may believe that teenagers should be treated as adults by criminal courts. A recent study in the journal *Science* found that, faced with a hypothetical situation in which a defendant suffered from brain damage, judges reduced the length of the sentence by about 7 percent.[21]

Often, a judge's personal philosophy will place her or him at odds with prosecutors. In July 2014, for example, teenager Latrez Cummings pleaded guilty in Detroit for participating in a violent attack on a man who accidentally struck a ten-year-old child with his pickup truck. Prosecutors wanted Cummings to receive a one-to-three-year sentence, but Judge James Callahan decided that the defendant should spend only six months behind bars. The judge's ruling seemed to be influenced, at least in part, by sympathy for the defendant's fatherless upbringing. "That's what you have needed in your life is a father," he told Cummings, "somebody to beat the hell out of you when you made a mistake."[22]

9-3 WHAT ARE SOME PROBLEMS WITH SENTENCING?

For some, the natural differences in judicial philosophies, when combined with a lack of institutional control, raise important questions. Why should a bank robber in South Carolina and a bank robber in Michigan receive different sentences? Even federal indeterminate sentencing guidelines seem overly vague: a bank robber can receive a prison term from one day to twenty years, depending almost entirely on the judge.[23] Furthermore, if judges have freedom to use their discretion, do they not also have the freedom to misuse it?

Aggravating Circumstances Any circumstances accompanying the commission of a crime that may justify a harsher sentence.

Purported improper judicial discretion is often the first reason given for two phenomena that plague the criminal justice system: *sentencing disparity* and *sentencing discrimination*. Though the two terms are often used interchangeably, they describe different statistical occurrences—the causes of which are open to debate.

LO9-3

9-3a Sentencing Disparity

Justice would seem to demand that those who commit similar crimes should receive similar punishments. **Sentencing disparity** occurs when this expectation is not met in one of three ways:

1. Criminals receive similar sentences for different crimes of unequal seriousness.
2. Criminals receive different sentences for similar crimes.
3. Mitigating or aggravating circumstances have a disproportionate effect on sentences.

Most of the blame for sentencing disparities is placed at the feet of the judicial profession. Even with the restrictive presence of the sentencing reforms we will discuss shortly, judges have a great deal of influence over the sentencing decision, whether they are making that decision themselves or instructing the jury on how to do so. Like other members of the criminal justice system, judges are individuals, and their discretionary sentencing decisions reflect that individuality.

For offenders, the amount of time spent in prison often depends as much on where the crime was committed as on the crime itself. A comparison of the sentences for drug trafficking reveals that someone convicted of the crime in Oregon faces an average of 69 months in prison, whereas a similar offender in eastern North Carolina can expect an average of 128 months.[24] The average sentences imposed in the Fourth Circuit, which includes North Carolina, South Carolina, Virginia, and West Virginia, are consistently harsher than those in the

Ninth Circuit, comprising most of the western states: 42 months longer for convictions related to firearms and 43 months longer for all offenses.[25]

Such disparities can be attributed to a number of different factors, including local attitudes toward crime and financial resources available to cover the expenses of incarceration. Also, because of different sentencing guidelines, which we will discuss later in the chapter, the punishment for the same crime in federal and state courts can be dramatically different. Figure 9.2 shows the sentencing disparities for certain crimes in the two systems.

9-3b Sentencing Discrimination

Sentencing discrimination occurs when disparities can be attributed to extralegal variables such as the defendant's gender, race, or economic standing.

RACE AND SENTENCING At first glance, racial discrimination would seem to be rampant in sentencing practices. Research by Cassia Spohn of Arizona State University and David Holleran of the College of New Jersey suggests that minorities pay a "punishment penalty" when it comes to sentencing.[26] In Chicago, Spohn and Holleran found that convicted African Americans were 12.1 percent more likely and convicted Hispanics were 15.3 percent more likely to go to prison than convicted non-Hispanic whites. Another report, released by the Illinois Disproportionate Justice Impact Study Commission, found that African Americans were nearly five times more likely to be sentenced to prison than whites for low-level drug crimes in that state.[27]

Nationwide, about 38 percent of all inmates in state and federal prisons are African American,[28] even though members of that minority group make up only about 13 percent of the country's population and represent 28 percent of those arrested.[29] In federal prisons, nearly seven out of every ten inmates is either African American or Hispanic.[30]

Interestingly, Spohn and Holleran found that the rate of imprisonment rose significantly for minorities who were young and unemployed. This led them to conclude that the disparities between races were not the result of "conscious" discrimination on the part of the sentencing judges. Rather, faced with limited time to make decisions and limited information about the offenders, the judges would resort to stereotypes, considering not just race, but age and unemployment as well.[31] Another study, published in 2006, found that older judges and judges who were members of minority groups in Pennsylvania were less likely to send offenders

Sentencing Disparity A situation in which those convicted of similar crimes do not receive similar sentences.

Sentencing Discrimination A situation in which the length of a sentence appears to be influenced by a defendant's race, gender, economic status, or other factor not directly related to the crime he or she committed.

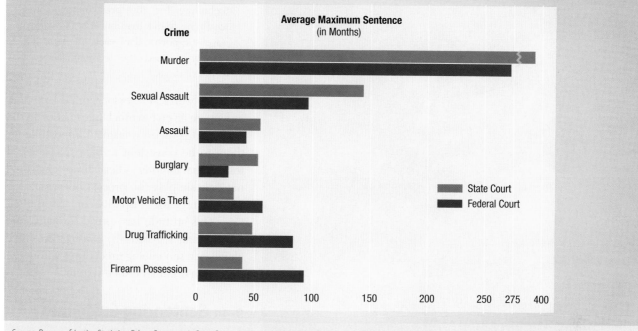

Source: Bureau of Justice Statistics, *Felony Sentences in State Courts, 2006—Statistical Tables* (Washington, D.C.: U.S. Department of Justice, December 2009), Table 1.6, page 9.

to prison, regardless of their race.[32] Such research findings support the argument in favor of diversity among judges, discussed in Chapter 7.

WOMEN AND SENTENCING Few would argue that race or ethnicity should be a factor in sentencing decisions—the system should be "color-blind." Does the same principle apply to women? In other words, should the system be "gender-blind" as well—at least on a policy level? Congress answered that question in the Sentencing Reform Act of 1984, which emphasized the ideal of gender-neutral sentencing.[33]

Gender Differences In practice, however, this has not occurred. Women who are convicted of crimes are less likely to go to prison than men, and those who are incarcerated tend to serve shorter sentences. According to government data, on average, a woman receives a sentence that is twenty-nine months shorter than that of a man for a violent crime and nine months shorter for a property crime.[34] When adjusting for comparable arrest offenses, criminal histories, and other presentencing factors, Sonja B. Starr of the University of Michigan Law School found that male convicts receive sentences that are 60 percent more severe than those for women.[35] One study attributes these differences to the elements of female criminality: in property crimes,

women are usually accessories, and in violent crimes, women are usually reacting to physical abuse. In both situations, the mitigating circumstances lead to lesser punishment.[36]

The Chivalry Effect Other evidence suggests that a *chivalry effect,* or the idea that women should be treated more leniently than men, plays a large role in sentencing decisions. Several self-reported studies have shown that judges may treat female defendants more "gently" than males and that with women, judges are influenced by mitigating factors such as marital status and family background that they would ignore with men.[37]

In certain situations, however, a woman's gender can work against her. Several years ago, for example, seventy-five-year-old Sandra Layne was convicted of second degree murder for fatally shooting her seventeen-year-old grandson. According to state sentencing guidelines, discussed in the next section, Layne, who had no criminal history, deserved to spend twelve to twenty years in prison. Oakland County (Michigan) judge Denise Langford, however, sentenced Layne to twenty to forty years behind bars, saying, "Grandmothers are supposed to protect."[38] According to Keith Crew, a professor of sociology and criminology at the University of Northern Iowa, defendants who are seen as bad mothers (or grandmothers) often "get the hammer" from judges and juries.[39]

A judge in Pontiac, Michigan, gave seventy-five-year-old Sandra Layne a harsher sentence than required by state guidelines for the second-degree murder of her seventeen-year-old grandson. *How might a woman's gender work against her in sentencing situations involving family-related violent crimes?*

AP Images/Rich Pedroncelli

CAREER TIP When a mother becomes involved with the criminal justice system, the state can decide to place her children in a foster home. The professionals who oversee this process and look out for the best interests of the children, and their families, are called *foster care case workers.*

9-4 HOW HAVE POLITICIANS TRIED TO "FIX" SENTENCING?

Judicial discretion, then, has both positive and negative aspects. Although it allows judges to impose a wide variety of sentences to fit specific criminal situations, it appears to fail to rein in a judge's subjective biases, which can lead to disparity and perhaps discrimination. Critics of judicial discretion believe that its costs (the lack of equality) outweigh its benefits (providing individualized justice). As Columbia law professor John C. Coffee noted:

Sentencing Guidelines Legislatively determined guidelines that judges are required to follow when sentencing those convicted of specific crimes.

If we wish the sentencing judge to treat "like cases alike," a more inappropriate technique for the presentation could hardly be found than one that stresses a novelistic portrayal of each offender and thereby overloads the decisionmaker in a welter of detail.[40]

In other words, Professor Coffee feels that judges are given too much information in the sentencing process, making it impossible for them to be consistent in their decisions. It follows that limiting judicial discretion would not only simplify the process but lessen the opportunity for disparity or discrimination. This attitude has spread through state and federal legislatures, causing extensive changes in sentencing procedures within the American criminal justice system.

9-4a Sentencing Guidelines

In an effort to eliminate the inequities of disparity by removing judicial bias from the sentencing process, many states and the federal government have turned to **sentencing guidelines,** which require judges to dispense legislatively determined sentences based on factors such as the seriousness of the crime and the offender's prior record.

STATE SENTENCING GUIDELINES In 1978, Minnesota became the first state to create a Sentencing Guidelines Commission with a mandate to construct and monitor the use of a determinate sentencing structure. The Minnesota Commission left no doubt as to the philosophical justification for the new sentencing statutes, stating unconditionally that retribution was its primary goal.[41] Today, about twenty states employ some form of sentencing guidelines with similar goals.

In general, these guidelines remove discretionary power from state judges by turning sentencing into a mathematical exercise. Members of the courtroom work group are guided by a *grid,* which helps them determine the proper sentence. Figure 9.3 shows the grid established by the Massachusetts sentencing commission. As in the grids used by most states, one axis ranks the type of crime, while the other refers to the offender's criminal history. In the grid for Massachusetts, the red boxes indicate the "incarceration zone." A prison sentence is required for crimes in this zone. The yellow boxes delineate a "discretionary zone," in which the judge can decide between incarceration or intermediate sanctions, which you will learn about in the next chapter.

FIGURE 9.3 A PORTION OF MASSACHUSETTS SENTENCING GUIDELINES

Sentencing Guidelines Grid

Level	Illustrative Offenses	Sentence Range				
6	Manslaughter (Involuntary) Armed Robbery (No Gun) A&B DW* (Significant Injury)	40–60 Months	45–67 Months	50–75 Months	60–90 Months	80–120 Months
5	Unarmed Robbery Unarmed Burglary Stalking in Violation of Order Larceny ($50,000 and over)	12–36 Months IS-IV IS-III IS-II	24–36 Months IS-IV IS-III IS-II	36–54 Months	48–72 Months	60–90 Months
	Criminal History Scale	**A** No/Minor Record	**B** Moderate Record	**C** Serious Record	**D** Violent/Repetitive	**E** Serious Violent

Intermediate Sanction Levels

IS-IV	24-Hour Restriction
IS-III	Daily Accountability
IS-II	Standard Supervision

*A&B DW = Assault and Battery, Dangerous Weapon

The numbers in each cell represent the range from which the judge selects the maximum sentence (Not More Than). The minimum sentence (Not Less Than) is two-thirds of the maximum sentence and constitutes the initial parole eligibility date.

www.mass.gov/courts/formsandguidelines/sentencing/grid.html

FEDERAL SENTENCING GUIDELINES In 1984, Congress passed the Sentencing Reform Act (SRA),[42] paving the way for federal sentencing guidelines that went into effect three years later. Similar in many respects to the state guidelines, the SRA also eliminated parole for federal prisoners and severely limited early release from prison due to good behavior.[43] The impact of the SRA and the state guidelines has been dramatic. Sentences have become harsher—by 2004, the average federal prison sentence was fifty months, more than twice as long as in 1984.[44]

Much to the disappointment of supporters of sentencing reform, a series of United States Supreme Court decisions handed down midway though the first decade of the 2000s held that federal sentencing guidelines were advisory only.[45] Five years after these Court decisions, according to the U.S. Sentencing Commission, African American defendants were receiving sentences about 20 percent longer than white males that were convicted of similar crimes.[46] Similarly, a 2012 study by the Transactional Records Access Clearinghouse found widespread sentencing disparities in federal courts, particularly in drug, weapons, and white-collar cases.[47]

JUDICIAL DEPARTURES In essence, the Supreme Court decisions just mentioned returned to federal judges the ability to "depart" from federal sentencing guidelines. Federal judges are taking advantage of this discretion, deviating from sentencing guidelines in almost half of all cases before them.[48] This "escape hatch" of judicial discretion is called a **departure,** and is available to state judges as well as their federal counterparts. Judges in Massachusetts, for example, can depart from the grid in Figure 9.3 if a case involves mitigating or aggravating circumstances.[49]

9-4b Mandatory Sentencing Guidelines

In an attempt to close even the limited loophole of judicial discretion offered by departures, politicians (often urged on by their constituents) have passed sentencing laws even more contrary to the idea of individualized justice. These **mandatory** (minimum) **sentencing guidelines** further limit a judge's power to deviate from determinate sentencing laws by setting firm standards for certain crimes.

STATE AND FEDERAL MANDATORY MINIMUMS The mandatory minimum "movement" started in the early 1970s in New York state, which was experiencing a wave of heroin-related crime. Governor Nelson Rockefeller pushed through a series of mandatory drug

Departure A stipulation in many federal and state sentencing guidelines that allows a judge to adjust his or her sentencing decision based on the special circumstances of a particular case.

Mandatory Sentencing Guidelines Statutorily determined punishments that must be applied to those who are convicted of specific crimes.

sentences, the most draconian being a fifteen-years-to-life punishment for anyone convicted of possessing four ounces of any illegal narcotic other than marijuana.[50] Today, nearly every state has mandatory sentencing laws, most related to crimes involving the sale or possession of illegal drugs.

The federal government passed its Anti-Drug Abuse Act[51] in the mid-1980s, in response to the cocaine overdose death of a well-known basketball player named Len Bias. Federal mandatory minimums are guided by a set of "triggers" based on the amount of drugs involved, the offender's criminal history, and many other attendant circumstances (see Chapter 3). These triggers include selling drugs to someone under twenty-one

years of age, using a minor as part of "drug operations," and carrying a firearm during the drug-related crime.[52] This legislation has given a great deal of power to federal prosecutors, who, by using their discretion to add penalty enhancements, are able to coerce defendants into plea bargaining rather than risking a lengthy prison sentence.[53]

"THREE-STRIKES" LEGISLATION Habitual offender laws are a form of mandatory sentencing found in twenty-six states and used by the federal government. Also known as "three-strikes-and-you're-out" laws, these statutes require that any person convicted of a third felony must serve a lengthy prison sentence. In many cases, the crime does not have to be of a violent or dangerous nature.

The Supreme Court validated the most punitive aspects of habitual offender laws with its decision in *Lockyer v. Andrade* (2003).[54] That case involved

Habitual Offender Laws Statutes that require lengthy prison sentences for those who are convicted of multiple felonies.

GANG INVESTIGATOR

CareerPrep

Job Description:

▶ Conduct assessments and refer at-risk youth to appropriate activities, programs, or agencies as an alternative to their becoming involved in criminal activity. Also, counsel troubled youths and their families.

▶ Serve as a liaison between the police department and schools and community organizations regarding gangs and other youth-related matters.

What Kind of Training Is Required?

▶ At a minimum, a high school diploma and any combination of training, education, and experience equivalent to three to five years' social service employment involving youth. A law enforcement background is also very helpful.

▶ Preferred candidates will have a bachelor's degree in counseling, criminal justice, or another social science field. Bilingual (English/Spanish) skills are desired.

Annual Salary Range?

▶ $50,000–$60,000

Pressmaster/ShutterStock.com

GETTING LINKEDIN

"Gang intelligence" is a growing field in both the public and private sectors. A recent LinkedIn posting for a gang SME (subject-matter expert) by a private company in Sacramento, California, required "Experience in identifying emerging threats or trends related to gangs operating inside and outside of prisons and their effect on communities."

the sentencing under California's "three-strikes" law of Leandro Andrade to fifty years in prison for stealing $153 worth of videotapes. Writing for the majority in a bitterly divided 5–4 decision, Justice Sandra Day O'Connor concluded that Andrade's punishment was not so "objectively" unreasonable that it violated the Constitution.[55] Basically, the justices who upheld the law said that if the California legislature—and by extension the California voters—felt that the law was reasonable, then the judicial branch was in no position to disagree.

REFORMING MANDATORY MINIMUMS Somewhat ironically, in 2012 California voters decided that the state's three-strikes law was indeed unreasonable. That year, by a two-thirds vote, Californians passed a ballot initiative revising the law. Now, a life sentence will be imposed only when the third felony conviction is for a serious or violent crime. Furthermore, the measure authorizes judges to resentence those approximately three thousand inmates who are serving life prison terms in California prisons because of a nonviolent "third strike."[56]

The California ballot initiative reflects nationwide discontent with mandatory minimum sentencing statutes. As we saw at the beginning of the chapter, in the comments of the judge who was forced to sentence Scott Walker to life in prison, these laws are often unpopular with judges. They are also seen as contributing heavily to the explosive, and costly, growth of the U.S. prison population since the 1980s, which we will discuss in Chapter 11. In addition, the country's minority population seems to have borne the brunt of harsh sentencing legislation—nearly 70 percent of all convicts subject to mandatory minimum sentences are African American or Hispanic.[57]

In response to these issues, nearly thirty states have reformed their mandatory sentencing laws since 2000. In general, these reforms take one of three approaches:[58]

1. *Expanding judicial discretion.* In Connecticut, judges can depart from mandatory minimum sentences for certain drug crimes when no violence or threat of violence was present.[59]

2. *Limiting habitual offender "triggers."* In Nevada, misdemeanor convictions no longer count toward a five-year mandatory minimum sentence for a third conviction.[60]

3. *Repealing or revising mandatory minimum sentences.* In 2009, New York repealed the "Rockefeller drug laws," eliminating mandatory minimum sentences for low-level drug offenders.[61]

On the federal level, the U.S. Congress is considering several bills that would allow federal judges to depart from mandatory minimum sentences for nonviolent drug offenses.[62] Absent legislative reform, the U.S. Department of Justice has asked federal prosecutors to avoid charging nonviolent drug offenders with the penalty enhancements that lead to long prison terms.[63]

9-4c Victim Impact Evidence

The final piece of the sentencing puzzle involves victims and victims' families. As mentioned in Chapter 2, crime victims traditionally were banished to the peripheries of the criminal justice system. This situation has changed dramatically with the emergence of the victims' rights movement over the past few decades. Victims are now given the opportunity to testify—in person or through written testimony—during sentencing hearings about the suffering they experienced as the result of the crime. These **victim impact statements (VISs)** have proved extremely controversial, however, and legal experts have had a difficult time determining whether they cause more harm than good.

LO9-4 **BALANCING THE PROCESS** The Crime Victims' Rights Act provides victims the right to be reasonably heard during the sentencing process,[64] and many state victims' rights laws contain similar provisions.[65] In general, these laws allow a victim (or victims) to tell his or her "side of the story" to the sentencing body, be it a judge, jury, or parole officer. In nonmurder cases, the victim can personally describe the physical, financial, and emotional impact of the crime. When the charge is murder or manslaughter, relatives or friends can give personal details about the victim and describe the effects of her or his death. In almost all instances, the goal of the VIS is to increase the harshness of the sentence.

Most of the debate surrounding VISs centers on their use in the sentencing phases of death penalty cases. Supporters point out that the defendant has always been allowed to present character evidence in the hopes of dissuading a judge or jury from capital punishment. According to some, a VIS balances the equation by giving survivors a voice in the process. Presenting a VIS is also said to have psychological benefits for victims,

Victim Impact Statement (VIS) A statement to the sentencing body (judge, jury, or parole board) in which the victim is given the opportunity to describe how the crime has affected her or him.

who are no longer forced to sit in silence as decisions that affect their lives are made by others.[66] Finally, on a purely practical level, a VIS may help judges and juries make informed sentencing decisions by providing them with an understanding of all of the consequences of the crime.

THE RISKS OF VICTIM EVIDENCE Opponents of the use of VISs claim that they interject dangerously prejudicial evidence into the sentencing process, which should be governed by reason, not emotion. The inflammatory nature of VISs, they say, may distract judges and juries from the facts of the case, which should be the only basis for a sentence.[67] Furthermore, critics contend that a VIS introduces the idea of "social value" into the courtroom. In other words, judges and juries may feel compelled to base the punishment on the "social value" of the victim (his or her standing in the community, role as a family member, and the like) rather than the circumstances of the crime.

In fact, research has shown that hearing victim impact evidence makes jurors more likely to impose the death penalty.[68] The Supreme Court, however, has given its approval to the use of VISs, allowing judges to decide whether the statements are admissible on a case-by-case basis, just as they do with any other type of evidence.[69]

9-5 WHAT IS THE STATUS OF CAPITAL PUNISHMENT IN THE UNITED STATES?

Few topics in the criminal justice system inspire such heated debate as **capital punishment.** Death penalty opponents such as legal expert Stephen Bright wonder whether "there comes a time when a society gets beyond some of the more primitive forms of punishment."[70] They point out that only twenty-three countries still employ the death penalty and that the United States is the sole Western democracy that continues the practice. Critics also claim that a process whose subjects are chosen by "luck and money and race" cannot serve the interests of justice.[71] Proponents believe that the death penalty serves as the ultimate deterrent for

violent criminal behavior and that the criminals who are put to death are the "worst of the worst" and deserve their fate.

Today, about three thousand convicts are living on "death row" in American prisons, meaning they have been sentenced to death and are awaiting execution. In the 1940s, as many as two hundred people were put to death in the United States in one year. As Figure 9.4 shows, the most recent high-water mark was ninety-eight in 1999. Despite declines since then, certain states and the federal government still regularly seek the death penalty for those offenders convicted of capital crimes. Consequently, the questions that surround the death penalty—Is it fair? Is it humane? Does it deter crime?—will continue to mobilize both its supporters and its detractors.

9-5a Methods of Execution

In its early years, when the United States adopted the practice of capital punishment from England, it also adopted English methods, which included drawing and quartering and boiling the convict alive. By the nineteenth century, these techniques had been deemed "barbaric" and were replaced by hanging. Indeed, the history of capital punishment in America is marked by attempts to make the act more humane. The 1890s saw the introduction of electrocution as a less painful method of execution than hanging, and in 1890 in Auburn Prison, New York, William Kemmler became the first American to die in an electric chair.

The "chair" remained the primary form of execution until 1977, when Oklahoma became the first state to adopt lethal injection. Today, this method dominates executions in all thirty-one states that employ the death penalty. Fourteen states authorize at least two different methods of execution, meaning that electrocution (eight states), lethal gas (three states), hanging (three states), and the firing squad (two states) are still used on very rare occasions.[72]

For most of the past three decades, states have used a similar three-drug process to carry out lethal injections. The process—which involves a sedative, a paralyzing agent, and a drug that induces heart failure—was designed to be as painless as possible for the condemned convict. Over the past five years, however, the companies that manufacture these three drugs have increasingly refused to sell them for execution purposes. This has forced state officials to experiment with untested replacement drugs, a development that—as we shall soon see—has added an element of uncertainty to capital punishment in the United States.

Capital Punishment The use of the death penalty to punish wrongdoers for certain crimes.

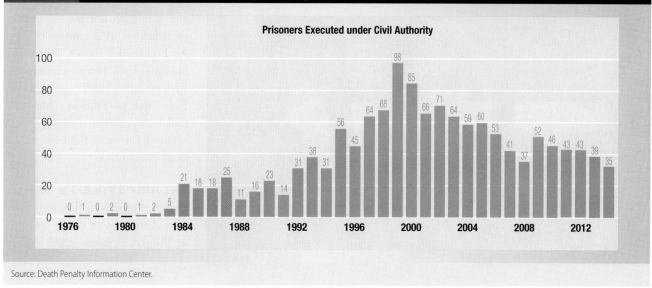

FIGURE 9.4 EXECUTIONS IN THE UNITED STATES, 1976 TO 2014

Prisoners Executed under Civil Authority

Source: Death Penalty Information Center.

9-5b The Death Penalty and the Supreme Court

The United States Supreme Court's attitude toward the death penalty has been shaped by two decisions made more than a century ago. First, in 1890, the Court established that as long as they are not carried out in an "inhuman" or "barbarous" fashion, executions are not forbidden by the Eighth Amendment.[73] Since that case, the Court has never ruled that any *method* of execution is unconstitutionally "cruel and unusual."

Then, in *Weems v. United States* (1910),[74] the Court made a ruling that further clarified the meaning of "cruel and unusual" as prohibited by the Eighth Amendment, though the facts of the case did not involve capital punishment. The defendant had been sentenced to fifteen years of hard labor, a heavy fine, and a number of other penalties for the relatively minor crime of falsifying official records. The Court overturned the sentence, ruling that the penalty was too harsh considering the nature of the offense. Ultimately, in the *Weems* decision, the Court set three important precedents concerning sentencing:

1. Cruel and unusual punishment is defined by the changing norms and standards of society and therefore is not based on historical interpretations.

2. Courts may decide whether a punishment is unnecessarily cruel with regard to physical pain.

3. Courts may decide whether a punishment is unnecessarily cruel with regard to psychological pain.[75]

"CRUEL AND UNUSUAL" CONCERNS In *Baze v. Rees* (2008),[76] the Supreme Court ruled that the mere possibility of pain "does not establish the sort of 'objectively intolerable risk of harm' that qualifies as cruel and unusual" punishment. That ruling, however, applied to the three-drug process described earlier, which has become difficult to implement because of supply issues.

Furthermore, there is some evidence that the replacement lethal injection methods used by various states, most of which use a drug called midazolam, may carry a "risk of harm." In January 2014, Michael Lee Wilson said, "I feel my whole body burning" as he was executed in Oklahoma.[77] Four months later, Oklahoma officials appeared to botch the execution of Clayton Lockett, who writhed in evident discomfort for forty-three minutes before dying. As a result, in early 2015 the Supreme Court agreed to determine whether the state's new midazolam-based lethal drug "cocktail" is a constitutionally acceptable method of execution.[78]

REFORMING THE DEATH PENALTY In the 1960s, the Supreme Court became increasingly concerned about what it saw as serious flaws in the way the states administered capital punishment. Finally, in 1967, the Court put a moratorium on executions until it could "clean up" the process. The chance to do so came with the *Furman v. Georgia* case, decided in 1972.[79]

The Bifurcated Process In its *Furman* decision, by a 5–4 margin, the Supreme Court essentially held that the death penalty, as administered by the states, violated the Eighth Amendment. Justice Potter Stewart was particularly eloquent in his concurring opinion, stating

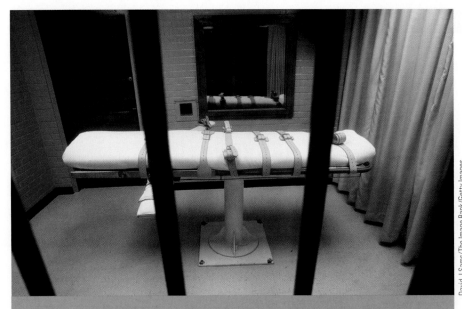

David J Sams/The Image Bank/Getty Images

Do you think that offenders convicted of capital crimes are entitled to a pain-free execution, allegedly provided in lethal injection death chambers such as those in Texas (pictured here)? Why or why not?

Even a cursory glance at the data shows that the death penalty states do not impose capital punishment at a consistent rate. As Figure 9.5 shows, a convict's likelihood of being executed is strongly influenced by geography. Five states—Florida, Missouri, Oklahoma, Texas, and Virginia—account for more than two-thirds of all executions.

THE JURY'S ROLE The Supreme Court reaffirmed the important role of the jury in death penalties in *Ring v. Arizona* (2002).[81] The case involved Arizona's bifurcated process: after the jury determined a defendant's guilt or innocence, it would be dismissed, and the judge alone would decide whether execution was warranted. The Court found that this procedure violated the defendant's Sixth Amendment right to a jury trial, ruling that juries must be involved in *both* stages of the bifurcated process. The decision invalidated death penalty laws in Arizona, Colorado, Idaho, Montana, and Nebraska, forcing legislatures in those states to hastily revamp their procedures. (To learn how a jury makes this difficult decision, see the feature *Discretion in Action—Life or Death?*)

Alabama is the only state that routinely allows a measure of judicial discretion when it comes to capital punishment. Alabama juries only *recommend* a sentence of death or life in prison. If the judge feels that the sentence is unreasonable, he or she can override the jury. This unusual policy has come under criticism because, between 1976 and 2013, Alabama judges rejected a life sentence in favor of execution ninety-five times (compared to only nine overrides in the other direction).[82] The Supreme Court recently refused to accept a case challenging the practice, however, ensuring that it will continue.[83]

MITIGATING CIRCUMSTANCES Several mitigating circumstances will prevent a defendant found guilty of first degree murder from receiving the death penalty. In 1986, the United States Supreme Court held that the Constitution prohibits the execution of a person who is insane. Sixteen years later, in *Atkins v. Virginia* (2002),[84] the Court similarly ended the death penalty for mentally handicapped defendants. This later decision underscored the continuing importance of the *Weems* test, discussed earlier in this section. In 1989, the Court

LO9-5 that the sentence of death was so arbitrary as to be comparable to "being struck by lightning."[80] Although the *Furman* ruling invalidated the death penalty for more than six hundred offenders on death row at the time, it also provided the states with a window to make the process less arbitrary, therefore bringing their death penalty statutes up to constitutional standards.

The result was a two-stage, or *bifurcated*, procedure for capital cases. In the first stage, a jury determines the guilt or innocence of the defendant for a crime that has, by state statute, been determined to be punishable by death. If the defendant is found guilty, the jury reconvenes in the second stage and considers all aggravating and mitigating factors to decide whether the death sentence is in fact warranted. Therefore, even if a jury finds the defendant guilty of a crime, such as first degree murder, that *may be* punishable by death, in the second stage it can decide that the circumstances surrounding the crime justify only a punishment of life in prison.

The Extent of Capital Punishment Today, thirty-one states and the federal government have capital punishment laws based on the bifurcated process. State governments are responsible for almost all executions in this country. The federal government has carried out only three death sentences since 1963, and usually seeks capital punishment only for high-profile defendants such as Dzhokhar Tsarnaev, convicted of planting bombs at the Boston Marathon in April 2013.

FIGURE 9.5 EXECUTIONS BY STATE, 1976–2014

WA 5
MT 3
ND
OR 2
ID 3
WY 1
SD 3
MN
WI
MI
NH*
VT
ME
NY
MA
RI
CT^c 1
NJ
DE 17
MD^d 5
D.C.
PA 3
NV 12
Utah 7
CO 1
NE^e 3
IA
IL^b 12
IN 20
OH 53
CA 13
KS*
MO 80
KY 3
WV
VA 110
AZ 37
NM^a 1
OK 111
AR 27
TN 6
NC 43
SC 43
TX 518
LA 28
MS 21
AL 56
GA 55
FL 89
AK
HI

■ States with the death penalty
▨ States without the death penalty

* Jurisdictions with no executions since 1976
a Repealed the use of the death penalty in 2009
b Repealed the use of the death penalty in 2011
c Repealed the use of the death penalty in 2012
d Repealed the use of the death penalty in 2013
e Repealed the use of the death penalty in 2015

Source: Death Penalty Information Center.

had rejected the argument that execution of a mentally handicapped person was "cruel and unusual" under the Eighth Amendment.[85] At the time, only two states barred execution of the mentally handicapped. Thirteen years later, eighteen states had such laws, and the Court decided that this increased number reflected "changing norms and standards of society."

Following the *Atkins* case, many observers, including four Supreme Court justices, hoped that the same reasoning would be applied to the question of whether convicts who committed the relevant crime when they were juveniles may be executed. These hopes were realized in 2005 when the Court issued its *Roper v. Simmons* decision, which effectively ended the execution of those who committed crimes as juveniles.[86] As in the *Atkins* case, the Court relied on the "evolving standards of decency" test, noting that a majority of the states, as well as every other civilized nation, prohibited the execution of offenders who committed their crimes before the age of eighteen. The *Roper* ruling required that seventy-two convicted murderers in twelve states be resentenced and took the death penalty "off the table" for dozens of pending cases in which prosecutors were seeking capital punishment for juvenile criminal acts.

9-5c The Future of the Death Penalty

As noted earlier in the chapter, the number of executions carried out each year in the United States has decreased dramatically since 1999. Other statistics also indicate a decline in death penalty activity. In 2014, only 72 people were sentenced to death, compared with 277 in 1999.[87] Also in 1999, Texas, the most active state when it comes to capital punishment, executed thirty-five convicts and sentenced another forty-eight to death. By 2014, those numbers had dropped to ten and eleven, respectively.[88]

THE DECLINE IN EXECUTIONS We have already addressed some of the reasons for the diminishing presence of executions in the criminal justice system. With its decisions in the *Atkins* (2002) and *Roper* (2005) cases, the United States Supreme Court removed the possibility that hundreds of mentally handicapped and juvenile offenders could be sentenced to death. The availability and reliability of drugs used in lethal injections have also become an issue. In 2015, at least four states—Arizona, Florida, Ohio, and Oklahoma— temporarily shut down their death chambers, either to

Discretion in Action

LIFE OR DEATH?

THE SITUATION In a fit of extreme jealousy, twenty-seven-year-old Jodi drove one thousand miles to the home of her thirty-year-old ex-boyfriend, Travis. After the couple had sex, Jodi stabbed Travis twenty-seven times and left him for dead in the shower. You are part of the jury that found Jodi guilty of first degree murder. You and your fellow jurors must now decide whether she should receive the death penalty, or, alternately, life in prison without parole, as punishment for her crime.

THE LAW Jurors must weigh aggravating factors against mitigating factors during the death penalty phase of criminal trials. If you believe that the aggravating factors surrounding Jodi's crime outweigh the mitigating factors, you must vote for her to be executed.

WHAT WOULD YOU DO? In arguing for her client's life, Jodi's attorney raises a number of mitigating factors, including the childhood abuse that Jodi

suffered, her borderline personality disorder, and her lack of a prior criminal record. Jodi also addresses the jury, telling you that her death would devastate her family. "I'm asking you, please, please don't do that to them. I've already hurt them so badly," Jodi says. Finally, Jodi describes several volunteer prison programs she would like to participate in, and speaks of her desire to bring "people together in a positive and constructive way" behind bars. The prosecutor counters that the violent nature of Jodi's crime outweighs any mitigating factors, and members of Travis's family ask you to sentence her to death. Do you think Jodi should receive the death penalty or life in prison? Why?

[To see whether an Arizona jury chose the death sentence in similar circumstances, go to Example 9.1 in Appendix A.]

*For more information on the death penalty, visit **www.death penaltyinfo.org/aggravating-factors-capital-punishment-state**.

---

reassess their drug protocols or in anticipation of the Supreme Court's ruling on Oklahoma's lethal injection procedures.

Other factors in the declining use of capital punishment in the United States include:

1. *The life-without-parole alternative.* In the early 1970s, only seven states allowed juries to sentence offenders to life in prison without parole instead of death. Now, every state provides this option, and juries seem to prefer this form of incapacitation to execution.[89]

2. *Plummeting murder rates.* The number of murders committed in this country is currently half what it was in the early 1990s.[90] As murder is the most common capital crime, this reduction has led to a decline in the number of offenders eligible for the death penalty.

3. *High costs.* Because of the costs of intensive law enforcement investigations, extensive *voir dire* (see Chapter 8), and lengthy appellate reviews, pursuing capital punishment can be very expensive for states. Nevada recently determined that its death penalty cases cost twice as much as similar cases without the death penalty, resulting in a $76 million price tag for state taxpayers since 1976.[91]

PUBLIC OPINION AND THE DEATH PENALTY In July 2014, a federal judge declared that California's death penalty system had become so arbitrary and unpredictable that it was unconstitutional. The state has the nation's largest death row population at around 750, but—because of procedural problems—has not carried out an execution since 2006. As a result, said the judge, those on California's death row are experiencing a punishment that "no rational jury or legislature could ever impose: life in prison, with the remote possibility of death."[92]

As a consequence of this ruling, California joined the four states mentioned earlier in suspending its death penalty operations in 2015. Furthermore, also in 2015, Nebraska became the seventh state in eight years to end capital punishment, along with Connecticut, Illinois, Maryland, New Jersey, New Mexico, and New York. Does this mean society's "standards of decency" are changing to the point that the death sentence could be completely abolished in the United States? Probably not. The Supreme Court has shown no interest in holding that the death penalty itself is unconstitutional. In addition to its *Baze* decision (discussed earlier in this section), in 2007 the Court made it easier for prosecutors to seek the death penalty by allowing them to remove potential jurors who express reservations about the practice.[93]

Although public support for the death penalty has been steadily dropping since the mid-1990s, one poll taken in 2014 showed that 63 percent of Americans still favor the practice. (That percentage does, however, drop to about 50 percent when the choice is between execution and a sentence of life in prison without parole.)[94] Taking a closer look at the numbers, however, it becomes evident that support for capital punishment is stronger among older, white Americans than it is among younger generations and members of minority groups.[95] Thus, in the future, the continued use of the death penalty in the United States may come under threat from a new generation of voters who oppose this method of criminal punishment.

CAREER TIP *Pollsters,* who conduct surveys of public opinion, play a crucial role in measuring the national mood concerning controversial criminal justice issues such as capital punishment.

STUDY TOOLS 9

READY TO STUDY? IN THE BOOK, YOU CAN:

☐ Rip out the Chapter Review Card, which includes key terms and chapter summaries.

ONLINE AT WWW.CENGAGEBRAIN.COM, YOU CAN:

☐ Learn about sentencing in adult versus juvenile crimes.

☐ Explore the Death Penalty Information Center (DPIC) Web site and Twitter feed.

☐ Interact with figures from the text, and watch quick animation clips.

☐ Prepare for tests with quizzes.

☐ Review the key terms with Flash Cards.

Quiz

1. The goal of the sentencing doctrine called _____ is to prevent future crimes by "setting an example" with punishments for convicted criminals.

2. A sentencing doctrine known as _____ suggests that offenders can be "treated" for their criminal tendencies and possibly "cured" of them.

3. _____ sentences set a minimum and maximum amount of time a convict must spend behind bars, giving corrections officials the discretion to release the inmate within that time period.

4. A determinate sentence indicates the exact length of incapacitation, minus possible reductions for _____ _____.

5. _____ circumstances can allow for a lighter sentence, while aggravating circumstances can lead to the imposition of a harsher penalty.

6. Sentencing _____ occurs when similar crimes are punished with dissimilar sentences.

7. Sentencing _____ is the result of judicial consideration of extralegal variables such as the defendant's race or gender.

8. With the aim of limiting judicial discretion, many states and the federal government have enacted sentencing _____.

9. By a large margin, _____ _____ is the most widespread method of execution in the United States today.

10. Following the "norms and standards" guidelines it established with the *Weems* decision, in 2005 the United States Supreme Court prohibited the execution of persons who were _____ at the time of their crime.

Answers can be found in the Answers section in the back of the book.

YOUR FEED-BACK YOUR BOOK

Our research never ends. Continual feedback from you ensures that we keep up with your changing needs.

10 Probation, Parole, and Intermediate Sanctions

Travis Dove/The New York Times/Redux

LEARNING OBJECTIVES

After studying this chapter, you will be able to . . .

10-1 Explain the justifications for community-based corrections programs.

10-2 Describe the three general categories of conditions placed on a probationer.

10-3 Identify the main differences between probation and parole.

10-4 Explain which factors influence the decision to grant parole.

10-5 List the three levels of home monitoring.

After you finish this chapter, go to **PAGES 225–226** for **STUDY TOOLS**

Returning home from a barbecue at 3 A.M. in rural Philo, Illinois, twenty-four-year-old Katie Daly skidded on wet gravel and lost control of the all-terrain vehicle she was driving. Her nineteen-year-old cousin, Annie Daly, was thrown from the passenger seat and died in a hospital four hours later. At the time of the accident, Katie's blood alcohol level was well over the state's legal limit, and she was charged with felony aggravated driving under the influence (DUI). Given her family connection to the victim, local prosecutors agreed to a plea deal in which Katie would be spared prison, instead receiving a punishment of probation for her crime.

Champaign County judge Richard Klaus had other ideas. Despite impassioned pleas for leniency from Annie's parents and brother, Klaus rejected the plea bargain and sentenced Katie to three and a half years in prison for reckless homicide. "Under the law, it is not a mitigating factor that a family member died. The loss to society is the same whether Annie was killed by a family member or a stranger," Klaus explained. "This is absolutely a deterrable crime and it must be deterred. It is the duty of the court to see that it is deterred."

Prosecutors and Katie's defense attorneys joined forces to appeal Klaus's decision. Noting Katie's youth, her lack of a criminal record, and the effect of the incarceration on her family, including her infant son, the appeals brief stated, "A prison sentence in this case would not be of any benefit to society, the defendant, or to our system of justice." In December 2014, an Illinois appellate court agreed, ruling that Klaus had abused his discretion by putting the defendant behind bars. After six months in prison, Katie was freed and resentenced to thirty months of probation. According to state's attorney Julia Reitz, the intent of the appellate court "was not to minimize the seriousness of the DUI aspect but more to focus on Katie's rehabilitative potential."

Katie Daly was eventually sentenced to probation for killing her cousin Annie in an alcohol-related accident involving an all-terrain vehicle such as the one shown here. What is your opinion of Judge Richard Klaus's justification for initially sentencing Daly to a prison term?

zhu difeng/ShutterStock.com

10-1 WHY DO WE NEED COMMUNITY CORRECTIONS?

In overturning Judge Richard Klaus's sentence of Katie Daly, the Fourth District Appellate Court of Illinois scolded the judge for focusing on incarceration and ignoring the "range of sentencing possibilities" called for by the facts of the case.[1] As this chapter will make clear, the range of sentencing possibilities for American judges includes numerous options that keep offenders out of prison and jail. For instance, about 3.9 million offenders such as Daly are presently serving their sentences in the community on *probation* rather than behind bars. In addition, approximately 850,000 convicts in the United States have been *paroled,* meaning that they are finishing their prison sentences "on the outside" under the supervision of correctional officers.[2]

America, says University of Minnesota law professor Michael Tonry, is preoccupied with the "absolute severity of punishment" and the "widespread view that only imprisonment counts."[3] Consequently, **community corrections** such as probation and parole are often considered a less severe, and therefore a less worthy, alternative to imprisonment. In reality, community corrections are crucial to our criminal justice system. One in fifty adults in this country is living under community

Community Corrections The correctional supervision of offenders in the community as an alternative to prison or jail terms.

supervision,[4] and few criminal justice matters are more pressing than the need to successfully reintegrate these offenders into society.

10-1a Reintegration

LO10-1 A very small percentage of all convicted offenders have committed crimes that warrant life imprisonment or capital punishment. Most, at some point, will return to the community. Consequently, according to one group of experts, the task of the corrections system

> includes building or rebuilding solid ties between the offender and the community, integrating or reintegrating the offender into community life—restoring family ties, obtaining employment and an education, securing in the larger sense a place for the offender in the routine functioning of society.[5]

Considering that some studies have shown higher recidivism rates for offenders who are subjected to prison culture, a frequent justification of community-based corrections is that they help to reintegrate the offender into society.

Reintegration has a strong theoretical basis in rehabilitative theories of punishment. An offender is generally considered to be "rehabilitated" when he or she no longer represents a threat to other members of the community and therefore is believed to be fit to live in that community. In the context of this chapter and the two that follow, it will also be helpful to see reintegration as a process through which criminal justice officials such as probation and parole officers provide the offender with incentives to follow the rules of society.

These incentives can be positive, such as enrolling the offender in a drug treatment program. They can also be negative—in particular, the threat of return to prison or jail for failure to comply. In all instances, criminal justice professionals must carefully balance the needs of the individual offender against the rights of law-abiding members of the community.

Reintegration A goal of corrections that focuses on preparing the offender for a return to the community unmarred by further criminal behavior.

Diversion In the context of corrections, a strategy to divert those offenders who qualify away from prison and jail and toward community-based and intermediate sanctions.

10-1b Diversion

Another justification for community-based corrections, based on practical considerations, is **diversion.** As you are already aware, many criminal offenses fall into the category of "petty," and it is well-nigh impossible, as well as unnecessary, to imprison every offender for every offense. Community-based corrections are an important means of diverting criminals to alternative modes of punishment so that scarce incarceration resources are consumed by only the most dangerous criminals.

In his "strainer" analogy, corrections expert Paul H. Hahn likens this process to the workings of a kitchen strainer. With each "shake" of the corrections "strainer," the less serious offenders are diverted from incarceration. At the end, only the most serious convicts remain in prison.[6]

The diversionary role of community-based punishments has become more pronounced as prisons and jails have filled up over the past three decades. In fact, probationers and parolees now account for about 70 percent of all adults in the American corrections systems.[7]

CAREER TIP In Nevada, judges can sentence problem gamblers to treatment rather than prison for gambling-related wrongdoing. This option has created a statewide demand for *pathological gambling therapists*, who help problem gamblers overcome their addictions.

AP Images/LM Otero

In Dallas, street prostitutes such as the two shown here are often treated as crime victims and offered access to treatment and rehabilitation programs. *How might society benefit if such offenders are kept out of jail or prison through these kinds of diversion programs?*

10-1c The "Low-Cost Alternative"

Not all of the recent expansion of community corrections can be attributed to acceptance of its theoretical underpinnings. Many politicians and criminal justice officials who do not look favorably on ideas such as reintegration and diversion have embraced programs to keep nonviolent offenders out of prison. The reason is simple: economics. The cost of constructing and maintaining prisons and jails, as well as housing and caring for inmates, has placed a great deal of pressure on corrections budgets across the country. States spend an estimated $52 billion a year on their corrections systems, most of which goes to prison operating costs.[8]

Community corrections offer an enticing financial alternative to imprisonment. The Bureau of Prisons estimates that the federal government saves about $25,600 annually by shifting a nonviolent offender from incarceration to supervised release.[9] The average yearly cost of housing an inmate in Nebraska is $35,169, compared with $3,760 for community corrections.[10] Prison admissions in North Carolina declined by 21 percent from 2011 to 2014, as state corrections officials moved nonviolent offenders to probation and parole. In the process, the state's annual corrections budget shrank by $50 million.[11]

10-2 HOW DOES PROBATION WORK?

As Figure 10.1 shows, **probation** is the most common form of punishment in the United States. Although it is administered differently in various jurisdictions, probation can be generally defined as

> the legal status of an offender who, after being convicted of a crime, has been directed by the sentencing court to remain in the community under the supervision of a probation service for a designated period of time and subject to certain conditions imposed by the court or by law.[12]

The theory behind probation is that certain offenders can be treated more economically and humanely by putting them under controls while still allowing them to live in the community. One of the advantages of probation has been that it provides for the rehabilitation of the offender while saving society the costs of incarceration. Despite probation's widespread use, certain participants in the criminal justice system question its ability to reach its rehabilitative goals. Critics point to the immense

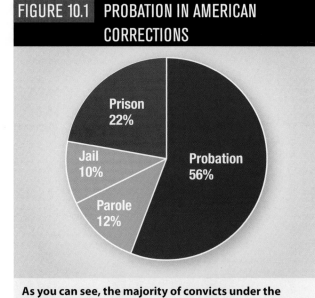

FIGURE 10.1 PROBATION IN AMERICAN CORRECTIONS

Prison 22%

Jail 10%

Parole 12%

Probation 56%

As you can see, the majority of convicts under the control of the American corrections system are on probation.

Source: Bureau of Justice Statistics, *Correctional Populations in the United States, 2013* (Washington, D.C.: U.S. Department of Justice, December 2014), Table 1, page 2.

number of probationers and the fact that many of them are violent felons as evidence that the system is "out of control." Supporters contend that nothing is wrong with probation in principle, but admit that its execution must be adjusted to meet the goals of modern corrections.[13]

10-2a Sentencing and Probation

Probation is basically an arrangement between sentencing authorities and the offender. In traditional probation, the offender agrees to comply with certain terms for a specified amount of time in return for serving the sentence in the community. One of the primary benefits for the offender, besides not being sent to a correctional facility, is that the length of the probationary period is usually considerably shorter than the length of a prison term (see Figure 10.2).

ALTERNATIVE SENTENCING ARRANGEMENTS The traditional form of probation is not the only arrangement that can be made. A judge can hand down a **suspended sentence,** under which a defendant who

Probation A criminal sanction in which a convict is allowed to remain in the community rather than be imprisoned.

Suspended Sentence A judicially imposed condition in which an offender is sentenced after being convicted of a crime, but is not required to begin serving the sentence immediately.

FIGURE 10.2 AVERAGE LENGTH OF SENTENCE: PRISON VERSUS PROBATION

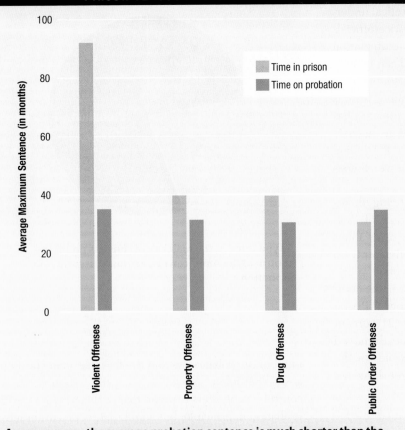

As you can see, the average probation sentence is much shorter than the average prison sentence for most crimes.

Source: Bureau of Justice Statistics, *Felony Defendants in State Courts, 2009—Statistical Tables* (Washington, D.C.: U.S. Department of Justice, December 2013), Table 25, page 30; and Table 27, page 31.

has been convicted and sentenced to be incarcerated is not required to serve the sentence. Instead, the judge puts the offender on notice, keeping open the option of reinstating the original sentence and sending the offender to prison or jail if he or she reoffends. In practice, suspended sentences are quite similar to probation.

Judges can also combine probation with incarceration. Such sentencing arrangements include:

▶ *Split sentences.* In **split sentence probation,** also known as *shock probation,* the offender is sentenced to a specific amount of time in prison or jail, to be followed by a period of probation.

▶ *Shock incarceration.* In this arrangement, an offender is sentenced to prison or jail with the understanding that after a period of time, she or he may petition the

court to be released on probation. Shock incarceration is discussed more fully later in the chapter.

▶ *Intermittent incarceration.* With intermittent incarceration, the offender spends a certain amount of time each week, usually during the weekend, in a jail, workhouse, or other government institution.

Split sentences are popular with judges, as they combine the "treatment" aspects of probation with the "punishment" aspects of incarceration. According to the U.S. Department of Justice, about a fifth of all probationers are also sentenced to some form of incarceration.[14]

CHOOSING PROBATION Generally, research has shown that offenders are most likely to be denied probation if they:

▶ Are convicted on multiple charges.

▶ Were on probation or parole at the time of the arrest.

▶ Have two or more prior convictions.

▶ Are addicted to narcotics.

▶ Seriously injured the victim of the crime.

▶ Used a weapon during the commission of the crime.[15]

As might be expected, the chances of a felon being sentenced to probation are highly dependent on the seriousness of his or her crime. Only 19 percent of probationers in the United States have committed a violent crime, including domestic violence and sex offenses. The majority of probationers have been convicted of property crimes, drug offenses, or public order crimes such as drunk driving.[16]

Probation permits the judicial system to recognize that some offenders are less blameworthy than others. Several years ago, for example, a judge in Arizona found himself with the difficult task of punishing eighty-six-year-old George Sanders for fatally shooting Virginia, his eighty-one-year-old wife. Virginia, who was suffering from a painful health condition, had begged George to end her life. In handing down his sentence of two years' probation, Judge John Ditsworth said that his decision tempered "justice with mercy."[17]

Split Sentence Probation A sentence that consists of incarceration in a prison or jail, followed by a probationary period in the community.

10-2b Conditions of Probation

A judge may decide to impose certain conditions as part of a probation sentence. These conditions represent a "contract" between the judge and the offender, in which the latter agrees that if she or he does not follow certain rules, probation may be *revoked*. **Revocation** is the formal process by which probation is ended and a probationer is punished for his or her wrongdoing, often by being sent to jail or prison for the original term decided by the court.

Judges have a great deal of discretion to impose any terms of probation that they feel are necessary. In the case that opened this chapter, for example, Champaign County (Illinois) judge Tom Difanis ordered Katie Daly not to use any alcohol or illegal drugs during her thirty-month probationary period. He also prohibited her from entering an establishment whose primary purpose is selling alcohol, and required her to wear an alcohol-monitoring device for the first year of her supervised sentence.

PRINCIPLES OF PROBATION A judge's personal philosophy is often reflected in the probation conditions that she or he creates for probationers. In *In re Quirk* (1997),[18] for example, the Louisiana Supreme Court upheld the ability of a trial judge to impose church attendance as a condition of probation. Though judges have a great deal of discretion in setting the conditions of probation, they do operate under several guiding principles. First, the conditions must be related to the dual purposes of probation, which most federal and state courts define as (1) the rehabilitation of the probationer and (2) the protection of the community. Second, the conditions must not violate the U.S. Constitution, as probationers are generally entitled to the same constitutional rights as other prisoners.[19]

Of course, probationers do give up certain constitutional rights when they consent to the terms of probation. Most probationers, for example, agree to spot checks of their homes for contraband such as drugs or weapons, and they therefore have a diminished expectation of privacy.

In *United States v. Knights* (2001),[20] the United States Supreme Court upheld the actions of deputy sheriffs in Napa County, California, who searched a probationer's home without a warrant or probable cause. The unanimous decision was based on the premise that because those on probation are more likely to commit crimes, law enforcement agents "may therefore justifiably focus on probationers in a way that [they do] not on the ordinary citizen."[21]

TYPES OF CONDITIONS Obviously, probationers who break the law are very likely to have their probation revoked. Other, less serious infractions may also result in revocation. The

LO10-2

conditions placed on a probationer fall into three general categories:

▶ *Standard conditions*, which are imposed on all probationers. These include reporting regularly to the probation officer, notifying the agency of any change of address, not leaving the jurisdiction without permission, and remaining employed.

▶ *Punitive conditions*, which usually reflect the seriousness of the offense and are intended to increase the punishment of the offender. Such conditions include fines, community service, restitution, drug testing, and home confinement (discussed later).

▶ *Treatment conditions*, which are imposed to reverse patterns of self-destructive behavior. Such treatment generally includes counseling for drug and alcohol abuse, anger management, and mental health issues, and is a component of approximately 27 percent of probation sentences in this country.[22]

Some observers feel that judges have too much discretion in imposing overly restrictive conditions that no person, much less one who has exhibited antisocial tendencies, could meet. Citing prohibitions on drinking liquor, gambling, and associating with "undesirables," as well as requirements such as meeting early curfews, the late University of Delaware professor Carl B. Klockars claimed that if probation rules were taken seriously, "very few probationers would complete their terms without violation."[23]

As the majority of probationers do complete their terms successfully,[24] Klockars's statement suggests that either probation officers are unable to determine that violations are taking place, or many of them are exercising a great deal of discretion in reporting minor probation violations. Perhaps the officers realize that violating probationers for every single "slip-up" is unrealistic and would add to the already significant problem of jail and prison overcrowding.

10-2c The Supervisory Role of the Probation Officer

The probation officer has two basic roles. The first is investigative and consists of conducting the presentence investigation (PSI), which was discussed in Chapter 9. The second is supervisory and begins as soon as the offender has been sentenced to probation. In smaller probation

Revocation The formal process that follows the failure of a probationer or parolee to comply with the terms of his or her probation or parole, often resulting in the probationer's incarceration.

CareerPrep

Job Description:

▶ Work with offenders or clients who have been sentenced to probation and will not go to prison or jail for their offenses. In some departments, investigate offender backgrounds, write presentence reports, and recommend sentences.

▶ Includes extensive fieldwork to meet with and monitor offenders. May be required to carry a firearm or other weapon for protection.

What Kind of Training Is Required?

▶ A bachelor's degree in criminal justice, social work, psychology, or a related field.

▶ Must be at least twenty-one years old, have no felony convictions, and have strong writing and interview skills. Experience in multicultural outreach is a plus.

Annual Salary Range?

▶ $30,000–$80,000

Stephen Coburn/ShutterStock.com

GETTING LINKEDIN

A recent LinkedIn posting for a deputy chief probation officer in Alameda County, California, focuses on the importance of community-relations skills in this profession. The "ideal candidate" for the post has passion and sensitivity for the needs of Alameda County's "ethnically/culturally diverse urban population" and a "track record of building trust and consensus" among coworkers and clients.

---

agencies, individual officers perform both tasks. In larger jurisdictions, the trend has been toward separating the responsibilities, with *investigating officers* handling the PSI and *line officers* concentrating on supervision.

Supervisory policies vary and are often a reflection of whether the authority to administer probation services is *decentralized* (under local, judicial control) or *centralized* (under state, administrative control). In any circumstance, however, certain basic principles of supervision apply. Starting with a preliminary interview, the probation officer establishes a relationship with the offender. This relationship is based on the mutual goal of both parties: the successful completion of the probationary period. Just because the line officer and the offender have the same goal, however, does not necessarily mean that cooperation will be a feature of probation.

Authority   The power designated to an agent of the law over a person who has broken the law.

THE USE OF AUTHORITY Not surprisingly, research shows that the ideal officer-offender relationship is based on mutual respect, honesty, and trust.[25] In reality, these qualities are often hard to maintain between probation officers and their clients. Any incentive an offender might have to be completely truthful with a line officer is marred by one simple fact: self-reported wrongdoing can be used to revoke probation. Even probation officers whose primary mission is to rehabilitate are under institutional pressure to punish their clients for violating conditions of probation. One officer deals with this situation by telling his clients

> that I'm here to help them, to get them a job, and whatever else I can do. But I tell them too that I have a family to support and that if they get too far off track, I can't afford to put my job on the line for them. I'm going to have to violate them.[26]

In the absence of trust, most probation officers rely on their **authority** to guide an offender successfully through the sentence. An officer's authority, or ability to influence a person's actions without resorting to force, is based partially on her or his power to revoke probation. It also reflects her or his ability to impose a number of lesser sanctions. For example, if a probationer fails to attend a required alcohol treatment program, the officer can send him or her to a "lockup," or detention center, overnight. To be successful, a probation officer must establish this authority early in the relationship because it is the primary tool for persuading the probationer to behave in an acceptable manner.

THE CASELOAD DILEMMA Even the most balanced, "firm but fair" approach to probation can be defeated by the problem of excessive *caseloads*. A **caseload** is the number of clients a probation officer is responsible for at any one time. Heavy probation caseloads seem inevitable: unlike a prison cell, a probation officer can always take "just one more" client. Furthermore, the ideal caseload size is very difficult to determine because different offenders require different levels of supervision.[27]

The consequences of disproportionate probation officer–probationer ratios are self-evident, however. When burdened with large caseloads, probation officers find it practically impossible to rigorously enforce the conditions imposed on their clients. Lack of surveillance leads to lack of control, which can undermine the very basis of a probationary system.

Between 2003 and 2014, the number of federal probation officers declined by 5 percent. Due to the stricter federal sentencing guidelines discussed in the previous chapter, the number of federal probationers increased by 19 percent over that time period. Furthermore, the rolls of federal probationers with mental health treatment conditions and substance abuse treatment conditions expanded significantly, placing even more time pressure on federal probation officers.[28]

10-2d **Revocation of Probation**

The probation period can end in one of two ways. Either the probationer successfully fulfills the conditions of the sentence, or the probationer misbehaves and probation is revoked, resulting in a prison or jail term. The decision of whether to revoke after a **technical violation**—such as failing to report a change of address or testing positive for drug use—is often made at the discretion of the probation officer and is therefore the focus of controversy. (See the feature *Discretion in Action—A Judgment Call* to learn more about the issues surrounding revocation.)

As we have seen, probationers do not always enjoy the same protections under the U.S. Constitution as other members of society. The United States Supreme Court has not stripped these offenders of all rights, however. In *Mempa v. Rhay* (1967),[29] the Court ruled that probationers are entitled to an attorney during the revocation process. Then, in *Morrissey v. Brewer* (1972) and *Gagnon v. Scarpelli* (1973),[30] the Court established a three-stage procedure by which the "limited" due process rights of probationers must be protected in potential revocation situations:

▶ *Preliminary hearing.* In this appearance before a "disinterested person" (often a judge), the facts of the violation or arrest are presented, and it is determined whether probable cause for revoking probation exists. This hearing can be waived by the probationer.

▶ *Revocation hearing.* During this hearing, the probation agency presents evidence to support its claim of violation, and the probationer can attempt to refute this evidence. The probationer has the right to know the charges being brought against him or her. Furthermore, probationers can testify on their own behalf and present witnesses in their favor, as well as confront and cross-examine adverse witnesses. A "neutral and detached" body must hear the evidence and rule on the validity of the proposed revocation.

▶ *Revocation sentencing.* If the presiding body rules against the probationer, then the judge must decide whether to impose incarceration and for what length of time. In a revocation hearing dealing with technical violations, the judge will often reimpose probation with stricter terms or intermediate sanctions.

In effect, this is a "bare-bones" approach to due process. Most of the rules of evidence that govern regular trials do not apply to revocation hearings. Probation officers are not, for example, required to read offenders their *Miranda* rights before questioning them about crimes they may have committed during probation. In *Minnesota v. Murphy* (1984),[31] the Supreme Court ruled that a meeting between probation officer and client does not equal custody and, therefore, the Fifth Amendment protection against self-incrimination does not apply, either.

Caseload The number of individual probationers or parolees under the supervision of a probation or parole officer.

Technical Violation An action taken by a probationer or parolee that, although not criminal, breaks the terms of probation or parole as designated by the court.

A JUDGMENT CALL

THE SITUATION You are a probation officer. Your client, Alain, was convicted of selling drugs and given a split sentence—three years in prison and three years on probation. You meet Alain for the first time two days after his release, and you are immediately concerned about his mental health. His mother confirms your worries, telling you that Alain needs help. You refer him to a psychiatric hospital, but the officials there determine that he "does not require mental health treatment at this time." Several weeks later, Alain's mother tells you that he is staying out late at night and "hanging out with the wrong crowd," both violations of his probation agreement. After he tests positive for marijuana, you warn Alain that, after one more violation, you will revoke his probation and send him back to prison. He tells you that he is "feeling agitated" and "having intermittent rage." You refer him to a substance abuse and mental health treatment facility, where he tests positive for marijuana once again.

THE LAW For any number of reasons, but particularly for the failed drug tests, you can start revocation proceedings against Alain. These proceedings will almost certainly conclude with his return to prison.

WHAT WOULD YOU DO? On the one hand, Alain has violated the terms of his probation agreement numerous times. On the other hand, he has been convicted of only one crime—a drug violation—and you have no evidence that he is behaving violently or poses a danger to himself or others. Furthermore, Alain has strong family support and is willing to enter treatment for his substance abuse problems. Do Alain's technical violations cause you to begin the revocation process? Why or why not?

[To see how a Fairfield County, Connecticut, probation officer dealt with a similar situation, go to Example 10.1 in Appendix A.]

10-2e Does Probation Work?

On March 11, 2014, police in Berkeley County, West Virginia, arrested William Jackson for placing a plastic bag over seventy-two-year-old Martha Tyler's head and suffocating her to death. At the time of the murder, Jackson was on probation for drug charges and grand larceny. Indeed, probationers are responsible for a significant amount of crime. According to recent data, 11 percent of all suspects arrested for violent crimes (and 13 percent of those arrested for murder) were on probation at the time of their apprehension.[32] Such statistics raise a critical question—is probation worthwhile?

To measure the effectiveness of probation, one must first establish its purpose. Generally, as we saw earlier, the goal of probation is to reintegrate

A Wareham, Massachusetts, probation officer checks her appointment schedule. *Why is mutual trust between probation officers and their clients often difficult to achieve?*

Boston Globe/Getty Images

and divert as many offenders as possible while at the same time protecting the public. Specifically, probation and other community corrections programs are evaluated by their success in preventing *recidivism*—the eventual rearrest of the probationer.[33] Given that most probationers are first-time, nonviolent offenders, the system is not designed to prevent relatively rare outbursts of violence, such as the murder committed by William Jackson.

RISK FACTORS FOR RECIDIVISM About 15 percent of all probationers are returned to prison or jail before the end of their probationary terms.[34] There are several risk factors that make a probationer more likely to recidivate, including the following:

> 1. *Antisocial personality patterns,* meaning that the probationer is impulsive, pleasure seeking, restlessly aggressive, or irritable.
>
> 2. *Procriminal attitudes,* such as negative opinions of authority and the law, as well as a tendency to rationalize prior criminal behavior.
>
> 3. *Social supports for crime,* including friends who are offenders and a living environment lacking in positive role models.[35]

Other important risk factors for recidivism include substance abuse and unemployment. By concentrating resources on those probationers who exhibit these risk factors, probation departments can succeed in lowering caseloads and overall recidivism rates.

"SWIFT AND CERTAIN" One of the problems with traditional methods of sanctioning probation violations is the length of the proceedings. If, for example, a probationer fails a drug test, it may take months before a penalty is enforced, weakening the link between wrongdoing and punishment. As criminologist James Q. Wilson pointed out, one does not discipline a child by saying, "Because [you've misbehaved], you have a 50-50 chance nine months from now of being grounded."[36]

A number of probation departments have implemented strategies that operate on the principle of providing "swift and certain" sanctions for probation violations. Perhaps the most successful of these strategies is Hawaii's Opportunity Probation with Enforcement (HOPE) program. The rules of HOPE are simple. Each substance abuse probationer must call the courthouse every day to learn if she or he is required to come in for urine tests for drugs, or *urinalysis.* If drugs are found in the probationer's system during one of these frequent tests, a short jail term—one to two weeks—is automatically served. HOPE has resulted in large reductions in positive drug tests by probationers, and its fifteen hundred participants are significantly less likely to be rearrested than those not in the program.[37]

10-3 HOW DOES PAROLE WORK?

At any given time, about 850,000 Americans are living in the community on **parole,** or the *conditional* release of a prisoner after a portion of his or her sentence has been served behind bars. Parole allows the corrections system to continue to supervise an offender who is no longer incarcerated. As long as parolees follow the conditions of their parole, they are allowed to finish their terms outside the prison. If parolees break the terms of their early release, however, they face the risk of being returned to a penal institution.

Parole is based on three concepts:[38]

> 1. *Grace.* The prisoner has no right to be given an early release, but the government has granted her or him that privilege.
>
> 2. *Contract of consent.* The government and the parolee enter into an arrangement whereby the latter agrees to abide by certain conditions in return for continued freedom.
>
> 3. *Custody.* Technically, though no longer incarcerated, the parolee is still the responsibility of the state. Parole is an extension of corrections.

Because of good-time credits and parole, most prisoners do not serve their entire sentence in prison. In fact, the average felon serves only about half of the term handed down by the court.

10-3a Comparing Probation and Parole

LO10-3 Both probation and parole operate under the basic assumption that the offender serves her or his time in the community rather than in a prison or jail. The main differences between the two concepts—which sound confusingly similar—involve their circumstances.

Parole The conditional release of an inmate before his or her sentence has expired.

Probation is a sentence handed down by a judge following conviction and usually does not include incarceration. Parole is a conditional release from prison and occurs after an offender has already served some time in a correctional facility. (See Figure 10.3 for clarification.)

CONDITIONS OF PAROLE In many ways, parole supervision is similar to probation supervision. Like probationers, offenders who are granted parole are placed under the supervision of community corrections officers and required to follow certain conditions. Parole conditions often mirror probation conditions. All parolees, for example, must comply with the law, and they are generally responsible for reporting to their parole officer at certain intervals.

The frequency of these visits, along with the other terms of parole, is spelled out in the **parole contract,** which sets out the agreement between the state and the paroled offender. Under the terms of the contract, the state agrees to conditionally release the inmate, and the future parolee agrees that her or his conditional release will last only as long as she or he abides by the contract.

Parole Contract An agreement between the state and the offender that establishes the conditions of parole.

PAROLE REVOCATION About a quarter of parolees return to prison before the end of their parole period, most because they were convicted of a new offense or had their parole revoked.[39] Property crimes are the most common reason that both male and female parolees return to incarceration, and men on parole are twice as likely as their female counterparts to have their parole revoked for a violent crime.[40] Parole revocation is similar in many aspects to probation revocation. If the parolee commits a new crime, then a return to prison is very likely. If, however, the individual commits a technical violation by breaking a condition of parole, then parole authorities have discretion as to whether revocation proceedings should be initiated. A number of states, including Michigan, Missouri, and New York, have taken steps to avoid reincarcerating parolees for technical violations as part of their continuing efforts to reduce prison populations.[41]

When authorities do attempt to revoke parole for a technical violation, they must provide the parolee with a revocation hearing.[42] Although this hearing does not provide the same due process protections as a criminal trial, the parolee does have the right to be notified of the charges, to present witnesses, to speak in his or her defense, and to question any hostile witnesses (so long as such questioning would not place these witnesses

FIGURE 10.3 PROBATION VERSUS PAROLE

	Probation	Parole
Basic Definition	An **alternative to imprisonment** in which a person who has been convicted of a crime is allowed to serve his or her sentence in the community subject to certain conditions and supervision by a probation officer.	An **early release** from a correctional facility, in which the convicted offender is given the chance to spend the remainder of her or his sentence under supervision in the community.
Timing	The offender is sentenced to a probationary term in place of a prison or jail term. If the offender breaks the conditions of probation, he or she is sent to prison or jail. Therefore, **probation generally occurs** *before* **imprisonment.**	Parole is a form of early release. Therefore, **parole occurs** *after* **an offender has spent time behind bars.**
Authority	**Probation is under the domain of the judiciary.** A judge decides whether to sentence a convict to probation, and a judge determines whether a probation violation warrants revocation and incarceration.	**Parole often falls under the domain of the parole board.** This administrative body determines whether the prisoner qualifies for early release and the conditions under which the parole must be served.
Characteristics of Offenders	As a number of studies have shown, probationers are normally less involved in the criminal lifestyle. Most of them are **first-time offenders who have committed nonviolent crimes.**	Many parolees have **spent months or even years in prison** and, besides abiding by conditions of parole, must make the difficult transition to "life on the outside."

Probation and parole have many aspects in common. In fact, probation and parole are so similar that many jurisdictions combine them into a single agency. There are, however, some important distinctions between the two systems, as noted above.

in danger). In the first stage of the hearing, the parole authorities determine whether there is probable cause to believe that a violation occurred. Then, they decide whether to return the parolee to prison.

PROBATION AND PAROLE OFFICERS Unlike police officers or sheriffs' deputies, probation and parole officers generally do not wear uniforms. Instead, they have badges that identify their position and agency. The duties of probation officers and parole officers are so similar that many small jurisdictions combine the two posts into a single position.

Given the supervisory nature of their professions, probation and parole officers are ultimately responsible for protecting the community by keeping their clients from committing crimes. There is also an element of social work in their duties, and these officers must constantly balance the needs of the community with the needs of the offender. Parole officers in particular are expected to help the parolee readjust to life outside the correctional institution by helping her or him find a place to live and a job, and seeing that she or he receives any treatment that may be necessary.

10-3b Discretionary Release

As you may recall from Chapter 9, corrections systems are classified by sentencing procedure—indeterminate or determinate. Indeterminate sentencing occurs when the legislature sets a range of punishments for particular crimes, and the judge and the parole board exercise discretion in determining the actual length of the prison term. For that reason, states with indeterminate sentencing are said to have systems of **discretionary release.**

ELIGIBILITY FOR PAROLE Under indeterminate sentencing, parole is not a right but a privilege. This is a crucial point, as it establishes the terms of the relationship between the inmate and the corrections authorities during the parole process. In *Greenholtz v. Inmates of the Nebraska Penal and Correctional Complex* (1979),[43] the United States Supreme Court ruled that inmates do not have a constitutionally protected right to expect parole, thereby giving states the freedom to set their own standards for determining parole eligibility. In most states that have retained indeterminate sentencing, a prisoner is eligible to be considered for parole release after serving a legislatively determined percentage of the minimum sentence—usually one-half or two-thirds—less any good time or other credits.

Not all convicts are eligible for parole. As we saw in Chapter 9, offenders who have committed the most serious crimes often receive life sentences without the possibility of early release. In general, life without parole is reserved for those who have committed first degree murder or are defined by statute as habitual offenders. As was also discussed in Chapter 9, however, more than 3,200 inmates convicted of nonviolent drug and property crimes have also received this sentence.[44] Today, about one-third of convicts serving life sentences have no possibility of parole.[45]

PAROLE PROCEDURES A convict does not apply for parole. Rather, different jurisdictions have different procedures for determining discretionary release dates. In many states, the offender is eligible for discretionary release at the end of his or her minimum sentence minus any good-time credits the offender has earned. In 2014, for example, Glenwood Carr was sentenced to six to twelve years in prison for fleeing the scene of a fatal accident that he caused by driving drunk in Clay, New York. This means that Carr will become eligible for parole after serving six years, less good time. In other states, parole eligibility is measured at either one-third or one-half of the maximum sentence, or it is a matter of discretion for the parole authorities.

In most, but not all, states, the responsibility for making the parole decision falls to the **parole board,** whose members are generally appointed by the governor. According to the American Correctional Association, the parole board has four basic roles:

1. To decide which offenders should be placed on parole.

2. To determine the conditions of parole and aid in the continuing supervision of the parolee.

3. To discharge the offender when the conditions of parole have been met.

4. If a violation occurs, to determine whether parole privileges should be revoked.[46]

Most parole boards are small, made up of three to seven members. In many jurisdictions, board members' terms are limited to between four and six years. The

Discretionary Release The release of an inmate into a community supervision program at the discretion of the parole board within limits set by state or federal law.

Parole Board A body of appointed civilians that decides whether a convict should be granted conditional release before the end of his or her sentence.

requirements for board members vary. Nearly half the states have no prerequisites, while others require a bachelor's degree or some expertise in the field of criminal justice.

LO10-4 **THE PAROLE DECISION** Parole boards use a number of criteria to determine whether a convict should be given discretionary release. These criteria include the nature of the underlying offense, the threat the offender would pose to the community if released, any prior criminal record, and the inmate's behavior behind bars. The attitude of the victim or the victim's family is also taken into consideration. In a system that uses discretionary parole, the actual release decision is made at a **parole grant hearing.** During this hearing, the entire board or a subcommittee reviews relevant information on the convict. Sometimes, but not always, the offender is interviewed.

Because the board members have only limited knowledge of each offender, key players in the case are often notified in advance of the parole hearing and asked to provide comments and recommendations. These participants include the sentencing judge, the attorneys at the trial, the victims, and any law enforcement officers who may be involved. After these preparations, the typical parole hearing itself is very short—usually lasting just a few minutes.

As parole has become a more important tool for reducing prison populations, corrections authorities are making greater efforts to ensure that the process does not endanger the community. Four-fifths of the parole boards in the United States now use risk-assessment software to help with the parole decision.[47] The use of such programs generally increases a state's number of parolees, as parole board members—left to their own devices—may hesitate to grant parole if there is even the slightest hint that an offender will recidivate. Texas, for example, released ten thousand more inmates on parole in 2012 than in 2005 as a result of using risk-assessment software. Similarly, with the aid of this technology, Michigan decreased its prison population by more than 15 percent between 2007 and 2013.[48]

PAROLE DENIAL When parole is denied, the reasons usually involve poor prison behavior by the offender and/or the severity of the underlying crime.[49] After a parole denial, the entire process will generally be replayed at the next "action date," which depends on the nature of the offender's crimes and all relevant laws. In February 2014, for example, Herman Bell was denied parole for the sixth time. More than four decades earlier, Bell had been convicted of murder and sentenced to twenty-five years to life in prison for his involvement in the execution-style killings of two New York City police officers. Although Bell was sixty-six years old at the time of his latest parole grant hearing, the state parole board told him that "if released at this time, there is a reasonable probability that you would not live and remain at liberty without again violating the law."[50]

On rare occasions, a state governor will veto the decision of a parole board to grant supervised release. In 2014, for example, a California parole board granted the release of seventy-one-year-old Bruce Davis, who had spent forty-three years behind bars for a double murder that took place in 1960. The board cited Davis's age, his religious conversion, and his role as a counselor to other inmates as factors in its decision. California governor Jerry Brown blocked Davis's parole, however, calling him an "unreasonable danger to society."[51]

AP Images/Jim Cole

A parole board discusses the fate of a parolee in Concord, New Hampshire. *What role should crime victims have in the parole process, if any? Explain your answer.*

Parole Grant Hearing A hearing in which the entire parole board or a subcommittee reviews information, meets the offender, and hears testimony from relevant witnesses to determine whether to grant parole.

10-3c Parole Guidelines

Nearly twenty states have moved away from discretionary release systems to procedures that provide for **mandatory release.** Under mandatory release, offenders leave prison only when their prison terms have expired, minus adjustments for good time. No parole board is involved in this type of release, which is designed to eliminate discretion from the process.

Instead, in mandatory release, corrections officials rely on **parole guidelines** to determine the early release date. Similar to sentencing guidelines (see Chapter 9), parole guidelines determine a potential parolee's risk of recidivism using a mathematical equation. Under this system, inmates and corrections authorities know the *presumptive parole date* soon after the inmate enters prison. So long as the offender does not experience any disciplinary or other problems while incarcerated, he or she can be fairly sure of the time of release.

Note that a number of states and the federal government claim to have officially "abolished" parole through truth-in-sentencing laws. (As described in Chapter 9, this form of legislation requires certain statutorily determined offenders to serve at least 85 percent of their prison terms.) For the most part, however, these laws simply emphasize prison terms that are "truthful," not necessarily "longer." Mechanisms for parole, by whatever name, are crucial to the criminal justice system for several reasons. First, they provide inmates with an incentive to behave properly in the hope of an early release. Second, they reduce the costs related to incarceration by keeping down the inmate population, a critical concern for prison administrators.[52]

10-4 WHAT ARE SOME TYPES OF INTERMEDIATE SANCTIONS?

Many observers feel that the most widely used sentencing options—imprisonment and probation—fail to reflect the immense diversity of crimes and criminals. **Intermediate sanctions** provide a number of additional sentencing options for those wrongdoers who require stricter supervision than that supplied by probation, but for whom imprisonment would be unduly harsh and counterproductive. The intermediate sanctions discussed in this section are designed to match the specific punishment and treatment of an individual offender with a corrections program that reflects that offender's situation.

Dozens of different variations of intermediate sanctions are handed down each year. To cover the spectrum succinctly, this section will discuss two general categories of sanctions: those administered primarily by the courts and those administered primarily by corrections departments. The latter include day reporting centers, intensive supervision probation, shock incarceration, and home confinement. Remember that these sanctions are not exclusive. They are often combined with imprisonment, with probation or parole, and with each other.

10-4a Judicially Administered Sanctions

The lack of sentencing options is most frustrating for the person who, in the majority of cases, does the sentencing— the judge. Consequently, when judges are given the discretion to "color" a punishment with intermediate sanctions, they will often do so. In addition to imprisonment and probation, a judge has five sentencing options:

1. **Fines.**
2. **Community service.**
3. **Restitution.**
4. **Pretrial diversion programs.**
5. **Forfeiture.**

Fines, community service, and restitution were discussed in Chapter 9. In the context of intermediate sanctions, it is important to remember that these punishments are generally combined with incarceration or probation. For that reason, some critics feel the retributive or deterrent impact of such punishments is severely limited. Many European countries, in contrast, rely heavily on fines as the sole sanctions for a variety of crimes.

PRETRIAL DIVERSION PROGRAMS Not every criminal violation requires the courtroom process. Consequently, some judges have the discretion to order an

---

Mandatory Release Release from prison that occurs when an offender has served the full length of his or her sentence, minus any adjustments for good time.

Parole Guidelines Standards that are used in the parole process to measure the risk that a potential parolee will recidivate.

Intermediate Sanctions Sanctions that are more restrictive than probation and less restrictive than imprisonment.

Job Description:

▶ Assess the background and needs of patients suffering from substance abuse and addiction, and craft and execute a plan for recovery.

▶ Lead group and one-on-one counseling sessions geared toward providing the patient with a sense of accountability and a desire to change the direction of her or his life.

Monkey Business/Fotolia

What Kind of Training Is Required?

▶ A bachelor's degree from a counselor program, often found in the department of education or psychology in undergraduate institutions, as well as two years of counseling in a related field or equivalent life experience.

▶ For licensing and employment with a government agency, a master's degree in substance abuse counseling or rehabilitation counseling is often required.

Annual Salary Range?

▶ $30,000–$60,000

SOCIAL MEDIA CAREER TIP
Manage your online reputation—or someone else will do it for you. Monitor your profile using tools such as iSearch, Pipl, and ZabaSearch. Check BoardTracker, BoardReader, and Omgili for information on what people are saying about you on message boards.

offender into a **pretrial diversion program** during the preliminary hearing. (Prosecutors can also offer an offender the opportunity to join such a program in return for reducing or dropping the initial charges.) These programs represent an "interruption" of the criminal proceedings and are generally reserved for young or first-time offenders who have been arrested on charges of illegal drug use, child or spousal abuse, or sexual misconduct. Pretrial diversion programs usually include extensive counseling, often in a treatment center. If the offender successfully follows the conditions of the program, the criminal charges are dropped.

PROBLEM-SOLVING COURTS Many judges have found opportunities to divert low-level offenders by presiding over problem-solving courts. In these comparatively informal courtrooms, judges attempt to address problems such as drug addiction, mental illness, and homelessness that often lead to the eventual rearrest of the offender. About three thousand problem-solving courts are operating in the United States. Although these specialized courts cover a wide variety of subjects, from domestic violence to juvenile crime to mental illness, the most common problem-solving courts are drug courts.

Although the specific procedures of drug courts vary widely, most follow a general pattern. Either after arrest or on conviction, the offender is given the option of entering a drug court program or continuing through the standard courtroom process. Those who choose the former come under the supervision of a judge who will oversee a mixture of treatment and sanctions designed to cure their addiction. When offenders successfully complete the program, the drug court rewards them by dropping all charges. Drug courts operate on the assumption that when a criminal addict's drug use is reduced, his or her drug-fueled criminal activity will also decline.

Pretrial Diversion Program An alternative to trial offered by a judge or prosecutor, in which the offender agrees to participate in a specified counseling or treatment program in return for withdrawal of the charges.

The success of drug courts has led state legislatures to target other areas of criminality for similar treatment. In 2013, new state laws were passed allowing prostitutes access to mental health courts (Illinois), authorizing problem-solving courts as a condition of a misdemeanor sentence (Indiana), and permitting any jurisdiction in the state to create a problem-solving court (Washington).[53]

> **CAREER TIP** If you want to influence how intermediate-sanction legislation and other criminal laws are written in your state, you should consider running for office as a *state legislator* at some point in your career.

FORFEITURE In 1970, Congress passed the Racketeer Influenced and Corrupt Organizations Act (RICO) in an attempt to prevent the use of legitimate business enterprises as shields for organized crime.[54] As amended, RICO and other statutes give judges the ability to implement *forfeiture* proceedings in certain criminal cases. **Forfeiture** is a process by which the government seizes property gained from or used in criminal activity. For example, if a person is convicted for smuggling cocaine into the United States from South America, a judge can order the seizure of not only the narcotics, but also the speedboat the offender used to deliver the drugs to a pickup point off the coast of South Florida. In *Bennis v. Michigan* (1996),[55] the Supreme Court ruled that a person's home or car could be forfeited even though the owner was unaware that the property was connected to illegal activity.

Once property is forfeited, the government has several options. It can sell the property, with the proceeds going to the state and/or federal law enforcement agencies involved in the seizure. Alternatively, the government agency can use the property directly in further crime-fighting efforts or award it to a third party, such as an informant. In Harris County, Texas, for example, law enforcement officials purchased about eight hundred body-worn cameras for local police officers (discussed in Chapter 5) using funds from civil forfeitures.

Forfeiture is financially rewarding for both federal and local law enforcement agencies. The U.S. Marshals Service manages about

$2.2 billion worth of contraband and property impounded from criminals and criminal suspects. In 2014, the agency shared about $487 million of these funds with state and local law enforcement agencies, with an additional $1.9 billion going to crime victims.[56]

10-4b Day Reporting Centers

First used in Great Britain, **day reporting centers (DRCs)** are mainly tools to reduce jail and prison overcrowding. Although the offenders are allowed to live in the community rather than jail or prison, they must spend all or part of each day at a reporting center. In general, being sentenced to a DRC is an extreme form of supervision. With offenders under a single roof, they are much more easily monitored and controlled. (According to critics of DRCs, they are also more easily able to "network" with other individuals who have criminal histories and drug and alcohol abuse issues.)[57]

DRCs are instruments of rehabilitation as well. They often feature treatment programs for drug and alcohol abusers and provide counseling for a number of

Forfeiture The process by which the government seizes private property attached to criminal activity.

Day Reporting Center (DRC) A community-based corrections center to which offenders report on a daily basis for treatment, education, and rehabilitation.

In Pinellas County, Florida, Judge Dee Anna Farnell congratulates graduates of her drug court program. *How does society benefit when an offender successfully completes a drug court program rather than being sent to prison or jail?*

Scott Keeler/*Tampa Bay Times*/ZUMAPRESS.com/Newscom

psychological problems, such as depression and anger management. Many of those found guilty in the Roanoke (Virginia) Drug Court, for example, are ordered to participate in a yearlong day reporting program. At the center, offenders meet with probation officers, submit to urine tests, and attend counseling and education programs, such as parenting and life-skills classes. After the year has passed, if the offender has completed the program to the satisfaction of the judge and has found employment, the charges will be dropped.

10-4c Intensive Supervision Probation

Over the past several decades, a number of jurisdictions have turned to **intensive supervision probation (ISP)** to solve the problems associated with burdensome caseloads we discussed earlier in the chapter. ISP offers a more restrictive alternative to regular probation, with higher levels of face-to-face contact between offenders and officers and frequent modes of control such as urine tests for drugs. In New Jersey, for example, ISP officers have caseloads of only 20 offenders (compared with 115 for other probation officers in the state) and are provided with additional resources to help them keep tabs on their charges.[58] Different jurisdictions have different methods of determining who is eligible for ISP, but a majority of states limit ISP to offenders who do not have prior probation violations.

The main goal of ISP is to provide prisonlike control of offenders while keeping them out of prison. Critics of ISP believe that it "causes" high failure rates, as more supervision increases the chances that an offender will be caught breaking conditions of probation.[59] One comparison of ISP with DRCs, however, found the intensive supervision of ISP to be more effective. In the six months following termination of the program, DRC participants were more likely to be convicted for a new offense and to test positive for drugs than their ISP counterparts. The study suggests that when combined with services such as outpatient drug treatment and educational training, ISP can be effective in producing low rates of recidivism.[60]

10-4d Shock Incarceration

As the name suggests, **shock incarceration** is designed to "shock" criminals into compliance with the law. Following conviction, the offender is first sentenced to a prison or jail term. Then, usually within ninety days, he or she is released and resentenced to probation. The theory behind shock incarceration is that by getting a taste of the brutalities of the daily prison grind, the offender will be shocked into a crime-free existence.

THE VALUE OF SHOCK In the past, shock incarceration was targeted primarily toward youthful, first-time offenders, who were thought to be more likely to be "scared straight" by a short stint behind bars. Recent data show, however, that 20 percent of all adults sentenced to probation spend some time in jail or prison before being released into the community.[61] Critics of shock incarceration are dismayed by this trend. They argue that the practice needlessly disrupts the lives of low-level offenders who would not otherwise be eligible for incarceration and exposes them to the mental and physical hardships of prison life (which we will discuss in Chapter 12).[62] Furthermore, there is little evidence that shock probationers fare any better than regular probationers when it comes to recidivism rates.[63]

BOOT CAMPS Impact incarceration programs, or *boot camps,* are a variation on traditional shock incarceration. Instead of spending the "shock" period of incarceration in prison or jail, offenders are sent to a boot camp. Modeled on military basic training, these camps are generally located within prisons and jails, though some can be found in the community. The programs emphasize strict discipline, manual labor, and physical training. They are designed to instill self-responsibility and self-respect in participants, thereby lessening the chances that they will return to a life of crime. More recently, boot camps have also emphasized rehabilitation, incorporating such components as drug and alcohol treatment programs, anger-management courses, and vocational training.

Intensive Supervision Probation (ISP) A punishment-oriented form of probation in which the offender is placed under stricter and more frequent surveillance and control than in conventional probation.

Shock Incarceration A short period of incarceration that is designed to deter further criminal activity by "shocking" the offender with the hardships of imprisonment.

CAREER TIP Although boot camps have fallen out of public favor somewhat, wilderness therapy programs for teenagers with behavioral problems such as drug or alcohol abuse or antisocial tendencies are flourishing. These programs rely *on field guides, outdoor instructors,* and *youth counselors* to succeed.

10-4e Home Confinement and Electronic Monitoring

Various forms of **home confinement**—in which offenders serve their sentences not in a government institution but at home—have existed for centuries. It has often served, and continues to serve, as a method of political control, used by totalitarian regimes to isolate and silence dissidents. For purposes of general law enforcement, home confinement was impractical until relatively recently. After all, one could not expect offenders to keep their promises to stay at home, and the personnel costs of guarding them were prohibitive.

In the 1980s, however, with the advent of **electronic monitoring,** or using technology to guard the prisoner, home confinement became more viable. Today, all fifty states and the federal government have home monitoring programs, with about 200,000 offenders, including probationers and parolees, participating at any one time.[64]

THE LEVELS OF HOME MONITORING

LO10-5 Home monitoring has three general levels of restriction:

1. *Curfew,* which requires offenders to be in their homes at specific hours each day, usually at night.

2. *Home detention,* which requires that offenders remain home at all times, with exceptions being made for education, employment, counseling, and other specified activities, such as the purchase of food or, in some instances, attendance at religious services.

3. *Home incarceration,* which requires the offender to remain home at all times, save for medical emergencies.

Under ideal circumstances, home confinement serves many of the goals of intermediate sanctions. It protects the community. It saves public funds and space in correctional facilities by keeping convicts out of institutional incarceration. It meets public expectations of punishment for criminals. Uniquely, home confinement also recognizes that convicts, despite their crimes, play important roles in the community, and allows them to

StockSolutions/Getty Images

How does an electronic monitoring device such as the one shown here meet many of the goals of intermediate sanctions?

continue in those roles. An offender, for example, may be given permission to leave confinement to care for elderly parents.

Home confinement is also lauded for giving sentencing officials the freedom to match the punishment with the needs of the offender. In 2014, for example, a sixty-four-year-old Maine businessman was sentenced to six months of home confinement for tax fraud. He was, however, allowed to return to his office during the day to earn the money needed to pay nearly $140,000 in court-ordered fines. The offender was also allowed to leave home for doctor's appointments and to buy groceries.

TYPES OF ELECTRONIC MONITORING According to some reports, the inspiration for electronic monitoring was a *Spider-Man* comic book in which the hero was trailed by the use of an electronic device on his arm. In 1979, a New Mexico judge named Jack Love, having read the comic, convinced an executive at Honeywell, Inc., to begin developing similar technology to supervise convicts.[65]

Home Confinement A community-based sanction in which offenders serve their terms of incarceration in their homes.

Electronic Monitoring A technique of supervision in which the offender's whereabouts are kept under surveillance by an electronic device.

Two major types of electronic monitoring have grown out of Love's initial concept. The first is "programmed contact," in which the offender is contacted periodically by voice or text to verify his or her whereabouts. Verification is obtained via a computer that uses voice or visual identification techniques or by requiring the offender to enter a code in an electronic box when called. The second is a "continuously signaling" device, worn around the convict's wrist, ankle, or neck. A transmitter in the device sends out a continuous signal to a "receiver-dialer" device located in the offender's dwelling. If the receiver device does not detect a signal from the transmitter, it informs a central computer, and the police are notified.

TECHNOLOGICAL ADVANCES IN ELECTRONIC MONITORING As electronic monitoring technology has evolved, the ability of community corrections officials to target specific forms of risky behavior has greatly increased. Michigan courts, for example, routinely place black boxes in the automobiles of repeat traffic law violators. Not only do these boxes record information about the offenders' driving habits for review by probation officers, but they also emit a loud beep when the car

GLOBAL POSITIONING SYSTEM (GPS)

CJ and Technology

Global positioning system (GPS) technology is a form of tracking technology that relies on twenty-four military satellites orbiting thousands of miles above the earth. The satellites transmit signals to each other and to a receiver on the ground, allowing a monitoring station to determine the location of a receiving device to within a few feet. GPS provides a much more precise level of supervision than regular electronic monitoring. The offender wears a transmitter, similar to a traditional electronic monitor, around his or her ankle or wrist. This transmitter communicates with a portable tracking device, a small box that uses military satellites to determine the offender's movements.

GPS technology can be used either "actively" to constantly monitor the subject's whereabouts, or "passively" to ensure that the offender remains within the confines of a limited area determined by a judge or probation officer. Inclusion and exclusion zones are also important to GPS supervision. Inclusion zones are areas such as a home or workplace where the offender is expected to be at certain times. Exclusion zones are areas such as parks, playgrounds, and schools where the offender is not permitted to go. GPS-linked computers can alert officials immediately

Sergey Nivens/ShutterStock.com

when an exclusion zone has been breached and create a computerized record of the offender's movements for review at a later time. Despite the benefits of this technology, it is rarely implemented. According to the Bureau of Justice Statistics, only about eight thousand offenders are currently being tracked by GPS.

Thinking about GPS
How might GPS monitoring be used to improve and overhaul the American bail system, covered in Chapter 8?

Explain the possible connection between higher levels of surveillance by probation and parole officers and greater numbers of probationers and parolees being incarcerated.

With access to intermediate sanctions, the judge may add a period of home confinement to the sentence. Critics contend that such practices **widen the net** of the corrections system by augmenting the number of citizens who are under the control and surveillance of the state and also *strengthen the net* by increasing the government's power to intervene in the lives of its citizens.[67] Technological advances—such as the black boxes in automobiles, sweat-testing ankle bracelets, and GPS devices mentioned in this chapter—will only accelerate the trend.

> **Widen the Net** The criticism that intermediate sanctions designed to divert offenders from prison actually increase the number of citizens who are under the control and surveillance of the American corrections system.

goes too fast or stops too quickly. Another device—an ankle bracelet—is able to test a person's sweat for alcohol levels and transmit the results over the Internet.

10-4f Widening the Net

As we have seen, most of the convicts chosen for intermediate sanctions are low-risk offenders. From the point of view of the corrections official doing the choosing, this makes sense. Such offenders are less likely to commit crimes and attract negative publicity. This selection strategy, however, appears to invalidate one of the primary reasons intermediate sanctions exist: to reduce prison and jail populations. If most of the offenders in intermediate sanctions programs would otherwise have received probation, then the effect on these populations is nullified. Indeed, studies have shown this to be the case.[66]

At the same time, intermediate sanctions broaden the reach of the corrections system. In other words, they increase rather than decrease the amount of control the state exerts over the individual. Suppose a person is arrested for a misdemeanor such as shoplifting and, under normal circumstances, would receive probation.

STUDY TOOLS 10

READY TO STUDY? IN THE BOOK, YOU CAN:

- [ ] Rip out the Chapter Review Card, which includes key terms and chapter summaries.

ONLINE AT WWW.CENGAGEBRAIN.COM, YOU CAN:

- [ ] Learn about forfeiture in a short video.
- [ ] Dig deeper into the world of the probation officer on Twitter: Probation officers@Probationnews.
- [ ] Interact with figures from the text, and watch quick animation clips.
- [ ] Prepare for tests with quizzes.
- [ ] Review the key terms with Flash Cards.

Quiz

1. Supporters of community corrections point to the role these programs play in _____ nonviolent offenders from prison and jail.

2. Offenders sentenced to _____ serve their sentence in the community under the supervision of the corrections system.

3. To a large extent, the effectiveness of community corrections programs is measured by _____, or the rate at which participants are rearrested and/or reincarcerated.

4. _____ refers to the conditional release of an inmate before the end of his or her sentence.

5. A _____ violation of the terms of probation or parole makes the offender eligible to be sent, or returned, to prison.

6. In jurisdictions that have systems of discretionary release, a _____ _____ makes the parole decision.

7. In jurisdictions with _____ release, offenders leave prison only when their prison terms have expired, minus adjustments for good time.

8. Judicially administered sanctions include fines, restitution, and _____, a process in which the government seizes property connected to illegal activity.

9. Boot camps, or militaristic programs designed to instill self-responsibility, are a form of _____ incarceration.

10. Home confinement has become more effective in recent years thanks to technology known as _____ _____.

Answers can be found in the Answers section in the back of the book.

ONE APPROACH.
70 UNIQUE SOLUTIONS.

www.cengage.com/4ltrpress

11 Prisons and Jails

Pla2na/ShutterStock.com

LEARNING OBJECTIVES

After studying this chapter, you will be able to . . .

11-1 Contrast the Pennsylvania and New York penitentiary theories of the 1800s.

11-2 List and briefly explain the four types of prisons.

11-3 List the factors that have caused the prison population to grow dramatically in the last several decades.

11-4 Describe the arguments for and against private prisons.

11-5 Summarize the distinction between jails and prisons, and indicate the importance of jails in the American corrections system.

After you finish this chapter, go to **PAGES 247–248** for **STUDY TOOLS**

A Trend Indeed?

The ballot initiative offered a dramatic solution to the problem of California's overcrowded prisons and jails. Called Proposition 47, it proposed to downgrade a number of nonviolent felonies involving less than $950—including grand theft, shoplifting, writing bad checks, receiving stolen property, and drug possession—to misdemeanors. As a result of this change, offenders convicted of these crimes would probably not wind up behind bars. In November 2014, nearly 60 percent of California voters approved Proposition 47. Three months after the new law went into effect, the jail populations of Los Angeles, Orange, and San Diego counties dropped by 20 percent, 22 percent, and 16 percent, respectively.

California is hardly the only state that recently has taken steps to reduce both its inmate population and the costs associated with its corrections system. In 2013, six states closed correctional facilities, with North Carolina alone estimating $40 million in savings. In 2014, thirty states passed legislation designed to lower incarceration rates, often by steering nonviolent offenders to community supervision. These policy choices reflect a small but significant trend in American corrections: fewer inmates. Before a slight (0.3 percent) rise in 2013, the total U.S. prison population declined each year from 2010 to 2012, the first time that had happened in nearly four decades.

To be sure, these decreases do little to threaten our nation's title as "the globe's leading incarcerator." About 2.2 million Americans are in prison and jail. The United States locks up six times as many of its citizens as Canada does, and eight times as many as a number of European democracies.

About 2.2 million inmates are incarcerated in the United States. *Economic considerations aside, what is your opinion of America's dramatically high incarceration rates?*

Still, the fact that politicians are willing to accept policies that reduce the number of inmates represents a sea change in the country's corrections strategies. "People want their government to make a distinction in the public safety area between those who have to be locked up and those who can serve their sentence in less expensive, more humane, and more effective ways," says former California state representative Darrel Steinberg, who pushed for Proposition 47's approval. "That's what the people want."

Sam Hodgson/Bloomberg/Getty Images

11-1 HOW HAVE AMERICAN PRISONS EVOLVED?

Today's high rates of imprisonment—often referred to as evidence of "mass incarceration" in the United States—are the result of many criminal justice strategies that we have discussed in this textbook. These include truth-in-sentencing guidelines, relatively long sentences for gun and drug crimes, "three-strikes" habitual offender laws, and judicial freedom to incarcerate convicts for relatively minor criminal behavior.

At the base of all these policies is a philosophy that sees prisons primarily as instruments of punishment. The loss of freedom imposed on inmates is the penalty for the crimes they have committed. Punishment has not, however, always been the main reason for incarceration in this country.

CAREER TIP Just as criminologists study crime, *penologists* study the corrections system, often with a focus on prison management and inmate rehabilitation.

11-1a English Roots

The prisons of eighteenth-century England, known as "bridewells" after London's Bridewell Palace, had little to do with punishment. These facilities were mainly used to hold debtors or those awaiting trial, execution, or banishment from the community. (In many ways, as will be made clear, these facilities resembled the modern jail.) English courts generally imposed one of two sanctions on convicted felons: they turned them loose, or they executed them.[1] Most felons were released, pardoned either by the court or the clergy after receiving a whipping or a branding.

The correctional system in the American colonies differed very little from that of their motherland. If anything, colonial administrators were more likely to use corporal punishment than their English counterparts, and the death penalty was not uncommon in early America. The one dissenter was William Penn, who adopted the "Great Law" in Pennsylvania in 1682. Based on Quaker ideals of humanity and rehabilitation, this criminal code forbade the use of torture and mutilation as forms of punishment. Instead, felons were ordered to pay restitution of property or goods to their victims. If the offenders did not have sufficient property to make restitution, they were placed in a prison, which was primarily a "workhouse."[2] The death penalty was still allowed under the "Great Law," but only in cases of premeditated murder. Penn proved to be an exception, however, and the path to reform was much slower in the colonies than in England.

11-1b Walnut Street Prison: The First Penitentiary

On William Penn's death in 1718, the "Great Law" was rescinded in favor of a harsher criminal code, similar to those of the other colonies. At the time of the American Revolution, however, the Quakers were instrumental in the first broad swing of the incarceration pendulum from punishment to rehabilitation. In 1776, Pennsylvania passed legislation ordering that offenders be reformed through treatment and discipline rather than simply beaten or executed.[3] Several states, including Massachusetts and New York, quickly followed Pennsylvania's example.

Pennsylvania continued its reformist ways by opening the country's first **penitentiary** in a wing of Philadelphia's Walnut Street Jail in 1790. The penitentiary

Penitentiary An early form of correctional facility that emphasized separating inmates from society and from each other.

Separate Confinement A nineteenth-century penitentiary system developed in Pennsylvania in which inmates were kept separate from each other at all times, with daily activities taking place in individual cells.

operated on the assumption that silence and labor provided the best hope of rehabilitating the criminal spirit. Remaining silent would force the prisoners to think about their crimes, and eventually the weight of conscience would lead to repentance. At the same time, enforced labor would attack the problem of idleness—regarded as the main cause of crime by penologists of the time.[4] Consequently, inmates at Walnut Street were isolated from one another in solitary rooms and kept busy with constant menial chores.

Eventually, the penitentiary at Walnut Street succumbed to the same problems that continue to plague institutions of confinement: overcrowding and excessive costs. As an influx of inmates forced more than one person to be housed in a room, maintaining silence became nearly impossible. By the early 1800s, officials could not find work for all of the convicts, so many were left idle.

11-1c The Great Penitentiary Rivalry: Pennsylvania versus New York

LO11-1 The apparent lack of success at Walnut Street did little to dampen enthusiasm for the penitentiary concept. Throughout the first half of the nineteenth century, a number of states reacted to prison overcrowding by constructing new penitentiaries. Each state tended to have its own peculiar twist on the roles of silence and labor, and two such systems—those of Pennsylvania and New York—emerged to shape the debate over the most effective way to run a prison.

THE PENNSYLVANIA SYSTEM After the failure of Walnut Street, Pennsylvania constructed two new prisons: the Western Penitentiary near Pittsburgh (opened in 1826) and the Eastern Penitentiary in Cherry Hill, near Philadelphia (1829). The Pennsylvania system took the concept of silence as a virtue to new extremes. Based on the idea of **separate confinement,** these penitentiaries were constructed with back-to-back cells facing outward from the center. (See Figure 11.1 for the layout of the original Eastern Penitentiary.) To protect each inmate from the corrupting influence of the others, prisoners worked, slept, and ate alone in their cells. Their only contact with other human beings came in the form of religious instruction from a visiting clergyman or prison official.[5]

THE NEW YORK SYSTEM If Pennsylvania's prisons were designed to transform wrongdoers into honest citizens, those in New York focused on obedience. When New York's Newgate Prison (built in 1791) became overcrowded, the state authorized the construction of Auburn Prison, which opened in 1816. Auburn initially operated under many of the same assumptions that guided the penitentiary at Walnut Street. Solitary confinement, however, seemed to lead to an inordinate amount of sickness, insanity, and even suicide among inmates, and it was abandoned in 1822. Nine years later, Elam Lynds became warden at Auburn and instilled the **congregate system,** also known as the Auburn system. Like Pennsylvania's separate confinement system, the congregate system was based on silence and labor. At Auburn, however, inmates worked and ate together, with silence enforced by prison guards.[6]

If either state can be said to have "won" the debate, it was New York. The Auburn system proved more popular, and a majority of the new prisons built during the first half of the nineteenth century followed New York's lead, though mainly for economic reasons rather than philosophical ones. New York's penitentiaries were cheaper to build because they did not require so much space. Furthermore, inmates in New York were employed in workshops, whereas those in Pennsylvania toiled alone in their cells. Consequently, the Auburn system was better positioned to exploit prison labor in the early years of widespread factory production.

11-1d The Reformers and the Progressives

The Auburn system did not go unchallenged. In the 1870s, a group of reformers argued that fixed sentences, imposed silence, and isolation did nothing to improve prisoners. These critics proposed that penal institutions should offer the promise of early release as a prime tool for rehabilitation. Echoing the views of the Quakers a century earlier, the reformers presented an ideology that would heavily influence American corrections for the next century.

This "new penology" was put into practice at New York's Elmira Reformatory in 1876. At Elmira, good behavior was rewarded by early release, and misbehavior was punished with extended time under a three-grade system of classification. On entering the institution, the offender was assigned a grade of 2. If the inmate followed the rules and completed work and school assignments, after six months he was moved up to grade 1, the necessary grade for release. If, however, the inmate broke institutional rules, he was lowered to grade 3. A grade 3 inmate needed to behave properly for three months before he could return to grade 2 and begin to work back toward grade 1 and eventual release.[7]

Although other penal institutions did not adopt the Elmira model, its theories came into prominence in the first two decades of the twentieth century thanks to the Progressive movement in criminal justice. The

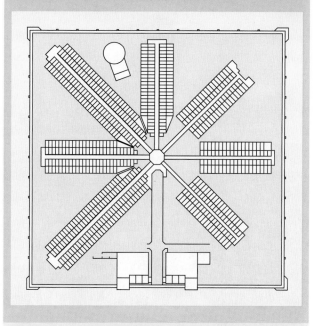

FIGURE 11.1 THE EASTERN PENITENTIARY

As you can see, the Eastern Penitentiary was designed in the form of a "wagon wheel," known today as the radial style. The back-to-back cells in each "spoke" of the wheel faced outward from the center to limit contact between inmates.

Progressives believed that criminal behavior was caused by social, economic, and biological factors and, therefore, a corrections system should have a goal of treatment, not punishment. Consequently, they trumpeted a **medical model** for prisons, which held that institutions should offer a variety of programs and therapies to cure inmates of their "ills," whatever the root causes. The Progressives were largely responsible for the spread of indeterminate sentences (Chapter 9), probation (Chapter 10), intermediate sanctions (Chapter 10), and parole (Chapter 10) in the first half of the twentieth century.

11-1e The Reassertion of Punishment

Even though the Progressives had a great influence on the corrections system as a whole, their theories had little impact on the prisons themselves. Many of these

Congregate System A nineteenth-century penitentiary system developed in New York in which inmates were kept in separate cells during the night but worked together in the daytime under a code of enforced silence.

Medical Model A model of corrections in which the psychological and biological roots of an inmate's criminal behavior are identified and treated.

11-1f The Role of Prisons in Modern Society

Inmates of the Elmira Reformatory in New York attend a presentation at the prison auditorium. *To what extent do you believe that treatment should be a part of the incarceration of criminals?*

For reasons that we will explain later in the chapter, the number of federal and state prisoners quadrupled between 1980 and 2010.[11] This increase reflects the varied demands placed on the modern American penal institution. As University of Connecticut sociologist Charles Logan once noted, Americans expect prisons to "correct the incorrigible, rehabilitate the wretched, . . . restrain the dangerous, and punish the wicked."[12] Basically, prisons exist to make society a safer place. Whether this is to be achieved through retribution, deterrence, incapacitation, or rehabilitation—the four justifications of corrections introduced in Chapter 9—depends on the operating philosophy of the individual penal institution.

Three general models of prisons have emerged to describe the different schools of thought behind prison organization:

▶ The *custodial model* is based on the assumption that prisoners are incarcerated for reasons of incapacitation, deterrence, and retribution. All decisions within the prison—such as what form of recreation to provide the inmates—are made with an eye toward security and discipline, and the daily routine of the inmates is highly controlled. The custodial model has dominated the most restrictive prisons in the United States since the 1930s.

▶ The *rehabilitation model* stresses the ideals of individualized treatment that we discussed in Chapter 9. Security concerns are often secondary to the well-being of the individual inmate, and a number of treatment programs are offered to aid prisoners in changing their criminal and antisocial behavior. The rehabilitation model came into prominence during the 1950s and enjoyed widespread popularity until it began to lose general acceptance in the 1970s and 1980s.

facilities had been constructed in the nineteenth century and were impervious to change. More important, prison administrators usually did not agree with the Progressives and their followers, so the day-to-day lives of most inmates varied little from the congregate system of Auburn Prison.

Academic attitudes began to shift away from the Progressives in the mid-1960s. Then, in 1974, the publication of Robert Martinson's famous "What Works?" essay provided opponents of the medical model with statistical evidence that rehabilitation efforts did nothing to lower recidivism rates.[8] This is not to say that Martinson's findings went unchallenged. A number of critics argued that rehabilitative programs could be successful.[9] In fact, Martinson himself retracted most of his claims in a little-noticed article published five years after his initial report.[10] Attempts by Martinson and others to "set the record straight" went largely unnoticed, however, as crime rose sharply in the early 1970s. This trend led many criminologists and politicians to champion "get tough" measures to deal with criminals they now considered "incurable." By the end of the 1980s, the legislative, judicial, and administrative strategies that we have discussed throughout this text had positioned the United States for an explosion in inmate populations and prison construction unparalleled in the nation's history.

▶ In the *reintegration model*, the correctional institution serves as a training ground for the inmate to prepare for existence in the community. Prisons that have adopted this model give the prisoners more responsibility during incarceration and offer halfway houses and work programs (both discussed in Chapter 12) to help them reintegrate into society. This model is becoming more influential, as corrections officials react to problems such as prison overcrowding.[13]

More critical views of the prison's role in society are at odds with these three "ideal" perspectives. Professor Alfred Blumstein argues that prisons create new criminals, especially with regard to nonviolent drug offenders. Not only do these nonviolent felons become socialized to the criminal lifestyle while in prison, but the stigma of incarceration makes it more difficult for them to obtain employment on release. Their only means of sustenance "on the outside" is to apply the criminal methods they learned in prison.[14] A study by criminal justice professors Cassia Spohn of Arizona State University and David Holleran of the College of New Jersey found that convicted drug offenders who were sentenced to prison were 2.2 times more likely to be incarcerated for a new offense than those sentenced to probation.[15]

11-2 HOW ARE PRISONS ORGANIZED AND MANAGED?

The United States has a dual prison system that parallels its dual court system, which we discussed in Chapter 7. The Federal Bureau of Prisons (BOP) currently operates about one hundred confinement facilities, ranging from prisons to immigration detention centers to community corrections institutions.[16] In the federal corrections system, a national director, appointed by the president, oversees six regional directors and a staff of nearly forty thousand employees. All fifty states also operate state prisons, which number about seventeen hundred and make up more than 90 percent of the country's correctional facilities.[17] Governors are responsible for the organization and operation of state corrections systems, which vary widely based on each state's geography, *demographics* (population characteristics), and political culture.

Generally, those offenders sentenced in federal court for breaking federal law serve their time in federal prisons, and those offenders sentenced in state court for breaking state law serve their time in state prisons. As you can see in Figure 11.2, federal prisons hold relatively few violent felons, because relatively few federal laws involve violent crime. At the same time, federal prisons are much more likely to hold public order offenders, a group that includes violators of federal immigration law.

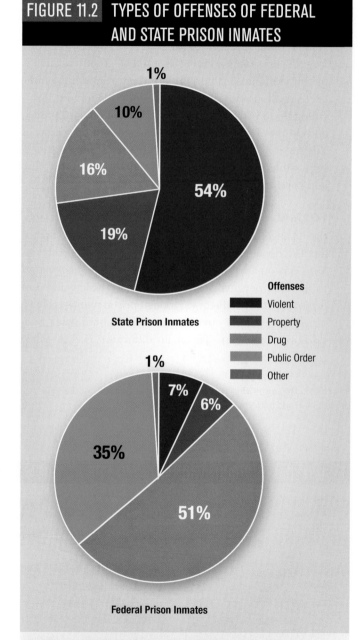

FIGURE 11.2 TYPES OF OFFENSES OF FEDERAL AND STATE PRISON INMATES

State Prison Inmates
1%
10%
16%
19%
54%

Offenses
- Violent
- Property
- Drug
- Public Order
- Other

Federal Prison Inmates
1%
7%
6%
35%
51%

As the comparison above shows, state prisoners are most likely to have been convicted of violent crimes, while federal prisoners are most likely to have been convicted of drug and public order offenses.

Source: Bureau of Justice Statistics, *Prisoners in 2013* (Washington, D.C.: U.S. Department of Justice, September 2014), Table 13, page 5; and Table 16, page 17.

11-2a Prison Administration

Whether the federal government or a state government operates a prison, its administrators have the same general goals, summarized by Charles Logan as follows:

> The mission of a prison is to keep prisoners—to keep them in, keep them safe, keep them in line, keep them healthy, and keep them busy—and to do it with fairness, without undue suffering and as efficiently as possible.[18]

Considering the environment of a prison—an enclosed world inhabited by people who are generally violent and angry and would rather be anywhere else—Logan's mission statement is somewhat unrealistic. A prison staff must supervise the daily routines of hundreds or thousands of inmates, a duty that includes providing them with meals, education, vocational programs, and different forms of leisure. The smooth operation of this supervision is made more difficult—if not, at times, impossible—by budgetary restrictions, overcrowding, and continual inmate turnover.

FORMAL PRISON MANAGEMENT In some respects, the management structure of a prison is similar to that of a police department, as discussed in Chapter 5. Both systems rely on a hierarchical (top-down) *chain of command* to increase personal responsibility. Both assign different employees to specific tasks, though prison managers have much more direct control over their subordinates than do police managers. The main difference is that police

Warden The prison official who is ultimately responsible for the organization and performance of a correctional facility.

departments have a *continuity of purpose* that is sometimes lacking in prison organizations. All members of a police force are, at least theoretically, working to reduce crime and apprehend criminals. In a prison, this continuity is less evident. An employee in the prison laundry service and one who works in the visiting center have little in common. In some instances, employees may even have cross-purposes: a prison guard may want to punish an inmate, while a counselor in the treatment center may want to rehabilitate her or him.

Consequently, a strong hierarchy is crucial for any prison management team that hopes to meet Charles Logan's expectations. As Figure 11.3 shows, the **warden** (also known as a superintendent) is ultimately responsible for the operation of a prison. He or she oversees deputy wardens, who in turn manage the various organizational lines of the institution. The custodial employees, who deal directly with the inmates and make up more than half of a prison's staff, operate under a militaristic hierarchy, with a line of command passing from the deputy warden to the captain to the correctional officer.

GOVERNING PRISONS The implications of prison mismanagement can be severe. While studying a series of prison riots, sociologists Bert Useem and Peter Kimball found that breakdown in managerial control commonly preceded such acts of mass violence.[19] During the 1970s, for example, conditions at the State Penitentiary in New Mexico deteriorated significantly. Inmates were increasingly the targets of random and harsh treatment at the hands of the prison staff, while at the same time a reduction in structured activities left prison life "painfully boring."[20] The result, in 1980, was one of the most violent prison riots in the nation's history.

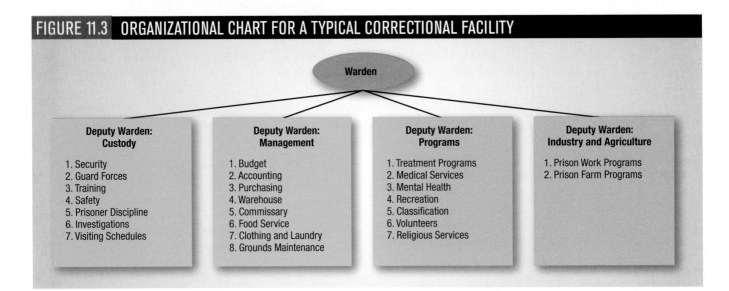

FIGURE 11.3 ORGANIZATIONAL CHART FOR A TYPICAL CORRECTIONAL FACILITY

Deputy Warden: Custody	**Deputy Warden: Management**	**Deputy Warden: Programs**	**Deputy Warden: Industry and Agriculture**
1. Security	1. Budget	1. Treatment Programs	1. Prison Work Programs
2. Guard Forces	2. Accounting	2. Medical Services	2. Prison Farm Programs
3. Training	3. Purchasing	3. Mental Health	
4. Safety	4. Warehouse	4. Recreation	
5. Prisoner Discipline	5. Commissary	5. Classification	
6. Investigations	6. Food Service	6. Volunteers	
7. Visiting Schedules	7. Clothing and Laundry	7. Religious Services	
	8. Grounds Maintenance		

Warden

What sort of prison management is most suited to avoid such situations? Most prisons in the United States operate under an authoritarian management structure, characterized by a strong leader, extensive control of the prison environment, and harsh discipline for misbehaving inmates.[21] Political scientist John DiIulio believes that, in general, the sound governance of correctional facilities is a matter of order, amenities, and services:

▶ *Order* can be defined as the absence of misconduct such as murder, assault, and rape. Many observers, including DiIulio, believe that, having incarcerated a person, the state has a responsibility to protect that person from disorder in the correctional institution.

▶ *Amenities* are those comforts that make life "livable," such as clean living conditions, acceptable food, and entertainment. One theory of incarceration holds that inmates should not enjoy a quality of life comparable to life outside prison. Without the basic amenities, however, prison life becomes unbearable, and inmates are more likely to lapse into disorder.

▶ *Services* include programs designed to improve an inmate's prospects on release, such as vocational training, remedial education, and drug treatment. Again, many feel that a person convicted of a crime does not deserve to participate in these kinds of programs, but they have two clear benefits. First, they keep the inmate occupied and focused during her or his sentence. Second, they reduce the chances that the inmate will go back to a life of crime after she or he returns to the community.[22]

According to DiIulio, in the absence of order, amenities, and services, inmates will come to see their imprisonment as not only unpleasant but unfair, and they will become much more difficult to control.[23] Furthermore, weak governance encourages inmates to come up with their own methods of regulating their lives. As we shall see in the next chapter, the result is usually high levels of violence and the expansion of prison gangs and other unsanctioned forms of authority.

CAREER TIP For spiritual guidance behind bars, inmates of all faiths turn to *prison chaplains*, who coordinate religious services in correctional facilities.

CLASSIFICATION One of the most important aspects of prison administration occurs soon after a defendant has been convicted of a crime and sentenced to be incarcerated. In this **classification** process, an inmate's

mental, physical, and security needs are evaluated to help determine the best correctional facility "fit." The classification process usually takes four to eight weeks and is overseen by a corrections counselor, also known as a case manager. During this period, the inmate undergoes numerous tests and interviews to identify education levels, medical issues, drug/alcohol addictions, and any behavioral "red flags."

Taking the results of the process into consideration, prison administrators generally rely on three broad criteria for classification purposes:

1. **The seriousness of the crime committed.**

2. **The risk of future criminal or violent conduct.**

3. **The need for treatment and rehabilitation programs.[24]**

Classification is not a one-time operation. Inmates can, and often do, change their behavior patterns during the course of their incarceration. If an inmate acts more violently, or, conversely, shows an increasingly positive attitude, that inmate will need to be *reclassified*. Furthermore, the successful completion of prison rehabilitation programs may require an adjustment in the inmate's release plan, discussed in the next chapter.[25]

11-2b Types of Prisons

Following the classification process, an inmate is assigned a **custody level.** Corrections officials rely on this custody level to place the inmate in the appropriate correctional facility. In the federal prison system and a number of state prison systems, an offender's custody level determines whether she or he is sent to one of six different types of prisons. Inmates in level 1 facilities are usually nonviolent and require the least amount of security, while inmates in level 6 facilities are the most dangerous and require the harshest security measures.

To simplify matters, most correctional facilities are designated as operating at one of three security levels—minimum, medium, or maximum. A fourth level—the supermaximum-security prison,

LO11-2

Classification The process through which prison officials screen each incoming inmate to best determine that inmate's security and treatment needs.

Custody Level As a result of the classification process, the security designation given to new inmates, crucial in helping corrections officials determine which correctional facility is best suited to the individual offender.

WARDEN

Job Description:

▶ As chief managing officer of an adult correctional institution, the warden is responsible for the custody, feeding, clothing, housing, care, treatment, discipline, training, employment, rehabilitation, and well-being of inmates.

▶ The warden provides institutional staff with effective communications, training, and leadership.

What Kind of Training Is Required?

▶ A bachelor's degree in criminal justice, social work, psychology, or a related field.

▶ One or more years of work experience in the management of a major division of a correctional institution.

Annual Salary Range?

▶ $38,000–$100,000 (depending on size of institution and geographic region)

Micah May, 2000/Used under license from ShutterStock.com

SOCIAL MEDIA CAREER TIP
Regularly reevaluate your social media tools and the methods you use to keep up to date in your fields of interest. If you are still using the same tools as a year ago, you probably aren't keeping up with the latest developments in Internet technology.

---

known as the "supermax"—is relatively rare and extremely controversial due to its hyper-harsh methods of punishing and controlling the most dangerous prisoners.

MAXIMUM-SECURITY PRISONS In a certain sense, the classification of prisoners today owes a debt to the three-grade system developed at the Elmira Reformatory, discussed earlier in the chapter. Once wrongdoers enter a corrections facility, they are constantly graded on behavior. Those who serve "good time," as we have seen, are often rewarded with early release. Those who compile extensive misconduct records are usually housed, along with violent and repeat offenders, in **maximum-security prisons.** The names of these institutions—Folsom, San Quentin, Sing Sing, Attica—conjure up foreboding images of concrete and steel jungles, with good reason.

Maximum-Security Prison A correctional institution designed and organized to control and discipline dangerous felons, as well as prevent escape.

Maximum-security prisons are designed with full attention to security and surveillance. In these institutions, inmates' lives are programmed in a militaristic fashion to keep them from escaping or from harming themselves or the prison staff. About a quarter of the prisons in the United States are classified as maximum security, and these institutions house about a third of the country's prisoners.

The Design Maximum-security prisons tend to be large—holding more than a thousand inmates—and they have similar features. The entire operation is usually surrounded by concrete walls that stand twenty to thirty feet high and have also been sunk deep into the ground to deter tunnel escapes. Fences reinforced with razor-ribbon barbed wire that can be electrically charged may supplement these barriers. The prison walls are studded with watchtowers, from which guards armed with shotguns and rifles survey the movement of prisoners below.

Inmates live in cells, most of them with dimensions similar to those found in the Topeka Correctional Facility, a maximum-security prison in Topeka, Kansas: eight feet by fourteen feet with cinder block walls. The space contains bunks, a toilet, a sink, and possibly a cabinet or closet. Cells are located in rows of *cell blocks,* each of which forms its own security unit, set off by a series of gates and bars. A maximum-security institution is essentially a collection of numerous cell blocks, each constituting its own prison within a prison.

Most prisons, regardless of their design, have cell blocks that open into sprawling prison yards, where the inmates commingle daily. The "prison of the future," however, rejects this layout. Instead, it relies on a podular design, as evident at the Two Rivers Correctional Institution in Umatilla, Oregon. At Two Rivers, which opened in 2007, fourteen housing pods contain ninety-six inmates each. Each unit has its own yard, so inmates rarely, if ever, interact with members of other pods. This design gives administrators the flexibility to, for example, place violent criminals in pod A and white-collar criminals in pod B without worrying about mixing the two different security levels.[26]

Security Measures Within maximum-security prisons, inmates' lives are dominated by security measures. Whenever they move from one area of the prison to another, they do so in groups and under the watchful eye of armed correctional officers. Television surveillance cameras may be used to monitor their every move, even when sleeping, showering, or using the toilet. They are subject to frequent pat-downs or strip searches at the guards' discretion. Constant "head counts" ensure that every inmate is where he or she should be. Tower guards—many of whom have orders to shoot to kill in the case of a disturbance or escape attempt—constantly look down on the inmates as they move around outdoor areas of the facility.

SUPERMAX PRISONS About thirty states and the Federal Bureau of Prisons (BOP) operate **supermax** (short for super-maximum security) **prisons,** which are supposedly reserved for the "worst of the worst" of America's corrections population. Many of the inmates in these facilities are deemed high risks to commit murder behind bars—about a quarter of the occupants of the BOP's U.S. Penitentiary Administrative Maximum (ADX) in Florence, Colorado, have killed other prisoners or assaulted correctional officers elsewhere.

Supermax Inmates Supermax prisons are also used as punishment for offenders who commit serious disciplinary infractions in maximum-security prisons, or for those inmates who become involved with prison gangs. In addition, a growing number of supermax occupants are either high-profile individuals who would be at constant risk of attack in a general prison population or convicted terrorists. Although different jurisdictions have different definitions of what constitutes a supermax, the most reliable surveys estimate that about sixty such facilities exist in the United States, holding approximately 25,000 inmates.[27]

The main purpose of a supermax prison is to strictly control the inmates' movement, thereby limiting (or eliminating) situations that could lead to breakdowns in discipline. The conditions at California's Security Housing Unit (SHU) at Pelican Bay State Prison are representative of most supermax institutions. Prisoners are confined to their one-person cells for twenty-three hours each day under video camera surveillance. They receive

AP Images/Matt York

What security measures can you identify from this photo of a cell block at a state prison in Arizona?

meals through a slot in the door. The cells measure eight by ten feet in size and are windowless. Fluorescent lights are continuously on, day and night, making it difficult for inmates to enjoy any type of privacy or sleep.[28]

For the most part, supermax prisons operate in a state of perpetual **lockdown,** in which all inmates are confined to their cells and social activities such as meals, recreational sports, and treatment programs are nonexistent. For the sixty minutes of each day that SHU inmates are allowed out of their cells (compared with twelve to sixteen hours in regular maximum-security prisons), they may either shower or exercise in an enclosed, concrete "yard" covered by plastic mesh. Prisoners are strip-searched before and after leaving their cells, and are placed in waist restraints and handcuffs on their way to and from the "yard" and showers.[29]

MEDIUM- AND MINIMUM-SECURITY PRISONS Medium-security prisons hold about 45 percent of the prison population and minimum-security prisons 20 percent. Inmates at **medium-security prisons** have for the most part committed less serious crimes than those housed in maximum-security prisons and are not considered high risks for escaping or causing harm. Consequently, medium-security institutions are not designed for control to the same extent as maximum-security prisons and have a more relaxed atmosphere. These facilities also offer more educational and treatment programs and allow for more contact between inmates. Medium-security prisons are rarely walled, relying instead on

Supermax Prison A highly secure, freestanding correctional facility—or such a unit within a correctional facility—that manages offenders who would pose a threat to the security and safety of other inmates and staff members if housed in the general inmate population.

Lockdown A disciplinary action taken by prison officials in which all inmates are ordered to their quarters and nonessential prison activities are suspended.

Medium-Security Prison A correctional institution that houses less dangerous inmates and therefore uses less restrictive measures to prevent violence and escapes.

high fences. Prisoners have more freedom of movement within the structures, and the levels of surveillance are much lower. Living quarters are less restrictive as well—many of the newer medium-security prisons provide dormitory housing.

A **minimum-security prison** seems at first glance to be more like a college campus than an incarceration facility. Most of the inmates at these institutions are first-time offenders who are nonviolent and well behaved. A high percentage are white-collar criminals. Indeed, inmates are often transferred to minimum-security prisons as a reward for good behavior in other facilities. Therefore, security measures are lax compared with even medium-security prisons. Unlike medium-security institutions, minimum-security prisons do not have armed guards. Prisoners are provided with amenities such as televisions and computers in their rooms. They also enjoy freedom of movement and are allowed off prison grounds for educational or employment purposes to a much greater extent than those held in more restrictive facilities.

CAREER TIP **Many colleges now offer degrees in recreation management. Although geared toward corporate fitness/wellness programs, this discipline also has a place in the corrections system. For example, Danbury Women's Prison has a track and a gymnasium that is used for Pilates and yoga classes.**

11-3 WHAT TRENDS ARE DRIVING THE AMERICAN PRISON POPULATION?

As Figure 11.4 shows, the number of Americans in prison or jail has increased dramatically in the past three decades. This growth can be attributed to a number of factors, starting with the enhancement and stricter enforcement of the nation's illegal drug laws.

11-3a Factors in Prison Population Growth

LO11-3 There are more people in prison and jail for drug offenses today than there were for *all* offenses in the early 1970s.[30] In 1980, about 19,000 drug offenders were incarcerated in state prisons and 4,800 drug offenders were in federal prisons. Thirty-three years later, state prisons held about 210,000 inmates who had been arrested for drug offenses, and the number of drug offenders in federal prisons had risen to approximately 98,000 (representing about half of all inmates in federal facilities).[31]

Minimum-Security Prison A correctional institution designed to allow inmates, most of whom pose low security risks, a great deal of freedom of movement and contact with the outside world.

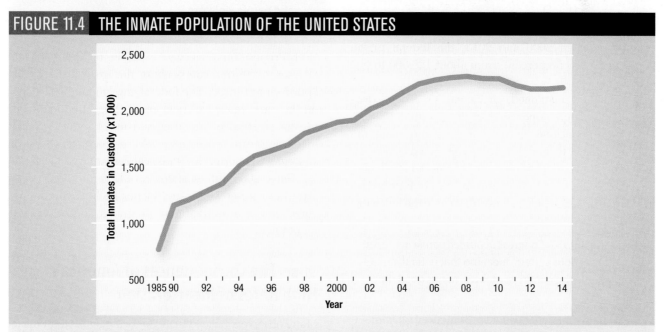

FIGURE 11.4 THE INMATE POPULATION OF THE UNITED STATES

The total number of inmates in the United States has risen from 744,208 in 1985 to about 2.2 million in 2014.

Source: U.S. Department of Justice.

INCREASED PROBABILITY OF INCARCERATION

The growth of America's inmate population also reflects the reality that the chance of someone who is arrested going to prison today is much greater than it was thirty years ago. Most of this growth took place in the 1980s, when the likelihood of incarceration in a state prison after arrest increased fivefold for drug offenses, three-fold for weapons offenses, and twofold for crimes such as sexual assault, burglary, auto theft, and larceny.[32] For federal crimes, the proportion of convicted defendants being sent to prison rose from 54 percent in 1988 to 88 percent in 2013.[33]

INMATES SERVING MORE TIME In Chapter 9, we discussed a number of "get tough" sentencing laws passed in reaction to the crime wave of the 1970s and 1980s. These measures, including sentencing guidelines, mandatory minimum sentences, and truth-in-sentencing laws, have significantly increased the length of prison terms in the United States.[34] Overall, inmates released from state prison in 2009 spent an average of nine months—about 36 percent—longer behind bars than those inmates released in 1990.[35] On the federal level, in the fifteen years after the passage of the Sentencing Reform Act of 1984, the average time served in federal prison increased more than 50 percent.[36]

FEDERAL PRISON GROWTH Even though, as noted earlier in the chapter, the overall U.S. prison population rose slightly in 2013, the number of federal prisoners dropped—by about 2,000—for the first time in thirty-four years.[37] This decrease is too small, however, to offset the earlier expansion of the federal corrections system. Between 2000 and 2013, the federal prison population grew 56 percent, from about 125,000 to just over 195,000.[38]

As already mentioned, an increase in federal drug offenders is largely responsible for the growth of the federal prison population. Because of mandatory minimum sentencing laws, federal drug traffickers spend an average of seventy-four months behind bars, considerably longer than those sentenced to state prisons.[39] Other factors driving federal prison population growth include the following:

1. Starting in 1987, Congress *abolished parole* in the federal corrections system, meaning that federal inmates must serve their entire sentences, minus good time credits.[40]

2. The number of federal inmates sentenced for *immigration violations* (covered by federal law rather

than state law) increased by 30 percent from 2001 to 2013.[41]

3. In 2015, approximately fourteen thousand *female offenders* were behind bars in federal prison, about double their numbers in 1995.[42] Indeed, there were about the same number of women in federal prison for drug offenses in 2012 as there were for all offenses in 1995.[43]

11-3b Decarceration

As recently as 2007, one expert lamented the unwillingness of corrections authorities in the United States to reduce their prison populations, calling such efforts "practically virgin territory."[44] This is no longer the case. The high cost of imprisonment—which reached $52.4 billion for the fifty states in 2012[45]—has caused policymakers to embrace strategies of *decarceration,* or the lowering of incarceration rates. In general, decarceration policies rely on three methods to reduce the number of offenders in prison:

1. Decreasing the probability that nonviolent offenders will be sentenced to prison.

2. Increasing the rate of release of nonviolent offenders from prison.

3. Decreasing the rate of imprisonment for probation and parole violators.[46]

With Proposition 47, as we saw at the beginning of this chapter, California voters chose the first decarceration approach just listed. The federal government is focusing on the early release of nonviolent drug offenders from prisons, a strategy we discussed in Chapter 9. States increasingly are relying on *evidence-based strategies,* or strategies supported by statistical research, to decarcerate. Since 2005, fifteen states have lowered their recidivism rates using well-tested tactics such as community corrections, prison treatment programs, and risk assessment planning.[47]

11-3c The Consequences of America's High Rates of Incarceration

Many observers believe that America's high rate of incarceration has contributed significantly to the drop in the country's crime rates.[48] Even so, criminologists are well

What are some of the possible consequences of having a parent behind bars for the affected child and for society as a whole?

"ripple effect on their communities and on the next generation of kids, growing up with their fathers in prison, will certainly be with us for at least a generation."[54]

11-4 WHAT ARE PRIVATE PRISONS?

As the prison population soared at the end of the twentieth century, state corrections officials faced a serious problem: too many inmates, not enough prisons. "States couldn't build space fast enough," explains corrections expert Martin Horn. "And so they had to turn to the private sector."[55] With corrections exhibiting all appearance of "a recession-proof industry," American businesses eagerly entered the market.

Today, **private prisons,** or prisons run by private firms to make a profit, are an important part of the criminal justice system. About two dozen private companies operate more than two hundred facilities across the United States. The two largest corrections firms, Corrections Corporation of America (CCA) and the GEO Group, Inc., manage approximately 160 correctional facilities and generate about $2.5 billion in annual revenue combined.[56] By 2013, private penal institutions housed about 133,000 inmates, representing 8.4 percent of all prisoners in the state and federal corrections systems.[57]

11-4a Why Privatize?

It would be a mistake to automatically assume that private prisons are less expensive to run than public ones. Nevertheless, the incentive to privatize is primarily financial.

aware of a number of negative consequences related to this country's immense prison and jail population.

For one, incarceration can have severe social repercussions for communities and the families that make up those communities. About 2.7 million minors in this country—one in twenty-eight—have a parent in prison.[49] These children are at an increased risk of suffering from poverty, depression, and academic problems, as well as higher levels of juvenile delinquency and eventual incarceration themselves.[50] Studies also link high imprisonment rates to increased incidence of sexually transmitted diseases and teenage pregnancy, as the separation caused by incarceration wreaks havoc on interpersonal relationships.[51] Incarceration also has a harmful impact on offenders themselves. After being released from prison or jail, these men and women suffer from a higher rate of physical and mental health problems than the rest of the population, and are more likely to struggle with addiction, unemployment, and homelessness.[52]

Because of the demographics of the U.S. prison population, these problems have a disproportionate impact on members of minority groups. African American males are incarcerated at a rate more than six times that of white males and about two and a half times that of Hispanic males.[53] With more black men behind bars than enrolled in the nation's colleges and universities, Marc Mauer of the Sentencing Project, a nonprofit research group in Washington, D.C., believes that the

Private Prisons Correctional facilities operated by private corporations instead of the government and, therefore, reliant on profits for survival.

LO11-4 **COST EFFICIENCY** In the 1980s and 1990s, a number of states and cities reduced operating costs by transferring government-run services such as garbage collection and road maintenance to the private sector. Similarly, private prisons can often be run more cheaply and efficiently than public ones for the following reasons:

▶ *Labor costs.* The wages of public employees account for nearly two-thirds of a prison's operating expenses. Although private corrections firms pay base salaries comparable to those enjoyed by public prison employees, their nonunionized staffs receive lower levels of overtime pay, workers' compensation claims, sick leave, and health-care insurance.

▶ *Competitive bidding.* Because of the profit motive, private corrections firms have an incentive to buy goods and services at the lowest possible price.

▶ *Less red tape.* Private corrections firms are not part of the government bureaucracy and therefore do not have to contend with the massive amount of paperwork that can clog government organizations.[58]

In 2005, the National Institute of Justice released the results of a five-year study comparing low-security public and private prisons in California. The government agency found that private facilities cost taxpayers between 6 and 10 percent less than public ones.[59] More recent research conducted at Vanderbilt University found that states saved about $15 million annually when they supplemented their corrections systems with privately managed institutions.[60]

OVERCROWDING AND OUTSOURCING Private prisons are becoming increasingly attractive to state governments faced with the competing pressures of tight budgets and overcrowded corrections facilities. Lacking the funds to alleviate overcrowding by building more prisons, state officials are turning to the private institutions for help.

In Oklahoma, for example, where corrections officials are sending prison inmates to local jails due to lack of prison space, more than a quarter of the state's prisoners—about 5,800 inmates—are housed in private facilities.[61] Often, the private prison is out of state, which leads to the "outsourcing" of inmates. California has alleviated its chronic overcrowding problems by sending about 9,000 inmates to private institutions in Arizona, Mississippi, and Oklahoma.[62]

11-4b The Argument against Private Prisons

The assertion that private prisons offer economic benefits is not universally accepted. A number of studies have found that private prisons are no more cost-effective than public ones.[63] Furthermore, opponents of private prisons worry that, despite the assurances of corporate executives, private corrections companies will "cut corners" to save costs, denying inmates important security guarantees in the process.

SAFETY CONCERNS Various studies have also uncovered disturbing patterns of misbehavior at private prisons. For example, in the year after CCA took over operations of Ohio's Lake Erie Correctional Institution from the state corrections department, the number of assaults against correctional officers and inmates increased by over 40 percent.[64] In addition, research conducted by Curtis R. Blakely of the University of South Alabama and Vic W. Bumphus of the University of Tennessee at Chattanooga found that a prisoner in a private correctional facility was twice as likely to be assaulted by a fellow inmate as a prisoner in a public one.[65]

PHILOSOPHICAL CONCERNS Other critics see private prisons as inherently unjust, even if they do save tax dollars or provide enhanced services. These observers believe that corrections is not simply another industry, like garbage collection or road maintenance, and that only the government has the authority to punish wrongdoers. In the words of John DiIulio:

> It is precisely because corrections involves the deprivation of liberty, precisely because it involves the legally sanctioned exercise of coercion by some citizens over others, that it must remain wholly within public hands.[66]

Furthermore, some observers note, if a private corrections firm receives a fee from the state for each inmate housed in its facility, does that not give management an incentive to increase the amount of time each prisoner serves? Though government parole boards make the final decision on an inmate's release from private prisons, the company could manipulate misconduct and good behavior reports to maximize time served and, by extension, increase profits.[67] "You can put a dollar figure on each inmate that is held at a private prison," says Alex Friedmann of *Prison Legal News.* "They are treated as commodities. And that's very dangerous and troubling when a company sees the people it incarcerates as nothing more than a money stream."[68]

11-4c The Future of Private Prisons

The number of inmates in private prisons declined by 3 percent from 2012 to 2013,[69] largely as a result of a reduction in the number of federal prisoners noted earlier in the chapter. Still, the private prison industry will continue to play an important role in American corrections, for two reasons. First, states experiencing shrinking corrections budgets and congested prisons rely on private correctional institutions to handle their inmate population overflow. Second, the federal government houses about 25,000 noncitizens—many of whom have violated immigration laws—in thirteen privately operated "Criminal Alien Requirement" correctional facilities across the country.[70]

11-5 WHY ARE JAILS SO IMPORTANT?

LO11-5 Although prisons and prison issues dominate the public discourse on corrections, there is an argument to be made that jails are the dominant penal institutions in the United States. In general, a prison is a facility designed to house people convicted of felonies for lengthy periods of time, while a **jail** is authorized primarily to hold pretrial detainees and offenders who have committed misdemeanors. On any given day, about 730,000 inmates are in jail in this country, and jails admit approximately 11.7 million persons over the course of an entire year.[71] Nevertheless, jail funding is often the lowest priority for the tight budgets of local governments, leading to severe overcrowding and other dismal conditions.

Many observers see this negligence as having far-reaching consequences for criminal justice. Jail is often the first contact that citizens have with the corrections system. It is at this point that treatment and counseling have the best chance to deter future criminal behavior. By failing to take advantage of this opportunity, says Professor Franklin Zimring of the University of California at Berkeley School of Law, corrections officials have created a situation in which "today's jail folk are tomorrow's prisoners."[72] (To better understand the role that these two correctional institutions play in the criminal justice system, see Figure 11.5.)

11-5a The Jail Population

Like their counterparts in state prisons, jail inmates are overwhelmingly young male adults. About 47 percent of jail inmates are white, 36 percent are African American, and 15 percent are Hispanic.[73] The main difference between state prison and jail inmates involves their criminal activity. As Figure 11.6 shows, jail inmates are more likely to have been convicted of nonviolent crimes than their counterparts in state prison.

> **Jail** A facility, usually operated by the county government, used primarily to hold persons awaiting trial and those who have been found guilty of misdemeanors.

FIGURE 11.5 THE MAIN DIFFERENCES BETWEEN PRISONS AND JAILS

	Prisons	Jails
1.	. . . are operated by the federal and state governments.	. . . are operated by county and city governments.
2.	. . . hold inmates who may have lived quite far away before being arrested.	. . . hold mostly inmates from the local community.
3.	. . . house only those who have been convicted of a crime.	. . . house those who are awaiting trial or have recently been arrested, in addition to convicts.
4.	. . . generally hold inmates who have been found guilty of serious crimes and received sentences of longer than one year.	. . . generally hold inmates who have been found guilty of minor crimes and are serving sentences of less than a year.
5.	. . . often offer a wide variety of rehabilitation and educational programs for long-term prisoners.	. . . due to smaller budgets, tend to focus only on the necessities of safety, food, and clothing.

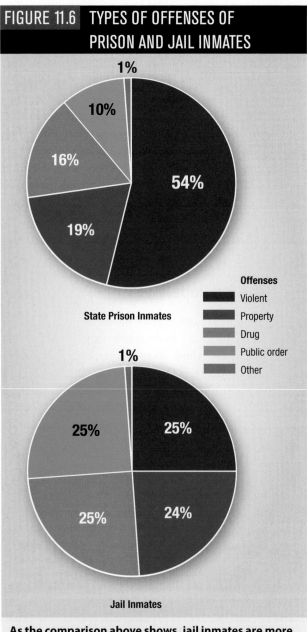

FIGURE 11.6 TYPES OF OFFENSES OF PRISON AND JAIL INMATES

State Prison Inmates

- 54%
- 1%
- 10%
- 16%
- 19%

Offenses
- Violent
- Property
- Drug
- Public order
- Other

Jail Inmates

- 1%
- 25%
- 25%
- 25%
- 24%

As the comparison above shows, jail inmates are more likely than state prisoners to have been convicted of nonviolent crimes. This underscores the main function of jails: to house less serious offenders for a relatively short period of time.

Source: Bureau of Justice Statistics, *Prisoners in 2013* (Washington, D.C.: U.S. Department of Justice, September 2014), Table 13, page 15; and Bureau of Justice Statistics, *Profile of Jail Inmates, 2002* (Washington, D.C.: U.S. Department of Justice, July 2004), 1.

Pretrial Detainees Individuals who cannot post bail after arrest and are therefore forced to spend the time prior to their trial incarcerated in jail.

Time Served The period of time a person denied bail (or unable to pay it) has spent in jail prior to his or her trial.

PRETRIAL DETAINEES A significant number of those detained in jails technically are not prisoners. They are **pretrial detainees** who have been arrested by the police and, for a variety of reasons that we discussed in Chapter 8, are unable to post bail. Pretrial detainees are, in many ways, walking legal contradictions. According to the U.S. Constitution, they are innocent until proved guilty. At the same time, by being incarcerated while awaiting trial, they are denied a number of personal freedoms and are subjected to the poor conditions of many jails.

In *Bell v. Wolfish* (1979), the Supreme Court rejected the notion that this situation is inherently unfair by refusing to give pretrial detainees greater legal protections than sentenced jail inmates have.[74] In essence, the Court recognized that treating pretrial detainees differently from convicted jail inmates would place too much of a burden on corrections officials and was therefore impractical.[75]

SENTENCED JAIL INMATES According to the U.S. Department of Justice, about 40 percent of those in jail have been convicted of their current charges.[76] In other words, they have been found guilty of a crime, usually a misdemeanor, and sentenced to time in jail. The typical jail term lasts between thirty and ninety days, and rarely does a prisoner spend more than one year in jail for any single crime. Often, a judge will credit the length of time the convict has spent in detention waiting for trial—known as **time served**—toward his or her sentence. This practice acknowledges two realities of jails:

1. Terms are generally too short to allow the prisoner to gain any benefit (that is, rehabilitation) from the jail's often limited or nonexistent treatment facilities. Therefore, the jail term can serve no purpose except to punish the wrongdoer. (Judges who believe jail time can serve purposes of deterrence and incapacitation may not agree with this line of reasoning.)

2. Jails are chronically overcrowded, and judges need to clear space for new offenders.

OTHER JAIL INMATES Pretrial detainees and those convicted of misdemeanors make up the majority of the jail population. Jail inmates also include probation and parole violators, the mentally ill, juveniles awaiting transfer to juvenile authorities, and immigration law violators being held for the federal government.

Increasingly, jails are also called on to handle the overflow from state prisons. To comply with a United States Supreme Court order to reduce its prison population, California corrections officials diverted thousands of low-level offenders from its prisons to its jails. This strategy, in turn, led to such severe overcrowding of local jails that, by 2014, these institutions were releasing 13,500 inmates a month, a 34 percent increase from three years earlier.[77]

11-5b Jail Administration

About 3,300 jails are in operation in the United States. The vast majority of these are managed on a county level by an elected sheriff. Most of the remainder are under the control of the federal government or local municipalities, and six state governments (Alaska, Connecticut, Delaware, Hawaii, Rhode Island, and Vermont) also manage jails. The capacity of jails varies widely. The Los Angeles County Men's Central Jail holds nearly seven thousand people, but jails that large are the exception rather than the rule. Forty percent of all jails in this country house fewer than fifty inmates.[78]

THE FEE SYSTEM Many jails operate on the principle of a **fee system,** in which a government agency reimburses the sheriff's department for the daily cost of housing and feeding each inmate. This practice is often problematic, because once the daily fee per inmate has been established (at, say $8), the sheriff is free to divert some of those funds to other areas of need in her or his department. Also, it is not uncommon for sheriffs'

> **Fee System** A system in which the sheriff's department is reimbursed by a government agency for the costs of housing jail inmates.

DEPUTY SHERIFF/JAIL DIVISION

CareerPrep

Job Description:

▶ Be responsible for supervising jail inmates by ensuring that order, discipline, safety, and security are maintained.

▶ Transport or escort inmates and defendants from jail to courtrooms, attorneys' offices, or medical facilities.

What Kind of Training Is Required?

▶ Depending on the jurisdiction, possession of a high school diploma or bachelor's degree, as well as successful completion of written and physical examinations, training, and a probationary period.

▶ Some states require completion of a "jail academy" training course of up to sixteen weeks, including field training.

Annual Salary Range?

▶ $44,000–$70,000

iStockPhoto.com/kaupok

GETTING LINKEDIN

In a recent LinkedIn posting, the Dane County (Wisconsin) Sheriff's Office highlighted "supervision of jail inmates" as part of its job description for a potential deputy sheriff hire. Indeed, in many counties, a sheriff deputy's main duties involve keeping order at the county jail rather than traffic control or law enforcement.

How does the layout of this direct supervision jail differ from that of the maximum-security prison pictured earlier in the chapter? What do these differences tell you about the security precautions needed for jail inmates as opposed to prison inmates?

departments to charge inmates "pay-to-stay" fees for aspects of their incarceration such as food, clothing, and medical and dental care.

THE "BURDEN" OF JAIL ADMINISTRATION Given that the public's opinion of jails ranges from negative to indifferent, some sheriffs neglect their jail management duties. Instead, they focus on high-visibility issues such as putting more law enforcement officers on the streets and improving security in schools. In fact, a jail usually receives publicity only after an escape or an incident in which inmates are abused by jailers. Nonetheless, with their complex and diverse populations, jails are often more difficult to manage than prisons. Jails hold people who have never been incarcerated before and who exhibit a range of behavior—from nonviolent to extremely violent—that only adds to the unpredictable atmosphere. Jail inmates have a number of other problems, including:

1. *Mental illness.* About 60 percent of jail inmates have a history of mental illness, including symptoms of schizophrenia, depression, hallucinations, and suicidal tendencies.[79]

2. *Physical health problems.* More than one-third of jail inmates report having a current medical problem such as an injury or ailments such as arthritis, asthma, or sexually transmitted diseases.[80]

3. *Substance abuse and dependency.* About two-thirds of jail inmates are dependent on alcohol or other drugs, and half of all convicted jail inmates were under the influence of drugs or alcohol at the time of their arrest.[81]

Because most jails lack the resources and facilities to properly deal with these problems, the task of managing jail inmate populations falls disproportionately on untrained prison staff. Speaking of mentally ill inmates at Rikers Island, New York City's main jail complex, one corrections official said, "They need medication, treatment, psychological help. They don't need a corrections officer."[82]

11-5c New-Generation Jails

For most of the nation's history, the architecture of a jail was secondary to its purpose of keeping inmates safely locked away. Consequently, most jails in the United States continue to resemble those from the days of the Walnut Street Jail in Philadelphia. In this *traditional*, or *linear*, *design*, jail cells are located along a corridor. To supervise the inmates while they are in their cells, custodial officers must walk up and down the corridor, so the number of prisoners they can see at any one time is severely limited. With this limited supervision, inmates can more easily break institutional rules.

PODULAR DESIGN In the 1970s, planners at the Bureau of Federal Prisons decided to upgrade the traditional jail design with the goal of improving conditions for both the staff and the inmates. The result was the **new-generation jail,** which differs significantly from its predecessors.[83] The layout of the new facilities makes it easier for the staff to monitor cell-confined inmates. The basic structure of the new-generation jail is based on a podular design. Each "pod" contains "living units" for individual prisoners. These units, instead of lining up along a straight corridor, are often situated in a triangle so that a staff member in the center of the triangle has visual access to nearly all the cells.

Daily activities such as eating and showering take place in the pod, which also has an outdoor exercise area. Treatment facilities are also located in the pod, allowing greater access for the inmates. During the day, inmates stay out in the open and are allowed back in their cells only when given permission. The officer locks the door to the cells from his or her control terminal.

DIRECT SUPERVISION APPROACH The podular design also enables a new-generation jail to be managed using a **direct supervision approach.**[84] One or more jail officers are stationed in the living area of the pod and are therefore in constant interaction with all prisoners in that particular pod. Some new-generation

jails even provide a desk in the center of the living area, which sends a very different message to the prisoners than the traditional control booth. Theoretically, jail officials who have constant contact with inmates will be able to stem misconduct quickly and efficiently, and will also be able to recognize "danger signs" from individual inmates and stop outbursts before they occur. (As noted earlier in the chapter, corrections officials are using aspects of podular design when building new prisons, for many of the same reasons that the trend has been popular in jails.)

New-Generation Jail A type of jail that is distinguished architecturally from its predecessors by a design that encourages interaction between inmates and jailers and that offers greater opportunities for treatment.

Direct Supervision Approach A process of prison and jail administration in which correctional officers are in continuous visual contact with inmates during the day.

STUDY TOOLS 11

READY TO STUDY? IN THE BOOK, YOU CAN:

☐ Rip out the Chapter Review Card, which includes key terms and chapter summaries.

ONLINE AT WWW.CENGAGEBRAIN.COM, YOU CAN:

☐ Learn about private sector prison problems in a short video.

☐ Explore the Web site and Facebook page of the nation's largest jail: Los Angeles County Sheriff's Department.

☐ Interact with figures from the text, and watch quick animation clips.

☐ Prepare for tests with quizzes.

☐ Review the key terms with Flash Cards.

Quiz

1. In the second half of the 1800s, the Progressive movement introduced the _____ model of prison management, which focused on rehabilitation rather than punishment.

2. The _____ (also known as a superintendent) is at the top of a prison's command structure.

3. Using a process called _____, prison administrators determine which correctional facility provides the best "fit" for the offender, based mostly on security concerns.

4. Offenders who have been convicted of violent crimes and repeat offenders are likely to be sent to _____-security prisons.

5. If a prisoner assaults another inmate or a correctional officer, prison officials may decide to transfer that prisoner to a _____ prison designed to hold the "worst of the worst."

6. Double the number of _____ offenders are in federal prisons today than was the case two decades ago, due in large part to increased federal prosecution and incarceration of drug offenders.

7. Many states are adopting strategies of _____ designed to reduce their inmate populations and the costs associated with their corrections systems.

8. Prison officials often feel pressure to send inmates to private prisons to alleviate _____ of public correctional facilities.

9. Rather than having been convicted of any crime, a significant number of jail inmates are _____ _____ who are unable to post bail.

10. Most jails are operated on a local level by the county _____.

Answers can be found in the Answers section in the back of the book.

ONE APPROACH.
70 UNIQUE SOLUTIONS.

12 The Prison Experience and Prisoner Reentry

John Moore/Getty Images News/Getty Images

LEARNING OBJECTIVES

After studying this chapter, you will be able to . . .

12-1 Explain the concept of prison as a total institution.

12-2 Indicate some of the reasons for violent behavior in prisons.

12-3 Describe the hands-off doctrine of prisoner law and indicate two standards used to determine if prisoners' rights have been violated.

12-4 Contrast parole, expiration release, pardon, and furlough.

12-5 Explain the goal of prisoner reentry programs.

After you finish this chapter, go to **PAGES 270–271** for **STUDY TOOLS**

The "Wildest Show in the South"

Two of the inmates sitting at the poker table had been convicted of murder. Two others were doing time for armed robbery. The fifth player in the "game"—a large, angry bull—rammed the table, and then turned its attention to the inmates, kicking its hind legs and swinging its massive horns with violent intent. The last prisoner of the four brave enough to remain seated during the bull's rampage was declared the winner, taking $200 back to his cell for his troubles.

"Convict Poker" is one of the most popular competitions at the Angola Prison Rodeo, which celebrated its fiftieth anniversary in 2014. Dubbed the "Wildest Show in the South," the tournament draws thousands of spectators to the Louisiana State Penitentiary each year and raises millions of dollars for the prison's educational and recreational programs. Warden Burl Cain promotes the rodeo as a highly anticipated perk for the inmates, who spend most of their days working in the prison's farming operations picking wheat, corn, and cotton. The rodeo also encourages discipline at the nation's largest maximum security prison, which houses most of Louisiana's violent offenders. Inmates know that, if they misbehave, they won't be allowed to participate in the event, which includes an arts-and-crafts fair open to the public.

Critics of the rodeo see it as an unseemly ritual in which untrained inmates are subjected to the risk (and reality) of serious injury for the amusement of tourists and the profit of the penitentiary. At a time when many prisoners across the country are denied amenities such as weightlifting, television, magazines, and conjugal visits, however, the Angola Prison Rodeo is a rare exception to the "no frills" movement in American corrections. Furthermore, the inmates are eager to take part. "[The rodeo] make me feel like somebody," says one who is serving a life sentence for murder. "It gives me a chance . . . to entertain the people and just have fun."

Are there any ethical problems with allowing prisoners to entertain paying customers by participating in competitions involving dangerous animals (such as this bull)? Why or why not?

Shawn Hine/ShutterStock.com

12-1 HOW DO INMATES ADJUST TO LIFE IN PRISON?

In this chapter, we will look at the life of the imprisoned convict, starting with the realities of an existence behind bars and finishing with the challenges of returning to free society. Along the way, we will discuss violence in prison, correctional officers, women's prisons, different types of release, and several other issues that are at the forefront of American corrections today. To start, we must understand the forces that shape prison culture and how those forces affect the overall operation of the correctional facility.

Any institution, whether a school, a bank, or a police department, has an organizational culture—a set of values that help the people in the organization understand what actions are acceptable and what actions are unacceptable. According to a theory put forth by the influential sociologist Erving Goffman, prison cultures are unique because prisons are **total institutions** that encompass every aspect of an inmate's life. Unlike a student or a bank teller, a prisoner cannot leave the institution or have any meaningful interaction with outside communities. Others arrange every aspect of daily life,

LO12-1 and all prisoners are required to follow this schedule in the same manner.[1]

Inmates develop their own argot, or language (see Figure 12.1). They create their own economy, which, in the absence of currency, is based on the barter of valued

> **Total Institution** An institution, such as a prison, that provides all of the necessities for existence to those who live within its boundaries.

FIGURE 12.1 PRISON SLANG

All day A life sentence, as in "I'm here all day."

All day and a night A life-without-parole sentence.

Bit Prison sentence, usually relatively short, as in "I've got a three-year bit."

Carga Heroin.

Catch a ride A request to another inmate to get high.

Cakero Description of a convict who rapes weaker inmates.

Fire on the line A warning that a correctional officer is in the area.

Fish A new arrival, unschooled in the ways of prison life.

Grandma's (or Grandma's House) A prison gang's meeting place, or the cell of the gang leader.

Mud Coffee.

Mule Someone who smuggles drugs into the institution.

N.G. "No good," as in "He's N.G." (meaning the inmate in question is not trustworthy).

Neutron Term used by gang members to describe an inmate not affiliated with a gang.

Old School Description of an older prisoner, usually with respect.

Square Cigarette.

Three knee deep To stab someone so that they're injured, but not killed, as a warning.

---

items such as food, contraband, and sexual favors. They establish methods of determining power, many of which, as we shall see, involve violence. Isolated and heavily regulated, prisoners create a social existence that is, out of both necessity and design, separate from the outside world.

12-1a Adapting to Prison Society

On arriving at prison, each convict attends an orientation session and receives a "Resident's Handbook." The handbook provides information such as meal and official count times, disciplinary regulations, and visitation guidelines. The norms and values of the prison society, however, cannot be communicated by the staff or learned from a handbook. As first described by Donald Clemmer in his classic 1940 work, *The Prison Community*, the process of **prisonization**—or adaptation to the prison culture—advances as the inmate gradually understands what constitutes acceptable behavior in the institution, as defined not by the prison officials but by other inmates.[2]

In studying prisonization, criminologists have focused on two areas: how prisoners change their behavior to adapt to life behind bars, and how life behind bars has changed because of inmate behavior. Sociologist John Irwin has identified several patterns of inmate behavior, each one driven by the inmate's personality and values:

1. **Professional criminals adapt to prison by "doing time."** In other words, they follow the rules and generally do whatever is necessary to speed up their release and return to freedom.

2. **Some convicts, mostly state-raised youths or those frequently incarcerated in juvenile detention centers, are more comfortable inside prison than outside.** These inmates serve time by "jailing," or establishing themselves in the power structure of prison culture.

3. **Other inmates take advantage of prison resources such as libraries or drug treatment programs by "gleaning,"** or working to improve themselves to prepare for a return to society.

4. Finally, **"disorganized" criminals exist on the fringes of prison society.** These inmates may have mental impairments or low levels of intelligence, and find it impossible to adapt to prison culture on any level.[3]

The process of categorizing prisoners has a theoretical basis, but it serves a practical purpose as well, allowing administrators to reasonably predict how different inmates will act in certain situations. An inmate who is "doing time" generally does not present the same security risk as one who is "jailing."

12-1b Who Is in Prison?

The culture of any prison is heavily influenced by its inmates. Their values, beliefs, and experiences will be reflected in the social order that exists behind bars. As we noted in the last chapter, the past three decades have seen incarceration rates of women and minority groups

---

Prisonization The socialization process through which a new inmate learns the accepted norms and values of the prison culture.

rise sharply. Furthermore, the arrest patterns of inmates have changed over that time period. A prisoner today is much more likely to have been incarcerated on a drug charge or immigration violation than was the case in the 1980s. Today's inmate is also more likely to behave violently behind bars—a situation that will be addressed shortly.

AN AGING INMATE POPULATION In recent years, the most significant demographic change in the prison population involves age. Though the majority of inmates are still under thirty-four years old, the number of state and federal prisoners over the age of forty has increased dramatically since the mid-1990s. Several factors have contributed to this upsurge, including longer prison terms, mandatory prison terms, recidivism, and higher levels of crimes—particularly violent crimes—committed by older offenders.[4] For example, in Angola State Prison, featured at the beginning of this chapter, the average sentence for those inmates not serving life-without-parole is ninety-one years.[5]

Corrections budgets are straining under the financial pressures caused by the health-care needs of aging inmates. Nationwide, an inmate aged fifty years or older is three times more expensive to incarcerate than a younger prisoner.[6] In Virginia, inmates fifty years or older have average annual medical expenses of about $5,372, compared with an average annual medical expense of $795 for those prisoners under fifty.[7] Given the burden of inmate medical costs, state corrections officials may be tempted to cut such services whenever possible. As we will see later in the chapter, however, prisoners have a constitutional right to adequate health care.

CAREER TIP Due to the increase in the number of ailing prison and jail inmates, *registered nurses* are in high demand in the corrections system.

MENTAL ILLNESS BEHIND BARS Another factor in rising correctional health-care costs is the high incidence of mental illness in American prisons and jails. During the 1950s and 1960s, nearly 600,000 mental patients lived in public hospitals, often against their will. A series of scandals spotlighting the poor medical services and horrendous living conditions in these institutions led to their closure and the elimination of much of the nation's state-run mental health infrastructure.[8] Many mentally ill people now receive no supervision whatsoever, and some inevitably commit deviant or criminal acts.

As a result, in the words of criminal justice experts Katherine Stuart van Wormer and Clemens Bartollas, jails and prisons have become "the dumping grounds for people whose bizarre behavior lands them behind bars."[9] On any given day, for example, the Cook County Jail in Chicago houses between 2,000 and 2,500 inmates who have been diagnosed with a mental illness.[10] Nearly 10 percent of all federal inmates receive medications to treat illnesses such as depression and bipolar disorder.[11] As with aging and ailing prisoners, correctional facilities are required by law to provide treatment to mentally ill inmates, thus driving the costs associated with their confinement well above the average. For reasons that should become clear over the course of this chapter, correctional facilities are not designed to foster mental well-being. Indeed, inmates with mental illnesses often find that their problems are exacerbated by the prison environment.[12]

12-1c Rehabilitation and Prison Programs

In Chapter 9, we saw that rehabilitation is one of the basic theoretical justifications for punishment. **Prison programs,** which include any organized activities designed to foster rehabilitation, benefit inmates in several ways. On a basic level, these programs get prisoners out of their cells and alleviate the boredom that marks prison and jail life. The programs also help inmates improve their health and skills, giving them a better chance of reintegration into society after release. Consequently, nearly every federal and state prison in the United States offers some form of rehabilitation.[13]

SUBSTANCE ABUSE TREATMENT As we have seen throughout this textbook, there is a strong link between crime and abuse of drugs and alcohol. According to the National Center on Addiction and Substance Abuse (CASA) at New York's Columbia University, 1.5 million prison and jail inmates in the United States meet the medical criteria for substance abuse or addiction. Also according to CASA, only 11 percent of these inmates have received any type of professional treatment behind bars.[14]

The most effective substance abuse programs for prisoners require trained staff, lengthy periods of therapy, expensive medication, and community aftercare, but such programs carry a price tag of nearly $10,000 per inmate. If every eligible prisoner in the United States

Prison Programs Organized activities for inmates that are designed to improve their physical and mental health, provide them with vocational skills, or simply keep them busy while incarcerated.

received such treatment, the cost would be $12.6 billion. Researchers at CASA contend, however, that "the nation would break even in a year" if just one in ten of these inmates remained substance and crime free and employed for one year after release from prison.[15]

VOCATIONAL AND EDUCATIONAL PROGRAMS
Even if an ex-convict does stay substance free, he or she will have a difficult time finding a steady paycheck. Employers are only about half as likely to hire job applicants with criminal records as they are those with "clean sheets."[16] To overcome this handicap, more than half of all American prisons offer *vocational* training, or prison programs that provide inmates with skills necessary to find a job. Such programs commonly provide instruction in blue-collar fields such as landscaping, automobile repair, and electrical work. Nine out of ten prisons also attempt to educate their inmates, offering literacy training, GED (general equivalency degree) programs, and other types of instruction.[17]

Some evidence suggests that such efforts can have a positive effect on rates of reoffending. A recent study by the nonprofit Rand Corporation, summarizing thirty years of research, found that ex-inmates who participated in education programs from behind bars had a 43 percent lower chance of reoffending within three years after release than those who did not.[18] In addition, the same study found that participation in vocational training improved an inmate's chances of finding post-release employment by 28 percent.[19]

CAREER TIP Most *prison teachers* are either corrections employees who have obtained the necessary certification or civilians with teaching credentials and previous career experience.

12-2 HOW VIOLENT IS LIFE BEHIND BARS?

Prisons and jails are dangerous places to live. Prison culture is predicated on violence—one observer calls the modern institution an "unstable and violent jungle."[20] Correctional officers use the threat of violence (and, at times, actual

Deprivation Model A theory that inmate aggression is the result of the frustration inmates feel at being deprived of freedom, consumer goods, sex, and other staples of life outside the institution.

violence) to control the inmate population. Sometimes, the inmates strike back. According to the National Institute of Justice, about two thousand correctional officers are injured by inmates annually in the United States.[21]

Among the prisoners, violence is used to establish power and dominance. On occasion, this violence leads to death. About seventy inmates in state prisons and twenty inmates in local jails are murdered by fellow inmates each year.[22] (Note, though, that this homicide rate is lower than the national average.) With nothing but time on their hands, prisoners have been known to fashion deadly weapons out of everyday items such as toothbrushes and mop handles. Many inmates also bring the "code of the street," with its fixation on "respect, toughness, and retribution," into prison, making them likely both to engage in violent acts behind bars and to be victims of such violence.[23]

12-2a Violence in Prison Culture

LO12-2 Until the 1970s, prison culture emphasized "noninterference" and did not support inmate-on-inmate violence. Prison "elders" would themselves punish any of their peers who showed a proclivity toward assaulting fellow inmates. Today, in contrast, violence is used to establish the prisoner hierarchy by separating the powerful from the weak. Humboldt State University's Lee H. Bowker has identified several other reasons for violent behavior:

▶ It provides a deterrent against being victimized, as a reputation for violence may eliminate an inmate as a target of assault.

▶ It enhances self-image in an environment that does not respect other attributes, such as intelligence.

▶ In the case of rape, it gives sexual relief.

▶ It serves as a means of acquiring material goods through extortion or outright robbery.[24]

The **deprivation model** can be used to explain the high level of prison violence. According to this model, the stressful and oppressive conditions of prison life lead to aggressive behavior on the part of inmates. Prison researcher Stephen C. Light found that when conditions such as overcrowding worsen, inmate misconduct often increases.[25] In these circumstances, the violent behavior may not have any express purpose—it may just be a means of relieving tension.

12-2b Riots

The deprivation model is helpful, though less convincing, in searching for the roots of collective violence. As far back as the 1930s, sociologist Frank Tannenbaum noted that

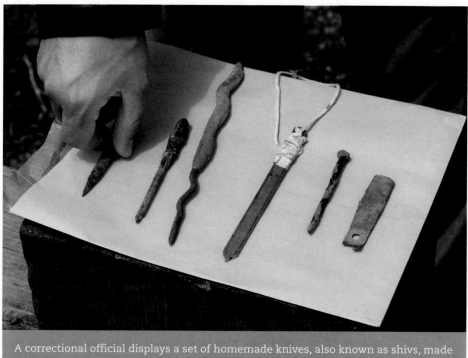

A correctional official displays a set of homemade knives, also known as shivs, made by inmates at Attica Correctional Facility in Attica, New York. *What are some of the reasons that violence flourishes behind bars?*

harsh prison conditions can cause tension to build among inmates until it eventually explodes in the form of mass violence.[26] Living conditions among prisons are fairly constant, however, so how can the seemingly spontaneous outbreak of prison riots be explained?

Researchers have addressed the seeming randomness of prison violence by turning to the concept of **relative deprivation.** These theories focus on the gap between what is expected in a certain situation and what is achieved. Criminologist Peter C. Kratcoski has argued that because prisoners enjoy such meager privileges to begin with, any further deprivation can spark disorder.[27] A number of prison experts have noted that collective violence occurs in response to heightened measures of security at corrections facilities.[28] Thus, the violence is primarily a reaction to additional reductions in freedom for inmates, who enjoy very little freedom to begin with.

Riots, which have been defined as situations in which a number of prisoners are beyond institutional control for a significant amount of time, are relatively rare. These incidents are marked by extreme levels of inmate-on-inmate violence and can often be attributed, at least in part, to poor living conditions and inadequate prison administration. For example, a 2012 riot at the Adams County Correctional Center in Natchez, Mississippi, that left one correctional officer dead and twenty others injured was sparked by inmate protests over poor

food and lack of medical care. Afterwards, a prisoner said, "The guard that died yesterday was a sad tragedy, but the situation is simple: if you treat a human as an animal for over two years, the response will be as an animal."[29]

12-2c Prison Rape

In contrast to riots, the problem of sexual assault in prisons receives relatively little attention from corrections officials and media sources. To remedy this situation, in 2003 Congress passed the Prison Rape Elimination Act, which mandates that prison officials collect data on the extent of the problem in their facilities.[30] According to a recent survey conducted because of this legislation, about 8,800 state prisoners reported having been sexually victimized by other inmates or prison staff during the previous year.[31]

Prison rape, like rape in general, is considered primarily an act of violence rather than sex. Inmates subject to rape ("punks") are near the bottom of the prison power structure and, in some instances, may accept rape by one particularly powerful inmate in return for protection from others.[32] Abused inmates often suffer from rape trauma syndrome and a host of other psychological ailments, including suicidal tendencies. Many prisons do not offer sufficient medical treatment for rape victims, nor does the prison staff take the necessary measures to protect obvious targets of rape—young, slightly built, nonviolent offenders. Furthermore, correctional officials are rarely held responsible for inmate-on-inmate violence.

12-2d Issues of Race and Ethnicity

On the morning of March 11, 2014, a melee involving two hundred African American and Mexican American inmates broke out in the yard of Calipatria State Prison in Calipatria, California. Race plays a major role in prison

Relative Deprivation The theory that inmate aggression is caused when freedoms and services that inmates have come to accept as normal are decreased or eliminated.

AP Images/David Duprey

life, and prison violence is often an outlet for racial tension. As prison populations have changed over the past three decades, with African Americans and Hispanics becoming the majority in many penal institutions, issues of race and ethnicity have become increasingly important to prison administrators and researchers.

SEPARATE WORLDS As early as the 1950s, researchers were noticing different group structures in inmate life. At that time, for example, prisoners at California's Soledad Prison informally segregated themselves according to geography as well as race: Tejanos (Mexicans raised in Texas), Chicanos, blacks from California, blacks from the South and Southwest, and the majority whites all formed separate social worlds.[33]

Khomkrit Phonsai/ShutterStock.com

What are some of the reasons that an inmate would join a prison gang?

Leo Carroll, professor of sociology at the University of Rhode Island, has written extensively about how today's prisoners are divided into hostile groups, with race determining nearly every aspect of an inmate's life, including friends, job assignments, and cell location.[34]

PRISON GANGS In many instances, racial and ethnic identification is the primary focus of the **prison gang**—a clique of inmates who join together in an organizational structure to engage in illegal activity. Gang affiliation is often the cause of inmate-on-inmate violence. For decades, the California prison system has been plagued by feuds involving various gangs such as the Mexican Mafia, composed of U.S.-born inmates of Mexican descent, and their enemies, a spin-off organization called La Nuestra Familia.

In part, the prison gang is a natural result of life in the modern prison. As one expert says of these gangs:

Their members have done in prison what many people do elsewhere when they feel personally powerless,

threatened, and vulnerable. They align themselves with others, organize to fight back, and enhance their own status and control through their connection to a more powerful group.[35]

In addition to their important role in the social structure of correctional facilities, prison gangs participate in a wide range of illegal economic activities within these institutions, including prostitution, drug selling, gambling, and loan sharking. A study released in 2011 by Alan J. Drury and Matt DeLisi of Iowa State University found that gang members were more likely to be involved in prison misconduct than those inmates who had been convicted of murder.[36]

The Prevalence of Prison Gangs The most recent research places the rate of gang membership at 11.7 percent in federal prisons, 13.4 percent in state prisons, and 15.6 percent in jails.[37] When the National Gang Crime Research Center surveyed prison administrators, however, almost 95 percent said that gang recruitment took place at their institutions, so the overall prevalence of gangs is probably much higher.[38] Los Angeles correctional officials believe that eight out of every ten inmates in their city jails are gang affiliated.

Prison Gang A group of inmates who band together within the corrections system to engage in criminal activities.

Combating Prison Gangs In their efforts to combat the influence of prison gangs, over the past decade correctional officials have increasingly turned to the **security threat group (STG)** model. Generally speaking, an STG is an identifiable group with three or more individuals and a leadership structure that poses a threat to the safety of other inmates or members of the corrections community. About two-thirds of all prisons have a correctional officer who acts as an STG coordinator.[39] This official is responsible for classifying individuals who are likely to be involved in STG (though not necessarily prison gang) activity and for taking measures to protect the prison community from these individuals.

In many instances, these measures are punitive. Prison officials, for example, have reduced overall levels of violence significantly by putting gang members in solitary confinement, away from the general prison population. Other punitive measures include restrictions on privileges such as family visits and prison program participation, as well as delays of parole eligibility.[40] Treatment philosophies also have a place in these strategies.

New York prison administrators have increased group therapy and anger-management classes for STGs, a decision they credit for low murder rates in their state prisons.[41]

12-3 HOW DO CORRECTIONAL OFFICERS MAINTAIN DISCIPLINE?

Ideally, the presence of correctional officers—the standard term used to describe prison guards—has the effect of lessening violence in American correctional institutions. Practically speaking, this is indeed the case.

> **Security Threat Group (STG)** A group of three or more inmates who engage in activity that poses a threat to the safety of other inmates or the prison staff.

CONTRABAND CELL PHONES

CJ and Technology

One piece of technology has made the task of controlling prison gangs extremely difficult: the cell phone. Although inmates are prohibited from possessing these devices, cell phones are routinely used to arrange attacks, plan escapes, and operate illegal money-making schemes from behind bars. The phones are usually smuggled in by visitors, who hide them in locations as varied as babies' diapers, food packages, soda cans, and body cavities. Each year, Florida corrections staff confiscate more than four thousand cell phones from prisoners and, as one state official points out, "We know that's not all of them."

Several years ago, forty-four inmates and correctional officers at the Baltimore City Detention Center were arrested for helping to operate the Black Guerrilla Family gang from within the prison using cell phones. In response, the state of Maryland started a managed access program to deal with the problem. This "cellular umbrella" antenna technology is designed to analyze all calls made from the prison and instantly block any that originate from a contraband phone. During a test run

Denis Vrublevski/ShutterStock.com

at a California prison, over the course of eleven days a managed access system blocked 24,190 call attempts from 2,593 unauthorized devices.

Thinking about Contraband Cell Phones
How might correctional officials use confiscated contraband cell phones to combat criminal activity by inmates?

Without correctional officers, the prison would be a place of anarchy. But in the highly regulated, oppressive environment of the prison, correctional officers must use the threat of violence (and, at times, actual violence) to instill discipline and keep order. Thus, the relationship between prison staff and inmates is marked by mutual distrust. Consider the two following statements, the first made by a correctional officer and the second by a prisoner:

> [My job is to] protect, feed, and try to educate scum who raped and brutalized women and children . . . who, if I turn my back, will go into their cell, wrap a blanket around their cellmate's legs, and threaten to beat or rape him if he doesn't give sex, carry contraband, or fork over radios, money, or other goods willingly. And they'll stick a shank in me tomorrow if they think they can get away with it.[42]

> The pigs in the state and federal prisons . . . treat me so violently, I cannot possibly imagine a time I could ever have anything but the deepest, aching, searing hatred for them. I can't begin to tell you what they do to me. If I were weaker by a hair, they would destroy me.[43]

It may be difficult for an outsider to understand the emotions that fuel such sentiments. French philosopher Michel Foucault points out that discipline, both in prison and in the general community, is a means of social organization as well as punishment.[44] Discipline is imposed when a person behaves in a manner that is contrary to the values of the dominant social group. Correctional officers and inmates have different concepts of the ideal structure of prison society, and, as the two quotations just cited demonstrate, this conflict generates intense feelings of fear and hatred, which often lead to violence.

12-3a Rank and Duties of Correctional Officers

The custodial staff at most prisons is organized according to four general ranks—captain, lieutenant, sergeant, and officer. In keeping with the militaristic model, captains are primarily administrators who deal directly with the warden on custodial issues. Lieutenants are the

CORRECTIONAL OFFICER

CareerPrep

Job Description:

▶ Ensure the safety of inmates and other employees of the correctional facility. This includes escorting inmates from their prison cells to other areas of the prison, standing guard over inmates after they have been removed from their cells, searching inmates for forbidden items, and patrolling the prison grounds.

What Kind of Training Is Required?

▶ At the state level, a high school diploma. At the federal level, a bachelor's degree or three years of full-time experience in counseling and supervision.

▶ Written, physical, and psychological examinations and a training period that can last up to six months, depending on the size of the correctional facility.

Annual Salary Range?

▶ $27,000–$70,000

Thinkstock Images/Getty Images

SOCIAL MEDIA CAREER TIP
Don't misrepresent facts or tell lies of omission online. Doing so in front of millions of online viewers ensures that you will almost certainly be caught, and such untruths can fatally damage career possibilities.

disciplinarians of the prison, responsible for policing and transporting the inmates. Sergeants oversee platoons of officers in specific parts of the prison, such as various cell blocks or work spaces.

Lucien X. Lombardo, professor of sociology and criminal justice at Old Dominion University, has identified six general job categories among correctional officers:[45]

1. *Block officers.* These employees supervise cell blocks containing as many as four hundred inmates, as well as the correctional officers on block guard duty. In general, the block officer is responsible for the well-being of the inmates. He or she tries to ensure that the inmates do not harm themselves or other prisoners and also acts as something of a camp counselor, dispensing advice and seeing that inmates understand and follow the rules of the facility.

2. *Work detail supervisors.* In many penal institutions, the inmates work in the cafeteria, the prison store, the laundry, and other areas. Work detail supervisors oversee small groups of inmates as they perform their tasks.

3. *Industrial shop and school officers.* These officers perform maintenance and security functions in workshop and educational programs. Their primary responsibility is to make sure that inmates are on time for these programs and do not cause any disturbances during the sessions.

4. *Yard officers.* Officers who work the prison yard usually have the least seniority, befitting the assignment's reputation as dangerous and stressful. These officers must be constantly on alert for breaches in prison discipline or regulations in the relatively unstructured environment of the prison yard.

5. *Tower guards.* These officers spend their entire shifts, which usually last eight hours, in isolated, silent posts high above the grounds of the facility. Although their only means of communication are walkie-talkies or cellular devices, the safety benefits of the position can outweigh the loneliness that comes with the job.

6. *Administrative building assignments.* Officers who hold these positions provide security at prison gates, oversee visitation procedures, act as liaisons for civilians, and handle administrative tasks such as processing the paperwork when an inmate is transferred from another institution.

12-3b Discipline

As Erving Goffman noted in his essay on the "total institution," in the general society adults are rarely placed in a position where they are "punished" as a child would be.[46] Therefore, the strict disciplinary measures imposed on prisoners come as something of a shock and can provoke strong defensive reactions. Correctional officers who must deal with these responses often find that disciplining inmates is the most difficult and stressful aspect of their job.

SANCTIONING PRISONERS As mentioned earlier, one of the first things that an inmate receives on entering a correctional facility is a manual that details the rules of the prison or jail, along with the punishment that will result from rule violations. These handbooks can be quite lengthy—running one hundred pages in some instances—and specific. Not only will a prison manual prohibit obvious misconduct such as violent or sexual activity, gambling, and possession of drugs or currency, but it also addresses matters of daily life such as personal hygiene, dress codes, and conduct during meals.

Correctional officers enforce the prison rules in much the same way that a highway patrol officer enforces traffic regulations. For a minor violation, the inmate may be "let off easy" with a verbal warning. More serious infractions will result in a "ticket," or a report forwarded to the institution's disciplinary committee.[47] The disciplinary committee generally includes several correctional officers and, in some instances, outside citizens or even inmates. Although, as we shall see, the United States Supreme Court has ruled that an inmate must be given a "fair hearing" before being disciplined, the Court denied inmates the ability to confront adverse witnesses or to consult a lawyer during these hearings.[48] In practice, then, an inmate has very little ability to challenge the committee's decision.

SOLITARY CONFINEMENT Depending on the seriousness of the violation, sanctions can range from a loss of privileges such as visits from family members to the extreme unpleasantness of **solitary confinement.** Although conditions may vary, in general this term refers to the confinement of an inmate alone in a small cell with minimal environmental stimulation or social interaction. In the past, solitary confinement was primarily a disciplinary tool. Today, however, prison officials use it as a form of

Solitary Confinement A disciplinary practice that involves placing the punished inmate in a separate cell to isolate him or her from human contact.

preventive detention for inmates, such as gang members, who are deemed a security risk to themselves or others.

Although critics contend that solitary confinement causes severe damage to the mental health of prisoners, no federal laws control its use. Only one state, Washington, places a limit—twenty days—on the length of time an inmate may be kept in isolation. According to estimates, at least 25,000 inmates—and probably significantly more—are in solitary confinement in American prisons at any given time.[49]

USE OF FORCE Most correctional officers prefer to rely on the "you scratch my back and I'll scratch yours" model for controlling inmates. In other words, as long as the prisoner makes a reasonable effort to conform to institutional rules, the correctional officer will refrain from taking disciplinary steps. Of course, the staff-inmate relationship is not always marked by cooperation, and correctional officers often find themselves in situations where they must use force.

Legitimate Security Interests Generally, courts have been unwilling to put too many restrictions on the use of force by correctional officers. As we saw with police officers in Chapter 5, correctional officers are given great leeway to use their experience to determine when force is warranted. In *Whitley v. Albers* (1986),[50] the Supreme Court held that the use of force by prison officials violates an inmate's Eighth Amendment protections only if the force amounts to "the unnecessary and wanton infliction of pain." Excessive force can be considered "necessary" if the legitimate security interests of the penal institution are at stake.

Courts have found that the "legitimate security interests" of a prison or jail justify the use of force when the correctional officer is

1. **Acting in self-defense.**

2. **Acting to defend the safety of a third person, such as a member of the prison staff or another inmate.**

3. **Upholding the rules of the institution.**

4. **Preventing a crime such as assault, destruction of property, or theft.**

5. **Preventing an escape effort.**[51]

In addition, most prisons and jails have written policies that spell out the situations in which their employees may use force against inmates. (The feature *Discretion in Action—Spitting Mad* describes a use-of-force situation

Discretion in Action

SPITTING MAD

THE SITUATION During a fit of depression caused by the breakup of his marriage, a state prison inmate named Schmidt purposefully tears at a previous wound in his arm. Correctional officers, following the orders of Deputy Warden Wasserman, strap Schmidt into a chair that restricts the inmate's ability to move. As he is being restrained, Schmidt becomes agitated and curses the correctional officers. Then, he spits at a nurse trying to treat his injuries. Wasserman reacts by discharging a can of pepper spray at Schmidt. (When aimed at the face, pepper spray is a nonlethal weapon that causes a sensation similar to having sand or needles in the eyes.) Wasserman then places a spit mask on Schmidt, which traps the chemicals against the offender's skin. Schmidt is not allowed to clean his eyes and nose for nearly half an hour but suffers no lasting physical harm as a result of the pepper spray.

THE LAW In most cases, correctional officers are justified in using force against inmates so long as that force does not cause "unnecessary and wanton" pain. (*Wanton* means "deliberate and unprovoked.")

WHAT WOULD YOU DO? Suppose you are the warden at the prison where this incident took place. Would you discipline Deputy Warden Wasserman for his use of force against Schmidt? Do you think that the steps Wasserman took to restrain Schmidt were justified? What about the use of pepper spray? Keep in mind that a spitting inmate may pose a danger to correctional officers if the inmate has a communicable disease.

[To see how state prison officials in Maine handled a similar situation, go to Example 12.1 in Appendix A.]

involving correctional officers in which an officer's action, though nonlethal, is bound to come under scrutiny.)

The "Malicious and Sadistic" Standard The judicial system has not, however, given correctional officers total freedom of discretion to apply force. In *Hudson v. McMillan* (1992),[52] the Supreme Court ruled that minor injuries suffered by a convict at the hands of a correctional officer following an argument did violate the inmate's rights, because there was no security concern at the time of the incident.

In other words, the issue is not *how much* force was used, but whether the officer used the force as part of a good faith effort to restore discipline or acted "maliciously and sadistically" to cause harm. This "malicious and sadistic" standard has been difficult for aggrieved prisoners to meet: in the ten years following the *Hudson* decision, only about 20 percent of excessive force lawsuits against correctional officials were successful.[53]

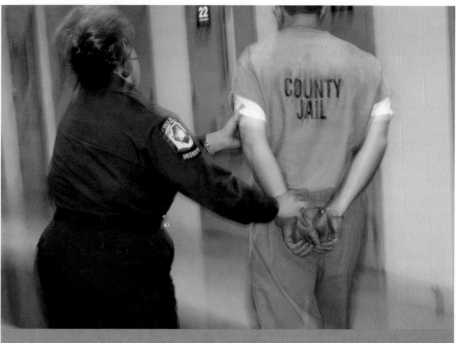

What are some of the challenges that face female correctional officers who work in men's prisons?

12-3c Female Correctional Officers

Security concerns were the main reason that, for many years, prison administrators refused to hire women as correctional officers in men's prisons. The consensus was that women were not physically strong enough to subdue violent male inmates and that their mere presence in the predominantly masculine prison world would cause disciplinary breakdowns.[54] As a result, in the 1970s a number of women brought lawsuits against state corrections systems, claiming that they were being discriminated against on the basis of their gender. For the most part, these legal actions were successful in opening the doors to men's prisons for female correctional officers (and vice versa).[55] Today, more than 150,000 women work in correctional facilities, many of them in constant close contact with male inmates.[56]

As it turns out, female correctional officers have proved just as effective as their male counterparts in maintaining discipline in men's prisons. Furthermore, evidence shows that women prison staff can have a calming influence on male inmates, thus lowering levels of prison violence.[57]

The primary problem caused by women working in male prisons, it seems, involves sexual misconduct. According to the federal government, nearly 55 percent of prison staff members who engage in sexual misconduct are female, with an estimated 84 percent of those sexual encounters considered consensual.[58] As we will see in the next section, similar issues exist between male correctional officers and female inmates, though in those cases the sexual contact is much more likely to be coerced.

12-3d Protecting Prisoners' Rights

The general attitude of the law toward inmates is summed up by the Thirteenth Amendment to the U.S. Constitution:

> Neither slavery nor involuntary servitude, except as a punishment for crime whereof the party shall have been duly convicted, shall exist within the United States.

LO12-3 In other words, inmates do not have the same guaranteed rights as other Americans. For most of the nation's history, courts have followed the spirit of this amendment by applying the **"hands-off" doctrine** of prisoner law. This (unwritten) doctrine

"Hands-Off" Doctrine The unwritten judicial policy that favors noninterference by the courts in the administration of prisons and jails.

assumes that the care of inmates should be left to prison officials and that it is not the place of judges to intervene in penal administrative matters.

At the same time, the United States Supreme Court has stated that "[t]here is no iron curtain between the Constitution and the prisons of this country."[59] Consequently, like so many other areas of the criminal justice system, the treatment of prisoners is based on a balancing act—here, between the rights of prisoners and the security needs of the correctional institutions. Of course, as just noted, inmates do not have the same civil rights as do other members of society. In 1984, for example, the Supreme Court ruled that arbitrary searches of prison cells are allowed under the Fourth Amendment because inmates have no reasonable expectation of privacy[60] (see Chapter 6 for a review of this expectation).

THE "DELIBERATE INDIFFERENCE" STANDARD As for those constitutional rights that inmates do retain, in 1976 the Supreme Court established the **"deliberate indifference"** standard. In the case in question, *Estelle v. Gamble,*[61] an inmate had claimed to be the victim of medical malpractice. As part of his majority opinion, Justice Thurgood Marshall wrote that prison officials violated a convict's Eighth Amendment rights if they "deliberately" failed to provide him or her with necessary medical care. At the time, the decision was hailed as a victory for prisoners' rights, and it continues to ensure that a certain level of health care is provided. Several years ago, for example, a U.S. district court ruled that prison officials at the Louisiana State Penitentiary, site of the prison rodeo discussed at the beginning of the chapter, were "deliberately indifferent" in allowing the heat in that facility's death row to reach levels causing "cruel and unusual" punishment.[62]

In general, however, courts have found it difficult to define "deliberate" in this context. Does it mean that prison officials "should have known" that an inmate was placed in harm's way, or does it mean that officials purposefully placed the inmate in that position?

The Supreme Court seems to have taken the latter position. In *Wilson v. Seiter* (1991),[63] for example, inmate Pearly L. Wilson filed a lawsuit alleging that certain conditions of his confinement—including overcrowding; excessive noise; inadequate heating, cooling, and ventilation; and unsanitary bathroom and dining facilities—were cruel and unusual. The Court ruled against Wilson, stating that he had failed to prove that these conditions, even if they existed, were the result of "deliberate indifference" on the part of prison officials.

"IDENTIFIABLE HUMAN NEEDS" In its *Wilson* decision, the Supreme Court created the **"identifiable human needs"** standard for determining Eighth Amendment violations. The Court asserted that a prisoner must show that the institution has denied her or him a basic need such as food, warmth, or exercise.[64] The Court mentioned only these three needs, however, forcing the lower courts to determine for themselves what other needs, if any, fall into this category.

Because of the Supreme Court's *Estelle* decision described above, prisoners do have a well-established right to "adequate" medical care. "Adequate" has been interpreted to mean a level of care comparable to what the inmate would receive if he or she were not behind bars.[65] This concept has not always proved popular with the general public. In 2012, a federal judge in Boston commanded Massachusetts to cover the costs of gender reassignment surgery for a male inmate who had murdered his wife twelve years earlier. After numerous complaints from taxpayers, the judge rescinded his order. Furthermore, several years ago the Supreme Court asserted, controversially, that the overcrowding of California's state prisons was so severe that it denied inmates satisfactory levels of health care.[66]

12-4 ARE WOMEN'S PRISONS DIFFERENT?

When the first women's prison in the United States opened in 1839 on the grounds of New York's Sing Sing institution, the focus was on rehabilitation. Prisoners were prepared for a return to society with classes on reading, knitting, and sewing. Early women's reformatories had few locks or bars, and several included nurseries for the inmates' young children. Today, the situation is dramatically different. "Women's institutions are literally men's institutions, only we pull out the urinals," remarks Meda Chesney-Lind, a criminologist at the University of Hawaii.[67] Given the different circumstances surrounding male and female incarceration, this uniformity can have serious consequences for the women imprisoned in this country.

"Deliberate Indifference" The standard for establishing a violation of an inmate's Eighth Amendment rights, requiring that prison officials were aware of harmful conditions in a correctional institution *and* failed to take steps to remedy those conditions.

"Identifiable Human Needs" The basic human necessities that correctional facilities are required by the Constitution to provide to inmates.

12-4a Characteristics of Female Inmates

Male inmates outnumber female inmates by approximately nine to one, and there are only about a hundred women's correctional facilities in the United States. Consequently, most research concerning the American corrections system focuses on male inmates and men's prisons. Enough data exist, however, to provide a useful portrait of women behind bars.

Female inmates are typically low income and undereducated, and have a history of unemployment. Female offenders are much less likely than male offenders to have committed a violent offense. Most are incarcerated for a nonviolent drug or property crime.[68] As Figure 12.2 shows, the demographics of female prisoners are similar to those of their male counterparts. That is, the majority of female inmates are under the age of forty, and the population is disproportionately African American.

The single factor that most distinguishes female prisoners from their male counterparts is a history of physical or sexual abuse. A self-reported study conducted by the federal government indicates that 55 percent of female jail inmates have been abused at some point in their lives, compared with only 13 percent of male jail inmates.[69] Fifty-seven percent of women in state prisons and 40 percent of women in federal prisons report some form of past abuse—both figures are significantly higher than those for male prisoners.[70] Health experts believe that these levels of abuse are related to the significant amount of drug and/or alcohol addiction that plagues the female prison population, as well as to the mental illness problems that such addictions can cause or exacerbate.[71]

12-4b The Motherhood Problem

Drug and alcohol use within a women's prison can be a function of the anger and depression many inmates experience due to being separated from their children. An estimated seven out of every ten female prisoners have at least one minor child. About 1.7 million American children have a mother who is under correctional supervision.[72] Given the scarcity of women's correctional facilities, inmates are often housed at great distances

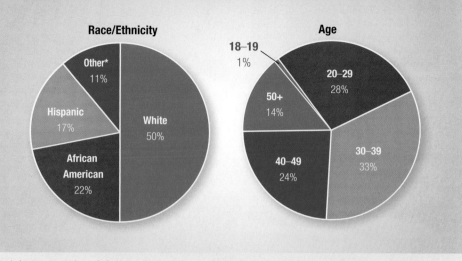

FIGURE 12.2 FEMALE PRISONERS IN THE UNITED STATES BY RACE, ETHNICITY, AND AGE

Race/Ethnicity
- White 50%
- African American 22%
- Hispanic 17%
- Other* 11%

Age
- 18–19 1%
- 20–29 28%
- 30–39 33%
- 40–49 24%
- 50+ 14%

*Includes American Indians, Alaska Natives, Native Hawaiians, other Pacific Islanders, and persons identifying two or more races.
Source: Bureau of Justice Statistics, *Prisoners in 2013* (Washington, D.C.: U.S. Department of Justice, September 2014), Table 7, page 8.

from their children. One study found that almost two-thirds of women in federal prison are more than five hundred miles from their homes.[73]

Further research indicates that an inmate who serves her sentence more than fifty miles from her residence is much less likely to receive phone calls or personal visits from family members. For most inmates and their families, the costs of "staying in touch" are too high.[74]

This kind of separation can have serious consequences for the children of inmates. When a father goes to prison, his children are likely to live with their mother. When a mother is incarcerated, however, her children are likely to live with other relatives or, in about 11 percent of the cases, be sent to foster care.[75] Only nine states provide facilities where inmates and their infant children can live together, and even in these facilities nursery privileges generally end once the child is eighteen months old.

12-4c The Culture of Women's Prisons

After spending five years visiting female inmates in the Massachusetts Correctional Institution (MCI) at Framingham, journalist Cristina Rathbone observed that the medium-security facility seemed "more like a high school than a prison."[76] The prisoners were older and tougher than high school girls, but they still divided into cliques, with the "lifers" at the top of the hierarchy and "untouchables" such as child abusers at the bottom. Unlike in men's prisons, where the underground economy revolves around drugs and weapons, at MCI-Framingham the most treasured contraband items are clothing, food, and makeup.[77]

Explain how a women's prison is typically different from a men's prison when it comes to levels of violence and social interactions between inmates.

engage in sexual activity are not automatically labeled homosexual, and lesbians are not hampered in their social-climbing efforts.[82]

SEXUAL VIOLENCE AND PRISON STAFF Compared with men's prisons, women's prisons have extremely low levels of race-based, gang-related physical aggression.[83] Furthermore, though rates of sexual victimization can be high, most such episodes involve abusive sexual contacts such as unwanted touching rather than sexual assault or rape.[84]

One form of serious prison violence that does plague women prisoners, however, is sexual misconduct by prison staff. Although no large-scale study on sexual abuse of female inmates by male correctional officers exists, a number of state-level studies suggest that it is widespread.[85] Dr. Kerry Kupers, who has studied the effects of prison sexual assault, believes that it contributes to depression, anxiety, and other mental illnesses suffered by so many women prisoners.[86]

THE PSEUDO-FAMILY Although both men's and women's prisons are organized with the same goals of control and discipline, the cultures within the two institutions are generally very different. As we have seen, male prison society operates primarily on the basis of power. Deprived of the benefits of freedom, male prisoners tend to create a violent environment that bears little relation to life on the outside.[78]

In contrast, researchers have found that women prisoners prefer to re-create their outside identities by forming social networks that resemble, as noted earlier, high school cliques or, more commonly, the traditional family structure.[79] In these pseudo-families, inmates often play specific roles, with the more experienced convicts acting as "mothers" to younger, inexperienced "daughters." As one observer noted, the younger women rely on their "moms" for emotional support, companionship, loans, and even discipline.[80]

Such a family unit may have a "married" couple at its head, sometimes with a lesbian assuming the role of the father figure. Indeed, homosexuality in women's prisons often manifests itself through the formation of another traditional family model: the monogamous couple.[81] For the most part, sex between inmates plays a different role in women's prisons than in men's prisons. In the latter, rape is an act of aggression and power rather than sex, and "true" homosexuals are relegated to the lowest rungs of the social hierarchy. By contrast, women inmates who

12-5 WHAT HAPPENS TO EX-INMATES?

On June 16, 2014, police arrested Gary Moran for killing a priest with a handgun in the courtyard of the Mother of Mercy Mission in Phoenix, Arizona. Moran, homeless, had been released from prison only six weeks earlier after serving eight years for aggravated assault with a deadly weapon. In contrast, on his release from California's San Quentin State Prison in 2013, multiple drug offender Eddie Griffin earned an internship with a software firm in San Francisco. After a year of working with him, Griffin's boss praised the ex-inmate's "great work ethic, strong progress, and positive attitude."[87]

Each year, about 630,000 inmates are released from American prisons. The challenge for ex-inmates is to ensure that their post-release experience mirrors that of Eddie Griffin rather than that of Gary Moran. More so

RJ Sangosti/Getty Images

than in the past, however, ex-convicts are not facing this challenge alone. Given the benefits to society of reducing recidivism, corrections officials and community leaders are making unprecedented efforts to help newly released prisoners establish crime-free lives.

12-5a Types of Prison Release

The majority of all inmates leaving prison—about two-thirds—do so through one of the parole mechanisms discussed in Chapter 10. Of the remaining third, most are given an **expiration release.**[88] Also known as "maxing out," expiration release occurs when an inmate has served the maximum amount of time on the initial sentence, minus reductions for good-time credits. On release, the inmate is not subjected to community supervision.

Another, quite rare unconditional release is a **pardon,** a form of executive clemency. The president (on the federal level) and the governor (on the state level) can grant a pardon, or forgive a convict's criminal punishment. Most states have a board of pardons—affiliated with the parole board—that makes recommendations to the governor in cases in which its members believe a pardon is warranted. The majority of pardons involve obvious miscarriages of justice, though sometimes a governor will pardon an individual to remove the stain of conviction from her or his criminal record.

LO12-4

Certain temporary releases also exist. Some inmates, who qualify by exhibiting good behavior and generally proving that they do not represent a risk to society, are allowed to leave the prison on **furlough** for a certain amount of time, usually between a day and a week. At times, a furlough is granted because of a family emergency, such as a funeral. Furloughs can be particularly helpful for an inmate who is nearing release and can use them to ease the readjustment period. Finally, *probation release* occurs following a short period of incarceration at the back end of shock probation, which we discussed in Chapter 10. Generally, however, as you have seen, probationers experience community supervision in place of a prison term.

12-5b The Challenges of Reentry

What steps can corrections officials take to lessen the possibility that ex-convicts will reoffend following their release? Efforts to answer that question have focused on programs that help inmates make the transition from prison to the outside. In past years, these programs would have come under the general heading of "rehabilitation," but today corrections officials and criminologists refer to them as part of the strategy of **prisoner reentry.**

The concept of reentry has come to mean many things to many people. For our purposes, keep in mind the words of Joan Petersilia of the University of California at Irvine, who defines *reentry* as encompassing "all activities and programming conducted to prepare ex-convicts to return safely to the community and to live as law abiding citizens."[89] In other words, whereas rehab is focused on the individual offender, *reentry* encompasses the released convict's relationship with society.

12-5c Barriers to Reentry

Perhaps the largest obstacle to successful prisoner reentry is the simple truth that life behind bars is very different from life on the outside. As one inmate explains, the "rules" of prison survival are hardly compatible with good citizenship:

> An unexpected smile could mean trouble. A man in uniform was not a friend. Being kind was a weakness. Viciousness and recklessness were to be respected and admired.[90]

The prison environment also insulates inmates. They are not required to make the day-to-day decisions that characterize a normal existence beyond prison bars. Depending on the length of incarceration, a released inmate must adjust to an array of economic, technological, and social changes that took place while she or he was behind

Expiration Release The release of an inmate from prison at the end of his or her sentence without any further correctional supervision.

Pardon An act of executive clemency that overturns a conviction and erases mention of the crime from the person's criminal record.

Furlough Temporary release from a prison for purposes of vocational or educational training, to ease the shock of release, or for personal reasons.

Prisoner Reentry A corrections strategy designed to prepare inmates for a successful return to the community and to reduce their criminal activity after release.

bars. Common acts such as using an ATM or a smartphone may be completely alien to someone who has just completed a long prison term.

CHALLENGES OF RELEASE Other obstacles hamper reentry efforts. Housing can be difficult to secure, as many private property owners refuse to rent to someone with a criminal record, and federal and state laws restrict public housing options for ex-convicts. A criminal past also limits the ability to find employment, as does the lack of job skills of someone who has spent a significant portion of his or her life in prison. Research conducted by the Urban Institute found that only about 45 percent of ex-inmates are able to secure employment eight months after being released.[91] Furthermore, these released offenders generally have no means of transporation and no place to live.

These economic barriers can be complicated by the physical and mental condition of the freed convict. We have already discussed the high incidence of substance abuse among prisoners and the health-care needs of aging inmates. In addition, one study concluded that as many as one in five Americans leaving jail or prison is seriously mentally ill.[92] (See Figure 12.3 for a list of the hardships commonly faced by former inmates in their first year out of prison.)

THE THREAT OF RELAPSE All of these problems conspire to make successful reentry difficult to achieve. Perhaps it is not surprising that research conducted by the Pew Center on the States found that 43 percent of ex-prisoners are back in prison or jail within three years of their release dates.[93] These figures highlight the problem of recidivism among those released from incarceration.

Even given the barriers to reentry we have discussed, these rates of recidivism seem improbably high. Regardless of their ability to find a job or housing, many ex-convicts are fated to run afoul of the criminal justice system. Psychologists Edward Zamble and Vernon Quinsey explain the phenomenon as a *relapse process*.[94] Take the hypothetical example of an ex-convict who gets in a minor automobile accident while driving from his home to his job one morning. The person in the other car gets out and starts yelling at the ex-convict, who "relapses" and reacts just as he would have in prison—by punching the other person in the face. The ex-convict is then convicted of assault and battery and given a harsh prison sentence because of his criminal record.

12-5d Promoting Desistance

One ex-inmate compared the experience of being released to entering a "dark room, knowing that there are steps in front of you and waiting to fall."[95] The goal of reentry is to act as a flashlight for convicts by promoting **desistance,** a general term used to describe the continued abstinence from offending and the reintroduction of offenders into society. Certainly, the most important

Desistance The process through which criminal activity decreases and reintegration into society increases over a period of time.

FIGURE 12.3 PRISONER REENTRY ISSUES

1. *Housing.* Nearly two-thirds of the men were living with family members, and about half considered their housing situation "temporary." Many were concerned about their living environment: half said that drug dealing was a major problem in their neighborhoods, and almost 25 percent were living with drug and alcohol abusers.

2. *Employment.* After one year, only about one-third of the former inmates had a full-time job, and another 11 percent were working part-time.

3. *Family and friends.* One in four of the men identified family support as the most important thing keeping them from returning to criminality. Another 16 percent said that avoiding certain people and situations was the most crucial factor in their continued good behavior.

4. *Programs and services.* About two-thirds of the former inmates had taken part in programs and services such as drug treatment and continuing education.

5. *Health.* More than half of the men reported suffering from a chronic health condition, and 29 percent showed symptoms of depression.

6. *Substance use.* About half of the men admitted to weekly drug use or alcohol intoxication. Men who had strong family ties and those who were required to maintain telephone contact with their parole officers were less likely to engage in frequent substance use.

7. *Parole violation and recidivism.* More than half of the former inmates reported that they had violated the conditions of their parole, usually by drug use or having contact with other parolees. Fifteen percent of the men returned to prison in the year after release. Four out of five of the returns were the result of a new crime.

Researchers from the Urban Institute in Washington, D.C., asked nearly three hundred former prisoners (all male) in the Cleveland, Ohio, area about the most pressing issues they faced in their first year after release. The answers provide a useful snapshot of the many challenges of reentry.

Source: Christy A. Visher and Shannon M. E. Courtney, *One Year Out: Experience of Prisoners Returning to Cleveland* (Washington, D.C.: Urban Institute, April 2007), 2.

factor in the process is the individual convict. She or he has to *want* to desist and take steps to do so. In most cases, however, ex-inmates are going to need help—help getting an education, help finding and keeping a job, and help freeing themselves from harmful addictions to drugs and alcohol. Corrections officials are in a good position to offer this assistance, and their efforts in doing so form the backbone of the reentry movement.

Reentry planning starts behind bars. In addition to the rehabilitation-oriented prison programs discussed **LO12-5** earlier in the chapter, most correctional facilities offer "life skills" classes to inmates. This counseling covers topics such as finding and keeping a job, locating a residence, understanding family responsibilities, and budgeting. After release, however, former inmates often find it difficult to continue with educational programs and counseling as they struggle to readjust to life outside prison. Consequently, parole supervising agencies operate a number of programs to facilitate offenders' desistance efforts while, at the same time, protecting the community to the greatest extent possible.

WORK RELEASE As is made clear in Figure 12.3, work and lodging are crucial components of desistance. Corrections officials have several options in helping certain parolees—usually low-risk offenders—find employment and a place to live during the supervision period. Nearly a third of correctional facilities offer **work release programs,** in which prisoners nearing the end of their sentences are given permission to work at paid employment in the community.[96]

HALFWAY HOUSES Inmates on work release either return to the correctional facility in the evening or, under certain circumstances, live in community

Work Release Program Temporary release of convicts from prison for purposes of employment. The offenders may spend their days on the job, but must return to the correctional facility at night and during the weekend.

HALFWAY HOUSE PROGRAM MANAGER

CareerPrep

Job Description:

▸ Coordinate recreational, educational, and vocational counseling and other programs for residents. Also, maintain the security of the house and the residents.

▸ Serve as a mediator between the residents and the community and as an advocate for the halfway house with community groups.

What Kind of Training Is Required?

▸ A bachelor's degree or master's degree in social work, career counseling, criminal justice, or psychology.

▸ Also helpful are internships, volunteer work with a halfway house, or community service work through an agency.

Annual Salary Range?

▸ $41,000–$61,000

Oleksiy Mark/ShutterStock.com

GETTING LINKEDIN

Halfway house employees are expected to be quite versatile. Among the requirements listed in a recent LinkedIn posting for a resident counselor in Des Moines, Iowa, was the ability to provide "education and treatment support" in the areas of "chemical dependency, daily living skills, parenting, self-sufficiency, behavioral/mental health, and relationships."

residential facilities known as **halfway houses.** These facilities, also available to other parolees and those who have finished their sentences, are often remodeled hotels or private homes. They provide a less institutionalized living environment than a prison or jail for a small number of offenders (usually between ten and twenty-five). Halfway houses can be tailored to the needs of the former inmate. Many communities, for example, offer substance-free transitional housing for those whose past criminal behavior was linked to drug or alcohol abuse.

12-5e The Special Case of Sex Offenders

Despite the beneficial impact of reentry efforts, one group of wrongdoers has consistently been denied access to such programs: those convicted of sex crimes. The eventual return of these offenders to society causes such high levels of community anxiety that the criminal justice system has not yet figured out what to do with them.

FEAR OF SEX OFFENDERS When sixty-three-year-old Christopher Hubbart, called the "Pillowcase Rapist" because he used that item to muffle the screams of his nearly forty victims, was released in Antelope Valley, California, in 2014, community members were outraged. "It scares the hell out of me," said one resident. "He's going to attack somebody again, and he's going to take someone's life."[97] To a large degree, this attitude reflects the widespread belief that convicted sex offenders cannot be "cured" of their criminality and therefore are destined to continue committing sex offenses after their release from prison.

It is true that the medical health profession has had little success in treating the "urges" that lead to sexually deviant or criminal behavior.[98] This has not, however, translated into rampant recidivism among sex offenders when compared to other types of criminals. According to the U.S. Department of Justice, the rearrest rates of rapists (46 percent) and those convicted of other forms of sexual assault (41 percent) are among the lowest for all offenders.[99]

Halfway House A community-based form of early release that places inmates in residential centers and allows them to reintegrate with society.

Furthermore, after analyzing eighty-two recidivism studies, Canadian researchers R. Karl Hanson and Kelly Morton-Bourgon found that only 14 percent of sex offenders were apprehended for another sex crime after release from prison or jail. On average, such offenders were significantly more likely to be rearrested for nonsexual criminal activity, if they were rearrested at all.[100]

CONDITIONS OF RELEASE Whatever their recidivism rates, sex offenders are subject to extensive community supervision after being released from prison. Generally, they are supervised by parole officers and live under the same threat of revocation as other parolees. Specifically, many sex offenders—particularly child molesters—have the following special conditions of release:

▸ No contact with children under the age of eighteen.

▸ Psychiatric treatment.

▸ Must stay a certain distance from schools or parks where children are present.

▸ Cannot own toys that may be used to lure children.

▸ Cannot have a job or participate in any activity that involves children.

Furthermore, more than half of the states and hundreds of municipalities have passed *residency restrictions* for convicted sex offenders. These laws ban sex offenders from living within a certain distance of places where children naturally congregate.

SEX OFFENDER NOTIFICATION LAWS Perhaps the most dramatic step taken by criminal justice authorities to protect the public from sex crimes involves *sex offender registries,* or databases that contain sex offenders' names, addresses, photographs, and other information. The movement to register sex offenders started about two decades ago, after seven-year-old Megan Kanka of Hamilton Township, New Jersey, was raped and murdered by a twice-convicted pedophile (an adult sexually attracted to children) who had moved into her neighborhood after being released from prison on parole.

The next year, in response to public outrage, the state passed a series of laws known collectively as the New Jersey Sexual Offender Registration Act, or "Megan's Law."[101] Today, all fifty states and the federal government have their own version of Megan's Law, or a

Residents of Phelan, California, protest the opening of a proposed group home for sex offenders in their neighborhood. *What are some of the reasons that community members fear the nearby presence of freed sex offenders? Are these fears justified? Why or why not?*

their midst. In general, the laws demand that a paroled sex offender notify local law enforcement authorities on taking up residence in a state. In Georgia, for example, paroled sex offenders are required to present themselves to both the local sheriff and the superintendent of the public school district where they plan to live.[102] This registration process must be renewed every time the parolee changes address.

The authorities, in turn, notify the community of the sex offender's presence through the use of one of two models. Under the "active" model, the authorities directly notify the community or community representatives. Traditionally, this notification has taken the form of bulletins or posters, distributed and posted within a certain distance from the offender's home. Now, however, a number of states use e-mail alerts to fulfill notification obligations. In the "passive" model, information on sex offenders is made open and available for public scrutiny.

Prevalence of Sex Offender Registries In 2006, Congress passed the Adam Walsh Child Protection and Safety Act, which established a national registry of sex offenders.[103] In addition, all fifty states operate sex offender registries with data on registered sex offenders in their jurisdictions. (For an idea of how this process works, you can visit the Federal Bureau of Investigation's Sex Offender Registry Web site.) The total number of registered sex offenders in the United States is about 800,000.

CIVIL CONFINEMENT To many, any type of freedom, even if encumbered by notification requirements, is too much freedom for a sex offender. "The issue is, what can you do short of putting them all in prison for the rest of their lives?" complained one policymaker.[104]

sex offender notification law, which requires local law authorities to alert the public when a sex offender has been released into the community.

Active and Passive Notification No two sex offender notification laws have exactly the same provisions, but all are designed with the goal of allowing the public to learn the identities of convicted sex offenders living in

> **Sex Offender Notification Law** Legislation that requires law enforcement authorities to notify people when convicted sex offenders are released into their neighborhood or community.

In fact, a number of states have devised a legal method to keep sex offenders off the streets for, if not their entire lives, then close to it. These **civil confinement** laws allow corrections officials to keep sex offenders locked up in noncorrectional facilities such as psychiatric hospitals after the conclusion of their prison terms. Under these laws, sexual criminals deemed a "danger to society" do not enjoy the same rights as other offenders regarding release from incarceration. In practice, civil confinement laws essentially give the state the power to detain this class of criminal indefinitely—a power upheld by the United States Supreme Court in 2010.[105]

Civil Confinement The practice of confining individuals against their will in noncorrectional facilities if they present a danger to the community.

STUDY TOOLS 12

READY TO STUDY? IN THE BOOK, YOU CAN:

☐ Rip out the Chapter Review Card, which includes key terms and chapter summaries.

ONLINE AT WWW.CENGAGEBRAIN.COM, YOU CAN:

☐ Learn about women who have committed identity theft in a short video.

☐ Dig deeper into social media by viewing a few tweets from staff at America's prisons and jails.

☐ Interact with figures from the text, and watch quick animation clips.

☐ Prepare for tests with quizzes.

☐ Review the key terms with Flash Cards.

Quiz

1. Prison culture is different from the cultures of schools or workplaces because prison is a _____ _____ that dominates every aspect of the inmate's life.

2. In recent decades, the prison culture has been affected by the increased average age of inmates, which has led to skyrocketing _____-_____ costs for federal and state corrections systems.

3. The concept of _____ _____, based on the gap between an inmate's expectations and reality, is used to explain the conditions that lead to prison riots.

4. Correctional officers may use force against inmates when a _____ security interest is being served.

5. Courts will not accept any force on the part of correctional officers that is "_____ and sadistic."

6. To prove that prison officials violated constitutional prohibitions against cruel and unusual punishment, the inmate must first show that the officials demonstrated "_____ indifference" in taking or not taking an action.

7. While levels of physical violence are relatively low in women's prisons, female inmates do face a greater threat of sexual assault from _____ _____ than male inmates do.

8. One way in which the corrections system tries to help inmates prepare for release is by offering _____ programs that include job training and work release opportunities.

9. Corrections officials promote desistance by allowing certain low-risk offenders to live in _____ houses, where they can receive specialized attention and treatment.

10. Sex offender _____ laws mandate that law enforcement officials alert the public when a sex offender has moved into the community.

Answers can be found in the Answers section in the back of the book.

13 The Juvenile Justice System

LEARNING OBJECTIVES

After studying this chapter, you will be able to . . .

 13-1 List the four major differences between juvenile courts and adult courts.

13-2 Identify and briefly describe the single most important United States Supreme Court case with respect to juvenile justice.

13-3 Describe the reasoning behind recent United States Supreme Court decisions that have lessened the harshness of sentencing outcomes for violent juvenile offenders.

 13-4 Describe the one variable that always correlates highly with juvenile crime rates.

13-5 Describe the four primary stages of pretrial juvenile justice procedure.

After you finish

this chapter, go

to **PAGES**

292–293 for

STUDY TOOLS

Life Lessened

When Ronald Salazar's mother and father left their native El Salvador to come to the United States, they decided that their son was too young to make the journey. So, they left him behind. For next the twelve years, Salazar was raised by grandparents who abused him, living in dire poverty and running with street gangs. By the time he finally joined his parents in Miami, they had three daughters and seemingly little affection for the long-lost "black sheep" of the family. Salazar responded by acting violently and, at the age of fourteen, was briefly hospitalized for a psychological evaluation after threatening to kill himself and his three sisters.

In 2005, on returning home from the hospital, Salazar did kill his eleven-year-old sister, Marina, strangling and raping her before slitting her throat. He was convicted of first degree murder and, under Florida law, given an automatic sentence of life in prison without the possibility of parole. Salazar seemed fated to spend the rest of his days behind bars until 2012, when the United States Supreme Court banned mandatory life sentences without parole for juvenile murderers. With its ruling, the Court opened the possibility that all such sentences could be reevaluated to determine whether the offender deserved a lesser punishment.

Consequently, in 2015, a tearful twenty-four-year-old Salazar found himself back in state court, telling Circuit Judge Ellen Sue Venzer, "My whole life has been messed up." Prosecutors argued strenuously against showing Salazar any leniency, comparing him to a character from a "bad slasher movie" who should never be let "loose on the streets." Following the hearing, however, Judge Venzer reduced Salazar's sentence to forty years in prison, meaning that he will likely go free in his mid-fifties. "You would have to admit that [this] fourteen-year-old kid had a horrific first fourteen years," said the judge, explaining her decision.

In 2015, a Florida judge reduced the sentence of Ronald Salazar, shown here, from life without parole to forty years for raping and killing his sister when he was fourteen years old. *What is your opinion of the judge's decision in this case?*

Peter Andrew Bosch/*Miami Herald*/MCT/Tribune News Service/Getty Images

13-1 WHY DO WE HAVE A SEPARATE JUSTICE SYSTEM FOR JUVENILES?

A difficult question—asked every time a younger offender such as Ronald Salazar commits a heinous act of violence—lies at the heart of the juvenile justice debate: Should such acts by youths be given the same weight as those committed by adults, or should they be seen as "mistakes" that can be corrected by care and counseling?

From its earliest days, the American juvenile justice system has operated as an uneasy compromise between "rehabilitation and punishment, treatment and custody."[1] At the beginning of the 1800s, juvenile offenders were treated the same as adult offenders—they were judged by the same courts and sentenced to the same severe penalties. This situation began to change soon after, as urbanization and industrialization created an immigrant underclass that was, at least in the eyes of many reformers, predisposed to deviant activity. Certain members of the Progressive movement, known as the child savers, began to take steps to "save" children from these circumstances, introducing the idea of rehabilitating delinquents in the process.

13-1a The Child-Saving Movement

In general, the child savers favored the doctrine of *parens patriae,* which holds that the state has not only a right but also a duty to care for children who are neglected, delinquent, or in some other way disadvantaged. Juvenile offenders, the child savers believed, required treatment, not punishment, and they were horrified at the thought of placing children in prisons with hardened adult criminals. In 1967, then Supreme Court justice Abe Fortas said of the child savers:

> They believed that society's role was not to ascertain whether the child was "guilty" or "innocent," but "What is he, how has he become what he is, and what had best be done in his interest and in the interest of the state to save him from a downward career." The child—essentially good, as they saw it—was made "to feel that he is the object of [the government's] care and solicitude," not that he was under arrest or on trial.[2]

Child-saving organizations convinced local legislatures to pass laws that allowed them to take control of children who exhibited criminal tendencies or had been neglected by their parents. To separate these children from the environment in which they were raised, the organizations created a number of institutions, the best known of which was New York's House of Refuge.

Opening in 1825, the House of Refuge implemented many of the same reformist measures popular in the penitentiaries of the time, meaning that its charges were subjected to the healthful influences of hard study and labor. Although the House of Refuge was criticized for its harsh discipline (which caused many boys to run away), similar institutions sprang up throughout the Northeast during the middle of the 1800s.

13-1b The Illinois Juvenile Court

The efforts of the child savers culminated with the passage of the Illinois Juvenile Court Act in 1899. The Illinois legislature created the first court specifically for juveniles, guided by the principles of *parens patriae* and based on the belief that children are not fully responsible for criminal conduct and are capable of being rehabilitated.[3]

The Illinois Juvenile Court and those in other states that followed in its path were (and, in many cases, remain) drastically different from adult courts:

LO13-1

▶ *No juries.* The matter was decided by judges who wore regular clothes instead of black robes and sat at a table with the other participants rather than behind a bench. Because the primary focus of the court was on the child and not the crime, the judge had wide discretion in disposing of each case.

▶ *Different terminology.* To reduce the stigma of criminal proceedings, "petitions" were issued instead of "warrants." The children were not "defendants," but "respondents," and they were not "found guilty" but "adjudicated delinquent."

▶ *No adversarial relationship.* Instead of trying to determine guilt or innocence, the parties involved in the juvenile court worked together in the best interests of the child, with the emphasis on rehabilitation rather than punishment.

▶ *Confidentiality.* To avoid "saddling" the child with a criminal past, juvenile court hearings and records were kept sealed, and the proceedings were closed to the public.

By 1945, every state had a juvenile court system modeled after the first Illinois court. For the most part, these courts were able to operate without interference until the 1960s and the onset of the juvenile rights movement.

13-1c Status Offending

After the first juvenile court was established in Illinois, the Chicago Bar Association described its purpose as, in part, to "exercise the same tender solicitude and care over its neglected wards that a wise and loving parent would exercise with reference to his [or her] own children under similar circumstances."[4] In other words, the state was given the responsibility of caring for those minors whose behavior seemed to show that they could not be controlled by their parents.

As a result, many **status offenders** found themselves in the early houses of refuge and continue to be placed in state-run facilities today. A status offense is an act that, if committed by a juvenile, is considered illegal and grounds for possible state custody. The same act, if committed by an adult, does not warrant law enforcement action. (See Figure 13.1 for an idea of which status offenses are most commonly brought to the attention of authorities.)

CAREER TIP Most states have attendance laws that require students to be in school during school hours. These states employ *truancy officers* to enforce such laws by working with parents and investigating suspicious patterns of absence.

Parens Patriae A doctrine that holds that the state has a responsibility to look after the well-being of children and to assume the role of parent if necessary.

Status Offender A juvenile who has engaged in behavior deemed unacceptable for those under a certain statutorily determined age.

FIGURE 13.1 STATUS OFFENSES

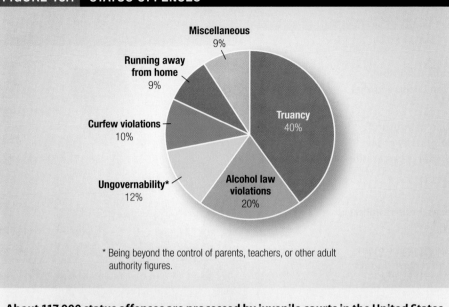

Miscellaneous 9%

Running away from home 9%

Curfew violations 10%

Ungovernability* 12%

Truancy 40%

Alcohol law violations 20%

* Being beyond the control of parents, teachers, or other adult authority figures.

About 117,000 status offenses are processed by juvenile courts in the United States each year. The most common, as this graph shows, are truancy (skipping school) and liquor-related offenses.

Source: Sarah Hockenberry and Charles Puzzanchera, *Juvenile Court Statistics, 2011* (Pittsburgh, Pa.: National Center for Juvenile Justice, July 2014), 66.

13-1d Juvenile Delinquency

In contrast to status offending, **juvenile delinquency** refers to conduct that would also be criminal if committed by an adult. According to federal law and the laws of most states, a juvenile delinquent is someone who has not yet reached his or her eighteenth birthday—the age of adult criminal responsibility—at the time of the offense in question. In two states (New York and North Carolina), persons aged sixteen are considered adults, and twelve other states confer adulthood on seventeen-year-olds for purposes of criminal law.

Under certain circumstances, discussed later in this chapter, children under these ages can be tried in adult courts and incarcerated in adult prisons and jails. Remember that Ronald Salazar was fourteen years old when he was charged as an adult for the rape and murder of his eleven-year-old sister, described in the opening of the chapter. By contrast, in 2013, high school football players Trent Mays, aged seventeen, and Ma'lik Richmond, aged sixteen, were found to be *delinquent beyond a reasonable doubt* of sexually assaulting an intoxicated sixteen-year-old girl in Steubenville, Ohio. Because they were adjudicated as juveniles, Mays and Richmond cannot be incarcerated past their twenty-first birthdays. Salazar, charged as an adult, faced the possibility of spending the rest of his life behind bars.

13-1e Constitutional Protections and the Juvenile Court

Though the ideal of the juvenile court seemed to offer the "best of both worlds" for juvenile offenders, in reality the lack of procedural protections led to many children being arbitrarily punished not only for crimes, but for status offenses as well. Juvenile judges were treating all violators similarly, which led to many status offenders being incarcerated in the same institutions as violent delinquents. In response to a wave of lawsuits demanding due process rights for juveniles, the United States Supreme Court issued several rulings in the 1960s and 1970s that significantly changed the juvenile justice system.

KENT V. UNITED STATES The first decision to extend due process rights to children in juvenile courts was *Kent v. United States* (1966).[5] The case concerned sixteen-year-old Morris Kent, who had been arrested for breaking into a woman's house, stealing her purse, and raping her. Because Kent was on juvenile probation, the state sought to transfer his trial for the crime to an adult court (a process to be discussed later in the chapter).

Without giving any reasons for his decision, the juvenile judge consented to this strategy, and Kent was sentenced in the adult court to a thirty- to ninety-year prison term. The Supreme Court overturned the sentence, ruling that juveniles have a right to counsel and a hearing in any instance in which the juvenile judge is considering sending the case to an adult court. The Court stated that, in such cases, a child receives "the worst of both worlds," getting neither the "protections accorded to adults" nor the "solicitous care and regenerative treatment" offered in the juvenile system.[6]

Juvenile Delinquency Behavior that is illegal under federal or state law that has been committed by a person who is under an age limit specified by statute.

Job Description:

▶ Provide safety, security, custodial care, discipline, and guidance for youths held in juvenile correctional facilities.

▶ Play a critical role in the rehabilitation of youthful offenders and, as a result, have a potentially great impact on their success during and after incarceration.

What Kind of Training Is Required?

▶ A bachelor's degree in human services, behavioral science, or a related field.

▶ Professional communication skills and commitment and dedication to the needs of adolescent offenders and their families.

Annual Salary Range?

▶ $33,000–$52,000

iStockPhoto.com/lisafx

SOCIAL MEDIA CAREER TIP
Potential employers want information about you, but they do not want your life story. To capitalize on two primary benefits of social media, personalize your message and be concise.

LO13-2 **IN RE GAULT** The *Kent* decision provided the groundwork for *In re Gault* one year later. Considered by many to be the single most important case concerning juvenile justice, *In re Gault* involved a fifteen-year-old boy who was arrested for allegedly making a lewd phone call while on probation.[7] In its decision, the Supreme Court held that juveniles facing a loss of liberty were entitled to many of the same basic procedural safeguards granted to adult offenders in this country. These safeguards include notice of charges, the right to counsel, the privilege against self-incrimination, and the right to confront and cross-examine witnesses.

OTHER IMPORTANT COURT DECISIONS Over the next ten years, the Supreme Court handed down three more important rulings on juvenile court procedure. The ruling in *In re Winship* (1970)[8] required the government to prove "beyond a reasonable doubt" that a juvenile had committed an act of delinquency, raising the burden of proof from a "preponderance of the evidence."

In *Breed v. Jones* (1975),[9] the Court held that the Fifth Amendment's double jeopardy clause prevented a juvenile from being tried in an adult court for a crime that had already been adjudicated in juvenile court. In contrast, the decision in *McKeiver v. Pennsylvania* (1971)[10] represented an instance in which the Court did not move the juvenile court further toward the adult model. In that case, the Court ruled that the Constitution did not give juveniles the right to a jury trial.

13-2 HOW IS DELINQUENCY DETERMINED?

In the eyes of many observers, the net effect of the Supreme Court decisions during the 1966–1975 period was to move juvenile justice away from the ideals of the child savers. As a result of these decisions, many young offenders would find themselves in a formalized system that is often indistinguishable from its adult counterpart. At the same time, though the Court has recognized that minors charged with crimes possess certain constitutional rights, it has failed to dictate at what age these rights should be granted. Consequently, the legal status of children in the United States varies depending on where they live, with each state making its own policy decisions on the crucial questions of age and competency.

13-2a The Age Question

On the morning of May 31, 2014, two twelve-year-old girls invited a friend to go with them to a park in Waukesha, Wisconsin. The pair proceeded to stab the other girl nineteen times with a kitchen knife, leaving her for dead among the trees. Afterward, the two girls explained their actions as an attempt to impress Slender Man, a fictional horror character popular on the Internet. "Many people do not believe Slender Man is real," one of the girls told the police. "[We] wanted to prove the skeptics wrong."[11]

In Chapter 3, we saw that early American criminal law recognized infancy as a defense against criminal charges. On attaining fourteen years of age, a youth was considered an adult and treated accordingly by the criminal justice system. Today, as Figure 13.2 shows, the majority of states (as well as the District of Columbia) allow for the prosecution of juveniles under the age of fourteen as adults. Even though Wisconsin does not allow for the prosecution of twelve-year-olds as adults, prosecutors decided to charge the Waukesha girls with attempted first degree homicide, which automatically placed them in adult court regardless of their ages.

In March 2015, a circuit judge upheld this decision, meaning that both girls faced up to sixty-five years in prison if found guilty. Their lawyers had argued that, due to their age, the girls should have been charged as juveniles with attempted second degree homicide. When young offenders who remain in juvenile court are found guilty, they receive "limited" sentences that usually expire when they turn eighteen or twenty-one. Under Wisconsin law, such offenders cannot be incarcerated in a juvenile corrections facility past their twenty-fifth birthdays.[12]

13-2b The Culpability Question

Many researchers believe that by the age of fourteen, an adolescent has the same ability as an adult to make a competent decision. Nevertheless, according to some observers, a juvenile's capacity to understand the difference between "right" and "wrong" does not mean that she or he should be held to the same standards of competency as an adult.

JUVENILE BEHAVIOR A study released in 2003 by the Research Network on Adolescent Development and Juvenile Justice found that 33 percent of juvenile defendants in criminal courts had the same low level of understanding of legal matters as mentally ill adults who had been found incompetent to stand trial.[13] Legal psychologist Richard E. Redding believes that

> adolescents' lack of life experience may limit their real-world decision-making ability. Whether we call it wisdom, judgment, or common sense, adolescents may not have nearly enough.[14]

Juveniles are generally more impulsive, more likely to engage in risky behavior, and less likely to calculate the long-term consequences of any particular action. Furthermore, adolescents are far more likely to respond to peer pressure than are adults. The desire for acceptance and approval may drive them to commit crimes: juveniles are arrested as part of a group at much higher rates than adults.[15] Furthermore, juveniles are less likely than adults to display remorse immediately following a violent act. As a result, they are often penalized by the courts for showing "less grief than the system demands."[16]

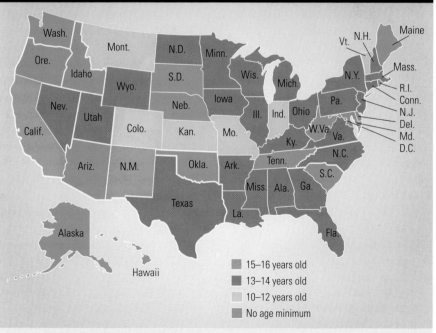

FIGURE 13.2 THE MINIMUM AGE AT WHICH A JUVENILE CAN BE TRIED AS AN ADULT

- 15–16 years old
- 13–14 years old
- 10–12 years old
- No age minimum

Source: Patrick Griffin, et al., *Trying Juveniles as Adults: An Analysis of State Transfer Laws and Reporting* (Washington, D.C.: Office of Juvenile Justice and Delinquency Prevention, September 2011).

LO13-3 **DIMINISHED GUILT** The "diminished culpability" of juveniles was one of the reasons given by the United States Supreme Court in its landmark decision in *Roper v. Simmons* (2005).[17] As we saw in Chapter 9, that case forbade the execution of offenders who were under the age of eighteen when they committed their crimes. In his majority opinion, Justice Anthony Kennedy wrote that because minors cannot fully comprehend the consequences of their actions, the two main justifications for the death penalty—retribution and deterrence—do not "work" with juvenile wrongdoers.[18]

The Graham Case The Supreme Court applied the same reasoning in two later cases that have dramatically affected the sentencing of violent juvenile offenders. First, in *Graham v. Florida* (2010),[19] the Court held that juveniles who commit crimes that do not involve murder may not be sentenced to life in prison without the possibility of parole. According to Justice Kennedy, who wrote the majority opinion, state officials must give these inmates "some meaningful opportunity to obtain release based on demonstrated maturity and rehabilitation."[20]

The Miller Case Then, with *Miller v. Alabama* (2012),[21] the Court banned laws in twenty-eight states that made life-without-parole sentences *mandatory* for juveniles

In 2014, Trenton Barnes, center, was sentenced to fifty years in prison without parole for committing murder as a juvenile. *According to the Supreme Court's* Miller *ruling, could the South Carolina judge have sentenced Barnes to life in prison without parole? Why or why not?*

convicted of murder. The case focused on the fate of Evan Miller, who was fourteen years old when he killed a neighbor with a baseball bat. The ruling did not signify that juvenile offenders such as Miller could not, under any circumstances, be sentenced to life without parole. Rather, the Court stated that judges must have the discretion to weigh the mitigating factors in each individual case.

For example, Miller had been abused by his stepfather and neglected by his alcoholic and drug-addicted mother, had spent most of his life in foster care, and had tried to commit suicide four times.[22] According to the Court, this type of personal history must be taken into account when determining the proper sentence for a juvenile murderer. Such mitigating factors may indicate that the offender has the potential to be rehabilitated and therefore should be afforded the possibility of parole.

13-3 HOW MUCH JUVENILE DELINQUENCY IS THERE IN THE UNITED STATES?

When asked, juveniles will admit to a wide range of illegal or dangerous behavior, including carrying weapons, getting involved in physical fights, driving after drinking alcohol, and stealing or deliberately damaging school property.[23] Has the juvenile justice system been effective in controlling and preventing this kind of misbehavior, as well as more serious acts?

To answer this question, many observers turn to the Federal Bureau of Investigation's Uniform Crime Report (UCR), initially covered in Chapter 2. Because the UCR breaks down arrest statistics by age of the arrestee, it has been considered the primary source of information on the presence of juveniles in America's justice system.

13-3a Delinquency by the Numbers

Generally speaking, UCR findings give a useful account of the extent of juvenile delinquency in the United States. In 2013, juveniles accounted for 11.1 percent of violent crime arrests and 9.7 percent of criminal activity arrests in general.[24] According to the UCR, that year juveniles were responsible for

The State/Getty Images

- 7 percent of all murder arrests.
- 9 percent of all aggravated assault arrests.
- 15 percent of all forcible rapes.
- 15 percent of all weapons arrests.
- 20 percent of all robbery arrests.
- 16 percent of all Part I property crimes.
- 8 percent of all drug offenses.

13-3b The Rise and Fall of Juvenile Crime

As Figure 13.3 shows, juvenile arrest rates for violent crimes have fluctuated dramatically over the past three decades. In the 2000s, with a few exceptions, juvenile crime in the United States has decreased at a rate similar to that of adult crime, as discussed earlier in this textbook. From 2002 to 2011, juvenile court delinquency caseloads declined by 26 percent.[25] Not surprisingly, the drop in juvenile arrests and court appearances has led to fewer juveniles behind bars. The national population of juvenile inmates decreased 18 percent between 2008 and 2010, allowing officials in some states, including California, Ohio, and Texas, to close juvenile detention facilities.[26]

A number of theories have been put forth to explain this downturn in juvenile offending. Some observers point to the increase in police action against "quality-of-life" crimes such as loitering, which they believe stops juveniles before they have a chance to commit more serious crimes. Similarly, about 80 percent of American municipalities enforce juvenile curfews, which restrict the movement of minors during certain hours, usually after dark.[27] In 2013, law enforcement made about 56,000 arrests for curfew and loitering law violations.[28]

Furthermore, hundreds of local programs designed to educate children about the dangers of drugs and crime operate across the country. Though the results of such community-based efforts are difficult, if not impossible, to measure—it cannot be assumed that children would have become delinquent if they had not participated—these programs are generally considered a crucial element of keeping youth crime under control.[29]

13-3c Girls in the Juvenile Justice System

Although overall rates of juvenile offending have been dropping, arrest rates for girls are declining more slowly than those for boys. Between 1997 and 2011, the number of cases involving males in delinquency courts declined 38 percent, while the female caseload in such courts declined by 22 percent.[30] Self-reported studies show, however, that there has been little change in girls' violent behavior over the past few decades.[31] How, then, do we explain why arrest rates for girls have changed and why the change is different from that for boys?

A GROWING PRESENCE Although girls have for the most part been treated more harshly than boys for status offenses,[32] a "chivalry effect" has traditionally existed in other areas of the juvenile justice system. In the past, police were likely to arrest offending boys while allowing girls engaging in similar behavior to go home to the care of their families. This is no longer the case. According

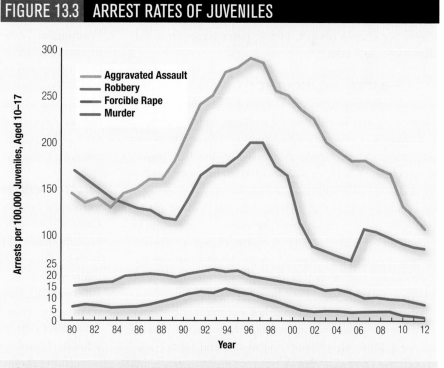

FIGURE 13.3 ARREST RATES OF JUVENILES

Aggravated Assault
Robbery
Forcible Rape
Murder

Arrests per 100,000 Juveniles, Aged 10–17

Year

After rising dramatically in the mid-1990s, juvenile arrest rates for violent crimes have—with a few exceptions—continued to drop steadily in the 2000s.

Source: Office of Juvenile Justice and Delinquency Prevention, *Statistical Briefing Book*, at **ojjdp.gov/ojstatbb/crime/JAR.asp.**

A police officer interviews two teenage girls who were involved in a fight in Tucson, Arizona. *Do you think that law enforcement is likely to treat girls more harshly than boys for this type of misbehavior? Why?*

that such behavior is considered normal for boys, but is seen as deviant for girls and therefore more deserving of punishment.[38]

13-3d School Violence and Bullying

One late Friday morning in October 2014, fourteen-year-old Jaylen Fryberg brought a .40 caliber Beretta handgun into the cafeteria of Marysville-Pilchuck High School in Marysville, Washington. Fryberg opened fire, killing four friends before fatally turning the weapon on himself. The incident was every student's (and teacher's and parent's) worst nightmare. Like other episodes of school violence, it received heavy media coverage, fanning fears that our schools are unsafe.

to the Office of Juvenile Justice and Delinquency Prevention, juvenile courts handled 55 percent more cases involving girls in 2011 as they did in 1985.[33] A particular problem area for girls appears to be the crime of assault. In 2013, females accounted for 23 percent of all juvenile arrests for aggravated assault and 28 percent of those arrests for simple assault, higher percentages than for other violent crimes.[34]

FAMILY-BASED DELINQUENCY Criminologists disagree on whether rising arrest rates for female juveniles reflect a change in behavior or a change in law enforcement practices. A significant amount of data supports the latter proposal, especially research showing that police are much more likely to make arrests in situations involving domestic violence than they were even a decade ago. Experts have found that girls are four times more apt to fight with parents or siblings than are boys, who usually engage in violent encounters with strangers. Consequently, a large percentage of female juvenile arrests for assault arise out of family disputes—arrests that until relatively recently would not have been made.[35]

Evidence also shows that law enforcement agents continue to treat girls more harshly for some status offenses. More girls than boys are arrested for the status offense of running away from home,[36] for example, even though studies show that male and female juveniles run away from home with equal frequency.[37] Criminologists who focus on issues of gender hypothesize

SAFE SCHOOLS Research does show that juvenile victimization and delinquency rates increase during the school day, and the most common juvenile crimes, such as simple assaults, are most likely to take place on school grounds.[39] In spite of well-publicized mass shootings such as the one carried out by Jaylen Fryberg in Marysville, Washington, however, violent crime is not commonplace in American schools. In fact, school-age youths are more than fifty times more likely to be murdered away from school than on a campus.[40] Furthermore, despite a slight increase in recent years, between 1995 and 2013 victimization rates of students for nonfatal crimes at school declined significantly, meaning that, in general, schools are safer today than they were in the recent past.[41]

Security Measures For the most part, these statistics mirror the downward trend of all criminal activity in the United States since the mid-1990s. In addition, since the fatal shootings of fourteen students and a teacher at Columbine High School near Littleton, Colorado, in 1999, many schools have improved security measures. From 1999 to 2013, the percentage of American schools using security cameras to monitor their campuses increased from 19 to 64 percent. Today, 88 percent of public schools control access to school buildings by locking or monitoring their doors.[42] Furthermore, about half of all public schools rely on law enforcement officers to patrol school grounds, although this is a controversial practice that many observers feel does more harm than good.

Disciplinary Measures The Columbine shootings also led many schools to adopt "zero tolerance" policies when it comes to student behavior. These policies require strict punitive measures, such as suspension, expulsion, or referral to the police, for *any* breach of the school's disciplinary code. As a result, according to research conducted by the Vera Institute of Justice, one in nine secondary school students are suspended or expelled each year.[43]

The many critics of zero-tolerance policies point out that only 5 percent of serious school disciplinary actions involve possession of a weapon.[44] Examples of less serious student behavior resulting in expulsion include incidents in which a seven-year-old ate a Pop-Tart into the shape of a gun, a young boy fired an imaginary bow-and-arrow, and a six-year-old boy kissed a six-year-old girl's hand.[45] This trend of reacting harshly to minor infractions may have serious repercussions for society. Students who have been expelled for any amount of time are at a much greater risk for future involvement in the juvenile justice system than those who have not faced such disciplinary measures.[46]

BULLIED STUDENTS A disproportionate number of young people who do bring guns or other weapons to school report that they have been *bullied* by other students.[47] **Bullying** can be broadly defined as repeated, aggressive behavior that contains at least one of the following elements:

1. *Physical abuse,* such as hitting, punching, or damaging the subject's property.

2. *Verbal abuse,* such as teasing, name calling, intimidation, or homophobic or racist remarks.

3. *Social and emotional abuse,* such as spreading false rumors, social exclusion, or playing jokes designed to humiliate.

4. *Cyber abuse,* which includes any form of bullying that takes place online or through the use of devices such as smartphones.

Changing Perspectives Bullying has traditionally been seen more as an inevitable rite of passage among adolescents than as potentially criminal behavior. In recent years, however, society has become more aware of the negative consequences of bullying, underscored by a number of high-profile "bullycides." In September 2013, for example, twelve-year-old Rebecca Sedwick jumped to her death at an abandoned concrete plant in Lakeland, Florida. Sedwick had been relentlessly bullied online and face-to-face by two other girls who, among other things, told her that she was "ugly" and that she should "drink bleach and die."[48] Furthermore, between 2009 and 2012, at least five American teenage boys committed suicide after being bullied about their sexuality.

Legal Responses According to data gathered by the federal government, 28 percent of students aged twelve to eighteen have been victims of bullying.[49] In particular, gay students are targeted—nine out of ten report being bullied within the previous year.[50] As a response to this problem, nearly every state has passed anti-bullying legislation. These laws focus mostly on "soft" measures, such as training school personnel how to recognize and respond to bullying.[51]

State legislatures have been reluctant to take "harder" measures such as specifically defining bullying as a crime. Returning to our previous example, in October 2013 Polk County Sheriff Grady Judd arrested the two girls who had bullied Rebecca Sedwick prior to her death and charged them with felony aggravated stalking. The state attorney's office quickly dropped the charges, however, after determining that the girls' behavior, while reprehensible, was not criminal.

13-4 WHY DO JUVENILES COMMIT CRIMES?

An influential study conducted by Professor Marvin Wolfgang and several colleagues in the early 1970s introduced the "chronic 6 percent" to criminology. The researchers found that out of one hundred boys, six will become chronic offenders, meaning that they are arrested five or more times before their eighteenth birthdays. Furthermore, Wolfgang and his colleagues determined that these chronic offenders are responsible for half of all crimes and two-thirds of all violent crimes within any given cohort (a group of persons who have similar characteristics).[52]

Does this "6 percent rule" mean that no matter what steps society takes, six out of every hundred juveniles are "bad seeds" and will act delinquently? Or does it point to a situation in which a small percentage of children may be more likely to commit crimes under certain circumstances?

Bullying Overt acts taken by students with the goal of intimidating, harassing, or humiliating other students.

Although it is not clear whether bullying in general is more prevalent now than in the past, one form of bullying is definitely on the rise. As the Internet, texting, and social media outlets such as Facebook, Instagram, and Snapchat have become integral parts of youth culture, so, it seems, has cyberbullying. Apps such as Yik Yak allow young people to make anonymous rude, cruel, and sexually suggestive comments about peers. In a recent poll, 85 percent of American and Canadian students said that they had been subject to cyberbullying at least once during the previous year.

To many, cyberbullying can be even more devastating than "old school" bullying. Not only does the anonymity of cyberspace seem to embolden perpetrators, causing them to be more vicious than they might be in person, but, as one expert points out, when bullying occurs online, "you can't get away from it." Still, as the example of Rebecca Sedwick in the text highlights, criminal law does not yet cover most forms

Cheryl E. Davis/Shutterstock.com

of cyberbullying. The consensus seems to be that children should not be charged with a crime for vicious behavior online unless that behavior contains a "specific threat of bodily harm or death." Another suggestion, that parents be held legally responsible for their child's online bullying, has also been ruled out as an unworkable solution to the problem.

Thinking about Cyberbullying
How should the criminal justice system respond to cyberbullying, if at all?

Most criminologists favor the second interpretation. In this section, we will examine the four factors that have traditionally been used to explain juvenile criminal behavior and violent crime rates: age, substance abuse, family problems, and gangs. Keep in mind, however, that the factors influencing delinquency are not limited to these topics (see Figure 13.4). Researchers are constantly interpreting and reinterpreting statistical evidence to provide fresh perspectives on this very important issue.

13-4a The Age-Crime Relationship

LO13-4 Crime statistics are fairly conclusive on one point: the older a person is, the less likely he or she will exhibit criminal behavior. Self-reported studies

Aging Out A term used to explain the fact that criminal activity declines with age.

Age of Onset The age at which a juvenile first exhibits delinquent behavior.

confirm that most people are involved in some form of criminal behavior—however "harmless"—during their early years. In fact, Terrie Moffitt of Duke University has said that "it is statistically aberrant to refrain from crime during adolescence."[53] So, why do the vast majority of us not become chronic offenders?

AGING OUT According to many criminologists, particularly Travis Hirschi and Michael Gottfredson, any group of at-risk persons—regardless of gender, race, intelligence, or class—will commit fewer crimes as they grow older.[54] This process is known as **aging out** (or, sometimes, *desistance*, a term we first encountered in the previous chapter). Professor Robert J. Sampson and his colleague John H. Laub believe that this phenomenon is explained by certain events, such as marriage, employment, and military service, which force delinquents to "grow up" and forgo criminal acts.[55]

AGE OF ONSET Another view sees the **age of onset,** or the age at which the youth begins delinquent behavior, as a consistent predictor of future criminal behavior.

One study compared recidivism rates between juveniles first judged to be delinquent before the age of fifteen and those first adjudicated delinquent after the age of fifteen. Of the seventy-one subjects who made up the first group, 32 percent became chronic offenders. Of the sixty-five who made up the second group, none became chronic offenders.[56]

Furthermore, according to the Office of Juvenile Justice and Delinquency Prevention, the earlier a youth enters the juvenile justice system, the more likely he or she will become a violent offender.[57] This research suggests that juvenile justice resources should be concentrated on the youngest offenders, with the goal of preventing crime and reducing the long-term risks for society.

13-4b Substance Abuse

As we have seen throughout this textbook, substance abuse plays a strong role in criminal behavior for adults. The same can certainly be said for juveniles. According to the University of Michigan's Institute for Social Research, 24 percent of American tenth-graders and 37 percent of American twelfth-graders are regular alcohol drinkers, increasing their risks for violent behavior, delinquency, academic problems, and unsafe sexual behavior.[58] Close to 40 percent of high school seniors report using marijuana at least once in the past twelve months, and just under 20 percent admit to using an illegal drug other than marijuana during that time period.[59]

A STRONG CORRELATION As with adults, substance abuse among juveniles seems to play a major role in offending. Drug use is associated with a wide range of antisocial and illegal behaviors by juveniles, from school suspensions to large-scale theft.[60] Nearly all young offenders (94 percent) entering juvenile detention self-report drug use at some point in their lives, and 85 percent have used drugs in the previous six months.[61]

According to the Arrestee Drug Abuse Monitoring Program, nearly 60 percent of male juvenile detainees and 46 percent of female juvenile detainees test positive for drug use at the time of their offense.[62] Drug use is a particularly strong risk factor for girls: 75 percent of young women incarcerated in juvenile facilities report regular drug and alcohol use—starting at the age of fourteen—and one study found that 87 percent of female teenage offenders need substance abuse treatment.[63]

FIGURE 13.4 RISK FACTORS FOR JUVENILE DELINQUENCY

Family	• Single parent/lack of parental role model • Parental or sibling drug/alcohol abuse • Extreme economic deprivation • Family members in a gang or in prison
School	• Academic frustration/failure • Learning disability • Negative labeling by teachers • Disciplinary problems
Community	• Social disorganization (refer to Chapter 2) • Presence of gangs and obvious drug use in the community • Availability of firearms • High crime/constant feeling of danger • Lack of social and economic opportunities
Peers	• Delinquent friends • Friends who use drugs or who are members of gangs • Lack of "positive" peer pressure
Individual	• Mental illness • Tendency toward aggressive behavior • Inability to concentrate or focus/easily bored/hyperactive • Alcohol or drug use • Fatalistic/pessimistic viewpoint

The characteristics listed here are generally accepted as "risk factors" for juvenile delinquency. In other words, if one or more of these factors are present in a juvenile's life, he or she has a greater chance of exhibiting delinquent behavior—though such behavior is by no means a certainty.

STRONG CAUSATION? The correlation between substance abuse and offending for juveniles seems obvious. Does this mean that substance abuse *causes* juvenile offending? Researchers make the point that most youths who become involved in antisocial behavior do so before their first experience with alcohol or drugs. Therefore, it would appear that substance abuse is a form of delinquent behavior rather than its cause.[64] Still, a 2011 study of adolescent offenders did find that substance abuse treatment reduces criminal behavior in the short term, suggesting that, at the least, the use of illegal drugs is an integral component of the juvenile delinquent lifestyle.[65]

13-4c Child Abuse and Neglect

Abuse by parents also plays a substantial role in juvenile delinquency. **Child abuse** can be broadly defined as the infliction of physical, emotional, or sexual damage on a child. **Child neglect** is a form of abuse that occurs when

Child Abuse Mistreatment of a child resulting in physical, emotional, or sexual damage.

Child Neglect A form of child abuse in which the child is denied certain necessities such as shelter, food, care, and love.

caregivers deprive a child of necessities such as love, shelter, food, and proper care. According to the National Survey of Children's Exposure to Violence, one in ten children in the United States experience mistreatment at the hands of a close family member.[66]

Children in homes characterized by violence or neglect suffer from a variety of physical, emotional, and mental health problems at a much greater rate than their peers.[67] This, in turn, increases their chances of engaging in delinquent behavior. One survey of violent juveniles showed that 75 percent had been subjected to severe abuse by a family member and 80 percent had witnessed violence in their homes.[68] Nearly half of all juveniles—and 80 percent of girls—sentenced to life in prison suffered high rates of abuse.[69]

Cathy Spatz Widom, currently a professor of psychology at John Jay College of Criminal Justice, compared the arrest records of two groups of subjects—one made up of 908 cases of substantiated parental abuse and neglect, and the other made up of 667 children who had not been abused or neglected. Widom found that those who had been abused or neglected were 53 percent more likely to be arrested as juveniles than those who had not.[70] Simply put, according to researchers Janet Currie of Columbia University and Erdal Tekin of Georgia State University, "child maltreatment roughly doubles the probability that an individual engages in many types of crime."[71]

13-4d Gangs

When youths cannot find the stability and support they require in the family structure, they will often turn to their peers. This is just one explanation for why juveniles join **youth gangs.** Although jurisdictions may have varying definitions, for general purposes a youth gang is viewed as a group of three or more persons who (1) self-identify as an entity separate from the community by special clothing, vocabulary, hand signals, and names and (2) engage in criminal activity. According to

Youth Gang A self-formed group of youths with several identifiable characteristics, including a gang name and other recognizable symbols, a geographic territory, and participation in illegal activities.

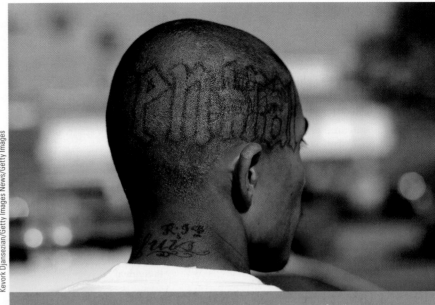

In Los Angeles, a gang member signifies his allegiance to the "Street Villains" through a series of elaborate tattoos. *What role does identity play in a juvenile's decision to join a gang?*

an exhaustive survey of law enforcement agencies, there are probably around 30,000 gangs with approximately 850,000 members in the United States.[72]

Juveniles who have experienced the risk factors discussed in this section are more likely to join a gang, and once they have done so, they are more likely to engage in delinquent and violent behavior than nongang members.[73] Statistics show high levels of gang involvement in most violent criminal activities in the United States.[74] About 80 percent of fatal shootings in Chicago are attributed to gangs, and mini-gangs of teenagers known as "crews" account for 30 percent of all shootings in New York City.[75]

Furthermore, a study of criminal behavior among juveniles in Seattle found that gang members were considerably more likely to commit crimes than at-risk youths who shared many characteristics with gang members but were not affiliated with any gang.[76]

WHO JOINS GANGS? The average gang member is eighteen years old, though members tend to be older in cities with long traditions of gang activity, such as Chicago and Los Angeles. Although it is difficult to determine with any certainty the makeup of gangs as a whole, one recent survey found that 46 percent of all gang members in the United States are Hispanic, 35 percent are African American, and 11 percent are white, with the remaining 8 percent belonging to other racial or ethnic backgrounds.[77]

Though gangs tend to have racial or ethnic characteristics—that is, one group predominates in each gang—many researchers do not believe that race or ethnicity is the dominant factor in gang membership. Indeed, gang members seem to come from lower-class or working-class communities, mostly in urban areas but with an increasing number from the suburbs and rural counties.

WHY JOIN GANGS? The decision to join a gang, like the decision to engage in any sort of antisocial or criminal behavior, is a complex one, and the factors that go into it vary depending on the individual. Generally, however, the reasons for gang membership involve one or more of the following:

1. *Identity.* Being part of a gang often confers a status that the individual feels he or she could not attain outside the gang.

2. *Protection.* Many gang members live in neighborhoods marked by high levels of crime and violence, and a gang guarantees support and retaliation in case of an attack.

3. *Fellowship.* The gang often functions as an extension of the family and provides companionship that may not be available at home.

4. *Criminal activity.* Many gang members enjoy financial rewards because of the gang's profits and protection.

5. *Intimidation.* Some gang members are pressured or forced to join the gang, often to act as "foot soldiers" in the gang's criminal enterprises.[78]

To help gang members leave their gang, "desistance experts" often focus on countering the same pressures that initially led to gang membership. For example, gang members with intimate partners and children are encouraged to commit to their "real family" rather than their "gang family." Help in gaining legal employment can also reduce some of the financial incentives for gang members to continue their illegal activities.[79]

13-5 WHAT HAPPENS AFTER A JUVENILE IS ARRESTED?

As part of the Juvenile Robbery Intervention Program, New York City detectives spend hours monitoring the Facebook pages and Twitter accounts of teenagers at risk for gang involvement and violent crime. Most commonly, however, contact between juvenile offenders and law enforcement takes place on the streets, initiated by a police officer on patrol who either apprehends the juvenile while he or she is committing a crime or answers a call for service. (See Figure 13.5 for an overview of the juvenile justice process.) The youth is then passed on to an officer of the juvenile court, who must decide how to handle the case.

13-5a Police Discretion and Juvenile Crime

Police arrest about 660,000 youths under the age of eighteen each year.[80] In most states, police officers must have probable cause to believe that the minor has committed an offense, just as they would if the suspect was an adult. Police power with regard to juveniles is greater than with adults, however, because police can take youths into custody for status offenses, such as possession of alcohol or truancy. In these cases, the officer is acting *in loco parentis,* or in the place of the parent. The officer's role is not necessarily to punish the youths, but to protect them from harmful behavior.

Police officers also have a great deal of discretion in deciding what to do with juveniles who have committed crimes or status offenses. Juvenile justice expert Joseph Goldstein labels this discretionary power **low-visibility decision making** because it relies on factors that the public is not generally in a position to understand or criticize. When a grave offense has taken place, a police officer may decide to formally arrest the juvenile, send him or her to juvenile court, or place the youth under the care of a social-service organization. In less serious situations, the officer may simply issue a warning or take the offender to the police station and release the child into the custody of her or his parents.

In making these discretionary decisions, police generally consider the following factors:

▶ The nature of the child's offense.

▶ The offender's past history of involvement with the juvenile justice system.

▶ The setting in which the offense took place.

▶ The ability and willingness of the child's parents to take disciplinary action.

▶ The attitude of the offender.

▶ The offender's race and gender.

Low-Visibility Decision Making A term used to describe the discretionary power police have in determining what to do with misbehaving juveniles.

FIGURE 13.5 THE JUVENILE JUSTICE PROCESS

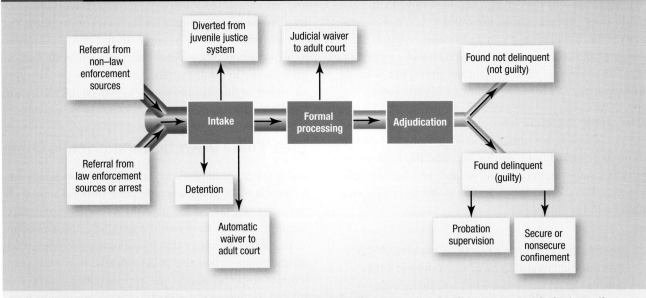

This diagram shows the possible tracks that a young person may take after her or his first contact with the juvenile justice system (usually a police officer).

Source: Office of Juvenile Justice and Delinquency Prevention.

Law enforcement officers notify the juvenile court system that a particular young person requires its attention through a process known as a **referral.** Anyone with a valid reason, including parents, relatives, welfare agencies, and school officials, can refer a juvenile to the juvenile court. The vast majority of cases in juvenile courts, however, are referred by the police.[81]

13-5b Intake

As noted earlier, if, following arrest, a police officer feels the offender warrants the attention of the juvenile justice process, the officer will refer the youth to juvenile court. Once this step has been taken, a complaint is filed with a special division of the juvenile court, and the **intake** process begins. Intake may be followed by

diversion to a community-based program, transfer to an adult court, or detention to await trial in juvenile court. Thus, intake, diversion, transfer, and detention are the four primary stages of pretrial juvenile justice procedure.

During intake, an official of the juvenile court—usually a probation officer, but sometimes a judge—must decide, in effect, what to do with the offender. The intake officer has several options during intake.

LO13-5

1. **Simply dismiss the case, releasing the offender without taking any further action. This occurs in about one in five cases, usually because the judge cannot determine a sufficient reason to continue.[82]**

2. **Divert the offender to a social-services program, such as drug rehabilitation or anger management.**

3. **File a petition for a formal court hearing. The petition is the formal document outlining the charges against the juvenile.**

4. **Transfer the case to an adult court, where the offender will be tried as an adult.**

With regard to status offenses, judges have sole discretion to decide whether to process the case or *divert* the youth to another juvenile service agency.

Referral The notification process through which a law enforcement officer or other concerned citizen makes the juvenile court aware of a juvenile's unlawful or unruly conduct.

Intake The process by which an official of the court must decide whether to file a petition, release the juvenile, or place the juvenile under some other form of supervision.

Petition The document filed with a juvenile court alleging that the juvenile is a delinquent or a status offender and requesting that the court either hear the case or transfer it to an adult court.

13-5c Pretrial Diversion

In the early 1970s, Congress passed the first Juvenile Justice and Delinquency Prevention (JJDP) Act, which ordered the development of methods "to divert juveniles from the traditional juvenile justice system."[83] Within a few years, hundreds of diversion programs had been put into effect. Today, diversion refers to the process of removing low-risk offenders from the formal juvenile justice system by placing them in community-based rehabilitation programs.

Diversion programs vary widely, but fall into three general categories:

1. *Probation.* In this program, the juvenile is returned to the community, but placed under the supervision of a juvenile probation officer. If the youth breaks the conditions of probation, he or she can be returned to the formal juvenile system.

2. *Treatment and aid.* Many juveniles have behavioral or medical conditions that contribute to their delinquent behavior, and many diversion programs offer remedial education, drug and alcohol treatment, and other forms of counseling to alleviate these problems.

3. *Restitution.* In these programs, the offender "repays" her or his victim, either directly or symbolically through community service.

Proponents of diversion programs include many labeling theorists, who believe that contact with the formal juvenile justice system "labels" the youth a delinquent, which leads to further delinquent behavior.

13-5d Transfer to Adult Court

One side effect of diversionary programs is that the youths who remain in the juvenile courts are more likely to be seen as "hardened" and thus less amenable to rehabilitation. This, in turn, increases the likelihood that the offender will be transferred to an adult court, a process in which the juvenile court waives jurisdiction over the youth. In the 1980s and 1990s, when the American juvenile justice system shifted away from ideals of treatment and toward punishment, transfer to adult court was one of the most popular means of "getting tough" on delinquents.

INCIDENCE OF TRANSFER The proportion of juveniles waived to adult court for property crimes has decreased steadily in the past two decades. About 5,400 delinquent cases are now waived to adult criminal court each year—less than 1 percent of all cases that reach juvenile court. This figure is down significantly from 1994, when the number of such cases peaked at 13,600.[84] Today, the majority of transfer cases involve juveniles who have committed a violent offense, such as Ronald Salazar of Florida and the two twelve-year-old girls from Wisconsin, discussed earlier in the chapter.[85]

METHODS OF TRANSFER There are three types of transfer laws, and most states use more than one of them depending on the jurisdiction and the seriousness of the offense. Juveniles are most commonly transferred to adult courts through **judicial waiver,** in which the juvenile judge is given the power to determine whether a young offender's case will be waived to adult court. The judge makes this decision based on the offender's age, the nature of the offense, and any criminal history. All but five states employ judicial waiver.

Twenty-nine states have taken the waiver responsibility out of judicial hands through **automatic transfer,** also known as *legislative waiver.* In these states, the legislatures have designated certain conditions—usually involving serious crimes such as murder and rape—under which a juvenile case is automatically "kicked up" to adult court. In Rhode Island, for example, a juvenile aged sixteen or older with two prior felony adjudications will automatically be transferred on being accused of a third felony.[86]

Fifteen states also allow for **prosecutorial waiver,** in which prosecutors are allowed to choose whether to initiate proceedings in juvenile or criminal court when certain age and offense conditions are met. (See *Discretion in Action—Juvenile Drunk Driving* for further insight into prosecutorial waiver procedures.)

13-5e Detention

Once the decision has been made that the offender will face adjudication in a juvenile court, the intake official must decide what to do with him or her until the start

Judicial Waiver The process in which the juvenile judge, based on the facts of the case at hand, decides that the alleged offender should be transferred to adult court.

Automatic Transfer The process by which a juvenile is transferred to adult court as a matter of state law.

Prosecutorial Waiver A procedure used in situations where the prosecutor has discretion to decide whether a case will be heard by a juvenile court or an adult court.

JUVENILE DRUNK DRIVING

THE SITUATION James, a seventeen-year-old high school senior, gets behind the wheel of his father's car with a blood alcohol concentration of .12, well over the state limit for driving under the influence (DUI). He slams headfirst into another car, killing the driver. Initially, he is charged with vehicular homicide as a juvenile.

THE LAW In this state, prosecutors have the discretion to waive juvenile offenders to adult court if the alleged offender is sixteen years old or older at the time of the alleged offense and is charged with a felony, such as vehicular manslaughter.

WHAT WOULD YOU DO? You are a prosecutor with the discretionary power to transfer James from juvenile court to adult court. On the one hand, James has no previous criminal record, did not intend to kill his victim, and has shown extreme remorse for his actions. Furthermore, he is a juvenile and, as such, is seen by the law as less culpable than an adult. On the other hand, his careless actions resulted in a homicide, and trying him as an adult might deter other juveniles from committing DUI crimes. Do you keep James in juvenile court or waive him to adult court? Why?

[To learn what a prosecutor in Denver, Colorado, did in a similar situation, see Example 13.1 in Appendix A.]

---

of the trial. Generally, the juvenile is released into the custody of parents or a guardian—most jurisdictions favor this practice in lieu of setting money bail for youths. The intake officer may also place the offender in **detention,** or temporary custody in a secure facility, until the disposition process begins. Once a juvenile has been detained, most jurisdictions require that a **detention hearing** be held within twenty-four hours. During this hearing, the offender has several due process safeguards, including the right to counsel, the right against self-incrimination, and the right to cross-examine and confront witnesses.

In justifying its decision to detain, the court will usually address one of three issues:

1. **Whether the child poses a danger to the community.**

2. **Whether the child will return for the adjudication process.**

3. **Whether detention will provide protection for the child.**

Detention The temporary custody of a juvenile in a secure facility after a petition has been filed and before the adjudicatory process begins.

Detention Hearing A hearing to determine whether a juvenile should be detained, or remain detained, while waiting for the adjudicatory process to begin.

The Supreme Court upheld the practice of preventive detention (see Chapter 8) for juveniles in *Schall v. Martin* (1984)[87] by ruling that youths can be detained if they are deemed a "risk" to the safety of the community or to their own welfare. Partly as a result, the number of juveniles detained for acts of violence increased 84 percent between 1985 and 2011.[88]

13-6 HOW ARE JUVENILES TRIED AND PUNISHED?

In just over half of all referred cases, the juvenile is eventually subject to formal proceedings in juvenile court.[89] As noted earlier, changes in the juvenile justice system since *In re Gault* (1967) have led many to contend that juvenile courts have become indistinguishable, both theoretically and practically, from adult courts. About half the states, for example, permit juveniles to request a jury trial under certain circumstances. Juvenile justice proceedings may still be distinguished from the adult system of criminal justice, however, and these differences are evident in the adjudication and disposition of the juvenile trial.

13-6a Adjudication

During the adjudication stage of the juvenile justice process, a hearing is held to determine whether the offender is delinquent or in need of some form of court supervision. Most state juvenile codes dictate a specific set of procedures that must be followed during the **adjudicatory hearing,** with the goal of providing the respondent with "the essentials of due process and fair treatment." Consequently, the respondent in an adjudicatory hearing has the right to notice of charges, counsel, and confrontation and cross-examination, and the privilege against self-incrimination.

Furthermore, "proof beyond a reasonable doubt" must be established to find the child delinquent. When the child admits guilt—that is, admits to the charges of the initial petition—the judge must ensure that the admission was voluntary.

At the close of the adjudicatory hearing, the judge is generally required to rule on the legal issues and evidence that have been presented. Based on this ruling, the judge determines whether the respondent is delinquent or in need of court supervision. Alternatively, the judge can dismiss the case based on a lack of evidence. It is important to remember that finding a child delinquent is *not* the same as convicting an adult of a crime. A delinquent does not face the same restrictions imposed on adult convicts in some states, such as limits on the right to vote and to run for political office.

13-6b Disposition

Once a juvenile has been adjudicated delinquent, the judge must decide what steps will be taken toward treatment and/or punishment. Most states provide for a *bifurcated* process in which a separate **disposition hearing** follows the adjudicatory hearing. Depending on state law, the juvenile may be entitled to counsel at the disposition hearing.

SENTENCING JUVENILES In an adult trial, the sentencing phase is primarily concerned with protecting the community from the convict. In contrast, a juvenile judge uses the disposition hearing to determine a sentence that will serve the needs of the child. For assistance in this crucial process, the judge will order the probation department to gather information on the juvenile and present it in the form of a **predisposition report.** The report usually contains information concerning the respondent's family background, the facts surrounding the delinquent act, and interviews with social workers, teachers, and other important figures in the child's life.

JUDICIAL DISCRETION In keeping with the rehabilitative tradition of the juvenile justice system, juvenile judges generally have a great deal of discretion in choosing one of several disposition possibilities. A judge can tend toward leniency, delivering only a stern reprimand or warning before releasing the juvenile into the custody of parents or other legal guardians. Otherwise, the choice is among incarceration in a juvenile correctional facility, probation, or community treatment. In most cases, the seriousness of the offense is the primary factor used in determining whether to incarcerate a juvenile, though history of delinquency, family situation, and the offender's attitude are all relevant.

13-6c Juvenile Corrections

In general, juvenile corrections are based on the concept of **graduated sanctions**—that is, the severity of the punishment should fit the crime. Consequently, status and first-time offenders are diverted or placed on probation, repeat offenders find themselves in intensive community supervision or treatment programs, and serious and violent offenders are placed in correctional facilities.

As society's expectations of the juvenile justice system have changed, so have the characteristics of its corrections programs. In some cities, for example, juvenile probation officers join police officers on the beat. Because the former are not bound by the same search and seizure restrictions as other law enforcement officials, this interdepartmental teamwork provides more opportunities to fight youth crime aggressively.

JUVENILE PROBATION The most common form of juvenile corrections is probation—33 percent of all delinquency cases disposed of by juvenile courts result in conditional diversion. The majority of all adjudicated delinquents (64 percent) will never receive a disposition more severe than being placed on probation.[90] These statistics reflect a general understanding among juvenile

Adjudicatory Hearing The process through which a juvenile court determines whether there is sufficient evidence to support the initial petition.

Disposition Hearing Similar to the sentencing hearing for adults, a hearing in which the juvenile judge or officer decides the appropriate punishment for a youth found to be delinquent or a status offender.

Predisposition Report A report prepared during the disposition process that provides the judge with relevant background material to aid in the disposition decision.

Graduated Sanctions The practical theory in juvenile corrections that a delinquent or status offender should receive a punishment that matches in seriousness the severity of the wrongdoing.

A bailiff tells a juvenile who has just completed his community service to tuck in his shirt at a City of Houston Municipal Court hearing. *Why do juvenile court judges favor community service and probation, when appropriate, as sentencing options for juveniles?*

CONFINING JUVENILES About 68,000 American youths (down from approximately 107,000 in 1995) are incarcerated in public and private juvenile correctional facilities in the United States.[91] Most of these juveniles have committed crimes against people or property, but a significant number (about 14 percent) have been incarcerated for technical violations of their probation or parole agreements.[92] After deciding that a juvenile needs to be confined, the judge has two sentencing options: nonsecure juvenile institutions and secure juvenile institutions.

Nonsecure Confinement Some juvenile delinquents do not require high levels of control and can be placed in **residential treatment programs.** These programs, run by either probation departments or social-services departments, allow their subjects freedom of movement in the community. Generally, this freedom is predicated on the juveniles following certain rules, such as avoiding alcoholic beverages and returning to the facility for curfew. Residential treatment programs can be divided into four categories:

court judges and other officials that a child should normally be removed from her or his home only as a last resort.

The organization of juvenile probation is very similar to adult probation (see Chapter 10), and juvenile probationers are increasingly subjected to electronic monitoring and other supervisory tactics. The main difference between the two programs lies in the attitude toward the offender. Adult probation officers have an overriding responsibility to protect the community from the probationer, while juvenile probation officers are expected to take the role of a mentor or a concerned relative in looking after the needs of the child.

1. *Foster care programs,* in which the juveniles live with couples who act as surrogate parents.

2. *Group homes,* which generally house between twelve and fifteen youths and provide treatment, counseling, and education services by a professional staff.

3. *Family group homes,* which combine aspects of foster care and group homes, meaning that a single family, rather than a group of professionals, looks after the needs of the young offenders.

4. *Rural programs,* which include wilderness camps, farms, and ranches where between thirty and fifty children are placed in an environment that provides recreational activities and treatment programs.

CAREER TIP Besides needing a bachelor's degree in a field such as criminal justice, psychology, or social work, applicants for the post of *juvenile probation officer* often need experience working with young people. Such experience can be gained by volunteering with organizations such as the Boys & Girls Club, YMCA, and Big Brothers Big Sisters.

Residential Treatment Program A government-run facility for juveniles whose offenses are not deemed serious enough to warrant incarceration in a training school.

Secure Confinement Secure facilities are comparable to the adult prisons and jails we discussed in Chapters 11 and 12. These institutions go by a confusing array of names depending on the state in which they are located, but the two best known are boot camps and training schools.

PhotoDisc

Job Description:

▶ Oversee the detention of juvenile offenders being held in temporary custody before the adjudicatory process begins. Observe the behavior of and, when necessary, counsel the juvenile offenders to ensure their safety during the detention period.

▶ Maintain personal relationships with the juvenile offenders so as to supervise their progress in educational, recreational, and therapeutic activities while housed at the detention center.

What Kind of Training Is Required?

▶ A high school diploma plus at least three years of work experience involving children of school age (seven to seventeen years) or one year of college education for each year of experience lacking.

▶ Physical agility and strength, as well as a firm manner in dealing with juveniles who may present severe disciplinary problems.

Annual Salary Range?

▶ $29,000–$62,000

GETTING LINKEDIN

Increasingly, juvenile detention centers are used to house undocumented non-citizen children who are in the United States illegally without their parents. As a result, a number of juvenile detention centers are advertising on LinkedIn for "bilingual detention specialists" to coordinate cases involving these young people.

A **boot camp** is the juvenile variation of shock probation. As we noted in Chapter 10, boot camps are modeled after military training for new recruits. Boot camp programs are based on the theory that by giving wayward youths a taste of the "hard life" of military-like training for short periods of time, usually no longer than 180 days, they will be "shocked" out of a life of crime. At a typical youth boot camp, inmates are grouped in platoons and live in dormitories. They spend eight hours a day training, drilling, and doing hard labor, and also participate in programs such as basic adult education and job skills training.

No juvenile correctional facility is called a "prison." This does not mean they lack a strong resemblance to prisons. The facilities that most closely mimic the atmosphere at an adult correctional facility are **training schools,** alternatively known as youth camps, youth development centers, industrial schools, and several other similar titles. Whatever the name, these institutions claim to differ from their adult countparts by offering a variety of programs to treat and rehabilitate the young offenders. In reality, training schools

Boot Camp A variation on traditional shock incarceration in which juveniles (and some adults) are sent to secure confinement facilities modeled on military basic training camps instead of prison or jail.

Training School A correctional institution for juveniles found to be delinquent or status offenders.

are plagued by many of the same problems as adult prisons and jails, including high levels of inmate-on-inmate violence, substance abuse, gang wars, and overcrowding.

Aftercare The variety of therapeutic, educational, and counseling programs made available to juvenile delinquents (and some adults) after they have been released from a correctional facility.

STUDY TOOLS 13

READY TO STUDY? IN THE BOOK, YOU CAN:

☐ Rip out the Chapter Review Card, which includes key terms and chapter summaries.

ONLINE AT WWW.CENGAGEBRAIN.COM, YOU CAN:

☐ Learn about one teen girl sentenced to life without parole in a short video.

☐ Dig into social media in criminal justice by exploring the Facebook page of the Coalition for Juvenile Justice (CJJ).

☐ Interact with figures from the text, and watch quick animation clips.

☐ Prepare for tests with quizzes.

☐ Review the key terms with Flash Cards.

AFTERCARE Juveniles leave correctional facilities through an early release program or because they have served the length of their sentences. Juvenile corrections officials recognize that many of these children, like adults, need assistance readjusting to the outside world. Consequently, released juveniles are often placed in **aftercare** programs. Based on the same philosophy that drives the prisoner reentry movement (discussed in the previous chapter), aftercare programs are designed to offer services for the juveniles, while at the same time supervising them to reduce the chances of recidivism.

The ideal aftercare program includes community support groups, education and employment aid, and continued monitoring to ensure that the juvenile is able to deal with the demands of freedom. Statistics suggest, however, that the aftercare needs of young offenders often go unmet. Nearly 60 percent of those who have been referred to juvenile court are "re-referred" before turning eighteen years old.[93] More troubling is the notion that many juvenile offenders are likely, if not destined, to become adult offenders. A report on Illinois's juvenile justice system criticized it as "a 'feeder system' to the adult criminal justice system and a cycle of crime, victimization, and incarceration."[94]

CAREER TIP *Aftercare coordinators* help juvenile offenders during the critical transitional period immediately after discharge from a youth correctional facility, when past temptations, acquaintances, and stresses pose the greatest threat to rehabilitation.

Quiz

1. At its inception, the American juvenile justice system was guided by the principles of *parens patriae,* which holds that the _____ has a responsibility to look after children when their parents cannot do so.

2. When a juvenile engages in wrongdoing that would not be a crime if done by an adult, she or he has committed a _____ _____.

3. The U.S. Supreme Court relied on the concept of "diminished culpability" when, in 2005, it prohibited the _____ _____ for offenders who were juveniles when they committed their crimes.

4. Experts focus on the process of _____ _____ to explain why young people commit fewer offenses as they grow older.

5. Youth who become involved in _____ are more likely to engage in criminal activity than those who do not.

6. If the circumstances are serious enough, a police officer can formally _____ an offending juvenile.

7. In less serious circumstances, a police officer can _____ the juvenile to the juvenile court system.

8. If a juvenile court judge believes that the seriousness of the offense so warrants, he or she can transfer the juvenile into the adult court system through a process called judicial _____.

9. A juvenile offender's delinquency is determined during the _____ hearing, which is similar in many ways to an adult trial.

10. If the juvenile is found to be delinquent, her or his sentence is determined during the _____ hearing.

Answers can be found in the Answers section in the back of the book.

14 Today's Challenges in Criminal Justice

Eugene Sergeev/ShutterStock.com

LEARNING OBJECTIVES

After studying this chapter, you will be able to . . .

14-1 Summarize the three federal laws that have been particularly influential on our nation's counterterrorism strategies.

14-2 Distinguish verbal threats that are protected by the Constitution from verbal threats that can be prosecuted as "true threats."

14-3 Outline the three major reasons why the Internet is conducive to the dissemination of child pornography.

14-4 Explain how background checks, in theory, protect the public from firearm-related violence.

14-5 Indicate some of the ways that white-collar crime is different from violent or property crime.

After you finish this chapter, go to **PAGES 314–315** for **STUDY TOOLS**

Teen Dreams

Shannon Maureen Conley first showed up on the homeland security radar when, in the fall of 2013, she was seen wandering outside the Faith Bible Church in Arvada, Colorado, wearing a large backpack and taking notes. A pastor notified local police, and, within days, an agent from the Federal Bureau of Investigation (FBI) asked the teenager to explain her behavior. "I hate those people," said Conley, a convert to Islam, referring to church officials. "If they think I'm a terrorist, I'll give them something to think I am," she told the FBI agent.

Over the next year and a half, federal authorities kept watch on Conley, interviewing her numerous times and opening a line of communication with her parents. After she signed up with U.S. Army Explorers, a group that trains young people in military tactics and firearm use, she admitted to the FBI that she intended to aid Muslim extremists in their efforts to wage *jihad* against the United States. Conley also said that overseas U.S. military bases and government employees living abroad were "legitimate targets of attack."

Finally, on April 8, 2014, the FBI arrested nineteen-year-old Conley at the Denver Airport as she was preparing to board a flight to Adana, Turkey. She had planned to make her way into Syria, which borders Turkey, and marry a Tunisian man she met online who was affiliated with the terrorist group known as the Islamic State of Iraq and the Levant (ISIL). A certified nurse's aide, Conley apparently intended to provide medical assistance to ISIL fighters, who have killed a number of Americans in the Middle East. Conley eventually pleaded guilty to providing material support to a foreign terrorist organization, and, in January 2015, a federal judge sentenced her to four years in prison. "Even though I was committed to the idea of *jihad*, I didn't want to hurt anyone," Conley told the judge at her sentencing hearing. "I do not believe that I am a threat to society."

In 2014, American teenager Shannon Conley was convicted of providing material support to ISIL, represented by the banners shown here. *Do you think that Conley actually committed a crime? If so, what was it? Explain your answers.*

Steve Allen/ShutterStock.com

14-1 HOW IMPORTANT IS PRIVACY IN THE AGE OF TERRORISM?

At the time of Shannon Conley's arrest, U.S. officials were uncertain exactly how many American citizens had traveled to the Middle East to join ISIL and similar extremist organizations. Few of these homegrown terrorists, whose numbers were estimated at about one hundred, had been as forthcoming as Conley about their plans. For example, before Moner Mohammad Abusalha blew himself up in May 2014 as part of a suicide attack in Syria, the government was unsure if the twenty-two-year-old Floridian had gone abroad to fight for ISIL or to provide humanitarian aid.[1]

Since the attacks of September 11, 2001, on New York, Washington, D.C., and rural Pennsylvania, homeland security officials have placed paramount importance on tracking communications among suspected terrorists. To do so, the federal government has greatly enhanced the capabilities of law enforcement and intelligence agencies to collect and store information on these suspects. At the same time, the federal government has angered many Americans who feel that their privacy rights have been ignored or discarded for the sake of national security. "You can't have 100 percent security and also then have 100 percent privacy," remarked President Barack Obama,[2] succinctly summarizing an ongoing balancing act that goes to the heart of American ideals of fairness and justice.

First responders mark the thirteenth anniversary of the September 11, 2001, terrorist attacks at a memorial in New York City. *What strategies do you think the federal government should implement to prevent similar large-scale attacks in the future?*

a katz/ShutterStock.com

14-1a National Security and Privacy

As has been noted several times in this textbook, our Constitution upholds the premise that Americans should not be subjected to the unreasonable use of government power. As we have also pointed out, *reasonableness* is a highly subjective concept, and Americans are often willing to give their government more leeway in times of national crisis. When it comes to antiterrorism efforts and homeland security, this flexibility has manifested itself in the form of federal legislation that expands the government's ability to locate, observe, prosecute, and punish suspected terrorists. The first legislative step in this direction, however, took place decades before September 11, 2001, and was designed primarily to weaken the office of the presidency.

LO14-1 **FOREIGN SURVEILLANCE** Until the 1970s, policies regarding **surveillance,** or the governmental monitoring of individuals or groups that posed national security threats to the United States,

were primarily the domain of the executive branch. That is, the president and his advisors decided who the federal government would target for its spy operations. Following President Richard Nixon's abuse of this discretion to eavesdrop on political opponents during the 1974 presidential campaign, in 1978 Congress passed the Foreign Intelligence Surveillance Act (FISA).[3] This legislation provided a legal framework for the government's electronic monitoring of suspected criminals or national security threats.

Under FISA, federal agents are able to eavesdrop on the communications of foreign persons or foreign entities, without a court order, for up to a year, as long as the purpose of the surveillance is national security and not law enforcement. If this surveillance uncovers wrongdoing by an American citizen, the government has seventy hours to gain judicial authorization to continue to monitor this suspect's activities.[4]

If the target is a "foreign agent" operating within the United States, FISA requires permission from a special court to engage in surveillance. This court, known as the Foreign Intelligence Surveillance Court, or FISA Court, is made up of eleven federal judges assigned by the chief justice of the Supreme Court. The FISA warrant application must identify the target of the surveillance, the nature of the information sought, and the monitoring method. The government agency must also certify that the goal of the surveillance is to "obtain foreign intelligence information."[5]

MATERIAL SUPPORT Another crucial piece of counterterrorism legislation was passed in response to the 1995 truck bombing of the Alfred P. Murrah Federal Building in Oklahoma City, Oklahoma, which killed 168 people. The primary goal of this legislation, the Antiterrorism and Effective Death Penalty Act (AEDPA), is to hamper terrorist organizations by cutting off their funding. The law prohibits persons from "knowingly providing *material support* or resources" to any group that the United States has designated a "foreign terrorist organization."[6]

Material support is defined very broadly in the legislation, covering funding, financial services, lodging, training, expert advice or assistance, communications

Surveillance The close observation of a person or group by government agents, in particular to uncover evidence of criminal or terrorist activities.

Material Support In the context of federal antiterrorism legislation, the act of helping a terrorist organization by engaging in a wide range of activity that includes providing financial support, training, and expert advice or assistance.

equipment, transportation, and other physical assets.[7] For example, Shannon Conley—discussed at the beginning of this chapter—was convicted for providing "material support" to ISIL even though she never actually left the United States or had any in-person contact with any members of that organization.

Furthermore, the AEDPA does not require that a suspect *intend* to aid the terrorist organization in question.[8] About a decade ago, Javed Iqbal was successfully prosecuted in New York for offering a satellite television package that included a channel operated by Hezbollah, a government-designated terrorist organization based in Lebanon. Even though there was no evidence that Iqbal intended to further the goals of Hezbollah, the fact that his conduct provided material support to the organization was sufficient to allow his prosecution under the law.[9]

THE PATRIOT ACT Enacted six weeks after the September 11, 2001, terrorist attacks, the **Patriot Act**[10] greatly strengthened the ability of federal law enforcement agents to investigate and incarcerate terrorist suspects. At 342 pages, the Patriot Act covered numerous areas related to homeland security, including immigration law and border protection, grants to local police departments, and compensation for the victims of the September 11 attacks. Here, we will focus on the legislation's rules regarding surveillance, summarized in Figure 14.1. Critics of the Patriot Act have focused on Sections 213 and 215, which allow government agents to conduct searches and seizures without many of the Fourth Amendment protections discussed in Chapter 6.

Specifically, Section 215 provides the National Security Agency (NSA), a federal agency that focuses on foreign intelligence operations, with the authority to collect the telephone billing records of Americans who have made calls to other countries, as those records are considered reasonably "relevant" to the agency's counterterrorism investigations.[11] Furthermore, the Patriot Act requires third parties such as telephone companies and Internet providers to turn over records of stored electronic communications to the federal government without notice to persons making those communications.

FIGURE 14.1 THE PATRIOT ACT AND ELECTRONIC SURVEILLANCE

- *Section 201:* Enables government agents to wiretap the communications of any persons suspected of terrorism or the dissemination of chemical weapons.
- *Section 204:* Makes it easier for government agents to get a warrant to search stored e-mail communications held by Internet service providers (ISPs).
- *Section 206:* The "roving wiretap" provision removes the requirement that government agents specify the particular places or things to be searched when obtaining warrants for surveillance of suspected terrorists.
- *Section 210:* Gives government agents enhanced authority to access the duration and timing of phone calls, along with phone numbers and credit cards used to pay for cell phone service.
- *Section 213:* The "sneak and peak" provision removes the requirement that government agents give notice to a target when they have searched her or his property.*
- *Section 214:* Removes the requirement that government agents prove that the subject of a FISA search, discussed earlier in the section, is actually the "agent of a foreign power."
- *Section 215:* The "business records" provision permits government agents to access "business records, medical records, educational records and library records" without showing probable cause of wrongdoing if the investigation is related to terrorism activities.

Under Title II of the Patriot Act, the sections summarized above greatly expanded the ability of federal intelligence operatives and law enforcement agents to conduct electronic surveillance operations on suspected terrorists.

* In 2012, this rule was revised to require notice within thirty days of the search in most circumstances.

Government agents do not need judicial permission to issue **national security letters,** as such requests are called. The agents only need to show, after the fact, that the targeted communications are relevant to a terrorism investigation.[12] These national security letters can be used to collect:

1. **Credit information from banks and loan companies.**

2. **Telephone and Internet data, including names, call times, physical addresses, and e-mail addresses.**

3. **Financial records such as money transfers and bank accounts.**

4. **Travel records held by "any commercial entity."[13]**

As we will soon see, widespread use of such surveillance tactics has led to a great deal of controversy over the federal government's information-gathering practices.

Patriot Act Legislation passed in the wake of the September 11, 2001, terrorist attacks that greatly expanded the ability of government agents to monitor and apprehend suspected terrorists.

National Security Letters Legal notices that compel the disclosure of customer records held by banks, telephone companies, Internet service providers, and other companies to the agents of the federal government.

14-1b Mass Surveillance

Following a series of controversies concerning the ability of the NSA to wiretap telephone and e-mail communications of suspected terrorists, in 2008 Congress passed an amended version of FISA. This legislative action did not, however, place greater limits on the NSA, which had amassed a massive database by secretly keeping track of millions of phone calls made by Americans who were not under suspicion of any wrongdoing. Instead, it essentially legalized government surveillance tactics that had previously been illegal by giving the NSA more freedom to act without oversight by the FISA court.[14]

FOURTH AMENDMENT AND HOMELAND SECURITY

The problem with the original FISA, according to some observers, was that it required a lengthy review process before the FISA court would issue a warrant allowing government agents to monitor a terrorist suspect. In an environment where individuals can rapidly change their e-mail addresses and mode of Internet communication, or use multiple cell phone numbers, this procedure was seen by these critics as too slow and cumbersome for effective intelligence gathering.[15] The NSA, FBI, and other government agencies argued that they needed more freedom to quickly collect massive amounts of information without judicial oversight.

This need, of course, must be tempered by the Fourth Amendment, which broadly requires that the government have probable cause of wrongdoing before intruding on a citizen's reasonable expectation of privacy. The amended FISA's authorization of large-scale warrantless electronic eavesdropping, in which hundreds of millions of phone and Internet records have been collected and stored in databases, created concerns that the federal government aimed to "write off the Fourth Amendment as technologically obsolete."[16]

METADATA COLLECTION In 2013, an NSA contractor named Edward Snowden revealed that, under the revised FISA, the NSA has monitored the cell phone and Internet activity of approximately 113 million Americans without probable cause or a warrant from the FISA court. Through a program known as Prism, the NSA gained access to the information collected by sending national security letters to several major telephone companies and ISPs, including Apple, Facebook, Google, Microsoft, Skype, Verizon, Yahoo, and YouTube.[17] By storing this "metadata," the government agency has gained unprecedented knowledge of whom Americans are communicating with, when these communications are taking place, and for how long.

"Red Flagging" Agents of the federal government had not been listening to actual phone conversations or reading hundreds of millions of e-mails. Rather, warrantless metadata collection and storage—justified, according to the FISA court, under Section 215 of the Patriot Act (see Figure 14.1)[18]—were designed to retroactively determine communications patterns that might raise a "red flag" of terrorist activity. If the NSA was able to uncover a pattern of communication that suggested such activity, it would apply for a FISA warrant and undertake further investigations of the individuals involved. Using this process, the FISA court was issuing about eighteen hundred orders each year for domestic surveillance.[19]

"Connecting the Dots" Proponents of the NSA metadata program argued that it was the only effective method for monitoring terrorist activity over the many communications systems that exist in the United States and elsewhere. In approving the strategy, a district court noted, "Without all the data points, the government cannot be certain it has connected

Do you agree with these protesters that the federal government should not be allowed to collect information about the telephone habits of U.S. citizens without first obtaining permission from a court? Why or why not?

Rena Schild/ShutterStock.com

the pertinent ones."[20] For example, in 2009 Najibullah Zazi was planning to bomb the New York subway system. After the FBI established Zazi as a suspect, the NSA sifted through its database and found a series of phone calls to Adis Medunjanin, one of his accomplices.

Much to the dismay of its supporters, however, in 2015 Congress overhauled the NSA's metadata collection program, revising Section 215 of the Patriot Act in the process. Now, only phone companies, not the NSA, have the authority to store metadata, and government agencies such as the NSA and the FBI must petition a special court for access to that information.[21]

EXPECTATIONS OF PRIVACY Critics of the NSA's metadata program have pointed out that, by the government's own admission, while it has contributed to about a dozen cases such as Najibullah Zazi's, the program has not directly uncovered any significant terrorist plots.[22] This limited impact, they successfully argued, does not justify the significant *invasion of privacy* involved.

Privacy Precedents As you may recall from Chapter 6, an individual usually has no expectation of privacy with regard to information voluntarily disclosed to third parties. So, for example, a person does not have an expectation of privacy for writing on the outside of an envelope given to the U.S. Postal Service or garbage left on the curb for collection.[23] As a result, government agents can search and seize that "information" without a warrant.

Several federal appeals courts have held that defendants have no reasonable expectation of privacy over information "voluntarily" provided to a telephone company or an ISP. In 2013, a federal judge refused to grant a new trial to defendants convicted of providing material support in the form of funds to an African terrorist organization. Federal agents admitted that they initially became interested in the defendants' behavior because of telephone records contained in the NSA database. The judge ruled that the agents did not need a warrant to obtain such information from the telephone company because individuals have "no legitimate expectation of privacy" in phone call data.[24]

CUSTOMS AND BORDER PROTECTION AGENT

CareerPrep

Job Description:

▶ Ensure that laws are observed when goods and people enter the United States. Work at ports of entry and along the U.S. borders with Canada and Mexico to prevent smuggling and the entrance of illegal aliens.

▶ Conduct surveillance along the border using electronic sensors, infrared scopes, low-light television systems, and aircraft.

What Kind of Training Is Required?

▶ Be fluent in Spanish or be able to learn the Spanish language.

▶ Pass a thorough background investigation, medical examination, fitness test, and drug test.

Annual Salary Range?

▶ $38,000–$93,000

Jim Parkin/ShutterStock.com

SOCIAL MEDIA CAREER TIP

Consider setting up personal and career-oriented Facebook pages or Twitter accounts and keeping your posts separated. Remember, though, that material on your "personal" page or account may still be seen by others outside your network.

In general, these judicial decisions rely on the precedent set by the United States Supreme Court in its *Smith v. Maryland* (1979)[25] decision. That case involved the police's warrantless seizure of phone numbers dialed from the home of a robbery suspect. The Court ruled that the defendant had voluntarily turned over the phone numbers to a third party—the phone company—for billing purposes and therefore had no reasonable expectation of privacy in the matter.

Privacy and Technology One federal judge has gone against the tide with regard to metadata and expectations of privacy. In 2013, U.S. District Judge Richard Leon of the District of Columbia found that the NSA's phone-data collection program "almost certainly" violated the Fourth Amendment.[26] Judge Leon argued that the Supreme Court's *Maryland* case involved a "one-time" search of phone calls emanating from the home of a single criminal suspect. In contrast, the NSA metadata program has been a "daily, all-encompassing indiscriminate dump" of information from "the phones of people who are not suspected of any wrongdoing."[27]

Judge Leon's opinion raises an interesting question: have our reasonable expectations of privacy changed because of technological innovations? As proof that such expectations have changed, the judge referred to a 2012 decision in which the Supreme Court ruled that it is unconstitutional for police to use a GPS device to track a suspect's movements without a warrant. He noted that justices who made the *Maryland* ruling in 1979 could not "have ever imagined how the citizens of [today] would interact with their phones."[29]

FOREIGN SURVEILLANCE TARGETS Foreign citizens do not enjoy the same protections under the Fourth Amendment as U.S. citizens. This distinction is important to the operation of a separate NSA data-collection program—mandated under the revised FISA of 2008—that gives the government the ability to monitor non–U.S. citizens believed to be located in another country. Section 702 of the FISA Amendment Act permits eavesdropping (not merely metadata collection) without a warrant on foreign persons to obtain information related to any of the following:

1. National security, such as details of an "actual or potential attack" or "other grave hostile acts [by a] foreign power or agent of a foreign power."

2. Foreign "intelligence activities."

3. "The conduct of the foreign affairs of the United States."[30]

The broad language of this amended law allowed the NSA to target nearly ninety thousand foreign people and organizations for surveillance in 2013.[31] This figure is significant because the law also permits eavesdropping without a warrant of a person who communicates with the target of foreign surveillance, even if that person is an American citizen. According to a detailed analysis of the NSA's global surveillance practices, the agency intercepts communications of nine incidental "bystanders" for every single "legally targeted" foreigner.[32]

This loophole has allowed the NSA to gather highly personal information such as baby pictures, medical records, and flirtatious Webcam chats from innocent persons, including Americans.[33] At the same time, it provides a valuable tool to uncover terrorist operations on U.S. soil, a growing concern that we will examine in the following section.

14-1c National Security and Speech

After the arrest of Shannon Conley at the Denver airport, discussed at the beginning of the chapter, FBI director James Comey distinguished the "mouth runners"—those who merely talk about their anti-American or violent beliefs—from potential terrorists. "This is a great country with lots of traditions of protecting mouth-running," said Comey. "We should continue that. But those who are inclined to cross the line, I've got to focus on them."[34]

How do our federal intelligence and law enforcement agencies tell the "mouth runners," protected by the American tradition of free speech, from the true threats? This question took on added urgency after a series of deadly terrorist attacks in Europe in early 2015, carried out by citizens of countries such as France and Belgium who had returned home after receiving training and support in the Middle East. This type of "small-scale attack" by a homegrown terrorist is "what keeps me up at night," says U.S. representative Michael McCaul, a Republican from Texas who chairs the House Homeland Security Committee.[35]

TRUE THREAT LAW In Chapter 1, we examined the situation involving Anthony Elonis, who was convicted for making violent threats against his wife in the form of rap lyrics he posted online. Elonis claimed that he never intended to actually harm his wife, and that his threats were not crimes but rather expressions of art.

The crucial United States Supreme Court case for differentiating "mere speech," which is protected by the First Amendment of the U.S. Constitution, from a *true threat,* which is not protected, concerned the racially charged issue of cross burning. In *Virginia v. Black* (2003),[36] the Court struck down part of a Virginia law that prohibited *all* forms of cross burning. The statute assumed that any person who would burn a cross would only do so with the intent to frighten or intimidate specific African American targets.

The Court ruled that the act of burning a cross was not enough to constitute a crime. The state must also prove that the act was done to place a specific victim "in fear of bodily harm or death." [37] So, burning a cross on the front lawn of an African American family is a **true threat,** and therefore a crime. By the same measure, burning a cross on one's own property as a general expression of racial hatred, out of sight of any members of minority groups, is not. (See the feature *Discretion in Action—Bragging about Bombing* for an example of how true threat doctrine works in the context of domestic terrorism.)

FINDING AND CAPTURING "KNOWN WOLVES" As a rule, individuals who intend to offer material support to terrorist organizations do not enjoy First Amendment protections. That is, they cannot claim to be harmless "mouth runners." Rather, by statute, many of the activities that constitute material support are considered true threats.[38] Sometimes, the true threat is legally obvious. In 2015, for example, six Bosnian immigrants living in Illinois, Missouri, and New York were indicted for providing material support to terrorist organizations in Syria and Iraq after they sent $8,000 worth of U.S. military uniforms, technical gear, and weapons to those

> **True Threat** An act of speech or expression that is not protected by the First Amendment because it is done with the intention of placing a specific victim or group of victims in fear of unlawful violence.

Discretion in Action

BRAGGING ABOUT BOMBING

THE SITUATION On his last night in prison after serving a short stint for marijuana distribution, Steven has a long conversation with his cellmate, who is wearing a recording device. First, Steven discusses his skill as a bomb builder, giving as an example an explosive device he designed to be hidden in the face-cream container of an ex-girlfriend. Steven then specifically outlines his plans to pose as a delivery man and blow up the Reuss Federal Plaza in Milwaukee with a truck bomb. His detailed explanation includes the number of detonators and drums of explosives he would use, where he would park, and how he would deflect suspicion. Steven describes his desire to kill as many government agents as possible, and, when pressed, tells his cellmate that there is "no doubt" that "someone's gonna get it."

THE LAW Steven's statements can be considered a "true threat," and therefore a criminal act, if they represent "a serious expression of an intent to commit an act of unlawful violence to a particular individual or group of individuals." There is no requirement that the targets of the action be aware of the threat.

WHAT WOULD YOU DO? As soon as he leaves prison, Steven is arrested by police for threatening to use a weapon of mass destruction against a government building. Steven tells police that he was joking, and never intended to actually destroy the Reuss Federal Plaza. After hearing a tape of the conversation, Steven's lawyer points out that his client bragged he would carry out the attack after he finished his probation—in eight years. If you are the prosecutor in this case, do you bring charges against Steven for making a "true threat?" Why or why not? What additional information would you need to make this decision?

[To see what happened in a similar situation involving an inmate in Milwaukee, Wisconsin, see Example 14.1 in Appendix A.]

countries. It would be difficult, if not impossible, to claim that such behavior was a protected form of free speech.

Often, however, the true threat is not as evident. In the introduction to this chapter, we saw how Shannon Conley spoke openly to the FBI about her intentions to aid terrorist fighters in Syria. Do those statements, along with purchasing an airline ticket to the Middle East, constitute a true threat? Her parents and attorney certainly did not think so. In recent years, however, federal authorities have erred on the side of caution by arresting numerous "known wolves," who, like Conley, took concrete steps to travel abroad and join anti-American terrorist organizations. As of yet, courts have proved unwilling to overturn the convictions of these defendants on First Amendment grounds.

14-2 WHAT IS CYBER CRIME?

Foreign terrorist organizations such as the Islamic State of Iraq and the Levant (ISIL) are using the Internet for activities other than recruitment and propaganda. In March 2015, the home Web sites of the Dublin Rape Crisis Center in Ireland, the Southwest Montana Community Federal Credit Union, and the Montauk Manor hotel in Suffolk County, New York, were replaced by a picture of the black ISIL flag and the words "hacked by ISIL, we are everywhere."[39]

Homeland security experts worry that such relatively harmless incidents are a precursor to a much more serious **cyberattack** by a terrorist organization. Such attacks are designed to damage a nation's infrastructure, such as power companies, water treatment plants, airports, chemical plants, and oil refineries. In a worst-case scenario, a cyberattack could allow a terrorist organization to seize control of the federal air traffic control system, or shut down national power grids. "This is a much bigger threat over time than losing some credit cards to cyber criminals," said one security expert.[40]

Of course, "losing some credit cards" is hardly a small concern, particularly if one of the credit cards in question happens to be your own. Furthermore, the Internet has proved reasonably secure from a "cyber 9/11," while being disturbingly susceptible to financial attacks. Several years ago, for example, a harmful piece of software created in Russia called GameOver Zeus was used to steal login details from computers belonging to thousands of small businesses and drain over $100 million from their bank accounts. "Robbing one person at a time using a knife or a gun doesn't scale well," notes Marc Goodman of the Future Crimes Institute. "But now one person can rob millions at the click of a button."[41]

14-2a Computer Crime and the Internet

Nearly every business in today's economy relies on computers to conduct its daily affairs and to provide consumers with easy access to its products and services. Furthermore, more than 600 million American household devices are now connected to the Internet, and the proliferation of handheld Internet devices has made it possible to be online at almost any time or place. In short, the Internet has become a place where large numbers of people interact socially and commercially. In any such environment, wrongdoing has an opportunity to flourish. Throughout this section, we will be using the

Cyberattack An attempt to damage or disrupt computer systems or electronic networks operated by computers.

P. C. Vey/The New Yorker Collection/Cartoonbank.com

"You know, you can do this just as easily online."

broad term **cyber crime** to describe any criminal activity occurring via a computer in the virtual community of the Internet.

ONLINE CRIME The example of *child pornography* shows how cyber crime has raised the stakes for the criminal justice system. (Child pornography is the illegal production and sale of material depicting sexually explicit conduct involving a child.) In the late 1970s, about 250 child pornography magazines were circulating in the United States, and it was relatively easy for law enforcement to confiscate hard copies of these publications.[42] With the advent of the Internet, however, child

LO14-3 pornography became much easier to disseminate. The reasons for this include:

1. *Speed.* The Internet is a quick means of sending visual material over long distances. Child pornographers can deliver their material faster online than through regular mail.

2. *Security.* Any illegal material that passes through the hands of a mail carrier is inherently in danger of being discovered. This risk is significantly reduced with e-mail. Furthermore, Internet sites that offer child pornography can protect their customers with passwords, which keep random Web surfers (or law enforcement agents) from stumbling on the site of chat rooms.

3. *Anonymity.* Obviously, anonymity is the most important protection offered by the Internet for sellers and buyers of child pornography, as it is for any person engaged in illegal behavior in cyberspace.[43]

Because of these three factors, courts and lawmakers have had a difficult time controlling not only child pornography but also a wide variety of other online wrongdoing.

THE INCIDENCE OF CYBER CRIME It is difficult, if not impossible, to determine how much cyber crime actually takes place. Often, people never know that they have been the victims of this type of criminal activity. Furthermore, businesses sometimes fail to report such crimes for fear of losing customer confidence. Nonetheless, in 2013, the Internet Crime Complaint Center (IC3), operated as a partnership between the FBI and the National White Collar Crime Center, received about 260,000 complaints representing just over $780 million in victim losses.[44] According to the Norton Cybercrime

Report, nearly 50 percent of all adults who use the Internet have been victimized by cyber crime, with annual global losses exceeding $113 billion.[45]

14-2b Cyber Crimes against Persons and Property

Most cyber crimes are not "new" crimes. Rather, they are existing crimes in which the Internet is the instrument of wrongdoing. The challenge for law enforcement is to apply traditional laws, which were designed to protect persons from physical harm or to safeguard their physical property, to crimes committed in cyberspace. Here, we look at several types of activity that constitute "updated" crimes against persons and property—online consumer fraud, cyber theft, and cyberstalking.

CYBER CONSUMER FRAUD The expanding world of e-commerce has created many benefits for consumers. It has also led to some challenging problems, including fraud conducted via the Internet. In general, fraud is any misrepresentation knowingly made with the intention of deceiving another person. Furthermore, the victim must reasonably rely on the fraudulent information to her or his detriment. **Cyber fraud,** then, is fraud committed over the Internet. Scams that were once conducted solely by mail or phone can now be found online, and new technology has led to increasingly more creative ways to commit fraud.

Online dating scams, for example, have increased dramatically in recent years, with fraudsters creating fake profiles to deceive unwitting romantic partners. According to the IC3, in 2013 online romance scam artists defrauded victims out of more than $80 million.[46] In one case, a Galesburg, Illinois, woman defrauded twenty-three men she met on dating Web sites out of hundreds of thousands of dollars by asking them to help pay for her mother's fictitious medical expenses.

As you can see in Figure 14.2, fraud accounts for the largest percentage of losses related to consumer cyber crime. Two widely reported forms of cyber crime are *advance fee fraud* and *online auction fraud.* In the

Cyber Crime A crime that occurs online, in the virtual community of the Internet, as opposed to in the physical world.

Cyber Fraud Any misrepresentation knowingly made over the Internet with the intention of deceiving another and on which a reasonable person would and does rely to his or her detriment.

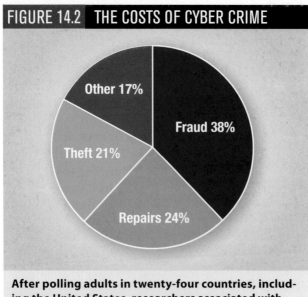

FIGURE 14.2 THE COSTS OF CYBER CRIME

Other 17%

Fraud 38%

Theft 21%

Repairs 24%

After polling adults in twenty-four countries, including the United States, researchers associated with the American security software company Symantec estimated that more than 1.5 million computer users worldwide are victims of cyber crime each day. As the graph shows, 83 percent of the financial costs associated with cyber crime are the result of fraud, theft, or computer repairs made necessary by the wrongdoing.

Source: *2013 Norton Report* (Mountain View, Calif.: Symantec, 2014), 8.

CYBER THEFT In cyberspace, thieves are not subject to the physical limitations of the "real" world. A thief can steal data stored in a networked computer with network access from anywhere on the globe. Only the speed of the connection and the thief's computer equipment limit the quantity of data that can be stolen.

Identity Theft This freedom from physical limitations has led to a marked increase in **identity theft,** which occurs when the wrongdoer steals a form of identification—such as a name, date of birth, or Social Security number—and uses the information to access the victim's financial resources. Once a Social Security number has been stolen, for example, it has proved fairly simple for the wrongdoer to commit tax fraud by filing false paperwork with the Internal Revenue Service (IRS) using that number. The defense attorney for one such tax fraud perpetrator—who accumulated $3 million before her arrest—expressed hope that the "IRS will figure out a way to prevent this from happening in the future, so someone with a sixth-grade education can't defraud them so easily."[47]

According to the federal government, about 7 percent of American households have at least one member who has been the victim of identity theft.[48] More than half of identity thefts involve the misappropriation of an existing credit-card account.[49] In the "real world," this is generally accomplished by stealing an actual credit card. Online, an identity thief can steal financial information by fooling Web sites into thinking that he or she is the true account holder. For example, important personal information such as one's birthday, hometown, or employer, often available on social media sites such as Facebook, can be used to convince a third party to reveal the victim's Social Security or bank account number.

Password Protection The more personal information a cyber criminal obtains, the easier it is for him or her to find a victim's online user name. Once the online user name has been compromised, it is easier to steal the victim's password, which is often the last line of defense to financial information. Numerous software programs aid identity thieves in illegally obtaining passwords. A technique called *keystroke logging,* for example, relies on software that embeds itself in a victim's computer and records every keystroke made on that computer. User names and passwords are then recorded and sold to the highest bidder. Internet users should also be wary of any links contained within e-mails sent from an unknown source, as these links can sometimes be used to illegally obtain personal information. (See Figure 14.3 for some hints on how to protect your online passwords.)

simplest form of advance fee fraud, consumers order and pay for items such as automobiles or antiques that are never delivered. Online auction fraud is also fairly straightforward. A person lists an item for auction, on either a legitimate or a fake auction site, and then refuses to send the product after receiving payment. Several years ago, for example, U.S. Immigration and Customs Enforcement uncovered a scheme in which a group of Romanians set up a fraudulent eBay site and convinced five American victims to send them $120,000 for nonexistent items such as boats and cars.

CAREER TIP Online auction companies hire *Internet fraud investigators* to ensure the authenticity of their services. In some instances, investigators must travel to countries with a reputation for harboring cyber criminals, such as Romania, Russia, and Ukraine. "The fraudsters need to know we're coming after them," says the head of eBay's Trust and Safety Division.

Identity Theft The theft of personal information, such as a person's name, driver's license number, or Social Security number.

FIGURE 14.3 PROTECTING ONLINE PASSWORDS

1. **Don't** use existing words such as your pet's name or your hometown. Such words are easy for computer identity theft programs to decode.
2. **Do** use at least eight characters in your passwords, with a nonsensical combination of upper- and lower-case letters, numbers, and symbols. A weak password is "scout1312." A strong password is "4X$dQ%3Z9j."
3. **Don't** use the same username and password for different Web accounts. If you do, then each account is in danger if one account is compromised.
4. **Do** use a different password for each Web account. If necessary, write down the various passwords and keep the list in a safe place.
5. **Don't** use information that can be easily found online or guessed at in choosing the questions that Web sites use to verify your password. That is, don't select questions such as "What is your birthday?" or "What is your city of birth?" Instead, choose questions with obscure answers that you are certain to remember or can easily look up.
6. **Don't** log on to any Web site if you are connected to the Internet via a wireless network (Wi-Fi) that is not itself password protected.

Once an online password has been compromised, the information on the protected Web site is fair game for identity thieves. By following these simple rules, you can strengthen the protection provided by your online passwords.

Phishing A distinct form of identity theft known as **phishing** adds a different wrinkle to this particular form of cyber crime. In a phishing attack, the perpetrators "fish" for financial data and passwords from consumers by posing as a legitimate business such as a bank or credit-card company. The "phisher" sends an e-mail asking the recipient to "update" or "confirm" vital information, often with the threat that an account or some other service will be discontinued if the information is not provided. Once the unsuspecting target enters the information, the phisher can use it to masquerade as the person or to extract funds from his or her bank or credit account.

The preferred method of phishing is through the use of **spam,** or unsolicited "junk e-mails" that flood virtual mailboxes with advertisements, solicitations, and other messages. By sending millions or even billions of these fraudulent e-mails, phishers need only entice a few users to "take the bait" to ensure a successful and lucrative operation. Phishing scams have also spread to other areas, such as text messaging and social-networking sites. About 22 percent of all phishing, for example, takes place on Facebook.[50]

Another form of phishing, called *spear phishing,* is much more difficult to detect because the messages seem to have come from co-workers, friends, or family members. In 2015, a cybergang infiltrated the security systems of a number of banks worldwide by sending bank employees e-mails containing links to news clips, apparently sent by colleagues. When the employees clicked on the links, they inadvertently downloaded software onto their computers that allowed the cyber thieves to drain hundreds of millions of dollars from accounts in the affected banks.

CYBER AGGRESSION AND SOCIAL MEDIA The
growing use of mobile devices such as smartphones and tablets has added another outlet for online criminal activity. According to Norton Security, only a quarter of the owners of such devices use security software for protection. As a result, nearly 40 percent of these users have experienced cybercrime such as vishing (phishing by phone) and smishing (phishing by SMS/text message).[51] In particular, widespread smartphone use seems to have exacerbated cyberbullying, which we discussed in the context of school crime in the previous chapter. According to one survey, American teenagers who consider themselves "heavy users" of their cell phones are much more likely to experience cyberbullying than those who consider themselves "normal users" of the devices.[52]

In Chapter 3's *CJ and Technology* feature, we discussed "revenge porn," a form of cyberbullying that involves the nonconsensual publication online of explicit sexual images. Revenge porn is often a component of **cyberstalking,** which occurs when one person uses e-mail, text messages, or some other form of electronic communication to cause a victim to reasonably fear for her or his safety or the safety of the victim's immediate family. According to the most recent federal data on the subject, about 850,000 Americans are targets of cyberstalking each year.[53]

Nearly every state and the federal government have passed laws to combat this form of criminal behavior. For instance, in April 2014, Adam Savader of Great

Phishing Sending an unsolicited e-mail that falsely claims to be from a legitimate organization in an attempt to acquire sensitive information from the recipient.

Spam Bulk e-mails, particularly of commercial advertising, sent in large quantities without the consent of the recipient.

Cyberstalking The crime of stalking, committed in cyberspace through the use of e-mail, text messages, or another form of electronic communication.

Neck, New York, was sentenced to thirty months in federal prison for cyberstalking fifteen different women. Besides sending his victims sexually explicit e-mails, Savader stole nude photos of the women by hacking into various social media sites. He then threatened to release the photos to the victims' relatives if they did not provide him with more such images.

14-2c Cyber Crimes in the Business World

Just as cyberspace can be a dangerous place for consumers, it presents a number of hazards for businesses that wish to offer their services on the Internet. Almost as soon as Apple, Inc., introduced a new mobile-payment system in late 2014, cyber thieves began using the company's smartphones and tablets to make purchases with stolen credit-card numbers.

The same circumstances that enable companies to reach a large number of consumers also leave them vulnerable to cyber crime. For example, at about the same time Apple was experiencing troubles with its new mobile-pay technology, cyber criminals were stealing the credit-card data of at least 60 million Home Depot customers and illegally accessing the financial information of 76 million JPMorgan Chase clients.

HACKERS The individuals who breached security at Home Depot and JPMorgan Chase are known as *hackers*. A **hacker** is a person who uses one computer to illegally access another. The danger posed by hackers has increased significantly because of **botnets,** or networks of computers that have been appropriated by hackers without the knowledge of their owners. A hacker will secretly install a program on large numbers of personal computer "robots," or "bots," that allows him or her to forward transmissions to an even larger number of systems. The program attaches itself to the host computer when someone operating the computer opens a fraudulent e-mail.

Brand X Pictures/Jupiter Images

According to several studies, someone who is a victim of a cyber crime such as identity theft has a relatively high risk of being a victim of the same crime again. *Why do you think this is the case?*

Programs that create botnets are forms of *malware,* a term that refers to any program that is harmful to a computer or, by extension, a computer user. A **worm,** for example, is a software program that is capable of reproducing itself as it spreads from one computer to the next. A **virus,** another form of malware, is also able to reproduce itself, but must be attached to an "infested" host file to travel from one computer network to another. Worms and viruses can be programmed to perform a number of functions, such as prompting host computers to continually "crash" and reboot, or otherwise infect the system.

Malware is often used to target specific companies or organizations. During the 2013 holiday season, for example, a group of Eastern European hackers managed to gain access to the computer system of the retail giant Target. Once "inside," these hackers infected the in-store devices that Target customers use to swipe their credit and debit cards with a "memory scraper" malware nicknamed Kaptoxa. Over the course of several weeks, the malware was used to steal credit and debit card data, as well as passwords, phone numbers, and addresses, from at least 70 million Target customers. Experts estimate that the Kaptoxa virus was used to steal more than $4 billion in unrecoverable losses from these unfortunate consumers.[54]

Hacker A person who uses one computer to break into another.

Botnet A network of computers that have been appropriated without the knowledge of their owners and used to spread harmful programs via the Internet; short for *robot network.*

Worm A computer program that can automatically replicate itself and interfere with the normal use of a computer. A worm does not need to be attached to an existing file to move from one network to another.

Virus A computer program that can replicate itself and interfere with the normal use of a computer. A virus cannot exist as a separate entity and must attach itself to another program to move through a network.

PIRATING INTELLECTUAL PROPERTY ONLINE Most people think of wealth in terms of houses, land, cars, stocks, and bonds. Wealth, however, also includes **intellectual property,** which consists of the products that result from intellectual, creative processes. The government provides various forms of protection for intellectual property, such as copyrights and patents. These protections ensure that a person who writes a book or a song or creates a software program is financially rewarded if that product is sold in the marketplace.

Intellectual property such as books, films, music, and software is vulnerable to "piracy"—the unauthorized copying and use of the property. In the past, copying intellectual products was time consuming, and the quality of the pirated copies was clearly inferior. In today's online world, however, things have changed. Simply clicking a mouse can now reproduce millions of unauthorized copies, and pirated duplicates of copyrighted works obtained via the Internet are often exactly the same as the original, or close to it. The Business Software Alliance estimates that 43 percent of all business software is pirated, costing software makers more than $62 billion in 2013.[55]

Intellectual Property Property resulting from intellectual, creative processes.

COMPUTER FORENSIC SPECIALIST

Job Description:

▶ Investigate misbehavior on computer systems by collecting and analyzing computer-related evidence. Retrieve data that have been encrypted or electronically stored on a commercial or personal computer.

▶ Work for a law enforcement or homeland security agency to investigate crimes or terrorists' activities, or for a private company to protect commercial data and defend against worms, viruses, and other malware.

What Kind of Training Is Required?

▶ An extensive knowledge of computers, computer programming, and data retrieval is essential. A number of colleges, universities, and online educational organizations offer computer forensic courses that provide the skills necessary for this career.

▶ A complete understanding of the rules of evidence in criminal courts and the ability to establish a proper chain of custody for all evidence retrieved from targeted computer databases.

Annual Salary Range?

▶ $50,000–$90,000

debra hughes, 2010/Used under license from ShutterStock.com

GETTING LINKEDIN

Most of the postings on LinkedIn for forensic computer specialists have been posted by banks and other financial institutions. A recent internship offered by a bank in Medford, Massachusetts, for example, promises the opportunity to gain experience in the field of "incident response"—that is, security breaches and bank robberies.

14-2d Fighting Cyber Crime

After Target suffered the extensive hacking attack described earlier, the company hired private contractors to plug its security holes and erase the malware from its compromised systems. Ideally, of course, corporations should have software already in place to prevent hacking operations, and most do. Businesses spend billions of dollars a year to *encrypt* their vital information. **Encryption** is the process of encoding information stored in computers in such a way that only authorized parties will have access to it.

Companies also hire outside experts to act as hackers and attempt to gain access to their systems, a practice known as "penetration testing." Even the most thorough private protection services often lag behind the ingenuity of the hacker community, however. In the Target attack, for example, the malware was programmed to constantly erase itself, making it practically impossible to detect. "The dynamics of the Internet and cyberspace are so fast that we have a hard time staying ahead of the adversary," admits former U.S. Secret Service agent Robert D. Rodriguez.[56]

THE "ZERO DAYS" PROBLEM The Internet was designed to promote connectivity, not security. As more and more online threats to companies such as Target have developed, those businesses have had to respond with increasingly novel defenses. Facebook, for example, has constructed ThreatData, a defense system that monitors new worms, viruses, and malicious Web sites to create a constantly updated "blacklist" of blocked malware. Still, it is virtually impossible to protect against "zero days," the industry term for new vulnerabilities that security software cannot detect and for which there are no defenses. According to the most recent State of Cyber Crime Survey, in 2013 at least three thousand companies were unaware of cyber intrusions until notified of the problem by the FBI.[57]

Clearly, private industry needs government help to fight off cyber criminals. With hundreds of millions of users in every corner of the globe transferring unimaginable amounts of information almost instantaneously, the Internet has proved resistant to government regulation. In addition, although a number of countries have tried to "control" the Internet, the U.S. government has generally adopted a hands-off attitude to better promote the free flow of ideas and encourage the growth of electronic commerce. Thus, in this country cyberspace is, for the most part, unregulated, making efforts to fight cyber crime all the more difficult.

CHALLENGES FOR LAW ENFORCEMENT "In the eighties, if there was a bank robbery, the pool of suspects was limited to the people who were in the vicinity at the time," says Shawn Henry, former head of the FBI's Cyber Division. "Now when a bank is robbed the pool of suspects is limited to the number of people in the world with access to a five-hundred dollar laptop and an Internet connection. Which . . . is two and a half billion people."[58] The difficulty of finding suspects is just one of the challenges that law enforcement officers face in dealing with online crime. Another is gathering evidence in cyberspace.

Cyber Forensics Police officers cannot put yellow tape around a computer screen or dust a Web site for fingerprints. The best, and often the only, way to fight computer crime is with technology that gives law enforcement agencies the ability to "track" hackers and other cyber criminals through the Internet. These efforts are complicated by the fact that digital evidence can be altered or erased even as the cyber crime is being committed. In Chapter 5, we discussed forensics, or the application of science to find evidence of criminal activity. Within the past two decades, a branch of this science known as **cyber forensics** has evolved to gather evidence of cyber crimes.

The main goal of cyber forensics is to gather **digital evidence,** or information of value to a criminal investigation that is stored on, received by, or transmitted by an electronic device such as a computer. Sometimes, this evidence is not particularly difficult to find. In the Social Security identity theft scheme mentioned earlier, the offender bragged about buying a $92,000 car and being the "queen of IRS tax fraud" on her Facebook page.

CYBER SLEUTHING More sophisticated cyber criminals employ technology such as Tor to cover their tracks. Tor is a form of software that allows users to mask their IP addresses (codes that identify individual computers on the Internet) and the IP addresses of anyone with whom they communicate. To counteract such efforts,

---

Encryption The encoding of computer data with the goal of protecting the data from unauthorized parties.

Cyber Forensics The application of computer technology to finding and utilizing evidence of cyber crimes.

Digital Evidence Information or data of value to a criminal investigation that is either stored on, received by, or transmitted by electronic means.

When it released the iPhone 6 in 2014, Apple, Inc., used a marketing pitch perfect for the times. The device, Apple promised, was government snoop-proof. Consumers would be given the option to create a security code unique to each iPhone—a code that Apple did not possess and therefore could not pass along to the federal government, regardless of the legal procedures discussed earlier in the chapter. The mathematical algorithm used on the phone to encrypt information such as e-mails, photos, and contacts is so complex, Apple claims, that it would take five and a half years to hack.

Thinking about Encrypted Smartphones
FBI director James B. Comey criticized Apple's encryption efforts for the iPhone 6, saying that companies should not market "something that expressly [allows] people to hold themselves beyond the law." Do you agree with Comey's statement? How might an encrypted smartphone benefit terrorists and criminals who operate on the Internet? Explain your answers.

Hemanta Kumar Raval/ShutterzStock.com

experts in cyber forensics have created tools such as the search engine Memex, which has the ability to bypass Tor's encryption codes by tracing past Internet activity. Memex has been particularly helpful in uncovering online sex trafficking operations, as it is able to determine the time and location of the photos that these criminal enterprises use to advertise sex workers on the Internet.[59]

Cyber sleuths can also create a digital duplicate of a targeted hard drive, enabling them to break access codes, determine passwords, and search files. "Short of taking your hard drive and having it run over by a Mack truck," says one expert, "you can't be sure that anything is truly deleted from your computer."[60] The latest challenge to cyber investigators is posed by *cloud computing*, in which data are stored not in a physical location but in a virtual, shared computing platform that is linked simultaneously to a number of different computers. Therefore, law enforcement officers investigating wrongdoing in the "cloud" may not have full control of the "crime scene." (The growing importance of cyber crime has led

a number of universities to offer graduate certificates in cyber forensics. To learn about one of the programs, go to the Web site of the Marshall University Forensic Science Center.)

14-3 WHAT IS THE DEBATE OVER GUN CONTROL?

Federal law regarding firearm sales online is fairly strict. The seller cannot simply mail a gun to the buyer. Instead, the seller must send the gun to a store or dealer that has been licensed by the federal government, and the buyer must pick up the gun in person. Several years ago, however, libertarian activist Cody Wilson uploaded instructions for making a plastic gun (using a 3-D printer) to the Internet. Within forty-eight hours, blueprints for this firearm—which fires .380 caliber bullets and is effective at short range—were downloaded 100,000 times and shared across the expanse of the Web.[61]

Being plastic, this gun can pass through metal detectors at airports, schools, and government buildings without notice. Consequently, some observers called for the federal government to ban it. Others insisted that the plastic gun should be regulated like any other firearm, meaning that it would be widely available to the public. Thus, this new type of weapon became another flashpoint in the debate over **gun control,** the shorthand term for policies that the government implements to regulate firearm ownership.

14-3a Firearms in the United States

Gun ownership is widespread in the United States, with about one-third of American households possessing at least one firearm.[62] According to the Congressional Research Service, there are about 310 million guns in the United States, not counting weapons on military bases.[63] Furthermore, there are nearly 130,000 federally licensed firearms dealers in this country, compared with about 144,000 gas stations and 14,000 McDonald's restaurants.[64]

The vast majority of gun owners are law-abiding citizens who use firearms for self-protection or recreational activities. Still, about 31,000 people are killed by gunfire in the United States each year, and firearms are used in 69 percent of the nation's murders and 41 percent of its robberies.[65] Furthermore, illegally obtained firearms are a constant concern for law enforcement officials and, apparently, many citizens. A recent poll showed that about half of Americans favor stricter measures by the government to control gun ownership.[66]

14-3b Regulating Gun Ownership

The Second Amendment to the U.S. Constitution states, "A well regulated Militia, being necessary to the security of a free State, the right of the people to keep and bear Arms, shall not be infringed." Because this language is somewhat archaic and vague, the United States Supreme Court has attempted to clarify the amendment's modern meaning. Over the course of two separate rulings, the Court stated that the Second Amendment provides

Lori Martin/ShutterStock.com

Do you think that increasing restrictions on the legal sale of firearms would reduce violent crime in the United States? Explain your answer.

individuals with a constitutional right to bear arms and that this right must be recognized at all levels of government—federal, state, and local.[67]

LO14-4 **BACKGROUND CHECKS** In both its Second Amendment cases, the Supreme Court emphasized that, to promote public safety, the government could continue to prohibit certain individuals—such as criminals and the mentally ill—from legally purchasing firearms. The primary method for doing so involves **background checks** of individuals who purchase firearms from federally licensed gun dealers.

The mechanics of background checks are regulated by the Brady Handgun Violence Prevention Act, enacted in 1993.[68] Known as the Brady Bill, this legislation requires a person wishing to purchase a gun from a licensed firearms dealer to apply for the privilege of doing so. The application process includes a background check by a law enforcement agency, usually the FBI. The applicant can be prohibited from purchasing a firearm if his or her record contains one of a number of "red flags," including a previous felony conviction, evidence of illegal drug addiction, or wrongdoing associated with domestic violence.[69]

Gun Control Efforts by a government to regulate or control the sale of firearms.

Background Check An investigation of a person's history to determine whether that person should be allowed a certain privilege, such as the ability to possess a firearm.

The Brady Bill has been criticized for requiring background checks only for those consumers who purchase guns from federally licensed firearms dealers. It does not cover purchases made at gun shows or from private citizens, which make up a significant percentage of the market.

MENTAL-HEALTH ISSUES Crucially, any person who has been involuntarily committed to a "mental institution" or "adjudicated as a mental defective" is also barred from purchasing or possessing firearms. The designation of being "mentally defective" is given to a person whom a court or other legal entity determines

1. Is a danger to herself or himself or others,
2. Lacks the mental capacity to manage her or his own affairs, or
3. Has been found insane or incompetent to stand trial by a criminal or military court.[70]

One problem with the background check system is that it relies on states to provide the federal government with mental-health information about their citizens. When states fail to do so, a background check is somewhat meaningless. In one well-known example of a background check failure, in 2005 a Virginia judge declared Virginia Tech student Seung-Hui Cho to be mentally ill. The state did not, however, submit Cho's name to the FBI, as required by federal law. Consequently, Cho was able to pass a background check and purchase several handguns. On April 16, 2007, he used the weapons to kill thirty-two people and injure seventeen others on the Virginia Tech campus in Blacksburg.

LEGISLATIVE GUN CONTROL EFFORTS Because of federal inaction, it has been left to the individual states to pass stricter gun control measures, if their elected officials choose to do so. So, in 2013, following several highly publicized mass shootings, states passed thirty-nine laws tightening gun ownership regulations. The New York Secure Firearms Enforcement Act, for example, requires background checks for private gun transactions and for the sale of ammunition. The law also makes it more difficult to purchase semiautomatic weapons and easier to keep firearms out of the hands of the mentally ill within state limits.[71]

During that year, states also passed seventy laws removing restrictions on the sale and use of firearms. Eight of these new laws allow guns on grade school grounds, two allow guns on college campuses, and several others allow people to carry firearms in churches

and bars.[72] If such contradictory legislative efforts are any indication, the issue of gun control will remain divisive and unresolved for the near future.

CAREER TIP A number of states require individuals to undergo firearms training in a classroom and on a target range before purchasing a handgun. Experts called *certified handgun instructors* administer such training to those individuals who want a gun permit.

14-4 WHAT IS WHITE-COLLAR CRIME?

A travel agent in Saco, Maine, takes thousands of dollars from clients for trips she never books. A man in Oakland, California, prepares federal loan applications for "straw students" who have no intention of attending school, pocketing $500,000 in the process. Employees of a Framingham, Massachusetts, pharmacy dispense tainted meningitis drugs that cause sixty-four deaths. A member of the United States House of Representatives from Illinois spends eighteen months behind bars for using campaign contributions to buy more than $750,000 worth of personal luxury items.

These cases represent a variety of criminal behavior with different motives, different methods, and different victims. Yet they all fall into the category of *white-collar crime*, an umbrella term for wrongdoing marked by deceit and scandal rather than violence. As we mentioned in Chapter 1, white-collar crime has a broad impact on the global economy, causing American businesses alone hundreds of billions of dollars in losses each year. Despite its global and national importance, however, white-collar crime has consistently challenged a criminal justice system that struggles to define the problem, much less effectively combat it.

14-4a Defining White-Collar Crime

LO14-5 White-collar crime is not an official category of criminal behavior measured by the federal government in the Uniform Crime Report. Rather, it covers a broad range of illegal acts involving "lying, cheating, and stealing," according to the FBI's Web site on the subject.[73] To give a more technical definition, white-collar crimes are financial activities characterized by deceit and concealment that do not involve physical force or violence. Figure 14.4 lists and describes some common types of white-collar crime.

FIGURE 14.4 WHITE-COLLAR CRIMES

Embezzlement

Embezzlement is a form of employee fraud in which an individual uses his or her position within an organization to *embezzle,* or steal, the employer's funds, property, or other assets. Pilferage is a less serious form of employee fraud in which the individual steals items from the workplace.

Tax Evasion

Tax evasion occurs when taxpayers underreport (or do not report) their taxable income or otherwise purposely attempt to evade a tax liability.

Credit-Card and Check Fraud

Credit-card fraud involves obtaining credit-card numbers through a variety of schemes (such as stealing them from the Internet) and using the numbers for personal gain. Check fraud includes writing checks that are not covered by bank funds, forging checks, and stealing traveler's checks.

Mail and Wire Fraud

This umbrella term covers all schemes that involve the use of mail, radio, television, the Internet, or a telephone to intentionally deceive in a business environment.

Securities Fraud

Securities fraud covers illegal activity in the stock market. Stockbrokers who steal funds from their clients are guilty of securities fraud, as are those who engage in *insider trading,* which involves buying or selling securities on the basis of information that has not been made available to the public.

Bribery

Also known as *influence peddling,* bribery occurs in the business world when somebody within a company or government sells influence, power, or information to a person outside the company or government who can benefit. A county official, for example, could give a construction company a lucrative county contract to build a new jail. In return, the construction company would give some of the proceeds, known as a *kickback,* to the official.

Consumer Fraud

This term covers a wide variety of activities designed to defraud consumers, from selling counterfeit art to offering "free" items, such as electronic devices or vacations, that include a number of hidden charges.

Insurance Fraud

Insurance fraud involves making false claims in order to collect insurance payments. Faking an injury in order to receive payments from a workers' compensation program, for example, is a form of insurance fraud.

DIFFERENT TECHNIQUES To differentiate white-collar crime from "regular" crime, criminologists Michael L. Benson of the University of Cincinnati and Sally S. Simpson of the University of Maryland focus on technique. For example, in an ordinary burglary, a criminal uses physical means, such as picking a lock, to get somewhere he or she should not be—someone else's home—to do something that is clearly illegal. Furthermore, the victim is a specific identifiable individual—the homeowner. In contrast, white-collar criminals usually (1) have legal access to the place where the crime occurs; (2) are spatially separated from the victim, who is often unknown; and (3) behave in a manner that is, at least superficially, legitimate.[74]

Benson and Simpson also identify three main techniques used by white-collar criminals to carry out their crimes:[75]

1. *Deception.* White-collar crime almost always involves a party who deceives and a party who is deceived. The nation's federal Medicare system, which provides health insurance for those sixty-five years of age and older, is a frequent target of deceptive practices. For example, from 1999 to 2014, the federal government paid billions of dollars to medical-supply companies as reimbursement for expensive wheelchairs that the companies provided to Medicare patients. Because the patients either did not exist or did not actually need wheelchairs, employees at the companies kept the reimbursed funds for themselves.[76]

2. *Abuse of trust.* A white-collar criminal often operates in a position of trust and misuses that trust for personal benefit. In 2015, for example, a financial advisor from Rockville, Maryland, was sentenced to forty-two months in prison for secretly withdrawing $1.2 million from the bank account of an elderly client to deposit in various personal accounts.

3. *Concealment and conspiracy.* To continue their illegal activities, white-collar criminals need to conceal those activities. In *odometer fraud,* for example, an automobile dealership "rolls back" the odometers of used cars so that a higher price can be charged for the vehicles. As soon as the fraud is discovered, the scheme can no longer succeed.

VICTIMS OF WHITE-COLLAR CRIME As the above examples show, sometimes the victim of a white-collar crime is obvious. A dishonest financial advisor is stealing directly from his or her clients, and odometer fraud denies consumers the actual value of their purchased automobiles. But who was victimized in the fraudulent Medicare wheelchair scheme? In that instance, the "victims" were the U.S. taxpayers, who collectively had to cover the cost of the unwarranted items. Such health-care scams defraud U.S. taxpayers out of at least $82 billion each year.[77] Often, white-collar crime does not target individuals but rather large groups or even abstract concepts such as "society" or "the environment."

14-4b Regulating and Policing White-Collar Crime

For legal purposes, a corporation can be treated as a person capable of forming the intent necessary to commit a crime. Thus, in March 2015, Freedom Industries pleaded guilty to three water-pollution crimes and agreed to pay about $900,000 in fines after accepting responsibility for a chemical leak that had contaminated drinking water in the Kanawha Valley of West Virginia thirteen months earlier. About ten thousand gallons of a coal-cleaning substance called 4-methylcyclohexane methanol were erroneously dumped in the Elk River, sickening hundreds of local residents.

The aftermath of the Elk River chemical spill, caused by Freedom Industries' negligence, is an example of *corporate violence*. In contrast to assaults committed by individual people, **corporate violence** is a result of policies or actions undertaken by a corporation. In the United States, parallel regulatory and criminal systems have evolved to prevent corporate violence and other forms of white-collar crime.

THE REGULATORY JUSTICE SYSTEM Although most white-collar crimes cause harm, these harms are not necessarily covered by criminal statutes. Indeed, more often they are covered by *administrative* laws, which we first encountered in Chapter 3. Such laws make up the backbone of the U.S. regulatory system, through which the government attempts to control the actions of individuals, corporations, and other institutions. The goal of **regulation** is not prevention or punishment as much as **compliance,** or the following of regulatory guidelines.

For example, more than a decade ago the Food and Drug Administration (FDA) approved use of the antipsychotic drug Risperdal—produced by Johnson & Johnson—to treat schizophrenia, a condition we discussed in Chapter 2. Violating these guidelines, representatives of Johnson & Johnson marketed Risperdal as medication for elderly nursing home patients and children who suffered from attention deficit hyperactivity disorder and autism. In 2013, the corporation agreed to pay $2.2 billion in penalties stemming from its lack of compliance, which placed Risperdal users at risk of stroke and other health problems.

The FDA—which protects the public health by regulating food products and a wide variety of drugs and medical practices—is one of the federal administrative agencies whose compliance oversight brings them into contact with white-collar crime. Other important federal regulatory agencies with regard to white-collar crime include:

1. **The Environmental Protection Agency (EPA),** which regulates air quality, water quality, and toxic waste. The EPA was intricately involved in the federal government's response to the Elk River chemical spill, described earlier in the section.

2. **The Occupational Safety and Health Administration (OSHA),** which enforces workplace health and safety standards.

3. **The Securities and Exchange Commission (SEC),** which ensures that financial markets such as the New York Stock Exchange operate in a fair manner.

In 2015, the Federal Communications Commission voted to regulate the Internet as a *public utility* (a company that provides a public service, such as electricity or telephone communications). This move may eventually impact federal law enforcement efforts to combat the various forms of cyber crime we discussed in the previous section.

LAW ENFORCEMENT AND WHITE-COLLAR CRIME In general, when officials at a regulatory agency find that criminal prosecution is needed to punish a particular violation, they will refer the matter to the U.S. Department of Justice. Either through such referrals or at their own discretion, federal officials prosecute white-collar crime using the investigatory powers of several different federal law enforcement agencies.

The FBI has become the lead agency when it comes to white-collar crime, particularly in response to recent financial scandals, as we shall soon see. The U.S. Postal Inspection Service is also quite active in such investigations, as fraudulent activities often involve the U.S. mail. In addition, the Internal Revenue Service's Criminal Investigative Division has jurisdiction over a wide variety of white-collar crimes, including tax fraud, and operates perhaps the most effective white-collar crime lab in the country.[78]

Corporate Violence Physical harm to individuals or the environment that occurs as the result of corporate policies or decision making.

Regulation A governmental order or rule having the force of law that is usually implemented by an administrative agency.

Compliance The state of operating in accordance with governmental standards.

14-4c White-Collar Crime in the 21st Century

The decade that ended in 2010 was marked by two periods of financial scandal. First, in 2001 and 2002, fraudulent accounting practices led to the demise of giant corporations such as Enron and Worldcom, costing investors tens of billions of dollars. Then, near the end of the decade, the collapse of the subprime mortgage market caused millions of Americans to lose their homes to foreclosure and led to the collapse of

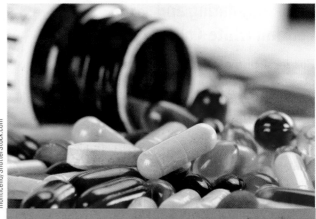

Suppose a drug manufacturer mislabels the ingredients of a particular supplement, and, as a result, a person who takes the supplement dies. *Has the drug manufacturer committed a white-collar crime? Does it matter if the mislabeling was accidental? Explain your answers.*

major financial institutions such as Lehman Brothers and Washington Mutual. In the latter period, headlines focused on widespread *mortgage fraud,* or dishonest practices relating to home loans, along with the misdeeds of Bernard Madoff. Before his 2008 arrest, Madoff managed to defraud thousands of investors out of approximately $65 billion.

As has often occurred in U.S. history, these scandals and the concurrent economic downturns led to greater regulation and criminalization of white-collar crime. In 1934, for example, in the wake of the Great Depression, Congress established the SEC to watch over the American economy.[79] Similarly, in 2002 Congress passed legislation which, among other things, enhanced the penalties for those convicted of white-collar crimes.[80] Bernard Madoff, for example, received a 150-year prison term for his illegal actions, and in June 2012 Allen Stanford was sentenced to 110 years in prison for stealing more than $7 billion from investors over the course of two decades.

Furthermore, in response to the "Great Recession" of 2008 and 2009, the FBI created the National Mortgage Fraud Team and began to crack down on a variety of white-collar crimes. Indeed, FBI agents are increasingly using aggressive tactics such as going undercover, planting wiretaps, and raiding offices—tactics previously reserved for drug dealers, mobsters, and terrorists—against white-collar criminals.

Quiz

1. A person who contributes funds to a "foreign terrorist organization" runs the risk of being prosecuted for the federal crime of providing _____ _____ under federal law.

2. The controversy over whether federal agents need a warrant before collecting metadata concerning phone and Internet activity hinges on a person's _____ _____ of privacy when using her or his telephone or going online.

3. Someone who makes a "true threat" that places a victim in fear of unlawful violence is not always protected by the First Amendment's guarantee of freedom of _____.

4. Web thieves have opportunities to practice _____ theft because of the large amount of personal financial information that is stored on the Internet.

5. Hackers sometimes employ _____, or networks of hijacked computers, to carry out various illegal online activities.

6. _____ _____ such as films and music is vulnerable to being "pirated" by unauthorized users on the Internet.

7. The Brady Bill requires a person who wants to purchase a firearm from a licensed dealer to undergo a _____ _____ to determine whether he or she is eligible for gun ownership.

8. The United States Supreme Court has ruled that a government body can prohibit gun ownership for those with a criminal record or a history of _____ _____.

9. White-collar criminals often use deception, concealment, and the abuse of _____ to perpetrate theft without violence.

10. Regulatory agencies require _____ with various guidelines to protect individuals from corporate violence.

Answers can be found in the Answers section in the back of the book.

ENDNOTES

1

1. "Don't Shoot," *The Economist* (December 13, 2014), 27.

2. Missouri Revised Statutes, Section 563.046.2 (August 28, 2014).

3. Quoted in Ashby Jones, "Why Ferguson Officer Wasn't Charged: A Look at the 'Use of Force' Doctrine," *Wall Street Journal* (November 24, 2014), at **blogs.wsj.com/law/2014/11/24/why -ferguson-officer-wasnt-charged-a-look-at-use -of-force-doctrine.**

4. Herman Bianchi, *Justice as Sanctuary: Toward a New System of Crime Control* (Bloomington: Indiana University Press, 1994), 72.

5. Tanzina Vega and Megan Thee-Brenan, "Polls Show National Unease with Missouri Unrest," *New York Times* (August 22, 2014), A14.

6. *2014 Report to the Nations: Occupational Fraud and Abuse* (Austin, Tex.: Association of Certified Fraud Examiners, 2014), 4.

7. Megan Kurlychek, "What Is My Left Hand Doing? The Need for Unifying Purpose and Policy in the Criminal Justice System," *Criminology & Public Policy* (November 2011), 909.

8. Quoted in Paula Mejia, "Supreme Court to Tackle Rap-Inspired Online Threats," *Newsweek .com* (November 30, 2014), at **www.newsweek .com/supreme-court-tackle-rap-inspired-online -threats-288060.**

9. *Gonzales v. Oregon,* 546 U.S. 243 (2006). Many United States Supreme Court cases will be cited in this book, and it is important to understand these citations. *Gonzales v. Oregon* refers to the parties in the case that the Court is reviewing. "U.S." is the abbreviation for *United States Reports,* the official publication of United States Supreme Court decisions. "546" refers to the volume of the *United States Reports* in which the case appears, and "243" is the page number. The citation ends with the year the case was decided, in parentheses. Most, though not all, Supreme Court case citations in this book will follow this formula.

10. Steve Nelson, "Bipartisan Task Force Looks to Cut List of 4,500 Federal Crimes," *U.S. News & World Report* (June 14, 2013), at **www.usnews .com/news/newsgram/articles/2013/06/14 /bipartisan-task-force-looks-to-cut-list-of-4500 -federal-crimes.**

11. President's Commission on Law Enforcement and Administration of Justice, *The Challenge of Crime in a Free Society* (Washington, D.C.: Government Printing Office, 1967), 7.

12. John Heinz and Peter Manikas, "Networks among Elites in a Local Criminal Justice System," *Law and Society Review* 26 (1992), 831–861.

13. James Q. Wilson, "What to Do about Crime: Blaming Crime on Root Causes," *Vital Speeches* (April 1, 1995), 373.

14. Herbert Packer, *The Limits of the Criminal Sanction* (Stanford, Calif.: Stanford University Press, 1968), 154–173.

15. *Ibid.*

16. Daniel Givelber, "Meaningless Acquittals, Meaningful Convictions: Do We Reliably Acquit the Innocent?" *Rutgers Law Review* 49 (Summer 1997), 1317.

17. Donna Evans, "Police Crackdown on Jaywalking Means Tickets of Up to $250," *DT News* (December 9, 2013), at **www.ladowntownnews .com/news/police-crackdown-on-jaywalking -means-tickets-of-up-to/article_f7ebf922-5ec6 -11e3-b537-001a4bcf887a.html.**

18. George P. Fletcher, "Some Unwise Reflections about Discretion," *Law & Contemporary Problems* (Autumn 1984), 279.

19. "ACLU Asks Justice Department to Investigate Racially-Biased Police Practices in Saginaw," *aclu.org* (September 19, 2013), at **www.aclu.org/criminal -law-reform-prisoners-rights-racial-justice/aclu -asks-justice-department-investigate.**

20. Antonin Scalia, "The Rule of Law as a Law of Rules," *University of Chicago Law Review* 56 (1989), 1178–1180.

21. John Kleinig, *Ethics and Criminal Justice: An Introduction* (New York: Cambridge University Press, 2008), 33–35.

22. Packer, *op. cit.,* 154–173.

23. Givelber, *op. cit.,* 1317.

24. Federal Bureau of Investigation, *Crime in the United States 2013* (Washington, D.C.: U.S. Department of Justice, 2014) at **www.fbi.gov/about -us/cjis/ucr/crime-in-the-u.s/2013/crime-in-the -u.s.-2013/cius-home.**

25. James Alan Fox, quoted in Donna Leinwand Leger, "Violent Crime Rises for 2nd Year," *USA Today* (October 25–27, 2013), 1A.

26. Vega and Thee-Brennan, *op. cit.,* A14.

27. Quoted in Richard A. Oppel, Jr., "National Questions over Police Hit Home in Cleveland," *New York Times* (December 9, 2014), A16.

28. Pew Research Center for the People & the Press, "Few See Adequate Limits on NSA Surveillance Program" (July 26, 2013), at **www.people -press.org/2013/07/26/few-see-adequate-limits -on-nsa-surveillance-program.**

29. Quoted in Timothy M. Phelps, "Terrorist Threat in U.S. Declining, FBI Directory Says," *Arizona Daily Star* (November 15, 2013), A15.

30. Bureau of Justice Statistics, *Correctional Populations in the United States,* 2013 (Washington, D.C.: U.S. Department of Justice, December 2014), Table 1, page 1.

31. "One Nation, Behind Bars," *The Economist* (August 17, 2013), 12.

32. Quoted in Erica Goode, "U.S. Prison Populations Decline, Reflecting New Approach to Crime," *New York Times* (July 26, 2013), A11.

33. Death Penalty Information Center, "Size of Death Row by Year—1968 to Present," at **www .deathpenaltyinfo.org/death-row-inmates-state -and-size-death-row-year#year.**

34. Death Penalty Information Center, "National Statistics on Death Penalty and Race," at **www .deathpenaltyinfo.org/race-death-rowinmates -executed-1976.**

35. Bureau of Justice Statistics, *Prisoners in 2013* (Washington, D.C.: U.S. Department of Justice, September 2014), Table 7, page 8.

36. Federal Bureau of Prisons, "Inmate Ethnicity," at **www.bop.gov/about/statistics/statistics _inmate_ethnicity.jsp.**

37. *A Guide to Mental Illness and the Criminal Justice System* (Arlington, Va.: National Alliance on Mental Illness, 1993), iii.

38. Doris J. James and Lauren E. Glaze, *Mental Health Problems of Prison and Jail Inmates* (Washington, D.C.: U.S. Department of Justice, December 2006), 1.

39. Liz Szabo, "The Cost of Not Caring," *USA Today* (May 13, 2014), 1A.

40. Quoted in *ibid.*

41. *Fact Sheet: Assertive Community Treatment* (Arlington, Va.: National Alliance on Mental Illness, September 2007), 1.

2

1. Quoted in Adam Nagourney, et al., "Before Brief, Deadly Spree, Trouble since Age 8," *New York Times* (June 2, 2014), A1.

2. Scott E. Wolfe and David C. Pyrooz, "Rolling Back Prices and Raising Crime Rates? The Walmart Effect on Crime in the United States," *The British Journal of Criminology* (March 2014), 199–221.

3. Matthew Larson and Gary Sweeten, "Breaking Up Is Hard to Do: Romantic Dissolution, Offending, and Substance Abuse During the Transition to Adulthood," *Criminology* (August 2012), 605–635.

4. James Q. Wilson and Richard J. Hernstein, *Crime and Human Nature: The Definitive Study of the Causes of Crime* (New York: Simon & Schuster, 1985), 44.

5. Jack Katz, *Seductions of Crime: Moral and Sensual Attractions of Doing Evil* (New York: Basic Books, 1988).

6. Quoted in Matt Pearce, "Police: 'Bored' Oklahoma Teens Randomly Kill Australian Student," *Los Angeles Times* (August 20, 2013), A5.

7. David C. Rowe, *Biology and Crime* (Los Angeles: Roxbury, 2002), 2.

8. L. E. Kreuz and R. M. Rose, "Assessment of Aggressive Behavior and Plasma Testosterone in Young Criminal Population," *Psychosomatic Medicine* 34 (1972), 321–332.

9. H. Persky, K. Smith, and G. Basu, "Relation of Psychological Measures of Aggression and Hostility to Testosterone Production in Men," *Psychosomatic Medicine* 33 (1971), 265, 276.

10. Cindy-Lee Dennis and Simone N. Vigod, "The Relationship between Postpartum Depression, Domestic Violence, Childhood Violence, and Substance Use: Epidemiologic Study of a Large Community Sample," *Violence against Women* (April 2013), 503–517.

11. Quoted in Pam Belluck, "'Thinking of Ways to Harm Her': New Findings on Timing and Range of Maternal Mental Illness," *New York Times* (June 16, 2014), A1.

12. Bureau of Justice Statistics, *Health Problems of Prison and Jail Inmates* (Washington, D.C.: U.S. Department of Justice, September 2006), 1.

13. Quoted in Eileen Sullivan, "Loners Like Tucson Gunman 'Fly below the Radar,'" *Associated Press* (January 17, 2011).

14. Herman Bianchi, *Justice as Sanctuary: Toward a New System of Crime Control* (Bloomington: Indiana University Press, 1994), 72.

15. Richard Friedman, "Why Can't Doctors Identify Killers?" *New York Times* (May 28, 2014), A21.

16. Philip Zimbardo, "Pathology of Imprisonment," *Society* (April 1972), 4–8.

17. David Canter and Laurence Alison, "The Social Psychology of Crime: Groups, Teams, and Networks," in *The Social Psychology of Crime: Groups, Teams, and Networks,* ed. David Canter and Laurence Alison (Hanover, N.H.: Dartmouth, 2000), 3–4.

18. Quoted in Lizette Alvarez, "Club Shooting in Rough Miami Neighborhood Continues a Cycle of Violence," *New York Times* (September 30, 2014), A15.

19. Clifford R. Shaw and Henry D. McKay, *Report on the Causes of Crime,* vol. 2: *Social Factors in Juvenile Delinquency* (Washington, D.C.: National Commission on Law Observance and Enforcement, 1931).

20. Emile Durkheim, *The Rules of Sociological Method,* trans. Sarah A. Solovay and John H. Mueller (New York: Free Press, 1964).

21. Robert K. Merton, *Social Theory and Social Structure* (New York: Free Press, 1957). See the chapter on "Social Structure and Anomie."

22. Richard Quinney, *The Social Reality of Crime* (Boston: Little, Brown, 1970).

23. Philip G. Zimbardo, "The Human Choice: Individuation, Reason, and Order versus Deindividuation, Impulse, and Chaos," in *Nebraska Symposium on Motivation,* ed. William J. Arnold and David Levie (Lincoln: University of Nebraska Press, 1969), 287–293.

24. Edwin H. Sutherland, *Criminology,* 4th ed. (Philadelphia: Lippincott, 1947).

25. Michael E. Roettger and Raymond Swisher, "Associations of Fathers' History of Incarceration with Sons' Delinquency and Arrest among Black, White, and Hispanic Males in the United States," *Criminology* (November 2011), 1109–1147.

26. Lindsay A. Robertson, Helena M. McAnally, and Robert J. Hancox, "Childhood and Adolescent Television Viewing and Antisocial Behavior in Early Adulthood," *Pediatrics* (March 2013), 439–446.

27. Travis Hirschi, *Causes of Delinquency* (Berkeley: University of California Press, 1969).

28. James Q. Wilson and George L. Kelling, "Broken Windows," *Atlantic Monthly* (March 1982), 29.

29. Francis T. Cullen and Robert Agnew, *Criminological Theory, Past to Present: Essential Readings,* 2d ed. (Los Angeles: Roxbury Publishing Co., 2003), 443.

30. Michael R. Gottfredson and Travis Hirschi, *A General Theory of Crime* (Stanford, Calif.: Stanford University Press, 1990).

31. *Ibid.,* 90.

32. *Ibid.*

33. Terrie Moffitt, "Adolescent-Limited and Life-Course-Persistent Antisocial Behavior: A Developmental Taxonomy," *Psychological Review* 100 (1993), 679–680.

34. *Ibid.,* 674.

35. Howard S. Becker, *Outsiders: Studies in the Sociology of Deviance* (New York: Free Press, 1963).

36. David G. Myers, *Psychology,* 7th ed. (New York: Worth Publishers, 2004), 576–577.

37. Peter B. Kraska, "The Unmentionable Alternative: The Need for and Argument against the Decriminalization of Drug Laws," in *Drugs, Crime, and the Criminal Justice System,* ed. Ralph Weisheit (Cincinnati, Ohio: Anderson Publishing, 1990).

38. Bureau of Justice Statistics, *Fact Sheet: Drug Related Crimes* (Washington, D.C.: U.S. Department of Justice, September 1994), 1.

39. *ADAM II: 2013 Annual Report* (Washington, D.C.: Office of National Drug Policy, January 2014), xi.

40. Bureau of Justice Statistics, "Alcohol and Crime: Data from 2002 to 2008," at **bjs.ojp.usdoj .gov/content/acf/29_prisoners_and_alcoholuse .cfm and bjs.ojp.usdoj.gov/content/acf/30_jails _and_alcoholuse.cfm.**

41. Friedman, *op. cit.*

42. James A. Inciardi, *The War on Drugs: Heroin, Cocaine, and Public Policy* (Palo Alto, Calif.: Mayfield, 1986), 148.

43. Federal Bureau of Investigation, *Uniform Crime Reporting Handbook* (Washington, D.C.: U.S. Department of Justice, 2004), 74.

44. Federal Bureau of Investigation, *Crime in the United States 2013* (Washington, D.C.: U.S. Department of Justice, 2014), at **www.fbi.gov /about-us/cjis/ucr/crime-in-the-u.s/2013/crime -in-the-u.s.-2013/about-cius.**

45. *Ibid.*

46. *Ibid.,* Table 1.

47. Jeffrey Reiman, *The Rich Get Richer and the Poor Get Prison,* 4th ed. (Boston: Allyn & Bacon, 1995), 59–60.

48. *Crime in the United States 2013, op. cit.,* Expanded Homicide Data Table 10.

49. *Ibid.,* Table 1.

50. *Ibid.,* Offense Definitions.

51. *Ibid.,* Table 29.

52. Marcus Felson, *Crime in Everyday Life* (Thousand Oaks, Calif.: Pine Forge Press, 1994), 3.

53. *Crime in the United States 2013, op. cit.,* at **www.fbi.gov/about-us/cjis/ucr/nibrs/2013 /resources/nibrs-participation-by-state.**

54. *Ibid.,* at **www.fbi.gov/about-us/cjis/ucr/nibrs /2013/data-tables.**

55. David Lisak and Paul M. Miller, "Repeat Rape and Multiple Offending among Undetected Rapists," *Violence & Victims* (2002), 73–84.

56. Lois H. Harrington et al., *President's Task Force on Victims of Crime: Final Report* (Washington, D.C.: U.S. Department of Justice, December 1982), viii.

57. 18 U.S.C. Section 3771 (2006).

58. Susan Herman, *Parallel Justice for Victims of Crime* (Washington, D.C.: The National Center for Victims of Crime, 2010), 45–48.

59. Chris E. Kubrin, et al., "Does Fringe Banking Exacerbate Neighborhood Crime Rates?" *Criminology and Public Policy* (May 2011), 437–464.

60. Larry Cohen and Marcus Felson, "Social Change and Crime Rate Trends: A Routine Activity Approach," *American Sociological Review* (1979), 588–608.

61. Kubrin, et al., *op. cit.,* 441.

62. Cohen and Felson, *op. cit.*

63. Herman, *op. cit.,* 13–16.

64. R. Barry Ruback, Valerie A. Clark, and Cody Warner, "Why Are Crime Victims at Risk of Being Victimized Again? Substance Use, Depression, and Offending as Mediators of the Victimization-Revictimization Link," *Journal of Interpersonal Violence* (January 2014), 157–185.

65. Quoted in Kevin Johnson, "Criminals Target Each Other, Trend Shows," *USA Today* (August 31, 2007), 1A.

66. Franklin E. Zimring, *The Great American Crime Decline* (New York: Oxford University Press, 2007), 45–72.

67. James Q. Wilson, "Concluding Essay in Crime," in James Q. Wilson and Joan Petersilia, eds., *Crime* (San Francisco: Institute for Contemporary Studies Press, 1995), 507.

68. Zimring, *op. cit.,* 6.

69. *Ibid.,* 197–198.

70. *Crime in the United States 2013, op. cit.,* Table 1.

71. Andrew Mach, "Violent Crime Rates in the U.S. Drop, Approach Historical Lows," *msnbc.com* (June 11, 2012), at **usnews.nbcnews.com/_news /2012/06/11/12170947-fbi-violent-crime-rates -in-the-us-drop-approach-historic-lows?lite.**

72. "Where Have All the Burglars Gone?" *The Economist* (July 20, 2013), 21–23.

73. Erica L. Smith and Alexia Cooper, *Homicide in the U.S. Known to Law Enforcement, 2011* (Washington, D.C.: U.S. Department of Justice, December 2013), 1.

74. *Crime in the United States 2013, op. cit.,* Expanded Homicide Data Table 3.

75. Michael Planty and Jennifer L. Truman, *Firearm Violence, 1993–2011* (Washington, D.C: U.S. Department of Justice, May 2013), 5.

76. *Crime in the United States 2013, op. cit.,* Expanded Homicide Data Table 6.

77. *Ibid.,* Table 43.

78. Mark Males and Lizzie Buchen, *Reforming Marijuana Laws: Which Approach Best Reduces the Harms of Criminalization* (San Francisco: Center of Juvenile and Criminal Justice, September 2014), 5–6.

79. Sarah Hockenberry and Charles Puzzanchera, *Juvenile Court Statistics, 2013* (Washington, D.C.: National Center for Juvenile Justice, July 2014), 20.

80. Ruth D. Peterson, "The Central Place of Race in Crime and Justice—The American Society of Criminology's 2011 Sutherland Address," *Criminology* (May 2012), 303–327.

81. Patricia Y. Warren, "Inequality by Design: The Connection between Race, Crime, Victimization, and Social Policy," *Criminology & Public Policy* (November 2010), 715.

82. Eric A. Stewart, Ronald L. Simons, and Rand D. Donger, "Assessing Neighborhood and Social Psychological Influence on Childhood Violence in an African American Sample," *Criminology* (November 2002), 801–829.

83. William Alex Pridemore, "A Methodological Addition to the Cross-National Empirical Literature on Social Structure and Homicide: A First Test of the Poverty-Homicide Thesis," *Criminology* (February 2008), 133.

84. Caroline Wolf Harlow, *Education and Correctional Populations* (Washington, D.C.: Bureau of Justice Statistics, January 2003), 1.

85. *Crime in the United States, op. cit.,* Expanded Homicide Table 6.

86. Bureau of Justice Statistics, *Jail Inmates at Midyear 2013—Statistical Tables* (Washington, D.C.: U.S. Department of Justice, May 2014), Table 2, page 6; Bureau of Justice Statistics, *Prisoners in 2013* (Washington, D.C.: U.S. Department of Justice, September 2014), Table 1, page 2; and *Crime in the United States 2013, op. cit.,* Table 33.

87. Federal Bureau of Justice, *Crime in the United States, 2000* (Washington, D.C.: U.S.

Department of Justice, 2001), Table 33, page 221; and *Crime in the United States 2013, op. cit.*, Table 33.

88. *Prisoners in 2013, op. cit.*, Table 1, page 2.

89. Jennifer Schwartz and Bryan D. Rookey, "The Narrowing Gender Gap in Arrests: Assessing Competing Explanations Using Self-Report, Traffic Fatality, and Official Data on Drunk Driving, 1980–2004," *Criminology* (August 2008), 637–638.

90. Quoted in Barry Yeoman, "Violent Tendencies: Crime by Women Has Skyrocketed in Recent Years," *Chicago Tribune* (March 15, 2000), 3.

91. *Crime in the United States 2013, op. cit.*, Table 42.

92. Schwarz and Rookey, *op. cit.*, 637–671.

93. Meda Chesney-Lind, "Patriarchy, Prisons, and Jails: A Critical Look at Trends in Women's Incarceration," *Prison Journal* (Spring/Summer 1991), 57.

94. Erika Harrell, *Violent Victimization Committed by Strangers, 1993–2010* (Washington, D.C.: U.S. Department of Justice, December 2012), Table 1, page 2.

95. Bureau of Justice Statistics, *Female Victims of Violence* (Washington, D.C.: U.S. Department of Justice, September 2009), Table 2, page 5.

96. Bonnie S. Fisher, Francis T. Cullen, and Michael G. Turner, *The Sexual Victimization of College Women* (Washington, D.C.: U.S. Department of Justice, December 2000), 10.

97. Eve S. Buzawa, "Victims of Domestic Violence," in Robert C. Davis, Arthur Lurigio, and Susan Herman, eds., *Victims of Crime*, 4th ed. (Los Angeles: Sage, 2013), 36–37.

98. Shannan Catalano, *Stalking Victims in the United States—Revised* (Washington, D.C.: U.S. Department of Justice, September 2012), 1, 5.

3

1. John S. Baker, Jr., *Measuring the Explosive Growth of Federal Crime Legislation* (Washington, D.C.: The Federalist Society for Law and Public Policy Studies, 2008), 1.

2. "US Court Records Show Nearly 500 Years in Prison Time for Medical Marijuana Offenses," *California NORML* (June 13, 2013), at **www.canorml.org/costs/Nearly_500_Years_Prison_Time_for_Medical_Marijuana_Offenses**.

3. Quoted in "Judge: Federal Law Trumps Montana's Medical Pot Law," *Associated Press* (January 23, 2012).

4. *Texas v. Johnson,* 491 U.S. 397 (1989).

5. *States of Nebraska and Oklahoma v. State of Colorado* (December 2014), at **www.scribd.com/doc/250506006/Nebraska-Oklahoma-lawsuit**.

6. Clean Water Act Section 309, 33 U.S.C.A. Section 1319 (1987).

7. *Bowers v. Hardwick,* 478 U.S. 186 (1986).

8. *Lawrence v. Texas,* 539 U.S., 558, 578 (2003).

9. Joel Feinberg, *The Moral Limits of the Criminal Law: Harm to Others* (New York: Oxford University Press, 1984), 221–232.

10. Henry M. Hart, Jr., "The Aims of the Criminal Law," *Law & Contemporary Problems* 23 (1958), 405–406.

11. John L. Diamond, "The Myth of Morality and Fault in Criminal Law Doctrine," *American Criminal Law Review* 34 (Fall 1996), 111.

12. Kentucky Statutes Section 437.060; and New Hampshire Revised Statutes Section 207:61.

13. Robby Korth and Jessica Boehm, "Butt Out: State Legislatures Move to Nullify Federal Gun Laws," *NBCNews.com* (August 21, 2014), at **www.nbcnews.com/news/investigations/butt-out-state-legislatures-move-nullify-federal-gun-laws-n185326**.

14. Idaho Senate Bill 1332 (March 19, 2014), at **legislature.idaho.gov/legislation/2014/S1332.htm**.

15. Lawrence M. Friedman, *Crime and Punishments in American History* (New York: Basic Books, 1993), 10.

16. *Federal Criminal Rules Handbook*, Section 2.1 (West 2008).

17. 625 Illinois Compiled Statutes Annotated Section 5/16-104 (West 2002).

18. Johannes Andenaes, "The Moral or Educative Influence of Criminal Law," *Journal of Social Issues* 27 (Spring 1971), 17, 26.

19. Thomas A. Mullen, "Rule without Reason: Requiring Independent Proof of the *Corpus Delicti* as a Condition of Admitting Extrajudicial Confession," *University of San Francisco Law Review* 27 (1993), 385.

20. *Hawkins v. State,* 219 Ind. 116, 129, 37 N.E.2d 79 (1941).

21. David C. Biggs, "'The Good Samaritan Is Packing': An Overview of the Broadened Duty to Aid Your Fellowman, with the Modern Desire to Possess Concealed Weapons," *University of Dayton Law Review* 22 (Winter 1997), 225.

22. Terry Halbert and Elaine Ingulli, *Law and Ethics in the Business Environment*, 6th ed. (Mason, Ohio: South-Western Cengage Learning, 2009), 8.

23. Model Penal Code Section 2.02.

24. Model Penal Code Section 2.02(c).

25. California Penal Code Section 189.

26. *Black's Law Dictionary*, 1423.

27. *United States v. Dotterweich,* 320 U.S. 277 (1943).

28. *State v. Stiffler,* 763 P.2d 308, 311 (Idaho Ct.App. 1988).

29. *State v. Harrison,* 425 A.2d 111 (1979).

30. Richard G. Singer and John Q. LaFond, *Criminal Law: Examples and Explanations* (New York: Aspen Law & Business, 1997), 322.

31. *State v. Linscott,* 520 A.2d 1067 (1987).

32. *Morissette v. United States,* 342 U.S. 246, 251–252 (1952).

33. Federal Bank Robbery Act, 18 U.S.C.A. Section 2113.

34. Bureau of Justice Statistics, *Hate Crime Victimization, 2004–2012, Statistical Tables* (Washington, D.C.: U.S. Department of Justice, February 2014), 1.

35. *United States v. Jiminez Recio,* 537 U.S. 270 (2003).

36. Paul H. Robinson, *Criminal Law Defenses* (St. Paul, Minn.: West, 2008), Section 173, Ch. 5Bl.

37. *M'Naghten's* Case, 10 Cl.&F. 200, Eng.Rep. 718 (1843). Note that the name is also spelled M'Naughten and McNaughten.

38. Model Penal Code Section 401 (1952).

39. Joshua Dressler, *Cases and Materials on Criminal Law,* 2d ed. (St. Paul, Minn.: West Group, 1999), 599.

40. Ronald Schouten, "The Insanity Defense: An Intersection of Morality, Public Policy, and Science," *Psychology Today* (August 16, 2012), at **www.psychologytoday.com/blog/almost-psychopath/201208/the-insanity-defense**.

41. Lawrence P. Tiffany and Mary Tiffany, "Nosologic Objections to the Criminal Defense of Pathological Intoxication: What Do the Doubters Doubt?" *International Journal of Law and Psychiatry* 13 (1990), 49.

42. *City of Missoula v. Paffhausen,* 289 P.3d 149–150 (Mont. 2012).

43. 518 U.S. 37 (1996).

44. Quoted in Gary Fields and John R. Emshwiller, "As Criminal Laws Proliferate, More Are Ensnared," *Wall Street Journal* (July 23, 2011), at **online.wsj.com/article/SB10001424052748703749504576172714184601654.html**.

45. *Lambert v. California,* 335 U.S. 225 (1957).

46. Federal Bureau of Investigation, *Crime in the United States 2013* (Washington, D.C.: U.S. Department of Justice, 2014), at **www.fbi.gov/about-us/cjis/ucr/crime-in-the-u.s/2013/crime-in-the-u.s.-2013,** Expanded Homicide Table 14 and Expanded Homicide Table 15.

47. Craig L. Carr, "Duress and Criminal Responsibility," *Law and Philosophy* 10 (1990), 161.

48. Arnold N. Enker, "In Supporting the Distinction between Justification and Excuse," *Texas Tech Law Review* 42 (2009), 277.

49. *United States v. May,* 727 F.2d 764 (1984).

50. *People v. Murillo,* 587 N.E.2d 1199, 1204 (Ill. App.Ct. 1992).

51. Florida Statutes Section 776.03 (2005).

52. *Ibid.*

53. Molly Hennessy-Fiske and Michael Muskal, "Jury Finds George Zimmerman Not Guilty," *Los Angeles Times* (July 13, 2013), A1.

54. Michael Bloomberg, quoted in "A Lethal Right to Self-Defense," *The Week* (May 4, 2012), 13.

55. Kevin Schwaller, "Justifiable Homicides Rise in Texas," *KXAN.com* (January 8, 2015), at kxan.com/2015/01/08/justifiable-homicides-rise-in-texas.

56. "Man Acquitted of Concealed Weapon Charge on 'Necessity' Defense," *San Francisco Examiner* (July 10, 2011), at **www.sfexaminer.com/local/crime/2011/07/man-acquitted-concealed-weapon-charge-necessity-defense**.

57. 287 U.S. 435 (1932).

58. Henry J. Abraham, *Freedom and the Court: Civil Liberties in the United States,* 7th ed. (New York: Oxford University Press, 1998), 38–41.

59. Bureau of Justice Statistics, *Capital Punishment, 2012—Statistical Tables* (Washington, D.C.: U.S. Department of Justice, May 2014), Table 10, page 14.

60. *Skinner v. Oklahoma,* 316 U.S. 535, 546–547 (1942).

4

1. Kate Zernike, "Camden Turns Around with New Police Force," *New York Times* (September 1, 2014), A1.

2. Egon Bittner, *The Functions of Police in a Modern Society*, Public Health Service Publication No. 2059 (Chevy Chase, Md.: National Institute of Mental Health, 1970), 38–44.

3. Carl Klockars, "The Rhetoric of Community Policing," in *Community Policing: Rhetoric or Reality*, ed. Jack Greene and Stephen Mastrofski (New York: Praeger Publishers, 1991), 244.

4. Jack R. Greene and Carl B. Klockars, "What Do Police Do?" in *Thinking about Police*, 2d ed.,

ed. Carl B. Klockars and Stephen D. Mastrofski (New York: McGraw-Hill, 1991), 273–284.

5. John S. Dempsey and Linda S. Forst, *An Introduction to Policing*, 6th ed. (Clifton Park, N.Y.: Delmar Cengage Learning, 2012), 380–381.

6. Federal Bureau of Investigation, *Crime in the United States 2013* (Washington, D.C.: U.S. Department of Justice, 2014), at **www.fbi.gov/about-us/cjis/ucr/crime-in-the-u.s/2013/crime-in-the-u.s.-2013,** Table 29.

7. Reprinted in *The Police Chief* (January 1990), 18.

8. Jason Busch, "Shots Fired: When a Police Car Becomes an Ambulance," *Law Enforcement Technology* (September 2013), 8–10.

9. Jerome H. Skolnick, "Police: The New Professionals," *New Society* (September 5, 1986), 9–11.

10. Quoted in Nancy Ritter, ed., "LAPD Chief Bratton Speaks Out: What's Wrong with Criminal Justice Research—and How to Make It Right," *National Institute of Justice Journal* 257 (2007), 29.

11. Gary Kleck and J.C. Barnes, "Do More Police Lead to More Crime Deterrence?" *Crime & Delinquency* (August 2014), 716–738.

12. Klockars, *op. cit.*, 250.

13. James Q. Wilson, *Varieties of Police Behavior: The Management of Law and Order in Eight Communities* (Cambridge, Mass.: Harvard University Press, 1968).

14. Quoted in Ronnie Garrett, "Predict and Serve," *Law Enforcement Technology* (January 2013), 19.

15. Scott Harris, "Product Feature: Predictive Policing Helps Law Enforcement 'See Around the Corners'," *The Police Chief* (October 2014), 44–45.

16. Charlie Beck and Colleen McCue, "Predictive Policing: What Can We Learn from Wal-Mart and Amazon about Fighting Crime in a Recession?" *The Police Chief* (November 2009), 19.

17. Gary LaFree, *Policing Terrorism* (Washington, D.C.: The Police Foundation, 2012), 1.

18. Federal Emergency Management Agency, "Information Bulletin No. 398: Fiscal Year 2014 DHS Preparedness Grant Programs Allocation Announcement" (July 25, 2014), at **www.fema.gov/media-library-data/1406300071406-69f388acb175b5226b828476d462a5ce/GPD%20IB%20Allocation%20Announcement_Final.pdf.**

19. *How Are Innovations in Technology Transforming Policing?* (Washington, D.C.: Police Executive Research Forum, January 2012), 2.

20. Joseph Goldstein and J. David Goodman, "Frisking Tactic Yields to a Focus on Youth Gangs," *New York Times* (September 13, 2013), A1.

21. Quoted in Joel Rubin, "Stopping Crime before It Starts," *Los Angeles Times* (August 21, 2010), A17.

22. James H. Chenoweth, "Situational Tests: A New Attempt at Assessing Police Candidates," *Journal of Criminal Law, Criminology and Police Science* 52 (1961), 232.

23. Yossef S. Ben-Porath et al., "Assessing the Psychological Suitability of Candidates for Law Enforcement Positions," *The Police Chief* (August 2011), 64–70.

24. D. P. Hinkle, "College Degree: An Impractical Prerequisite for Police Work," *Law and Order* (July 1991), 105.

25. Quoted in *How Are Innovations in Technology Transforming Policing?, op. cit.*, 10.

26. Bureau of Justice Statistics, *Local Police Departments, 2007* (Washington, D.C.: U.S.

Department of Justice, December 2010), Table 5, page 11.

27. Kevin Johnson, "Police Agencies Find It Hard to Require Degrees," *USA Today* (September 18, 2006), 3A.

28. Hinkle, *op. cit.*

29. *Local Police Departments, 2007, op. cit.*, 12.

30. Bureau of Justice Statistics, *State and Local Law Enforcement Training Academies, 2006* (Washington, D.C.: U.S. Department of Justice, February 2009), 7.

31. National Advisory Commission on Civil Disorder, *Report* (Washington, D.C.: U.S. Government Printing Office, 1968), Chapter 11.

32. *Crime in the United States 2013, op. cit.*, Table 74.

33. Marisa Silvestri, "Doing Time: Becoming a Police Leader," *International Journal of Police Science & Managements* (November 2005), 266–281.

34. Dorothy Schulz, quoted in Talk of the Nation, "What Changes as Women Rise through Law Enforcement's Ranks," *NPR* (April 2, 2013), at **www.npr.org/2013/04/02/176037643/what-changes-as-women-rise-through-law-enforcements-ranks.**

35. Gene L. Scaramella, Steven M. Cox, and William P. McCamey, *Introduction to Policing* (Thousand Oaks, Calif.: Sage Publications, 2011), 318.

36. Kenneth J. Novak, Robert A. Brown, and James Frank, *Women on Patrol: An Analysis of Differences in Officer Arrest Behavior* (Bingley, United Kingdom: Emerald Group Publishing Ltd., 2006), 21–27.

37. Quoted in Robin N. Haarr and Merry Morash, "The Effect of Rank on Police Women Coping with Discrimination and Harassment," *Police Quarterly* (December 2013), 403.

38. Quoted in Talk of the Nation, *op. cit.*

39. Katherine Stuart van Wormer and Clemens Bartollas, *Women and the Criminal Justice System*, 3d ed. (Upper Saddle River, N.J.: Pearson Education, 2011), 318–319.

40. Quoted in Teresa Lynn Wertsch, "Walking the Thin Blue Line: Policewomen and Tokenism Today," *Women and Criminal Justice* (1998), 35–36.

41. Quoted in Kimberly A. Lonsway, Rebecca Paynich, and Jennifer N. Hall, "Sexual Harassment in Law Enforcement: Incidence, Impact, and Perception," *Police Quarterly* (June 2013), 196.

42. The Cato Institute, "National Police Misconduct Statistics and Reporting Project: 2010 Quarterly Q3 Report," at **www.policemisconduct.net/statistics/2010-quarterly-q3-report.**

43. Lonsway, Paynich, and Hall, *op. cit.*, 179–180.

44. *Local Police Departments, 2007, op. cit.*, 14.

45. David Alan Sklansky, "Not Your Father's Police Department: Making Sense of the New Demographics of Law Enforcement," *Journal of Criminal Law and Criminology* (Spring 2006), 1209–1243.

46. Peter C. Moskos, "Two Shades of Blue: Black and White in the Blue Brotherhood," *Law Enforcement Executive Forum* (2008), 57.

47. Scaramella, Cox, and McCamey, *op. cit.*, 324.

48. Dempsey and Forst, *op. cit.*, 183.

49. *Wygant v. Jackson Board of Education*, 476 U.S. 314 (1986).

50. Bureau of Justice Statistics, *Census of State and Local Law Enforcement Agencies, 2008* (Washington, D.C.: U.S. Department of Justice, July 2011), 1; and Bureau of Justice Statistics, *Federal*

Law Enforcement Officers, 2008 (Washington, D.C.: U.S. Department of Justice, June 2012), 1.

51. *Census of State and Local Law Enforcement Agencies, 2008, op. cit.*, 3.

52. *Local Police Departments, 2007, op. cit.*, Table 3, page 9.

53. *Census of State and Local Law Enforcement Agencies, 2008, op. cit.*, 4.

54. *Ibid.*, Table 4, page 5.

55. Bureau of Justice Statistics, *Sheriffs' Offices, 2003* (Washington, D.C.: U.S. Department of Justice, May 2006), 15–18.

56. Bureau of Justice Statistics, *Sheriffs' Departments, 1997* (Washington, D.C.: U.S. Department of Justice, February 2000), 14.

57. Doris Meissner et al., *Immigration Enforcement in the United States: The Rise of a Formidable Machinery* (Washington, D.C.: Migration Policy Institute, January 2013), 2.

58. United States Border Patrol, "Nationwide Illegal Alien Apprehensions Fiscal Years 1925–2014," at **www.cbp.gov/sites/default/files/documents/BP%20Total%20Apps%20FY1925-FY2014_0.pdf.**

59. Julia Preston, "Border Patrol Seeks to Add Digital Eyes to Its Ranks," *New York Times* (March 22, 2014), A11.

60. John Hudson, "FBI Drops Law Enforcement as 'Primary' Mission," *Foreign Policy* (January 5, 2014), at **foreignpolicy.com/2014/01/05/fbi-drops-law-enforcement-as-primary-mission.**

61. United States Marshals Service, "Fact Sheet," at **www.justice.gov/marshals/duties/factsheets/general-1209.html.**

62. *The United States Security Industry* (Alexandria, Va.: ASIS International, 2013), 1.

63. John B. Owens, "Westec Story: Gated Communities and the Fourth Amendment," *American Criminal Law Review* (Spring 1997), 1138.

64. *Local Police Departments, 2007, op. cit.*, Table 8, page 13.

65. Seattle Police Department, Seattle Police Manual, "5.120—Secondary Employment" (Updated March 19, 2014), at **www.seattle.gov/police/publications/manual.**

66. William C. Cunningham, John J. Strauchs, and Clifford W. Van Meter, *The Hallcrest Report II: Private Security Trends, 1970 to 2000* (Boston: Butterworth-Heinemann, 1990), 236.

5

1. Kenneth Culp David, *Police Discretion* (St. Paul, Minn.: West Publishing Co., 1975).

2. C. E. Pratt, "Police Discretion," *Law and Order* (March 1992), 99–100.

3. "More than a Hunch," *Law Enforcement News* (September 2004), 1.

4. Bureau of Justice Statistics, *Local Police Departments, 2003* (Washington, D.C.: U.S. Department of Justice, May 2006), 24.

5. Jack Richter, "Number of Police Pursuits Drop Dramatically in Los Angeles," *Los Angeles Police Department Press Release* (August 30, 2003).

6. Quoted in Ryan Boetel, "APD Chief, IRO Often at Odds over Lapel Video," *Albuquerque Journal* (December 27, 2014), A1.

7. Nicole Perez, "Officer Who Shot Mary Hawkes Fired for Insubordination," *Albuquerque Journal* (December 1, 2014), at **www.abqjournal**

.com/503875/news/lawyer-albuquerque-officer -in-shooting-fired.html.

8. Samuel Walker, *The Police in America: An Introduction*, 2d ed. (New York: McGraw-Hill, 1992), 16.

9. George L. Kelling and Mark H. Moore, "From Political to Reform to Community: The Evolving Strategy of Police," in *Community Policing: Rhetoric or Reality*, ed. Jack Greene and Stephen Mastrofski (New York: Praeger Publishers, 1988), 13.

10. Michael White, *Controlling Officer Behavior in the Field* (New York: John Jay College of Criminal Justice, 2011), 19.

11. Henry M. Wrobleski and Karen M. Hess, *Introduction to Law Enforcement and Criminal Justice*, 7th ed. (Belmont, Calif.: Wadsworth/ Thomson Learning, 2003), 119.

12. Bureau of Justice Statistics, *Local Police Departments, 2007* (Washington, D.C.: U.S. Department of Justice, December 2010), 6.

13. Connie Fletcher, "What Cops Know," *On Patrol* (Summer 1996), 44–45.

14. David H. Bayley, *Police for the Future* (New York: Oxford University Press, 1994), 20.

15. Walker, *op. cit.*, 103.

16. Eric J. Scott, *Calls for Service: Citizens Demand an Initial Police Response* (Washington, D.C.: National Institute of Justice, 1981), 28–30.

17. Vivian B. Lord, et al., "Factors Influencing the Response of Crisis Intervention Team-Certified Law Enforcement Officers," *Police Quarterly* (December 2011), 388.

18. E. Fuller Torrey, *Justifiable Homicides by Law Enforcement Officers: What Is the Role of Mental Illness?* (Arlington, Va.: Treatment Advocacy Center, September 2013), 3.

19. Lord, et al., *op. cit.*, 390–391.

20. *Ibid.*, 391–392.

21. William G. Gay, Theodore H. Schell, and Stephen Schack, *Routine Patrol: Improving Patrol Productivity*, vol. 1 (Washington, D.C.: National Institute of Justice, 1977), 3–6.

22. Boetel, *op. cit.*

23. Gary W. Cordner, "The Police on Patrol," in *Police and Policing: Contemporary Issues*, ed. Dennis Jay Kenney (New York: Praeger Publishers, 1989), 60–71.

24. Quoted in Sarah Stillman, "The Throwaways," *New Yorker* (September 3, 2012), 38–39.

25. Center on Law and Security, *Terrorist Trial Report Card: September 11, 2001–September 11, 2009* (New York: New York University School of Law, January 2010), 42–44.

26. "Dad Accuses FBI of Setting Up 'Mommy's Boy' Son in Bomb Plot," *ABC News* (January 15, 2015), at **abcnews.go.com/US/dad-accuses-fbi -setting-son-bomb-plot/story?id=28240751.**

27. Federal Bureau of Investigation, *Crime in the United States 2013* (Washington, D.C.: U.S. Department of Justice, 2014), at **www.fbi.gov /about-us/cjis/ucr/crime-in-the.u.s/2013/crime -in-the.u.s.-2013/cius-home,** Table 25.

28. James M. Cronin, Gerard R. Murphy, Lisa L. Spahr, Jessica I. Toliver, and Richard E. Weger, *Promoting Effective Homicide Investigations* (Washington, D.C.: Police Executive Research Forum, August 2007), 102–103.

29. Robert C. Davis, Carl Jenses, and Karin E. Kitchens, *Cold Case Investigations: An Analysis of Current Practices and Factors Associated with Successful Outcomes* (Santa Monica, Calif.: RAND Corporation, 2011), xii.

30. Ronald F. Becker, *Criminal Investigations*, 2d ed. (Sudbury, Mass.: Jones & Bartlett, 2004), 7.

31. Bureau of Justice Statistics, *Census of Publicly Funded Forensic Crime Laboratories, 2009* (Washington, D.C.: U.S. Department of Justice, August 2012), 1.

32. Joseph Peterson, Ira Sommers, Deborah Baskin, and Donald Johnson, *The Role and Impact of Forensic Evidence in the Criminal Justice Process* (Washington, D.C.: National Institute of Justice, September 2010), 8–9.

33. Simon A. Cole, "More Than Zero: Accounting for Error in Latent Fingerprinting Identification," *Journal of Criminal Law and Criminology* (Spring 2005), 985–1078.

34. Quoted in "New DNA Database Helps Crack 1979 N.Y. Murder Case," *Miami Herald* (March 14, 2000), 18A.

35. Judith E. Lewter, "The Use of Forensic DNA in Criminal Cases in Kentucky as Compared with Other Selected States," *Kentucky Law Journal* (1997–1998), 223.

36. "CODIS—NDIS Statistics," at **www.fbi.gov /about-us/lab/biometric-analysis/codis/ndis -statistics.**

37. *Maryland v. King*, 133 S.Ct. 1980 (2013).

38. Wrobleski and Hess, *op. cit.*, 173.

39. Stephen J. Blumberg and Julian V. Luke, "Wireless Substitution: Early Release of Estimates from the National Health Interview Survey, July–December 2013," *National Health Interview Survey* (Centers for Disease Control and Prevention, July 2014), 1.

40. *Local Police Departments, 2007, op. cit.*, Table 12, page 15.

41. Jerry H. Ratcliffe, et al., "The Philadelphia Foot Patrol Experiment: A Randomized Controlled Trial of Police Patrol Effectiveness in Violent Crime Hotspots," *Criminology* (August 2011), 795–830.

42. David Weisburd and Cynthia Lum, "The Diffusion of Computerized Crime Mapping in Policing: Linking Research and Practice," *Police Practice and Research* 6 (2005), 419–434.

43. Quoted in "New Model Police," *The Economist* (June 9, 2007), 29.

44. Lawrence W. Sherman, "Policing for Crime Prevention," in *Contemporary Policing: Controversies, Challenges, and Solutions*, ed. Quint C. Thurman and Jihong Zhao (Los Angeles: Roxbury Publishing Co., 2004), 63–66.

45. *Ibid.*, 65.

46. Dennis Rosenbaum, quoted in Jon Schuppe, "Can Smarter Police Work Prevent Another Ferguson?" *NBC News* (August 15, 2014), at **www .nbcnews.com/storyline/michael-brown -shooting/can-smarter-police-work-prevent -another-ferguson-n180841.**

47. Herman Goldstein, "Improving Policing: A Problem-Oriented Approach," *Crime and Delinquency* 25 (1979), 236–258.

48. Bureau of Justice Assistance, *Problem-Oriented Drug Enforcement: A Community-Based Approach for Effective Policing* (Washington, D.C.: Office of Justice Programs, 1993), 5.

49. Larry Celona, et al., "Gunman Executes 2 NYPD Cops in Garner 'Revenge,'" *New York Post* (December 20, 2014), at **nypost.com/2014/12 /20/2-nypd-cops-shot-execution-style-in -brooklyn.**

50. Quoted in Al Baker and J. David Goodman, "New Fight for a Police Bullhorn after 2 Killings," *New York Times* (December 24, 2012), A1.

51. Al Baker and J. David Goodman, "Arrests and Summonses Rise in New York City, but Fall Short of Pre-Slowdown Levels," *New York Times* (January 13, 2015), A21.

52. Quoted in Benjamin Mueller, "Outcome of Eric Garner Case Bares a Staten Island Divide," *New York Times* (December 5, 2014), A30.

53. Harry J. Mullins, "Myth, Tradition, and Ritual," *Law and Order* (September 1995), 197.

54. William Westly, *Violence and the Police: A Sociological Study of Law, Custom, and Morality* (Cambridge, Mass.: MIT Press, 1970).

55. Officer Down Memorial Page, at **www.odmp .org/search/year?year=2014.**

56. Federal Bureau of Investigation, *Law Enforcement Officers Killed and Assaulted, 2011* (Washington, D.C.: U.S. Department of Justice, 2012), at **www.fbi.gov/about-us/cjis/ucr/leoka /2013/officers-assaulted/assaults_topic_page _-2013.**

57. John S. Dempsey and Linda S. Forst, *An Introduction to Policing*, 7th ed. (Clifton Park, N.Y.: Delmar Cengage Learning, 2014), 180.

58. Steven G. Brandl and Meghan S. Stroshine, "The Physical Hazards of Police Work Revisited," *Police Quarterly* (September 2012), 263.

59. Officer Down Memorial Page, *op cit.*; and Craig W. Floyd and Kevin P. Morrison, "Officer Safety on Our Roadways: What the Numbers Say about Saving Lives," *The Police Chief* (July 2010), 28.

60. National Highway Traffic Safety Administration, *Characteristics of Law Enforcement Officers' Fatalities in Motor Vehicle Crashes* (Washington, D.C.: U.S. Department of Transportation, January 2011), Figure 15, page 25.

61. Gail A. Goolsakian, et al., *Coping with Police Stress* (Washington, D.C.: National Institute of Justice, 1985).

62. Kim S. Ménard and Michael L. Arter, "Stress, Coping, Alcohol Use, and Posttraumatic Stress Disorder among an International Sample of Police Officers: Does Gender Matter," *Police Quarterly* (December 2014), 309–310.

63. University at Buffalo, "Impact of Stress on Police Officers' Physical and Mental Health, *Science Daily* (September 29, 2009), at **www.buffalo .edu/news/releases/2008/09/9660.html.**

64. James F. Ballenger, et al., "Patterns and Predictors of Alcohol Use in Male and Female Urban Police Officers," *American Journal on Addictions* (January–February 2011), 21–29.

65. Daniel W. Clark, Elizabeth K. White, and John M. Violanti, "Law Enforcement Suicide: Current Knowledge and Future Directions," *The Police Chief* (May 2012), 48.

66. Bureau of Justice Statistics, *Contacts between Police and the Public, 2008* (Washington, D.C.: U.S. Department of Justice, October 2011), 14.

67. Bureau of Justice Statistics, *Arrest-Related Deaths, 2003–2009, Statistical Tables* (Washington, D.C.: U.S. Department of Justice, November 2011), 1.

68. David J. Spotts, "Reviewing Use-of-Force Practices," *The Police Chief* (August 2012), 12.

69. H. Range Hutson, Deirdre Anglin, Phillip Rice, Demetrious N. Kyriacou, Michael Guirguis, and Jared Strote, "Excessive Use of Force by Police: A Survey of Academic Emergency Physicians," *Emergency Medicine Journal* (January 2009), 20–22.

70. Columbia Law School, "Professors Fagan and Harcourt Provide Facts on Grand Jury Practice after Staten Island Decision" (January 23, 2015), at

www.law.columbia.edu/media_inquiries/news
_events/2014/december2014/garner-grand
-jury-facts.

71. *Scott v. Harris*, 127 S.Ct. 1779 (2007).

72. 471 U.S. 1 (1985).

73. 471 U.S. 1, 11 (1985).

74. 490 U.S. 386 (1989).

75. *Brosseau v. Haugen*, 543 U.S. 194 (2004).

76. Frank Newport, "Gallup Review: Black and White Attitudes Toward Police," *Gallup.com* (August 20, 2014), at **www.gallup.com/poll /175088/gallup-review-black-white-attitudes -toward-police.aspx.**

77. Missouri Attorney General Chris Koster, "MO Stops Report," at **ago.mo.gov/VehicleStops /Reports.php?lea=161.**

78. Drake Bennett, "Building a Better Police Department," *Businessweek* (December 15– December 21, 2014), 27.

79. Knapp Commission, *Report on Police Corruption* (New York: Brazilier, 1973).

80. Jocelyn M. Pollock and Ronald F. Becker, "Ethics Training Using Officers' Dilemmas," *FBI Law Enforcement Bulletin* (November 1996), 20–28.

81. Quoted in Thomas J. Martinelli, "Dodging the Pitfalls of Noble Cause Corruption and the Intelligence Unit," *The Police Chief* (October 2009), 124.

82. Pollock and Becker, *op. cit.*, 20–28.

83. Brandon V. Zuidema and H. Wayne Duff, "Organizational Ethics through Effective Leadership," *Law Enforcement Bulletin* (March 2009), 8–9.

6

1. *Florida v. Jardines*, 569 U.S. _____ (2013).

2. *United States v. Place*, 462 U.S. 696 (1983); and *Illinois v. Caballes*, 543 U.S. 405 (2005).

3. *Jardines, op. cit.*, at _____.

4. *Michigan v. Summers*, 452 U.S. 692 (1981).

5. *Brinegar v. United States*, 338 U.S. 160 (1949).

6. Rolando V. del Carmen, *Criminal Procedure for Law Enforcement Personnel* (Monterey, Calif.: Brooks/Cole Publishing Co., 1987), 63–64.

7. *Maryland v. Pringle*, 540 U.S. 366 (2003).

8. 500 U.S. 44 (1991).

9. *United States v. Leon*, 468 U.S. 897 (1984).

10. Thomas Y. Davis, "A Hard Look at What We Know (and Still Need to Learn) about the 'Costs' of the Exclusionary Rule: The NIJ Study and Other Studies of 'Lost' Arrests," *A.B.F. Research Journal* (1983), 680.

11. 430 U.S. 387 (1977).

12. 467 U.S. 431 (1984).

13. 468 U.S. 897 (1984).

14. 514 U.S. 1 (1995).

15. *California v. Greenwood*, 486 U.S. 35 (1988).

16. *Ibid.*

17. 389 U.S. 347 (1967).

18. *Ibid.*, 361.

19. 486 U.S. 35 (1988).

20. *Ibid.*

21. *Kentucky v. King*, 563 U.S. _____ (2011).

22. *Jardines, op. cit.*, at _____.

23. *Coolidge v. New Hampshire*, 403 U.S. 443, 467 (1971).

24. *Millender v. Messerschmidt*, 620 F.3d 1016 (9th Cir. 2010).

25. del Carmen, *op. cit.*, 158.

26. *Katz v. United States*, 389 U.S. 347, 357 (1967).

27. *Brigham City v. Stuart*, 547 U.S. 398 (2006).

28. 414 U.S. 234–235 (1973).

29. 395 U.S. 752 (1969).

30. *Ibid.*, 763.

31. Carl A. Benoit, "Questioning 'Authority': Fourth Amendment Consent Searches," *FBI Law Enforcement Bulletin* (July 2008), 24.

32. *Bumper v. North Carolina*, 391 U.S. 543 (1968).

33. *State v. Stone*, 362 N.C. 50, 653 S.E.2d 414 (2007).

34. 267 U.S. 132 (1925).

35. *United States v. Ross*, 456 U.S. 798, 804–809 (1982); and *Chambers v. Maroney*, 399 U.S. 42, 44, 52 (1970).

36. 453 U.S. 454 (1981).

37. *Arizona v. Gant*, 556 U.S. 332 (2009).

38. Adam Liptak, "Justices Significantly Cut Back Officers' Searches of Cars of People They Arrest," *New York Times* (April 22, 2009), A12.

39. Dale Anderson and Dave Cole, "Search and Seizure after *Arizona v. Gant*," *Arizona Attorney* (October 2009), 15.

40. *Whren v. United States*, 517 U.S. 806 (1996).

41. 403 U.S. 443 (1971).

42. *Kyollo v. United States*, 533 U.S. 27 (2001).

43. 388 U.S. 42 (1967).

44. 18 U.S.C. Sections 2510(7), 2518(1)(a), 2516 (1994).

45. Christopher K. Murphy, "Electronic Surveillance," in "Twenty-Sixth Annual Review of Criminal Procedure," *Georgetown Law Journal* (April 1997), 920.

46. *United States v. Nguyen*, 46 F.3d 781, 783 (8th Cir. 1995).

47. Joseph Siprut, "Privacy through Anonymity: An Economic Argument for Expanding the Right of Privacy in Public Places," *Pepperdine Law Review* 33 (2006), 311, 320.

48. *California v. Riley*, 134 S.Ct. 2473 (2014).

49. *Ibid.*, 2485.

50. *Ibid.*, 2473.

51. Karen M. Hess and Henry M. Wroblewski, *Police Operation: Theory and Practice* (St. Paul, Minn.: West Publishing Co., 1997), 122.

52. 392 U.S. 1 (1968).

53. *Ibid.*, 20.

54. *Ibid.*, 21.

55. See *United States v. Cortez*, 449 U.S. 411 (1981); and *United States v. Sokolow*, 490 U.S. 1 (1989).

56. *United States v. Arvizu*, 534 U.S. 266 (2002).

57. *Ibid.*, 270.

58. *United States v. Place*, 462 U.S. 696 (1983).

59. *Hibel v. Sixth Judicial District Court*, 542 U.S. 177 (2004).

60. *Ibid.*, 182.

61. *Minnesota v. Dickerson*, 508 U.S. 366 (1993).

62. *People v. Powell*, IL App.1st 122275 (2014).

63. *Arizona v. Johnson*, 555 U.S. 328 (2009).

64. Rolando V. del Carmen and Jeffrey T. Walker, *Briefs of Leading Cases in Law Enforcement*, 2d ed. (Cincinnati, Ohio: Anderson, 1995), 38–40.

65. *Florida v. Royer*, 460 U.S. 491 (1983).

66. See also *United States v. Mendenhall*, 446 U.S. 544 (1980).

67. del Carmen, *op. cit.*, 97–98.

68. 514 U.S. 927 (1995).

69. Linda J. Collier and Deborah D. Rosenbloom, *American Jurisprudence*, 2d ed. (Rochester, N.Y.: Lawyers Cooperative Publishing, 1995), 122.

70. 547 U.S. 586 (2006).

71. *United States v. Banks*, 540 U.S. 31, 41 (2003).

72. *Hudson v. Michigan*, 547 U.S. 586, 593 (2006).

73. Tom Van Dorn, "Violation of Knock-and-Announce Rule Does Not Require Suppression of All Evidence Found in Search," *The Police Chief* (October 2006), 10.

74. "Warrantless Searches and Seizures," in *Georgetown Law Journal Annual Review of Criminal Procedure, 2011* (Washington, D.C.: Georgetown Law Journal, 2011), 955.

75. *Atwater v. City of Lago Vista*, 532 U.S. 318, 346–347 (2001).

76. 445 U.S. 573 (1980).

77. *Steagald v. United States*, 451 U.S. 204 (1981).

78. *Brown v. Mississippi*, 297 U.S. 278 (1936).

79. *Miranda v. Arizona*, 384 U.S. 436 (1966).

80. H. Richard Uviller, *Tempered Zeal* (Chicago: Contemporary Books, 1988), 188–198.

81. *Orozco v. Texas*, 394 U.S. 324 (1969); *Oregon v. Mathiason*, 429 U.S. 492 (1977); and *California v. Beheler*, 463 U.S. 1121 (1983).

82. *Orozco, op. cit.*, 325.

83. *Pennsylvania v. Muniz*, 496 U.S. 582 (1990).

84. del Carmen, *op. cit.*, 267–268.

85. *New York v. Quarles*, 467 U.S. 649 (1984).

86. Ethan Bronner and Michael S. Schmidt, "In Questions at First, No *Miranda* for Suspect," *New York Times* (April 23, 2013), A13.

87. *Moran v. Burbine*, 475 U.S. 412 (1986).

88. *Michigan v. Mosley*, 423 U.S. 96 (1975).

89. *Fare v. Michael C.*, 442 U.S. 707, 723–724 (1979).

90. 512 U.S. 452 (1994).

91. 560 U.S. 370 (2010).

92. Richard A. Leo, "Inside the Interrogation Room," *Journal of Criminal Law and Criminology* (1996), 266.

93. Saul M. Kassin and Lawrence S. Wrightsman, "Prior Confessions and Mock Juror Verdicts," *Journal of Social Psychology* (1980), 133–146.

94. The Innocence Project, "False Confessions & Mandatory Recording of Interrogations," at **www .innocenceproject.org/fix/False-Confessions .php.**

95. Saul M. Kassin, "Internalized False Confessions," in Michael P. Toglia, et al., eds., *Handbook of Eyewitness Psychology, Vol. 1* (New York: Psychology Press, 2007), 171.

96. Douglas Starr, "The Interview: Do Police Interrogation Techniques Produce False Confessions?" *The New Yorker* (December 9, 2013), 43–44.

97. *Ibid.*, 44.

98. "Death Row Interview with Henry McCollum," *News and Observer* (Raleigh, N.C.) (August 30, 2014), at **www.youtube.com/watch?v=NxV6 PWfa7i8.**

99. The Innocence Project, *op. cit.*

100. Jennifer L. Mnookin, "Can a Jury Believe What It Sees?" *New York Times* (July 14, 2014), A19.

7

1. Quoted in Carol Rosenberg, "Guantanamo Trial Delays Frustrate 9/11 Relatives," *Miami Herald* (April 17, 2014), A1.

2. Roscoe Pound, "The Administration of Justice in American Cities," *Harvard Law Review* 12 (1912).

3. Russell Wheeler and Howard Whitcomb, *Judicial Administration: Text and Readings* (Englewood Cliffs, N.J.: Prentice Hall, 1977), 3.

4. Larry J. Siegel, *Criminology: Instructor's Manual,* 6th ed. (Belmont, Calif.: West/Wadsworth Publishing Co., 1998), 440.

5. Gerald F. Velman, "Federal Sentencing Guidelines: A Cure Worse Than the Disease," *American Criminal Law Review* 29 (Spring 1992), 904.

6. Wayne R. LaFave, "Section 4.6. Multiple Jurisdiction and Multiple Prosecution," *Substantive Criminal Law,* 2d ed. (C.J.S. Criminal Section 254), 2007.

7. 18 U.S.C. Section 3231; and *Solorio v. United States,* 483 U.S. 435 (1987).

8. 18 U.S.C.A. Section 1951.

9. 372 U.S. 335 (1963).

10. 384 U.S. 436 (1966).

11. 408 U.S. 238 (1972).

12. 428 U.S. 153 (1976).

13. 18 U.S.C.A. Section 704.

14. *U.S. v. Alvarez,* 132 S.Ct. 2537 (2012).

15. 18 U.S.C.A. Section 704(a).

16. Public Law Number 103-322, Section 16001, 108 Statute 2036 (1994), codified as amended at 18 U.S.C. Section 2259.

17. *Paroline v. United States,* 134 S.Ct. 1710 (2014).

18. *Navarette v. California,* 562 U.S. ___ (2014).

19. David R. Stras and James F. Spriggs II, "Explaining Plurality Opinions," *Georgetown Law Journal* 99 (March 2010), 519.

20. Harlington Wood, Jr., "Judiciary Reform: Recent Improvements in Federal Judicial Administration," *American University Law Review* 44 (June 1995), 1557.

21. Pub. L. No. 76-299, 53 Stat. 1223, codified as amended at 28 U.S.C. Sections 601–610 (1988 & Supp. V 1993).

22. James E. Lozier, "The Missouri Plan a.k.a. Merit Selection Is the Best Solution for Selecting Michigan's Judges," *Michigan Bar Journal* 75 (September 1996), 918.

23. Ron Malega and Thomas H. Cohen, *State Court Organization, 2011* (Washington, D.C.: U.S. Department of Justice, November 2013), 8.

24. Ciara Torres-Spelliscy, Monique Chase, and Emma Greenman, *Improving Judicial Diversity,* 2d ed. (New York: Brennan Center for Justice, 2010), 1.

25. Ibid.

26. Maura Dolan, "Diversity Rises among California Judges," *Los Angeles Times* (February 28, 2013), at **articles.latimes.com/2013/feb/28/local/la-me-judges-20130301.**

27. New York State Bar Association Executive Committee, *Judicial Diversity: A Work in Progress* (Albany: New York State Bar Association, September 2014), Table 1, page 5.

28. Federal Judicial Center, "Diversity on the Bench," at **www.fjc.gov/history/home.nsf/page/judges_diversity.html.**

29. 295 U.S. 78 (1935).

30. *Brady v. Maryland,* 373 U.S. 83 (1963).

31. Brendan Kirby, "Judge Overturns 13-Year-Old Capital Murder Conviction of Mobile-Based State Trooper," *AL.com* (September 4, 2013), at **blog.al.com/live/2013/09/judge_overturns_13-year-old_ca.html.**

32. Celesta Albonetti, "Prosecutorial Discretion: The Effects of Uncertainty," *Law and Society Review* 21 (1987), 291–313.

33. *Gideon v. Wainwright,* 372 U.S. 335 (1963); *Massiah v. United States,* 377 U.S. 201 (1964); *United States v. Wade,* 388 U.S. 218 (1967); *Argersinger v. Hamlin,* 407 U.S. 25 (1972); and *Brewer v. Williams,* 430 U.S. 387 (1977).

34. Larry Siegel, *Criminology,* 6th ed. (Belmont, Calif.: West/Wadsworth Publishing Co., 1998), 487–488.

35. Center for Professional Responsibility, *Model Rules of Professional Conduct* (Washington, D.C.: American Bar Association, 2003), Rules 1.6 and 3.1.

36. *United States v. Wade,* 388 U.S. 218, 256–258 (1967).

37. 372 U.S. 335 (1963).

38. 387 U.S. 1 (1967).

39. 407 U.S. 25 (1972).

40. Laurence A. Benner, "Eliminating Excessive Public Defender Workloads," *Criminal Justice* (Summer 2011), 25.

41. American Bar Association, "Providing Defense Services," Standard 5-7.1, at **www.abanet.org/crimjust/standards/defsvcs_blk.html#7.1.**

42. Robert C. Boruchowitz, "The Right to Counsel: Every Accused Person's Right," *Washington State Bar Association Bar News* (January 2004), at **www.wsba.org/media/publications/barnews/2004/jan-04-boruchowitz.htm.**

43. Bureau of Justice Statistics, *County-Based and Local Public Defender Offices, 2007* (Washington, D.C.: U.S. Department of Justice, September 2010), 3.

44. "State-by-State Court Fees," *npr.org* (May 19, 2014), at **www.npr.org/2014/05/19/312455680/state-by-state-court-fees.**

45. Alicia Bannon, Mitali Nagrecha, and Rebekah Diller, *Criminal Justice Debt: A Barrier to Reentry* (New York: Brennan Center for Justice, October 2010), 12.

46. Randolph Braccialarghe, "Why Were Perry Mason's Clients Always Innocent?" *Valparaiso University Law Review* (Fall 2004), 65.

47. John Kaplan, "Defending Guilty People," *University of Bridgeport Law Review* (1986), 223.

48. 491 U.S. 554 (1989).

8

1. Lawrence M. Friedman and Robert V. Percival, *The Roots of Justice* (Chapel Hill: University of North Carolina Press, 1981).

2. *Riverside County, California v. McLaughlin,* 500 U.S. 44 (1991).

3. Michael R. Jones, *Unsecured Bonds: The As Effective and Most Efficient Pretrial Release Option* (Washington, D.C.: Pretrial Justice Institute, October 2013), 10–20.

4. Quoted in Julie Bosman, et al., "Amid Conflicting Accounts, Trusting Darren Wilson," *New York Times* (November 26, 2014), A1.

5. New York Court of Appeals Judge Sol Wachtler, quoted in David Margolik, "Law Professor to Administer Courts in State," *New York Times* (February 1, 1985), B2.

6. Sam Skolnick, "Grand Juries: Power Shift?" *The Legal Times* (April 12, 1999), 1.

7. Milton Hirsh and David Oscar Markus, "Fourth Amendment Forum," *Champion* (December 2002), 42.

8. Bruce Frederick and Don Stemen, *The Anatomy of Discretion: An Analysis of Prosecutorial Decision Making—Summary Report* (New York: Vera Institute of Justice, December 2012), 4–16.

9. Tom Lininger, "Evidentiary Issues in Federal Prosecutions of Violence against Women," *Indiana Law Review* 36 (2003), 709.

10. 18 U.S.C. Section 3553(e) (2006).

11. 404 U.S. 257 (1971).

12. Fred C. Zacharias, "Justice in Plea Bargaining," *William and Mary Law Review* 39 (March 1998), 1121.

13. Bureau of Justice Statistics, *Prosecutors in State Courts, 2007—Statistical Tables* (Washington, D.C.: U.S. Department of Justice, December 2011), 2.

14. Milton Heumann, *Plea Bargaining: The Experiences of Prosecutors, Judges, and Defense Attorneys* (Chicago: University of Chicago Press, 1978), 58.

15. Albert W. Alschuler, "The Defense Attorney's Role in Plea Bargaining," *Yale Law Journal* 84 (1975), 1200.

16. Stephen J. Schulhofer, "Plea Bargaining as Disaster," *Yale Law Journal* 101 (1992), 1987.

17. North Carolina General Statutes Section 15A-832(f) (2003).

18. 18 U.S.C. Section 3771 (2004).

19. Quoted in John Beauge, "Widow to Pa. Craigslist Killer: 'No Punishment Will Ever Be Long Enough,'" *PennLive* (September 18, 2014), at **www.pennlive.com/midstate/index.ssf/2014/09/widows_says_craigslist_killers.html#incart_story_package.**

20. John Beauge, "Couple Avoid Death Penalty, Face Life in Prison for Pleading Guilty to Craigslist Murder," *PennLive* (August 26, 2014), at **www.pennlive.com/midstate/index.ssf/2014/08/couple_pleads_guilty_in_sunbur_1.html.**

21. 407 U.S. 514 (1972).

22. 391 U.S. 145 (1968).

23. *Blanton v. Las Vegas,* 489 U.S. 538 (1989).

24. *Apodaca v. Oregon,* 406 U.S. 404 (1972); and *Lee v. Louisiana,* No. 07-1523 (2008).

25. 332 U.S. 46 (1947).

26. *Salinas v. Texas,* 570 U.S. _____ (2013).

27. Judy Clarke, quoted in Katharine Q. Seelye, "Boston Bombing Suspect Seeking Change of Trial Venue," *New York Times* (June 19, 2014), A16.

28. Quoted in Milton J. Valencia, "Judge Denies Tsarnaev Request for Change of Venue," *Boston Globe* (September 25, 2014), A1.

29. 397 U.S. 358 (1970).

30. 380 U.S. 224 (1965).

31. 476 U.S. 79 (1986).

32. Eric L. Muller, "Solving the *Batson* Paradox: Harmless Error, Jury Representation, and the Sixth Amendment," *Yale Law Journal* 106 (October 1996), 93.

33. 499 U.S. 400 (1991).

34. 502 U.S. 1056 (1992).

35. *Snyder v. Louisiana,* 552 U.S. 472 (2008).

36. 511 U.S. 127 (1994).

37. Harry Kalven and Hans Zeisel, *The American Jury* (Boston: Little, Brown, 1966), 163–167.

38. Donald E. Shelton, "Juror Expectations for Scientific Evidence in Criminal Cases: Perceptions and Reality about the 'CSI Effect' Myth," *Thomas M. Cooley Law Review* 27 (2010), at **www.npr.org /documents/2011/feb/shelton-CSI-study.pdf.**

39. Thomas J. Reed, "Trial by Propensity: Admission of Other Criminal Acts Evidenced in Federal Criminal Trials," *University of Cincinnati Law Review* 50 (1981), 713.

40. *Ibid.*

41. *People v. Zackowitz,* 254 N.Y. 192 (1930).

42. Federal Rules of Procedure, Rule 804(b)(2).

43. Arthur Best, *Evidence: Examples and Explanations,* 4th ed. (New York: Aspen Law & Business, 2001), 89–90.

44. David W. Broeder, "The University of Chicago Jury Project," *Nebraska Law Review* 38 (1959), 744–760.

45. 164 U.S. 492 (1896).

46. *United States v. Fioravanti,* 412 F.2d 407 (3d Cir. 1969).

47. Bureau of Justice Statistics, *Federal Justice Statistics, 2010* (Washington, D.C.: U.S. Department of Justice, December 2013), 17, 26.

48. The Innocence Project, "Know the Cases," at **www.innocenceproject.org/know.**

49. Michigan Law School & Northwestern Law School, "The National Registry of Exonerations," at **www.law.umich.edu/special/exoneration/Pages /browse.aspx.**

50. "Brief for the American Psychological Association as Amici Curiae Supporting Petitioner," *Perry v. New Hampshire,* 132 S. Ct. 716 (2012).

51. *District Attorney's Office v. Osborne,* 557 U.S. 52 (2009).

52. Theresa Hsu Schriever, "In Our Own Backyard: Why California Should Care about Habeas Corpus," *McGeorge Law Review* 45 (2014), 764–798.

9

1. Herbert L. Packer, "Justification for Criminal Punishment," in *The Limits of Criminal Sanction* (Palo Alto, Calif.: Stanford University Press, 1968), 36–37.

2. Frank O. Bowman III, "Playing '21' with Narcotics Enforcement: A Response to Professor Carrington," *Washington and Lee Law Review* 52 (1995), 972.

3. James Q. Wilson, *Thinking about Crime* (New York: Basic Books, 1975), 235.

4. Ashley Nellis, *Life Goes On: The Historic Rise of Life Sentences in America* (Washington, D.C.: The Sentencing Project, September 2013), 1.

5. Isaac Ehrlich, "Participation in Illegitimate Activities: A Theoretical and Empirical Investigation," *Journal of Political Economy* 81 (May/June 1973), 521–564.

6. Avinash Singh Bhati, *An Information Theoretic Method for Estimating the Number of Crimes Averted by Incapacitation* (Washington, D.C.: Urban Institute, July 2007), 18–33.

7. Todd Clear, *Harm in Punishment* (Boston: Northeastern University Press, 1980).

8. Patricia M. Clark, "An Evidence-Based Intervention for Offenders," *Corrections Today* (February/March 2011), 62–64.

9. Robert V. Wolf, *Widening the Circle: Can Peacemaking Work Outside of Tribal Communities?* (New York: Center for Court Innovation, 2012), 2–8.

10. Quoted in *ibid.,* 8.

11. Kimberly S. Burke, *An Inventory and Examination of Restorative Justice Practices for Youth in Illinois* (Chicago: Illinois Criminal Justice Information Authority, April 2013), 6–7.

12. Gregory W. O'Reilly, "Truth-in-Sentencing: Illinois Adds Yet Another Layer of 'Reform' to Its Complicated Code of Corrections," *Loyola University of Chicago Law Journal* (Summer 1996), 986, 999–1006.

13. David E. Olson, et al., *Final Report: The Impact of Illinois' Truth-in-Sentencing Law on Sentence Lengths, Time to Serve and Disciplinary Incidents of Convicted Murderers and Sex Offenders* (Chicago: Illinois Criminal Justice Information Authority, June 2009), 4–5.

14. Paul W. Keve, *Crime Control and Justice in America: Searching for Facts and Answers* (Chicago: American Library Association, 1995), 77.

15. Adam Ferrise, "Man Ordered by Judge to Hold Sign Saying He Bullied Disabled Children Starts His Five-Hour Shift," *Cleveland.com* (April 13, 2014), at **www.cleveland.com/metro/index .ssf/2014/04/man_ordered_by_judge_to_hold _s.html.**

16. Danielle A. Alvarez, "Flowers, Dinner, Bowling—and Counseling—Ordered by Broward Judge in Domestic Case," *Sunsentinel.com* (February 7, 2012), at **articles.sun-sentinel.com/2012 -02-07/news/fl-flowers-food-bowling-20120207 _1_red-lobster-broward-judge-judge-johnjay -hurley.**

17. Kate Stith and José A. Cabranes, "Judging under the Federal Sentencing Guidelines," *Northwestern University Law Review* 91 (Summer 1997), 1247.

18. Mark M. Lanier and Claud H. Miller III, "Attitudes and Practices of Federal Probation Officers towards Pre-Plea/Trial Investigative Report Policy," *Crime & Delinquency* 41 (July 1995), 365–366.

19. Nancy J. King and Rosevelt L. Noble, "Felony Jury Sentencing in Practice: A Three-State Study," *Vanderbilt Law Review* (2004), 1986.

20. Julie R. O'Sullivan, "In Defense of the U.S. Sentencing Guidelines Modified Real-Offense System," *Northwestern University Law Review* 91 (1997), 1342.

21. Lisa G. Aspinwall, Teneille R. Brown, and James Tabery, "The Double-Edged Sword: Does Biomechanism Increase or Decrease Judges' Sentencing of Psychopaths?" *Science* (August 2012), 846–849.

22. Quoted in Robert Allen, "6-Month Sentence for Driver's Attacker Angers Prosecutor," *Detroit Free Press* (July 17, 2014), at **www.usatoday.com /story/news/nation/2014/07/17/steven-utash -detroit-beating-sentencing/12783233/.**

23. 18 U.S.C. Section 2113(a) (1994).

24. U.S. Sentencing Commission, "Statistical Information Packet, Fiscal Year 2013, Oregon," Table 7, at **www.ussc.gov/sites/default/pdf /research-and-publications/federal-sentencing -statistics/state-district-circuit/2013/or13.pdf;** and "Statistical Information Packet, Fiscal Year 2013, Eastern District of North Carolina," Table 7, at **www.ussc.gov/sites/default/pdf/research -and-publications/federal-sentencing-statistics /state-district-circuit/2013/nce13.pdf.**

25. U.S. Sentencing Commission, "Statistical Information Packet, Fiscal Year 2012, First Circuit," Table 7, at **www.ussc.gov/sites/default /files/pdf/research-and-publications/federal -sentencing-statistics/state-district-circuit/2013 /4c13.pdf;** and "Statistical Information Packet, Fiscal Year 2012, Ninth Circuit," Table 7, at **www .ussc.gov/sites/default/files/pdf/research-and -publications/federal-sentencing-statistics /state-district-circuit/2013/9c13.pdf.**

26. Cassia Spohn and David Holleran, "The Imprisonment Penalty Paid by Young, Unemployed Black and Hispanic Male Offenders," *Criminology* 35 (2000), 281.

27. Illinois Disproportionate Justice Impact Study Commission, "Key Findings and Recommendations" (2011), at **www.illinoissenatedemocrats .com/phocadownload/PDF/Attachments/2011 /djisfactsheet.pdf.**

28. Bureau of Justice Statistics, *Prisoners in 2013* (Washington, D.C.: U.S. Department of Justice, September 2014), Table 14, page 16.

29. Nellis, *op. cit.,* 10.

30. Bureau of Justice Statistics, *Federal Statistics, 2010* (Washington, D.C.: U.S. Department of Justice, December 2013), Table 14, page 24.

31. Spohn and Holleran, *op. cit.,* 301.

32. Brian Johnson, "The Multilevel Context of Criminal Sentencing: Integrating Judge- and County-Level Influences," *Criminology* (May 2006), 259–298.

33. 28 U.S.C. Section 991 (1994).

34. Bureau of Justice Statistics, *Felony Sentences in State Courts, 2006—Statistical Tables* (Washington, D.C.: U.S. Department of Justice, December 2009), Table 3.5, page 20.

35. Sonja B. Starr, "Estimating Gender Disparities in Federal Criminal Cases," *University of Michigan Law and Economics Research Paper* (August 29, 2012), at **papers.ssrn.com/sol3/papers.cfm ?abstract_id=2144002.**

36. Clarice Feinman, *Women in the Criminal Justice System,* 3d ed. (Westport, Conn.: Praeger, 1994), 35.

37. Darrell Steffensmeier, John Kramer, and Cathy Streifel, "Gender and Imprisonment Decisions," *Criminology* 31 (1993), 411.

38. Quoted in L. L. Brasier, "Sandra Layne Sentenced to 20–40 Years in Death of Grandson," *Detroit Free Press* (April 18, 2013), at **archive .freep.com/article/20130418/NEWS03/3041 80154/sandra-layne-sentencing-oakland -county-jonathan-hoffman-west-bloomfield.**

39. Quoted in Kareem Fahim and Karen Zraick, "Seeing Failure of Mother as Factor in Sentencing," *New York Times* (November 17, 2008), A24.

40. John C. Coffee, "Repressed Issues of Sentencing," *Georgetown Law Journal* 66 (1978), 987.

41. J. S. Bainbridge, Jr., "The Return of Retribution," *ABA Journal* (May 1985), 63.

42. Pub. L. No. 98-473, 98 Stat. 1987, codified as amended at 18 U.S.C. Sections 3551–3742 and 28 U.S.C. Sections 991–998 (1988).

43. Julia L. Black, "The Constitutionality of Federal Sentences Imposed under the Sentencing Reform Act of 1984 after *Mistretta v. United States,*" *Iowa Law Review* 75 (March 1990), 767.

44. *Fifteen Years of Guidelines Sentencing: An Assessment of How Well the Federal Criminal Justice System Is Achieving the Goals of Sentencing Reform* (Washington, D.C.: U.S. Sentencing Commission, November 2004), 46.

45. *Blakely v. Washington,* 542 U.S. 296 (2004); *United States v. Booker,* 543 U.S. 220 (2005); and *Gall v. United States,* 552 U.S. 38 (2007).

46. *Demographic Differences in Federal Sentencing Practices: An Update of the Booker Report's Multivariate Regression Analysis* (Washington,

D.C.: U.S. Sentencing Commission, March 2010), C-3.

47. Transactional Records Access Clearinghouse, "Wide Variations Seen in Federal Sentencing" (March 5, 2012), at **trac.syr.edu/whatsnew/email .120305.html.**

48. U.S. Sentencing Commission, "Table N: National Comparison of Sentence Imposed and Position Relative to the Guideline Range, Fiscal Year 2013," *FY 2013 Sourcebook,* at **www.ussc .gov/Research_and_Statistics/Annual_Reports _and_Sourcebooks/2012/TableN.pdf.**

49. Neal B. Kauder and Brian J. Ostrom, *State Sentencing Guidelines: Profiles and Continuum* (Williamsburg, Va.: National Center for State Courts, 2008), 15.

50. N.Y. Penal Law Sections 220.21, 60.5, 70.0(3) (1973).

51. Public Law Number 99–570 (1986).

52. 21 U.S.C. Section 859(b) (1986); 21 U.S.C. Section 861(a) (1986); and 18 U.S.C. Section 924(c)(1)(A)(i) (1998).

53. Todd R. Clear, George F. Cole, and Michael D. Reisig, *American Corrections,* 7th ed. (Belmont, Calif.: Thomson Wadsworth, 2006), 68–69.

54. *Lockyer v. Andrade,* 270 F.3d 743 (9th Cir. 2001).

55. *Ibid.,* 76.

56. Marisa Lagos and Ellen Huet, "'Three Strikes' Law Changes Approved by Wide Margin," *San Francisco Chronicle* (November 7, 2012), A14.

57. *United States Sentencing Commission, Report to Congress: Mandatory Minimum Penalties in the Federal Criminal Justice System* (Washington, D.C.: United States Sentencing Commission, October 2011), xxviii.

58. Ram Subramanian and Ruth Delaney, *Playbook for Change? States Reconsider Mandatory Sentences* (New York: Vera Institute of Justice, February 2014), 8–12.

59. Connecticut Senate Bill Number 1160 (2001).

60. Nevada House Bill Number 239 (2009).

61. Jim Parsons, et al., *End of an Era? The Impact of Drug Reform in New York City* (New York: Vera Institute of Justice, 2015).

62. Evan Bernick and Paul J. Larkin, Jr., *Reconsidering Mandatory Minimum Sentences: The Arguments for and against Potential Reforms* (Washington, D.C.: The Heritage Foundation, February 10, 2014), 1.

63. Erick Eckhold, "Prosecutors Draw Fire for Sentences Called Harsh," *New York Times* (December 6, 2013), A19.

64. Justice for All Act of 2004, Pub. L. No. 108-405, 118 Stat. 2260.

65. Paul G. Cassell, "In Defense of Victim Impact Statements," *Ohio State Journal of Criminal Law* (Spring 2009), 614.

66. Edna Erez, "Victim Voice, Impact Statements, and Sentencing: Integrating Restorative Justice and Therapeutic Jurisprudence Principles in Adversarial Proceedings," *Criminal Law Bulletin* (September/October 2004), 495.

67. Bryan Myers and Edith Greene, "Prejudicial Nature of Impact Statements," *Psychology, Public Policy, and Law* (December 2004), 493.

68. Bryan Myers and Jack Arbuthnot, "The Effects of Victim Impact Evidence on the Verdicts and Sentencing Judgments of Mock Jurors," *Journal of Offender Rehabilitation* (1999), 95–112.

69. *Payne v. Tennessee,* 501 U.S. 808 (1991).

70. Comments made at the Georgetown Law Center, "The Modern View of Capital Punishment,"

American Criminal Law Review 34 (Summer 1997), 1353.

71. David Bruck, quoted in Bill Rankin, "Fairness of the Death Penalty Is Still on Trial," *Atlanta Journal-Constitution* (July 29, 1997), A13.

72. Bureau of Justice Statistics, *Capital Punishment, 2012* (Washington, D.C.: U.S. Department of Justice, May 2014), Table 2, page 6.

73. *In re Kemmler,* 136 U.S. 447 (1890).

74. 217 U.S. 349 (1910).

75. Pamela S. Nagy, "Hang by the Neck until Dead: The Resurgence of Cruel and Unusual Punishment in the 1990s," *Pacific Law Journal* 26 (October 1994), 85.

76. 553 U.S. 35 (2008).

77. Quoted in Dan Frosch and Sabrina Tavernise, "Judge Rejects Execution Delay over Use of Compounded Drug," *New York Times* (January 27, 2014), A11.

78. Adam Liptak and Erik Eckholm, "Justices to Hear Case over Drugs Used in Executions," *New York Times* (January 23, 2015), A1.

79. 408 U.S. 238 (1972).

80. 408 U.S. 309 (1972) (Stewart, concurring).

81. 536 U.S. 584 (2002).

82. Adam Liptak, "Alabama Judges Retain the Right to Override Juries in Capital Sentencing," *New York Times* (November 19, 2013), A15.

83. *Woodward v. Alabama,* 134 S.Ct. 405 (2013).

84. 536 U.S. 304 (2002).

85. *Penry v. Lynaugh,* 492 U.S. 302 (1989).

86. 543 U.S. 551 (2005).

87. *The Death Penalty in 2014: Year End Report* (Washington, D.C.: Death Penalty Information Center, December 2014), 1.

88. *Ibid.,* 2.

89. "The Slow Death of the Death Penalty," *The Economist* (April 26, 2014), 27.

90. Federal Bureau of Investigation, *Crime in the United States 2013* (Washington, D.C.: U.S. Department of Justice, 2014), at **www.fbi.gov /about-us/cjis/ucr/crime-in-the-u.s/2013/crime -in-the-u.s.-2013,** Table 1.

91. Legislative Auditor, *Performance Audit: Fiscal Costs of the Death Penalty* (Carson City: State of Nevada, 2014), 1.

92. *Jones v. Chappell* (C.D. Cal. 2014), available at **documents.latimes.com/judge-orders -californias-death-penalty-unconstitutional/.**

93. *Uttecht v. Brown,* 551 U.S. 1 (2007).

94. Gallup, "Americans' Support for Death Penalty Stable" (October 23, 2014), at **www.gallup .com/poll/178790/americans-support-death -penalty-stable.aspx.**

95. Pew Research Center, "Shrinking Majority of Americans Support Death Penalty" (March 28, 2014), at **www.pewforum.org/2014/03/28 /shrinking-majority-of-americans-support -death-penalty/.**

10

1. Mary Schenk and Michael Howie, "Reckless Homicide Sentence Reduced to Probation," *The News-Gazette* (Champaign, Ill.) (December 2, 2014), at **www.news-gazette.com/news/local /2014-12-02/reckless-homicide-sentence -reduced-probation.html.**

2. Bureau of Justice Statistics, *Correctional Populations in the United States, 2013* (Washington,

D.C.: U.S. Department of Justice, December 2014), Table 1, page 2.

3. Michael Tonry, *Sentencing Matters* (New York: Oxford Press, 1996), 28.

4. *Correctional Populations in the United States, 2013, op. cit.,* 1.

5. Corrections Task Force of the President's Commission on Law Enforcement and Administration of Justice (1967).

6. Paul H. Hahn, *Emerging Criminal Justice: Three Pillars for a Proactive Justice System* (Thousand Oaks, Calif.: Sage Publications, 1998), 106–108.

7. *Correctional Populations in the United States, 2013, op. cit.,* Table 1, page 2.

8. Pew Center on the States, *State of Recidivism: The Revolving Door of America's Prisons* (Washington, D.C.: The Pew Charitable Trusts, April 2011).

9. "Supervision Costs Significantly Less than Incarceration in Federal System," *United States Courts* (July 18, 2013), at **news.uscourts.gov /supervision-costs-significantly-less -incarceration-federal-system.**

10. Ram Subramanian and Rebecca Tublitz, *Realigning Justice Resources: A Review of Population Spending Shifts in Prison and Community Corrections* (New York: Vera Institute of Justice, 2012), 32, 33.

11. Erik Eckholm, "North Carolina Cuts Prison Time for Probation Violators, and Costs," *New York Times* (September 12, 2014), A14.

12. Paul W. Keve, *Crime Control and Justice in America* (Chicago: American Library Association, 1995), 183.

13. Gerald Bayens and John Ortiz Smykla, *Probation, Parole, and Community-Based Corrections* (New York: McGraw-Hill, 2013), 186–217.

14. Bureau of Justice Statistics, *Probation and Parole in the United States, 2010* (Washington, D.C.: U.S. Department of Justice, December 2011), Appendix table 3, page 31.

15. Joan Petersilia and Susan Turner, *Prison versus Probation in California: Implications for Crime and Offender Recidivism* (Santa Monica, Calif.: RAND Corporation, 1986).

16. Bureau of Justice Statistics, *Probation and Parole in the United States, 2013* (Washington, D.C.: U.S. Department of Justice, October 2014), Appendix table 3, page 17.

17. Brian Skoloff, "George Sanders Gets Probation in Mercy Killing," *Associated Press* (March 29, 2013).

18. 705 So.2d 172 (La. 1997).

19. Neil P. Cohen and James J. Gobert, *The Law of Probation and Parole* (Colorado Springs, Colo.: Shepard's/McGraw-Hill, 1983), Section 5.01, 183–184; Section 5.03, 191–192.

20. 534 U.S. 112 (2001).

21. *Ibid.,* 113.

22. Bureau of Justice Statistics, *Felony Defendants in Large Urban Counties, 2009—Statistical Tables* (Washington, D.C.: U.S. Department of Justice, December 2013), Table 28, page 32.

23. Carl B. Klockars, Jr., "A Theory of Probation Supervision," *Journal of Criminal Law, Criminology, and Police Science* 63 (1972), 550–557.

24. *Probation and Parole in the United States, 2013, op. cit.,* Table 4, page 5.

25. Gwen Robinson, "What Works in Offender Management?" *The Howard Journal of Criminal Justice* 44 (2005), 307–318.

26. Klockars, *op. cit.,* 551.

27. Matthew T. DeMichele, *Probation and Parole's Growing Caseloads and Workload Allocation: Strategies for Managerial Decision Making* (Lexington, Ky.: American Probation and Parole Association, May 2007).

28. "Rise in Number of Serious Offenders Takes Toll on Supervision Resources," *United States Courts* (October 15, 2014), at **news.uscourts.gov /rise-numbers-serious-offenders-takes-toll -supervision-resources.**

29. 389 U.S. 128 (1967).

30. *Morrissey v. Brewer,* 408 U.S. 471 (1972); and *Gagnon v. Scarpelli,* 411 U.S. 778 (1973).

31. 465 U.S. 420 (1984).

32. *Felony Defendants in Large Urban Counties, 2009—Statistical Tables, op. cit.,* Table 6, page 10.

33. Jennifer L. Skeem and Sarah Manchak, "Back to the Future: From Klockars' Model of Effective Supervision to Evidence-Based Practice in Probation," *Journal of Offender Rehabilitation* 47 (2008), 231.

34. *Probation and Parole in the United States, 2013, op. cit.,* Table 4, page 5.

35. Pamela M. Casey, Roger K. Warren, and Jennifer K. Elek, *Using Offender Risk and Needs Assessment Information at Sentencing* (Williamsburg, Va.: National Center for State Courts, 2011), Table 1, page 5.

36. James Q. Wilson, "Making Justice Swifter," *City Journal* 7 (1997), 4.

37. Angela Hawken and Mark Kleiman, *Managing Drug Involved Probationers and Swift and Certain Sanctions: Evaluating Hawaii's HOPE* (Washington, D.C.: U.S. Department of Justice, December 2009), 4.

38. Todd R. Clear, George F. Cole, and Michael D. Reisig, *American Corrections,* 9th ed. (Belmont, Calif.: Wadsworth Cengage Learning, 2011), 408.

39. *Probation and Parole in the United States, 2013, op. cit.,* Appendix table 7, page 21.

40. Bureau of Justice Statistics, *Probation and Parole in the United States, 2012* (Washington, D.C.: U.S. Department of Justice, December 2013), Table 7, page 9.

41. Joseph Walker, "Rules May Help Parolees Avoid Jail for Small Errors," *New York Times* (January 5, 2012), at **cityroom.blogs.nytimes.com/2012 /01/05/rating-a-parolees-risk-before-a-return -to-prison.**

42. *Morrissey v. Brewer,* 408 U.S. 471 (1972).

43. 442 U.S. 1 (1979).

44. American Civil Liberties Union, *A Living Death: Life without Parole for Nonviolent Offenses* (November 2013), 2.

45. Marie Gottschalk, "Days without End: Life Sentences and Penal Reform," *Prison Legal News* (April 11, 2013), at **www.prisonlegalnews.org /24102_displayArticle.aspx.**

46. William Parker, *Parole: Origins, Development, Current Practices, and Statutes* (College Park, Md.: American Correctional Association, 1972), 26.

47. "Prison Breakthrough," *The Economist* (April 19, 2014), 29.

48. Joseph Walker, "State Parole Boards Use Software to Decide Which Inmates to Release," *Wall Street Journal* (October 11, 2013), A8.

49. Clear, Cole, and Reisig, *op. cit.,* 389.

50. Quoted in Thomas Tracy, "Cop-Killer Herman Bell Denied Parole in Murder of Two NYPD Officers in 1971," *New York Daily News* (February 25, 2014), at **www.nydailynews.com/new-york /nyc-crime/cop-killer-herman-bell-denied -parole-article-1.1701111.**

51. Quoted in "Governor Denies Parole to a Follower of Manson," *Associated Press* (August 9, 2014).

52. Mark P. Rankin, Mark H. Allenbaugh, and Carlton Fields, "Parole's Essential Role in Bailing Out Our Nation's Criminal Justice Systems," *Champion* (January 2009), 47–48.

53. Ram Subramanian, Rebecka Moreno, and Sharyn Broomhead, *Recalibrating Justice: A Review of 2013 State Sentencing and Corrections Trends* (New York: Vera Institute of Justice, July 2014), 20–21.

54. 18 U.S.C. Sections 1961–1968.

55. 516 U.S. 442 (1996).

56. U.S. Marshals, "Fact Sheet: Asset Forfeiture 2015," at **www.usmarshals.gov/duties/factsheets /asset_forfeiture.pdf.**

57. Douglas J. Boyle, et al., "Overview of: 'An Evaluation of Day Reporting Centers for Parolees: Outcomes of a Randomized Trial,'" *Criminology & Public Policy* (February 2013), 136.

58. *ISP Fact Sheet: Intensive Supervision Program* (Trenton, N.J.: Administrative Office of the Courts, February 2015), 1–2.

59. Joan Petersilia and Susan Turner, "Intensive Probation and Parole," *Crime and Justice* 17 (1993), 281–335.

60. Douglas J. Boyle, et al., *Outcomes of a Randomized Trial of an Intensive Community Corrections Program—Day Reporting Center—for Parolees, Final Report for the National Institute of Justice* (Washington, D.C.: U.S. Department of Justice, October 2011), 3–4.

61. *Probation and Parole in the United States, 2010, op. cit.,* Appendix table 3, page 31.

62. Clear, Cole, and Reisig, *op. cit.,* 125.

63. Paul Stageberg and Bonnie Wilson, *Recidivism among Iowa Probationers* (Des Moines: Iowa Division of Criminal and Juvenile Justice Planning, July 2005); and Paul Koniceck, *Five Year Recidivism Follow-Up Offender Releases* (Columbus: Ohio Department of Rehabilitation and Correction, August 1996).

64. Todd R. Clear, et al., *American Corrections in Brief,* 2d ed. (Belmont, Calif.: Wadsworth Cengage Learning, 2014), 102.

65. Josh Kurtz, "New Growth in a Captive Market," *New York Times* (December 31, 1989), 12.

66. Michael Tonry and Mary Lynch, "Intermediate Sanctions," in *Crime and Justice,* vol. 20, ed. Michael Tonry (Chicago: University of Chicago Press, 1996), 99.

67. Dennis Palumbo, Mary Clifford, and Zoann K. Snyder-Joy, "From Net Widening to Intermediate Sanctions: The Transformation of Alternatives to Incarceration from Benevolence to Malevolence," in *Smart Sentencing: The Emergence of Intermediate Sanctions,* ed. James M. Byrne, Arthur Lurigio, and Joan Petersilia (Newbury Park, Calif.: Sage, 1992), 231.

11

1. James M. Beattie, *Crime and the Courts in England, 1660–1800* (Princeton, N.J.: Princeton University Press, 1986), 506–507.

2. Samuel Walker, *Popular Justice* (New York: Oxford University Press, 1980), 11.

3. Michael Meranze, *Laboratories of Virtue: Punishment, Revolution, and Authority in Philadelphia, 1760–1835* (Chapel Hill: University of North Carolina Press, 1996), 55.

4. Negley K. Teeters, *The Cradle of the Penitentiary: The Walnut Street Jail at Philadelphia, 1773–1835* (Philadelphia: Pennsylvania Prison Society, 1955), 30.

5. Negley K. Teeters and John D. Shearer, *The Prison at Philadelphia's Cherry Hill* (New York: Columbia University Press, 1957), 142–143.

6. Henry Calvin Mohler, "Convict Labor Policies," *Journal of the American Institute of Criminal Law and Criminology* 15 (1925), 556–557.

7. Zebulon Brockway, *Fifty Years of Prison Service* (Montclair, N.J.: Patterson Smith, 1969), 400–401.

8. Robert Martinson, "What Works? Questions and Answers about Prison Reform," *Public Interest* 35 (Spring 1974), 22.

9. See Ted Palmer, "Martinson Revisited," *Journal of Research on Crime and Delinquency* (1975), 133; and Paul Gendreau and Bob Ross, "Effective Correctional Treatment: Bibliotherapy for Cynics," *Crime & Delinquency* 25 (1979), 499.

10. Robert Martinson, "New Findings, New Views: A Note of Caution Regarding Sentencing Reform," *Hofstra Law Review* 7 (1979), 243.

11. Byron Eugene Price and John Charles Morris, eds., *Prison Privatization: The Many Facets of a Controversial Industry, Volume 1* (Santa Barbara, Calif.: Praeger, 2012), 58.

12. Charles H. Logan, *Criminal Justice Performance Measures in Prisons* (Washington, D.C.: U.S. Department of Justice, 1993), 5.

13. Todd R. Clear and George F. Cole, *American Corrections,* 4th ed. (Belmont, Calif.: Wadsworth Publishing Co., 1997), 245–246.

14. Alfred Blumstein, "Prisons," in *Crime,* ed. James Q. Wilson and Joan Petersilia (San Francisco: ICS Press, 1995), 392.

15. Cassia Spohn and David Holleran, "The Effect of Imprisonment on Recidivism Rates of Felony Offenders: A Focus on Drug Offenders," *Criminology* (May 1, 2002), 329–357.

16. Bureau of Justice Statistics, *Census of State and Federal Correctional Facilities, 2005* (Washington, D.C.: U.S. Department of Justice, October 2008), 2.

17. *Ibid.*

18. Charles H. Logan, "Well Kept: Comparing Quality of Confinement in a Public and Private Prison," *Journal of Criminal Law and Criminology* 83 (1992), 580.

19. Bert Useem and Peter Kimball, *Stages of Siege: U.S. Prison Riots, 1971–1986* (New York: Oxford University Press, 1989).

20. Bert Useem, "Disorganization and the New Mexico Prison Riot of 1980," *American Sociology Review* 50 (1985), 685.

21. Peter M. Carlson and John J. DiIulio, Jr., "Organization and the Management of the Prison," in *Prison and Jail Administration: Practice and Theory,* 3d ed., ed. Peter M. Carlson (Burlington, Mass.: Jones & Bartlett Learning, 2015), 272.

22. John J. DiIulio, *Governing Prisons* (New York: Free Press, 1987), 12.

23. *Ibid.*

24. Todd R. Clear, George F. Cole, and Michael D. Reisig, *American Corrections,* 9th ed. (Belmont, Calif.: Wadsworth Cengage Learning, 2010), 162.

25. Peter M. Carlson, "Inmate Classification," in *Prison and Jail Administration: Practice and Theory, op. cit.,* 53–57.

26. Douglas Page, "The Prison of the Future," *Law Enforcement Technology* (January 2012), 11–13.

27. Daniel P. Mears, "Supermax Prisons: The Policy and the Evidence," *Criminology and Public Policy* (November 2013), 684.

28. Keramet Reiter, *Parole, Snitch, or Die: California's Supermax Prisons and Prisoners, 1987–2007* (Berkeley: University of California Institute for the Study of Social Change, 2010), 1.

29. "Facts about Pelican Bay's SHU," *California Prisoner* (December 1991).

30. Steven D. Levitt, "Understanding Why Crime Fell in the 1990s: Four Factors That Explain the Decline and Six That Do Not," *Journal of Economic Perspectives* (Winter 2004), 177.

31. Bureau of Justice Statistics, *Prisoners in 2013* (Washington, D.C.: U.S. Department of Justice, September 2014), Table 13, page 15; and Table 16, page 17.

32. Allen J. Beck, "Growth, Change, and Stability in the U.S. Prison Population, 1980–1995," *Corrections Management Quarterly* (Spring 1997), 9–10.

33. U.S. District Courts, "Criminal Defendants Sentenced after Conviction, by Offense, during the 12-Month Period Ending September 30, 2013" at **www.uscourts.gov/uscourts/Statistics /JudicialBusiness/2013/appendices/D05 Sep13.pdf.**

34. Joan Petersilia, "Beyond the Prison Bubble," *Wilson Quarterly* (Winter 2011), 27.

35. *Time Served: The High Cost, Low Return of Longer Prison Terms* (Washington, D.C.: The Pew Center on the States, June 2012), 2.

36. *Fifteen Years of Guidelines Sentencing: An Assessment of How Well the Federal Criminal Justice System Is Achieving the Goals of Sentencing Reform* (Washington, D.C.: U.S. Sentencing Commission, November 2004), 46.

37. *Prisoners in 2013, op. cit.,* Table 1, page 2.

38. *Ibid.,* Table 3, page 4.

39. Julie Samuels, Nancy La Vigne, and Samuel Taxy, *Stemming the Tide: Strategies to Reduce the Growth and Cut the Cost of the Federal Prison System* (Washington, D.C.: Urban Institute, November 2013), 1.

40. Comprehensive Crime Control Act of 1984, Public Law Number 98-473.

41. *Prisoners in 2013, op. cit.,* Table 15, page 17.

42. Federal Bureau of Prisons, "Inmate Gender" (January 25, 2015), at **www.bop.gov/about /statistics/statistics_inmate_gender.jsp.**

43. Bureau of Justice Statistics, *Prisoners in 2012: Trends in Admissions and Releases, 1991–2012* (Washington, D.C.: U.S. Department of Justice, December 2013), Appendix table 10, page 43; and Bureau of Justice Statistics, *Prison and Jail Inmates 1995* (Washington, D.C.: U.S. Department of Justice, August 1996), Table 6, page 6.

44. James B. Jacobs, "Finding Alternatives to the Carceral State," *Social Research* (Summer 2007), 695.

45. *State Spending for Corrections: Long Term Trends and Recent Criminal Justice Policy Reforms* (Washington, D.C.: The National Association of State Budget Officers, September 2013), 1.

46. Rosemary Gartner, Anthony N. Doob, and Franklin E. Zimring, "The Past as Prologue? Decarceration in California Then and Now," *Criminology & Public Policy* (May 2011), 294–296.

47. Council of State Governments Justice Center, *Reducing Recidivism: States Deliver Results* (New York: Council of State Governments Justice Center, June 2014), 1–23.

48. Dan Seligman, "Lock 'Em Up," *Forbes* (May 23, 2005), 216–217.

49. Bruce Western and Becky Pettit, *Collateral Costs: Incarceration's Effect on Economic Mobility* (Washington, D.C.: The Pew Charitable Trusts, 2010), 4.

50. John Tierney, "Prison and the Poverty Trap," *New York Times* (February 19, 2013), D1.

51. *Ibid.*

52. *Rethinking the Blues: How We Police in the U.S. and at What Cost* (Washington, D.C.: Justice Policy Institute, May 2012), 34.

53. *Prisoners in 2012: Trends in Admissions and Releases, 1991–2012, op. cit.,* Table 18, page 25.

54. Quoted in Fox Butterfield, "Study Finds 2.6% Increase in U.S. Prison Population," *New York Times* (July 28, 2003), A8.

55. Quoted in Scott Cohn, "Private Prison Industry Grows Despite Critics," *cnbc.com* (October 18, 2011), at **www.nbcnews.com/id/44936562/ns /business-cnbc_tv/t/private-prison-industry -grows-despite-critics/#.UW6vC7_zdzU.**

56. Thierry Godard, "The Economics of the American Prison System," *SmartAsset.com* (January 23, 2015), at **smartasset.com/insights/the -economics-of-the-american-prison-system.**

57. *Prisoners in 2013, op. cit.,* Table 12, page 14.

58. "A Tale of Two Systems: Cost, Quality, and Accountability in Private Prisons," *Harvard Law Review* (May 2002), 1872.

59. Douglas C. McDonald and Kenneth Carlson, *Contracting for Imprisonment in the Federal Prison System: Cost and Performance of the Privately Operated Taft Correctional Institution* (Cambridge, Mass.: Abt Associates, Inc., October 2005), vii.

60. Vanderbilt University Law School, "New Study Shows Benefits of Having Privately and Publicly Managed Prisons in the Same State" (November 25, 2008), at **law.vanderbilt.edu/article-search /article-detail/index.aspx?nid=213.**

61. Clifton Adcock, "State Weighs Moving More Inmates to Private Prisons, or Buying a Private Prison," *Oklahoma Watch* (January 9, 2014), at **oklahomawatch.org/2014/01/09/with-over crowded-prisons-state-looks-at-moving-more -inmates-to-private-prisons-or-buying-a -private-prison.**

62. "California Prisoners Could Be Moved Out of State Due to Overcrowding," *Associated Press* (January 8, 2014).

63. Gerald G. Gaes, "The Current Status of Prison Privatization Research on American Prisons" (2012), at **works.bepress.com/gerald_gaes_1/.**

64. Gregory Geisler, *CIIC: Lake Erie Correctional Institution* (Columbus, Ohio: Correctional Institution Inspection Committee, January 2013), 16.

65. Curtis R. Blakely and Vic W. Bumphus, "Private and Public Sector Prisons," *Federal Probation* (June 2004), 27.

66. John DiIulio, "Prisons, Profits, and the Public Good: The Privatization of Corrections," in *Criminal Justice Center Bulletin* (Huntsville, Tex.: Sam Houston State University, 1986).

67. Richard L. Lippke, "Thinking about Private Prisons," *Criminal Justice Ethics* (Winter/Spring 1997), 32.

68. Quoted in Cohn, *op. cit.*

69. *Prisoners in 2013, op. cit.,* Table 12, page 14.

70. *Warehoused and Forgotten: Immigrants Trapped in Our Shadow Private Prison System* (New York: American Civil Liberties Union, June 2014), 6.

71. Bureau of Justice Statistics, *Jail Inmates at Midyear 2013—Statistical Tables* (Washington, D.C.: U.S. Department of Justice, May 2014), 1, 4.

72. Quoted in Fox Butterfield, "'Defying Gravity,' Inmate Population Climbs," *New York Times* (January 19, 1998), A10.

73. *Jail Inmates at Midyear 2013—Statistical Tables, op. cit.,* Table 2, page 6.

74. 441 U.S. 520 (1979).

75. *Ibid.,* at 546.

76. *Jail Inmates at Midyear 2013—Statistical Tables, op. cit.,* 1.

77. Paige St. John, "Early Jail Releases Have Surged Since California's Prison Realignment," *Los Angeles Times* (August 16, 2014), at **www.latimes .com/local/crime/la-me-ff-early-release-2014 0817-story.html#page=1.**

78. Bureau of Justice Statistics, *Census of Jail Facilities, 2006* (Washington, D.C.: U.S. Department of Justice, December 2011), 14.

79. Doris J. James and Lauren E. Glaze, *Bureau of Justice Statistics Special Report: Mental Health Problems of Prison and Jail Inmates* (Washington, D.C.: U.S. Department of Justice, September 2006), 1.

80. Laura M. Maruschak, *Bureau of Justice Statistics Special Report: Medical Problems of Jail Inmates* (Washington, D.C.: U.S. Department of Justice, November 2006), 1.

81. Jennifer C. Karberg and Doris J. James, *Bureau of Justice Statistics Special Report: Substance Dependence, Abuse, and Treatment of Jail Inmates, 2002* (Washington, D.C.: U.S. Department of Justice, July 2005), 1.

82. Quoted in Michael Schwirtz, "Rikers Island Struggles with a Surge in Violence and Mental Illness," *New York Times* (March 19, 2014), A1.

83. R. L. Miller, "New Generation Justice Facilities: The Case for Direct Supervision," *Architectural Technology* 12 (1985), 6–7.

84. David Bogard, Virginia A. Hutchinson, and Vicci Persons, *Direct Supervision Jails: The Role of the Administrator* (Washington, D.C.: National Institute of Corrections, February 2010), 1–2.

12

1. Erving Goffman, "On the Characteristics of Total Institutions," in *Asylums: Essays on the Social Situation of Mental Patients and Other Inmates* (New York: Doubleday, 1961), 6.

2. Donald Clemmer, *The Prison Community* (Boston: Christopher, 1940).

3. John Irwin, *Prisons in Turmoil* (Boston: Little, Brown, 1980), 67.

4. *Old Behind Bars: The Aging Prison Population in the United States* (New York: Human Rights Watch, 2012), 24–42.

5. "Life, Death, and Raging Bulls," *The Economist* (May 10, 2014), 30.

6. Kevin E. McCarthy and Carrie Rose, *State Initiatives to Address Aging Prisoners* (Hartford: Connecticut General Assembly, Office of Legislative Research, 2013), 3.

7. *Managing Prison Health Care Spending* (Philadelphia: The Pew Charitable Trusts, October 2013), 11.

8. Michael Vitiello, "Addressing the Special Problems of Mentally Ill Prisoners: A Small Piece of the Solution to Our Nation's Prison Crisis," *Denver University Law Review* (Fall 2010), 57–62.

9. Katherine Stuart van Wormer and Clemens Bartollas, *Women and the Criminal Justice System,*

3d ed. (Upper Saddle River, N.J.: Pearson Education, 2011), 143.

10. "Locked In," *The Economist* (August 3, 2013), 24.

11. Kevin Johnson, "Mentally Ill Fill Crowded Prisons," *USA Today* (July 25, 2014), 5A.

12. William Kanapaux, "Guilty of Mental Illness," *Psychiatric Times* (January 1, 2004), at **www.psychiatrictimes.com/forensic-psych/content/article/10168/47631.**

13. Bureau of Justice Statistics, *Census of State and Federal Correctional Facilities, 2005* (Washington, D.C.: U.S. Department of Justice, October 2008), 6.

14. *Behind Bars II: Substance Abuse and America's Prison Population* (New York: The National Center on Addiction and Substance Abuse at Columbia University, February 2010), 4.

15. *Ibid.*, 83–84.

16. Devah Pager and Bruce Western, *Investigating Prisoner Reentry: The Impact of Conviction Status on the Employment Prospects of Young Men* (Washington, D.C.: National Institute of Justice, October 2009), 6.

17. *Census of State and Federal Correctional Facilities, 2005, op. cit.*, 6.

18. Lois M. Davis, et al., *Evaluating the Effectiveness of Correctional Education* (Santa Monica, Calif.: The Rand Corporation, 2013), xvi.

19. *Ibid.*, xvii.

20. Robert Johnson, *Hard Time: Understanding and Reforming the Prison*, 2d ed. (Belmont, Calif.: Wadsworth, 1996), 133.

21. Paul J. Biermann, *Improving Correctional Officer Safety: Reducing Inmate Weapons* (Washington, D.C.: National Institute of Justice, 2007), 23.

22. Bureau of Justice Statistics, *Mortality in Local Jails and State Prisons, 2000–2012—Statistical Tables* (Washington, D.C.: U.S. Department of Justice, October 2014), Table 1, page 6; and Table 15, page 19.

23. Daniel P. Mears, et al., "The Code of the Street and Inmate Violence: Investigating the Salience of Imported Belief Systems," *Criminology* (August 2013), 695–728.

24. Lee H. Bowker, *Prison Victimization* (New York: Elsevier, 1981), 31–33.

25. Stephen C. Light, "The Severity of Assaults on Prison Officers: A Contextual Analysis," *Social Science Quarterly* 71 (1990), 267–284.

26. Frank Tannenbaum, *Crime and Community* (Boston: Ginn & Co., 1938).

27. Randy Martin and Sherwood Zimmerman, "A Typology of the Causes of Prison Riots and an Analytical Extension to the 1986 Virginia Riot," *Justice Quarterly* 7 (1990), 711–737.

28. Bert Useem, "Disorganization and the New Mexico Prison Riot of 1980," *American Sociological Review* 50 (1985), 677–688.

29. Quoted in R. L. Nave, "Private Prisons, Public Problems," *Jackson (Miss.) Free Press* (June 6, 2012), at **www.jacksonfreepress.com/news/2012/jun/06/private-prisons-public-problems.**

30. 42 U.S.C. Sections 15601–15609 (2006).

31. Bureau of Justice Statistics, *Sexual Victimization Reported by Adult Correctional Authorities, 2009–11* (Washington, D.C.: U.S. Department of Justice, January 2014), 1.

32. James E. Robertson, "The Prison Rape Elimination Act of 2003: A Primer," *Criminal Law Bulletin* (May/June 2004), 270–273.

33. Irwin, *op. cit.*, 47.

34. Leo Carroll, "Race, Ethnicity, and the Social Order of the Prison," in *The Pains of Imprisonment*, ed. R. Johnson and H. Toch (Beverly Hills, Calif.: Sage, 1982).

35. Craig Haney, "Psychology and the Limits of Prison Pain," *Psychology, Public Policy, and Law* (December 1977), 499.

36. Alan J. Drury and Matt DeLisi, "Gangkill: An Exploratory Empirical Assessment of Gang Membership, Homicide Offending, and Prison Misconduct," *Crime & Delinquency* (January 2011), 130–146.

37. *A Study of Gangs and Security Threat Groups in America's Adult Prisons and Jails* (Indianapolis: National Major Gang Task Force, 2002).

38. George W. Knox, "The Problem of Gangs and Security Threat Groups (STGs) in American Prisons Today: Recent Research Findings from the 2004 Prison Gang Survey," available at **www.ngcrc.com/corr2006.html.**

39. *Ibid.*

40. John Winterdyk and Rick Ruddell, "Managing Prison Gangs: Results from a Survey of U.S. Prison Systems," *Journal of Criminal Justice* 38 (2010), 733–734.

41. Alan Gomez, "States Make Prisons Far Less Deadly," *USA Today* (August 22, 2008), 3A.

42. Quoted in John J. DiIulio, Jr., *No Escape: The Future of American Corrections* (New York: Basic Books, 1991), 268.

43. Jack Henry Abbott, *In the Belly of the Beast* (New York: Vintage Books, 1991), 54.

44. Michel Foucault, *Discipline and Punish: The Birth of the Prison* (New York: Pantheon Books, 1977), 128.

45. Lucien X. Lombardo, *Guards Imprisoned: Correctional Officers at Work* (Cincinnati, Ohio: Anderson Publishing Co., 1989), 51–71.

46. Goffman, *op. cit.*, 7.

47. Todd R. Clear, George F. Cole, and Michael D. Reisig, *American Corrections*, 9th ed. (Belmont, Calif.: Wadsworth Cengage Learning, 2011), 333.

48. *Wolff v. McDonnell*, 418 U.S. 539 (1974).

49. Erica Goode, "Prisons Rethink Isolation, Saving Money, Lives, and Sanity," *New York Times* (March 11, 2012), A1.

50. 475 U.S. 312 (1986).

51. Christopher R. Smith, *Law and Contemporary Corrections* (Belmont, Calif.: Wadsworth, 1999), Chapter 6.

52. 503 U.S. 1 (1992).

53. Darrell L. Ross, "Assessing *Hudson v. McMillan* Ten Years Later," *Criminal Law Bulletin* (September/October 2004), 508.

54. Van Wormer and Bartollas, *op. cit.*, 387.

55. Cristina Rathbone, *A World Apart: Women, Prison, and a Life behind Bars* (New York: Random House, 2006), 46.

56. Carl Nink et al., *Women Professionals in Corrections: A Growing Asset* (Centerville, Utah: MTC Institute, August 2008), 1.

57. Michael H. Jaime and Armand R. Burruel, "Labor Relations in Corrections," in *Prison and Jail Administration: Practice and Theory*, 3d ed., ed. Peter M. Carlson (Burlington, Mass.: Jones & Bartlett Learning, 2015), 264.

58. *Sexual Victimization Reported by Adult Correctional Authorities, 2009–11, op. cit.*, Table 10, page 12; and page 17.

59. *Wolff v. McDonnell*, 539.

60. *Hudson v. Palmer*, 468 U.S. 517 (1984).

61. 429 U.S. 97 (1976).

62. "Judge Orders Air Conditioning for Angola Prison's Death Row," *Associated Press* (May 24, 2014).

63. 501 U.S. 294 (1991).

64. *Wilson v. Seiter*, 501 U.S. 294, 304 (1991).

65. *Woodall v. Foti*, 648 F.2d, 268, 272 (5th Cir. 1981).

66. *Brown v. Plata*, 563 U.S. ____ (2011).

67. Quoted in Alexandra Marks, "Martha Checks in Today," *Seattle Times* (October 8, 2004), A8.

68. Bureau of Justice Statistics, *Sourcebook of Criminal Justice*, 3d ed. (Washington, D.C.: U.S. Department of Justice, 2003), Table 6.56, page 519; and Bureau of Justice Statistics, *Prisoners in 2013* (Washington, D.C.: U.S. Department of Justice, September 2014), Table 13, page 15.

69. Bureau of Justice Statistics, *Profile of Jail Inmates, 2002* (Washington, D.C.: U.S. Department of Justice, July 2004), 10.

70. Bureau of Justice Statistics, *Prior Abuse Reported by Inmates and Probationers* (Washington, D.C.: U.S. Department of Justice, April 1999), 2.

71. *Caught in the Net: The Impact of Drug Policies on Women and Families* (Washington, D.C.: American Civil Liberties Union, 2004), 18–19.

72. Sarah Schirmer, Ashley Nellis, and Marc Mauer, *Incarcerated Parents and Their Children: Trends 1991–2007* (Washington, D.C.: The Sentencing Project, February 2009), 2.

73. Kelly Bedard and Eric Helland, "Location of Women's Prisons and the Deterrent Effect of 'Harder' Time," *International Review of Law and Economics* (June 2004), 152.

74. *Ibid.*

75. Schirmer, Nellis, and Mauer, *op. cit.*, 5.

76. Rathbone, *op. cit.*, 4.

77. *Ibid.*, 158.

78. Van Wormer and Bartollas, *op. cit.*, 137–138.

79. Barbara Bloom and Meda Chesney-Lind, "Women in Prison," in *It's a Crime: Women and Justice*, 4th ed., ed. Roslyn Muraskin (Upper Saddle River, N.J.: Prentice Hall, 2007), 542–563.

80. Piper Kerman, *Orange Is the New Black: My Year in a Women's Prison* (New York: Spiegal and Grau, 2011), 131.

81. Esther Heffernan, *Making It in Prison: The Square, the Cool, and the Life* (New York: Wiley, 1972), 91.

82. Leanne F. Alarid, "Female Inmate Subcultures," in *Corrections Contexts: Contemporary and Classical Readings*, ed. James W. Marquart and Jonathan R. Sorenson (Los Angeles: Roxbury Publishing Co., 1997), 136–137.

83. Barbara Owen et al., *Gendered Violence and Safety: A Contextual Approach to Improving Security in Women's Facilities*, December 2008, 12–14, at **www.ncjrs.gov/pdffiles1/nij/grants/225340.pdf.**

84. Nancy Wolff, Cynthia Blitz, Jing Shi, Jane Siegel, and Ronet Bachman, "Physical Violence inside Prisons: Rates of Victimization," *Criminal Justice and Behavior* 34 (2007), 588–604.

85. Van Wormer and Bartollas, *op. cit.*, 146–148.

86. Barbara Bloom, Barbara Owen, and Stephanie Covington, *Gender Responsive Strategies: Research, Practice, and Guiding Principles for Women Offenders* (Washington, D.C.: National Institute of Corrections, 2003), 26.

87. Hamed Aleaziz, "Optimism for Ex-Inmates' 2nd Chance at Redemption," *San Francisco Chronicle* (November 10, 2014), A1.

88. Bureau of Justice Statistics, *Prisoners in 2012: Trends in Admissions and Releases, 1991–2012* (Washington, D.C.: U.S. Department of Justice, December 2013), Table 2, page 4.

89. Joan Petersilia, *When Prisoners Come Home: Parole and Prisoner Reentry* (New York: Oxford University Press, 2003), 39.

90. Victor Hassine, *Life without Parole: Living in Prison Today,* ed. Thomas J. Bernard and Richard McCleary (Los Angeles: Roxbury Publishing Co., 1996), 12.

91. Christy Visher, Sara Debus, and Jennifer Yahner, *Employment after Prison: A Longitudinal Study of Releases in Three States* (Washington, D.C.: Urban Institute, October 2008), 1.

92. *Ill Equipped: U.S. Prisons and Offenders with Mental Illness* (New York: Human Rights Watch, 2003).

93. Pew Center on the States, *State of Recidivism: The Revolving Door of America's Prisons* (Washington, D.C.: The Pew Charitable Trusts, April 2011), 2.

94. Edward Zamble and Vernon Quinsey, *The Criminal Recidivism Process* (Cambridge, England: Cambridge University Press, 1997).

95. Quoted in Kevin Johnson, "After Years of Solitary, Freedom Is Hard to Grasp," *USA Today* (June 9, 2005), 2A.

96. *Census of State and Federal Correctional Facilities, 2005, op. cit.,* Table 6, page 5.

97. Quoted in "'Pillowcase Rapist' Released to Live in Los Angeles Community," *Associated Press* (July 9, 2014).

98. Belinda Brooks Gordon and Charlotte Bilby, "Psychological Interventions for Treatment of Adult Sex Offenders," *British Medical Journal* (July 2006), 5–6.

99. Bureau of Justice Statistics, *Recidivism of Prisoners Released in 1994* (Washington, D.C.: U.S. Department of Justice, June 2002), Table 9, page 8.

100. R. Karl Hanson and Kelly Morton-Bourgon, "The Characteristics of Persistent Sexual Offenders: A Meta-Analysis of Recidivism Studies, *Journal of Consulting and Clinical Psychology* 73 (2005), 1154–1163.

101. New Jersey Revised Statute Section 2C:7-8(c) (1995).

102. Georgia Code Annotated Section 42-9-44.1(b)(1).

103. Public Law Number 109-248, Section 116, 120 Statute 595 (2006).

104. Abby Goodnough, "After Two Cases in Florida, Crackdown on Molesters," *Law Enforcement News* (May 2004), 12.

105. *United States v. Comstock,* 560 U.S. 126 (2010).

13

1. Jennifer M. O'Connor and Lucinda K. Treat, "Getting Smart about Getting Tough: Juvenile Justice and the Possibility of Progressive Reform," *American Criminal Law Review* 33 (Summer 1996), 1299.

2. *In re Gault,* 387 U.S. 1, 15 (1967).

3. Samuel Davis, *The Rights of Juveniles: The Juvenile Justice System,* 2d ed. (New York: C. Boardman Co., 1995), Section 1.2.

4. Quoted in Anthony Platt, *The Child Savers* (Chicago: University of Chicago Press, 1969), 119.

5. 383 U.S. 541 (1966).

6. *Ibid.,* 556.

7. 387 U.S. 1 (1967).

8. 397 U.S. 358 (1970).

9. 421 U.S. 519 (1975).

10. 403 U.S. 528 (1971).

11. Quoted in David Lohr, "Police Reveal Dark Details about 12-Year-Olds Accused of Stabbing a Friend to Meet 'Slenderman,'" *The Huffington Post* (June 13, 2014), at **www.huffingtonpost.com /2014/06/03/slenderman-stabbing_n_5439667 .html.**

12. Christina D. Carmichael, *Juvenile Justice and Youth Aids Program: Informational Paper 57* (Madison: Wisconsin Legislative Fiscal Bureau, January 2013), 10.

13. Research Network on Adolescent Development and Juvenile Justice, *Youth on Trial: A Developmental Perspective on Juvenile Justice* (Chicago: John D. & Catherine T. MacArthur Foundation, 2003), 1.

14. Richard E. Redding, "Juveniles Transferred to Criminal Court: Legal Reform Proposals Based on Social Science Research," *Utah Law Review* (1997), 709.

15. Howard N. Snyder and Melissa Sickmund, *Juvenile Offenders and Victims: A National Report* (Washington, D.C.: U.S. Department of Justice, 1995), 47.

16. Martha Grace Duncan, "'So Young and So Untender': Remorseless Children and the Expectations of the Law," *Columbia Law Review* (October 2002), 1469.

17. 543 U.S. 551 (2005).

18. *Ibid.,* 567.

19. 130 S.Ct. 2011 (2010).

20. *Ibid.,* 2030.

21. 132 S. Ct. 2455 (2012).

22. *Ibid.,* at 2463.

23. *Surveillance Summaries: Youth Risk Behavior Surveillance—United States, 2013* (Washington, D.C.: Centers for Disease Control and Prevention, June 13, 2014).

24. Federal Bureau of Investigation, *Crime in the United States 2013* (Washington, D.C.: U.S. Department of Justice, 2014), Table 38, at **www .fbi.gov/about-us/cjis/ucr/crime-in-the-u.s/2013 /crime-in-the-u.s.-2013.**

25. Sarah Hockenberry and Charles Puzzanchera, *Juvenile Court Statistics 2011* (Washington, D.C.: National Center for Juvenile Justice, July 2014), 7.

26. Office of Juvenile Justice and Delinquency Prevention, *Juvenile Residential Facility Census, 2010: Selected Findings* (Washington, D.C.: U.S. Department of Justice, September 2013), 1; and Todd Richmond, "Fewer Young Criminals Push States to Close Prisons," *Associated Press* (June 7, 2010).

27. David McDowell, "Juvenile Curfew Laws and Their Influence on Crime," *Federal Probation* (December 2006), 58.

28. *Crime in the United States, 2013, op. cit.,* Table 29.

29. Office of Juvenile Justice and Delinquency Prevention, "Community Prevention Grants Program," at **www.ojjdp.gov/cpg.**

30. *Juvenile Court Statistics, 2011, op. cit.,* 12.

31. Sara Goodkind, et al., "Are Girls Really Becoming More Delinquent? Testing the Gender Convergence Hypothesis by Race and Ethnicity, 1976–2005," *Children and Youth Services Review* (August 2009), 885–889.

32. Kimberly Kempf-Leonard and Lisa Sample, "Disparity Based on Sex: Is Gender-Specific

Treatment Warranted?" *Justice Quarterly* 17 (2000), 89–128.

33. *Juvenile Court Statistics, 2011, op. cit.,* 12.

34. *Crime in the United States, 2013, op. cit.,* Table 33.

35. Margaret A. Zahn et al., "The Girls Study Group—Charting the Way to Delinquency Prevention for Girls," *Girls Study Group: Understanding and Responding to Girls' Delinquency* (Washington, D.C.: Office of Juvenile Justice and Delinquency Prevention, October 2008), 3.

36. *Juvenile Court Statistics, 2011, op. cit.,* 70.

37. Melissa Sickmund and Howard N. Snyder, *Juvenile Offenders and Victims: 1999 National Report* (Washington, D.C.: Office of Juvenile Justice and Delinquency Prevention, 1999), 58.

38. Meda Chesney-Lind, *The Female Offender: Girls, Women, and Crime* (Thousand Oaks, Calif.: Sage Publications, 1997).

39. Denise C. Gottfredson and David A. Soulé, "The Timing of Property Crime, Violent Crime, and Substance Abuse among Juveniles," *Journal of Research in Crime and Delinquency* (February 2005), 110–120.

40. National Center for Education Statistics and Bureau of Justice Statistics, *Indicators of School Crime and Safety: 2013* (Washington, D.C.: U.S. Department of Justice, June 2014), 6.

41. *Ibid.,* 10–15.

42. *Ibid.,* 86.

43. Jacob Kang-Brown, et al., *A Generation Later: What We've Learned about Zero-Tolerance in Schools* (New York: Vera Institute of Justice, December 2013), 2.

44. *Indicators of School Crime and Safety: 2013, op. cit.,* Table 22.2, page 159.

45. "The Perils of Peanut Tossing," *The Economist* (December 21, 2013), 35.

46. Kathryn C. Monahan, et al., "From the School Yard to the Squad Car: School Discipline, Truancy, and Arrest," *Journal of Youth and Adolescence* (July 2014), 1110–1122.

47. Lana Shapiro and Andrew Adesman, "Exponential, Not Additive, Increase in Risk of Weapons Carrying by Adolescents Who Themselves Are Frequent and Recurrent Victims of Bullying," *Developmental & Behavioral Pediatrics* (May 2014), at **www.abstracts 2view.com/pas/view.php?nu=PAS14L1_2725.3 &terms=.**

48. Quoted in "Online Bullying: Charging Kids with Felonies," *The Week* (November 1, 2013), 14.

49. *Indicators of School Crime and Safety: 2013, op. cit.,* 44.

50. Jessica Bennett, "From Lockers to Lockup," *Newsweek* (October 11, 2010), 39.

51. Adam J. Speraw, "No Bullying Allowed: A Call for a National Anti-Bullying Statute to Promote a Safer Learning Environment in American Public Schools," *Valparaiso University Law Review* (Summer 2010), 1151–1198.

52. Marvin E. Wolfgang, *From Boy to Man, from Delinquency to Crime* (Chicago: University of Chicago Press, 1987).

53. Quoted in John H. Laub and Robert J. Sampson, "Understanding Desistance from Crime," in *Crime and Justice: A Review of Research* (Chicago: University of Chicago Press, 2001), 6.

54. Travis Hirschi and Michael Gottfredson, "Age and the Explanation of Crime," *American Journal of Sociology* 89 (1982), 552–584.

55. Robert J. Sampson and John H. Laub, "A Life-Course View on the Development of Crime,"

Annals of the American Academy of Political and Social Science (November 2005), 12.

56. David P. Farrington, "Offending from 10 to 25 Years of Age," in *Prospective Studies of Crime and Delinquency,* ed. Katherine Teilmann Van Dusen and Sarnoff A. Mednick (Boston: Kluwer-Nijhoff Publishers, 1983), 17.

57. Office of Juvenile Justice and Delinquency Prevention, *Juveniles in Court* (Washington, D.C.: U.S. Department of Justice, June 2003), 29.

58. Lloyd D. Johnston, et al., *Monitoring the Future: National Survey Results on Drug Use, 1975–2014—2014 Overview; Key Findings on Adolescent Drug Use* (Ann Arbor, Mich.: Institute for Social Research, February 2015), 38.

59. *Ibid.,* 11, 13.

60. Carl McCurley and Howard Snyder, *Co-occurrence of Substance Abuse Behaviors in Youth* (Washington, D.C.: Office of Juvenile Justice and Delinquency Prevention, 2008).

61. Gary McClelland, Linda Teplin, and Karen Abram, "Detection and Prevalence of Substance Abuse among Juvenile Detainees," *Juvenile Justice Bulletin* (Washington, D.C.: Office of Juvenile Justice and Delinquency Prevention, June 2004), 10.

62. Arrestee Drug Abuse Monitoring Program, *Preliminary Data on Drug Use and Related Matters among Adult Arrestees and Juvenile Detainees* (Washington, D.C.: National Institute of Justice, 2003).

63. National Mental Health Association, "Mental Health and Adolescent Girls in the Justice System," at **www.nmha.org/children/justjuv/girlsjj.cfm.**

64. Larry J. Siegel and Brandon C. Welsh, *Juvenile Delinquency: The Core,* 4th ed. (Belmont, Calif.: Wadsworth Cengage Learning, 2011), 268.

65. Edward P. Mulvey, *Highlights from Pathways to Desistance: A Longitudinal Study of Serious Adolescent Offenders* (Washington, D.C.: Office of Juvenile Justice and Delinquency Prevention, March 2011), 1–3.

66. Sherry Hamby et al., *Juvenile Justice Bulletin: Children's Exposure to Intimate Partner Violence and Other Family Violence* (Washington, D.C.: Office of Juvenile Justice and Delinquency Prevention, October 2011), 1.

67. Kimberly A. Tyler and Katherine A. Johnson, "A Longitudinal Study of the Effects of Early Abuse on Later Victimization among High-Risk Adolescents," *Violence and Victims* (June 2006), 287–291.

68. Grover Trask, "Defusing the Teenage Time Bombs," *Prosecutor* (March/April 1997), 29.

69. Ashley Nellis, *The Lives of Juvenile Lifers: Findings from a National Survey* (Washington, D.C.: The Sentencing Project, March 2012), 2.

70. Cathy Spatz Widom, *The Cycle of Violence* (Washington, D.C.: National Institute of Justice, October 1992).

71. Janet Currie and Erdal Tekin, *Does Child Abuse Cause Crime?* (Atlanta: Andrew Young School of Policy Studies, April 2006), 27–28.

72. Arlen Egley, Jr., James C. Howell, and Meena Harris, "Highlights of the 2012 National Youth Gang Survey," *Office of Juvenile Justice and Delinquency Prevention Fact Sheet* (December 2014), 1.

73. Chris Melde and Finn-Aage Esbensen, "Gangs and Violence: Disentangling the Impact of Gang Membership on the Level and Nature of Offending," *Journal of Quantitative Criminology* (June 2013), 143–166.

74. *2013 National Gang Report* (Washington, D.C.: National Gang Intelligence Center, 2014), 3–5.

75. Tony Dokoupil, "'Small World of Murder': As Homicides Drop, Chicago Police Focus on Social Network of Gangs," *NBC News* (December 17, 2013), at **www.nbcnews.com/news/us-news /chicago-police-focus-small-world-murder -n281;** and Vivian Yeem, "An 8th Grader, a Gun and a Bus Rider in the Way," *New York Times* (March 14, 2014), A1.

76. Karl G. Hill, Christina Lui, and J. David Hawkins, *Early Precursors of Gang Membership: A Study of Seattle Youth* (Washington, D.C.: Office of Juvenile Justice and Delinquency Prevention, December 2001).

77. "National Youth Gang Survey Analysis," National Gang Center, at **www.nationalgang center.gov/survey-analysis/demographics.**

78. Los Angeles Police Department, "Why Young People Join Gangs" (2014), at **www.lapdonline .org/top_ten_most_wanted_gang_members /content_basic_view/23473.**

79. Michelle Arciaga Young and Victor Gonzalez, "Getting Out of Gangs, Staying Out of Gangs: Gang Intervention and Desistance Strategies," *National Gang Center Bulletin* (January 2013).

80. *Crime in the United States 2013, op. cit.,* Table 32.

81. *Juvenile Court Statistics, 2011, op. cit.,* 31.

82. Sarah Hockenberry and Charles Puzzanchera, *Delinquency Cases in Juvenile Court, 2011* (Washington, D.C.: Office of Juvenile Justice and Delinquency Prevention, December 2014), 3.

83. 42 U.S.C. Sections 5601–5778 (1974).

84. Office of Juvenile Justice and Delinquency Prevention, *Delinquency Cases Waived to Criminal Court, 2011* (Washington, D.C.: U.S. Department of Justice, December 2014), 1.

85. *Ibid.,* 2.

86. Rhode Island General Laws Section 14-1-7.1 (1994 and Supp. 1996).

87. 467 U.S. 253 (1984).

88. *Juvenile Court Statistics, 2011, op. cit.,* 32.

89. *Delinquency Cases in Juvenile Court, 2011, op. cit,* 3.

90. *Ibid.*

91. Sarah Hockenberry, *Juveniles in Residential Placement, 2011* (Washington, D.C.: Office of Juvenile Justice and Delinquency Prevention, August 2014), 3.

92. Melissa Sickmund and Charles Puzzanchera, eds., *Juvenile Offenders and Victims: 2014 National Report* (Washington, D.C.: National Center for Juvenile Justice, December 2014), 194.

93. Howard N. Snyder and Melissa Sickmund, *Juvenile Offenders and Victims: 2006 National Report* (Washington, D.C.: National Center for Juvenile Justice, March 2006), 235.

94. *Youth Reentry Improvement Report* (Springfield: Illinois Juvenile Justice Commission, November 2011), 9.

14

1. Michael S. Schmidt, "Syria Suicide Bombing Puts U.S. Face on *Jihad* Video," *New York Times* (June 15, 2014), A1.

2. Quoted in Anita Kumar and Michael Doyle, "Federal Watching Is Rampant These Days," *Arizona Daily Star* (June 8, 2013), A1.

3. 50 U.S.C. Sections 1801–1811.

4. 50 U.S.C. Sections 1801(a)(1)–(3).

5. 50 U.S.C. Section 1804(a)(6).

6. 18 U.S.C. Section 2339B(a)(1) (1996).

7. 18 U.S.C. Section 2339A(b) (Supp. I 2001).

8. 18 U.S.C. Section 2339B(a)(1) (2006).

9. William K. Rashbaum, "Law Put to Unusual Use in Hezbollah TV Case, Some Say," *New York Times* (August 26, 2006), B2.

10. Uniting and Strengthening America by Providing Appropriate Tools Required to Intercept and Obstruct Terrorism (USA PATRIOT) Act of 2001, Pub. L. No. 107-56, 115 Stat. 272 (2001).

11. 50 U.S.C. Section 1861(b)(2)(A) (2006).

12. 18 U.S.C. Section 2709 (2012).

13. John S. Dempsey and Linda S. Forst, *An Introduction to Policing,* 7th ed. (Clifton Park, N.Y.: Delmar Cengage Learning, 2014), 537.

14. FISA Amendment Act of 2008, Pub. L. No. 110-261, 122 Stat. 2436 (2008).

15. John Yoo, "The Legality of the National Security Agency's Bulk Data Surveillance Programs," *Harvard Journal of Law and Public Policy* (Summer 2014), at **papers.ssrn.com/sol3/papers.cfm ?abstract_id=2369192.**

16. Jay Bookman, "Which Do You Value? Privacy, or the Illusion of Security?" *AJC* (December 17, 2013), at **www.ajc.com/weblogs/jay-bookman /2013/dec/17/which-do-you-value-privacy-or -illusion-security/#_federated=1.**

17. Timothy B. Lee, "Here's Everything We Know about PRISM to Date," *Washington Post WonkBlog* (June 12, 2013), at **www.washingtonpost.com /blogs/wonkblog/wp/2013/06/12/heres -everything-we-know-about-prism-to-date/.**

18. Steven G. Bradbury, "Understanding the NSA Programs: Bulk Acquisition of Telephone Metadata under Section 215 and Foreign-Targeted Collection under Section 702," *Lawfare Research Paper Series* (September 1, 2013), 2.

19. Charlie Savage and Matt Apuzzo, "U.S. Spied on 5 American Muslims, a Report Says," *New York Times* (July 10, 2014), A17.

20. *ACLU v. Clapper,* 959 F.Supp.2d 724, 726 (S.D.N.Y. 2013).

21. Jennifer Steinhauer and Jonathan Weisman, "U.S. Surveillance in Place Since 9/11 Is Sharply Limited," *New York Times* (June 2, 2015), A1.

22. "Despite Outcry, Government Still Collects Your Phone Data," *USA Today* (October 22, 2014), 6A.

23. *Katz v. United States,* 389 U.S. 347, 351 (1967); and *California v. Greenwood,* 486 U.S. 35 (1988).

24. *United States v. Moalin et al.,* at **www .documentcloud.org/documents/902291 -moalin-131114-deny-new-trial.html.**

25. 442 U.S. 735 (1979).

26. *Klayman v. Obama,* 957 F.Supp.2d 825 (D.D.C. December 16, 2013).

27. Quoted in "A Powerful Rebuke of Mass Surveillance," *New York Times* (December 17, 2013).

28. *United States v. Jones,* 565 U.S. ____ (2012).

29. Quoted in "A Powerful Rebuke of Mass Surveillance," *op. cit.*

30. 50 U.S.C. Section 1881a (2011).

31. Ellen Nakashima, "Feds Report 90,000 Foreign Surveillance Targets," *Dallas Morning News* (June 28, 2014), 11A.

32. David E. Sanger and Matt Apuzzo, "Officials Defend N.S.A. after New Privacy Details Are Reported," *New York Times* (July 7, 2014), A9.

33. *Ibid.*

34. Quoted in "Colorado Teen Shannon Conley's Support of ISIS Raises Alarm about American *Jihadists,*" *Associated Press* (September 10, 2014).

35. Quoted in Stephen Collinson, "Paris Attack: The New Terror," *CNN.com* (January 8, 2015), at **www.cnn.com/2015/01/08/politics/paris-new-terror/**.

36. 538 U.S. 343 (2003).

37. *Ibid.*, at 358.

38. 18 U.S.C. Section 2339A(b)(1).

39. John Leyden, "Pro-ISIS Script Kiddies Deface Dublin Rape Crisis Centre Site," *The Register* (March 10, 2015), at **www.theregister.co.uk/2015/03/10/is_script_kiddies_defacement/**.

40. Derek Harp, quoted in Erin Kelly, "As Cyberthreats Rise, Push for Intelligence Heightened," *USA Today* (December 24, 2014), 3A.

41. Quoted in "Special Report Cyber-Security: Hackers Inc.," *The Economist* (July 12, 2014), 5.

42. William R. Graham, Jr., "Uncovering and Eliminating Child Pornography Rings on the Internet," *Law Review of Michigan State University Detroit College of Law* (Summer 2000), 466.

43. Richard Wortley and Stephen Smallbone, "The Problem of Internet Child Pornography," Center for Problem Oriented Policing (2006), at **www.popcenter.org/problems/child_pornography**.

44. Internet Crime Complaint Center, *IC3 2013 Internet Crime Report* (Glen Allen, Va.: National White Collar Crime Center, 2014), 3.

45. *2013 Norton Report* (Mountain View, Calif.: Symantec, 2014), 8, 11.

46. Internet Crime Complaint Center, *op. cit.*, 9.

47. Quoted in Michael Kranish, "IRS Is Overwhelmed by Identity Theft Fraud," *Boston Globe* (February 16, 2014), A1.

48. Bureau of Justice Statistics, *Identity Theft Reported by Households, 2005–2010* (Washington, D.C.: U.S. Department of Justice, November 2011), 1.

49. *Ibid.*, Table 4, page 5.

50. Nadezhda Demidova, "Social Network Frauds," *SecureList.com* (June 11, 2014), at **securelist.com/analysis/publications/63855/social-network-frauds/**.

51. *2013 Norton Report, op. cit.*, 7.

52. Openet, press release, "Openet-Sponsored Study Reveals 41 Percent of Teenagers Experience Cyber-bullying" (January 18, 2012), at **www.openet.com/company/news-events/pressreleases?id=482**.

53. Bureau of Justice Statistics, *Stalking Victimization in the United States* (Washington, D.C.: U.S. Department of Justice, January 2009), 1.

54. Elizabeth E. Harris, et al., "A Sneaky Path into Target Customers' Wallets," *New York Times* (January 18, 2014), A1.

55. *The Compliance Gap: BSA Global Software Survey* (Washington, D.C.: Business Software Alliance, June 2014), 2.

56. Quoted in Marc Santora, "In Hours, Thieves Took $45 Million in A.T.M. Scheme," *New York Times* (May 10, 2013), A1.

57. *US Cybercrime: Rising Risks, Reduced Readiness* (Los Angeles: PwC, June 2014), 7.

58. Quoted in John Seabrook, "Network Insecurity," *The New Yorker* (May 20, 2013), 64.

59. Elizabeth Dwoskin, "Sleuthing Search Engine: Even Better than Google?" *Wall Street Journal* (February 11, 2015), at **www.wsj.com/articles/sleuthing-search-engine-even-better-than-google-1423703464**.

60. Quoted in "Cybersleuths Find Growing Role in Fighting Crime," *HPC Wire*, at **www.hpcwire.com/hpc-bin/artread.pl?direction=Current&articlenumber=19864**.

61. "Downloading Guns: Firearms Go Digital," *The Week* (May 24, 2013), 4.

62. James Lindgren, "Fall from Grace: Arming America and the Bellesiles Scandal," *Yale Law Journal* 111 (2002), 2203.

63. Bureau of Alcohol, Tobacco, Firearms and Explosives, *Firearms Commerce in the United States 2011* (Washington, D.C.: U.S. Department of Justice, August 2011), 15.

64. Mathias H. Heck, Jr., "Section Offers Forum for Discussion of Gun Policy," *Criminal Justice* (Winter 2014), 1.

65. Federal Bureau of Investigation, *Crime in the United States 2012* (Washington, D.C.: U.S. Department of Justice, 2013), at **www.fbi.gov/about-us/cjis/ucr/crime-in-the-u.s./2012/crime-in-the-u.s.-2012/cius_home**, Expanded Homicide Data Table 7 and Table 15.

66. Lydia Saad, "U.S. Remains Divided over Passing Stricter Gun Laws," *Gallup Politics* (October 25, 2013), at **www.gallup.com/poll/165563/remains-divided-passing-stricter-gun-laws.aspx**.

67. *District of Columbia v. Heller*, 554 U.S. 570 (2008); and *McDonald v. Chicago,* 561 U.S. 3025 (2010).

68. 18 U.S.C. 922(t).

69. Ronald J. Frandsen et al., *Background Checks for Firearm Transfers, 2010—Statistical Tables* (Washington, D.C.: U.S. Department of Justice, February 2013), 1.

70. 27 C.F.R. Section 478.11 (2010).

71. "Governor Cuomo Signs NY Safe Act in Rochester" (January 16, 2013), at **www.governor.ny.gov/press/12162013cuomo-signs-safe-act-roch**.

72. Herbert Buchsbau, "Amid Wave of Pro-Gun Legislation, Georgia Proposes Sweeping Law," *New York Times* (March 25, 2014), A11.

73. Federal Bureau of Investigation, "White-Collar Crime," at **www.fbi.gov/about-us/investigate/white_collar/whitecollarcrime**.

74. Michael L. Benson and Sally S. Simpson, *White-Collar Crime: An Opportunity Perspective* (New York: Routledge, 2009), 79–80.

75. *Ibid.*, 81–87.

76. David A. Fahrenthold, "A Medicare Scam That Just Kept Rolling," *Washington Post* (August 16, 2014), at **www.washingtonpost.com/sf/national/2014/08/16/a-medicare-scam-that-just-kept-rolling/**.

77. "That's Where the Money Is," *The Economist* (May 31, 2014), 13.

78. David O. Friedrichs, *Trusted Criminals: White Collar Crime in Contemporary Society,* 4th ed. (Belmont, Calif.: Wadsworth Cengage Learning, 2010), 278–283.

79. 15 U.S.C. Sections 78a *et seq.*

80. White-Collar Crime Penalty Enhancement Act of 2002, 18 U.S.C. Sections 1341, 1343, 1349–1350.

DISCRETION IN ACTION CASE STUDIES

2.1 In the autumn of 2014, California passed the nation's first affirmative consent law. Under this law, all state colleges and universities must require "affirmative, conscious and voluntary agreement to engage in sexual activity," which can be verbal or communicated through actions. This agreement must be indicated at each stage of sexual activity. So, for example, consent to kissing cannot be taken to indicate consent for intercourse. If a California post-secondary school fails to implement an affirmative consent policy, the school will lose state financial aid.

Even those who support California's new law realize that, "unless every dorm room comes equipped with a court reporter," there will continue to be miscommunication between students regarding sex. Nor, they agree, will it necessarily stop sexual predators from targeting victims. Rather, the hope is that the new policy changes a student culture in which lack of protest or resistance is taken as confirmation of assent to sex.

3.1 After University of Virginia senior George Huguely was arrested for the death of his twenty-two-year-old ex-girlfriend Yeardley Love in 2010, prosecutors charged him with first degree murder, punishable by life in prison. The prosecutors asserted that Huguely was enraged because Love was dating someone else, and that he intended to kill her in a premeditated act. Huguely's lawyers insisted that, at worst, their client was guilty of involuntary manslaughter. At the time of the crime, they pointed out, he was drunk and had no intent to harm Love, much less kill her. Furthermore, they argued, Love died from suffocation well after Huguely left her apartment.

In 2012, a Charlottesville, Virginia, jury found Huguely guilty of second degree murder, reasoning that although he did not intend to kill Love, he did act with malice aforethought and his violent behavior was the cause of her death. A judge later sentenced Huguely to twenty-three years in prison.

5.1 Before Donald Rickar could flee from the West Memphis, Arkansas, parking lot, law enforcement officers fired fifteen shots at his car, killing him. Rickar's family sued, claiming that the officers had used excessive force in taking Rickar's life. The case reached the United States Supreme Court, which held unanimously in 2014 that the officers had acted reasonably under the circumstances.

The Court's decision echoed a 2007 case in which it ruled for a Georgia officer who had forced a suspect's vehicle off the road to end a high-speed pursuit, leaving the suspect partially paralyzed. In general, then, police officers are justified in using deadly force to terminate high-speed chases that threaten the lives of those involved in the chase, even if such force puts the fleeing suspect at risk of significant injury or death.

6.1 In 1996, two Washington, D.C., police officers pulled over Michael J. Wren—a young African American male who was driving a truck with temporary plates in a high-crime neighborhood—for failing to signal while making a right turn. They found two large bags of crack cocaine in Wren's possession, and arrested him. The United States Supreme Court upheld Wren's conviction, ruling that as long as police officers have probable cause to believe that a traffic violation has occurred, the "real" reason for making the stop is irrelevant.

As Justice Antonin Scalia put it, "Subjective intentions play no role in ordinary, probable-cause, Fourth Amendment analysis." In practical terms, this ruling gives law enforcement agents the ability to confirm "hunches" about serious illegal behavior as long as the target of these hunches commits even the most minor traffic violation. Such violations could include failing to properly signal during a turn, or making a rolling stop at a stop sign, or driving five miles over the posted speed limit.

7.1 In 2012, the Oregon Supreme Court ordered a new trial for Samuel Lawson and, in the process, established new procedures for determining the admissibility of eyewitness identification in state courts. Today, Oregon courts must consider all the factors that could contaminate eyewitness identifications, including the effects of suggestive comments made by law enforcement agents.

In this case, the Oregon Supreme Court noted that Sheryl had sustained a critical gunshot wound at the time of her husband's murder, only saw the assailant briefly in the dark, and did not identify Lawson until two years after the events at the campsite. At the least, the defendant's attorneys should have been able to address these factors during the trial, thus allowing jurors to decide for themselves whether Sheryl's eyewitness testimony was reliable.

8.1 Cody Cofer, Michelle Williams's defense attorney, focused his arguments on the fact that the evidence against his client was circumstantial. That is, there was no way to definitively prove how Greg Williams had died. Cofer also pointed out that Michelle had no financial motive to kill her husband, and that her explanation regarding a "cover-up" to protect her daughter from trauma was a reasonable one. "The worst thing our system can do is convict an innocent person," Cofer told the jurors. "That's a decision you'll have to live with for the rest of your lives."

Despite these efforts, the jury did indeed convict Michelle of murder and, in September 2014, a judge sentenced her to sixty years in prison. The evidence that nobody but Michelle could have killed Greg, though circumstantial, apparently was strong enough to overcome any reasonable doubt in the minds of the jurors.

9.1 The same Arizona jury that found Jodi Arias guilty of murdering Travis Alexander with such "exceptional cruelty" that she was eligible for the death penalty was unable to decide whether she should be executed. That is, the twelve jurors were unable to come to a unanimous decision on either execution or a life-in-prison sentence. Under state law, prosecutors were able to seat a second jury to make the sentencing decision, and, therefore, a second sentencing phase for Arias was scheduled to take place sixteen months after the first.

Following this second sentencing phase, which lasted nearly five months, the second jury deliberated for twenty-six hours over a period of six days before—again—deadlocking.

By state law, this meant that Arias' fate passed to the hands of Maricopa County Superior Court Judge Sherry Stephens. In April 2015, Judge Stephens sentenced the defendant to spend life in prison. Explaining his decision, the judge said that Arias' crime was "especially cruel" and that it "involved substantial planning and preparation. . . . The defendant destroyed evidence . . . and went to great lengths to conceal her involvement."

10.1 Alain LeConte's probation officer did not take any steps to revoke his probation. The issue became moot, however, when LeConte was arrested for killing a gas station attendant during an armed robbery in Norwalk, Connecticut. The crime took place between his first and second failed drug tests. LeConte's probation officer came under a great deal of criticism for failing to revoke his probation, but she received support from her supervisor. "We can only do so much," he said. "[LeConte's] probation officer went out of her way to assist this young man, but unfortunately it wasn't successful."

The supervisor also pointed out that LeConte had no known history of violent behavior and had been a generally cooperative probationer when it came to getting treatment. This case underscores the difficult aspects of a probation officer's job. A misjudgment, even if it was based on a reasonable evaluation of the situation, can end in tragedy.

12.1 Initially, state prison officials decided to fire a correctional officer named Welch following an incident at the Maine Correctional Center in Windham similar to the one described in the feature. Because of Welch's otherwise unblemished career, however, his punishment was eventually reduced to a thirty-day suspension without pay.

Following the incident, the Maine Department of Corrections instituted new guidelines regarding "cutters" (inmates who injure themselves) and "spitters" that promoted the use of pepper spray rather than other types of force by correctional officers. It seems that Welch's mistake was that he grew angry at the inmate's insults and let his anger influence the level of his response. "It's all right for [inmates] to have the last word, we have the last action," said a state prison official.

13.1 In 2008, a Denver, Colorado, prosecutor chose to charge seventeen-year-old James Stewart as an adult for vehicular homicide. After Stewart was moved to an adult jail, he tightened several bed sheets around his neck and hung himself. Stewart's suicide led to a change in state law that requires judges to review prosecutorial waivers in certain situations and makes it much less likely that a juvenile offender awaiting trial will be held in an adult jail.

In the first year after this law was passed, the number of juvenile offenders waived to state adult court dropped by nearly 85 percent. Nonetheless, Colorado prosecutors dislike the new law. One claims that he and his colleagues are in a better position than judges to decide whether a juvenile should be tried in adult court, due to a prosecutor's "experience" and "years and years of weighing one case against similarly situated cases."

14.1 In 2004, Steven Parr was convicted of threatening to blow up the Reuss Federal Plaza in Milwaukee and sentenced to ten years in prison. Before finding that Parr's bragging was a "true threat" and therefore not protected by the First Amendment, the jury heard a great deal of evidence in addition to the recording made by the prison whistleblower. A number of witnesses—including three ex-girlfriends and two former neighbors—testified that not only was Parr skilled in explosives, but also that he often spoke of his hatred for the federal government and his admiration for domestic terrorists such as Tim McVeigh, whose 1995 bombing of the Alfred P. Murrah Federal Building in Oklahoma City is mentioned in the text.

Prosecutors also showed the jury a number of books and notebooks in Parr's possession that indicated his obsession with bomb building. Because of this evidence, in 2008 an appeals court ruled that a reasonable jury could have found that Parr's words constituted a "true threat" and upheld his conviction.

ANSWERS TO CHAPTER QUIZ QUESTIONS

1

1. Violent
2. Property
3. Federalism
4. State
5. Discretion
6. Ethics
7. Crime control
8. Due process
9. Terrorism
10. Recidivism

2

1. Criminologists
2. Theory
3. Rational choice
4. Psychology
5. Disorganization
6. Learning
7. Abuse
8. Uniform Crime Report
9. Victim
10. Self-reported

3

1. Constitution
2. Case
3. Civil
4. Felony
5. Misdemeanor
6. Intent
7. Insanity
8. Self-defense
9. Entrapment
10. Due process

4

1. Enforce
2. Services
3. Intelligence
4. Probationary
5. Double
6. Sheriffs'
7. Highway
8. FBI (Federal Bureau of Investigation)
9. ATF (Bureau of Alcohol, Tobacco, Firearms and Explosives)
10. Deter

5

1. Policy
2. Deter/prevent
3. Forensics
4. DNA
5. Incident
6. Random
7. Community
8. Stress
9. Reasonable
10. Corruption

6

1. Probable cause
2. Exclusionary
3. Privacy
4. Consent
5. Reasonable
6. Frisk
7. Custody
8. Warrant
9. Before
10. Waive

7

1. Defendants
2. Crime control
3. Jurisdiction
4. Federal
5. *Certiorari*
6. Concurring
7. Governor
8. Prosecutors
9. Counsel
10. Public

8

1. Bail
2. Grand jury
3. Plea bargain
4. Bench
5. Reasonable doubt
6. *Voir dire*
7. Prejudice
8. Direct
9. Cross
10. Appeal

9

1. Deterrence
2. Rehabilitation
3. Indeterminate
4. Good time
5. Mitigating
6. Disparity
7. Discrimination
8. Guidelines
9. Lethal injection
10. Juveniles

10

1. Diverting
2. Probation
3. Recidivism
4. Parole
5. Technical
6. Parole board
7. Mandatory
8. Forfeiture
9. Shock
10. Electronic monitoring

11

1. Medical
2. Warden
3. Classification
4. Maximum
5. Supermax
6. Drug
7. Decarceration
8. Overcrowding
9. Pretrial detainees
10. Sheriff

12

1. Total institution
2. Health-care
3. Relative deprivation
4. Legitimate
5. Malicious
6. Deliberate
7. Correctional officers
8. Reentry
9. Halfway
10. Notification

13

1. Government/state
2. Status offense
3. Death penalty
4. Aging out
5. Gangs
6. Arrest
7. Refer
8. Waiver
9. Adjudicatory
10. Disposition

14

1. Material support
2. Reasonable expectation
3. Speech
4. Identity
5. Botnets
6. Intellectual property
7. Background check
8. Mental illness
9. Trust
10. Compliance

INDEX

STEPS OF THE CRIMINAL JUSTICE SYSTEM

Step 1:
Entry into the System

Step 2: Prosecution and Pretrial Services

Step 3: Adjudication

Step 4:
Sentencing and Sanctions

Step 5: Corrections

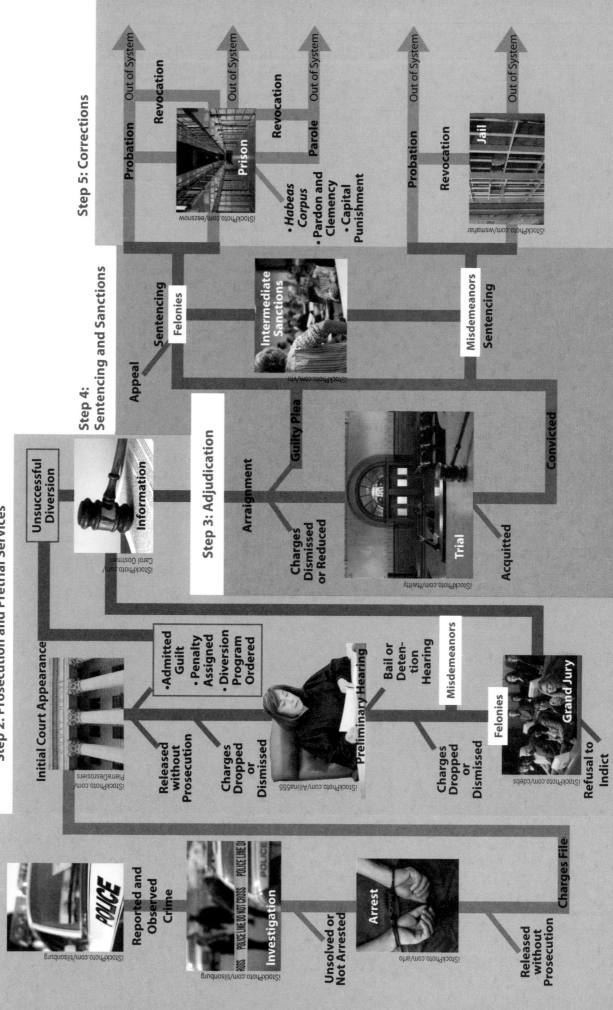

STEPS OF THE CRIMINAL JUSTICE SYSTEM

Step 1: Entry into the System

- Once a law enforcement agency has established that a crime has been committed, a suspect must be identified and apprehended for the case to proceed through the system.

- Sometimes a suspect is apprehended at the scene of the crime; at other times, however, identification of a suspect requires an extensive investigation.

- Often, no one is identified or apprehended. In some instances, a suspect is arrested, and later the police determine that no crime was committed and the suspect is released.

Step 2: Prosecution and Pretrial Services

- After an arrest, law enforcement agencies present information about the case and about the accused to the prosecutor, who will decide if formal charges will be filed with the court.

- A suspect charged with a crime must be taken before a judge without unnecessary delay.

- At the initial appearance, the judge informs the accused of the charges and decides whether there is probable cause to detain the accused person.

- If the offense is not serious, the determination of guilt and an assessment of a penalty may also occur at this stage.

- Often, the defense counsel is assigned at the initial appearance. All suspects charged with serious crimes have a right to be represented by an attorney. If the suspect cannot afford a defense attorney, the court will provide one for him or her at the public's expense.

- A pretrial release decision may also be made at the initial appearance. The court may decide that the suspect poses a threat to society and place him or her in jail until the trial.

- The court may decide to release the suspect with the understanding that he or she will return for the trial, or release the suspect on bail (meaning he or she must provide the court with monetary payment [bail], which will be returned when the suspect appears for the trial).

- In many jurisdictions, the initial appearance may be followed by a preliminary hearing. The main function of this hearing is to discover if there is probable cause to believe that the accused committed a known crime within the jurisdiction of the court. If the judge does find probable cause or the accused waives his or her right to the preliminary hearing, the case may be sent to a grand jury.

- A grand jury hears evidence against the accused presented by the prosecutor and decides if there is sufficient evidence to cause the accused to be brought to trial. If the grand jury finds sufficient evidence, it submits to the court an indictment, a written statement of the essential facts of the offense charged against the accused.

- Misdemeanor cases and some felony cases proceed by the issuance of an information, a formal, written accusation submitted to the court by a prosecutor.

- In some jurisdictions, defendants—often those without prior criminal records—may be eligible for diversion programs. In these programs, the suspect does not go to trial and instead must complete a rehabilitation program, such as drug treatment. If he or she is successful, the charges may be dropped, and his or her criminal record may remain clear.

Step 3: Adjudication

- Once an indictment or information has been filed with the trial court, the accused is scheduled for an arraignment.

- At the arraignment, the accused is informed of the charges, advised of his or her rights, and asked to enter a plea to the charges.

- Sometimes a plea of guilty is the result of negotiations between the prosecutor and the defendant. If the defendant pleads guilty and this plea is accepted by the judge, no trial is held and the defendant is sentenced.

- If the accused pleads not guilty, a date is set for the trial. A person accused of a serious crime is guaranteed a trial by jury.

- During the trial, the prosecution and defense present evidence, and the judge decides issues of law. The jury then decides whether the defendant will be acquitted (found not guilty) or convicted (found guilty of the initial charges or of other offenses).

- If the defendant is found guilty, he or she may request that the trial be reviewed by a higher court to assure that the rules of trial procedure were followed.

Step 4: Sentencing and Sanctions

- After a conviction, a sentence is imposed. In most cases, the judge decides the sentence, though sometimes the jury makes this decision.

- Some of the sentencing choices available to judges and juries include: the death penalty, incarceration in prison or jail, probation (allowing the convicted person to remain in the community as long as he or she follows certain rules), and fines. In many jurisdictions, persons convicted of certain types of offenses must serve a prison term.

Step 5: Corrections

- Offenders sentenced to incarceration usually serve time in a local jail or a prison. Offenders sentenced to less than one year usually go to jail, while those sentenced to more than one year go to prison.

- A prisoner may become eligible for parole after serving part of his or her sentence. Parole is the release of a prisoner before the full sentence has been served. If released under parole, the convict will be supervised in the community for the balance of his or her sentence.

CRIMINAL JUSTICE TIMELINE

	Supreme Court Criminal Justice Decisions	Legal Events
1900s	1903 Lottery ticket ban upheld	
1910s	1914 *Weeks v. U.S.:* Exclusionary rule adopted for federal courts 1919 *Schenck v. U.S.:* Socialist found guilty of obstructing war effort	1914 Harrison Narcotics Act passed 1919 Prohibition begins
1920s	1923 *Frye v. U.S.:* Scientific evidence admissible if it has gained general acceptance 1927 *Tumey v. Ohio:* Paying a judge only if defendant is found guilty is unconstitutional 1928 *Olmstead v. U.S.:* Wiretaps legal if no trespass	1921 William Taft becomes Chief Justice 1925 Federal Probation Act
1930s	1932 *Powell v. Alabama:* Limited right to counsel in capital cases established 1939 *U.S. v. Miller:* Right to bear arms limited to militia	1930 Charles Evans Hughes becomes Chief Justice 1931 National Commission on Law Observance and Enforcement—Wickersham Commission 1933 Prohibition ends 1935 199 executions in U.S.; highest rate in 20th century 1937 FDR's court packing plan defeated 1939 Administrative Office of U.S. Courts created
1940s		1941 Harlan Stone becomes Chief Justice 1946 Fred Vinson becomes Chief Justice
1950s	1956 *Griffin v. Illinois:* Indigents entitled to court-appointed attorney for first appeal	1953 Earl Warren becomes Chief Justice

1960s	1961 *Mapp v. Ohio:* Exclusionary rule required in state courts
	1963 *Fay v. Noia:* Right to *habeas corpus* expanded
	        Brady v. Maryland: Prosecutors must turn over evidence favorable to defense
	        Gideon v. Wainwright: Indigents have right to counsel
	1966 *Sheppard v. Maxwell:* Conviction reversed based on prejudicial pretrial publicity
	        Miranda v. Arizona: Suspects must be advised of rights before interrogation
	1967 *In re Gault:* Requires counsel for juveniles
		1966 Bail Reform Act favors pretrial release
		1967 President's Commission on Law Enforcement and Administration of Justice
		1969 Warren Burger becomes Chief Justice

1970s	1972 *Furman v. Georgia:* Declares state death penalty laws unconstitutional
	        Barker v. Wingo: Adopts flexible approach to speedy trial
	1975 *Gerstein v. Pugh:* Arrestee entitled to a prompt hearing
	1976 *Gregg v. Georgia:* Upholds death penalty
	        North v. Russell: Upholds non-lawyer judges
	1979 *Burch v. Louisiana:* Six-member juries must be unanimous
		1970 Organized Crime Control Act
		1971 Prison riot in Attica, New York
		1972 Break-in at Watergate
		1973 National Advisory Commission on Criminal Justice Standards and Goals
		1973 Nixon declares war on drugs
		1977 Determinate sentencing enacted in 4 states

1980s	1986 *Batson v. Kentucky:* Jurors cannot be excluded because of race 1987 *U.S. v. Salerno:* Preventive detention upheld 1989 *Mistretta v. U.S.:* U.S. sentencing guidelines upheld	1982 Victim and Witness Protection Act 1984 Bail Reform Act: judge may consider if defendant is a danger to the community 1985 DNA first used in criminal case 1986 William Rehnquist becomes Chief Justice 1987 U.S. Sentencing Guidelines begin

1990s	1991 *Payne v. Tennessee:* Victim impact statements admissible during sentencing
	        Burns v. Reed: Prosecutors have qualified immunity in civil lawsuits
	        Chisom v. Roemer: Voting Rights Act applies to elected judges
	1995 *U.S. v. Lopez:* Federal law barring guns in school unconstitutional
		1993 Three-strikes laws gain currency
		1994 New Jersey passes Megan's Law
		1995 U.S. prison population tops one million
		1996 Antiterrorism and Effective Death Penalty Act limits habeas petitions in federal court

2000s	2004 *Hamdi v. Rumsfeld:* U.S. citizens seized overseas during antiterror military operations must be given access to U.S. courts 2005 *Roper v. Simmons:* Capital punishment for crimes committed when the offender was under eighteen years of age is unconstitutional 2013 *Maryland v. King:* As part of the normal booking process, law enforcement officers may take DNA samples of those suspects arrested for serious crimes	2002 The Patriot Act enacted into law; Department of Homeland Security established 2005 John Roberts, Jr., becomes Chief Justice 2012 California voters modify the state's "three-strikes" law to allow for a life sentence only when the new felony conviction is "serious or violent" 2013 The U.S. prison and jail population levels off at approximately 2.3 million

CRIMINAL JUSTICE TIMELINE CONTINUED

	Famous Trials		Leading Crimes
1900s		1901	President McKinley assassinated by anarchist
		1908	Butch Cassidy and the Sundance Kid killed in Bolivia
1910s		1915	Anti-Semitic lynching of Leo Frank in Atlanta
		1919	Black Sox scandal in baseball
1920s	1921 Sacco and Vanzetti sentenced to death for murder	1921	Charles Ponzi sentenced to prison for pyramid scheme
	1925 Scopes "Monkey Trial"	1924	Leopold and Loeb plead guilty to thrill murder
	1927 Teapot Dome trials become symbol of government corruption	1929	St. Valentine's Day massacre ordered by Al Capone in Chicago
1930s	1931 Chicago mobster Al Capone found guilty of income tax evasion	1934	Bonnie and Clyde killed
	1935 Bruno Hauptman convicted of kidnapping Charles Lindbergh's young son		"Baby Face" Nelson and "Pretty Boy" Floyd killed
	1939 Crime boss "Lucky" Luciano found guilty of compulsory prostitution		
1940s	1941 Murder, Inc. trials	1945	Bank robber Willie Sutton escapes from prison
	1948 Caryl Chessman sentenced to death for kidnapping and robbery	1947	Hollywood hopeful Black Dahlia's mutilated body found
	1949 Alger Hiss found guilty of perjury in the onset of the Cold War		
1950s	1951 Julius and Ethel Rosenberg sentenced to death for espionage	1950	Brinks armored car robbery in Boston
	1954 Dr. Samuel Sheppard convicted of murder	1957	George Metesky confesses to a string of New York City bombings
	1958 Daughter of movie actress Lana Turner found not guilty of killing mom's hoodlum lover	1959	Murder of Kansas farm couple becomes basis of *In Cold Blood*
1960s	1964 Teamster President Jimmy Hoffa found guilty	1962	French Connection drug bust
	1966 Dr. Sam Sheppard acquitted in second trial	1963	President Kennedy assassinated
	1968 Black Panther Huey Newton found guilty of voluntary manslaughter	1964	Boston Strangler arrested
	1969 Chicago 7 found guilty of incitement to riot and conspiracy	1966	Richard Speck kills eight Chicago nurses
		1968	Martin Luther King, Jr., and Robert Kennedy assassinated
		1969	Manson family commits Helter Skelter murders
1970s	1971 Lt. William Calley found guilty of murder in My Lai massacre	1971	Skyjacker D.B. Cooper disappears
	1976 Heiress Patty Hearst found guilty of bank robbery	1974	Heiress Patty Hearst kidnapped by terrorists
	1977 Maryland governor Marvin Mandel found guilty of mail fraud	1974– 1978	Ted Bundy confesses to killing thirty women between these years; he also confesses to rape, kidnapping, and necrophilia; he dies by electric chair in 1989
		1975	Jimmy Hoffa disappears
		1977	Serial murderer Son of Sam arrested in New York
		1978	Jonestown massacre
		1978– 1991	Jeffrey Dahmer's killing and cannibalism spree; he is imprisoned in 1992, and is murdered while incarcerated in 1994
1980s	1980 John Wayne Gacy convicted of killing 33 boys	1980	Headmistress Jean Harris kills Scarsdale Diet Doctor
	1982 Automaker John DeLorean acquitted of cocaine trafficking	1981	President Ronald Reagan survives assassination attempt by John Hinckley
	1984 Mayflower Madam pleads guilty to misdemeanor of promoting prostitution	1984	21 killed at San Diego McDonald's
	1987 Subway vigilante Bernhard Goetz acquitted of attempted murder	1987	Savings and loan mogul Charles Keating accused of millions in fraud
	1989 Televangelist Jim Bakker found guilty of fraud	1989	Junk bond king Michael Milken pays $600 million fine
1990s	1993 L.A. police officers found guilty in federal court of civil rights violations against Rodney King	1992	Boxer Mike Tyson charged with rape
	1995 O. J. Simpson found not guilty of murdering his ex-wife Nicole and her friend, Ronald Goldman	1994	Fire in Waco kills Branch Davidians
	1996 During second trial, Menendez brothers found guilty of killing wealthy parents	1995	Oklahoma City bombing
	1997 Timothy McVeigh sentenced to death for Oklahoma City bombing	1997	Nanny in Boston charged with child murder
2000s	2000 NYPD officers acquitted for killing Amadou Diallo	2001	Terrorists strike targets in New York City and the Washington, D.C.-area, including Flight 93, which crashes in a Pennsylvania field
	2003 Washington State's Gary Ridgway sentenced as worst serial killer in U.S. history	2007	Student Cho Seung Hui murders five faculty members and twenty-seven students on the campus of Virginia Tech in Blacksburg, Virginia
	2006 Zacarias Moussaoui convicted for conspiring to kill U.S. citizens as part of the September 11, 2001, terrorist attacks	2009	Bernard Madoff pleads guilty to running a $65 billion Ponzi scheme
	2013 George Zimmerman found not guilty of second degree murder by reason of self-defense for killing teenager Trayvon Martin during an altercation in Sanford, Florida	2012	Adam Lanza kills twenty children and six adult staff members during a shooting spree at Sandy Hook Elementary School in Newtown, Connecticut

SUMMARY

1-1

Define crime, and identify the different types of crime. Crime is any action punishable under criminal statutes and is considered an offense against society. Types of crime include (a) violent crime, (b) property crime, (c) public order crime, (d) white-collar crime, (e) organized crime, and (f) high-tech crime.

1-2

Outline the three levels of law enforcement. Because we have a federal system of government, law enforcement occurs at the (a) national, or federal, level and the (b) state level and within the states at (c) local levels. Because crime is mostly a local concern, most employees in the criminal justice system work for local governments. Agencies at the federal level include the FBI, the DEA, and the U.S. Secret Service, among others.

1-3

List the essential elements of the corrections system. Criminal offenders are placed on probation, incarcerated in a jail or prison, transferred to community-based corrections facilities, or released on parole.

1-4

Define ethics, and describe the role that it plays in discretionary decision making. Ethics consist of the moral principles that guide a person's perception of right and wrong. Most criminal justice professionals have a great deal of discretionary leeway in their day-to-day decision making, and their ethical beliefs can help ensure that they make such decisions in keeping with society's established values.

1-5

Contrast the crime control and due process models. The crime control model assumes that the criminal justice system is designed to protect the public from criminals. Thus, its most important function is to punish and repress criminal conduct. The due process model presumes that the accused are innocent and provides them with the most complete safeguards, usually within the court system.

KEY TERMS

1-1

Assault A threat or an attempt to do violence to another person that causes that person to fear immediate physical harm. **6**

Battery The act of physically contacting another person with the intent to do harm, even if the resulting injury is insubstantial. **6**

Burglary The act of breaking into or entering a structure (such as a home or office) without permission for the purpose of committing a felony. **6**

Conflict Model A criminal justice model in which the content of criminal law is determined by the groups that hold economic, political, and social power in a community. **5**

Consensus Model A criminal justice model in which the majority of citizens in a society share the same values and beliefs. Criminal acts are acts that conflict with these values and beliefs and that are deemed harmful to society. **4**

Crime An act that violates criminal law and is punishable by criminal sanctions. **3**

Deviance Behavior that is considered to go against the norms established by society. **5**

Larceny The act of taking property from another person without the use of force with the intent of keeping that property. **6**

Morals Principles of right and wrong behavior, as practiced by individuals or by society. **4**

Murder The unlawful killing of one human being by another. **6**

CHAPTER REVIEW 1

Organized Crime Illegal acts carried out by illegal organizations engaged in the market for illegal goods or services, such as illicit drugs or firearms. **7**

Public Order Crime Behavior that has been labeled criminal because it is contrary to shared social values, customs, and norms. **6**

Robbery The act of taking property from another person through force, threat of force, or intimidation. **6**

Sexual Assault Forced or coerced sexual intercourse (or other sexual acts). **6**

White-Collar Crime Nonviolent crimes committed by business entities or individuals to gain a personal or business advantage. **7**

1-2

Criminal Justice System The interlocking network of law enforcement agencies, courts, and corrections institutions designed to enforce criminal laws and protect society from criminal behavior. **7**

Justice The quality of fairness that must exist in the processes designed to determine whether individuals are guilty of criminal wrongdoing. **7**

1-3

Federalism A form of government in which a written constitution provides for a division of powers between a central government and several regional governments. **9**

Formal Criminal Justice Process The model of the criminal justice process in which participants follow formal rules to create a smoothly functioning disposition of cases from arrest to punishment. **11**

System A set of interacting parts that, when functioning properly, achieve a desired result. **11**

1-4

Discretion The ability of individuals in the criminal justice system to make operational decisions based on personal judgment instead of formal rules or official information. **12**

FIGURE 1.3	DISCRETION IN THE CRIMINAL JUSTICE SYSTEM
Police	**Judges**
• Enforce laws	• Set conditions for pretrial release
• Investigate specific crimes	• Accept pleas
• Search people or buildings	• Dismiss charges
• Arrest or detain people	• Impose sentences
Prosecutors	**Correctional Officials**
• File charges against suspects brought to them by the police	• Assign convicts to prison or jail
• Drop cases	• Punish prisoners who misbehave
• Reduce charges	• Reward prisoners who behave well

Ethics The moral principles that govern a person's perception of right and wrong. **13**

Informal Criminal Justice Process A model of the criminal justice system that recognizes the informal authority exercised by individuals at each step of the criminal justice process. **12**

1-5

Capital Crime A criminal act that makes the offender eligible to receive the death penalty. **18**

Civil Liberties The basic rights and freedoms for American citizens guaranteed by the U.S. Constitution, particularly in the Bill of Rights. **17**

Crime Control Model A criminal justice model that places primary emphasis on the right of society to be protected from crime and violent criminals. **14**

Domestic Terrorism Acts of terrorism that take place on U.S. soil without direct foreign involvement. **17**

Due Process Model A criminal justice model that places primacy on the right of the individual to be protected from the power of the government. **14**

Homeland Security A concerted national effort to prevent terrorist attacks within the United States and reduce the country's vulnerability to terrorism. **17**

Recidivism The act of committing a new crime after a person has already been punished for a previous crime by being convicted and sent to jail or prison. **18**

Terrorism The use or threat of violence to achieve political objectives. **17**

SUMMARY

2-1

Discuss the difference between a hypothesis and a theory in the context of criminology. A hypothesis is a proposition, usually presented in an "If . . . , then . . ." format, that can be tested by researchers. If enough different authorities are able to test and verify a hypothesis, it will usually be accepted as a theory. Because theories can offer explanations for behavior, criminologists often rely on them when trying to determine the causes of criminal behavior.

2-2

Contrast the medical model of addiction with the criminal model of addiction. Those who support the former believe that addicts are not criminals, but mentally or physically ill individuals who are forced into acts of petty crime to "feed their habit." Those in favor of the criminal model of addiction believe that abusers and addicts endanger society with their behavior and should be treated like any other criminals.

2-3

Distinguish between the National Crime Victimization Survey (NCVS) and self-reported surveys. The NCVS involves an annual survey of more than 40,000 households conducted by the Bureau of the Census along with the Bureau of Justice Statistics. The survey queries citizens on crimes that have been committed against them. As such, the NCVS includes crimes not necessarily reported to police. Self-reported surveys, in contrast, involve asking individuals about criminal activity to which they may have been a party.

2-4

Describe the three ways that victims' rights legislation increases the ability of crime victims to participate in the criminal justice system. (a) The right to be informed of victims' rights in general and of specific information relating to the relevant criminal case; (b) the right to be present at court proceedings involving the victim; and (c) the right to be heard on matters involving the prosecution, punishment, and release of the offender.

2-5

Identify the three factors most often used by criminologists to explain changes in the nation's crime rate. (a) Levels of incarceration, because an offender behind bars cannot commit any additional crimes and the threat of imprisonment acts as a deterrent to criminal behavior; (b) the size of the youth population, because those under the age of twenty-four commit the majority of crimes in the United States; and (c) the health of the economy, because when income and employment levels fall, those most directly affected may turn to crime for financial gain.

KEY TERMS

2-1

Causation The relationship in which a change in one variable creates a recognizable change in another variable. **23**

Correlation The relationship between two variables that tend to move in the same direction. **23**

Criminology The scientific study of crime and the causes of criminal behavior. **23**

Hypothesis A possible explanation for an observed occurrence that can be tested by further investigation. **24**

Theory An explanation of a happening or circumstance that is based on observation, experimentation, and reasoning. **24**

2-2

Anomie A condition in which the individual feels a disconnect from society due to the breakdown or absence of social norms. **29**

Biology The science of living organisms, including their structure, function, growth, and origin. **26**

Control Theory A series of theories that assume that all individuals have the potential for criminal behavior, but are restrained by the damage that such actions would do to their relationships with family, friends, and members of the community. **31**

Hormone A chemical substance, produced in tissue and conveyed in the bloodstream, that controls certain cellular and body functions, such as growth and reproduction. **26**

CHAPTER REVIEW 2

Learning Theory The theory that delinquents and criminals must be taught both the practical and the emotional skills necessary to participate in illegal activity. **30**

Life Course Criminology The study of crime based on the belief that behavioral patterns developed in childhood can predict delinquent and criminal behavior later in life. **31**

Psychology The scientific study of mental processes and behavior. **26**

Rational Choice Theory A school of criminology that holds that wrongdoers act as if they weigh the possible benefits of criminal or delinquent activity against the expected costs of being apprehended. **25**

Social Conflict Theories A school of criminology that views criminal behavior as the result of class conflict. **30**

Social Process Theories A school of criminology that considers criminal behavior to be the predictable result of a person's interaction with his or her environment. **30**

Social Psychology The study of how individual behavior is influenced by the behavior of groups in social situations. **27**

Sociology The study of the development and functioning of groups of people who live together within a society. **28**

Strain Theory The assumption that crime is the result of frustration felt by individuals who cannot reach their financial and personal goals through legitimate means. **29**

Testosterone The hormone primarily responsible for the production of sperm and the development of male secondary sex characteristics, such as the growth of facial and pubic hair and the change of voice pitch. **26**

2-3

Criminal Model of Addiction An approach to drug abuse that holds that drug offenders harm society by their actions to the same extent as other criminals and should face the same punitive sanctions. **34**

Decriminalization The removal of criminal penalties associated with a product or act, which then becomes subject only to civil sanctions such as fines and citations. **34**

Drug Any substance that modifies biological, psychological, or social behavior; in particular, an illegal substance with those properties. **32**

Drug Abuse The use of drugs that results in physical or psychological problems for the user, as well as disruption of personal relationships and employment. **33**

Legalization To make a formerly illegal product or action lawful. In the context of marijuana, the process includes strict regulation, including a ban on sale to or use by minors. **34**

Medical Model of Addiction An approach to drug addiction that treats drug abuse as a mental illness and focuses on treating and rehabilitating offenders rather than punishing them. **34**

Psychoactive Drug A chemical that affects the brain, causing changes in emotions, perceptions, and behavior. **32**

2-4

Dark Figure of Crime A term used to describe the actual amount of crime that takes place. The "figure" is "dark," or impossible to detect, because a great number of crimes are never reported to the police. **37**

Part I Offenses Crimes reported annually by the FBI in its Uniform Crime Report. Part I offenses include murder, rape, robbery, aggravated assault, burglary, larceny, and motor vehicle theft. **35**

Part II Offenses All crimes recorded by the FBI that do not fall into the category of Part I offenses. These crimes include both misdemeanors and felonies. **35**

Self-Reported Survey A method of gathering crime data that relies on participants to reveal and detail their own criminal or delinquent behavior. **37**

Uniform Crime Report (UCR) An annual report compiled by the FBI to give an indication of criminal activity in the United States. **35**

Victim Surveys A method of gathering crime data that directly surveys participants to determine their experiences as victims of crime. **37**

2-5

Repeat Victimization The theory that certain people and places are more likely to be subject to repeated criminal activity and that past victimization is a strong indicator of future victimization. **40**

Victim Any person who suffers physical, emotional, or financial harm as the result of a criminal act. **38**

2-6

Domestic Violence Willful neglect or physical violence that occurs within a familial or other intimate relationship. **43**

Stalking The criminal act of causing fear in a person by repeatedly subjecting that person to unwanted or threatening attention. **44**

SUMMARY

3-1

List the four written sources of American criminal law. (a) The U.S. Constitution and state constitutions; (b) statutes passed by Congress and state legislatures (plus local ordinances); (c) administrative agency regulations; and (d) case law.

3-2

Discuss the primary goals of civil law and criminal law and explain how these goals are realized. Civil law is designed to resolve disputes between private individuals and other entities such as corporations. In these disputes, one party, called the plaintiff, tries to gain monetary damages by proving that the accused party, or defendant, is to blame for a tort, or wrongful act. In contrast, criminal law exists to protect society from criminal behavior. To that end, the government prosecutes defendants, or persons who have been charged with committing a crime.

3-3

List and briefly define the most important excuse defenses for crimes. Insanity—different tests of insanity can be used, including (a) the *M'Naghten* rule (right-wrong test); (b) the ALI/MPC test, also known as the substantial-capacity test; and (c) the irresistible-impulse test. **Intoxication**—voluntary and involuntary, the latter being a possible criminal defense. **Mistake**—sometimes valid if the law was not published or reasonably known or if the alleged offender relied on an official statement of the law that was erroneous. Also, a mistake of fact may negate the mental state necessary to commit a crime.

3-4

Describe the four most important justification criminal defenses. Duress—requires that (a) the threat is of serious bodily harm or death, (b) the harm is greater than that caused by the crime; (c) the threat is immediate and inescapable; and (d) the defendant became involved in the situation through no fault of his or her own. **Justifiable use of force**—the defense of one's person, dwelling, or property, or the prevention of a crime. **Necessity**—justifiable if the harm sought to be avoided is greater than that sought to be prevented by the law defining the offense charged. **Entrapment**—that the criminal action was induced by certain governmental persuasion or trickery.

3-5

Explain the importance of the due process clause in the criminal justice system. The due process clause acts to limit the power of government. In the criminal justice system, the due process clause requires that certain procedures be followed to ensure the fairness of criminal proceedings and that all criminal laws be reasonable and in the interest of the public good.

KEY TERMS

3-1

Administrative Law The body of law created by administrative agencies (in the form of rules, regulations, orders, and decisions) in order to carry out their duties and responsibilities. **49**

Ballot Initiative A procedure in which the citizens of a state, by collecting enough signatures, can force a public vote on a proposed change to state law. **49**

Case Law The rules of law announced in court decisions. **50**

Constitutional Law Law based on the U.S. Constitution and the constitutions of the various states. **48**

Precedent A court decision that furnishes an example of authority for deciding subsequent cases involving similar facts. **49**

Rule of Law The principle that the rules of a legal system apply equally to all persons, institutions, and entities—public or private—that make up a society. **47**

Stare Decisis (pronounced *ster-*ay dih-*si-ses*). A legal doctrine under which judges are obligated to follow the precedents established in prior decisions. **50**

Statutory Law The body of law enacted by legislative bodies. **48**

Supremacy Clause A clause in the U.S. Constitution establishing that federal law is the "supreme law of the land" and shall prevail when in conflict with state constitutions or statutes. **48**

3-3

Beyond a Reasonable Doubt The degree of proof required to find the defendant in a criminal trial guilty of committing the crime. The defendant's guilt must be the only reasonable explanation for the criminal act before the court. **53**

Civil Law The branch of law dealing with the definition and enforcement of all private or public rights, as opposed to criminal matters. **52**

Defendant In a civil court, the person or institution against whom an action is brought. In a criminal court, the person or entity who has been formally accused of violating a criminal law. **52**

Liability In a civil court, legal responsibility for one's own or another's actions. **52**

CHAPTER REVIEW 3

Plaintiff The person or institution that initiates a lawsuit in civil court proceedings by filing a complaint. **52**

Preponderance of the Evidence The degree of proof required to decide in favor of one side or the other in a civil case. In general, this requirement is met when a plaintiff shows that a claim more likely than not is true. **53**

3-4

Felony A serious crime, usually punishable by death or imprisonment for a year or longer. **53**

Infraction In most jurisdictions, a noncriminal offense for which the penalty is a fine rather than incarceration. **54**

Mala in Se A descriptive term for acts that are inherently wrong, regardless of whether they are prohibited by law. **54**

Mala Prohibita A descriptive term for acts that are made illegal by criminal statute and are not necessarily wrong in and of themselves. **54**

Misdemeanor A criminal offense that is not a felony; usually punishable by a fine and/or a jail term of less than one year. **53**

3-5

Actus Reus (pronounced *ak-*tus *ray-*uhs). A guilty (prohibited) act. **55**

Attempt The act of taking substantial steps toward committing a crime while having the ability and the intent to commit the crime, even if the crime never takes place. **56**

Attendant Circumstances The facts surrounding a criminal event that must be proved to convict the defendant of the underlying crime. **59**

Conspiracy A plot by two or more people to carry out an illegal or harmful act. **60**

Corpus Delicti The body of circumstances that must exist for a criminal act to have occurred. **54**

Felony-Murder An unlawful homicide that occurs during the attempted commission of a felony. **59**

Hate Crime Law A statute that provides for greater sanctions against those who commit crimes motivated by bias against an individual or a group based on race, ethnicity, religion, gender, sexual orientation, disability, or age. **60**

Inchoate Offense Conduct deemed criminal without actual harm being done, provided that the harm that would have occurred is a harm the law tries to prevent. **60**

Involuntary Manslaughter A homicide in which the offender had no intent to kill her or his victim. **58**

Mens Rea (pronounced mehns ray-uh). Mental state, or intent. A wrongful mental state is usually as necessary as a wrongful act to establish criminal liability. **56**

Negligence A failure to exercise the standard of care that a reasonable person would exercise in similar circumstances. **56**

Recklessness The state of being aware that a risk does or will exist and nevertheless acting in a way that consciously disregards this risk. **56**

Statutory Rape A strict liability crime in which an adult engages in a sexual act with a minor. **58**

Strict Liability Crimes Certain crimes, such as traffic violations, in which the defendant is guilty regardless of her or his state of mind at the time of the act. **58**

Voluntary Manslaughter A homicide in which the intent to kill was present in the mind of the offender, but malice was lacking. **57**

3-6

Competency Hearing A court proceeding to determine whether the defendant is mentally well enough to understand the charges filed against him or her and cooperate with a lawyer in presenting a defense. **62**

Duress Unlawful pressure brought to bear on a person, causing the person to perform an act that he or she would not otherwise perform. **64**

Duty to Retreat The requirement that a person claiming self-defense prove that she or he first took reasonable steps to avoid the conflict that resulted in the use of deadly force. **64**

Entrapment A defense in which the defendant claims that he or she was induced by a public official—usually an undercover agent or police officer—to commit a crime that he or she would otherwise not have committed. **66**

Infancy The status of a person who is below the legal age of majority. Under early American law, infancy excused young wrongdoers of criminal behavior because presumably they could not understand the consequences of their actions. **61**

Insanity A defense for criminal liability that asserts a lack of criminal responsibility due to mental instability. **61**

Intoxication A defense for criminal liability in which the defendant claims that the taking of intoxicants rendered him or her unable to form the requisite intent to commit a criminal act. **62**

Irresistible-Impulse Test A test for the insanity defense under which a defendant who knew his or her action was wrong may still be found insane if he or she was unable, as a result of a mental deficiency, to control the urge to complete the act. **61**

M'Naghten Rule A common law test of criminal responsibility, derived from *M'Naghten*'s Case in 1843, that relies on the defendant's inability to distinguish right from wrong. **61**

Necessity A defense against criminal liability in which the defendant asserts that circumstances required her or him to commit an illegal act. **65**

Self-Defense The legally recognized privilege to protect one's self or property from injury by another. **64**

Substantial-Capacity Test (ALI/MPC Test) A test for the insanity defense that states that a person is not responsible for criminal behavior when he or she "lacks substantial capacity" to understand that the behavior is wrong or to control the behavior. **61**

3-7

Bill of Rights The first ten amendments to the U.S. Constitution. **66**

Due Process Clause The provisions of the Fifth and Fourteenth Amendments to the Constitution that guarantee that no person shall be deprived of life, liberty, or property without due process of law. **67**

Procedural Criminal Law Rules that define the manner in which the rights and duties of individuals may be enforced. **66**

Procedural Due Process A provision in the Constitution that states that the law must be carried out in a fair and orderly manner. **67**

Substantive Criminal Law Law that defines the rights and duties of individuals with respect to one another. **66**

Substantive Due Process The constitutional requirement that laws used in accusing and convicting persons of crimes must be fair. **68**

SUMMARY

4-1

List the four basic responsibilities of the police. (a) To enforce laws, (b) to provide services, (c) to prevent crime, and (d) to preserve the peace.

4-2

Identify the differences between the police academy and field training as learning tools for recruits. The police academy is a controlled environment where police recruits learn the basics of policing from instructors in classrooms. In contrast, field training takes place in the "real world": the recruit goes on patrol with an experienced police officer.

4-3

Describe the challenges facing women who choose law enforcement as a career. Many male officers believe that their female counterparts are not physically or mentally strong enough for police work, which puts pressure on women officers to continually prove themselves. Female officers must also deal with tokenism, or the stigma that they were hired only to fulfill diversity requirements, and sexual harassment in the form of unwanted advances or obscene remarks.

4-4

Indicate some of the most important law enforcement agencies under the control of the Department of Homeland Security. (a) U.S. Customs and Border Protection, which polices the flow of goods and people across the United States' international borders and oversees the U.S. Border Patrol; (b) U.S. Immigration and Customs Enforcement, which investigates and enforces our nation's immigration and customs laws; and (c) the U.S. Secret Service, which protects high-ranking federal government officials and federal property.

4-5

Analyze the importance of private security today. In the United States, businesses and citizens spend billions of dollars each year on private security. Heightened fear of crime and increased crime in the workplace have fueled the growth in spending on private security.

KEY TERMS

4-1

Intelligence-Led Policing An approach that measures the risk of criminal behavior associated with certain individuals or locations so as to predict when and where such criminal behavior is most likely to occur in the future. **74**

4-2

Field Training The segment of a police recruit's training in which he or she is removed from the classroom and placed on the beat, under the supervision of a senior officer. **78**

Probationary Period A period of time at the beginning of a police officer's career during which she or he may be fired without cause. **77**

Recruitment The process by which law enforcement agencies develop a pool of qualified applicants from which to select new employees. **76**

4-3

Double Marginality The double suspicion that minority law enforcement officers face from their white colleagues and from members of the minority community to which they belong. **79**

Sexual Harassment A repeated pattern of unwelcome sexual advances and/or obscene remarks in the workplace. Under certain circumstances, sexual harassment is illegal and can be the basis for a civil lawsuit. **79**

4-4

Coroner The medical examiner of a county, usually elected by popular vote. **82**

CHAPTER REVIEW 4

Drug Enforcement Administration (DEA) The federal agency responsible for enforcing the nation's laws and regulations regarding narcotics and other controlled substances. **86**

Federal Bureau of Investigation (FBI) The branch of the Department of Justice responsible for combating terrorism and investigating violations of federal law. **85**

Infrastructure The services and facilities that support the day-to-day needs of modern life, such as electricity, food, transportation, and water. **85**

Private Security Security services, such as guard and patrol services, provided by private corporations or individuals rather than police officers. **88**

Sheriff The primary law enforcement officer in a county, usually elected by popular vote. **81**

U.S. Customs and Border Protection (CBP) The federal agency responsible for protecting U.S. borders and facilitating legal trade and travel across those borders. **84**

U.S. Immigration and Customs Enforcement (ICE) The federal agency that enforces the nation's immigration and customs laws. **84**

U.S. Secret Service A federal law enforcement organization with the primary responsibility of protecting the president, the president's family, the vice president, and other important political figures. **84**

FIGURE 4.3   FEDERAL LAW ENFORCEMENT AGENCIES

Department of Homeland Security

DEPARTMENT NAME	APPROXIMATE NUMBER OF OFFICERS	MAIN RESPONSIBILITIES
U.S. Customs and Border Protection (CBP)	37,000	(1) Prevent the illegal flow of people and goods across America's international borders; (2) facilitate legal trade and travel
U.S. Immigration and Customs Enforcement (ICE)	12,400	Uphold public safety and homeland security by enforcing the nation's immigration and customs laws
U.S. Secret Service	4,500	(1) Protect the president, the president's family, former presidents and their families, and other high-ranking politicians; (2) combat currency counterfeiters

Department of Justice

DEPARTMENT NAME	APPROXIMATE NUMBER OF OFFICERS	MAIN RESPONSIBILITIES
Federal Bureau of Investigation (FBI)	13,600	(1) Protect national security by fighting international and domestic terrorism; (2) enforce federal criminal laws such as those dealing with cyber crime, public corruption, and civil rights violations
Drug Enforcement Administration (DEA)	4,700	Enforce the nation's laws regulating the sale and use of drugs
Bureau of Alcohol, Tobacco, Firearms and Explosives (ATF)	2,500	(1) Combat the illegal use and trafficking of firearms and explosives; (2) investigate the illegal diversion of alcohol and tobacco products
U.S. Marshals Service	4,000	(1) Provide security at federal courts; (2) protect government witnesses; (3) apprehend fugitives from the federal court or corrections system

Department of the Treasury

DEPARTMENT NAME	APPROXIMATE NUMBER OF OFFICERS	MAIN RESPONSIBILITIES
Internal Revenue Service (IRS)	2,500	Investigate potential criminal violations of the nation's tax code

A number of federal agencies employ law enforcement officers who are authorized to carry firearms and make arrests. The most prominent ones are under the control of the U.S. Department of Homeland Security, the U.S. Department of Justice, and the U.S. Department of the Treasury.

SUMMARY

5-1

Explain why police officers are allowed discretionary powers. Police officers are considered trustworthy and able to make honest decisions. They have experience and training. They are knowledgeable in criminal behavior. Finally, they must have the discretion to take reasonable steps to protect themselves.

5-2

List the three primary purposes of police patrol. (a) The deterrence of crime, (b) the maintenance of public order, and (c) the provision of services that are not related to crime.

5-3

Describe how forensic experts use DNA fingerprinting to solve crimes. Law enforcement agents gather trace evidence such as blood, semen, skin, or hair from the crime scene. Because these items are rich in DNA, which provides a unique genetic blueprint for every living organism, crime labs can create a DNA profile of the suspect and test it against other such profiles stored in databases. If the profiles match, then law enforcement agents have found a strong suspect for the crime.

5-4

Determine when police officers are justified in using deadly force. Police officers must make a reasonable judgment in determining when to use force that will place the suspect in threat of injury or death. That is, given the circumstances, the officer must reasonably assume that the use of such force is necessary to avoid serious injury or death to the officer or someone else.

5-5

Explain what an ethical dilemma is and name four categories of ethical dilemmas that a police officer typically may face. An ethical dilemma is a situation in which police officers (a) do not know the right course of action, (b) have difficulty doing what they consider to be right, and/or (c) find the wrong choice very tempting. The four types of ethical dilemmas involve (a) discretion, (b) duty, (c) honesty, and (d) loyalty.

KEY TERMS

5-1

Policy A set of guiding principles designed to influence the behavior and decision making of police officers. **94**

5-2

Ballistics The study of firearms, including the firing of the weapon and the flight of the bullet. **100**

Broken Windows Theory Wilson and Kelling's theory that a neighborhood in disrepair signals that criminal activity is tolerated in the area. By cracking down on quality-of-life crimes, police can reclaim the neighborhood and encourage law-abiding citizens to live and work there. **105**

Bureaucracy A hierarchically structured administrative organization that carries out specific functions. **95**

Clearance Rate A comparison of the number of crimes cleared by arrest and prosecution with the number of crimes reported during any given time period. **99**

Cold Case A criminal investigation that has not been solved after a certain amount of time. **99**

Cold Hit The establishment of a connection between a suspect and a crime, often through the use of DNA evidence, in the absence of an ongoing criminal investigation. **102**

Community Policing A policing philosophy that emphasizes community support for and cooperation with the police in preventing crime. **105**

Computer-Aided Dispatch (CAD) A method of dispatching police patrols units to the site of 911 emergencies with the assistance of a computer program. **102**

CHAPTER REVIEW 5

Confidential Informant (CI) A human source for police who provides information concerning illegal activity in which he or she is involved. **99**

Crime Mapping Technology that allows crime analysts to identify trends and patterns of criminal behavior within a given area. **103**

Delegation of Authority The principles of command on which most police departments are based, in which personnel take orders from and are responsible to those in positions of power directly above them. **95**

Detective The primary police investigator of crimes. **98**

Directed Patrol A patrol strategy that is designed to focus on a specific type of criminal activity in a specific geographical location. **103**

DNA Fingerprinting The identification of a person based on a sample of her or his DNA, the genetic material found in the cells of all living things. **101**

Forensics The application of science to establish facts and evidence during the investigation of crimes. **100**

Hot Spots Concentrated areas of high criminal activity that draw a directed police response. **103**

Incident-Driven Policing A reactive approach to policing that emphasizes a speedy response to calls for service. **102**

Proactive Arrests Arrests that occur because of concerted efforts by law enforcement agencies to respond to a particular type of criminal or criminal behavior. **104**

Problem-Oriented Policing A policing philosophy that requires police to identify potential criminal activity and develop strategies to prevent or respond to that activity. **105**

Random Patrol A patrol strategy that relies on police officers monitoring a certain area with the goal of detecting crimes in progress or preventing crime due to their presence. Also known as *general* or *preventive patrol.* **103**

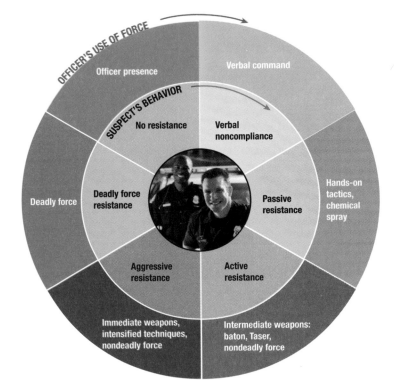

Source: Michael E. Miller, "Taser Use and the Use-of-Force Continuum," *Police Chief* (September 2010), 72.
Photo credit: iStockPhoto.com/Susan Chiang

Reactive Arrests Arrests that come about as part of the ordinary routine of police patrol and responses to calls for service. **104**

Trace Evidence Evidence such as a fingerprint, blood, or hair found in small amounts at a crime scene. **100**

5-3

Blue Curtain A metaphorical term used to refer to the value placed on secrecy and the general mistrust of the outside world shared by many police officers. **107**

Burnout A mental state that occurs when a person suffers from exhaustion and has difficulty functioning normally as a result of overwork and stress. **108**

Civil Rights Violation Any interference with a citizen's constitutional rights by a civil servant such as a police officer. **110**

Deadly Force Force applied by a police officer that is likely or intended to cause death. **109**

Police Subculture The values and perceptions that are shared by members of a police department

and, to a certain extent, by all law enforcement agents. **106**

Racial Profiling The practice of targeting people for police action based solely on their race, ethnicity, or national origin. **110**

Reasonable Force A degree of force that is appropriate to protect the police officer or other citizens and is not excessive. **109**

Socialization The process through which a police officer is taught the values and expected behavior of the police subculture. **106**

Stressors The conditions that cause stress. **107**

5-4

Duty The moral sense of a police officer that she or he should behave in a certain manner. **111**

Noble Cause Corruption Knowing misconduct by a police officer with the goal of attaining what the officer believes is a "just" result. **111**

Police Corruption The abuse of authority by a law enforcement officer for personal gain. **111**

SUMMARY

6-1

Outline the four major sources that may provide probable cause.
(a) Personal observation, usually due to an officer's personal training, experience, and expertise; (b) information, gathered from informants, eyewitnesses, victims, police bulletins, and other sources; (c) evidence, which often has to be in plain view; and (d) association, which generally must involve a person with a known criminal background who is seen in a place where criminal activity is openly taking place.

6-2

Explain when searches can be made without a warrant. Searches and seizures can be made without a warrant if they are incidental to an arrest (but they must be reasonable); when they are made with voluntary consent; when they involve the "movable vehicle" exception; when property has been abandoned; and when items are in plain view, under certain restricted circumstances (see *Coolidge v. New Hampshire*).

6-3

Distinguish between a stop and a frisk, and indicate the importance of the case *Terry v. Ohio*. Though the terms *stop* and *frisk* are often used in concert, a stop is the separate act of detaining a suspect when an officer reasonably believes that a criminal activity is about to take place. A frisk is the physical "pat-down" of a suspect. In *Terry v. Ohio*, the Supreme Court ruled that an officer must have "specific and articulable facts" before making a stop, but those facts may be "taken together with rational inferences."

6-4

List the four elements that must be present for an arrest to take place. (a) Intent, (b) authority, (c) seizure or detention, and (d) the understanding of the person that he or she has been arrested.

6-5

Indicate situations in which a *Miranda* warning is unnecessary.
(a) When no questions that are testimonial in nature are asked of the suspect; (b) when there is no suspect and witnesses in general are being questioned at the scene of a crime; (c) when a person volunteers information before the police ask anything; (d) when a suspect has given a private statement to a friend without the government orchestrating it; (e) during a stop and frisk when no arrests have been made; (f) during a traffic stop; and (g) when a threat to public safety exists.

KEY TERMS

6-1

Exclusionary Rule A rule under which any evidence that is obtained in violation of the accused's rights, as well as any evidence derived from illegally obtained evidence, will not be admissible in criminal court. **117**

Fruit of the Poisoned Tree Evidence that is acquired through the use of illegally obtained evidence and is therefore inadmissible in court. **118**

"Good Faith" Exception The legal principle that evidence obtained with the use of a technically invalid search warrant is admissible during trial if the police acted in good faith when they sought the warrant from a judge. **118**

"Inevitable Discovery" Exception The legal principle that illegally obtained evidence can be admissible in court if police using lawful means would "inevitably" have discovered it. **118**

Probable Cause Reasonable grounds to believe the existence of facts warranting certain actions, such as the search or arrest of a person. **116**

Searches and Seizures The legal term, as found in the Fourth Amendment to the U.S. Constitution, that generally refers to the searching for and the confiscating of evidence by law enforcement agents. **116**

6-2

Affidavit A written statement of facts, confirmed by the oath or affirmation of the party making it and made before a person having the authority to administer the oath or affirmation. **120**

Consent Searches Searches by police that are made after the subject of the search has agreed to the action. In these situations, consent, if given of free will, validates a warrantless search. **121**

Electronic Surveillance The use of electronic equipment by law enforcement agents to record private conversations or observe conduct that is meant to be private. **124**

Plain View Doctrine The legal principle that objects in plain view of a law enforcement agent who has the right to be in a position to have that view may be seized without a warrant and introduced as evidence. **123**

Search The process by which police examine a person or property to find evidence that will be used to prove guilt in a criminal trial. **119**

Searches Incidental to Arrests Searches for weapons and evidence that are conducted on persons who have just been arrested. **121**

Search Warrant A written order, based on probable cause and issued by a judge or magistrate, commanding that police officers or criminal investigators search a specific person, place, or property to obtain evidence. **120**

Seizure The forcible taking of a person or property in response to a violation of the law. **120**

6-3

Frisk A pat-down or minimal search by police to discover weapons. **127**

Stop A brief detention of a person by law enforcement agents for questioning. **127**

6-4

Arrest To deprive the liberty of a person suspected of criminal activity. **128**

Arrest Warrant A written order, based on probable cause and issued by a judge or magistrate, commanding that the person named on the warrant be arrested by the police. **129**

FIGURE 6.3 THE DIFFERENCE BETWEEN A STOP AND AN ARREST

	Stop	Arrest
Justification	Reasonable suspicion only	Probable cause
Warrant	None	Required in some, but not all, situations
Intent of Officer	To investigate suspicious activity	To make a formal charge against the suspect
Search	May frisk, or "pat down," for weapons	May conduct a full search for weapons or evidence
Scope of Search	Outer clothing only	Area within the suspect's immediate control or "reach"

Both stops and arrests are considered seizures because both police actions involve the restriction of an individual's freedom to "walk away." Both must be justified by a showing of reasonableness as well. You should be aware, however, of the differences between a stop and an arrest. *During a stop,* **police can interrogate the person and make a limited search of his or her outer clothing. In certain circumstances, such as the discovery of an illegal weapon during the stop, the officers may arrest the person.** *If an arrest is made,* **the suspect is now under police control and is protected by the U.S. Constitution.**

Exigent Circumstances Situations that require extralegal or exceptional actions by the police. **129**

Warrantless Arrest An arrest made without a prior warrant for the action. **130**

6-5

Coercion The use of physical force or mental intimidation to compel a person to do something—such as confess to committing a crime—against her or his will. **130**

Custodial Interrogation The questioning of a suspect after that person has been taken into custody. In this situation, the suspect must be read his or her *Miranda* rights before interrogation can begin. **131**

Custody The forceful detention of a person or the perception that a person is not free to leave the immediate vicinity. **131**

False Confession An admission of guilt when the confessor did not, in fact, commit the crime. **133**

Interrogation The direct questioning of a suspect to gather evidence of criminal activity and to try to gain a confession. **130**

Miranda **Rights** The constitutional rights of accused persons taken into custody by law enforcement officials, such as the right to remain silent and the right to counsel. **131**

SUMMARY

7-1

Define *jurisdiction* and contrast geographic and subject-matter jurisdiction. Jurisdiction relates to the power of a court to hear a particular case. Courts are typically limited in geographic jurisdiction—for example, to a particular state. Some courts are restricted in subject matter, such as a small claims court, which can hear only cases involving civil matters under a certain monetary limit.

7-2

Explain the difference between trial and appellate courts. Trial courts are courts of the first instance, where a case is first heard. Appellate courts review the proceedings of a lower court. Appellate courts do not have juries.

7-3

Explain briefly how a case is brought to the Supreme Court. Cases decided in U.S. courts of appeals, as well as cases decided in the highest state courts (when federal questions arise), can be appealed to the Supreme Court. If at least four justices approve of a case filed with the Supreme Court, the Court will issue a writ of *certiorari,* ordering the lower court to send the Supreme Court the record of the case for review.

7-4

List the different names given to public prosecutors and indicate the general powers that they have. At the federal level, the prosecutor is called the U.S. attorney. In state and local courts, the prosecutor may be referred to as the prosecuting attorney, state attorney, district attorney, county attorney, or city attorney. Prosecutors in general have the power to decide when and how the state will pursue an individual suspected of criminal wrongdoing. In some jurisdictions, the district attorney is also the chief law enforcement officer, holding broad powers over police operations.

7-5

Explain why defense attorneys must often defend clients they know to be guilty. In our criminal justice system, the most important responsibility of a defense attorney is to be an advocate for her or his client. This means ensuring that the client's constitutional rights are protected during criminal justice proceedings, regardless of whether the client is guilty or innocent.

KEY TERMS

7-2

Appellate Courts Courts that review decisions made by lower courts, such as trial courts; also known as *courts of appeals.* **141**

Concurrent Jurisdiction The situation that occurs when two or more courts have the authority to preside over the same criminal case. **139**

Dual Court System The separate but interrelated court system of the United States, made up of the courts on the national level and the courts on the state level. **141**

Extradition The process by which one jurisdiction surrenders a person accused or convicted of violating another jurisdiction's criminal law to the second jurisdiction. **140**

Jurisdiction The authority of a court to hear and decide cases within an area of the law or a geographic territory. **139**

Opinions Written statements by the judges expressing the reasons for the court's decision in a case. **141**

Trial Courts Courts in which most cases begin and in which questions of fact are examined. **141**

7-3

Magistrate A public civil officer or official with limited judicial authority within a particular geographic area, such as the authority to issue an arrest warrant. **142**

Problem-Solving Courts Lower courts that have jurisdiction over one specific area of criminal activity, such as illegal drugs or domestic violence. **142**

CHAPTER REVIEW 7

7-4

Concurring Opinions Separate opinions prepared by judges who support the decision of the majority of the court but who want to make or clarify a particular point or to voice disapproval of the grounds on which the decision was made. **147**

Dissenting Opinions Separate opinions in which judges disagree with the conclusion reached by the majority of the court and expand on their own views about the case. **147**

Judicial Review The power of a court—particularly the United States Supreme Court—to review the actions of the executive and legislative branches and, if necessary, declare those actions unconstitutional. **146**

Oral Arguments The verbal arguments presented in person by attorneys to an appellate court. Each attorney presents reasons why the court should rule in his or her client's favor. **147**

Rule of Four A rule of the United States Supreme Court that the Court will not issue a writ of *certiorari* unless at least four justices approve of the decision to hear the case. **146**

Writ of *Certiorari* A request from a higher court asking a lower court for the record of a case. In essence, the request signals the higher court's willingness to review the case. **146**

7-5

Docket The list of cases entered on a court's calendar and thus scheduled to be heard by the court. **148**

Missouri Plan A method of selecting judges that combines appointment and election. **149**

Nonpartisan Elections Elections in which candidates are presented on the ballot without any party affiliation. **149**

Partisan Elections Elections in which candidates are affiliated with and receive support from political parties. **149**

7-6

Attorney-Client Privilege A rule of evidence requiring that communications between a client and his or her attorney be kept confidential, unless the client consents to disclosure. **155**

Attorney General The chief law officer of a state; also, the chief law officer of the nation. **152**

Courtroom Work Group The social organization consisting of the judge, prosecutor, defense attorney, and other court workers. **150**

Defense Attorney The lawyer representing the defendant. **152**

Public Defenders Court-appointed attorneys who are paid by the state to represent defendants who cannot afford private counsel. **153**

Public Prosecutors Individuals, acting as trial lawyers, who initiate and conduct cases in the government's name and on behalf of the people. **150**

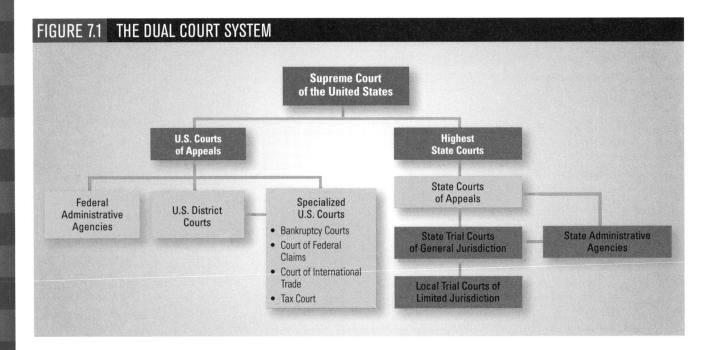

FIGURE 7.1 THE DUAL COURT SYSTEM

SUMMARY

8-1

Identify the steps involved in the pretrial criminal process. (a) Suspect taken into custody or arrested; (b) initial appearance before a magistrate; (c) the posting of bail or release on recognizance; (d) preventive detention, if deemed necessary to ensure the safety of other persons or the community, or regular detention, if the defendant is unable to post bail; (e) preliminary arraignment; (f) grand jury hearings, after which an indictment is issued against the defendant if the grand jury finds probable cause; (g) arraignment; and (h) plea bargaining.

8-2

Indicate why prosecutors, defense attorneys, and defendants often agree to plea bargains. For prosecutors, a plea bargain removes the risk of losing the case at trial, particularly if the evidence against the defendant is weak. For defense attorneys, the plea bargain may be the best deal possible for a potentially guilty client. For defendants, plea bargains give a measure of control over a highly uncertain future.

8-3

Identify the basic protections enjoyed by criminal defendants in the United States. According to the Sixth Amendment, a criminal defendant has the right to a speedy and public trial by an impartial jury in the physical location where the crime was committed. Additionally, a person accused of a crime must be informed of the nature of the crime and be confronted with the witnesses against him or her. Further, the accused must be able to summon witnesses in her or his favor and have the assistance of counsel.

8-4

Contrast challenges for cause and peremptory challenges during *voir dire*. A challenge for cause occurs when an attorney provides the court with a legally justifiable reason why a potential juror should be excluded. In contrast, peremptory challenges do not require any justification by the attorney and are usually limited to a small number. They cannot, however, be based, even implicitly, on race or gender.

8-5

List the standard steps in a criminal jury trial. (a) Opening statements by the prosecutor and the defense attorney; (b) presentation of evidence; (c) cross-examination by the defense attorney of the same witnesses; (d) presentation of the defendant's case; (e) cross-examination by the prosecutor; (f) after the defense closes its case, rebuttal by the prosecution; (g) cross-examination of the prosecution's new witnesses by the defense and introduction of new witnesses of its own, called the surrebuttal; (i) closing arguments by both the defense and the prosecution; (j) the charging of the jury by the judge; (k) jury deliberations; and (l) presentation of the verdict.

KEY TERMS

8-1

Bail The dollar amount or conditions set by the court to ensure that an individual accused of a crime will appear for further criminal proceedings. **160**

Bail Bond Agent A businessperson who agrees, for a fee, to pay the bail amount if the accused fails to appear in court as ordered. **161**

Initial Appearance An accused's first appearance before a judge or magistrate following arrest. **160**

Preventive Detention The retention of an accused person in custody due to fears that she or he will commit a crime if released before trial. **161**

Property Bond Property provided to the court by the defendant as an assurance that he or she will return for trial; an alternative to cash bail. **161**

Release on Recognizance (ROR) A judge's order that releases an accused from jail with the understanding that he or she will return of his or her own will for further proceedings. **161**

8-2

Case Attrition The process through which prosecutors, by deciding whether to prosecute each person arrested, effect an overall reduction in the number of persons prosecuted. **164**

Discovery Formal investigation by each side prior to trial. **162**

Grand Jury The group of citizens called to decide whether probable cause exists to believe that a suspect committed the crime with which she or he has been charged. **162**

Indictment A charge or written accusation, issued by a grand jury, that probable cause exists to believe that a named person has committed a crime. **162**

Information The formal charge against the accused issued by the prosecutor after a preliminary hearing has found probable cause. **162**

CHAPTER REVIEW 8

Preliminary Hearing An initial hearing in which a magistrate decides if there is probable cause to believe that the defendant committed the crime with which he or she is charged. **162**

8-3

Arraignment A court proceeding in which the suspect is formally charged with the criminal offense stated in the indictment. **164**

Nolo Contendere Latin for "I will not contest it." A plea in which a criminal defendant chooses not to challenge, or contest, the charges brought by the government. **164**

Plea Bargaining The process by which the accused and the prosecutor work out a mutually satisfactory conclusion to the case, subject to court approval. **165**

8-4

Acquittal A declaration following a trial that the individual accused of the crime is innocent in the eyes of the law and thus is absolved from the charges. **168**

Bench Trial A trial conducted without a jury, in which a judge makes the determination of the defendant's guilt or innocence. **167**

Jury Trial A trial before a judge and a jury. **167**

Statute of Limitations A law limiting the amount of time prosecutors have to bring criminal charges against a suspect after the crime has occurred. **167**

8-5

Challenge for Cause A *voir dire* challenge for which an attorney states the reason why a prospective juror should not be included on the jury. **170**

Master Jury List The list of citizens in a court's district from which a jury can be selected; compiled from voter-registration lists, driver's license lists, and other sources. **169**

Peremptory Challenges *Voir dire* challenges to exclude potential jurors from serving on the jury without any supporting reason or cause. **170**

Venire The group of citizens from which the jury is selected. **169**

Voir Dire The preliminary questions that the trial attorneys ask prospective jurors to determine whether they are biased or have any connection with the defendant or a witness. **169**

8-6

Circumstantial Evidence Indirect evidence that is offered to establish, by inference, the likelihood of a fact that is in question. **173**

Closing Arguments Arguments made by each side's attorney after the cases for the plaintiff and defendant have been presented. **177**

Confrontation Clause The part of the Sixth Amendment that guarantees all defendants the right to confront witnesses testifying against them during the criminal trial. **175**

Cross-Examination The questioning of an opposing witness during trial. **175**

Direct Evidence Evidence that establishes the existence of a fact that is in question without relying on inference. **172**

Direct Examination The examination of a witness by the attorney who calls the witness to the stand to testify. **174**

Evidence Anything that is used to prove the existence or nonexistence of a fact. **172**

Expert Witness A witness with professional training or substantial experience qualifying her or him to testify on a certain subject. **172**

Hearsay An oral or written statement made by an out-of-court speaker that is later offered in court by a witness (not the speaker) concerning a matter before the court. **175**

Lay Witness A witness who can truthfully and accurately testify on a fact in question without having specialized training or knowledge. **172**

Opening Statements The attorneys' statements to the jury at the beginning of the trial. **172**

Real Evidence Evidence that is brought into court and seen by the jury, as opposed to evidence that is described for a jury. **172**

Rebuttal Evidence given to counteract or disprove evidence presented by the opposing party. **177**

Relevant Evidence Evidence tending to make a fact in question more or less probable than it would be without the evidence. Only relevant evidence is admissible in court. **174**

Testimony Verbal evidence given by witnesses under oath. **172**

8-7

Allen Charge An instruction by a judge to a deadlocked jury with only a few dissenters that asks the jurors in the minority to reconsider the majority opinion. **178**

Appeal The process of seeking a higher court's review of a lower court's decision for the purpose of correcting or changing this decision. **178**

Charge The judge's instructions to the jury following the attorneys' closing arguments. **177**

Double Jeopardy The prosecution of a person twice for the same criminal offense; prohibited by the Fifth Amendment to the Constitution. **179**

Habeas Corpus An order that requires corrections officials to bring an inmate before a court or a judge and explain why he or she is being held in prison. **180**

Hung Jury A jury whose members are so irreconcilably divided in their opinions that they cannot reach a verdict. **178**

Sequestration The isolation of jury members during a trial to ensure that their judgment is not influenced by information other than what is provided in the courtroom. **177**

Verdict A formal decision made by the jury. **177**

Wrongful Conviction The conviction, either by verdict or by guilty plea, of a person who is factually innocent of the charges. **180**

SUMMARY

9-1

List and contrast the four basic philosophical reasons for sentencing criminals. (a) Retribution, (b) deterrence, (c) incapacitation, and (d) rehabilitation. Under the principle of retributive justice, the severity of the punishment is in proportion to the severity of the crime. Punishment is an end in itself. In contrast, the deterrence approach seeks to prevent future crimes by setting an example. Such punishment is based on its deterrent value and not necessarily on the severity of the crime. The incapacitation theory of punishment simply argues that a criminal in prison cannot inflict further harm on society. In contrast, the rehabilitation theory asserts that criminals can be rehabilitated in the appropriate prison environment.

9-2

Contrast indeterminate with determinate sentencing. Indeterminate sentencing follows from legislative penal codes that set minimum and maximum amounts of incarceration time. Determinate sentencing carries a fixed amount of time, although this may be reduced for "good time."

9-3

Explain some of the reasons why sentencing reform has occurred. One reason is sentencing disparity, which is indicative of a situation in which those convicted of similar crimes receive dissimilar sentences (often due to a particular judge's sentencing philosophy). Sentencing discrimination has also occurred on the basis of defendants' gender, race, or economic standing. An additional reason for sentencing reform has been a general desire to "get tough on crime."

9-4

Identify the arguments for and against the use of victim impact statements during sentencing hearings. Proponents of victim impact statements believe that they allow victims to provide character evidence in the same manner as defendants have always been allowed to do and that they give victims a therapeutic "voice" in the sentencing process. Opponents argue that the statements bring unacceptable levels of emotion into the courtroom and encourage judges and juries to make sentencing decisions based on the "social value" of the victim rather than the facts of the case.

9-5

Identify the two stages that make up the bifurcated process of death penalty sentencing. The first stage of the bifurcated process requires a jury to find the defendant guilty or not guilty of a crime that is punishable by execution. If the defendant is found guilty, then, in the second stage, the jury reconvenes to decide whether the death sentence is warranted.

KEY TERMS

9-1

Deterrence The strategy of preventing crime through the threat of punishment. **184**

Incapacitation A strategy for preventing crime by detaining wrongdoers in prison, thereby separating them from the community and reducing criminal opportunities. **184**

Just Deserts A sanctioning philosophy based on the assertion that criminal punishment should be proportionate to the severity of the crime. **184**

Rehabilitation The philosophy that society is best served when wrongdoers are provided the resources needed to eliminate criminality from their behavioral pattern. **185**

Restitution Monetary compensation for damages done to the victim by the offender's criminal act. **187**

Restorative Justice An approach to punishment designed to repair the harm done to the victim and the community by the offender's criminal act. **186**

Retribution The philosophy that those who commit criminal acts should be punished for breaking society's rules to the extent required by just deserts. **183**

9-2

Aggravating Circumstances Any circumstances accompanying the commission of a crime that may justify a harsher sentence. **191**

Determinate Sentencing Imposition of a sentence that is fixed by a sentencing authority and cannot be reduced by judges or other corrections officials. **187**

CHAPTER REVIEW 9

"Good Time" A reduction in time served by prisoners based on good behavior, conformity to rules, and other positive behavior. **188**

Indeterminate Sentencing Imposition of a sentence that prescribes a range of years rather than a definite period of years to be served. **187**

Mitigating Circumstances Any circumstances accompanying the commission of a crime that may justify a lighter sentence. **190**

Presentence Investigative Report An investigative report on an offender's background that assists a judge in determining the proper sentence. **189**

"Real Offense" The actual offense committed, as opposed to the charge levied by a prosecutor as the result of a plea bargain. **190**

Truth-in-Sentencing Laws Legislative attempts to ensure that convicts will serve approximately the terms to which they were initially sentenced. **188**

9-3

Sentencing Discrimination A situation in which the length of a sentence appears to be influenced by a defendant's race, gender, economic status, or other factor not directly related to the crime he or she committed. **192**

Sentencing Disparity A situation in which those convicted of similar crimes do not receive similar sentences. **192**

9-4

Departure A stipulation in many federal and state sentencing guidelines that allows a judge to adjust his or her sentencing decision based on the special circumstances of a particular case. **195**

Habitual Offender Laws Statutes that require lengthy prison sentences for those who are convicted of multiple felonies. **196**

Mandatory Sentencing Guidelines Statutorily determined punishments that must be applied to those who are convicted of specific crimes. **195**

Sentencing Guidelines Legislatively determined guidelines that judges are required to follow when sentencing those convicted of specific crimes. **194**

Victim Impact Statement (VIS) A statement to the sentencing body (judge, jury, or parole board) in which the victim is given the opportunity to describe how the crime has affected her or him. **197**

9-5

Capital Punishment The use of the death penalty to punish wrongdoers for certain crimes. **198**

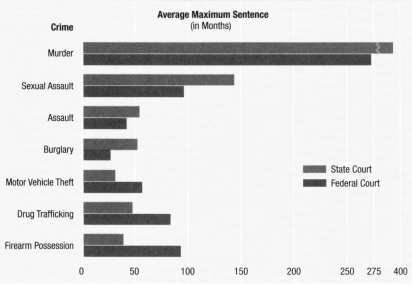

FIGURE 9.2 AVERAGE MAXIMUM SENTENCES FOR SELECTED CRIMES IN STATE AND FEDERAL COURTS

Source: Bureau of Justice Statistics, *Felony Sentences in State Courts, 2006—Statistical Tables* (Washington, D.C.: U.S. Department of Justice, December 2009), Table 1.6, page 9.

SUMMARY

10-1

Explain the justifications for community-based corrections programs. One justification involves reintegration of the offender into society. Reintegration restores family ties, encourages employment and education, and secures a place for the offender in the routine functioning of society. Other justifications involve diversion and cost savings. By diverting criminals to alternative modes of punishment, further overcrowding of jail and prison facilities can be avoided, as can the costs of incarcerating the offenders.

10-2

Describe the three general categories of conditions placed on a probationer. (a) Standard conditions, such as requiring that the probationer notify the agency of a change of address, not leave the jurisdiction without permission, and remain employed; (b) punitive conditions, such as restitution, community service, and home confinement; and (c) treatment conditions, such as required drug or alcohol treatment.

10-3

Identify the main differences between probation and parole. Probation is a sentence handed down by a judge that generally acts as an alternative to incarceration. Parole is a form of early release from prison determined by a parole authority, often a parole board. Probationers are usually first-time offenders who have committed nonviolent crimes, while parolees have often spent significant time in prison.

10-4

Explain which factors influence the decision to grant parole. In deciding whether to grant parole, parole board members primarily consider the severity of the underlying crime and the threat the offender will pose to the community if released. Other factors include the offender's level of remorse and his or her behavior while incarcerated.

10-5

List the three levels of home monitoring. (a) Curfew, which requires that the offender be at home during specified hours; (b) home detention, which requires that the offender be at home except for education, employment, and counseling; and (c) home incarceration, which requires that the offender be at home at all times except for medical emergencies.

KEY TERMS

10-1

Community Corrections The correctional supervision of offenders in the community as an alternative to prison or jail terms. **207**

Diversion In the context of corrections, a strategy to divert those offenders who qualify away from prison and jail and toward community-based and intermediate sanctions. **208**

Reintegration A goal of corrections that focuses on preparing the offender for a return to the community unmarred by further criminal behavior. **208**

10-2

Authority The power designated to an agent of the law over a person who has broken the law. **212**

Caseload The number of individual probationers or parolees under the supervision of a probation or parole officer. **213**

Probation A criminal sanction in which a convict is allowed to remain in the community rather than be imprisoned. **209**

Revocation The formal process that follows the failure of a probationer or parolee to comply with the terms of his or her probation or parole, often resulting in the probationer's incarceration. **211**

Split Sentence Probation A sentence that consists of incarceration in a prison or jail, followed by a probationary period in the community. **210**

CHAPTER REVIEW 10

Suspended Sentence A judicially imposed condition in which an offender is sentenced after being convicted of a crime, but is not required to begin serving the sentence immediately. **209**

Technical Violation An action taken by a probationer or parolee that, although not criminal, breaks the terms of probation or parole as designated by the court. **213**

10-3

Discretionary Release The release of an inmate into a community supervision program at the discretion of the parole board within limits set by state or federal law. **217**

Mandatory Release Release from prison that occurs when an offender has served the full length of his or her sentence, minus any adjustments for good time. **219**

Parole The conditional release of an inmate before his or her sentence has expired. **215**

Parole Board A body of appointed civilians that decides whether a convict should be granted conditional release before the end of his or her sentence. **217**

Parole Contract An agreement between the state and the offender that establishes the conditions of parole. **216**

Parole Grant Hearing A hearing in which the entire parole board or a subcommittee reviews information, meets the offender, and hears testimony from relevant witnesses to determine whether to grant parole. **218**

Parole Guidelines Standards that are used in the parole process to measure the risk that a potential parolee will recidivate. **219**

10-4

Day Reporting Center (DRC) A community-based corrections center to which offenders report on a daily basis for treatment, education, and rehabilitation. **221**

FIGURE 10.3	PROBATION VERSUS PAROLE	
	Probation	**Parole**
Basic Definition	An **alternative to imprisonment** in which a person who has been convicted of a crime is allowed to serve his or her sentence in the community subject to certain conditions and supervision by a probation officer.	An **early release** from a correctional facility, in which the convicted offender is given the chance to spend the remainder of her or his sentence under supervision in the community.
Timing	The offender is sentenced to a probationary term in place of a prison or jail term. If the offender breaks the conditions of probation, he or she is sent to prison or jail. Therefore, **probation generally occurs *before* imprisonment.**	Parole is a form of early release. Therefore, **parole occurs *after* an offender has spent time behind bars.**
Authority	**Probation is under the domain of the judiciary.** A judge decides whether to sentence a convict to probation, and a judge determines whether a probation violation warrants revocation and incarceration.	**Parole often falls under the domain of the parole board.** This administrative body determines whether the prisoner qualifies for early release and the conditions under which the parole must be served.
Characteristics of Offenders	As a number of studies have shown, probationers are normally less involved in the criminal lifestyle. Most of them are **first-time offenders who have committed nonviolent crimes.**	Many parolees have **spent months or even years in prison** and, besides abiding by conditions of parole, must make the difficult transition to "life on the outside."

Probation and parole have many aspects in common. In fact, probation and parole are so similar that many jurisdictions combine them into a single agency. There are, however, some important distinctions between the two systems, as noted above.

Electronic Monitoring A technique of supervision in which the offender's whereabouts are kept under surveillance by an electronic device. **223**

Forfeiture The process by which the government seizes private property attached to criminal activity. **221**

Home Confinement A community-based sanction in which offenders serve their terms of incarceration in their homes. **223**

Intensive Supervision Probation (ISP) A punishment-oriented form of probation in which the offender is placed under stricter and more frequent surveillance and control than in conventional probation. **222**

Intermediate Sanctions Sanctions that are more restrictive than probation and less restrictive than imprisonment. **219**

Pretrial Diversion Program An alternative to trial offered by a judge or prosecutor, in which the offender agrees to participate in a specified counseling or treatment program in return for withdrawal of the charges. **220**

Shock Incarceration A short period of incarceration that is designed to deter further criminal activity by "shocking" the offender with the hardships of imprisonment. **222**

Widen the Net The criticism that intermediate sanctions designed to divert offenders from prison actually increase the number of citizens who are under the control and surveillance of the American corrections system. **225**

SUMMARY

11-1

Contrast the Pennsylvania and New York penitentiary theories of the 1800s. Basically, the Pennsylvania system imposed total silence on its prisoners. Based on the concept of separate confinement, penitentiaries were constructed with back-to-back cells facing both outward and inward. Prisoners worked, slept, and ate alone in their cells. In contrast, New York used the congregate system: silence was imposed, but inmates worked and ate together.

11-2

List and briefly explain the four types of prisons. (a) Maximum-security prisons, which are designed mainly with security and surveillance in mind. Such prisons are usually large and consist of cell blocks, each of which is set off by a series of gates and bars. (b) Medium-security prisons, which offer considerably more educational and treatment programs and allow more contact between inmates. Such prisons are usually surrounded by high fences rather than by walls. (c) Minimum-security prisons, which permit prisoners to have television sets and computers and often allow them to leave the grounds for educational and employment purposes. (d) Supermaximum-security (supermax) prisons, in which prisoners are confined to one-person cells for up to twenty-three hours per day under constant video camera surveillance.

11-3

List the factors that have caused the prison population to grow dramatically in the last several decades. (a) The enhancement and stricter enforcement of the nation's drug laws; (b) increased probability of incarceration; (c) inmates serving more time for each crime; (d) federal prison growth; and (e) rising incarceration rates for women.

11-4

Describe the arguments for and against private prisons. Proponents of private prisons contend that they can be run more cheaply and efficiently than public ones. Opponents of prison privatization dispute such claims, and argue that private prisons are financially motivated to deny inmates the same protections and rights they receive in public correctional facilities.

KEY TERMS

11-1

Congregate System A nineteenth-century penitentiary system developed in New York in which inmates were kept in separate cells during the night but worked together in the daytime under a code of enforced silence. **231**

Medical Model A model of corrections in which the psychological and biological roots of an inmate's criminal behavior are identified and treated. **231**

Penitentiary An early form of correctional facility that emphasized separating inmates from society and from each other. **230**

Separate Confinement A nineteenth-century penitentiary system developed in Pennsylvania in which inmates were kept separate from each other at all times, with daily activities taking place in individual cells. **230**

11-2

Classification The process through which prison officials screen each incoming inmate to best determine that inmate's security and treatment needs. **235**

Custody Level As a result of the classification process, the security designation given to new inmates, crucial in helping corrections officials determine which correctional facility is best suited to the individual offender. **235**

Lockdown A disciplinary action taken by prison officials in which all inmates are ordered to their quarters and nonessential prison activities are suspended. **238**

CHAPTER REVIEW 11

Maximum-Security Prison A correctional institution designed and organized to control and discipline dangerous felons, as well as prevent escape. **236**

Medium-Security Prison A correctional institution that houses less dangerous inmates and therefore uses less restrictive measures to prevent violence and escapes. **238**

Minimum-Security Prison A correctional institution designed to allow inmates, most of whom pose low security risks, a great deal of freedom of movement and contact with the outside world. **239**

Supermax Prison A highly secure, freestanding correctional facility—or such a unit within a correctional facility—that manages offenders who would pose a threat to the security and safety of other inmates and staff members if housed in the general inmate population. **238**

Warden The prison official who is ultimately responsible for the organization and performance of a correctional facility. **234**

11-4

Private Prisons Correctional facilities operated by private corporations instead of the government and, therefore, reliant on profits for survival. **241**

11-5

Direct Supervision Approach A process of prison and jail administration in which correctional officers are in continuous visual contact with inmates during the day. **247**

Fee System A system in which the sheriff's department is reimbursed by a government agency for the costs of housing jail inmates. **245**

Jail A facility, usually operated by the county government, used primarily to hold persons awaiting trial and those who have been found guilty of misdemeanors. **243**

New-Generation Jail A type of jail that is distinguished architecturally from its predecessors by a design that encourages interaction between inmates and jailers and that offers greater opportunities for treatment. **247**

Pretrial Detainees Individuals who cannot post bail after arrest and are therefore forced to spend the time prior to their trial incarcerated in jail. **244**

Time Served The period of time a person denied bail (or unable to pay it) has spent in jail prior to his or her trial. **244**

11-5

Summarize the distinction between jails and prisons, and indicate the importance of jails in the American corrections system. Generally, a prison is for those convicted of felonies who will serve lengthy periods of incarceration, whereas a jail is for those who have been convicted of misdemeanors and will serve less than a year of incarceration. Jails also hold individuals awaiting trial, juveniles awaiting transfer to juvenile authorities, probation and parole violators, and the mentally ill. In any given year, approximately 11.7 million people are admitted to jails, and therefore jails often provide the best chance for treatment or counseling that may deter future criminal behavior by these low-level offenders.

FIGURE 11.5	THE MAIN DIFFERENCES BETWEEN PRISONS AND JAILS	
	Prisons	**Jails**
1.	. . . are operated by the federal and state governments.	. . . are operated by county and city governments.
2.	. . . hold inmates who may have lived quite far away before being arrested.	. . . hold mostly inmates from the local community.
3.	. . . house only those who have been convicted of a crime.	. . . house those who are awaiting trial or have recently been arrested, in addition to convicts.
4.	. . . generally hold inmates who have been found guilty of serious crimes and received sentences of longer than one year.	. . . generally hold inmates who have been found guilty of minor crimes and are serving sentences of less than a year.
5.	. . . often offer a wide variety of rehabilitation and educational programs for long-term prisoners.	. . . due to smaller budgets, tend to focus only on the necessities of safety, food, and clothing.

SUMMARY

12-1

Explain the concept of prison as a total institution. Though many people spend time in partial institutions—schools, companies where they work, and religious organizations—only in prison is every aspect of an inmate's life controlled, and that is why prisons are called total institutions. Every detail for every prisoner is fully prescribed and managed.

12-2

Indicate some of the reasons for violent behavior in prisons. (a) To separate the powerful from the weak and establish a prisoner hierarchy; (b) to minimize one's own probability of being a target of assault; (c) to enhance one's self-image; (d) to obtain sexual relief; and (e) to obtain material goods through extortion or robbery.

12-3

Describe the hands-off doctrine of prisoner law and indicate two standards used to determine if prisoners' rights have been violated. The hands-off doctrine assumes that the care of prisoners should be left to prison officials and that it is not the place of judges to intervene. Nonetheless, the Supreme Court has created two standards to be used by the courts in determining whether a prisoner's Eighth Amendment protections against cruel and unusual punishment have been violated. Under the "deliberate indifference" standard, prisoners must show that prison officials were aware of harmful conditions at the facility but failed to remedy them. Under the "identifiable human needs" standard, prisoners must show that they were denied a basic need such as food, warmth, or exercise.

12-4

Contrast parole, expiration release, pardon, and furlough. Parole is an early release program for those incarcerated. Expiration release occurs when the inmate has served the maximum time for her or his initial sentence minus good-time credits. A pardon can be given only by the president or one of the fifty governors. Furlough is a temporary release while in jail or prison.

12-5

Explain the goal of prisoner reentry programs. Based on the ideals of promoting desistance, these programs have two main objectives: (a) to prepare a prisoner for a successful return to the community, and (b) to protect the community by reducing the chances that the ex-convict will continue her or his criminal activity after release from prison.

KEY TERMS

12-1

Prisonization The socialization process through which a new inmate learns the accepted norms and values of the prison culture. **252**

Prison Programs Organized activities for inmates that are designed to improve their physical and mental health, provide them with vocational skills, or simply keep them busy while incarcerated. **253**

Total Institution An institution, such as a prison, that provides all of the necessities for existence to those who live within its boundaries. **251**

12-2

Deprivation Model A theory that inmate aggression is the result of the frustration inmates feel at being deprived of freedom, consumer goods, sex, and other staples of life outside the institution. **254**

Prison Gang A group of inmates who band together within the corrections system to engage in criminal activities. **256**

Relative Deprivation The theory that inmate aggression is caused when freedoms and services that inmates have come to accept as normal are decreased or eliminated. **255**

Security Threat Group (STG) A group of three or more inmates who engage in activity that poses a threat to the safety of other inmates or the prison staff. **257**

12-3

"Deliberate Indifference" The standard for establishing a violation of an inmate's Eighth Amendment rights, requiring that prison officials were aware of harmful conditions in a correctional institution *and* failed to take steps to remedy those conditions. **262**

"Hands-Off" Doctrine The unwritten judicial policy that favors noninterference by the courts in the administration of prisons and jails. **261**

"Identifiable Human Needs" The basic human necessities that correctional facilities are required by the Constitution to provide to inmates. **262**

Solitary Confinement A disciplinary practice that involves placing the punished inmate in a separate cell to isolate him or her from human contact. **259**

12-5

Civil Confinement The practice of confining individuals against their will in noncorrectional facilities if they present a danger to the community. **270**

Desistance The process through which criminal activity decreases and reintegration into society increases over a period of time. **266**

Expiration Release The release of an inmate from prison at the end of his or her sentence without any further correctional supervision. **265**

Furlough Temporary release from a prison for purposes of vocational or educational training, to ease the shock of release, or for personal reasons. **265**

Halfway House A community-based form of early release that places inmates in residential centers and allows them to reintegrate with society. **268**

| FIGURE 12.3 | PRISONER REENTRY ISSUES |

1. *Housing.* Nearly two-thirds of the men were living with family members, and about half considered their housing situation "temporary." Many were concerned about their living environment: half said that drug dealing was a major problem in their neighborhoods, and almost 25 percent were living with drug and alcohol abusers.

2. *Employment.* After one year, only about one-third of the former inmates had a full-time job, and another 11 percent were working part-time.

3. *Family and friends.* One in four of the men identified family support as the most important thing keeping them from returning to criminality. Another 16 percent said that avoiding certain people and situations was the most crucial factor in their continued good behavior.

4. *Programs and services.* About two-thirds of the former inmates had taken part in programs and services such as drug treatment and continuing education.

5. *Health.* More than half of the men reported suffering from a chronic health condition, and 29 percent showed symptoms of depression.

6. *Substance use.* About half of the men admitted to weekly drug use or alcohol intoxication. Men who had strong family ties and those who were required to maintain telephone contact with their parole officers were less likely to engage in frequent substance use.

7. *Parole violation and recidivism.* More than half of the former inmates reported that they had violated the conditions of their parole, usually by drug use or having contact with other parolees. Fifteen percent of the men returned to prison in the year after release. Four out of five of the returns were the result of a new crime.

Researchers from the Urban Institute in Washington, D.C., asked nearly three hundred former prisoners (all male) in the Cleveland, Ohio, area about the most pressing issues they faced in their first year after release. The answers provide a useful snapshot of the many challenges of reentry.

Source: Christy A. Visher and Shannon M. E. Courtney, *One Year Out: Experience of Prisoners Returning to Cleveland* (Washington, D.C.: Urban Institute, April 2007), 2.

Pardon An act of executive clemency that overturns a conviction and erases mention of the crime from the person's criminal record. **265**

Prisoner Reentry A corrections strategy designed to prepare inmates for a successful return to the community and to reduce their criminal activity after release. **265**

Sex Offender Notification Law Legislation that requires law enforcement authorities to notify people when convicted sex offenders are released into their neighborhood or community. **269**

Work Release Program Temporary release of convicts from prison for purposes of employment. The offenders may spend their days on the job, but must return to the correctional facility at night and during the weekend. **267**

SUMMARY

13-1
List the four major differences between juvenile courts and adult courts. (a) No juries, (b) different terminology, (c) limited adversarial relationship, and (d) confidentiality.

13-2
Identify and briefly describe the single most important United States Supreme Court case with respect to juvenile justice. The case was *In re Gault,* decided by the Supreme Court in 1967. In this case a minor was arrested for allegedly making an obscene phone call. His parents were not notified and were not present during the juvenile court judge's decision-making process. In this case, the Supreme Court held that juveniles are entitled to many of the same due process rights granted to adult offenders, including notice of charges, the right to counsel, the privilege against self-incrimination, and the right to confront and cross-examine witnesses.

13-3
Describe the reasoning behind recent United States Supreme Court decisions that have lessened the harshness of sentencing outcomes for violent juvenile offenders. In banning capital punishment and limiting the availability of life sentences without parole for offenders who committed their crimes as juveniles, the Supreme Court has focused on the concept of "diminished culpability." This concept is based on the notion that violent juvenile offenders cannot fully comprehend the consequences of their actions and are more deserving of the opportunity for rehabilitation than adult violent offenders.

13-4
Describe the one variable that always correlates highly with juvenile crime rates. The older a person is, the less likely he or she will exhibit criminal behavior. This process is known as aging out. Thus, persons in any at-risk group will commit fewer crimes as they get older.

13-5
Describe the four primary stages of pretrial juvenile justice procedure. (a) Intake, in which an official of the juvenile court engages in a screening process to determine what to do with the youthful offender; (b) pretrial diversion, which may consist of probation, treatment and aid, and/or restitution; (c) jurisdictional waiver to an adult court, in which case the youth leaves the juvenile justice system; and (d) some type of detention, in which the youth is held until the disposition process begins.

KEY TERMS

13-1
Juvenile Delinquency Behavior that is illegal under federal or state law that has been committed by a person who is under an age limit specified by statute. **275**

Parens Patriae A doctrine that holds that the state has a responsibility to look after the well-being of children and to assume the role of parent if necessary. **274**

Status Offender A juvenile who has engaged in behavior deemed unacceptable for those under a certain statutorily determined age. **274**

13-3
Bullying Overt acts taken by students with the goal of intimidating, harassing, or humiliating other students. **281**

13-4
Age of Onset The age at which a juvenile first exhibits delinquent behavior. **282**

Aging Out A term used to explain the fact that criminal activity declines with age. **282**

Child Abuse Mistreatment of a child resulting in physical, emotional, or sexual damage. **283**

Child Neglect A form of child abuse in which the child is denied certain necessities such as shelter, food, care, and love. **283**

Youth Gang A self-formed group of youths with several identifiable characteristics, including a gang name and other recognizable symbols, a geographic territory, and participation in illegal activities. **284**

CHAPTER REVIEW 13

13-5

Automatic Transfer The process by which a juvenile is transferred to adult court as a matter of state law. **287**

Detention The temporary custody of a juvenile in a secure facility after a petition has been filed and before the adjudicatory process begins. **288**

Detention Hearing A hearing to determine whether a juvenile should be detained, or remain detained, while waiting for the adjudicatory process to begin. **288**

Intake The process by which an official of the court must decide whether to file a petition, release the juvenile, or place the juvenile under some other form of supervision. **286**

Judicial Waiver The process in which the juvenile judge, based on the facts of the case at hand, decides that the alleged offender should be transferred to adult court. **287**

Low-Visibility Decision Making A term used to describe the discretionary power police have in determining what to do with misbehaving juveniles. **285**

Petition The document filed with a juvenile court alleging that the juvenile is a delinquent or a status offender and requesting that the court either hear the case or transfer it to an adult court. **286**

Prosecutorial Waiver A procedure used in situations where the prosecutor has discretion to decide whether a case will be heard by a juvenile court or an adult court. **287**

Referral The notification process through which a law enforcement officer or other concerned citizen makes the juvenile court aware of a juvenile's unlawful or unruly conduct. **286**

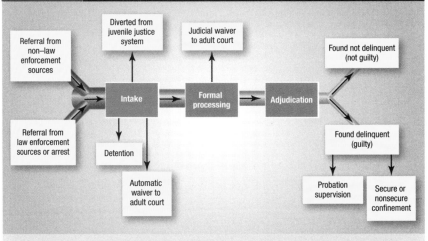

FIGURE 13.5 THE JUVENILE JUSTICE PROCESS

This diagram shows the possible tracks that a young person may take after her or his first contact with the juvenile justice system (usually a police officer).

Source: Office of Juvenile Justice and Delinquency Prevention.

13-6

Adjudicatory Hearing The process through which a juvenile court determines whether there is sufficient evidence to support the initial petition. **289**

Aftercare The variety of therapeutic, educational, and counseling programs made available to juvenile delinquents (and some adults) after they have been released from a correctional facility. **292**

Boot Camp A variation on traditional shock incarceration in which juveniles (and some adults) are sent to secure confinement facilities modeled on military basic training camps instead of prison or jail. **291**

Disposition Hearing Similar to the sentencing hearing for adults, a hearing in which the juvenile judge or officer decides the appropriate punishment for a youth found to be delinquent or a status offender. **289**

Graduated Sanctions The practical theory in juvenile corrections that a delinquent or status offender should receive a punishment that matches in seriousness the severity of the wrongdoing. **289**

Predisposition Report A report prepared during the disposition process that provides the judge with relevant background material to aid in the disposition decision. **289**

Residential Treatment Program A government-run facility for juveniles whose offenses are not deemed serious enough to warrant incarceration in a training school. **290**

Training School A correctional institution for juveniles found to be delinquent or status offenders. **291**

SUMMARY

14-1

Summarize the three federal laws that have been particularly influential on our nation's counterterrorism strategies. (a) The Foreign Intelligence Surveillance Act (FISA) lays the groundwork for electronically monitoring national security threats. (b) The Antiterrorism and Effective Death Penalty Act (AEDPA) prohibits the providing of material support to terrorist organizations. (c) The Patriot Act greatly strengthened the ability of law enforcement agents to investigate and prosecute suspected terrorists.

14-2

Distinguish verbal threats that are protected by the Constitution from verbal threats that can be prosecuted as "true threats." The First Amendment protects speech, including threats, that should not cause a person or group of people reasonably to fear for their safety. A "true threat," by contrast, expresses the viable intent of the speaker to harm potential victims, or to place those victims in reasonable fear of danger.

14-3

Outline the three major reasons why the Internet is conducive to the dissemination of child pornography. The Internet provides (a) a quick way to transmit child pornography from providers to consumers; (b) security such as untraceable e-mails and password-protected Web sites and chat rooms; and (c) anonymity for buyers and sellers of child pornography.

14-4

Explain how background checks, in theory, protect the public from firearm-related violence. Any person who wants to buy a firearm from a federally licensed dealer must go through an application process that includes a background check. This process is designed to keep firearms out of the hands of individuals who are deemed safety risks. Consequently, a person will fail the background check—and have the gun purchase denied—if he or she exhibits any one of a number of dangerous tendencies, including showing signs of mental illness, having a felony conviction, being addicted to illegal drugs, or engaging in domestic violence.

14-5

Indicate some of the ways that white-collar crime is different from violent or property crime. A wrongdoer committing a standard crime usually uses physical means to get somewhere he or she legally should not be in order to do something clearly illegal. Also, the victims of violent and property crimes are usually easily identifiable. In contrast, a white-collar criminal usually has legal access to the crime scene where he or she is doing something seemingly legitimate. Furthermore, victims of white-collar crimes are often unknown or unidentifiable.

KEY TERMS

14-1

Material Support In the context of federal antiterrorism legislation, the act of helping a terrorist organization by engaging in a wide range of activity that includes providing financial support, training, and expert advice or assistance. **296**

National Security Letters Legal notices that compel the disclosure of customer records held by banks, telephone companies, Internet service providers, and other companies to the agents of the federal government. **297**

Patriot Act Legislation passed in the wake of the September 11, 2001, terrorist attacks that greatly expanded the ability of government agents to monitor and apprehend suspected terrorists. **297**

Surveillance The close observation of a person or group by government agents, in particular to uncover evidence of criminal or terrorist activities. **296**

True Threat An act of speech or expression that is not protected by the First Amendment because it is done with the intention of placing a specific victim or group of victims in fear of unlawful violence. **301**

14-2

Botnet A network of computers that have been appropriated without the knowledge of their owners and used to spread harmful programs via the Internet; short for *robot network*. **306**

Cyberattack An attempt to damage or disrupt computer systems or electronic networks operated by computers. **302**

CHAPTER REVIEW 14

Cyber Crime A crime that occurs online, in the virtual community of the Internet, as opposed to in the physical world. **303**

Cyber Forensics The application of computer technology to finding and utilizing evidence of cyber crimes. **308**

Cyber Fraud Any misrepresentation knowingly made over the Internet with the intention of deceiving another and on which a reasonable person would and does rely to his or her detriment. **303**

Cyberstalking The crime of stalking, committed in cyberspace through the use of e-mail, text messages, or another form of electronic communication. **305**

Digital Evidence Information or data of value to a criminal investigation that is either stored on, received by, or transmitted by electronic means. **308**

Encryption The encoding of computer data with the goal of protecting the data from unauthorized parties. **308**

Hacker A person who uses one computer to break into another. **306**

Identity Theft The theft of personal information, such as a person's name, driver's license number, or Social Security number. **304**

Intellectual Property Property resulting from intellectual, creative processes. **307**

Phishing Sending an unsolicited e-mail that falsely claims to be from a legitimate organization in an attempt to acquire sensitive information from the recipient. **305**

Spam Bulk e-mails, particularly of commercial advertising, sent in large quantities without the consent of the recipient. **305**

Virus A computer program that can replicate itself and interfere with the normal use of a computer. A virus cannot exist as a separate entity and must attach itself to another program to move through a network. **306**

Worm A computer program that can automatically replicate itself and interfere with the normal use of a computer. A worm does not need to be attached to an existing file to move from one network to another. **306**

14-3

Background Check An investigation of a person's history to determine whether that person should be allowed a certain privilege, such as the ability to possess a firearm. **310**

Gun Control Efforts by a government to regulate or control the sale of firearms. **310**

14-4

Compliance The state of operating in accordance with governmental standards. **313**

Corporate Violence Physical harm to individuals or the environment that occurs as the result of corporate policies or decision making. **313**

Regulation A governmental order or rule having the force of law that is usually implemented by an administrative agency. **313**

FIGURE 14.4 WHITE-COLLAR CRIMES

Embezzlement
Embezzlement is a form of employee fraud in which an individual uses his or her position within an organization to *embezzle*, or steal, the employer's funds, property, or other assets. Pilferage is a less serious form of employee fraud in which the individual steals items from the workplace.

Tax Evasion
Tax evasion occurs when taxpayers underreport (or do not report) their taxable income or otherwise purposely attempt to evade a tax liability.

Credit-Card and Check Fraud
Credit-card fraud involves obtaining credit-card numbers through a variety of schemes (such as stealing them from the Internet) and using the numbers for personal gain. Check fraud includes writing checks that are not covered by bank funds, forging checks, and stealing traveler's checks.

Mail and Wire Fraud
This umbrella term covers all schemes that involve the use of mail, radio, television, the Internet, or a telephone to intentionally deceive in a business environment.

Securities Fraud
Securities fraud covers illegal activity in the stock market. Stockbrokers who steal funds from their clients are guilty of securities fraud, as are those who engage in *insider trading*, which involves buying or selling securities on the basis of information that has not been made available to the public.

Bribery
Also known as *influence peddling*, bribery occurs in the business world when somebody within a company or government sells influence, power, or information to a person outside the company or government who can benefit. A county official, for example, could give a construction company a lucrative county contract to build a new jail. In return, the construction company would give some of the proceeds, known as a *kickback*, to the official.

Consumer Fraud
This term covers a wide variety of activities designed to defraud consumers, from selling counterfeit art to offering "free" items, such as electronic devices or vacations, that include a number of hidden charges.

Insurance Fraud
Insurance fraud involves making false claims in order to collect insurance payments. Faking an injury in order to receive payments from a workers' compensation program, for example, is a form of insurance fraud.